W9-AXZ-999

Teaching with
The Bedford Handbook

Welcome to the ninth edition of *The Bedford Handbook*, now more useful and more relevant than ever. The realities of the college writing course are changing; for some of you, your teaching context is changing. Some of you are having to rethink what you assign and how you teach. In order to keep pace with change, we recently asked users of *The Bedford Handbook* to describe how their teaching lives are evolving.

 Some instructors responded by saying they're teaching online and teaching with media more than ever.

"More and more of the course work is ending up online."
— **Anne Marie Hubbell**, University of Maryland

"I am using video, audio, and game technology in my teaching."
— **Jenny Heil**, Emory University

"In my online course, students do not have the benefit of face-to-face, spontaneous interactions with me, so they need resources that allow them to quickly locate and readily understand solutions for writing issues they encounter when I am not available online."
— **Linda Darnell Stanley**, Santa Fe College

Others reported trying new pedagogies or adding a slightly different emphasis.

"I've begun to assign more sequenced writing. Careful sequencing helps to justify the usefulness of each small assignment within the broader context of the course's goals."
— **Alex Quinlan**, University of Tennessee at Chattanooga

"We have a much stronger emphasis on the revision process."
— **Luis Nazario**, Pueblo Community College

"A lot more time is devoted to peer review."
— **Angela Henning**, William Jessup University

 Many are finding that they teach even more from the handbook.

"We now spend time in class using the handbook; in the past, I'd just assign it as a 'recommended reading.'"
— **Carl Lindgren**, College of Saint Benedict/St. John's University

"The handbook allows me to give individual students different exercises. Class time is more productive; students work on areas they need to improve."
— **Erin Nunnally**, Northern Virginia Community College

"We spend time in class learning how to use the handbook to improve writing."
— **Tara King**, Pierce College

Revising *The Bedford Handbook* meant thinking through all such changes and offering a tool that is more relevant to the course, more useful in a variety of teaching and learning contexts, and more closely aligned with students' needs and practices.

As you look through the ninth edition of *The Bedford Handbook*, you may at first notice content changes—more coverage of critical reading, for example. The new edition is much more than a grammar reference or a citation guide. It's a real classroom tool with topics and models you'll find useful as you teach—thesis statements, evidence, analysis, synthesis, and more. You may also notice a change in how the handbook works. The ninth edition is much more than a print book. It's part of an integrated tool that combines instruction in print with interactivity and practice in an online setting. Bedford Integrated Media allows you to use the handbook more actively as a classroom tool and allows your students to use the handbook more actively as a learning tool.

These introductory pages provide suggestions for using the handbook's print pages and e-Pages to do the following:

- Support your goals and assignments
- Save time
- Engage students
- Teach good habits

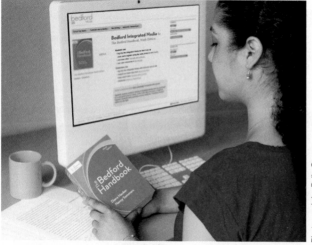

Photograph by Pelle Cass.

Assigning a handbook and using it as you teach saves you time, fosters good student habits, and opens up new teaching and learning possibilities.

Supporting your goals and assignments with *The Bedford Handbook*

When students routinely use their handbook in the course, they see its value, find it's a faster avenue to answers than Google or other Web search engines, are more likely to rely on it as a reference, and are more likely to achieve the goals of the course.

Many writing instructors find it helpful to review the goals of the course during the first or second class period. When you discuss goals (your school may use the word "outcomes" or "competencies"), talk with students about how the course materials you've assigned will reinforce those goals.

When you discuss this course goal...	You can point out this resource in the book or media...
Students will use critical thinking and reading skills to analyze topics and source texts.	Writing guide for an analytical essay on pages 122–23
Students will ethically integrate the words and ideas of others (direct quotations, summaries, and paraphrases) into their own writing.	Exercises on integrating sources in the e-Pages
Students will reflect on their own development as writers.	Advice about reflective writing and portfolio keeping in section 2

Other tips for reinforcing the goals of the course and specific assignments include the following:

- In your syllabus, inform students that the handbook's content will be useful in class and important for their success. Align specific sections of the handbook with specific course goals.

- Assign a scavenger hunt to help students familiarize themselves with the integrated media. Ask them to find print pages or e-Pages that support concepts you emphasize in your course (peer review, MLA style, or revising, for example).

- When you give assignments, build in cross-references to the handbook that give students a jump start in learning and fulfilling the expectations of the assignment.

Assignment Expectations: Your essay must be thesis driven (1c), as analyzing the text should produce an overall opinion of the effectiveness or persuasiveness of the essay itself. Your thesis should express your opinion on how the text was written — *not* on the topic of the essay. For example, your thesis would express whether the text was effective or not, well written or not, convincing or not, or a combination of these points.

You are also required to locate (50d) and use one additional source in this essay. This additional source may come from something we've already read this semester or a source you locate on your own. Remember to cite both the essay being analyzed and the additional source in proper MLA format (56).

Saving time with *The Bedford Handbook*

If you want to focus on working with students on larger rhetorical concepts and don't want to spend a lot of energy on sentence-level matters or on inventing content, let the handbook help.

Expect edited papers, but don't be the editor.

Using some of your comments to direct students to content in the handbook has the dual benefit of saving you time and teaching students how to find revision help in the handbook. You don't have to edit a student's subject-verb agreement errors; writing *21a* or *sv agr* in the margin will send the student to advice and examples that teach the lesson and will give you more time to comment at length on a more global concern. Be sure to have a conversation with students about how to use codes such as *21a* and *sv agr* before or as you return the first set of drafts.

Build skills through LearningCurve and other e-Pages resources.

If you find you need to cover grammar, style, and punctuation topics with the whole class or a few students, the online components of the Integrated Media for *The Bedford Handbook* will help. Students can build and practice skills on their own time, and you can easily keep track of their progress. The LearningCurve exercises (available for 17 common topics) are

---

hackerhandbooks.com/bedhandbook

e Grammatical sentences > Exercises: 19–3 to 19–7

✓ Grammatical sentences > LearningCurve: Sentence fragments

References in the print book direct students to exercises in the e-Pages for extra practice.

adaptive, which means the program personalizes the practice for students—offering more or less difficult items in response to an individual's progress through the exercise. Easy reporting gives you a view of success by student or by class.

Assign and give credit for editing logs.

When you ask your students to keep track of their learning by charting the errors they make and the corrections they try, you are encouraging a long-term writerly habit *and* saving yourself time. Students can create editing log pages where they record (a) an incorrect sentence from their own writing, (b) the handbook section number and rule that helps them revise the sentence, and (c) the corrected sentence. (For a sample, see p. 68.) As an end-of-course assignment, you can ask students to reflect on what they learned from keeping an editing log.

Engaging students with *The Bedford Handbook*

When it finally clicks for students that a particular resource is going to help them become stronger, more successful learners, they engage. They pay attention. You can help them realize the usefulness of their handbook, its power to help them collaborate with others, and the <*ahem!*> fun of adaptive learning.

Bring it to class; use it in class.

The Bedford Handbook is handy and portable. If you're using an e-book version of the book, it's even more so. Require that students have it in class with them. Here are three easy ways to engage students in an activity that teaches a rhetorical concept and draws on the handbook:

- **Try the "So what?" test (p. 33).** Pair students. Each student shares a draft of an opening paragraph with a thesis statement. Students discuss each other's draft by answering the "So what?" questions. Each writer makes notes about how to revise.

- **Try analyzing a sample paper (pp. 81–86).** In preparation for assigning a reflective essay, ask students to read the "Key features" of the genre and then, in pairs or small groups, identify those features in the sample by Lucy Bonilla.

- **Try the double-entry notebook experiment (p. 113).** Examine the sample notebook entries as a class. Discuss the differences between the content in the left column and that in the right column. For a reading you have assigned, give students 20 minutes to start on their own double-entry notebook.

For **more than 100 additional practical tips** for teaching writing with *The Bedford Handbook*, see the bottom panel of the pages in this book, the Instructor's Annotated Edition.

View video tutorials in class or assign them for homework.

We have included a series of video tutorials in the e-Pages to help students familiarize themselves with the topics in the handbook, the reference aids, and the ways in which a handbook will help them in their writing course and in any other college course that requires writing. In short, the tutorials help them to see the *value* in their purchase.

Use e-Pages activities to engage students in their own writing.

Students in a writing course should be doing writing instead of just reading about writing. The e-Pages offer students prompts and a space in which to write—a place to practice applying the lessons of the handbook to their own drafts. "As you write" prompts in the e-Pages make the handbook's content meaning-ful and useful.

As you write: Planning with sources

Read three sources that you are considering for your research project. Ask yourself how each source will function in your proj-ect. Consult 52a to understand the various ways to use sources to develop your points. In your research log, write brief notes about what role each source will play in your paper. Will it offer back-ground information, an explanation of a key term, an alternative interpretation, expert testimony, or something else?

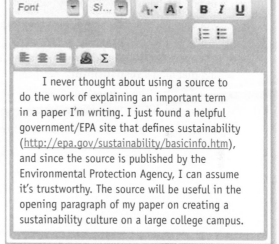

I never thought about using a source to do the work of explaining an important term in a paper I'm writing. I just found a helpful government/EPA site that defines sustainability (http://epa.gov/sustainability/basicinfo.htm), and since the source is published by the Environmental Protection Agency, I can assume it's trustworthy. The source will be useful in the opening paragraph of my paper on creating a sustainability culture on a large college campus.

Writing prompts in the e-Pages help students apply handbook lessons to their own writing.

Teaching good habits with *The Bedford Handbook*

A nationwide survey of more than 1,000 first-year student writers informed the theme of the ninth edition, habits of mind. These students—from two- and four-year colleges, enrolled in a wide variety of college programs, and with diverse levels of prior success with writing—wrote about the need to be curious, engaged, responsible, and reflective learners in order to succeed in college.

The Bedford Handbook includes content that supports your teaching of rhetorical skills, of course; what's more, it also teaches important academic habits.

- For advice about using **curiosity** to probe for writing topics, see page 514.

- For help with reading actively to foster **engagement** with texts, see page 128.

- For examples of notetaking, paraphrasing, and summarizing that model **responsibility**, see pages 531–37.

- For practice with **reflection**, assign any of the "As you write" activities in the e-Pages.

- For advice on **putting the habits together** for college research, see page 518.

res
518 **50b**   Thinking like a researcher; gathering sources

Thinking like a researcher

To develop your authority as a researcher, you need to think like a researcher — asking interesting questions, becoming well informed through reading and evaluating sources, and citing sources to acknowledge other researchers.

Be curious. What makes you angry, concerned, or perplexed? What topics and debates do you care about? What problems do you want to help solve? Explore your topic from multiple perspectives, and let your curiosity drive your project.

Be engaged. Talk with a librarian and learn how to use your library's research tools and resources. Once you find promising sources, let one source lead you to another; follow bibliographic clues to learn who else has written about your topic. Listen to the key voices in the research conversation you've joined — and then respond.

Be responsible. Use sources to develop and support your ideas rather than patching them together to let them speak for you. From the start of your research project, keep careful track of sources you read or view (see 51), place quotation marks around words copied from sources, and maintain accurate records for all bibliographic information.

Be reflective. Keep a research log, and use your log to explore various points you are developing and to pose counterarguments to your research argument. Research is never a straightforward path, so use your log to reflect on the evolution of your project as well as your evolution as a researcher.

The handbook helps students use the habits (curiosity, engagement, responsibility, and reflection) as college researchers.

Know that we support you.

Perhaps you've been teaching 20 years and would like a few fresh ideas. Or perhaps you're new to using media in the classroom. Then again, maybe you're entirely new to teaching. In any case, we can help. We offer a wide variety of support resources and services.

Instructor resources

Teaching with Hacker Handbooks

This collection of resources helps you answer the question *How can I integrate a handbook into my course?* Both novice and seasoned teachers who assign writing will benefit from the practical strategies and materials developed by master teachers and others in the field.

Part I of *Teaching with Hacker Handbooks* addresses larger teaching concerns in chapters such as "Designing Effective Assignments" and "Responding to Student Writing." Part II offers ten ready-to-use modules, such as "Teaching Students to Integrate Sources" and "Teaching Paragraphs," each including a discussion of common writing challenges, a single assignment or class activity, and a directory to additional resources. And Part III includes handouts, assignments, and sample syllabi drawn from the composition community.

hackerhandbooks.com

Visit **hackerhandbooks.com** for teaching advice, to learn about the different Hacker/Sommers handbooks, to download practical teaching materials, to view a video that shares students' thoughts about feedback, and to connect with Nancy Sommers through her blog, *Between the Drafts.*

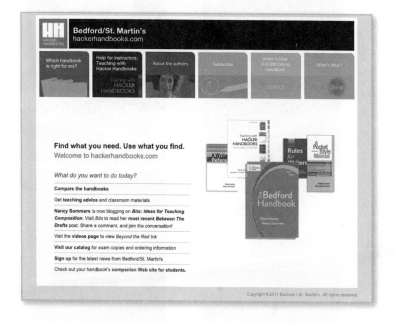

Professional resources

You can also request free professional resources such as the following at **bedfordstmartins.com/teachingcentral**.

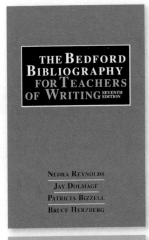

THE BEDFORD BIBLIOGRAPHY FOR TEACHERS OF WRITING SEVENTH EDITION

NEDRA REYNOLDS
JAY DOLMAGE
PATRICIA BIZZELL
BRUCE HERZBERG

Responding to Student Writers

Nancy Sommers

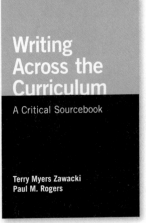

Writing Across the Curriculum

A Critical Sourcebook

Terry Myers Zawacki
Paul M. Rogers

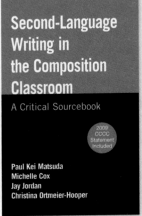

Second-Language Writing in the Composition Classroom

A Critical Sourcebook

2009 CCCC Statement Included

Paul Kei Matsuda
Michelle Cox
Jay Jordan
Christina Ortmeier-Hooper

Webinars and campus workshops

Because we are committed to supporting the teaching of composition, Bedford/St. Martin's can host online or live events for you and your colleagues if you want to learn more about a product or how you can use it effectively in your course. Contact your sales representative to schedule a workshop with an author, an editor, a media trainer, or other content expert.

Training & Support

Sign up for a training webinar from our **Support Team!**

SIGN UP NOW

"Thank you so very much for your workshop yesterday. Our faculty were truly inspired by the workshop, as was I. So many of our faculty came by my office afterwards to say how much they enjoyed the session. The one comment that I heard consistently was that they felt a renewed sense of purpose in their teaching. That is perhaps the best gift any WPA could ask for."

— **Christopher Minnix**, director of freshman composition and developmental studies, University of Alabama at Birmingham, in an e-mail message to author Nancy Sommers

The Bedford Handbook

Ninth
Edition

The Bedford Handbook

Diana Hacker

Nancy Sommers
Harvard University

BEDFORD/ST. MARTIN'S
BOSTON ◆ NEW YORK

For Bedford/St. Martin's

Executive Editor: Michelle M. Clark
Senior Editors: Barbara G. Flanagan and Mara Weible
Associate Editor: Kylie Paul
Senior Production Editor: Rosemary R. Jaffe
Assistant Production Manager: Joe Ford
Marketing Manager: Scott Berzon
Copy Editor: Linda McLatchie
Indexer: Ellen Kuhl Repetto
Photo Researcher: Sheri Blaney
Senior Art Director: Anna Palchik
Text Design: Claire Seng-Niemoeller
Cover Design: Donna Lee Dennison
Composition: Cenveo Publisher Services
Printing and Binding: RR Donnelley and Sons

President, Bedford/St. Martin's: Denise B. Wydra
Editorial Director for English and Music: Karen S. Henry
Director of Marketing: Karen R. Soeltz
Production Director: Susan W. Brown
Director of Rights and Permissions: Hilary Newman

Manufactured in the United States of America.

8   7   6   5   4   3
f   e   d   c   b   a

For information, write: Bedford/St. Martin's, 75 Arlington Street,
Boston, MA 02116   (617-399-4000)

ISBN 978-1-4576-0803-2 (Instructor's Annotated Edition)
ISBN 978-1-4576-0801-8 (hardcover Student Edition)
ISBN 978-1-4576-0802-5 (softcover Student Edition)

Acknowledgments

Preface for Instructors

Use a handbook. Start a habit.

Dear Colleagues:

Welcome to the ninth edition of *The Bedford Handbook.* Two questions guided my work on this edition: How do students *become* college writers? And how can a handbook help students learn the expectations of academic writing? We know that *becoming* a confident college writer is an apprenticeship, a process that takes practice and doesn't happen—for any student—in a single course or semester. And we also know that the more students rely on their handbook and learn from its lessons, the more effective they will become as writers.

So to prepare for the ninth edition, I did what we ask of our students—research—and surveyed more than 1,000 first-year writers at 35 colleges and universities to learn how students interpret their college writing assignments and read their teachers' comments, how they define revision and research, and how they endeavor to become good academic writers. I listened to

Nancy Sommers with college writers

students' questions and assumptions about college writing—as well as their advice for their fellow students.

The results of the survey clearly pointed to this conclusion: Students are more likely to become successful college writers if they develop good habits. In other words, good academic habits make good college writers. These habits—curiosity, engagement, responsibility, and reflection, often called *habits of mind*—develop over time and provide a foundation for academic success. This discovery reinforces what many of us have learned from the literature in composition (especially from the recent work of the Council of Writing Program Administrators[1]) and has allowed me to imagine, in response, practical handbook advice for students.

As you look through the ninth edition, you'll discover many innovations inspired by the survey to help your students become curious, engaged, responsible, and reflective readers and writers. All good writing, for instance, starts with curiosity, and in the ninth edition students are offered specific strategies that foster curiosity: asking questions, practicing inquiry, finding entry points in research conversations, and developing thesis statements to open up conversations with their readers. And to foster engagement, the new edition offers much more practical support for reading and conversing with texts in a variety of modes and genres and for reading drafts, both students' own work and the work of peers. To become engaged writers, students need to become thoughtful, engaged readers.

One of the most important habits students can learn is *how* to use a handbook to answer the basic question "How do I write a good college paper?" Using a trusted, authoritative reference

---

1. "Framework for Success in Postsecondary Writing" (2011), developed jointly by the Council of Writing Program Administrators, the National Council of Teachers of English, and the National Writing Project, offers a discussion of habits of mind as they relate to college readiness and college success and shares methods for relevant rhetorical instruction.

is a good academic habit that will serve your students throughout their college careers. Doing so demonstrates responsibility. To encourage students to use their handbooks, the ninth edition includes the topics, advice, and examples you'd expect in the print pages of the book—accompanied by many, many opportunities to practice its lessons online in the book's e-Pages.

In the new e-Pages, you'll find writing prompts, called *As you write*, that ask students to apply handbook advice to their own work and practice the skills they need for college writing—crafting and revising thesis statements, asking a research question, reading texts critically, writing in various genres, editing their work, and making revision suggestions to peers. You'll also find exercises on every grammar, style, and punctuation topic. These are in addition to the exercises offered in the print book. The e-Pages encourage students to develop habits of curiosity, engagement, responsibility, and reflection as they develop the habit of using their handbook.

The ninth edition serves your needs as well as your students' needs. The Instructor's Annotated Edition shares more than 100 tips from my own teaching—ways to integrate the handbook and facilitate your students' development as writers, editors, and researchers. And you'll find that having the handbook in a combined print and online format allows you to insert custom content, such as favorite assignments or handouts, as new e-Pages, easily and conveniently. The content becomes more useful, and teaching with the handbook becomes even easier.

I am eager to share the ninth edition of *The Bedford Handbook* with you and with your students.

Nancy Sommers

What's new in this edition?

- Research-based strategies for **becoming a college writer**. A new introduction and six new *Becoming a college writer* pages help students develop the academic habits that will foster their success as college writers: curiosity, engagement, responsibility, and reflection. The pages offer insights and advice from the more than 1,000 college writers surveyed, provide a writing prompt that helps students draw on earlier experiences with writing, and direct them to practical help in their handbook.

- Practical **writing guides**. Five new writing guides support students as they compose common college assignments: arguments, analyses, annotated

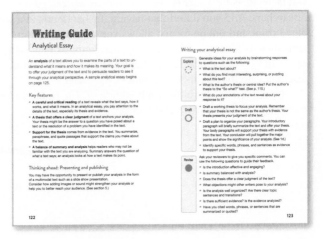

bibliographies, reflective cover letters, and literacy narratives. The guides help students understand the expectations of the genre and provide a path as they explore, draft, and revise.

- More strategies for **reading**. A completely revised Part II emphasizes reading as the foundation of every college research and writing assignment. The handbook teaches students to read traditional and multimodal texts, sources, their own work, and the work of their peers critically and reflectively.

- **New research coverage** that emphasizes engagement and responsibility. Substantially revised research advice emphasizes finding an entry point in a debate and developing authority as a researcher. Because some sources are difficult to cite, new practical how-to boxes address authorship and new types of sources such as course materials and reposted video content.

- An emphasis on **multimodal texts and composing in new genres**. A new chapter on reading and writing about multimodal texts introduces new genres and practical strategies for analysis. Throughout the book, writing guides for five different genres give tips for composing college assignments as podcasts, presentations, Web sites, and other alternatives to the traditional essay. New

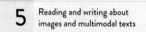

5   Reading and writing about images and multimodal texts

In many of your college classes, you'll have the opportunity to read and write about images, such as photographs or paintings, as well as multimodal texts, such as advertisements, maps, videos, or Web sites. Multimodal texts are those that combine one or more of the following modes: words, static images, moving images, and sound. You might, for instance, be asked to analyze an advertisement for a composition course, a map for a geology course, or a YouTube video for a sociology course.

Writing about images or multimodal texts differs from writing about written texts—a photograph is a different kind of text

discussions of genre and sample papers in new genres (literacy narrative, reflective portfolio letter) align the book more closely with the goals of writing programs.

• The handbook is now **Bedford Integrated Media**, with part of the book in print and part online. The e-Pages, online at hackerhandbooks.com/bedhandbook, extend the lessons of the print pages with interactive writing prompts and scorable practice exercises. And LearningCurve offers game-like adaptive quizzing for many handbook topics. Easy-to-spot cross-references on the print pages direct students to the e-Pages content.

> hackerhandbooks.com/bedhandbook
> e Grammatical sentences > Exercises: 19–3 to 19–7
> ✓ Grammatical sentences > LearningCurve: Sentence fragments

270 practice exercises help students build skills and strengthen their editing. The exercises report to a gradebook so you can keep track of progress if you choose.

36 "As you write" prompts encourage students to apply the lessons of the handbook to their own writing. Students complete brief writing assignments about organizing a paper, drafting thesis statements, working with peers, integrating sources, and other writing topics—and can submit their writing for assessment.

LearningCurve, game-like online quizzing, builds confidence with sentence-level skills by adapting to students' responses and adjusting the difficulty level of the quiz items.

And access is easy. Students who purchase a new copy of *The Bedford Handbook* will have access to the book's complete Integrated Media. To access the online components, students simply use the activation code from the card in the print book when they log in for the first time at hackerhandbooks.com/bedhandbook.

(Students who do not have a new book can purchase access to the online components of the Integrated Media at hackerhandbooks.com/bedhandbook.)

- An innovative **x-Book that helps you reimagine your course**. You can easily adapt the handbook to your course by reordering, hiding, or adding content. Assigning content and tracking progress is simple, too. Students do the work of the course—reading, writing, viewing, reflecting, sharing—right in the pages of the book. And when readers start discussions on a page, the handbook becomes a social space where writers can learn from each other. An x-Book version of *The Bedford Handbook*, fully online, helps you engage your students and keep the course organized. Learn more at bedfordstmartins.com/xbook.

- **135 new teaching tips**. The Instructor's Annotated Edition offers ideas for class activities, assignments, and ways to pair handbook content with your pedagogy and program goals.

What hasn't changed?

- The handbook **covers a lot of ground**. Even the most popular search engines can't give students the confidence that comes with a coherent, authoritative reference that covers the topics they need in a writing course. *The Bedford Handbook* supports students as they compose for different purposes and audiences and in a variety of genres, as they collaborate, revise, conduct research, document sources, format their writing, and edit for clarity.

- It's **easy to use, easy to understand**. The handbook's explanations are brief, accessible, and illustrated by examples, most by student writers. The book's many boxes, charts, checklists, and menus are designed to help users find what they need quickly.

- It's **affordable**. *The Bedford Handbook* is the most reasonably priced comprehensive handbook on the market. And when students hang on to their handbook for the writing they'll do in other college courses, the cost is divided by four or eight semesters, and the value is even higher.

- It's **coherent, authoritative, trustworthy**. Writing-related resources on the Web offer *information*, but they don't offer *instruction*. With the ninth edition of *The Bedford Handbook*, students have reference content that has been class-tested by hundreds of thousands of students and instructors.

Acknowledgments

I am grateful for the expertise, enthusiasm, and classroom experience that so many individuals brought to the ninth edition.

Reviewers

Pamela Adelman, Averett University; Nancy Sosna Bohm, Lake Forest College; Deborah D. Borchers, Pueblo Community College; Susan H. Bussey, Georgia Gwinnett College; Marsha Cline, Central New Mexico Community College; Jessica Damian, Georgia Gwinnett College; Anne Dearing, Hudson Valley Community College; Ryan Diehl, Hutchinson Community College; Rebecca Renée Eades, Volunteer State Community College; Nancy Enright, Seton Hall University; Angela Erickson-Grussing, College of St. Benedict/St. John's University; Barbara Fister, Gustavus Adolphus College; Michael Frisoli, University of Maryland, University College; Stephanie Gai, College of the Redwoods; Maria Gladys Garcia, California State University, Long Beach; Jan Geyer, Hudson Valley Community College; Lowell Habel, Chapman University; Jenny Heil, Emory University; Angela Henning, William Jessup University; Anne Marie Hubbell, University of Maryland, University College; Lauren Ingraham, University of Tennessee at Chattanooga; John Jebb,

University of Delaware; Tara King, Pierce College; John Kupersmith, University of California, Berkeley; Jessica Labbé, Greensboro College; Jeanne I. Lakatos, Western Connecticut University; Leslie R. Leach, College of the Redwoods; Naomi Leimsider, Hunter College/CUNY; Carl Lindgren, College of St. Benedict/St. John's University; Chad Eric Littleton, University of Tennessee at Chattanooga; Diana Matthews, Santa Fe College; Jennifer McArdle, Western State Colorado University; Catherine Meeks, University of Tennessee at Chattanooga; Tagonei L. Mharapara, College of St. Benedict/St. John's University; Ruth Mirtz, University of Mississippi; Amanda E. Mita, Cornell University; Luis Nazario, Pueblo Community College; Julie Nichols, Northwest Florida State College; Erin Nunnally, Northern Virginia Community College; Timothy Parker, University of Tennessee at Chattanooga; Roberta Proctor, Palm Beach State College; Alex Quinlan, University of Tennessee at Chattanooga; Erin Radcliffe, Central New Mexico Community College; John Ribar, Palm Beach State College; Patrick Ryan, Western Connecticut State University; Alyssa Sepinwall, California State University, San Marcos; William Sheldon, Hutchinson Community College; Linda Darnell Stanley, Santa Fe College; Maxine Sturdivant, Wallace Community College; Laurel Topken, Western Nevada College; Tom Treffinger, Greenville Technical College; Cheli J. Turner, Greenville Technical College; Sandra Van Pelt, Belhaven University; Joseph P. Wofford III, Meredith College; Barbara Wurtzel, Springfield Technical Community College; Xuan Zheng, University of Washington

Editorial advisers

I am grateful to the following individuals, fellow teachers of writing, for helping me shape a new edition that responds to students' needs and reflects current pedagogy and practices.

Regina Dilgen, Palm Beach State College
Africa Fine, Palm Beach State College

Maria Garcia-Landry, Palm Beach State College
Edward Glenn, Miami Dade College
Mickey Hall, Volunteer State Community College
Chad Hammett, Texas State University
Traci Klass, Palm Beach State College
Jeannine Morgan, St. Johns River State College
Susan North, University of Tennessee at Chattanooga
Jan Odom, Georgia Gwinnett College
Sharon Prince, Wharton County Junior College
Lisa Shaw, Miami Dade College
Nancy Wilson, Texas State University
Rita Wisdom, Tarrant County College, Northeast

Survey participants

More than 1,000 first-year college writers responded to a survey about making the transition from high school writing to college writing, revising drafts, understanding college assignments, and more. Their responses informed the ninth edition's emphasis on four habits necessary for college success: curiosity, engagement, responsibility, and reflection. The survey participants represent the following schools:

Austin Community College
Brandeis University
Brigham Young University
Bristol Community College
Carroll Community College
Centennial College
College of Marin
Columbus State University
Contra Costa College
Contra Costa High School
Elon University
Florida State College at Jacksonville
George Mason University
Hudson Valley Community College
Johns Hopkins University
John Tyler Community College
McKinley Technology High School
Miami Dade College

Montgomery College,
Rockville
Oklahoma City University
Palm Beach State College
Pima Community College
Rock Valley College
Southern Utah University
Syracuse High School
University of Alabama
University of Arizona
University of California,
San Diego
University of California,
Santa Barbara
University of Central
Missouri
University of Central
Oklahoma
University of Mississippi
University of New Mexico
University of the District
of Columbia
Utah Valley University
Wichita State University

Student reviewers and contributors

I would like to thank the following students who agreed to be interviewed by their instructors about their experiences with the previous edition of *The Bedford Handbook*: Randall Alexander, Pierce College; Elizabeth Campbell, University of Maryland, University College; Gloria Cavanaugh, College of the Redwoods; Thomas Craig, Chapman University; Zachary Drye, University of Tennessee at Chattanooga; Corlando Grant, Seton Hall University; Robert Hazelwood, Saint Johns River Community College; Victoria Hendricks, Hutchinson Community College; Irvin Hernandez, University of Tennessee at Chattanooga; Susana Ibañez, California State University, Long Beach; Christina Jeffries, Northwest Florida State College; Kanyanat Jongjaisu, Northern Virginia Community College, Alexandria; Eugenia Kincaid, Central New Mexico Community College; Lezlie Lee-French, California State University, San Marcos; Alexandra Lentz, College of Saint Benedict/Saint John's University; Caitlin Lingerfelt, William Jessup University; Kaitlyn Lounsbury, Hudson Valley Community College; Mary Katherine O'Donnell, Greensboro College; Jacquethia Robinson, Georgia Gwinnett College; Kelvin Sablan, Western Nevada College; Suzy Schenk, Belhaven

University; Yang Song, Emory University; Veronica Swaim, Cornell University; Kristine Ward, Georgia Gwinnett College.

Including sample student work in each edition of the handbook makes the resource useful for you and your students. I would like to thank the following students who have let us adapt their papers as models: Ned Bishop, Sam Jacobs, Luisa Mirano, Michelle Nguyen, Anna Orlov, Emilia Sanchez, Matt Watson, and Ren Yoshida.

Bedford/St. Martin's

A comprehensive handbook is a collaborative writing project, and it is my pleasure to acknowledge and thank the enormously talented Bedford/St. Martin's editorial team, whose deep commitment to students informs each new feature of *The Bedford Handbook*. Joan Feinberg, president of Macmillan Higher Education and Diana Hacker's first editor, offers her superb judgment on every aspect of this handbook. Denise Wydra, president of Bedford/St. Martin's, brings her editorial eye and visionary thinking to the ninth edition, inspiring the handbook's exciting new integrated media format.

Michelle Clark, executive editor, is the editor every author dreams of having—a treasured friend and colleague and an endless source of creativity and clarity. Michelle combines wisdom with patience, imagination with practicality, and hard work with good cheer. Barbara Flanagan, senior editor, who has worked on Diana Hacker's handbooks for more than 25 years, brings insistence on precision and clarity as well as unrivaled expertise in documentation. Mara Weible, senior editor, brings to the ninth edition her teacher's sensibility and editor's unerring eye. Thanks to Kylie Paul, associate editor, for expertly managing the review process, developing student papers, assisting with the survey of more than 1,000 students, and coordinating details related to both our Web and print projects. And many thanks to the media team—Harriet Wald, Rebecca Merrill, Sarah Ferguson,

Kimberly Hampton, and Allison Hart—who led the development effort behind the integrated media components and the x-Book.

The passionate commitment to *The Bedford Handbook* of many Bedford colleagues—Karen Henry, Leasa Burton, Scott Berzon, Nick Carbone, Jimmy Fleming, Jane Helms, and Karen Soeltz—ensures that the ninth edition remains the most innovative and practical comprehensive handbook on the market. Many thanks to Rosemary Jaffe, senior production editor, who keeps us on schedule and gracefully turns a manuscript into a handbook and who, with this edition, produced both the print pages and the e-Pages. And thanks to Linda McLatchie, copyeditor, for her thoroughness and attention to detail; to Claire Seng-Niemoeller, text designer, who crafted a lighter, more open, and more accessible ninth edition of the book; and to Donna Dennison, art director, who has given the book a strikingly beautiful cover.

Last, but never least, I offer thanks to my own students who, over many years, have shaped my teaching and helped me understand their challenges in becoming college writers. Thanks to my friends and colleagues Suzanne Lane, Maxine Rodburg, Laura Saltz, and Kerry Walk for sustaining conversations about the teaching of writing. And thanks to my family: to Joshua Alper, an attentive reader of life and literature, for his steadfastness across the drafts; to my parents, Walter and Louise Sommers, and my aunt Elsie Adler, who encouraged me to write and set me forth on a career of writing and teaching; to my extended family, Ron and Charles Mary, Sam and Kate, and Alexander, for their good humor and good cheer; and to Rachel and Curran, Alexandra and Brian, witty and wise beyond measure, always generous with their instruction and inspiration in all things that matter.

Nancy Sommers

For Students: How to Use *The Bedford Handbook*

Your handbook will help you answer most of the questions you are likely to have as you plan, draft, and revise a piece of writing:

> How do I choose and narrow a topic?
> How can I consider different audiences when I'm drafting?
> How do I know when to begin a new paragraph?
> Where should I use a comma if I'm listing things in a sentence?
> How can I cite online videos in my works cited list?
> How can I write a reflective essay?

Lucky for you, your handbook consists of Integrated Media: print pages and e-Pages.

YOUR HANDBOOK: BEDFORD INTEGRATED MEDIA

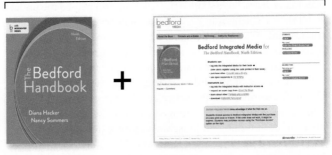

The print pages offer you advice, give you the rules to follow, and show you examples. The online e-Pages allow you to practice skills and apply the handbook's lessons to your own writing. The two work together — as a system. Visit hackerhandbooks .com/bedhandbook for short videos on how to use the system to help you be a confident college writer and for tutorials on how to use the print book's reference aids.

Contents

---

*   NEW TO THIS EDITION

Part I includes new help for college writers in *Becoming a college writer* pages. It offers two *Writing guides*: one for a literacy narrative, the other for a reflective letter.

* **NEW TO THIS EDITION**
  Part II includes a new section 5 on reading and writing about multimodal texts; *Becoming a college writer* pages; and *Writing guides* for an analytical essay and an argument.

✳ **NEW TO THIS EDITION**

All parts of the book include e-Pages 🄴, the online components of Integrated Media. Some sections also include LearningCurve ✅, game-like quizzing on grammar topics. See hackerhandbooks.com /bedhandbook.

✳ NEW TO THIS EDITION

Section 40 includes a new section on abbreviating units of measurement and a new section on the plural of abbreviations.

40d Units of measurement
40f Plural of abbreviations

✳   NEW TO THIS EDITION

Part X includes help for students with new *Becoming a college writer* pages; with a *Writing guide* for annotated bibliographies; and with additional support for managing a research project.

✻ NEW TO THIS EDITION

✻ NEW TO THIS EDITION
   The popular Citation at a glance pages have been expanded to include visual guidance for citing common sources in *Chicago* style.
   63d   *Chicago* documentation style

✻ NEW TO THIS EDITION
   The **appendix** provides eleven sample pages from a range of academic and professional genres.

Becoming a College Writer

Introduction: A letter from the author

"To become a college writer, practice, practice, practice. Just start writing. You will learn from the mistakes you make."
— **Maxime Duijist**, student, University of the District of Columbia

"Don't be afraid to write about something new, something you don't understand."
— **Amy Fortuna**, student, Brigham Young University

Dear Students:

Welcome to *The Bedford Handbook*—your handbook. Think of it as your guide to writing in college and beyond. Writing well helps you succeed in college courses and prepares you for the world of work. Becoming a confident writer, though, doesn't happen—for anyone—in a single course or semester. The students who are quoted throughout the handbook, your peers, are learning that it happens over time, in steps and in stages. You'll find that your confidence as a writer grows as you embrace new expectations—and as you "practice, practice, practice" being a college writer.

College offers many opportunities to write and to learn from the process of writing and revising. As you write, you will read and respond to what others have written, use evidence to support your ideas, and develop your ability to think carefully and creatively—no matter what discipline. In a sociology class, you might be asked to write a field report; in a nursing class, a case study; and in a literature class, a critical analysis. By writing in these disciplines, you contribute your ideas and join thinkers and writers who share interests, ideas, and ways of communicating with one another. *The Bedford Handbook* is designed

TEACHING TIP

This new introduction provides opportunities to talk about the expectations of college writing and to help students make the transition from high school writing. Students know that something more will be expected of them as college writers, but they are unsure what that might mean. You may find it useful to ask students: How do you think college writing will be different from high school writing?

to help you make the most of all your college writing experiences and to show you how to write successful college papers.

When college students are asked to reflect on why writing is important to them, many claim that writing helps them learn. One of my former students told me, "Once you write a paper, you begin to see so much more about the subject." Another student explained, "When you are not writing papers in a course, you take more of a tourist's view of a subject because you don't have to think in depth about any of the material." It is in the process of writing—of working in depth with your own thinking—that you find what's interesting in a subject and why you care about it. And it is through this process that you learn to figure out not just what you think, but *why* you think it.

Developing academic habits

Before developing the ninth edition of *The Bedford Handbook*, I wanted to figure out what the handbook needed and *why* it needed it. So I surveyed more than one thousand first-year students at thirty-five colleges and universities to learn more about the habits of effective college writers. I asked students how they planned, drafted, and revised their papers and what advice they would offer other writers to help them succeed. The students offered practical, *doable* advice that came to them through their own trial and error—advice such as "write drafts and ask people to give you feedback" and "the more you can take from a reading, the more you have to give as a writer." Their responses suggested that developing *curiosity*, *engagement*, *responsibility*, and *reflection*—in other words, good academic habits—makes good writers. These habits, often called *habits of mind*, develop over time, take practice and persistence, and require a willingness to learn from both successes and mistakes. This handbook will give you practice in developing these four key habits.

TEACHING TIP

Students are introduced to the idea that writing is a process that happens over time. Students will benefit from a discussion of the word *process*. How is the writing process similar to and different from other processes?

Throughout *The Bedford Handbook*, you will see several "Becoming a college writer" pages, which offer insights and advice from the college writers surveyed.

Curiosity   All good college writing starts with curiosity. What problems or issues intrigue you? What questions need to be explored? How could you solve a problem in a new way? Writing is much more interesting and rewarding when you explore questions you don't have answers to. Think of college writing not as a process of putting down on paper what you already know but as a way of discovering answers to what you can't explain.

> "Don't be afraid to ask questions. And make sure the questions you are asking are ones you and your readers care about."
>
> — **Dario Foroutan**, student, University of Arizona

BECOMING A CURIOUS WRITER

- Go beyond yes/no questions when deciding what to write about. You may start with a question such as *Do SAT scores predict students' academic success?* But you'll be able to dig a little deeper into your subject if you focus on a particular group of students—multilingual students, for instance—and ask *how* or *why* SAT scores predict academic success for this group.

- When you encounter perspectives that are different from yours, be open-minded. Ask classmates how they came to different interpretations about a reading or an idea or why they reached a different conclusion from looking at the same data.

- Read each assignment carefully, and note any questions you have. What is the purpose of the assignment? Is a specific genre expected? And who is the intended audience? Curious writers investigate the details of each assignment.

TEACHING TIP

Students are introduced to four habits—*curiosity*, *engagement*, *responsibility*, and *reflection*—and given practical steps for *becoming curious*, for *becoming responsible*, and so forth. The emphasis here is on *becoming* and specific ways to enact these habits. Try using this question to prompt a class discussion: What does it take for a habit to become habitual? Reflection, in particular, is a good habit to initiate at the start of the semester. You might encourage students, further, to reflect about their own writing habits, perhaps in a brief written response: How do they approach assignments? What are some effective habits they have developed as writers? And what are some less-than-effective habits—procrastination, for example, or staring at a blank computer screen?

Engagement   Writing is a social activity that brings you into conversations with scholars, instructors, classmates, and peers. Reading actively allows you to engage with other writers. Participating in classroom or online discussions deepens your thinking and gives you opportunities to engage with your instructors and classmates. Seeking feedback from and reaching out to others on campus who might support your learning allows you to engage with a wider learning community. Effective college writers have learned that active approaches to learning work much better than passive ones.

> "Find a purpose in your writing assignments. And try to write what you would sincerely be interested in reading."
>
> — **Nicole Zimmer**, student, Bristol Community College

BECOMING AN ENGAGED WRITER

- Write multiple drafts to pursue a subject in stages and to make the process manageable. You don't need to know *exactly* what you want to say at the outset; you may begin thinking and writing in one direction and then change course as you think and read more about your topic. Along the way, as you draft and revise your work, reach out to readers who can help you shape your work in progress.

- Knock on doors and ask for help with your writing. Make a habit of visiting your instructor during office hours. Use college resources — librarians, tutors, writing center consultants, and advisers — to talk through ideas, test arguments, and clarify your thinking. Good college writers seek feedback and use resources.

- Consider joining a writing group or a study group. Working with a small community of classmates or other students makes learning a productive exchange of ideas (you give something — and then get something in return), reduces stress, and boosts motivation.

Responsibility   Engaging with the ideas of other writers and thinkers requires responsibility—to represent their ideas accurately and honestly and to acknowledge their contributions to your work. By giving credit to your sources, you write with integrity, showing yourself as a responsible writer who should be taken seriously. And you show your readers the boundaries between your own ideas and those of your sources, acknowledging contributions to your thinking.

Being responsible also means being accountable to collaborators in team or group projects. Such projects often mirror real-world writing situations, and the practice you get working toward a common goal with peers is valuable.

> "Use your sources reliably without warping the original meanings of the words."
>
> — **James Thermitus**, student, Miami Dade College

BECOMING A RESPONSIBLE WRITER

- Understand the sources you use. Doing so will allow you to put your sources to work for you. In other words, you figure out what *you* want to say and then use sources to develop and support your ideas. Being responsible means avoiding patching together sources to let them speak for you.

- Use sources responsibly by developing key habits: Keep track of what you read or view, place quotation marks around words copied from sources, use your own words in paraphrases and summaries, maintain accurate records for all bibliographic information, and never copy and paste Web sources directly into drafts. Use the style (MLA, APA, *Chicago*) preferred in your discipline or by your instructor to cite sources.

- For group projects, attend all meetings, whether they happen in person or online. Take notes and contribute ideas. When members of the group disagree about how to proceed, try going back to the roots of the project: What is the purpose of the project? What genre are you producing? Who is your target audience? Collaborating on a project can bring stress, for sure, but it also fosters growth and responsibility.

Reflection   Reflection involves questioning experiences to learn from them. Being reflective in a writing class often means stopping to think about your own writing habits or approaches to writing tasks. By examining your decisions, successes, and challenges, you'll be able to figure out what's working and what's not, evaluate your writing process, participate in your own learning, and transfer skills from one writing assignment to the next.

> "Be passionate about learning to write. The more you learn about who you are as a writer, the easier it is to write successfully."
>
> — **Lorda Laurent**, student, Palm Beach State College

BECOMING A REFLECTIVE WRITER

- Track your writing development by keeping a journal or blog. Use your entries to ask questions about your habits and patterns as a writer and to build an awareness of yourself as a writer. For instance, how do you begin each assignment? Or how do you respond to feedback on your drafts? What types of comments help you revise?

- Take time to talk with your instructor after the first or second assignment. Make notes about what you are learning and where you're struggling. Taking time to examine your habits and approaches can be a valuable learning experience.

- Keep a portfolio, whether or not you're assigned to do so. A portfolio is simply a collection of your work and often includes drafts as well as final pieces. Taking the time to review previous projects—and especially the comments

TEACHING TIP

The "As you write" exercise gives students an opportunity to practice academic habits with their peers. It also gives students an opportunity to see the benefits of listening to and learning from their peers. If you are teaching an online course or a course with a significant online component, you might ask students to engage in a conversation about the photograph through the class discussion board.

you received on drafts or final copies — will provide direction for your next writing project and allow you to track your growth as a writer.

Best wishes for a successful year,

Nancy Sommers

As you write: Practicing academic habits

The e-Pages for *The Bedford Handbook* include writing prompts that will help you apply the handbook's advice to your own writing. References to the e-Pages occur throughout the book; they look like this:

hackerhandbooks.com/bedhandbook

e The writing process > As you write: Exploring a subject

The following writing prompt, the only one that appears here in the print book, gives you an opportunity to practice academic habits — curiosity, engagement, responsibility, and reflection. Spend time viewing the image on page 8, a photograph by David Sacks. Since the photograph doesn't speak for itself, you need to examine it closely to discover possible interpretations. Start by listing the details you notice (see 1b).

Be curious What details do you notice? What intrigues you about the image? What does or does not make sense? Brainstorm questions about the photograph. Select the question that seems most promising and write a paragraph response. Use your paragraph to offer a possible interpretation of the photograph.

Be engaged Discuss your questions and interpretation with two classmates. How are their questions and interpretations

---

TEACHING TIP

Part of becoming a college writer is learning *how* to use a handbook. *The Bedford Handbook* is a resource for students as they practice the habits and develop the skills they need to write successfully. You might ask students: Where in your handbook will you find help for asking questions, writing multiple drafts, becoming a peer reviewer, writing reflectively, or learning to use sources responsibly? Consider assigning a scavenger hunt targeted to content in the book.

Tororo School, Uganda

similar to or different from yours? As you listen to one another's interpretation of the photograph, ask questions and challenge classmates to explain their interpretations.

Be responsible Summarize the views and interpretations of your classmates. Ask them if you have stated their positions fairly.

Be reflective Reflect on the process. What did you learn from thinking about a photograph with several possible interpretations? What did you learn from listening to your classmates and engaging with their ideas? What was challenging about this exercise?

AN ADDITIONAL RESOURCE ON HABITS OF MIND

The Council of Writing Program Administrators, along with the National Council of Teachers of English and the National Writing Project, recently developed "Framework for Success in Postsecondary Writing" (2011). The "Framework" addresses college readiness in the context of the skills and "habits of mind" necessary to achieve success in college today. You can read the executive summary or the full text at wpacouncil.org/framework.

PART I

The Writing Process

Becoming a College Writer

Choose topics you care about

"Make connections between yourself and what you are learning. Care about what you are learning, and care about how you are learning." — **Shaye Heyman**, student, University of New Mexico

College writing can seem intimidating, especially when you first try to grasp how expectations for college writing differ from those for high school writing. Something more and something different are being asked of you, but what?

One way to approach each college writing assignment, as Shaye Heyman suggests, is to make the effort to find personal connections with what you are learning. Writing about a topic you care about enables you to write with more authority, confidence, and success. Even when you're not free to choose the topic, you can choose the angle by thinking, "What's at stake here for me (or my family, my community, my school)?"

- Remember a time when something you said or wrote had power or really mattered. What do you think made your words so powerful? Why?

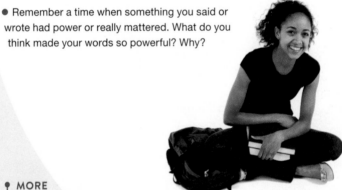

MORE
Choosing subjects, 1a
Understanding an assignment, page 17
Exploring subjects, 1b

TEACHING TIP

Use Shaye Heyman's quotation as a catalyst for class discussion. Ask students to think about situations when they wrote about topics that mattered to them. Some of these situations might have been at work; some might have been in school. Project Heyman's words to give students an opportunity to discuss her advice. Ask students: What does it mean to "make connections between yourself and what you are learning"? What does the phrase "how you are learning" mean? As an alternative to the prompt provided in the text, you could ask students to identify the writerly habits they need to develop to follow Heyman's advice.

Writing is a process of figuring out what you think, not a matter of recording already developed thoughts. Since it's not possible to think about everything all at once, most experienced writers handle a piece of writing in stages. You will generally move from planning to drafting to revising, but as your ideas develop, you will find yourself circling back and returning to earlier stages.

1 Exploring, planning, and drafting

Before composing a first draft, spend some time generating ideas. Mull over your subject while listening to music, taking a walk, or driving to work; or jot down inspirations or explore your questions with a willing listener. Consider these questions: What do you find puzzling, striking, or interesting about your subject? What would you like to know more about? Be curious and open to new ideas and different points of view. Explore questions you don't have answers to.

1a Assess the writing situation.

Begin by taking a look at your writing situation. The key elements of a writing situation include the following:

- subject
- purpose
- audience
- genre
- sources of information
- constraints (length, document design, reviewers, deadlines)

TEACHING TIP

To initiate a discussion about the writing process, present or project these three quotations from writers on writing:

Get it down. Take chances. It may be bad, but it's the only way you can do anything really good. — William Faulkner

The act of composition is a series of discoveries. — E. L. Doctorow

Convince yourself that you are working in clay, not marble, on paper, not eternal bronze: Let that first sentence be as stupid as it wishes.

— Jacques Barzun

It is likely that you will make final decisions about all of these matters later in the writing process—after a first draft, for example—but you can save yourself time by thinking about as many of them as possible in advance. For a quick checklist, see the following chart.

Checklist for assessing the writing situation

Subject

- Has the subject (or a range of possible subjects) been assigned to you, or are you free to choose your own?
- What interests you about your subject? What questions would you like to explore?
- Why is your subject worth writing about? How might readers benefit?
- Do you need to narrow your subject (because of length restrictions, for instance)?

Purpose and audience

- Why are you writing: To inform readers? To persuade them? To call them to action? To offer an interpretation of a text?
- Who are your readers? How well informed are they about the subject? What do you want them to learn?
- How interested and attentive are your readers likely to be? Will they resist any of your ideas? What possible objections will you need to anticipate and counter?
- What is your relationship to your readers: Student to instructor? Citizen to citizen? Expert to novice? Employee to supervisor?

Genre

- What genre (type of writing) does your assignment require: A report? A proposal? An analysis of data? An essay?
- If the genre is not assigned, what genre is appropriate for your subject, purpose, and audience?

TEACHING TIP

Many writing programs have developed outcomes, such as the WPA Outcomes Statement, to identify their program's writing goals. Many program outcomes focus on the writing process — students' abilities to write multiple drafts, learn to critique the work of others, and understand the collaborative and social aspects of the writing process. Present or project one or two key outcomes (from your writing program) for discussion. Ask students to find the specific pages and sections of their handbook that provide instruction for these outcomes.

TEACHING TIP

Some teachers like to use writing assignments from different disciplines to help students grasp how subject, purpose, audience, genre, and

CHECKLIST FOR ASSESSING THE WRITING SITUATION (*cont.*)

- What are the expectations and conventions of your assigned genre? For instance, what type of evidence is typically used in the genre?
- Does the genre require a specific design format or method of organization?
- Does the genre require or benefit from visuals, such as photos, drawings, or graphs?

Sources of information

- Where will your information come from: Reading? Research? Direct observation? Interviews? Questionnaires?
- What type of evidence suits your subject, purpose, audience, and genre?
- What documentation style is required: MLA? APA? *Chicago*?

Length and document design

- Do you have any length specifications? If not, what length seems appropriate, given your subject, purpose, audience, and genre?
- Is a particular document format required? If so, do you have guidelines to follow or examples to consult?
- How might visuals — charts, graphs, tables — help you convey information and support your purpose?

Reviewers and deadlines

- Who will be reviewing your draft: Your instructor? A writing center tutor? One or more classmates?
- What are your deadlines? How much time will you need to allow for the various stages of writing, including proofreading and printing or posting the final draft?
- Will you be sharing a draft electronically or in hard copy? If electronically, will your readers be able to handle your file's size and format?

expected evidence vary across disciplines. If you include this in your pedagogy, consider assigning students to read Part XI, Writing in the Disciplines, to supplement your instruction. Further, you might have students talk with faculty in their major or in another discipline to see what the expectations are for writers in that discipline.

TEACHING TIP

Students are familiar with various genres — poems, short stories, graphic novels, reports — but often they are unfamiliar with the term. Introduce students to works in a few different genres, and ask them to think about the similarities and differences among these genres. To guide the discussion, use the "Understanding genre" questions on page 21.

Academic English

What counts as good writing varies from culture to culture and even among groups within cultures. In some situations, you will need to become familiar with the writing styles — such as direct or indirect, personal or impersonal, plain or embellished — that are valued by the culture or discipline for which you are writing.

Subject

Frequently your subject will be given to you. In a psychology class, for example, you might be asked to explain Bruno Bettelheim's Freudian analysis of fairy tales. In a composition course, assignments often ask you to analyze texts and evaluate arguments. In the business world, you may be assigned to draft a marketing plan. When you are free to choose your own subject, let your own curiosity focus your choice. If you are studying television, radio, and the Internet in a communications course, for example, you might ask yourself which of these subjects interests you most. Perhaps you want to learn more about the role streaming video can play in activism and social change. Look through your readings and class notes to see if you can identify questions you'd like to explore further in an essay.

Make sure that you can reasonably investigate your subject in the space you have. If you are limited to a few pages, for example, you could not do justice to a broad subject such as "videos as agents of social change." You could, however, focus on one aspect of the subject — perhaps contradictory claims about the effectiveness of "narrowcasting," or creating video content for small, specific audiences.

If your interest in a subject stems from your personal experience, you will want to ask what it is about your experience that would interest your audience and why. For example, if you have volunteered at

> **MAKING THE MOST OF YOUR HANDBOOK**
>
> Effective research writers often start by asking a question.
>
> ▶ Posing questions for research: 50b

TEACHING TIP

Before students draft their first assignment, give them practice in narrowing a subject to a topic. As a class or small group activity, ask students to practice narrowing the subjects in Exercise 1–1 by asking a series of questions that they are curious to answer.

a homeless shelter, you might have spent some time talking to homeless children and learning about their needs. Perhaps you can use your experience to broaden your readers' understanding of the issues, to persuade an organization to fund an after-school program for homeless children, or to propose changes in legislation.

Whether or not you choose your own subject, it's important to be aware of the expectations of each writing situation. The chart on page 17 suggests ways to interpret assignments.

Purpose

Your purpose, or reason for writing, will often be dictated by your writing situation. Perhaps you have been asked to draft a proposal requesting funding for a student organization, to report the results of a psychology experiment, or to write about the controversy surrounding genetically modified (GM) foods for the school newspaper. Even though your overall purpose may be fairly obvious in such situations, a closer look at the assignment can help you make some necessary decisions. How detailed should the proposal be? How technical does your psychology professor expect your report to be? Do you want to inform students about the GM food controversy or to change their attitudes toward it?

In many writing situations, part of your challenge will be discovering a purpose. Asking yourself why readers should care about what you are saying can help you decide what your purpose might be. Perhaps your subject is magnet schools — schools that draw students from different neighborhoods because of features such as advanced science classes or a concentration on the arts. If you have discussed magnet schools in class, a description of how these schools work probably will not interest you or your readers. But maybe you have discovered that your county's magnet schools are not promoting diversity as had been planned, and you want to call your readers to action.

SCHOLARS ON THE TEACHING SITUATION

Skorczewski, Dawn. "From Playing the Role to Being Yourself: Becoming the Teacher in the Writing Classroom." *Teaching One Moment at a Time.* Amherst: U of Massachusetts P, 2005. 15–37. Print. Skorczewski uses her experiences as a new instructor and draws on the stories of several others as she examines how to be oneself and an authoritative teacher at the same time. The balance, she argues, is reached over time, with experience, by embracing the fear inherent in the teaching situation, and through a conscious effort on the teacher's part to "tell yourself who you are and who you are not in the classroom."

Although no precise guidelines will lead you to a purpose, you can begin by asking, "Why am I writing?" and "What is my goal?" Identify which one or more of the following aims you hope to accomplish.

PURPOSES FOR WRITING

to inform	to evaluate
to persuade	to recommend
to entertain	to request
to call readers to action	to propose
to change attitudes	to provoke thought
to analyze	to express feelings
to argue	to summarize

Writers often misjudge their own purposes, summarizing when they should be analyzing, or expressing feelings about problems instead of proposing solutions. Before beginning any writing task, pause to ask, "Why am I communicating with my readers?" This question will lead you to another important question: "Just who are my readers?"

Audience

Audience analysis, a process in which you identify your readers and their expectations, can often lead you to an effective strategy for reaching your readers. A writer whose purpose was to persuade first-year college students to recycle began by making some observations about her audience (see p. 18).

Her analysis led the writer to appeal to her readers' competitive nature and gaming experience — she invited college students to think about recycling as achieving different levels in a video game. Her audience analysis also warned her against adopting a preachy tone that her readers might find offensive. Instead of lecturing, she decided to draw examples from her own experience with the "levels" of being green — recycling paper and plastic, carrying a refillable water bottle, biking to campus, buying

SCHOLARS ON THE TEACHING SITUATION

Villanueva, Victor, and Kristin L. Arola, eds. *Cross-Talk in Comp Theory: A Reader*. 3rd ed. Urbana: NCTE, 2011. Print. The authors track the conversations within the composition community in forty-three essays by frequently cited scholars such as Mike Rose, Patricia Bizzell, David Bartholomae, and Richard Braddock. The third edition covers the new landscape of teaching and composing with technology, especially amid the rise of social media and the expectation that students can produce multimodally. A new chapter, "Virtual Talk: Composing beyond the Word," includes newer voices: Cynthia Selfe, Kathleen Blake Yancey, Diana George, and others.

Understanding an assignment

Determining the purpose of an assignment

The wording of an assignment may suggest its purpose. You might be expected to do one or more of the following in a college writing assignment:

- summarize information from textbooks, lectures, or research (See 4c.)
- analyze ideas and concepts (See 4d.)
- take a position on a topic and defend it with evidence (See 6.)
- synthesize (combine ideas from) several sources and create an original argument (See 55c and 60.)

Understanding how to answer an assignment's question

Many assignments will ask you to answer a *how* or *why* question. You cannot answer such questions using only facts; instead, you will need to take a position. For example, the question "*What* are the survival rates for leukemia patients?" can be answered with facts. The question "*Why* are the survival rates for leukemia patients in one state lower than those in a neighboring state?" must be answered with both facts and interpretation. If a list of questions appears in the assignment, be careful — instructors rarely expect you to answer all the questions in order. Look instead for topics or themes that will help you ask your own questions.

Recognizing implied questions

When you are asked to *discuss*, *analyze*, *agree or disagree with*, or *consider* a topic, your instructor will often expect you to answer a *how* or *why* question.

Discuss the effects of the No Child Left Behind Act on special education programs. =	*How* has the No Child Left Behind Act affected special education programs?
Consider the recent rise of attention deficit hyperactivity disorder diagnoses. =	*Why* are diagnoses of attention deficit hyperactivity disorder rising?

SCHOLARS ON THE TEACHING SITUATION

Logan, Shirley Wilson. "Changing Missions, Shifting Positions, and Breaking Silences." *College Composition and Communication* 55.2 (2003): 330–42. Print. In this version of her address as chair of the 2003 CCCC convention, Logan reviews eleven important position statements that the CCCC has made on professional standards and students' linguistic rights, beginning with the 1974 statement "Students' Right to Their Own Language" and ending with the 2001 "Statement on Second Language Writing and Writers." After her 2003 address, Logan appointed a committee to create the position statement "Teaching, Learning, and Assessing Writing in Digital Environments," which was adopted in February 2004.

AUDIENCE ANALYSIS

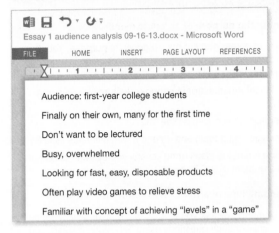

used clothing, taking notes on a laptop, and so on. The result was an essay that reached its readers instead of alienating them.

In some writing situations, the audience will not be defined for you. But the choices you make as you write will tell readers who you think they are (novices or experts, for example) and will show respect for your readers' perspectives.

For help with audience analysis when composing e-mail messages, see the chart on page 20.

Academic audiences In college writing, considerations of audience can be more complex than they seem at first. Your instructors will read your essay, of course, but most instructors play multiple roles while reading. Their first and most obvious roles are as coach and evaluator; but they are also intelligent and objective readers, the kind of people who might reasonably be informed, entertained, or called to action by what you have to say and who want to learn from your insights and ideas.

Some instructors specify an audience, such as readers of a local newspaper, a hypothetical supervisor, or peers in a particular field. Other instructors expect you to imagine an audience

ADDITIONAL RESOURCE ON THE TEACHING SITUATION

TeachingCentral (bedfordstmartins.com/teachingcentral). This Bedford/ St. Martin's collection offers free classroom materials and readings, a blog space for teachers to share ideas, new media materials for professional development, and a complete list of free print and online resources for instructors.

appropriate to your purpose, subject, and genre. Still others prefer that you write for a general audience of educated readers—nonspecialists who can be expected to read with a critical eye.

Business audiences Writers in the business world often find themselves writing for multiple audiences. A letter to a client, for instance, might be distributed to sales representatives as well. Readers of a report might include people with and without technical expertise, or readers who want details and those who prefer a quick overview.

To satisfy the demands of multiple audiences, business writers have developed a variety of strategies: attaching cover letters to detailed reports, adding boldface headings, placing summaries in the margin, and using abstracts or executive summaries to highlight important points.

Public audiences Writers in communities often write to a specific audience—a legislative representative, readers of a local newspaper, fellow members of a social group. With public writing, it is more likely that you are familiar with the views your readers hold and the assumptions they make, so you may be better able to judge how to engage those readers. If you are writing to a group of other parents to share ideas for lowering school bus transportation costs, for instance, you may have a good sense of whether to lead with a logical analysis of other school-related fees or with a fiery criticism of key decision makers.

Genre

When writing for a college course, pay close attention to the genre, or type of writing, assigned. Each genre is a category of writing meant for a specific purpose and audience, with its own set of agreed-upon expectations and conventions for style, structure, and document design. Sometimes an assignment specifies the genre—an essay in a writing class, a lab report or research proposal in a biology class, a policy memo in a criminal justice class, or an executive summary in a business class. Sometimes

SCHOLARS ON THE TEACHING SITUATION

Hacker, Diana. "Following the Tao." *Teaching English in the Two-Year College* 27.3 (2000): 297–300. Print. Hacker suggests that the Chinese classic *Tao Te Ching*, which offers advice to rulers, can benefit teachers as well. In fact, she says, many of the *Tao*'s insights have become accepted wisdom in the teaching of composition over the past twenty-five years. Hacker's article is organized around five of her favorite lines from the *Tao*: Practice nonaction. Yield and overcome; bend and be straight. In action, watch the timing. Give up learning and put an end to your troubles. Achieve greatness in little things.

Considering audience when writing e-mail messages

In academic, business, and public contexts, you will want to show readers that you value their time. Here are some strategies for writing effective e-mails:

- Use a concise, meaningful subject line to help readers sort messages and set priorities.
- Put the most important part of your message at the beginning so that your reader sees it without scrolling.
- Write concisely; keep paragraphs short.
- For long, detailed messages, provide a summary at the beginning.
- Avoid writing in all capital letters or all lowercase letters.
- Proofread for typos and obvious errors that are likely to slow down readers.

You will also want to follow conventions of etiquette and avoid violating standards of academic integrity. Here are some strategies for writing responsible e-mails:

- E-mail messages can easily be forwarded to others and reproduced. Do not write anything that you would not want attributed to you.
- Do not forward another person's message without asking his or her permission.
- If you write an e-mail message that includes someone else's words — opinions, statistics, song lyrics, and so forth — let your reader know the source for that material and where any borrowed material begins and ends.
- Choose your words carefully because e-mail messages can easily be misread. Without your voice, facial gestures, or body language, a message can be misunderstood.
- Pay careful attention to tone; avoid writing anything that you wouldn't be comfortable saying directly to a reader.

SCHOLARS ON THE WRITING SITUATION

Sommers, Nancy, and Laura Saltz. "The Novice as Expert: Writing the Freshman Year." *College Composition and Communication* 56.1 (2004): 124–49. Print. Using their findings from a longitudinal study of four hundred Harvard undergraduates, the authors describe the students' writing experiences in their first-year courses other than English. They discuss the teaching methods that helped successful students realize that they "get something" more than just a grade if the writing matters to them and that they have some knowledge to "give" to their readers. At two extremes on the spectrum of writing experience were students for whom the only value in writing was a grade or a means of personal expression and students who understood that writing is "the heart of what they know and learn."

the genre is yours to choose, and you need to decide if a particular genre—a poster presentation, an audio essay, a Web page, or a podcast, for example—will help you communicate your purpose and reach readers.

It is helpful to think of genre as an opportunity to enter a discipline and join a group of thinkers and writers who share interests, ideas, and ways of communicating with one another. For instance, if you are asked to write a lab report for a biology class or a case study for an education class, you have the opportunity to practice the methods used by scholars in these fields and to communicate with them. For the lab report, your purpose might be to present the results of an experiment; your evidence would be the data you collected while conducting your experiment, and you would use scientific terms expected by your audience. For the case study, your purpose might be to analyze student-teacher interactions in a single classroom; your evidence might be data collected from interviews and observations. (For a discussion of genres in various disciplines, see 65.)

To understand the expectations of different genres—and the opportunities present in different genres—you can begin by asking some of the following questions.

UNDERSTANDING GENRE

If the genre has been assigned, the following questions will help you focus on its expectations.

- Do you have access to samples of writing in the genre that has been assigned?
- Who is the audience? What interests, ideas, and beliefs do typical readers of the genre share?
- What type of evidence is usually required in the genre?
- What specialized vocabulary do readers expect in the genre?
- What citation style do readers expect?
- Does the genre require a specific format or organization?

If you are free to choose the genre, the following questions will help you focus on its expectations.

- What is your purpose for writing: To argue a position? To instruct? To present a process? To inspire? To propose?
- Who is your audience? What do you know about your readers or viewers?
- What method of presenting information would appeal to your audience: Reasoned paragraphs? Diagrams and pictures? Video? Slides?
- What are the advantages and disadvantages of the genre you have chosen, given your purpose, audience, and deadline?

Sources of information

Where will your evidence—facts, details, and examples—come from? What kind of reading, observation, or research is necessary to meet the expectations of your assignment?

Reading Reading is an important way to deepen your understanding of a topic and expand your perspective. It will be your primary source of information for many college assignments. For example, if you are assigned to write a literature review for a psychology or biology class, you will need to read and evaluate the research that has been published about a particular topic. Or if you are assigned to write a case study for a nursing class, you will read and analyze detailed information about a client's health issues.

Read with an open mind to learn from the insights and research of others. Take notes on your thoughts, impressions, and questions. Your notes can be a way to enter a conversation with the authors of the texts you read. (See 4.) And always keep careful records of any sources you read and consult.

Observation Observation is an excellent means of collecting information about a wide range of subjects, such as gender relationships on a popular television program, the clichéd language of sports announcers, or a current exhibit at the local art museum. For such subjects, do not rely on your memory alone;

your information will be fresher and more detailed if you actively collect it, with a notebook, laptop, or voice recorder.

Interviews and questionnaires   Interviews and questionnaires can supply detailed and interesting information on many subjects. A nursing student interested in the care of terminally ill patients might interview hospice nurses; a criminal justice major might speak with a local judge about alternative sentencing for first offenders; a future teacher might conduct a survey on the use of whiteboard technology in local elementary schools.

It is a good idea to record interviews to preserve any vivid quotations that you might want to weave into your essay. Circulating questionnaires by e-mail or on a Web site will facilitate responses. Keep questions simple, and specify a deadline to ensure that you get a reasonable number of replies. (See also 50e.)

Length and document design

Writers seldom have complete control over length requirements. Journalists usually write within strict word limits set by their editors, businesspeople routinely aim for conciseness, and most college assignments specify an approximate length.

Your writing situation may also require a certain document design. Specific formats are used in business for letters, memos, and reports. In the academic world, you may need to learn precise disciplinary and genre conventions for lab reports, critiques, research papers, and so on. For most undergraduate essays, a standard format is acceptable. (See the appendix, pp. 805–17.)

In some writing situations, you will be free to create your own design, complete with headings, displayed lists, and perhaps visuals such as charts and graphs.

Reviewers and deadlines

In college classes, the use of reviewers is common. Some instructors play the role of reviewer for you; others may suggest that you visit your college's writing center. Still others schedule peer review sessions in class or online. Such sessions give you a chance to hear what other students think about your draft in progress. (See 2a.)

Deadlines are a key element of any writing situation. They help you plan your time and map out what you can accomplish in that time. For complex writing projects, such as research papers, you'll need to plan your time carefully. By working backward from the final deadline, you can create a schedule of target dates for completing parts of the process. (See p. 517 for an example.)

> **MAKING THE MOST OF YOUR HANDBOOK**
>
> Peer review can benefit writers at any stage of the writing process.
>
> ▸ Guidelines for peer reviewers: page 58

EXERCISE 1–1   Narrow three of the following subjects into topics that would be manageable for an essay of two to five pages.

1. Treatments for mental illness
2. An experience with racism or sexism
3. Handheld electronic devices in the classroom
4. Images of women in video games
5. Mandatory drug testing in the workplace

EXERCISE 1–2   Suggest a purpose and an audience for three of the following subjects. *More practice:* e

1. Genetic modification of cash crops
2. Government housing for military veterans
3. The future of print magazines
4. Working with special needs children
5. Hybrid cars

1b Explore your subject.

Experiment with one or more techniques for exploring your subject and discovering your purpose:

hackerhandbooks.com/bedhandbook

e The writing process > Exercises: 1–3
e The writing process > As you write: Exploring a subject

TEACHING TIP

Some teachers find it helpful to give students practice in asking questions — in investigating a topic in detail. Students are often reluctant to take risks and experiment with questions they don't have answers to. Emphasize the writerly habit of *curiosity* — all good writing begins with being curious, asking questions, and caring about the answers to these questions. In class, try brainstorming a list of questions to ask about certain policies or practices at your school. You may even want to follow up by assigning teams to go out and find answers to those questions.

- talking and listening
- reading and annotating texts
- asking questions
- brainstorming (listing ideas)
- clustering
- freewriting
- keeping a journal
- blogging

Whatever technique you turn to, the goal is the same: to generate ideas that will lead you to a question, a problem, or a topic that you want to explore further.

Talking and listening

Because writing is a process of figuring out what you think about a subject, it is useful to try out your ideas on other people. Conversation can deepen and refine your ideas before you begin to write them down. By talking and listening to others, you can also discover what they find interesting, what they are curious about, and where they disagree with you. If you are writing an argument, you can try it out on listeners with other points of view.

Many writers begin a project by brainstorming ideas in a group, debating with friends, or chatting with an instructor. Others prefer to record themselves by talking through their thoughts. Some writers exchange ideas by sending e-mail or texts or by posting to blogs. You may be encouraged to share ideas with your classmates and instructor in an online workshop where you can begin to explore your thoughts before starting a draft.

Reading and annotating texts

Reading is an important way to deepen your understanding of a topic, learn from the insights and research of others, and expand your perspective. Books, articles, reports, and visuals such as photographs, cartoons, videos, and other Web content can be important sources to explore as you generate ideas. Annotating a text, written or visual, encourages you to read actively—to

SCHOLARS ON THE WRITING PROCESS

Dunn, Patricia A. *Talking, Sketching, Moving: Multiple Literacies in the Teaching of Writing.* Portsmouth: Boynton, 2001. Print. Dunn argues that too many students are excluded by our "print-loving pedagogies" and that we can all benefit if we make space for the multiple literacies students bring to our writing classrooms. In a lengthy and very useful third chapter, she describes a variety of strategies — visual, aural, and kinesthetic — that teachers can use to help even the most proficient writers generate ideas and organize their texts in more insightful ways. Strategies include "rhetorical proof cards"; sketching-to-learn and moving-to-learn activities; sketching to generate metaphors; and connecting ideas through oral outlines and oral journals.

highlight key concepts, to note contradictions in an argument, or to raise questions for further research and investigation. (See 4a for an annotated article and 5a for an annotated advertisement.)

Asking questions

When gathering material for a story, journalists routinely ask themselves Who? What? When? Where? Why? and How? In addition to helping journalists get started, these questions ensure that they will not overlook an important fact.

Whenever you are writing about ideas, events, or people, whether current or historical, asking questions is one way to get started. One student, whose topic was the negative reaction in 1915 to D. W. Griffith's silent film *The Birth of a Nation*, began exploring her topic with this set of questions:

- *Who* objected to the film?
- *What* were the objections?
- *When* were protests first voiced?
- *Where* were protests most strongly expressed?
- *Why* did protesters object to the film?
- *How* did protesters make their views known?

As often happens, the answers to these questions led to another question the writer wanted to explore. After she discovered that protesters objected to the film's racist portrayal of African Americans, she wondered whether their protests had changed attitudes. This question prompted an interesting topic for a paper: Did the film's stereotypes lead to positive, if unintended, consequences?

In academic writing, scholars often generate ideas by posing questions related to a specific discipline. If you are writing in a particular

> **MAKING THE MOST OF YOUR HANDBOOK**
>
> Effective college writers begin by asking questions.
>
> ▶ Asking questions in academic disciplines: 64b

WRITING CENTER DIRECTORS ON THE WRITING PROCESS

"Many regular users of the writing center recognize that they can integrate the way the tutors work with their own writing process, so that one step includes working with a draft or a series of ideas or an outline, another getting feedback. When feedback thus also becomes part of their writing process, they learn to build time into their long-range writing plans for tutor/peer interaction instead of trying to cram their paper into the keyboard at the last minute. This global state of mind — seeing one's writing as part of larger processes involving the writing center, the professor's expectations, the world of research and ideas, other audiences (real or imagined) — is a key factor in the development of effective writers."

— Scott Hendrix, director of writing, Albion College

discipline, try to find out which questions its scholars typically explore. Look for clues in assigned readings, assignments, and class discussions to understand how a discipline's questions help you understand its concerns. (See 64.)

Brainstorming

Brainstorming, or listing ideas, is a good way to figure out what you know and what questions you have. Here is a list one student writer jotted down for an essay about community service requirements for college students:

> Volunteered in high school.
>
> Teaching adults to read motivated me to study education.
>
> "The best way to find yourself is to lose yourself in the service of others." — Gandhi
>
> Volunteering helps students find interests and career paths.
>
> Is required volunteering a contradiction?
>
> Many students need to work to pay college tuition.
>
> Enough time to study, work, and volunteer?
>
> Can't students volunteer for their own reasons?
>
> What schools have community service requirements?
>
> What do students say about community service requirements?

The ideas and questions appear here in the order in which they first occurred to the writer. Later she rearranged them, grouped them under general categories, deleted some, and added others. These initial thoughts led the writer to questions that helped her narrow her topic. In other words, she treated her early list as a source of ideas and a springboard to new ideas, not as an outline.

Clustering

Clustering (sometimes called *mapping*) emphasizes relationships among ideas. To cluster ideas, write your subject in the center of

---

SCHOLARS ON THE WRITING PROCESS

Sommers, Nancy. "The Call of Research: A Longitudinal View of Writing Development." *College Composition and Communication* 60.1 (2008): 152–64. Print. Do students leave college as stronger writers than when they entered? This question frames Sommers's analysis of writing by four hundred Harvard freshmen over the course of their undergraduate education. She finds, however, that to answer the question requires focusing on outcomes, "endpoints," and that doing so ignores the process of writing development and the process of writing in favor of an unfortunate emphasis on the products students produce.

a sheet of paper, draw a circle around it, and surround the circle with related ideas connected to it with lines. Look for categories and connections among your ideas. The writer of the diagram below was exploring ideas for an essay on obesity in children.

Freewriting

In its purest form, freewriting is simply nonstop writing. You set aside ten minutes or so and write whatever comes to mind, without pausing to think about word choice, spelling, or even meaning. If you get stuck, you can write about being stuck, but you should keep your fingers moving. Freewriting lets you ask questions without feeling that you have to answer them. Sometimes a question that comes to mind at this stage will point you in an unexpected direction.

To explore ideas on a particular topic, consider using a technique known as *focused freewriting*. Again, you write quickly and

CLUSTER DIAGRAM

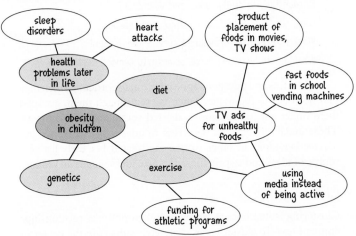

SCHOLARS ON FREEWRITING

Elbow, Peter. *Writing with Power: Techniques for Mastering the Writing Process.* 2nd ed. New York: Oxford UP, 1998. Print. In his first two chapters, Elbow describes prewriting strategies, including freewriting.

freely, but this time you focus on a specific subject and pay attention to the connections among your ideas.

Keeping a journal

A journal is a collection of informal, exploratory, sometimes experimental writing. In a journal, often meant for your eyes only, you can take risks. You might freewrite, pose questions, comment on an interesting idea from one of your classes, or keep a list of questions that occur to you while reading. You might imagine a conversation between yourself and your readers or stage a debate to understand opposing positions. A journal can also serve as a sourcebook of ideas to draw on in future essays.

Blogging

Although a blog is a type of journal, it is a public writing space rather than a private one. In a blog, you might express opinions, make observations, recap events, play with language, or interpret an image. You can explore an idea for a paper by blogging about it in different ways or from different angles. One post might be your frustrated comments about the lack of parking for commuter students at your school. Maybe the next post shares a compelling statistic about the competition for parking spaces at campuses nationwide. Since most blogs have a commenting feature, you can create a conversation by inviting readers to give you feedback—ask questions, make counterarguments, or suggest other sources on a topic.

1c Draft and revise a working thesis statement.

For many types of writing, you will be able to assert your central idea in a sentence or two. Such a statement, which ordinarily appears in the opening paragraph of your finished essay, is called a *thesis*.

TEACHING TIP

To become confident college writers, students need practice developing, evaluating, and revising thesis statements. As a class, draft a few working thesis statements related to a topic you've recently discussed as a class. Analyze these thesis statements by having students answer the questions in the chart "Putting your working thesis to the 'So what?' test" (p. 33). During a future class, when your students have complete drafts of a current paper, ask them to exchange drafts with a partner and use the questions in the chart to help them evaluate each other's thesis statements.

What makes an effective thesis statement?

A successful thesis statement is a central idea that requires supporting evidence; its scope is appropriate for the assigned length of the essay; and it is sharply and specifically focused. A thesis is a promise to readers. It is often one or more of the following:

- your answer to a question you have posed
- the resolution of a problem you have identified
- a statement that announces your position on a debatable topic

Drafting a working thesis

As you explore your topic and iden-tify questions to investigate, you will begin to see possible ways to focus your material. At this point, try to settle on a *tentative* central idea, or working thesis statement. The more complex your topic, the more your focus will change as your drafts evolve. Think of your working thesis as preliminary, open for consider-ation and revision, as you clarify your purpose and consider the expecta-tions of your audience. As your ideas

> **MAKING THE MOST OF YOUR HANDBOOK**
>
> The thesis statement is central to many types of writing.
>
> ▶ Writing arguments: 6
> ▶ Writing about texts: 4, 6f
> ▶ Writing about images and multimodal texts: 5
> ▶ Writing research papers: 53 (MLA), 58 (APA), 63 (*Chicago*)
> ▶ Writing literature papers: 7c

develop, you'll need to revisit your working thesis to see if it rep-resents the position you want to take or if it can be supported by the sources of evidence you have accumulated.

You'll find that the process of answering a question you have posed, resolving a problem you have identified, or taking a position on a debatable topic will focus your thinking and lead you to develop a working thesis. At the top of the next page, for example, are one student's efforts to pose a question and draft a working thesis for an essay in his ethics course.

TEACHING TIP

Students need language to talk about writing as writing. The language in 1c helps students move beyond thinking of their thesis statements as "good" or "bad" and gives them a way to see a thesis, for example, as an answer to a question, not a question itself, or as a solution to a problem, not a statement of the problem. You may find it useful to use the lan-guage in 1c in class discussions and when you respond to drafts.

TEACHING TIP

You may find it helpful to use a projector, a document camera, or pre-sentation software to project or present working thesis statements to give students practice in using the problem/strategy approach to evaluate and revise thesis statements.

QUESTION

Should athletes who enhance their performance through bio-technology be banned from athletic competition?

WORKING THESIS

Athletes who boost their performance through biotechnology should be banned from athletic competition.

The working thesis offers a useful place to start writing—a way to limit the topic and focus a first draft—but it doesn't take into consideration the expectations of readers who will ask "Why?" and "So what?" The student has taken a position—athletes should be banned—but he hasn't answered *why* athletes should be banned if they boost their performance through biotechnology. To fully answer his own question, he might push his own thinking with the word *because.*

STRONGER THESIS

Athletes who boost their performance through biotechnology should be banned from competition *because. . . .*

The *because* clause will allow the student to claim something specific in his thesis—for example, that biotechnology gives athletes an unfair advantage and disrupts the sense of fair play.

Here another student focuses a working thesis for a researched argument paper in her composition course by identifying a problem.

PROBLEM

Americans who earn average incomes cannot run effective national political campaigns.

WORKING THESIS

Congress should pass legislation that would make it possible for Americans who are not wealthy to be viable candidates in national political campaigns.

The student has roughed out language for solving the problem (by enacting federal legislation), which is a good starting point.

Readers, though, will want to know *why* legislation will resolve the problem and what specific legislation will address this problem. As the student researches and learns more about her topic and perhaps talks with a tutor or peer, she will be able to revise her working thesis and suggest a specific solution, such as federal restrictions on campaign spending.

Revising a working thesis

As you move to a clearer and more specific position you want to take, you'll start to see ways to revise your working thesis. You may find that the evidence you have collected supports a different thesis; you may find that your position has changed as you learned more about your topic. Revision is ongoing; as your ideas evolve, your working thesis will evolve, too. One effective way to revise a working thesis is to put it to the "So what?" test: Can you explain why readers will want to read an essay with this thesis? Can you respond when readers ask "So what?" or "Why does your thesis matter?" Such questions help you keep audience and purpose—and the expectations of your assignment—in mind as you revise.

Using a problem/strategy approach as you revise

Revising a working thesis is easier if you have a method or an approach. The following problem/strategy approach is an effective way to evaluate and revise a working thesis, especially if you tend to start out with thesis statements that are too factual, too broad, too narrow, too vague—or perhaps not even phrased as statements. (See "Unclear thesis" in 2a.)

A thesis should require proof or further development through facts and details; it cannot itself be a fact or a description.

hackerhandbooks.com/bedhandbook
 The writing process > As you write: Revising a thesis

TEACHING TIP

Consider assigning the "As you write" writing prompts, found in the handbook's Integrated Media at hackerhandbooks.com/bedhandbook. These activities, referenced at the bottoms of many pages in the handbook, help students to apply the handbook's lessons to the writing they are doing for the course.

Putting your working thesis to the "So what?" test

Use the following questions to help you revise your working thesis.

- Ask yourself why readers will want to read an essay with this thesis. How would you respond to a reader who hears your thesis and asks "So what?" or "Why does it matter?"

- Does your thesis answer a question, propose a solution to a problem, or take a position in a debate? Why will readers be interested in your answer, solution, or position?

- Will any readers disagree with this thesis? If so, what might they say?

- Is the thesis too obvious? If you cannot come up with interpretations different from your own, you may need to revise your thesis.

- Does the thesis require an essay's worth of development? Or will you run out of points too quickly?

- Can you provide enough support for your thesis with the evidence available?

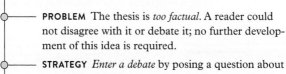

WORKING THESIS The first polygraph was developed by Dr. John A. Larson in 1921.

PROBLEM The thesis is *too factual*. A reader could not disagree with it or debate it; no further development of this idea is required.

STRATEGY *Enter a debate* by posing a question about your topic that has more than one possible answer. For example: Should the polygraph be used by private employers? Your thesis should be your answer to the question.

REVISED THESIS Because the polygraph has not been proved reliable, even under controlled conditions, its use by private employers should be banned.

SCHOLARS ON PREWRITING AND INVENTION

Shafer, Gregory. "Using Letters for Process and Change in the Basic Writing Class." *Teaching English in the Two-Year College* 27.3 (2000): 285–92. Print. Shafer asked his developmental writing students to write letters to one another and to him in an effort to help them overcome their fears, anxieties, and frustrations. Shafer explains his rationale for the assignments and shares his experience using one of his own letters as a model in class discussion.

Gorrell, Donna. "Central Question for Prewriting and Revising." *Teaching English in the Two-Year College* 23.1 (1996): 34–38. Print. Gorrell suggests that students begin their writing process not with a thesis statement but with a question. She offers examples and two lists: questions to develop a focus and questions to guide revisions.

A thesis should be an answer to a question, not a question itself.

WORKING THESIS Would John F. Kennedy have continued to escalate the war in Vietnam if he had lived?

PROBLEM The thesis is *a question*, not an answer to a question.

STRATEGY *Take a position* on your topic by answering the question you have posed. Your thesis should be your answer to the question.

REVISED THESIS Although John F. Kennedy sent the first American troops to Vietnam before he died, an analysis of his foreign policy suggests that he would not have escalated the war had he lived.

A thesis should be of sufficient scope for your assignment; it should not be too broad.

WORKING THESIS Mapping the human genome has many implications for health and science.

PROBLEM The thesis is *too broad*. Even in a very long research paper, you would not be able to discuss all the implications of mapping the human genome.

STRATEGY *Focus on a subtopic of your original topic.* Once you have chosen a subtopic, take a position in an ongoing debate and pose a question that has more than one answer. For example: Should people be tested for genetic diseases? Your thesis should be your answer to the question.

REVISED THESIS Although scientists can now detect genetic predisposition for specific diseases, policymakers should establish clear guidelines about whom to test and under what circumstances.

A thesis also should not be too narrow.

WORKING   A person who carries a genetic mutation linked to a
THESIS   particular disease might or might not develop that
           disease.

    PROBLEM The thesis is *too narrow*. It does not sug-
    gest any argument or debate about the topic.

    STRATEGY *Identify challenging questions* that readers
    might ask about your topic. Then pose a question
    that has more than one answer. For example: Do
    the risks of genetic testing outweigh its usefulness?
    Your thesis should be your answer to this question.

REVISED   Though positive results in a genetic test do not
THESIS   guarantee that the disease will develop, such results
           can cause psychological trauma; genetic testing
           should therefore be avoided if possible.

A thesis should be sharply focused, not too vague. Avoid fuzzy, hard-to-define words such as *interesting*, *good*, or *disgusting*.

WORKING   The Vietnam Veterans Memorial is an interesting
THESIS   structure.

    PROBLEM This thesis is *too fuzzy and unfocused*. It's
    difficult to define *interesting*, and the sentence doesn't
    give readers any cues about where the essay is going.

    STRATEGY *Focus your thesis with concrete language and
    a clear plan.* Pose a question about the topic that has
    more than one answer. For example: How does the
    physical structure of the Vietnam Veterans Memorial
    shape the experience of visitors? Your thesis—your
    answer to the question—should use specific language.

REVISED   By inviting visitors to see their own reflections in
THESIS   the wall, the Vietnam Veterans Memorial creates a
           link between the present and the past.

EXERCISE 1–4 In each of the following pairs, which sentence might work well as a thesis for a short paper? What is the problem with the other one? Is it too factual? Too broad? Too vague? Use the problem/strategy approach from pages 33–35 to evaluate each thesis. *More practice:* e

1. a. By networking with friends, a single parent can manage to strike a balance among work, school, a social life, and family.
   b. Single parents face many challenges as they try to juggle all of their responsibilities.

2. a. At the Special Olympics, athletes with disabilities show that, with hard work and support from others, they can accomplish anything — that they can indeed be winners.
   b. Working with the Special Olympics program is rewarding.

3. a. History 201, taught by Professor Brown, is offered at 10:00 a.m. on Tuesdays and Thursdays.
   b. Whoever said that history is nothing but polishing tombstones must have missed History 201, because in Professor Brown's class history is vibrantly alive.

4. a. So far, research suggests that zero-emissions vehicles are not a sensible solution to the problem of steadily increasing air pollution.
   b. Because air pollution is of serious concern to many people today, several US government agencies have implemented plans to begin solving the problem.

5. a. Anorexia nervosa is a dangerous and sometimes deadly eating disorder occurring mainly in young, upper-middle-class teens.
   b. The eating disorder anorexia nervosa is rarely cured by one treatment alone; only by combining drug therapy with psychotherapy and family therapy can the client begin the long journey to wellness.

1d Draft a plan.

Many writers draft a plan as part of the early process of drafting a paper. Listing and organizing supporting ideas can help a writer

hackerhandbooks.com/bedhandbook
e The writing process > Exercises: 1–5 to 1–7

EXERCISE 1–4 *Answers:*

1. a; b is too broad
2. a; b is too vague
3. b; a is too factual
4. a; b is too broad
5. b; a is too factual

figure out how to flesh out the thesis. Creating outlines, whether informal or formal, can help you make sure your writing is focused and logical and can help you identify any gaps in your support.

When to use an informal outline

You might want to sketch an informal outline to see how you will support your thesis and to figure out a tentative structure for your ideas. Informal outlines can take many forms. Perhaps the most common is simply the thesis followed by a list of major ideas.

> Working thesis: Television advertising should be regulated to help prevent childhood obesity.
>
> - Children watch more television than ever.
> - Snacks marketed to children are often unhealthy and fattening.
> - Childhood obesity can cause sleep disorders and other health problems.
> - Addressing these health problems costs taxpayers billions of dollars.
> - Therefore, these ads are actually costing the public money.
> - If advertising is free speech, do we have the right to regulate it?
> - We regulate alcohol and cigarette ads on television, so why not advertisements for soda and junk food?

If you began by jotting down a list of ideas (see p. 27), you can turn the list into a rough outline by crossing out some ideas, adding others, and putting the ideas in a logical order.

When to use a formal outline

Early in the writing process, rough outlines have certain advantages: They can be produced quickly, they are obviously tentative, and they can be revised easily. However, a formal outline may be useful later in the writing process, after you have written a rough draft, especially if your topic is complex. It can help you

TEACHING TIP

If you are looking for an alternative to traditional outlining as a planning step, ask your students to use storyboarding or mapping to help them visualize an organizational plan. Students can use note cards or sticky notes with key points and key pieces of evidence to help them organize their drafts. Check with the staff in your school's writing center, who may be able to give you samples of graphic organizers and other templates that emphasize the visual/spatial aspects of organizing information.

see whether the parts of your essay work together and whether your essay's structure is logical.

The following formal outline brought order to the research paper in 57b, on Internet surveillance in the workplace. The student's thesis statement is an important part of the outline. Everything else in the outline supports it, either directly or indirectly.

Thesis: Although companies often have legitimate concerns that lead them to monitor employees' Internet usage—from expensive security breaches to reduced productivity—the benefits of electronic surveillance are outweighed by its costs to employees' privacy and autonomy.

I. Although employers have always monitored employees, electronic surveillance is more efficient than other methods.
    A. Employers can gather data in large quantities.
    B. Electronic surveillance can be continuous.
    C. Electronic surveillance can be conducted secretly, with keystroke logging programs.

II. Some experts argue that employers have legitimate reasons to monitor employees' Internet usage.
    A. Unmonitored employees could accidentally breach security.
    B. Companies are legally accountable for the online actions of employees.

III. Despite valid concerns, employers should value employee morale and autonomy and avoid creating an atmosphere of distrust.
    A. Setting the boundaries for employee autonomy is difficult in the wired workplace.
        1. Using the Internet is the most popular way of wasting time at work.
        2. Employers can't easily determine if employees are working or surfing the Web.
    B. Surveillance can create resentment among employees.
        1. Web surfing can relieve stress, and restricting it can generate tension between managers and workers.
        2. Enforcing Internet usage can seem arbitrary.

WRITING CENTER DIRECTORS ON PLANNING

"One thing that seems to help less experienced writers a great deal is when they realize that most successful student writers don't just write their final draft the night before a paper is due and receive an A. Students who write A papers understand their own writing process and the elements of a good essay. And they spend quite a lot of time writing, thinking, revising, thinking some more, and revising again. I sometimes quote Michelangelo to discouraged students: 'If people knew how hard I worked, they wouldn't think I'm a genius.' The myth of the writer producing focused, clear, coherent, interesting prose all alone late at night is still alive and well. Students need to understand the reality of the good writer."

— Leslie R. Leach, writing center coordinator, College of the Redwoods

IV. Surveillance may not increase employee productivity, and trust may benefit productivity.
   A. A company shouldn't care how many hours salaried employees work as long as they get the job done.
   B. Casual Internet use can actually benefit companies.
      1. The Internet may spark business ideas.
      2. The Internet may suggest ideas about how to operate more efficiently.

V. Employees' rights to privacy are not well defined by the law.
   A. Few federal guidelines on electronic surveillance exist.
   B. Employers and employees are negotiating the boundaries without legal guidance.
   C. As technological capabilities increase, the need to define boundaries will also increase.

Planning with headings

When drafting a research paper or a business document, consider using headings to guide your planning and to help your readers follow the organization of your final draft. While drafting, you can insert your working thesis, experiment with possible headings, and type chunks of text beneath each heading. You may need to try grouping your ideas in a few different ways to suit your purpose and audience.

> **MAKING THE MOST OF YOUR HANDBOOK**
>
> Headings can help writers plan and readers understand a document.
>
> ▶ Using parallel form for headings: 9a
> ▶ Papers organized with headings: 62b, 63f

1e Draft an introduction.

Some writers, but not all, begin a paper by drafting the introduction, which introduces the writer's central idea. If you find it difficult to introduce a paper that you have not yet written, try drafting the body first and saving the introduction for later.

hackerhandbooks.com/bedhandbook

🄴 The writing process > As you write: Revising an introduction

---

TEACHING TIP

Spend a whole class period on hooks, the rhetorical devices writers use to motivate interest in their writing. Bring in a sampling of five to eight essays and articles that show a variety of ways to start a piece of writing. Discuss a few in depth as a class. Ask students to respond to questions such as these: What strategies have the writers used to hook their readers? Are these strategies effective? Why or why not?

Your introduction will usually be a paragraph of 50 to 150 words (in a longer paper, it may be more than one paragraph). Perhaps the most common strategy is to open with a few sentences that engage readers and establish your purpose for writing, your central idea. The statement of your central idea is called a *thesis*. (See also 1c.) In the following introduction, the thesis is highlighted.

> As the United States industrialized in the nineteenth century, using immigrant labor, social concerns took a backseat to the task of building a prosperous nation. The government did not regulate industries and did not provide an effective safety net for the poor or for those who became sick or injured on the job. Immigrants and the poor did have a few advocates, however. Settlement houses such as Hull-House in Chicago provided information, services, and a place for reform-minded individuals to gather and work to improve the conditions of the urban poor. Alice Hamilton was one of these reformers. Her work at Hull-House spanned twenty-two years and later expanded throughout the nation. Hamilton's efforts helped to improve the lives of immigrants and drew attention and respect to the problems and people that until then had been ignored.
>
> — Laurie McDonough, student

Each sentence leading to your thesis should hook readers by drawing them into the world of the essay and showing them why your essay is worth reading. The chart on page 41 provides strategies for drafting an introduction.

Whether you are writing for a scholarly audience, a professional audience, a public audience, or a general audience, you cannot assume your readers' interest in the topic. The hook should spark readers' curiosity and offer them a reason to continue.

Although the thesis frequently appears at the end of the introduction, it can just as easily appear at the beginning. Much work-related writing commonly begins with the thesis.

TEACHING TIP

Encourage students to develop a repertoire of strategies for drafting an introduction by asking them to write multiple opening paragraphs for each draft and then to write brief reflective responses. In their responses, they should assess which of the strategies is most effective for their draft and say why they think so. Remind them to consider their purpose and audience. You might even ask two or three students to share their introductions with the class (using a document camera) and then to defend their assessments.

Strategies for drafting an introduction

The following strategies can provide a hook for your reader, whether you are composing a traditional essay or a multimodal work such as a slide show presentation or a video.

Offer a startling statistic or an unusual fact

Ask a question

Introduce a quotation or a bit of dialogue

Provide historical background

Define a term or concept

Propose a problem, contradiction, or dilemma

Use a vivid example or image

Develop an analogy

Relate an anecdote

> Flextime scheduling, which has proved its effectiveness at the Library of Congress, should be introduced on a trial basis at the main branch of the Montgomery County Public Library. By offering its employees flexible work hours, the library can boost employee morale and cut down on absenteeism. Flextime scheduling would also allow the library to expand its hours of operation, a key benefit to the community.
>
> — David Warren, student

As you draft your introduction, think about your writing situation, especially your genre. For some types of writing, it may be difficult or impossible to express the central idea in a thesis statement; or it may be unwise or unnecessary to put a thesis statement in the essay itself. A literacy narrative, for example, may have a focus too subtle to be distilled in a single sentence. Strictly informative writing, like that found in many business memos or nursing reports, may be difficult to summarize in a thesis. In such instances, do not try to force the central idea into a thesis statement. Instead, think in terms of an overriding purpose and of the genre's conventions and expectations. (See 1a and 64d.)

SCHOLARS ON WRITER'S BLOCK

Rose, Mike. "Rigid Rules, Inflexible Plans, and the Stifling of Language: A Cognitivist Analysis of Writer's Block." *College Composition and Communication* 31.4 (1980): 389–401. Print. In a study of blocked and nonblocked writers, Rose discovered that the blocked writers were all working within a set of rigid rules and inflexible plans. One writer, for example, believed that an introduction must always dazzle readers, and another invariably planned her writing with a complex outline. The nonblocked writers worked with rules as well, but they viewed them quite differently — as guidelines or "rules of thumb" to be followed in most instances, but to be rejected when they conflicted with common sense.

> **Academic English**
>
> If you come from a culture that prefers an indirect approach in writing, you may feel that asserting a thesis early in an essay sounds unrefined and even rude. In the United States, however, readers appreciate a direct approach; when you state your point as directly as possible, you show that you understand your topic and value your readers' time.

1f Draft the body.

The body of your essay develops support for your thesis, so it's important to have at least a working thesis before you start writing. What does your thesis promise readers? What question are you trying to answer? What problem are you trying to solve? What is your position on the topic? Keep these questions in mind as you draft the body of your essay.

You may already have written an introduction that includes your working thesis. If not, as long as you have a draft thesis you can begin developing the body and return later to the introduction. If your thesis suggests a plan (see 1e) or if you have sketched a preliminary outline, try to organize your paragraphs accordingly.

Draft the body of your essay by writing at least one paragraph about each supporting point you listed in the planning stage. If you do not have a plan, pause for a few moments and sketch one (see 1d). As you draft the body, keep asking questions; keep anticipating what your readers may need to know.

Keep in mind that often you might not know what you want to say until you have written a draft. It is possible to begin without a plan—assuming you are prepared to treat your first attempt as a "discovery draft" that may be radically rewritten once you discover what you really want to say. Whether or not you have a plan when you begin drafting, you can often figure

---

WRITERS ON WRITING

The idea is to get the pencil moving quickly.   — Bernard Malamud

It is the lead that gives the writer control over his [or her] subject.
                                                        — Donald M. Murray

Once your mind is caught on the right snag, there's nothing so hard about the mechanics of writing.   — Anne Tyler

out a workable order for your ideas by stopping each time you start a new paragraph to think about what your readers will need to know to follow your train of thought.

For more detailed help with drafting and developing paragraphs, see 3.

USING SOURCES RESPONSIBLY: As you draft, keep careful notes and records of any sources you read and consult. If you quote, paraphrase, or summarize a source, include a citation, even in your draft (see 54b, 59b, and 63b). You will save time and avoid plagiarism if you follow the rules of citation while drafting.

Adding visuals as you draft

As you draft, you may decide that some of the support for your thesis could come from one or more visuals. Visuals can convey information concisely and powerfully. Charts, graphs, and tables, for example, can simplify complex numerical information. Images — including photographs and diagrams — often express an idea more vividly than words can. Keep in mind that if you download a visual — or use published information to create your own visual — you must credit your source. The chart on pages 44–45 describes eight types of visuals and their purposes.

Always consider how a visual supports your purpose and how your audience might respond to it. A student writing about electronic surveillance in the workplace, for example, used a cartoon to illustrate her point about employees' personal use of the Internet at work (see 57b). Another student, writing about treatments for childhood obesity, created a table to display data she had found in two different sources and discussed in her paper (see 62b). Note that these students use visuals to supplement their writing, not to substitute for it.

TEACHING TIP

Students benefit from being reminded to cite their sources when drafting. To illustrate the importance of using sources responsibly, project or present a sample student draft. Students need to understand why and how including citations in rough drafts *saves time* and avoids plagiarism. Direct students to the "Using sources responsibly" advice throughout *The Bedford Handbook* (for example, see p. 43). You may even facilitate a class discussion about what makes a responsible writer.

Choosing visuals to suit your purpose

Pie chart

Pie charts compare a part or parts to the whole. Segments of the pie represent percentages of the whole (and always total 100 percent).

Health insurance coverage in the United States (2007)
Uninsured 15%   Medicaid 13%
Medicare 12%
Individual 5%
Other public insurance 1%
Employer-insured 54%

Bar graph (or line graph)

Bar graphs highlight trends over a period of time or compare numerical data. Line graphs display the same data as bar graphs; the data are graphed as points, and the points are connected with lines.

THE PURSUIT OF PROPERTY
Home ownership rates in the United States
70% 60% 50% 40% 30% 20%
1930 1940 1950 1960 1970 1980 1990 2000

Infographic

An infographic presents data in a visually engaging form. The data are usually numerical, as in bar graphs or line graphs, but they are represented by a graphic element instead of by bars or lines.

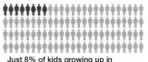

Just 8% of kids growing up in low-income communities graduate from college by age 24.

Table

Tables display numbers and words in columns and rows. They can be used to organize complicated numerical information into an easily understood format.

Prices of daily doses of AIDS drugs ($US)

Drug	Brazil	Uganda	Côte d'Ivoire	US
3TC (Lamuvidine)	1.66	3.28	2.95	8.70
ddC (Zalcitabine)	0.24	4.17	3.75	8.80
Didanosine	2.04	5.26	3.48	7.25
Efavirenz	6.96	n/a	6.41	13.13
Indinavir	10.32	12.79	9.07	14.93
Nelfinavir	4.14	4.45	4.39	6.47
Nevirapine	5.04	n/a	n/a	8.48
Saquinavir	6.24	7.37	5.52	6.50
Stavudine	0.56	6.19	4.10	9.07
ZDV/3TC	1.44	7.34	n/a	18.78
Zidovudine	1.08	4.34	2.43	10.12

Source: UNAIDS, 2000

Sources [top to bottom]: Kaiser Foundation; US Census Bureau; postsecondary .org; UNAIDS.

TEACHING TIP

If you encourage students to use visuals in their writing — photographs, charts, diagrams, drawings, and so on — plan to show some examples in class (or post them to the course Web site). Many students have never included visuals in their writing and need to see how visuals, when chosen purposefully and placed accurately, can provide support and engage readers. See pages 75, 170, and 659 in this handbook for examples of student essays that incorporate visual evidence.

44

Photograph

Photographs vividly depict people, scenes, or objects discussed in a text.

Diagram

Diagrams, useful in scientific and technical writing, concisely illustrate processes, structures, or interactions.

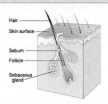

Flowchart

Flowcharts show structures (the hierarchy of employees at a company, for example) or steps in a process and their relation to one another. (See also p. 279 for another example.)

Map

Maps illustrate distances, historical information, or demographics and often use symbols for geographic features and points of interest.

Sources [top to bottom]: Fred Zwicky; NIAMS; Arizona Board of Regents; Lynn Hunt et al.

Considering design as you draft

Aside from planning visual evidence for your ideas, you will need to think about how to format your paper. Formatting, or designing, your document promotes readability and helps you meet the expectations of your readers and the requirements of the genre. The following questions will help you to keep your purpose and audience in mind as you design your document.

- What is the purpose of your document? How can your document design help you achieve this purpose?
- Who are your readers? What are their expectations?
- What format is required? What format options—layout, margins, line spacing, and font styles—will readers expect?
- How should you place and label any visuals you decide to use?

See the appendix, which starts on page 805, for sample pages from a variety of academic and business documents. Each is annotated to illustrate specific design guidelines.

USING SOURCES RESPONSIBLY: If you create a chart, table, or graph using information from your research, you must cite the source of the information even though the visual is your own. If you download a photograph from the Web or scan an image from a magazine or book, you must credit the person or organization that created it, just as you would cite any other source that you use in a college paper (see 54a, 59a, or 63b, depending on what documentation style your assignment requires).

1g Draft a conclusion.

A conclusion should remind readers of the essay's main idea without repeating it. Often the concluding paragraph can be relatively short. By the end of the essay, readers should already

---

TEACHING TIP

One way to emphasize the importance of conclusions is to show students a few brief speeches. (Ask your Bedford/St. Martin's sales rep to give you trial access to VideoCentral Plus.) In a speech, it is especially important to conclude with strength and purpose—either summarizing for an audience, inspiring an audience, calling audience members to action, or providing some coherent link to the ideas in the opening part of the speech. Ask students to study two or three brief speeches, perhaps viewing them a few times. In small groups, ask them to take notes on whether the conclusions were effective and then to give reasons why or why not. Finally, ask them to reflect on one lesson or one strategy they might be able to transfer to their writing as they prepare to write conclusions.

Strategies for drafting a conclusion

In addition to echoing your main idea, a conclusion might do any of the following:

- Briefly summarize your essay's key points
- Propose a course of action
- Offer a recommendation
- Discuss the topic's wider significance or implications
- Redefine a key term or concept
- Pose a question for future study

---

understand your main point; your conclusion drives it home and, perhaps, gives readers something more to consider.

To conclude an essay analyzing the shifting roles of women in the military services, one student discusses her topic's implications for society as a whole.

> As the military continues to train women in jobs formerly reserved for men, our understanding of women's roles in society will no doubt continue to change. And as news reports of women training for and taking part in combat operations become commonplace, reports of women becoming CEOs, police chiefs, and even president of the United States will cease to surprise us. Or perhaps we have already reached this point.
>
> — Rosa Broderick, student

To make the conclusion memorable and to give a sense of completion, you might include a detail, an example, a phrase, a quotation, or a statistic from the introduction to bring readers full circle. To conclude an essay explaining how credit card companies hook college students, one student brings readers full circle by echoing his thesis and ending with a familiar phrase borrowed from popular culture.

hackerhandbooks.com/bedhandbook

e The writing process > As you write: Revising a conclusion

Credit cards are a convenient part of life, and there is nothing wrong with having one or two of them. Before signing up for a particular card, however, college students should take time to read the fine print and do some comparison shopping. Students also need to learn to resist the many seductive offers that credit card companies extend to them after they have signed up. Students who can't "just say no" to temptations such as high credit limits and revolving balances could well become hooked on a cycle of debt from which there is no easy escape. — Matt Watson, student

Whatever concluding strategy you choose, keep in mind that an effective conclusion is decisive and unapologetic. Avoid introducing wholly new ideas at the end of an essay. And because the conclusion is so closely tied to the rest of the essay in both content and tone, be prepared to rework it (or even replace it) when you revise.

1h Manage your files.

Keeping track of all your notes, outlines, rough drafts, and final drafts can be challenging. Be sure to give your files distinct names that reflect the appropriate stage of your writing process, and store them in a logical place.

Writing online or in a word processing program can make drafting and revising easier. You can undo changes or return to an earlier draft if a revision misfires. Applying the following steps can help you explore drafting and revising possibilities with little risk.

- Create folders and subfolders for each assignment. Save notes, outlines, and drafts together. (See p. 49.)
- Label revised drafts with different file names and dates.

hackerhandbooks.com/bedhandbook

e The writing process > As you write: Managing your files

TEACHING TIP

Give students a template to use for file names, especially if you've found in the past that students are susceptible to overwriting files or losing work. You may want to adopt a file-naming convention and require that students use it. For instance, EN101.14_CriticalResponse_D2_FeeneyK.doc is a file name that gives the course (EN 101), section number (14), the assignment (critical response), the number of the student's draft (draft 2), and the student's name (Kristin Feeney). In addition, you might find it helpful to ask students to include a date in every file name: 092712 is September 27, 2012.

- Print hard copies, make backup copies, and press the Save button often (every five to ten minutes).

- Always record complete bibliographic information about any sources you might use, including visuals.

- Use a comment function to make notes to yourself or to respond to the drafts of peers.

MANAGING FILES

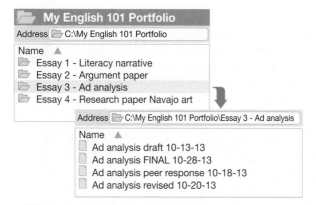

2   Revising, editing, and reflecting

Revising is rarely a one-step process. Global matters—thesis, purpose, organization, content, and overall strategy—generally receive attention first. Improvements in sentence structure, word choice, grammar, punctuation, and mechanics usually come later. As you ask questions about global matters, you can ask

SCHOLARS ON REVISING

Sommers, Nancy. "Revision Strategies of Student Writers and Experienced Adult Writers." *College Composition and Communication* 31.4 (1980): 378–88. Print. As Sommers explores perceptions about revision, she considers the central role revising plays in the composing process. Sommers shares her findings on the subject after questioning both student and adult writers, asking them to explain what revision means to them. The author illustrates how revision is an essential and fruitful tool that could and should be an important part of the writing process.

Becoming a College Writer

Form a community of readers around you

> "Don't be afraid to seek help with writing. Use all the resources available and ask people to read your drafts. Feedback gives you perspective." — **Donovan Castro**, student, University of Arizona

Have you ever tried writing an entire essay — blank page to final draft — in a single sitting? Was it your best work? Writing and revising multiple drafts allows you to write in stages, seek feedback, and make improvements. Giving yourself time to seek and receive feedback means that a first draft doesn't have to be perfect.

One effective way to approach revision is to form a community of readers around you. As Donovan Castro suggests, use "resources" — instructors, librarians, writing center tutors, classmates — to help you gain perspective on your draft's effectiveness. You might sense that something isn't working, but you don't know why or how to address it. Engage another reader who might help solve a problem. As you write in college, be open to readers' responses and be willing to learn from them.

- You may have had some experience with peer review or feedback groups in the past. Recall one experience that was particularly positive or negative. What do you think made it so?

MORE
Revising with comments, pages 51–57
Approaching global revision in cycles, 2b

TEACHING TIP

Use Donovan Castro's quotation as a catalyst for classroom discussion. What college resources are available to students — writing center tutors, for instance — to provide support and feedback? You may want to ask your students to find one detail or fact (such as the building that houses the mentor program or the hours of online chat with the library staff) about a college resource before you meet again. In addition, ask students what habits they need to develop to form a community of readers around them.

interested readers to help you see what's working and not working in your draft. You might want to visit your school's writing center, for instance, to review your draft with a writing tutor. Or you can enlist friends or family to be the audience for your draft. Simple questions such as "Do you understand my main idea?" and "Is my draft focused and organized?" will help you see your draft through readers' eyes. The checklist for global revision on page 64 may help you and your reviewers get started.

> **MAKING THE MOST OF YOUR HANDBOOK**
>
> Seeking feedback and using it are critical steps in revising a college paper.
>
> ► Checklist for global revision: page 64
> ► Guidelines for peer reviewers: page 58
> ► Guidelines for using reviewers' comments: page 59

Section 2a provides specific strategies to help you revise, using comments from your reviewers. Section 2b provides strategies for revising for global concerns, and section 2c offers strategies for revising and editing sentences.

2a Develop strategies for revising with comments.

To revise is to *re-see*, and the comments you receive from your reviewers—instructors, peers, and writing center tutors—will help you re-see your draft from your readers' point of view. As you write for college courses, find reviewers and seek their feedback. When you ask readers for their comments, revision becomes a social experience, connecting you with the questions and concerns of readers who help you shape your work in progress.

Sometimes the comments you'll receive are written as shorthand commands—"Be specific!"—and sometimes as questions—"What is your main point?" Such comments don't immediately show you *how* to revise, but they do identify places where global and sentence-level revisions can improve your draft. Sort through the comments you receive with your purpose and audience in mind. And don't hesitate to ask your reviewers to explain their comments if you don't understand them.

SCHOLARS ON FEEDBACK

Sommers, Nancy. "Across the Drafts." *College Composition and Communication* 58.2 (2006): 248–57. Print. Sommers examines the "role feedback plays in the complex story of why some students prosper as college writers while others lag." She explains that if teachers offer tough criticism with their comments but also treat their students like equals, students are more likely to become engaged in their work. With an enhanced sense of engagement, students not only can improve themselves with each assignment but also might carry what they've learned from their revisions and interactions with instructors outside of the classroom.

You may also want to keep a revision and editing log, a list of the global and sentence-level concerns that come up repeatedly in your reviewers' comments. For instance, if you frequently receive comments such as "Develop more" or "Avoid run-on sentences," you can use these comments to help you learn specific lessons and to transfer your learning from one assignment to the next. (See 2c.)

This section addresses common types of comments an instructor, a peer, or a writing center tutor might offer and suggests specific strategies for revising.

THE COMMENT: Narrow your introduction

SIMILAR COMMENTS: Unfocused intro · Too broad

UNDERSTANDING THE COMMENT   When readers point out that your introduction needs to be "narrowed," the comment often signals that the beginning sentences of your essay are not specific or focused.

> ; even believe that rituals
> actions influence the outcome
> e fans go beyond cheering, and
> ssment, and chanted slurs   Narrow
> your
> orts.   introduction

STRATEGIES FOR REVISING

- *Reread your introduction and ask questions.* Are the sentences leading to your thesis specific enough to engage readers and communicate your purpose? Do these sentences lead logically to your thesis? Do they spark your readers' curiosity and offer them a reason to continue reading? (See 1e.)

- *Try engaging readers with a "hook"* in your introduction — a question, a quotation, a vivid example, or an image. (See the chart on p. 41.)

hackerhandbooks.com/bedhandbook

e The writing process > As you write: Using reviewers' comments

---

SCHOLARS ON FEEDBACK

Treglia, Maria Ornella. "Feedback on Feedback: Exploring Student Responses to Teachers' Written Commentary." *Journal of Basic Writing* 27.1 (2008): 105–37. Print. Treglia's study found that students, especially L2 students, engage in more productive revision if they receive "mitigated" comments on drafts. This style of commentary, in which a specific critical directive is preceded by praise, appears to motivate writers, foster their confidence, and provide them with choices, according to the author. Treglia, whose study focused on two writing instructors and fourteen students at a single urban university, calls for continued study of the subject.

THE COMMENT: Unclear thesis

SIMILAR COMMENTS: Vague thesis · State your position · What is your main point?

UNDERSTANDING THE COMMENT When readers point out that your thesis is unclear, the comment often signals that they have a hard time identifying your essay's main point.

> the mother or other relatives.
> r drives to dance lessons,
> eball team, hosts birthday
> omework help. Do more *Unclear thesis*
> r hinder the development of

STRATEGIES FOR REVISING

- *Ask questions.* What is the thesis, position, or main point of the draft? Can you support it with the available evidence? (See 1c, 5c, and 5d.)

- *Reread your entire draft.* Because ideas develop as you write, you may find that your conclusion contains a clearer statement of your main point than does your working thesis. Or you may find your thesis elsewhere in your draft. (See 1e.)

- *Try framing your thesis* as an answer to a question you pose, the resolution of a problem you identify, or a position you take in a debate. And put your thesis to the "So what?" test: Why would a reader be interested in this thesis? (See 1c and 1e.)

THE COMMENT: Develop more

SIMILAR COMMENTS: Undeveloped · Give examples · Explain

UNDERSTANDING THE COMMENT When readers suggest that you "develop more," the comment often signals that you stopped short of providing a full and detailed discussion of your idea.

> nd his past (195). In his
> ited, he removed himself
> tanced himself from his *Develop more*
> he Achievement of Desire,"
> e separation from his family

SCHOLARS ON REVISING

Horning, Alice S. "Reflection and Revision: Intimacy in College Writing." *Composition Chronicle* 9 (1997): 4–7. Print. Horning, an advocate of portfolio teaching, suggests that we need to involve students in assessing their own writing processes and products. In Horning's classes, for each paper they write, students submit a "writing process statement" in which they reflect on some aspect of their drafting and revising process. Horning offers a number of prompts for reflective writing along with student examples of such writing.

STRATEGIES FOR REVISING

- *Read your paragraph to a peer or a tutor* and ask specific questions. What's missing? Do readers need more background information or examples to understand your point? Do they need more evidence to be convinced? Is it clear what point you're making with your details? (See 5d.)

- *Keep your purpose in mind.* Your assignment probably asks you to do more than summarize sources or list examples and evidence. Make sure to discuss the examples and illustrations you provide and analyze your evidence. (See 5e.)

- *Think about why your main point matters to your readers.* Take another look at your points and support, and answer the "So what?" question. (See p. 33.)

THE COMMENT: Be specific

SIMILAR COMMENTS: Need examples • Evidence?

UNDERSTANDING THE COMMENT When readers say that you need to "be specific," the comment often signals that you could strengthen your writing with additional details.

> cultural differences between the
> Italy. Italian citizens do not share
> attitudes or values as American   Be specific
> erences make it hard for some
> feel comfortable coming to the

STRATEGIES FOR REVISING

- *Reread your topic sentence* to understand the focus of the paragraph. (See 3a.)

- *Ask questions.* Does the paragraph contain claims that need support? Have you provided evidence — specific examples, vivid details and illustrations, statistics and facts — to help readers understand your ideas and find them persuasive? (See 5e.)

- *Interpret your evidence.* Remember that details and examples don't speak for themselves. You'll need to show readers how evidence supports your claims. (See 4d and 5e.)

TEACHING TIP

Spend time talking as a class about the purpose of feedback and the characteristics of useful feedback. To prepare students for the class, ask them to take some notes on their past experiences with feedback. What kind of feedback was particularly helpful for them? What kind of feedback was not at all helpful? Share your thoughts about feedback, and perhaps project or present examples of comments you've written on past students' drafts and final work.

THE COMMENT: Consider opposing viewpoints

SIMILAR COMMENTS: What about the other side? •
Counterargument?

UNDERSTANDING THE COMMENT When
readers suggest that you "consider opposing
viewpoints," the comment often signals that
you need to recognize and respond to possible
objections to your argument.

> ostile work environment
>
> rchers Shepard and Clifton
>
> es using drug-testing   Consider
> opposing
> ave lower productivity   viewpoints
>
> ve not adopted such

STRATEGIES FOR REVISING

- *Read more* to learn about the debates surrounding the topic.
  (See 50a and 50b.)

- *Ask questions.* Are there other sides to the issue? Would
  a reasonable person offer an alternative explanation for the
  evidence or provide counterevidence? (See 6i.)

- *Be open-minded.* Although it might seem illogical to introduce opposing arguments, you'll show your knowledge of
  the topic by recognizing that not everyone draws the same
  conclusion. (See 6f, 6g, and p. 561.)

- *Introduce and counter objections* with phrases like these:
  "Some readers might point out that . . ." or "Critics of this
  view argue that. . . ." (See p. 165.)

- *Revise your thesis,* if necessary, to account for other points of view.

THE COMMENT: Summarize less, analyze more

SIMILAR COMMENTS: Too much summary • Show, don't tell •
Go deeper

UNDERSTANDING THE COMMENT When readers point out that you need to include more
analysis and less summary, the comment often
signals that they are looking for your interpretation of the text.

> uages she speaks with
>
> For example, she speaks   Summarize
> cano Texas Spanish with her less,
> s English at school (327). analyze
> more
> r experience with speaking

AN ADDITIONAL RESOURCE ON COMMENTS

As a class, view the brief film *Beyond the Red Ink: Students Talk about
Teachers' Comments* (available online at hackerhandbooks.com).
Consult the brief user's guide, also online, for discussion topics
and activities.

TEACHING TIP

Ask students to read through the comments they've received on a recent
draft. Then ask them to write a one-page revision plan to explain what
they've learned from these comments and how they plan to use these
comments to revise.

STRATEGIES FOR REVISING

- *Reread your paragraph and highlight the sentences that summarize.* Then, in a different color, highlight the sentences that contain your analysis. (Summary describes what the text says; analysis offers a judgment or an interpretation of the text.) (See 4c and 4d.)

- *Reread the text* (or passages of the text) that you are analyzing. Pay attention to how the language and structure of the text contribute to its meaning. (See 4a.)

- *Ask questions.* What strategies does the author use, and how do those strategies help convey the author's message? What insights about the text can you share with your readers? How can you deepen your readers' understanding of the author's main points? (See 4a and 4d.)

THE COMMENT: Cite your sources

SIMILAR COMMENTS: Source? • Whose words? • Document

UNDERSTANDING THE COMMENT When readers point out that you need to "cite your sources," the comment often signals that you need to acknowledge and give proper credit to the contributions of others.

> end, Edna Pontellier is
> a "naked . . . new-born creature"
> act of ending her own life, *Cite*
> *your*
> ig a kind of rebirth. *sources*

STRATEGIES FOR REVISING

- *Reread your sentence and ask questions.* Have you properly acknowledged all the contributions—words, ideas, facts, or visuals—that you use as evidence? Have you given credit to the sources you quote, summarize, or paraphrase? Have you made it clear to readers how to locate the source if they want to consult it?

- *Ask your instructor* which documentation style you are required to use—MLA, APA, or *Chicago*.

SCHOLARS ON PEER REVIEW

Armstrong, Sonya L., and Eric J. Paulson. "Whither 'Peer Review'? Terminology Matters for the Writing Classroom." *Teaching English in the Two-Year College* 35.4 (2008): 398–407. Print. The authors make a case for the need for more precise terminology to describe peer sessions and argue that the terms in current practice — *peer review, peer response, peer editing, peer evaluation,* and *peer critique* — are not interchangeable. Their essay encourages instructors to reflect on peer session practices and to "clarify" the purposes of these activities for themselves and their students.

- *Revise* by including an in-text citation for any words, ideas, facts, or visuals you used as evidence and by using quotation marks around borrowed language from a source.

- *Review advice on citing sources:* 54 (MLA), 59 (APA), and 63b (*Chicago*).

2b Approach global revision in cycles.

Making major revisions can be difficult, especially when you've worked hard to write a first draft. Revising is a lot easier, though, when you ask reviewers and readers for suggestions. And revising is more effective when you approach it in cycles, rather than attempting to change everything all at once. Four common cycles of global revision are discussed in this section:

- Engaging the audience
- Sharpening the focus
- Improving the organization
- Strengthening the content

Engaging the audience

Sometimes a rough draft needs an overhaul because it is directed at no particular audience. Readers are put off by such writing because they aren't sure what's in it for them. A good question to ask yourself and your reviewers is the toughest question a reader might ask: "So what?" If your draft can't pass the "So what?" test, you may need to rethink your entire approach.

Once you have made sure that your draft is directed at an audience—readers who stand to benefit in some way by reading it—you may still need to refine your tone. The tone of a piece of writing expresses the writer's feelings toward the audience and the topic, so it is important to get it right. When you seek

hackerhandbooks.com/bedhandbook

e The writing process > Exercises: 2–1 and 2–2

SCHOLARS ON PEER REVIEW

Butts, Elizabeth A. "Overcoming Student Resistance to Group Work." *Teaching English in the Two-Year College* 28.1 (2000): 81–83. Print. Students resist group assignments, in part because assignments are not structured effectively and in part because teachers often don't help students get the most out of group work. Butts shares a specific assignment sequence she uses to help students succeed in a group environment.

Guidelines for peer reviewers

View yourself as a coach, not a judge.

Think of yourself as proposing possibilities, not dictating revisions. It is the writer, after all, who will have to grapple with the task of improving the essay. Work with the writer to identify the strengths and limitations of the draft.

Restate the writer's main ideas.

It's helpful for the writer to see if you understand the main point of the essay. Restate the thesis for the writer. And try to paraphrase each paragraph of the draft to help the writer see if the essay's points are clearly expressed.

Where possible, give specific compliments.

Vague compliments (such as "I liked your essay") sound insincere — and they aren't helpful. Point out specific successes. For example, you might mention that you particularly admire how the writer presents the opposing viewpoint in the second paragraph before challenging it in the third.

Link suggestions for improvement to the writer's goals.

Criticism is constructive when it is offered in the right spirit. For example, you might advise the writer to put the most dramatic example last, where it will have the maximum impact on readers.

Ask questions and tell the writer where you would like to hear more.

Note passages that you found either confusing or interesting. By asking for clarification, you will help the writer see what needs to be revised. Indicating an interest in hearing more about a topic will often inspire the writer to come up with useful and vivid details.

Express interest in reading the next draft.

When your interest is sincere, expressing it can be a powerful motivation for a writer.

SCHOLARS ON PEER REVIEW

Bruffee, Kenneth A. "Writing and Collaboration." *Collaborative Learning: Higher Education, Interdependence, and the Authority of Knowledge.* Baltimore: Johns Hopkins UP, 1993. 52–62. Print. Bruffee proposes that we view writing as a "social, collaborative, constructive conversational act," and he explains several ways in which conversation can help writers.

Bishop, Wendy. "Helping Peer Writing Groups Succeed." *Teaching English in the Two-Year College* 15.2 (1988): 120–25. Print. Bishop reviews research on writing groups and lists reasons for their success and failure. She also outlines what teachers should know before using groups and suggests strategies for training, monitoring, and evaluating groups.

Guidelines for using reviewers' comments

Don't take criticism personally.

Your reader is responding to your essay, not to you. It may be frustrating to hear that you still have more work to do, but taking feedback seriously will make your essay stronger.

Pay attention to ideas that contradict your own.

If comments show that a reviewer doesn't understand what you're trying to do, don't be defensive. Instead, consider why your reader is confused, and figure out how to clarify your point. Responding to readers' objections — instead of dismissing them — may strengthen your ideas and make your essay more persuasive.

Look for global concerns.

Your reviewers will probably make more suggestions than you can use. To keep things manageable, focus on the comments that relate to your thesis, organization, and evidence. Do your readers understand your main idea? Can they follow your train of thought? Are they looking for more supporting ideas or facts?

Weigh feedback carefully.

As you begin revising, you may find yourself sorting through suggestions from many people, including instructors, writing tutors, and peer reviewers. Sometimes these readers will agree, but often their advice will differ. It's important to sort through all the comments you receive with your original goals in mind — otherwise, you'll be facing the impossible task of trying to incorporate everyone's advice.

Keep a revision and editing log.

Make a clear and simple list of the global and sentence-level concerns that keep coming up in most of your reviewers' comments. That list can serve as a starting point each time you revise a paper. When you take charge of your own writing in this way, comments will become a valuable resource.

SCHOLARS ON THE WRITING PROCESS

Qualley, Donna. *Turns of Thought: Teaching Composition as Reflexive Inquiry*. Portsmouth: Boynton, 1997. Print. Qualley describes a method for teaching students to think about their reading and writing practices. She demonstrates by reflecting on her own practices and noting the ways she had to "unlearn" and revise some of her basic assumptions about teaching writing and responding to student writers.

responses to your draft, ask your readers about your tone. If they respond that your tone seems too self-centered or too flippant, bossy, patronizing, or hostile, you'll want to modify it to show respect for your readers.

The following paragraph was drafted by a student who hoped to persuade his audience to buy organic produce.

A PARAGRAPH THAT ALIENATES READERS

If you choose to buy organic produce, you are supporting local farmers as well as demonstrating your opposition to chemical pesticides. As more and more supermarkets carry organic fruits and vegetables, consumers have fewer reasons not to buy organic. Some consumers do not buy organic produce because they are not willing to spend the extra money. But if you care at all about the environment or the small farmer, you should be willing to support organic farms in your area.

When the student asked a classmate to review his draft, his classmate commented that the tone was harsh and alienating. His reviewer questioned why he assumed his readers didn't care about the environment. (See p. 61.)

A PARAGRAPH THAT RESPECTS READERS

By choosing to buy organic produce, you have the opportunity to support local farmers, to oppose the use of chemical pesticides, and to taste some of the freshest produce available. Because more supermarkets carry organic produce than ever, you won't even have to miss out on any of your favorite fruits or vegetables. Although organic produce can be more expensive than conventional produce, the costs are not prohibitive. For example, a pound of organic bananas at my local grocery store is eighty-nine cents, while the conventional bananas are sixty-nine cents a pound. If you can afford this small price difference, you will have the opportunity to make a difference for the environment and for the small farmer.   — Leon Nage, student

TEACHING TIP

Because they have difficulty distinguishing between sentence-level revision and global revision, students benefit from seeing and studying examples of global revisions. You may find it useful to present or project drafts from your own writing or drafts from former students to illustrate the cycles of global revision.

TEACHING TIP

If students find revising an overwhelming task, they might benefit from focusing on revising small units before tackling entire drafts. For instance, you might ask students to review the strategies for drafting an introduction and then to revise their introductions; or ask them to review material on topic sentences and then to revise by adding or sharpening topic sentences.

EXCERPT FROM AN ONLINE PEER REVIEW SESSION

> **Peer Reviewer:** I see your point, but it's harsh. You need to think about how to be more diplomatic.
>
> **Writer:** How is it harsh? What could I change?
>
> **Reviewer:** You accuse "some consumers" of being unwilling to spend extra money or being uninterested in helping the environment. What reader is motivated to read something that's insulting or alienating?
>
> **Writer:** Well. . . . It's true that people don't like to spend extra money. How else can I say this?
>
> **Reviewer:** What if you give more positive reasons for supporting the cause? That would be a little more inviting.
>
> **Writer:** That's a good idea. I'll try it.

Sharpening the focus

A clearly focused draft fixes readers' attention on one central idea and does not stray from that idea. You can sharpen the focus of a draft by clarifying the introduction (especially the thesis) and by deleting any text that is off the point.

Clarifying the introduction   Reread your introduction to see if it clearly states the essay's main idea. To help you revise, ask your reviewers questions such as the following:

- Does the introduction let readers know what to expect as they read on?

- Does it make the significance of the subject clear so that readers will want to keep reading?

- Can readers tell where the introduction stops and the body of the essay begins? Have you perhaps included material in the introduction that really belongs in the body? Is your introduction too broad or unfocused?

- Does the thesis accurately state the main idea of the essay?

SCHOLARS ON REVISING

Murray, Donald M. *The Craft of Revision*. 5th ed. Orlando: Harbrace, 2003. Print. Murray argues that "we build effective writing more from increasing the strengths of a text than from eliminating error." He shows how writers can increase strengths by paying attention to global matters such as focus, organization, development, and voice.

SCHOLARS ON CONFERENCING

Boynton, Linda. "See Me: Conference Strategies for Developmental Writers." *Teaching English in the Two-Year College* 30.4 (2003): 391–402. Print. Boynton describes twenty-five strategies that teachers can use with basic writers to help them feel at home in a college environment. She categorizes these according to what can be done before, during, and after a conference.

Deleting text that is off the point   Compare the introduction, especially the thesis statement, with the body of the essay. Does the body fulfill the promise of the introduction? If not, you will need to adjust one or the other. Either rebuild the introduction to fit the body or keep the introduction and delete body sentences or paragraphs that stray from its point.

Improving the organization

A draft is well organized when its major divisions are logical and easy to follow. To improve the organization of your draft, you may need to take one or more of the following actions: adding or sharpening topic sentences, moving blocks of text, and inserting headings.

Adding or sharpening topic sentences   Topic sentences state the main ideas of the paragraphs in the body of an essay. (See 3a.) You can review the organization of a draft by reading only the topic sentences. Do the topic sentences clearly support the essay's main idea? Can you turn them into a reasonable sentence outline of the paper? (See 1d.) If your draft lacks topic sentences, add them unless you have a good reason for omitting them.

Moving blocks of text   Improving the organization of a draft can be as simple as moving a few sentences from one paragraph to another or reordering paragraphs. You may also find that you can clarify the organization of a draft by combining choppy paragraphs or by dividing those that are too long for easy reading. (See 3e.) Often, however, the process is more complex. As you move blocks of text, you may need to supply transitions to make the text fit smoothly in the new positions; you may also need to rework topic sentences to make your new organization clear.

SCHOLARS ON CONFERENCING

Gay, Pamela. "Dialogizing Response in the Writing Classroom: Students Answer Back." *Journal of Basic Writing* 17.1 (1998): 3–17. Print. Gay points out that while composition teachers use interaction and dialogue among student writers to promote invention, revision, and evaluation of work in progress, these same teachers may not regularly invite students to discuss teachers' responses. She shares strategies that she uses in her classes to initiate a dialogue between teacher and writer.

Before moving text, consider sketching a revised outline. Divisions in the outline might become topic sentences in the restructured essay. (See 1d.)

Inserting headings In long documents, such as complex research papers or business reports, headings can help readers follow your organization. Typically, headings are presented as phrases, declarative or imperative sentences, or questions. To draw attention to headings, you can center them, put them in boldface, underline them, use all capital letters, or do some combination of these techniques. (See also 62a for use of headings in APA papers.)

Strengthening the content

In reviewing the content of a draft, first consider whether your argument is sound. You may need to rethink your argument as you revise. Second, consider whether any text (sentences or paragraphs) should be added or deleted, keeping in mind what your readers need to know to understand your ideas. If your purpose is to argue a point, consider how persuasively you have proved your point to an intelligent, thoughtful audience. If your purpose is to inform, be sure that you have presented your ideas clearly and with enough detail to meet your readers' needs.

Rethinking your argument A first draft presents you with an opportunity to rethink your argument. You can often deepen your ideas about a subject by asking yourself some hard questions:

- Is your claim more sweeping than the evidence supports?
- Have you left out an important step in the argument?
- Have you dealt fairly with opposing arguments?
- Is your draft free of faulty reasoning? (See 6a.)

WRITING CENTER DIRECTORS ON THE TUTOR'S ROLE

"Sometimes students make unspoken comparisons between writing center visits and visits to other services. Meeting with a tutor is not like a doctor's visit, with a tutor writing out a prescription to make the paper better. It's not like taking dirty clothes to the laundry, with the student dropping off the paper and picking it up later all cleaned up. Instead a writing tutor is a student's partner in improving either the written product or the processes involved in creating it or, most often, both. Students can be expected to *do* things in a session: practice a strategy, record ideas, mark their own papers for revision, rewrite sentences, ask and answer questions. And they should expect to apply the practices and information they've gained from the session on their own."

— Deanne Gute, writing specialist, University of Northern Iowa

Checklist for global revision

Purpose and audience

- Does the draft address a question, a problem, or an issue that readers care about?
- Is the draft appropriate for its audience? Does it address the audience's knowledge of and attitudes toward the subject?
- Is the tone respectful?

Focus

- Is the thesis clear? Is it prominently placed?
- Does the thesis answer a reader's "So what?" question?
- If the draft has no thesis, is there a good reason for omitting it?

Organization and paragraphing

- Is each paragraph unified around a main point?
- Does each paragraph support and develop the thesis?
- Have you provided organizational cues such as topic sentences and headings?
- Are ideas presented in a logical order?
- Are any paragraphs too long or too short for easy reading?

Content

- Is the supporting material relevant and persuasive?
- Which ideas need further development? Have you left your readers with any unanswered questions?
- Are the parts proportioned sensibly? Do major ideas receive enough attention?
- Where might redundant or irrelevant material be deleted?

Point of view

- Is the dominant point of view — first person (*I* or *we*), second person (*you*), or third person (*he, she, it, one,* or *they*) — appropriate for your purpose and audience? (See 13.)

ADDITIONAL RESOURCE ON THE TUTOR'S ROLE

Ryan, Leigh, and Lisa Zimmerelli. *The Bedford Guide for Writing Tutors.* 5th ed. Boston: Bedford, 2010. Print. The authors offer practical guidelines for conferencing with students at all stages of the writing process, helping students with varied backgrounds and learning styles, tutoring students who are writing in various disciplines, coping with difficult tutoring situations, and tutoring online or with computers.

Adding text   If any paragraphs or sections of the essay are too skimpy to be clear and convincing (a common problem in rough drafts), add specific facts, details, and examples. You may need to go back to the beginning of the writing process: listing specifics, brainstorming ideas with friends or classmates, perhaps doing more research. As you revise paragraphs, it's helpful to ask questions such as *Why?* and *How?*

Deleting text   Look for sentences and paragraphs that can be cut without serious loss of meaning. Ask your reviewers if they can show you sentences where you have repeated yourself or strayed from your point. Maybe you have given too much emphasis to minor ideas. Cuts may also be necessitated by word limits, such as those imposed by a college assignment or by the realities of the business world, where readers are often pressed for time.

2c   Revise and edit sentences; proofread a final draft.

When you revise sentences, you focus on effectiveness; when you edit, you check for correctness. Proofreading is a slow and careful reading in search of spelling errors, typos, and other obvious mistakes.

Revising and editing sentences

Much of this book offers advice on revising sentences for clarity and on editing them for grammar, punctuation, and mechanics.

Some writers handle sentence-level revisions directly at the computer, experimenting on-screen with a variety of possible improvements. Other writers prefer to print out a hard copy of the draft and mark it up before making changes in the file.

SCHOLARS ON WRITING CENTERS

Briggs, Lynn C., and Meg Woolbright, eds. *Stories from the Center: Connecting Narrative and Theory in the Writing Center*. Urbana: NCTE, 2000. Print. The essays in this collection focus on the stories writing center directors and tutors tell about their work with student writers, including the conflicts that occur when the writer and the tutor have different goals for the sessions or when a tutor encounters instructor comments or methods that seem misguided.

Here, for example, is a rough-draft paragraph as one student edited it on her computer for a variety of sentence-level problems.

> Although some cities have found creative ways to improve access to public transportation for passengers with physical disabilities, ~~and to fund other programs, there have been problems in~~ our city has struggled with ~~due to the need to address~~ budget constraints and competing ~~needs~~ priorities. ~~This~~ The budget crunch has led citizens to question how funds are distributed.~~?~~ For example, last year ~~when~~ city officials voted to use available funds to support ~~had to choose between allocating funds for accessible transportation or allocating funds to~~ after-school programs rather than transportation upgrades. ~~, they voted for the after-school programs.~~ It is not clear to some citizens why ~~these~~ after-school programs are more important.

The original paragraph was too wordy, a problem that can be addressed through any number of revisions. The following revision would also be acceptable.

> Some cities have funded improved access to public transportation for passengers with physical disabilities. Because of budget constraints, our city chose to fund after-school programs rather than transportation programs. As a result, citizens have begun to question how funds are distributed and why certain programs are more important than others.

Some of the improvements in the first revision do not involve choice and must be fixed in any revision. For example, the hyphen in *after-school programs* is necessary; a noun must be substituted for the pronoun *these* in the last sentence; and the question mark in the second sentence must be changed to a period.

SCHOLARS ON WRITING CENTERS

Thompson, Jan C. "Beyond Fixing Today's Paper: Promoting Metacognition and Writing Development in the Tutorial through Self-Questioning." *Writing Lab Newsletter* 23.6 (1999): 1–6. Print. Thompson discusses several ways to use questions to shape the tutorial dialogue and explains how tutors can help writers learn to use the same strategies independently. Thompson's strategies and suggestions are meant for all levels of students, including those who have learning disabilities.

Proofreading

After revising and editing, you are ready to prepare your final copy. (See the appendix for formatting guidelines for your particular paper.) Make sure to allow yourself enough time for proofreading.

Proofreading is a special kind of reading: a slow and methodical search for misspellings, typographical mistakes, and omitted words or word endings. Such errors can be difficult to spot in your own work because you may read what you intended to write, not what is actually on the page. To fight this natural tendency, try one or more of the following tips.

PROOFREADING TIPS

- Remove distractions and allow yourself ten to fifteen minutes of pure concentration; turn off the TV and your cell phone and find a quiet place, away from people who are talking.

- Proofread out loud, articulating each word as it is actually written.

- Proofread hard copy pages; mistakes can be difficult to catch on-screen.

- Don't rely too heavily on spell checkers and grammar checkers. Before automatically accepting their changes, consider their accuracy and appropriateness.

- Enlist a volunteer (a friend, roommate, or co-worker) to proofread after you.

Although proofreading may be slow, it is crucial. Errors strewn throughout an essay are distracting and annoying. If the writer doesn't care about this piece of writing, the reader might wonder, "Why should I?" A carefully proofread essay, however, sends a positive message: It shows that you value your writing and respect your readers.

hackerhandbooks.com/bedhandbook

e The writing process > As you write: Proofreading your work

TEACHING TIP

Your students might benefit from a discussion about the strengths and limitations of grammar checkers and spell checkers. These tools are useful, but they aren't always correct. If you are seeing strange mistakes in your students' drafts because they reflect the wayward advice of grammar checkers and spell checkers, you might want to present or project examples for your class and facilitate a discussion about relying too heavily on this kind of technology. Be sure to emphasize the need to read critically — always — even when it comes to grammar checker advice!

Creating a personal editing log

An important aspect of becoming a college writer is learning how to identify your grammar, punctuation, and spelling errors. You can use an editing log to keep a personal list of your common errors and learn the rules to correct the errors.

To begin your log, review all the errors identified on your last piece of writing. Use the following questions to guide the development of your personal editing log.

- What errors do you make most frequently?
- What pattern do you see in these errors?
- What rule(s) do you need to learn to correct the errors?
- Where in your handbook will you find the rules?

SAMPLE EDITING LOG PAGE

> **Original Sentence**
>
> Athletes who use any type of biotechnology give themselves an unfair advantage they should be banned from competition.
>
> **Edited Sentence**
>
> Athletes who use any type of biotechnology give themselves an unfair advantage ⌄, and they should be banned from competition.
>
> **Rule or Pattern Applied**
>
> To edit a run-on sentence, use a comma and a coordinating conjunction (and, but, or). Handbook, section 20a

TEACHING TIP

Try presenting or projecting examples of editing logs to show students how to develop their own. An editing log helps students become independent learners and encourages them to use their handbooks to correct their errors. It also saves you time. When students receive a draft back with an error marked, they should use their editing log to record the incorrect sentence from their draft, as well as the handbook section that gives advice about correcting the error, and then to write the revised sentence.

2d Sample student writing: Literacy narrative

Student writer Michelle Nguyen wrote the essay "A Place to Begin" (pp. 74–76) in response to the following assignment.

SAMPLE LITERACY NARRATIVE ASSIGNMENT

How have your experiences with writing, positive or negative, shaped you as a writer? Write a literacy narrative (500–1,000 words) to explore this question. Select one or more key experiences that you think best illustrate how you became the writer you are today. You might want to focus on a particular person who influenced you or on events, inside or outside of school, that shaped your writing attitudes and practices. In addition to telling a story, your narrative should make a larger point about learning to write that will be of interest to your readers.

When she received the assignment, Nguyen considered several possible directions before settling on her focus. To get started, she listed some people who had influenced her writing development and brainstormed about her experiences in ESL classrooms. As she reviewed her notes, she realized that she was most excited about focusing her story on one influential person, a kind old man whose home was a safe haven away from her noisy Hanoi neighborhood. Because the assignment asked her to make a larger point about learning to write, she decided that a good strategy would be to identify something surprising about these experiences, although she wasn't sure at first what that might be. Nguyen's notes in black (see p. 70) are her initial thoughts on the topic. The notes in color are the writer's further thoughts, written a few hours after the original list.

TEACHING TIP

The handbook offers a case study of one writer at work — Michelle Nguyen. Students see her writing process from rough notes to final draft. In pairs or small groups (this exercise would work in an online class, too), ask students to study the differences between Nguyen's rough and final drafts. Ask them to take notes on the following questions: What do they learn about composing and revising from the Nguyen case study? How did the writer's classmates' comments help her to revise? How did her revision goals focus her revision? You might conduct this class just before you hand back a set of drafts and have your students focus on writing revision goals of their own.

SAMPLE NOTES

Who and what has shaped me as a writer?

Possible people:

Uncle Bao gave me his diaries before he died. I didn't know anyone in my family kept a diary—but how did this diary influence me as writer? Not sure.

***Vietnam War veteran—damaged vocal cords—didn't talk much—but he taught me to read and how to take care of small pets. His home provided a safe haven away from my noisy, crime—swamped neighborhood and the first place I could hear myself think. He saw something in me—a writer?—and he encouraged me to write. What was surprising? He was worldly without words. —This looks like something I would like to try writing about.

ESL teacher—Ms. Melrose—made me feel comfortable in my new school, new city, new country. She gave me chocolate when I wrote my first English sentence. —Sounds sweet, but is there anything interesting or surprising about this one? Not sure.

Possible experiences:

Placed in ESL class when I arrived in America. The only Vietnamese speaker. Took a long time to think in English.

Here is the draft that Nguyen submitted, together with the comments she received from three of her classmates.

ROUGH DRAFT WITH PEER COMMENTS

Rough Draft

My family used to live in the heart of Hanoi, Vietnam. The neighborhood was small but swamped with crime. Drug addicts scoured the alleys and stole the most mundane things—old clothes, worn slippers, even license plates of motorbikes. Like anyone else in Vietnam in the '90s, we struggled with poverty. There was no entertainment device in our house aside from an 11" black-and-white television. Even then, electricity went off for hours on a weekly basis.

I was particularly close to a Vietnam War veteran. My parents were away a lot, so the old man became like a grandfather to me. He taught me how to ride a bicycle, how to read, how to take care of small pets. He worked sporadically from home, fixing bicycle tires and broken pedals. He was a wrinkly old man who didn't talk much. His vocal cords were damaged during the war, and it caused him pain to speak. In a neighborhood full of screaming babies and angry shop owners and slimy criminals, his home was my quiet haven. I could read and write and think and bond with someone whose worldliness came from his wordlessness.

The tiny house he lived in stood at the far end of our neighborhood. It always smelled of old clothes and forgotten memories. He was a slight man, but his piercing black eyes retained their intensity even after all these years. He must have made one fierce soldier.

"I almost died once," he said, dusting a picture frame. It was one of those rare instances he ever mentioned his life during the war. As he talked, I perched myself on the side of an armchair, rested my head on my tiny hands, and listened intently. I didn't understand much. I just liked hearing his low, humming voice. The concept

> **Comment [Alex F]:** Add a title to focus readers.

> **Comment [Brian S]:** You have great details here to set the scene in Hanoi, but why does it matter that you didn't have an "entertainment device"? Choose the most interesting among all these details.

> **Comment [Sameera K]:** I really like your introduction. It's so vivid. Think about adding a photo of your neighborhood so readers can relate. What does Hanoi look like?

> **Comment [Brian S]:** Worldliness came from wordlessness — great phrase! Is this part of your main idea? What is your main idea?

> **Comment [Sameera K]:** You do a good job of showing us why this Vietnam veteran was important to you, but it seems like this draft is more a story about the man and not about you.

of war for me was strictly confined to the classroom, and even then, the details of combat were always murky. The teachers just needed us to know that the communist troops enjoyed a glorious victory.

"I was the only survivor of my unit. 20 guys. All dead within a year. Then they let me go," he said. His voice cracked a little and his eyes misted over as he stared at pictures from his combatant past. "We didn't even live long enough to understand what we were fighting for."

He finished the sentence with a drawn-out sigh, a small set of wrinkles gathering at the end of his eyes. Years later, as I thought about his stories, I started to wonder why he referred to his deceased comrades by the collective pronoun "we." It was as if a little bit of him died on the battlefield with them too.

> **Comment [Alex F]:** I like reading about this man, but I'm not sure what point you are making about literacy. Is the point that writing happens in quiet, not in noise?

Three years after my family left the neighborhood, I learned that the old man became stricken with cancer. When I came home the next summer, I visited his house and sat by his sickbed. His shoulder-length mop of salt and pepper hair now dwarfed his rail-thin figure. We barely exchanged a word. He just held my hands tightly until my mother called for me to leave, his skeletal fingers leaving a mark on my pale palms. Perhaps he was trying to transmit to me some of his worldliness and his wisdom. Perhaps he was telling me to go out into the world and live the free life he never had.

> **Comment [Sameera K]:** I'm curious to hear more about you and why this man was so important to you. What did he teach you about writing? What did he see in you?

Some people say that writers are selfish and vain. The truth is, I learned to write because it gave me peace in the much too noisy world of my Vietnamese childhood. In the quiet of the old man's house, I gazed out the window, listened to my thoughts, and wrote them down. It all started with a story about a wrinkly Vietnam War veteran who didn't talk much.

> **Comment [Alex F]:** This sentence is confusing. Your draft doesn't seem to be about the selfishness or vanity of writers.

> **Comment [Brian S]:** What does "it" refer to? I think you're trying to say something important here, but I'm not sure what it is.

After reading her draft and considering the feedback from her classmates, Nguyen realized that she had chosen a good direction but that she hadn't focused her draft to meet the expectations of the assignment. As her classmates pointed out, her rough draft was more a portrait of the Vietnam War veteran and not really a literacy narrative. With her classmates' questions and suggestions in mind, Nguyen developed some goals for revising her draft.

MICHELLE NGUYEN'S REVISION GOALS

- Need a title.
- Revise introduction to set the scene more dramatically. Use Sameera's idea to include a photo of my Vietnamese neighborhood.
- Make the story my story, not the man's story. Answer Sameera's question: What did the man see in me and I in him? Delete extra material about the old man.
- Answer Brian's question: What is my main idea?
- Follow Alex's question about the contrast between quiet and noise and Brian's suggestion about the connection between wordlessness and worldliness. Make the contrasts sharper between the noisy neighborhood and the quiet of the man's house.
- Theme about literacy needs to be clearer. Figure out what main idea I'm trying to communicate. See if there is a possible idea in the various contrasts. The surprise was finding writing in silence, not in the noisy exchange of voices in my neighborhood.

On the following pages is Michelle Nguyen's final draft. For a guide to writing a literacy narrative, see pages 78–79.

hackerhandbooks.com/bedhandbook
🄴 The writing process > Sample student writing
   > Nguyen, Rough Draft (literacy narrative; peer-reviewed)
   > Nguyen, "A Place to Begin" (literacy narrative)

Michelle Nguyen

Professor Wilson

English 101

22 September 2012

A Place to Begin

I grew up in the heart of Hanoi, Vietnam—Nhà Dầu—a small but busy neighborhood swamped with crime. Houses, wedged in among cafés and other local businesses (see fig. 1), measured uniformly about 200 square feet, and the walls were so thin that we could hear every heated debate and impassioned disagreement. Drug addicts scoured the vicinity and stole the most mundane things—old clothes, worn slippers, even license plates of motorbikes. It was a neighborhood where dogs howled and kids ran amok and where the earth was always moist and marked with stains. It was the 1990s Vietnam in miniature, with all the turmoil and growing pains of a newly reborn nation.

In a city perpetually inundated with screaming children and slimy criminals, I found my place in the home of a Vietnam War veteran. My parents were away a lot, so the old man became like a grandfather to me. He was a slight man who didn't talk much. His vocal cords had been damaged during the war, and it caused him pain to speak. In his quiet home, I could read and write in the presence of someone whose worldliness grew from his wordlessness.

His tiny house stood at the far end of our neighborhood and always smelled of old clothes and forgotten memories. His wall was plastered with pictures from his combatant past, pictures that told his life story when his own voice couldn't. "I almost died once," he said, dusting a picture frame. It was one of those rare instances he ever mentioned his life during the war.

I perched myself on the side of the armchair, rested my head on

---

Vivid description and concrete details engage the reader.

Narrative is focused on one key story.

A thesis is not always required for a literacy narrative, but Nguyen uses one to capture her main idea.

Nguyen 2

Fig. 1. Nhà Dầu neighborhood in Hanoi (personal photograph by author).

my tiny hands, and listened intently. I didn't understand much. I just liked hearing his low, raspy voice.

> Photograph conveys physical details and provides authenticity.

"I was the only survivor of my unit. Twenty guys. All dead within a year. Then they let me go."

He finished the sentence with a drawn-out sigh, a small set of wrinkles gathering at the corner of his eye.

> Nguyen develops her narrative with dialogue.

I wanted to hear the details of that story yet was too afraid to ask. But the bits and pieces I did hear, I wrote down in a notebook. I wanted to make sure that there were not only photos but also written words to bear witness to the old veteran's existence.

Once, I caught him looking at the jumbled mess of sentences I'd written. I ran to the table and snatched my notebook, my cheeks warmed with a bright tinge of pink. I was embarrassed. But mostly, I was terrified that he'd hate me for stealing his life story and turning it into a collection of words and characters and ambivalent feelings.

"I'm sorry," I muttered, my gaze drilling a hole into the tiled floor.

Nguyen 3

A dramatic moment demonstrates the relationship between Nguyen and the veteran.

Quietly, he peeled the notebook from my fingers and placed it back on the table.

In his muted way, with his mouth barely twisted in a smile, he seemed to be granting me permission and encouraging me to keep writing. Maybe he saw a storyteller and a writer in me, a little girl with a pencil and too much free time.

The last time I visited Nhà Dầu was for the veteran's funeral two years ago. It was a cold November afternoon, but the weather didn't dampen the usual tumultuous spirit of the neighborhood. I could hear the jumble of shouting voices and howling dogs, yet it didn't bother me. For a minute I closed my eyes, remembering myself as a little girl with a big pencil, gazing out a window and scribbling words in my first notebook.

Circling back to the scene from the first paragraph gives the narrative coherence.

Many people think that words emerge from words and from the exchange of voices. Perhaps this is true. But the surprising paradox of writing for me is that I started to write in the presence of silence. It was only in the utter stillness of a Vietnam War veteran's house that I could hear my thoughts for the first time, appreciate language, and find the confidence to put words on a page. With one notebook and a pencil, and with the encouragement of a wordless man to tell his story, I began to write. Sometimes that's all a writer needs, a quiet place to begin.

Nguyen's main idea gives the story its significance.

2e Prepare a portfolio; reflect on your writing.

At the end of the semester, your instructor may ask you to submit a portfolio, or collection, of your writing. A writing portfolio often consists of drafts, revisions, and reflections that demonstrate a writer's thinking and learning processes or that showcase the writer's best work. Your instructor may give you the choice of submitting your portfolio on paper or electronically.

Your instructor also may distinguish between a *process portfolio* and an *evaluation portfolio* (sometimes called an *assessment portfolio*). A process portfolio allows you to demonstrate your development as a writer; in it you will collect notes, outlines, reflective journal or blog entries, multiple drafts—in short, the messy stuff. In an evaluation portfolio, you will include a few select final pieces that have perhaps been revised multiple times, along with early drafts of those pieces. Your instructor may assign a combination, asking at the end of the semester that you reshape your process portfolio into an evaluation portfolio.

As early in the course as possible, be sure you know the answers to the following questions:

- Should the portfolio be a paper collection or an electronic one? Is it your choice?
- Will the portfolio be a process portfolio, an evaluation portfolio, or a combination?
- Will the portfolio be checked or assessed before the end of the term? If so, when or how often?
- Are you free to choose any or all of the pieces to include?
- Are you free to include a variety of items (not just rough and final drafts of papers), such as outlines and notes, journal entries, photographs or other visuals, comments from reviewers, sound files, or video clips?
- Will your instructor be the primary or only audience for the portfolio? Or will the portfolio be shared with peers or with other instructors?
- Who will evaluate the portfolio?

TEACHING TIP

Keeping a portfolio helps students develop the academic habit of *reflection* so that they can recognize their growth as writers. Writing a reflective opening statement — cover letter, introduction, preface, or memo — provides a wonderful opportunity for students to look back and evaluate their strengths and challenges as a writer. If your program does not use a portfolio system, consider assigning a reflective memo or cover letter with one or more final drafts. Students can realize the benefits of reflecting if they are doing so about an entire semester's worth of work — or about the steps they took to write a single assignment.

Writing Guide
Literacy Narrative

A **literacy narrative** allows you to reflect on key reading or writing experiences and to ask: How have my experiences shaped who I am as a reader or writer? A sample literacy narrative begins on page 74.

Key features

- **A well-told narrative** shows readers what happened. Lively details present the sights, sounds, and smells of the world in which the story takes place. Dialogue and action add interest and energy.

- **A main idea or insight** about reading or writing gives a literacy narrative its significance and transforms it from a personal story to one with larger, universal interest.

- **A well-organized narrative**, like all essays, has a beginning, a middle, and an ending and is focused around a thesis or main idea. Narratives can be written in chronological order, reverse chronological order, or with a series of flashbacks.

- **First-person point of view (I)** gives a narrative immediacy and authenticity. Your voice may be serious or humorous, but it should be appropriate for your main idea.

Thinking ahead: Presenting or publishing

You may have some flexibility in how you present or publish your literacy narrative. If you have the opportunity to submit it as a podcast, video, or another genre, leave time in your schedule for recording or filming. Also, in seeking feedback, ask reviewers to comment on your plans for using sounds or images.

TEACHING TIP

Students enjoy the opportunity to write literacy narratives and learn about themselves as writers. When they ask themselves, "How have my key writing or reading experiences shaped who I am as a writer or reader?" they practice the writerly habits of curiosity and reflection. Consider assigning a literacy narrative — perhaps as a diagnostic essay — early in the semester.

Writing your literacy narrative

Explore

What story will you tell? You can't write about every reading or writing experience or every influential person. Find one interesting experience to focus your narrative. Generate ideas with questions such as the following:

- What challenges have you confronted as a reader or a writer?
- Who were the people who nurtured (or delayed) your reading or writing development?
- What are your best or worst childhood memories of reading or writing?
- What images do you associate with learning to read or write?
- What is significant about the story you want to tell? What larger point do you want readers to take away from your narrative?

Draft

Figure out the best way to tell your story. A narrative isn't a list of "this happened" and then "that happened." It is a focused story with its own logic and order. You don't need to start chronologically. Experiment: What happens if you start in the middle of the story or work in reverse? Try to come up with a tentative organization, and then start to draft.

Revise

Ask reviewers for specific feedback. Here are some questions to guide their comments:

- What main idea do readers take away from your story? Ask them to summarize this idea in one sentence.
- Is the narrative focused around the main idea?
- Are the details vivid? Sufficient? Where might you convey your story more clearly? Would it help to add dialogue? Would visuals deepen the impact of your story?
- Does your introduction bring readers into the world of your story?
- Does your conclusion provide a sense of the story's importance?

TEACHING TIP

Focus students' attention on the key features of the literacy narrative in preparation for writing their own. Ask them to annotate Michelle Nguyen's literacy narrative with the "Key features" from the writing guide for a literacy narrative by their side (see p. 78). Ask them to identify the main idea, the vivid details, and so on.

TIP: Save your notes, drafts, and reviewers' comments for possible use in your portfolio. The more you have assembled, the more you have to choose from to represent your best work. Keep your documents organized in a paper or electronic file system for easy access. (See 1h.)

Reflection—the process of stepping back periodically to examine your decisions, preferences, strengths, and challenges as a writer—helps you recognize your growth as a writer and is the backbone of portfolio keeping.

When you submit your portfolio for a final evaluation or reading, you may be asked to include a reflective opening statement—a cover letter, an introduction, a preface, a memo, or an essay. Whatever form your reflective piece takes, it could be your most important writing in the course. Reflective writing allows you to do the following:

- show that you can identify the strengths and weaknesses of your writing

- comment on the progress you've made in the course

- understand your own writing process

- demonstrate that you've made good writing decisions

- comment on how you might use skills developed in or experiences from your writing course in other courses where writing is assigned

Your instructor will expect you to reflect, too, on how *specific* pieces in the portfolio show your development as a writer.

Check with your instructor about the guidelines for your reflective opening statement.

hackerhandbooks.com/bedhandbook

e The writing process > Sample student writing
    > Bonilla, Sample Reflective Letter for a Portfolio (reflective writing)

ADDITIONAL RESOURCE ON PORTFOLIO TEACHING

Reynolds, Nedra, and Rich Rice. *Portfolio Teaching: A Guide for Instructors.* 2nd ed. Boston: Bedford, 2006. Print. In this professional resource, Reynolds and Rice provide the practical information instructors and writing program administrators need to use the portfolio method successfully in a writing course. Their brief guide includes sections on planning the portfolio course, encouraging reflective learning, and assessing portfolios and concludes with an annotated bibliography.

SAMPLE REFLECTIVE LETTER FOR A PORTFOLIO

Bonilla 1

December 11, 2012
Professor Todd Andersen
Humanities Department
Johnson State College

Dear Professor Andersen,

This semester has been more challenging than I had anticipated. I have always been a good writer, but I discovered this semester that I had to stretch myself in ways that weren't always comfortable. I learned that if I wanted to reach my readers, I needed to understand that not everyone sees the world the way I do. I needed to work with my peers and write multiple drafts to understand that a first draft is just a place to start. I have chosen three pieces of writing for my portfolio: "Negi and the Other Girl: Nicknames and Identity," "School Choice Is a Bad Choice," and "Flat-footed Advertising." Each shows my growth as a writer in different ways, and the final piece was my favorite assignment of the semester.

The peer review sessions that our class held in October helped me with my analytical response paper. My group and I chose to write about "Jíbara," by Esmeralda Santiago, for the Identity unit. My first and second drafts were unfocused. I spent my first draft basically retelling the events of the essay. I think I got stuck doing that because the details of Santiago's essay are so interesting—the biting termites, the burning metal, and the *jíbara* songs on the radio—and because I didn't understand the differences between summary and analysis. My real progress came when I decided to focus the essay on one image—the mirror hanging in Santiago's small house, a mirror that was hung too high

Reflective writing can take various forms. Bonilla wrote her reflection as a letter.

Reflective writing often calls for first person ("I").

Bonilla lists the pieces included in her portfolio by title.

Bonilla comments on a specific area of growth.

ADDITIONAL RESOURCE ON PORTFOLIO KEEPING

Reynolds, Nedra, and Rich Rice. *Portfolio Keeping: A Guide for Students.* 2nd ed. Boston: Bedford, 2006. Print. In its first edition, this was the first guide to provide all the information students need to use the portfolio method successfully in a writing course. In the second edition, Reynolds and Rice pay closer attention to electronic portfolios.

TEACHING TIP

Ask students to focus on the "Key features" from the writing guide for a reflective letter (see p. 84). As a class, annotate Lucy Bonilla's reflective letter to identify how the writer uses these features.

Bonilla 2

for her to look into. Finding a focus helped me move from listing the events of the essay to interpreting those events. I thought my peers would love my first draft, but they found it confusing. Some of their comments were hard to take, but their feedback (and all the peer feedback I received this semester) helped me see my words through a reader's eyes.

Even in the reflective document, Bonilla includes elements of good college writing, such as using transitions.

While my Identity paper shows my struggle with focus, my next paper shows my struggle with argument. For my argument essay, I wrote about charter schools. My position is that the existence of charter schools weakens the quality of public schools. In my first draft, my lines of argument were not in the best order. When I revised, I ended the paper with my most powerful argument: Because they refuse to adopt open enrollment policies and are unwilling to admit students with severe learning or behavior problems, charter schools are elitist. While revising, I also introduced a counterargument in my final draft because our class discussion showed me that many of my peers disagree with me. To persuade them, I needed to address their arguments in favor of charter schools. My essay is stronger because I acknowledged that both the proponents and opponents of abandoning charters want improved education for America's children. It took me a while to understand that including counterarguments would actually make my argument more convincing, especially to readers who don't already agree with

Bonilla reflects on how skills from her writing course will carry over to other courses.

me. Understanding the importance of counterargument helped me with other writing I did in this course, and it will help me in the writing I do for my major, political science.

Another stretch for me this semester was seeing visuals as texts that are worth more than a five-second response. The final assignment was my favorite because it involved a number of

Bonilla 3

surprises. I wasn't so much surprised by the idea that ads make arguments because I understand that they are designed to persuade consumers. What was surprising was being able to see all the elements of a visual and write about how they work together to convey a clear message. For my essay "Flat-footed Advertising," I chose the EAS Performance Nutrition ad "The New Theory of Evolution for Women." In my summary of the ad, I noted that the woman who follows the EAS program for twelve weeks and "evolves" is compared to modern humans and our evolution from apes as shown in the classic 1966 *March of Progress* illustration (Howell 41). It was these familiar poses of "Nicolle," the woman in the image, that drew me to study this ad.

In my first draft, I made all of the obvious points, looking only literally at the comparison and almost congratulating the company on such a clever use of a classic scientific drawing. Your comments on my draft were a little unsettling because you asked me "So what?"—why would my ideas matter to a reader? You pushed me to consider the ad's assumptions and to question the meaning of the word *evolve*. In my revised essay, I argue that even though Nicolle is portrayed as powerful, satisfied, and "fully evolved," the EAS ad campaign rests on the assumption that performance is best measured by physical milestones. In the end, an ad that is meant to pay homage to woman's strength is in fact demeaning. My essay evolved from draft to draft because I allowed my thinking to change and develop as I revised. I've never revised as much as I did with this final assignment. I actually cared about this essay and I wanted to show my readers why my argument mattered.

The expectations for college writing are different from those for high school writing. I believe that my portfolio pieces show that I

Bonilla mentions how comments on her draft helped her revise.

In her conclusion, Bonilla summarizes her growth in the course.

Writing Guide
Reflective Letter

A **reflective letter** gives you an opportunity to introduce yourself as a writer, to show your progress and key decisions, and to introduce the contents of a portfolio. A sample reflective letter begins on page 81.

Key features

- **First-person perspective (*I*)** gives a reflective statement its individuality and authenticity. You are the writer; you are introducing your work and explaining your choices.

- **A thoughtful tone** shows you examining and learning from your experiences and evaluating your strengths and limitations as a writer. Your honest assessment of your work shows that you are a trustworthy and sincere interpreter of your progress.

- **A focused opening statement** provides readers with specific details to understand the contents and organization of your portfolio.

- **Acknowledgment** of the assistance you received shows that you are responsible to readers and reviewers.

Thinking ahead: Presenting or publishing

You may have some flexibility in how you present or publish a reflective piece for your portfolio. Some instructors require a formal essay; others may ask for a letter. Still others may invite you to submit an audio file. If you are submitting an e-portfolio, chances are that your instructor will require your reflective statement in digital form. If you're publishing for the Web, you may want to insert headings for easier navigation.

Writing your reflective letter

Explore

Generate ideas by brainstorming responses to questions such as the following:

- Which piece of writing is your best entry? What does it illustrate about you as a writer, student, or researcher?
- How do the selections in your portfolio illustrate your strengths or challenges?
- What do you learn about your development when you compare your early drafts with your final drafts?
- What do your drafts reveal about your revision process? Examine in detail the revisions you made to one key piece and the changes you want readers to notice.
- How will you use the skills and experiences from your writing course in future courses?

Draft

Follow the guidelines given for the form of your reflective statement — an essay, a cover letter, a memo — and focus your reflections to avoid a list-like structure. Experiment with headings and various chronological or thematic groupings. Ask: What have I learned — and how?

Revise

Ask reviewers for specific feedback. Here are some questions to guide their comments:

- What major idea do readers take away from your reflective statement? Can they summarize it in one sentence?
- Where in your piece do readers want more reflection and more detailed explanations?
- Is your reflective statement focused and organized?
- Have you used specific passages from drafts, feedback, or other documents from your portfolio to illustrate your reflections?
- Have you explained how you will apply what you learned to future writing assignments?
- What added details might give readers a fuller perspective of your development and your accomplishments in the course?

finished this course as a stronger writer. I have learned to take risks in my writing and to use the feedback from you and my peers, and now I know how to acknowledge the points of view of my audience to be more persuasive. I'm glad to have had the chance to write a reflection at the end of the course. I hope you enjoy reading this portfolio and seeing the evolution of my work this semester.

Sincerely,

Lucy Bonilla

Lucy Bonilla

3 Building effective paragraphs

Except for special-purpose paragraphs, such as introductions and conclusions (see 1e and 1g), paragraphs are clusters of information supporting an essay's main point (or advancing a story's action). Aim for paragraphs that are clearly focused, well developed, organized, coherent, and neither too long nor too short for easy reading. Note that there is no ideal length for a paragraph, but your instructor may have specific guidelines.

3a Focus on a main point.

A paragraph should be unified around a main point. The point should be clear to readers, and all sentences in the paragraph should relate to it.

Stating the main point in a topic sentence

As readers move into a paragraph, they need to know where they are—in relation to the whole essay—and what to expect in the sentences to come. A good topic sentence, a one-sentence summary of the paragraph's main point, acts as a signpost pointing in two directions: backward toward the thesis of the essay and forward toward the body of the paragraph.

Like a thesis statement (see 1c), a topic sentence is more general than the material supporting it. Usually the topic sentence (highlighted in the following example) comes first in the paragraph.

hackerhandbooks.com/bedhandbook

e The writing process > As you write: Creating unity

TEACHING TIP

To initiate a discussion about building effective paragraphs, present or project the following statements about paragraphs. Ask students to talk about how they think about paragraphs and paragraphing and what challenges they face when they start to put their ideas in paragraph form.

All living creatures manage some form of communication. The dance patterns of bees in their hive help to point the way to distant flower fields or announce successful foraging. Male stickleback fish regularly swim upside-down to indicate outrage in a courtship contest. Male deer and lemurs mark territorial ownership by rubbing their own body secretions on boundary stones or trees. Everyone has seen a frightened dog put his tail between his legs and run in panic. We, too, use gestures, expressions, postures, and movement to give our words point.

— Olivia Vlahos, *Human Beginnings*

Sometimes the topic sentence is introduced by a transitional sentence linking it to earlier material. In the following paragraph, the topic sentence has been delayed to allow for a transition.

But flowers are not the only source of spectacle in the wilderness. An opportunity for late color is provided by the berries of wildflowers, shrubs, and trees. Baneberry presents its tiny white flowers in spring but in late summer bursts forth with clusters of red berries. Bunchberry, a ground-cover plant, puts out red berries in the fall, and the red berries of wintergreen last from autumn well into the winter. In California, the bright red, fist-sized clusters of Christmas berries can be seen growing beside highways for up to six months of the year.

— James Crockett et al., *Wildflower Gardening*

To hook readers, writers are sometimes tempted to begin paragraphs with vivid quotations or compelling statistics from a source. A topic sentence in the writer's own words, however, can remind readers of the claim of the paper, advance the argument, and introduce the evidence from a source. In the following paragraph on the effects of the 2010 oil spill in the Gulf of Mexico, the writer uses a topic sentence (highlighted) to state that the extent of the threat is unknown before quoting three sources that illustrate her point.

To date, the full ramifications [of the oil spill] remain a question mark. An August report from the National Oceanic

SCHOLARS ON PARAGRAPHS

Lindemann, Erika. *A Rhetoric for Writing Teachers*. 4th ed. New York: Oxford UP, 2001. 146–62. Print. Lindemann distinguishes among views of "paragraphs-as-products" and "paragraphing-as-process," arguing that the former view is less effective in helping students become better writers. Building on the work of Christensen and Winterowd, she offers a sequence of lessons for teaching paragraphing and advises teachers to focus on student writing whenever possible.

WRITING CENTER DIRECTORS ON COHERENCE

"Writing is meant to be read, and that understanding — that movement from writing for the self to writing for readers — is essential if students are to improve their writing. One key role tutors play is that of the

and Atmospheric Administration estimated that 75 percent of the oil had "either evaporated or been burned, skimmed, recovered from the wellhead, or dispersed." However, Woods Hole Oceanographic Institution researchers reported that a 1.2-mile-wide, 650-foot-high plume caused by the spill "had and will persist for some time." And University of Georgia scientists concluded that almost 80 percent of the released oil hadn't been recovered and "remains a threat to the ecosystem."

— Michele Berger, "Volunteer Army"

Occasionally the topic sentence may be withheld until the end of the paragraph—but only if the earlier sentences hang together so well that readers perceive their direction, if not their exact point.

Sticking to the point

Sentences that do not support the topic sentence destroy the unity of a paragraph. If the paragraph is otherwise focused, such sentences can simply be deleted or perhaps moved elsewhere. In the following paragraph describing the inadequate facilities in a high school, the information about the chemistry instructor (highlighted) is clearly off the point.

As the result of tax cuts, the educational facilities of Lincoln High School have reached an all-time low. Some of the books date back to 1990 and have long since shed their covers. The few computers in working order must share one printer. The lack of lab equipment makes it necessary for four or five students to work at one table, with most watching rather than performing experiments. Also, the chemistry instructor left to have a baby at the beginning of the semester, and most of the students don't like the substitute. As for the furniture, many of the upright chairs have become recliners, and the desk legs are so unbalanced that they play seesaw on the floor.

experienced reader, one who can point out what's clear, what needs support, what coheres, and so on. Once student writers get the concept of writing for a reader, they are likely to improve in all of those areas — clarity, unity, coherence — on their own."

— Leslie R. Leach, writing center coordinator, College of the Redwoods

WRITERS ON WRITING

The purpose of paragraphing is to give the reader a rest. The writer is saying: Have you got that? If so, I'll go to the next point.   — H. W. Fowler

Short paragraphs put air around what you write and make it look inviting, whereas one long chunk of type can discourage the reader from even starting to read.   — William Zinsser

EXERCISE 3–1 Underline the topic sentence in the following paragraph and cross out any material that does not clarify or develop the central idea. *More practice:* e

> Quilt making has served as an important means of social, political, and artistic expression for women. In the nineteenth century, quilting circles provided one of the few opportunities for women to forge social bonds outside of their families. Once a week or more, they came together to sew as well as trade small talk, advice, and news. They used dyed cotton fabrics much like the fabrics quilters use today; surprisingly, quilters' basic materials haven't changed that much over the years. Sometimes the women joined their efforts in support of a political cause, making quilts that would be raffled to raise money for temperance societies, hospitals for sick and wounded soldiers, and the fight against slavery. Quilt making also afforded women a means of artistic expression at a time when they had few other creative outlets. Within their socially acceptable roles as homemakers, many quilters subtly pushed back at the restrictions placed on them by experimenting with color, design, and technique.

3b Develop the main point.

Though an occasional short paragraph is fine, particularly if it functions as a transition or emphasizes a point, a series of brief paragraphs suggests inadequate development. How much development is enough? That varies, depending on the writer's purpose and audience.

For example, when health columnist Jane Brody wrote a paragraph attempting to convince readers that it is impossible to lose fat quickly, she knew that she would have to present a great deal of evidence because many dieters want to believe the opposite. She did *not* write only the following:

> When you think about it, it's impossible to lose—as many diets suggest—10 pounds of *fat* in ten days, even on a total

EXERCISE 3–1 *Answers:*

Topic sentence: Quilt making has served as an important means of social, political, and artistic expression for women. Eliminate the following sentence: They used dyed cotton fabrics much like the fabrics quilters use today; surprisingly, quilters' basic materials haven't changed that much over the years.

fast. Even a moderately active person cannot lose so much weight so fast. A less active person hasn't a prayer.

This three-sentence paragraph is too skimpy to be convincing. But the paragraph that Brody did write contains enough evidence to convince even skeptical readers.

> When you think about it, it's impossible to lose—as many . . . diets suggest—10 pounds of *fat* in ten days, even on a total fast. A pound of body fat represents 3,500 calories. To lose 1 pound of fat, you must expend 3,500 more calories than you consume. Let's say you weigh 170 pounds and, as a moderately active person, you burn 2,500 calories a day. If your diet contains only 1,500 calories, you'd have an energy deficit of 1,000 calories a day. In a week's time that would add up to a 7,000-calorie deficit, or 2 pounds of real fat. In ten days, the accumulated deficit would represent nearly 3 pounds of lost body fat. Even if you ate nothing at all for ten days and maintained your usual level of activity, your caloric deficit would add up to 25,000 calories. . . . At 3,500 calories per pound of fat, that's still only 7 pounds of lost fat.
>
> — Jane Brody, *Jane Brody's Nutrition Book*

3c Choose a suitable pattern of organization.

Although paragraphs (and indeed whole essays) may be patterned in any number of ways, certain patterns of organization occur frequently, either alone or in combination: examples and illustrations, narration, description, process, comparison and contrast, analogy, cause and effect, classification and division, and definition. These patterns (sometimes called *methods of development*) have different uses, depending on the writer's subject and purpose.

Examples and illustrations

Examples, perhaps the most common pattern of development, are appropriate whenever the reader might be tempted to ask,

---

TEACHING TIP

When students receive a comment such as "need a transition" or "missing connection," this comment signals that the reader is confused about the progression of the writer's ideas. To give students practice using transitions, distribute a number of paragraphs with missing transitions. These can be student pieces or professional pieces that you alter for the purpose of this activity. In small groups, ask students to talk through the examples and note what is missing or what connections the writers are missing. Then ask each group to revise one paragraph. As a final step, ask students to present their revisions to the class using a document camera.

"For example?" Though examples are just selected instances, not a complete catalog, they are enough to suggest the truth of many topic sentences, as in the following paragraph.

> Normally my parents abided scrupulously by "The Budget," but several times a year Dad would dip into his battered black strongbox and splurge on some irrational, totally satisfying luxury. Once he bought over a hundred comic books at a flea market, doled out to us thereafter at the tantalizing rate of two a week. He always got a whole flat of pansies, Mom's favorite flower, for us to give her on Mother's Day. One day a boy stopped at our house selling fifty-cent raffle tickets on a sailboat, and Dad bought every ticket the boy had left—three books' worth.
>
> — Connie Hailey, student

Illustrations are extended examples, frequently presented in story form. Because they require several sentences apiece, they are used more sparingly than examples. When well selected, however, they can be a vivid and effective means of developing a point. The writer of the following paragraph uses illustrations to demonstrate that Harriet Tubman, the underground railroad's most famous conductor, was a genius at eluding her pursuers.

> Part of [Harriet Tubman's] strategy of conducting was, as in all battle-field operations, the knowledge of how and when to retreat. Numerous allusions have been made to her moves when she suspected that she was in danger. When she feared the party was closely pursued, she would take it for a time on a train southward bound. No one seeing Negroes going in this direction would for an instant suppose them to be fugitives. Once on her return she was at a railroad station. She saw some men reading a poster and she heard one of them reading it aloud. It was a description of her, offering a reward for her capture. She took a southbound train to avert suspicion. At another time when Harriet heard men talking about her, she pretended to

WRITING CENTER DIRECTORS ON THE TUTOR'S ROLE

"Many students need emotional encouragement as much as specific writing instruction. They have not been successful writers in the past and are often literally afraid of writing. Before they can be successful, they need to identify themselves as writers who own the work they create rather than merely as students trying to get a good grade in a class. We try to help them achieve this goal by pointing out areas where they are strong and showing them how to build upon those strengths."

— Elizabeth Caulfield, student learning center director,
Palm Beach State College

read a book which she carried. One man remarked, "This can't be the woman. The one we want can't read or write." Harriet devoutly hoped the book was right side up.

— Earl Conrad, *Harriet Tubman*

Narration

A paragraph of narration tells a story or part of a story. Narrative paragraphs are usually arranged in chronological order, but they may also contain flashbacks, interruptions that take the story back to an earlier time. The following paragraph, from Jane Goodall's *In the Shadow of Man*, recounts one of the author's experiences in the African wild.

> One evening when I was wading in the shallows of the lake to pass a rocky outcrop, I suddenly stopped dead as I saw the sinuous black body of a snake in the water. It was all of six feet long, and from the slight hood and the dark stripes at the back of the neck I knew it to be a Storm's water cobra—a deadly reptile for the bite of which there was, at that time, no serum. As I stared at it an incoming wave gently deposited part of its body on one of my feet. I remained motionless, not even breathing, until the wave rolled back into the lake, drawing the snake with it. Then I leaped out of the water as fast as I could, my heart hammering.

> — Jane Goodall, *In the Shadow of Man*

Description

A descriptive paragraph sketches a portrait of a person, place, or thing by using concrete and specific details that appeal to one or more of our senses—sight, sound, smell, taste, and touch. Consider, for example, the following description of the grasshopper invasions that devastated the midwestern landscape in the United States in the late 1860s.

SCHOLARS ON THE HISTORY OF WRITING INSTRUCTION

Russell, David R. *Writing in the Academic Disciplines: A Curricular History.* 2nd ed. Carbondale: Southern Illinois UP, 2002. Print. Russell's book provides a useful parallel to histories of writing instruction in English departments. He examines "the broader, though largely tacit traditions students encounter in the whole curriculum" to understand the ways students learn to write in their fields. Writing, he argues, is not a single skill that can be taught once and for all in a general composition course; rather it is deeply embedded in the diverse practices of disciplinary discourse communities. His chapters trace the effects of increasingly specialized disciplines on writing instruction, the role of writing in general education reforms, the evolution of the writing across the curriculum (WAC) movement, and the distinction between and curricular models for WAC and writing in the disciplines (WID).

They came like dive bombers out of the west. They came by the millions with the rustle of their wings roaring overhead. They came in waves, like the rolls of the sea, descending with a terrifying speed, breaking now and again like a mighty surf. They came with the force of a williwaw and they formed a huge, ominous, dark brown cloud that eclipsed the sun. They dipped and touched earth, hitting objects and people like hailstones. But they were not hail. These were *live* demons. They popped, snapped, crackled, and roared. They were dark brown, an inch or longer in length, plump in the middle and tapered at the ends. They had transparent wings, slender legs, and two black eyes that flashed with a fierce intelligence.

— Eugene Boe, "Pioneers to Eternity"

Process

A process paragraph is structured in chronological order. A writer may choose this pattern either to describe how something is made or done or to explain to readers, step-by-step, how to do something. Here is a paragraph explaining how to perform a "roll cast," a popular fly-fishing technique.

Begin by taking up a suitable stance, with one foot slightly in front of the other and the rod pointing down the line. Then begin a smooth, steady draw, raising your rod hand to just above shoulder height and lifting the rod to the 10:30 or 11:00 position. This steady draw allows a loop of line to form between the rod top and the water. While the line is still moving, raise the rod slightly, then punch it rapidly forward and down. The rod is now flexed and under maximum compression, and the line follows its path, bellying out slightly behind you and coming off the water close to your feet. As you power the rod down through the 3:00 position, the belly of line will roll forward. Follow through smoothly so that the line unfolds and straightens above the water.

— *The Dorling Kindersley Encyclopedia of Fishing*

SCHOLARS ON THE HISTORY OF WRITING INSTRUCTION

Murphy, James J., ed. *A Short History of Writing Instruction: From Ancient Greece to Modern America*. Mahwah: Erlbaum, 2001. Print. This collection traces the development of writing instruction from its roots in ancient Greece, where it supplemented oral instruction and trained the mind in abstract thinking and self-reflection. The book then covers the instructional materials and methods of the Middle Ages and the Renaissance and the teaching practices that evolved in Britain and America. The discussion of the evolution of writing instruction in the United States begins in the seventeenth century and covers the emergence of rhetoric and composition as a discipline, its major theories, and the literacy "crises" to which it has responded over the last century.

Comparison and contrast

To compare two subjects is to draw attention to their similarities, although the word *compare* also has a broader meaning that includes a consideration of differences. To contrast is to focus only on differences.

Whether a paragraph stresses similarities or differences, it may be patterned in one of two ways. The two subjects may be presented one at a time, as in the following paragraph of contrast.

> So Grant and Lee were in complete contrast, representing two diametrically opposed elements in American life. Grant was the modern man emerging; beyond him, ready to come on the stage, was the great age of steel and machinery, of crowded cities and a restless, burgeoning vitality. Lee might have ridden down from the old age of chivalry, lance in hand, silken banner fluttering over his head. Each man was the perfect champion of his cause, drawing both his strengths and his weaknesses from the people he led.
> — Bruce Catton, "Grant and Lee: A Study in Contrasts"

Or a paragraph may proceed point by point, treating the two subjects together, one aspect at a time. The following paragraph uses the point-by-point method to contrast speeches given by Abraham Lincoln in 1860 and Barack Obama in 2008.

> Two men, two speeches. The men, both lawyers, both from Illinois, were seeking the presidency, despite what seemed their crippling connection with extremists. Each was young by modern standards for a president. Abraham Lincoln had turned fifty-one just five days before delivering his speech. Barack Obama was forty-six when he gave his. Their political experience was mainly provincial, in the Illinois legislature for both of them, and they had received little exposure at the national level—two years in the House of Representatives for Lincoln, four years in the Senate for Obama. Yet each was seeking his party's nomination against a New York senator of longer

SCHOLARS ON THE HISTORY OF WRITING INSTRUCTION

Connors, Robert J. "Personal Writing Assignments." *College Composition and Communication* 38.2 (1987): 166–83. Print. Connors tracks the shift in writing instruction from assignments on "impersonal," abstract topics, which asked students to draw from their own store of knowledge and reading, to assignments based on personal experience that became dominant in the late nineteenth century, when it was believed that students would write better essays if they wrote about themselves.

standing and greater prior reputation — Lincoln against Senator William Seward, Obama against Senator Hillary Clinton. They were both known for having opposed an initially popular war — Lincoln against President Polk's Mexican War, raised on the basis of a fictitious provocation; Obama against President Bush's Iraq War, launched on false claims that Saddam Hussein possessed WMDs [weapons of mass destruction] and had made an alliance with Osama bin Laden.

— Garry Wills, "Two Speeches on Race"

Analogy

Analogies draw comparisons between items that appear to have little in common. Writers turn to analogies for a variety of reasons: to make the unfamiliar seem familiar, to provide a concrete understanding of an abstract topic, to argue a point, or to provoke fresh thoughts or changed feelings about a subject. In the following paragraph, physician Lewis Thomas draws an analogy between the behavior of ants and that of humans.

Ants are so much like human beings as to be an embarrassment. They farm fungi, raise aphids as livestock, launch armies into wars, use chemical sprays to alarm and confuse enemies, capture slaves. The families of weaver ants engage in child labor, holding their larvae like shuttles to spin out the thread that sews the leaves together for their fungus gardens. They exchange information ceaselessly. They do everything but watch television.

— Lewis Thomas, "On Societies as Organisms"

Although analogies can be a powerful tool for illuminating a subject, they should be used with caution in arguments. Just because two things may be alike in one respect, we cannot conclude that they are alike in all respects. (See "false analogy," p. 146.)

SCHOLARS ON RESPONDING TO STUDENT WRITING

Sommers, Nancy. "Responding to Student Writing." *College Composition and Communication* 33.2 (1982): 148–56. Print. Sommers takes a look at the academic writing process from an unexpected angle as she discusses the meaning and the motive behind teacher comments. Just as students must expend a great deal of effort to craft a successful essay, the author reminds us that teachers must also strive to respond in ways that help students see the need to revise and that encourage students to see the "potential for development."

Cause and effect

When causes and effects are a matter of argument, they are too complex to be reduced to a simple pattern (see p. 146). However, if a writer wishes merely to describe a cause-and-effect relationship that is generally accepted, then the effect may be stated in the topic sentence, with the causes listed in the body of the paragraph.

> The fantastic water clarity of the Mount Gambier sinkholes results from several factors. The holes are fed from aquifers holding rainwater that fell decades — even centuries — ago, and that has been filtered through miles of limestone. The high level of calcium that limestone adds causes the silty detritus from dead plants and animals to cling together and settle quickly to the bottom. Abundant bottom vegetation in the shallow sinkholes also helps bind the silt. And the rapid turnover of water prohibits stagnation.
> — Hillary Hauser, "Exploring a Sunken Realm in Australia"

Or the paragraph may move from cause to effects, as in this paragraph from a student paper on the effects of the industrial revolution on American farms.

> The rise of rail transport in the nineteenth century forever changed American farming — for better and for worse. Farmers who once raised crops and livestock to sustain just their own families could now make a profit by selling their goods in towns and cities miles away. These new markets improved the living standard of struggling farm families and encouraged them to seek out innovations that would increase their profits. On the downside, the competition fostered by the new markets sometimes created hostility among neighboring farm families where there had once been a spirit of cooperation. Those farmers who couldn't compete with their neighbors left farming forever, facing poverty worse than they had ever known.
> — Chris Mileski, student

AN ADDITIONAL RESOURCE ON RESPONDING TO STUDENT WRITING

Sommers, Nancy. *Responding to Student Writers*. Boston: Bedford, 2012. Print. Sommers offers a model for thinking about response as a dialogue between students and teachers — and for thinking about the benefits of responding to *writers* as well as to their writing. In this resource, which is based on her research and her travels to two- and four-year colleges and universities, Sommers focuses on the roles that teacher feedback plays in writers' development and offers strategies for moving away from responding as correcting.

Classification and division

Classification is the grouping of items into categories according to some consistent principle. For example, an elementary school teacher might classify children's books according to their level of difficulty, but a librarian might group them by subject matter. The principle of classification that a writer chooses ultimately depends on the purpose of the classification. The following paragraph classifies species of electric fish.

> Scientists sort electric fishes into three categories. The first comprises the strongly electric species like the marine electric rays or the freshwater African electric catfish and South American electric eel. Known since the dawn of history, these deliver a punch strong enough to stun a human. In recent years, biologists have focused on a second category: weakly electric fish in the South American and African rivers that use tiny voltages for communication and navigation. The third group contains sharks, nonelectric rays, and catfish, which do not emit a field but possess sensors that enable them to detect the minute amounts of electricity that leak out of other organisms.
> — Anne and Jack Rudloe, "Electric Warfare: The Fish That Kill with Thunderbolts"

Division takes one item and divides it into parts. As with classification, division should be made according to some consistent principle. The following passage describes the components that make up a baseball.

> Like the game itself, a baseball is composed of many layers. One of the delicious joys of childhood is to take apart a baseball and examine the wonders within. You begin by removing the red cotton thread and peeling off the leather cover—which comes from the hide of a Holstein cow and has been tanned, cut, printed, and punched with holes. Beneath the cover is a thin layer of cotton string, followed by several hundred yards of woolen yarn, which makes up the bulk of the ball. Finally,

AN ADDITIONAL RESOURCE ON RESPONDING TO STUDENT WRITING

White, Edward M. *Assigning, Responding, Evaluating: A Writing Teacher's Guide.* 4th ed. Boston: Bedford, 2007. Print. White offers advice on developing assignments; on different methods of assessing, evaluating, and responding to student writing; and on conducting large-scale exit or proficiency exams.

in the middle is a rubber ball, or "pill," which is a little smaller than a golf ball. Slice into the rubber and you'll find the ball's heart—a cork core. The cork is from Portugal, the rubber from southeast Asia, the covers are American, and the balls are assembled in Costa Rica.

— Dan Gutman, *The Way Baseball Works*

Definition

A definition puts a word or concept into a general class and then provides enough details to distinguish it from others in the same class. In the following paragraph, the writer defines *envy* as a special kind of desire.

Envy is so integral and so painful a part of what animates behavior in market societies that many people have forgotten the full meaning of the word, simplifying it into one of the synonyms of desire. It is that, which may be why it flourishes in market societies: democracies of desire, they might be called, with money for ballots, stuffing permitted. But envy is more or less than desire. It begins with an almost frantic sense of emptiness inside oneself, as if the pump of one's heart were sucking on air. One has to be blind to perceive the emptiness, of course, but that's just what envy is, a selective blindness. *Invidia*, Latin for envy, translates as "non-sight," and Dante has the envious plodding along under cloaks of lead, their eyes sewn shut with leaden wire. What they are blind to is what they have, God-given and humanly nurtured, in themselves.

— Nelson W. Aldrich Jr., *Old Money*

3d Make paragraphs coherent.

When sentences and paragraphs flow from one to another without discernible bumps, gaps, or shifts, they are said to be

SCHOLARS ON RESPONDING TO STUDENT WRITING

Tobin, Lad. *Reading Student Writing: Confessions, Meditations, and Rants.* Portsmouth: Boynton, 2004. Print. Writing in an engagingly personal voice, Tobin discusses the way our identities, values, and assumptions shape the way we read and respond to our students' writing. He combines memoir, stories of the classroom, and self-reflection to argue that we can read even the most problematic student texts more generously if we reflect on our own experiences as student writers and if we recognize that teacher burnout and institutional attitudes toward student writing may be the cause, not the effect, of "bad" student writing.

coherent. Coherence can be improved by strengthening the ties between old information and new. A number of techniques for strengthening those ties are detailed in this section.

Linking ideas clearly

Readers expect to learn a paragraph's main point in a topic sentence early in the paragraph. Then, as they move into the body of the paragraph, they expect to encounter specific details, facts, or examples that support the topic sentence—either directly or indirectly.

If a sentence does not support the topic sentence directly, readers expect it to support another sentence in the paragraph and therefore to support the topic sentence indirectly. The following paragraph begins with a topic sentence. The highlighted sentences are direct supports, and the rest of the sentences are indirect supports.

> Though the open-space classroom works for many children, it is not practical for my son, David. First, David is hyperactive. When he was placed in an open-space classroom, he became distracted and confused. He was tempted to watch the movement going on around him instead of concentrating on his own work. Second, David has a tendency to transpose letters and numbers, a tendency that can be overcome only by individual attention from the instructor. In the open classroom he was moved from teacher to teacher, with each one responsible for a different subject. No single teacher worked with David long enough to diagnose the problem, let alone help him with it. Finally, David is not a highly motivated learner. In the open classroom, he was graded "at his own level," not by criteria for a certain grade. He could receive a B in reading and still be a grade level behind, because he was doing satisfactory work "at his own level."
> — Margaret Smith, student

Repeating key words

Repetition of key words is an important technique for gaining coherence. To prevent repetitions from becoming dull, you can use variations of a key word (*hike, hiker, hiking*), pronouns referring to

SCHOLARS ON RESPONDING TO STUDENT WRITING

Ransdell, D. R. "Directive versus Facilitative Commentary." *Teaching English in the Two-Year College* 26.3 (1999): 269–76. Print. Responding to work by Richard Straub, who recommends facilitative rather than directive comments on student writing, Ransdell argues that both styles of commentary can be useful. Ransdell showed her students each type of comment on side-by-side versions of the same draft and asked them which style they preferred. The students were divided in their preferences, offering good rationales for both styles.

the word (*gamblers . . . they*), and synonyms (*run, spring, race, dash*). In the following paragraph describing plots among indentured servants in the seventeenth century, historian Richard Hofstadter binds sentences together by repeating the key word *plots* and echoing it with a variety of synonyms (which are highlighted).

> Plots hatched by several servants to run away together occurred mostly in the plantation colonies, and the few recorded servant uprisings were entirely limited to those colonies. Virginia had been forced from its very earliest years to take stringent steps against mutinous plots, and severe punishments for such behavior were recorded. Most servant plots occurred in the seventeenth century: a contemplated uprising was nipped in the bud in York County in 1661; apparently led by some left-wing offshoots of the Great Rebellion, servants plotted an insurrection in Gloucester County in 1663, and four leaders were condemned and executed; some discontented servants apparently joined Bacon's Rebellion in the 1670's. In the 1680's the planters became newly apprehensive of discontent among the servants "owing to their great necessities and want of clothes," and it was feared they would rise up and plunder the storehouses and ships; in 1682 there were plant-cutting riots in which servants and laborers, as well as some planters, took part.
> — Richard Hofstadter, *America at 1750*

Using parallel structures

Parallel structures are frequently used within sentences to underscore the similarity of ideas (see 9). They may also be used to bind together a series of sentences expressing similar information. In the following passage describing folk beliefs, anthropologist Margaret Mead presents similar information in parallel grammatical form.

> Actually, almost every day, even in the most sophisticated home, something is likely to happen that evokes the memory of some old folk belief. The salt spills. A knife falls to the floor. Your nose tickles. Then perhaps, with a slightly embarrassed smile, the person who spilled the salt tosses a pinch over his left

SCHOLARS ON RESPONDING TO STUDENT WRITING

Smith, Summer. "The Genre of the End Comment: Conventions in Teacher Responses to Student Writing." *College Composition and Communication* 48.2 (1997): 249–68. Print. Examining more than three hundred end comments written on student writing, Smith identifies sixteen "primary genres" divided further into three categories: "judging genres," "reader response genres," and "coaching genres." Smith also examines the ways that teachers choose from among these genres — such as evaluation of style, of effort, of correctness — to construct end comments. Smith suggests that generic end comments are less helpful to students, while comments that focus on a writer's performance are more helpful.

shoulder. Or someone recites the old rhyme, "Knife falls, gentleman calls." Or as you rub your nose you think, That means a letter. I wonder who's writing?

— Margaret Mead, "New Superstitions for Old"

Maintaining consistency

Coherence suffers whenever a draft shifts confusingly from one point of view to another or from one verb tense to another. (See 13.) In addition, coherence can suffer when new information is introduced with the subject of each sentence. As a rule, a sentence's subject should echo a subject or an object in the previous sentence.

Providing transitions

Transitions help readers move from sentence to sentence; they also alert readers to more global connections of ideas—those between paragraphs or even larger blocks of text.

Sentence-level transitions Certain words and phrases signal connections between (or within) sentences. Frequently used transitions are included in the chart on page 104.

Skilled writers use transitional expressions with care, making sure, for example, not to use *consequently* when *also* would be more precise. They are also careful to select transitions with an appropriate tone, perhaps preferring *so* to *thus* in an informal piece, *in summary* to *in short* for a scholarly essay.

In the following paragraph, taken from an argument that dinosaurs had the "'right-sized' brains for reptiles of their body size," biologist Stephen Jay Gould uses transitions (highlighted) with skill.

I don't wish to deny that the flattened, minuscule head of large bodied Stegosaurus houses little brain from our subjective, top-heavy perspective, but I do wish to assert that we should not expect more of the beast. First of all, large animals have relatively smaller brains than related, small animals. The correlation of brain size with body size among kindred animals (all reptiles, all mammals, for example) is remarkably regular. As we move from

---

SCHOLARS ON COHERENCE

Lan, Haixia. "Contrastive Rhetoric: A Must in Cross-Cultural Inquiries." *ALT DIS: Alternative Discourses and the Academy.* Ed. Christopher Schroeder, Helen Fox, and Patricia Bizzell. Portsmouth: Boynton, 2002. 68–79. Print. Lan traces the cultural and discursive differences in Western and Chinese approaches to constructing analytical arguments. She shows how philosophically different views affect every aspect of written communication, from invention to the shape of a thesis to ways of reasoning and constructing coherent texts. Cultures shape texts, she argues, but discursive practices also shape cultural perspectives.

Choose transitions carefully and vary them appropriately. Each transition has a different meaning (see the chart on p. 104). If you do not use a transition with an appropriate meaning, you might confuse your readers.

▶ Although taking eight o'clock classes may seem

unappealing, coming to school early has its advantages.
For example,
~~Moreover,~~ students who arrive early typically avoid
∧
the worst traffic and find the best parking spaces.

small to large animals, from mice to elephants or small lizards to Komodo dragons, brain size increases, but not so fast as body size. In other words, bodies grow faster than brains, and large animals have low ratios of brain weight to body weight. In fact, brains grow only about two-thirds as fast as bodies. Since we have no reason to believe that large animals are consistently stupider than their smaller relatives, we must conclude that large animals require relatively less brain to do as well as smaller animals. If we do not recognize this relationship, we are likely to underestimate the mental power of very large animals, dinosaurs in particular.

— Stephen Jay Gould, "Were Dinosaurs Dumb?"

Paragraph-level transitions   Paragraph-level transitions usually link the *first* sentence of a new paragraph with the *first* sentence of the previous paragraph. In other words, the topic sentences signal global connections.

Look for opportunities to allude to the subject of a previous paragraph (as summed up in its topic sentence) in the topic sentence of the next one. In his essay "Little Green Lies," Jonathan

hackerhandbooks.com/bedhandbook

e The writing process > As you write: Using transitions
e The writing process > Exercises: 3–3

SCHOLARS ON COHERENCE

Powell, Malea. "Listening to Ghosts: An Alternative (Non)Argument." *ALT DIS: Alternative Discourses and the Academy*. Ed. Christopher Schroeder, Helen Fox, and Patricia Bizzell. Portsmouth: Boynton, 2002. 11–22. Print. In this evocative essay, which mixes stories and analysis, Powell, a Native American scholar, invites readers to rethink the logic of the traditional argument essay. She questions the assumptions that underlie notions of coherence and invites teachers, by her example, to imagine discourse practices that challenge inherited standards and to "reinvent our writings in another voice, another language."

Common transitions

To show addition: and, also, besides, further, furthermore, in addition, moreover, next, too, first, second

To give examples: for example, for instance, to illustrate, in fact, specifically

To compare: also, in the same manner, similarly, likewise

To contrast: but, however, on the other hand, in contrast, nevertheless, still, even though, on the contrary, yet, although

To summarize or conclude: in short, in summary, in conclusion, to sum up, therefore

To show time: after, as, before, next, during, later, finally, meanwhile, then, when, while, immediately

To show place or direction: above, below, beyond, nearby, opposite, close, to the left

To indicate logical relationship: if, so, therefore, consequently, thus, as a result, for this reason, because, since

H. Adler uses this strategy in the following topic sentences, which appear in a passage describing the benefits of plastic packaging.

> Consider aseptic packaging, the synthetic packaging for the "juice boxes" so many children bring to school with their lunch. One criticism of aseptic packaging is that it is nearly impossible to recycle, yet on almost every other count, aseptic packaging is environmentally preferable to the packaging alternatives. Not only do aseptic containers not require refrigeration to keep their contents from spoiling, but their manufacture requires less than one-10th the energy of making glass bottles.
>
> What is true for juice boxes is also true for other forms of synthetic packaging. The use of polystyrene, which is commonly (and mistakenly) referred to as "Styrofoam," can reduce food waste dramatically due to its insulating properties. (Thanks to these properties, polystyrene cups are much preferred over paper for that morning cup of coffee.) Polystyrene also requires significantly fewer resources to produce than its paper counterpart.

Transitions between blocks of text   In long essays, you will need to alert readers to connections between blocks of text that are more than one paragraph long. You can do this by inserting transitional sentences or short paragraphs at key points in the essay. Here, for example, is a transitional paragraph from a student research paper. It announces that the first part of the paper (about how apes demonstrate language skills) has come to a close and the second part (about whether they understand grammar) is about to begin.

> Although the great apes have demonstrated significant language skills, one central question remains: Can they be taught to use that uniquely human language tool we call grammar, to learn the difference, for instance, between "ape bite human" and "human bite ape"? In other words, can an ape create a sentence?

Another strategy to help readers move from one block of text to another is to insert headings in your essay. Headings, which usually sit above blocks of text, allow you to announce a new topic boldly, without the need for subtle transitions.

3e If necessary, adjust paragraph length.

Most readers feel comfortable reading paragraphs that range between one hundred and two hundred words. Shorter paragraphs require too much starting and stopping, and longer ones strain readers' attention span. There are exceptions to this guideline, however. Paragraphs longer than two hundred words frequently appear in scholarly writing, where scholars explore complex ideas. Paragraphs shorter than one hundred words occur in newspapers because of narrow columns; in informal essays to quicken the pace; and in business writing and Web sites, where readers routinely skim for main ideas.

In an essay, the first and last paragraphs will ordinarily be the introduction and the conclusion. These special-purpose paragraphs are likely to be shorter than the paragraphs in the body of the essay. Typically, the body paragraphs will follow the essay's outline: one paragraph per point in short essays, several paragraphs per point in longer ones. Some ideas require more development than others, however, so it is best to be flexible. If an idea stretches to a length unreasonable for a paragraph, you should divide the paragraph, even if you have presented comparable points in the essay in single paragraphs.

Paragraph breaks are not always made for strictly logical reasons. Writers use them for the following reasons as well.

REASONS FOR BEGINNING A NEW PARAGRAPH

- to mark off the introduction and the conclusion
- to signal a shift to a new idea
- to indicate an important shift in time or place
- to emphasize a point (by placing it at the beginning or the end, not in the middle, of a paragraph)
- to highlight a contrast
- to signal a change of speakers (in dialogue)
- to provide readers with a needed pause
- to break up text that looks too dense

Beware of using too many short, choppy paragraphs, however. Readers want to see how your ideas connect, and they become irritated when you break their momentum by forcing them to pause every few sentences. Here are some reasons you might have for combining some of the paragraphs in a rough draft.

REASONS FOR COMBINING PARAGRAPHS

- to clarify the essay's organization
- to connect closely related ideas
- to bind together text that looks too choppy

PART II

Academic Reading and Writing

Becoming a College Writer

curiosity **engagement** responsibility reflection

Engage with the texts you read

> "The best way to become a good writer is to become a good reader. The more you take from a reading, the more you have to give as a writer."
>
> — **Carolyn Cremona**, student, Austin Community College

In college, you'll read a range of texts, and you'll be asked to respond — to write analytically about the texts you read, to argue with their authors, and to offer your insights about what the texts mean. College reading and writing are intertwined. Becoming a college writer requires you to develop a new habit, as Carolyn Cremona suggests: Become an engaged reader.

You might ask, though, "How can I judge the work of a researcher who has spent decades studying a topic?" This is a natural question. After all, these expectations — entering academic conversations and taking positions on topics you are learning about — may be new to you. Commit yourself to reading carefully enough to understand an author's ideas and then reading skeptically enough to question those ideas and talk back to the author.

- Think back to a time when you felt strongly about something you read — in or out of school. What made you react so strongly: The topic? The author's message or method (way of communicating)? Your own values or beliefs?

MORE
Sample annotated reading, page 111
Asking the "So what?" question, page 115
Guidelines for active reading, page 114

TEACHING TIP

Use the student quotation as a discussion prompt. Ask students if they agree with Cremona. How are reading and writing related? It might help to share with them your thoughts about the relationship between these two academic tasks. If you assign a great deal of reading in your writing course, discuss your reasoning behind this. What are your goals for your students?

4 Reading and writing critically

To become a college writer, you need to become a critical, engaged reader—habitually questioning and conversing with the texts you read. When you read critically, you read with an open, curious, even skeptical mind to understand both what is said and why. You examine a text's assumptions, assess its evidence, and weigh its conclusions. You read and reread to comprehend an author's ideas and what those ideas mean to you. And when you write critically, you respond to a text and its author, with thoughtful questions and personal insights, offering your judgment of *how* the parts of a text contribute to its overall effect.

As you write across the disciplines, you will be asked to read, respond to, and analyze a wide range of complex texts—books, articles, essays, reports, case studies. To write about these texts, you need to read them actively.

4a Read actively.

Reading, like writing, is an active process that happens in steps. Most texts, such as the ones assigned in college, don't yield their meaning with one quick reading. Rather, they require you to read and reread to grasp the gist, the main point, and to comprehend a text's many layers of meaning.

When you read actively, you pay attention to details you would miss if you just skimmed a text and let its words slip past you. First, you read to understand the main ideas. Then you pay attention to your own reactions by making note of what interests, surprises, or puzzles you. Active readers preview a text, annotate it, and then converse with it.

hackerhandbooks.com/bedhandbook

e Academic reading and writing > As you write: Reading actively

TEACHING TIP

Ask students to read short pieces online—perhaps articles from the school's online newspaper or blog posts that relate to a topic you may be talking about in class. Then ask them to write brief summaries of these pieces so that they get practice reading online—and summarizing as well.

TEACHING TIP

If students' assigned readings include essays, articles, and posts written by contemporary writers—those who have blogs and other forums for comments—ask students to talk back, literally, to an author by posting a comment. With guidelines about audience awareness, this exercise can provide an opportunity for students to make a contribution to a real dialogue.

Previewing a text

Previewing—looking quickly through a text before you read—helps you understand its basic features and structure. A text's title, for example, may reveal an author's purpose; a text's format or design may reveal what kind of text it is—a book, a report, a policy memo, and so on. As you preview, you can browse for illustrations, scan headings, and gain a sense of the text's subsections. The more you know about a text before you read it, the easier it will be to dig deeper into it.

Annotating a text

Annotating helps you capture and record your responses to a text. As you annotate, you take notes—you jot down questions and reactions in the margins of the text or on electronic or paper sticky notes. You might circle or underline the author's main points or key ideas. Or you might develop your own system of annotating by placing question marks, asterisks, or stars by the text's thesis or major pieces of evidence. Annotating a text will help you make sense of it and answer the basic question "What is this text about?"

As you annotate and think about a text, you are starting to write about it. Responding with notes helps you frame what *you* want to say about the author's ideas or questions you want to address in response to the text. On a second or third reading, you may notice contradictions—statements the author makes that, put side-by-side, just don't seem to make sense—or surprising insights that may lead to further investigation. Each rereading will raise new questions and lead to a better understanding of the text.

The following example shows how one student, Emilia Sanchez, annotated an article from *CQ Researcher*, a newsletter about social and political issues.

TEACHING TIP

To initiate a discussion about reading actively, present or project this quotation, by playwright George Bernard Shaw: "As soon as I open [a book], I occupy the book, I stomp around in it. I underline passages, scribble in the margins, leave my mark. I like to be able to hear myself responding to a book, answering it, agreeing and disagreeing in a manner I recognize as peculiarly my own." Ask students what they think it means to "stomp around in" something that they read.

ANNOTATED ARTICLE

Big Box Stores Are Bad for Main Street

BETSY TAYLOR

Opening strategy — the problem is not x, it's y.

There is plenty of reason to be concerned about the proliferation of Wal-Marts and other so-called "big box" stores. The question, however, is not whether or not these types of stores create jobs (although several studies claim they produce a net job loss in local communities) or whether they ultimately save consumers money. The real concern about having a 25-acre slab of concrete with a 100,000 square foot box of stuff land on a town is whether it's good for a community's soul.

Sentimental — what is a community's soul? I would think job security and a strong economy are better for a community's "soul" than small stores that have to lay people off or close.

Lumps all big boxes together.

Assumes all small businesses are attentive.

The worst thing about "big boxes" is that they have a tendency to produce Ross Perot's famous "big sucking sound"—sucking the life out of cities and small towns across the country. On the other hand, small businesses are great for a community. They offer more personal service; they won't threaten to pack up and leave town if they don't get tax breaks, free roads and other blandishments; and small-business owners are much more responsive to a customer's needs. (Ever try to complain about bad service or poor quality products to the president of Home Depot?)

Logic problem? Why couldn't customer complain to store manager?

True?

Yet, if big boxes are so bad, why are they so successful? One glaring reason is that we've become a nation of hyper-consumers, and the big-box boys know this. Downtown shopping districts comprised of small businesses take some of the efficiency out of overconsumption. There's all that hassle of having to travel from store to store, and

---

TEACHING TIP

The Emilia Sanchez example on page 111 shows how one student annotated a text and conversed with its author. You may find that your students have relatively little experience engaging with a text and questioning its author. The Sanchez example shows one student "talking back" to a text with respect and insight. Using a brief article about a topic your students can sink their teeth into, practice this kind of critical annotation as a class. Ask students to identify and question the thesis of the text, an important step in the reading process, using the "So what?" question (see p. 33).

having to pull out your credit card so many times. Occasionally, we even find ourselves chatting with the shopkeeper, wandering into a coffee shop to visit with a friend or otherwise wasting precious time that could be spent on acquiring more stuff.

Taylor wishes for a time that is long gone or never was.

Author's either/ or thinking isn't working. Stores like Home Depot try to encourage a community feel.

But let's face it—bustling, thriving city centers are fun. They breathe life into a community. They allow cities and towns to stand out from each other. They provide an atmosphere for people to interact with each other that just cannot be found at Target, or Wal-Mart or Home Depot.

Community vs. economy. What about prices?

Is it anti-American to be against having a retail giant set up shop in one's community? Some people would say so. On the other hand, if you board up Main Street, what's left of America?

Ends with emotional appeal. This appeal seems too simplistic.

Conversing with a text

Conversing with a text—or talking back to a text and its author—helps you move beyond your initial notes to draw conclusions about what you've read. Perhaps you ask additional questions, point out something that doesn't make sense, or use the author's points to spark related ideas. As you talk back to a text, you dig a little deeper into it. You look more closely at how the author works through a topic, and you judge the author's evidence and conclusions. Conversing takes your notes to the next level—and is especially helpful when you have to write about a text. For example, student writer Emilia Sanchez noticed on a first reading that her assigned text closed with an emotional appeal. On a second reading, she questioned whether that emotional appeal worked or whether it was really too simplistic.

Many writers use a **double-entry notebook** to converse with a text and its author. To create one, draw a line down the

TEACHING TIP

The double-entry notebook is a useful tool for students not only when they are reading actively but also when they are viewing or listening. When students have to write about a film, a TV episode, a YouTube video, a campus lecture, or some other "text" that's not a print text, suggest that they use the double-entry notebook to record what the text says and their own questions and observations about the text. (For more on writing about images and multimodal texts, see section 5.)

center of a notebook page. On the left side, record what the author says; include quotations, sentences, and key terms from the text. On the right side, record your observations and questions. This is your opportunity to converse with an author and to generate ideas. With each rereading of a text, you can return to your notebook to add new insights or questions.

A double-entry notebook allows you to begin to see the difference between what a text says and what it means and to visualize the conversation between you and the author as it develops.

Here is an excerpt from student writer Emilia Sanchez's double-entry notebook.

Ideas from the text	My responses
"The question, however, is not whether or not these types of stores create jobs (although several studies claim they produce a net job loss in local communities) or whether they ultimately save consumers money" (1011).	Why are big-box stores bad if they create jobs or save people money? Taylor dismisses these possibilities without acknowledging their importance. My family needs to save money and needs jobs more than "chatting with the shopkeeper" (1011).
"The real concern. . . is whether [big-box stores are] good for a community's soul" (1011). "[S]mall businesses are great for a community" (1011).	Taylor is missing something here. Are all big-box stores bad? Are all small businesses great? Would getting rid of big-box stores save the "soul" of America? Is Main Street the "soul" of America? Taylor sounds overly sentimental. She assumes that people spend more money because they shop at big-box stores. And she assumes that small businesses are always better for consumers.

NOTE: To create a digital double-entry notebook, you can use a table or text boxes in a word processing program.

USING SOURCES RESPONSIBLY: Remember to put quotation marks around words you have copied and to keep an accurate record of page numbers for quotations as well as for ideas you have noted on the left side.

SCHOLARS ON ACADEMIC THINKING AND THE WEB

Sosnoski, James. "Hyper-Readers and Their Reading Engines." *Passions, Pedagogies, and Twenty-First Century Technologies.* Logan: Utah State UP, 1999. 161–77. Print. Critical reading of electronic texts—especially those found on the Web—requires specific reading strategies. Sosnoski explores the ways that reading on-screen has affected reading practices and describes a number of different ways of "hyper-reading" that have evolved. His discussion will be of interest to instructors who incorporate online texts in their teaching of critical thinking.

Guidelines for active reading

Preview a written text.

- Who is the author? What are the author's credentials?
- What is the author's purpose: To inform? To persuade? To call to action?
- Who is the expected audience?
- When was the text written? Where was it published?
- What kind of text is it: A book? A report? A scholarly article? A policy memo?
- Does the text have illustrations, charts, or photos? Is it divided into subsections?

Annotate a written text.

- What surprises, puzzles, or intrigues you about the text?
- What question does the text attempt to answer? Or what problem does it attempt to solve?
- What is the author's thesis, or central claim?
- What type of evidence does the author provide to support the thesis? How persuasive is this evidence?

Converse with a written text.

- What are the strengths and limitations of the text?
- Has the author drawn conclusions that you want to question? Do you have a different interpretation of the evidence?
- Does the text raise questions that it does not answer?
- Does the author consider opposing points of view? Does the author seem to treat sources fairly?

Ask the "So what?" question.

- Why does the author's thesis need to be argued, explained, or explored? What's at stake?
- What has the author overlooked or failed to consider in presenting this thesis? What's missing?

GUIDELINES FOR ACTIVE READING *(cont.)*

- Could a reasonable person draw different conclusions about the issue?
- To put an author's thesis to the "So what?" test, use phrases like the following: *The author overlooks this important point:* . . . and *The author's argument is convincing because.* . . .

Asking the "So what?" question

As you read and annotate a text, make sure you understand its thesis, or central idea. Ask yourself: "What is the author's thesis?" Then put the author's thesis to the "So what?" test: "Why does this thesis matter? Why does it need to be argued?" Perhaps you'll conclude that the thesis is too obvious and doesn't matter at all—or that it matters so much that you feel the author stopped short and overlooked key details. You'll be in a stronger position to analyze a text after putting its thesis to the "So what?" test.

4b Outline a text to identify main ideas.

You are probably familiar with using an outline as a planning tool to help you organize your ideas. An outline is a useful tool for reading, too. Outlining a text—identifying its main idea and major parts—can be an important step in your reading process.

As you outline, look closely for a text's thesis statement (main idea) and topic sentences because they serve as important signposts for readers. A thesis statement often appears in the introduction, usually in the first or second paragraph. Topic sentences often can be found at the beginning of body paragraphs, where they announce a shift to a new idea. (See 1e and 3a.)

Put the author's thesis and key points in your own words. Here, for example, are the points Emilia Sanchez identified as she prepared to write her summary and analysis of the text printed on page 111. Notice that Sanchez does not simply trace the author's ideas paragraph by paragraph; instead, she sums up the article's central points.

OUTLINE OF "BIG BOX STORES ARE BAD FOR MAIN STREET"

Thesis: Whether or not they take jobs away from a community or offer low prices to consumers, we should be worried about "big-box" stores like Wal-Mart, Target, and Home Depot because they harm communities by taking the life out of downtown shopping districts.

I.   Small businesses are better for cities and towns than big-box stores are.
   A. Small businesses offer personal service; big-box stores do not.
   B. Small businesses don't make demands on community resources as big-box stores do.
   C. Small businesses respond to customer concerns; big-box stores do not.

II. Big-box stores are successful because they cater to consumption at the expense of benefits to the community.
   A. Buying everything in one place is convenient.
   B. Shopping at small businesses may be inefficient, but it provides opportunities for socializing.
   C. Downtown shopping districts give each city or town a special identity.

Conclusion: Although some people say that it's anti-American to oppose big-box stores, actually these stores threaten the communities that make up America by encouraging buying at the expense of the traditional interactions of Main Street.

TEACHING TIP

Ask students to work in small groups to outline a text (preferably one that makes an argument). Give each group two highlighters. Ask them to highlight the author's thesis, or central idea, in one color and to highlight the supporting ideas in a second color. When your students do this, they are mapping out the major parts of the reading and creating a visual guide to the text's argument. You can also have students complete this kind of exercise with their own writing. This technique can help them identify gaps in their thesis and supporting evidence.

Reading online

For many college assignments, you will be asked to read online sources. Research has shown that readers tend to skim and browse online texts rather than read them carefully. On the Web, it is easy to become distracted. And when you skim a text, you are less likely to remember what you have read and less inclined to reread to grasp layers of meaning.

The following strategies will help you read critically online.

Read slowly. Focus and concentration are the goals of all reading, but online readers need to work against the tendency to skim. Instead of sweeping your eyes across the page, consciously slow down the pace of your reading to focus on each sentence.

Avoid multitasking. Close other applications, especially e-mail and social media. If you follow a link for background or the definition of a term, return to the text immediately.

Annotate electronically. You can take notes and record questions on electronic texts. In a print-formatted electronic document (such as a PDF version of an article), you can use the highlighting features in your PDF reader. You might also use electronic sticky notes or the comment feature in your word processing program.

Print the text. You may want to save a text to a hard drive, USB drive, or network and then print it (making sure to record information about the source for proper citation later). Once you print it, you can easily annotate it.

SCHOLARS ON ACADEMIC THINKING AND WRITING

Paul, Richard, and Linda Elder. "Critical Thinking: The Art of Socratic Questioning, Part III." *Journal of Developmental Education* 31.3 (2008): 34–35. Print. In this installment of their ongoing series on critical thinking, Paul and Elder discuss three modes of Socratic questioning useful in fostering student thinking: spontaneous, exploratory, and focused. The authors offer strategies for sparking students' curiosity and for modeling the intellectual moves that are required for college-level thinking and writing.

4c Summarize to deepen your understanding.

Your goal in summarizing a text is to state the work's main ideas and key points simply, objectively, and accurately in your own words. Writing a summary does not require you to judge the author's ideas; it requires you to *understand* the author's ideas.

MAKING THE MOST OF
YOUR HANDBOOK

Knowing how to summarize a
source is a key research skill.

▶ Using summaries in
researched writing: 51c

Whereas in an outline you x-ray a text to see its major parts, in a summary you flesh out the parts to demonstrate your understanding of what they say. In summarizing, you condense information, put an author's ideas in your own words, and test your understanding of what a text says. If you have sketched a brief outline of the text (see 4b), refer to it as you draft your summary.

Following is Emilia Sanchez's summary of the article that is printed on page 111.

> In her essay "Big Box Stores Are Bad for Main Street," Betsy Taylor argues that chain stores harm communities by taking the life out of downtown shopping districts. Explaining that a community's "soul" is more important than low prices or consumer convenience, she argues that small businesses are better than stores like Home Depot and Target because they emphasize personal interactions and don't place demands on a community's resources. Taylor asserts that big-box stores are successful because "we've become a nation of hyper-consumers" (1011), although the convenience of shopping in these stores comes at the expense of benefits to the community. She concludes by suggesting that it's not "anti-American" to oppose big-box stores because the damage they inflict on downtown shopping districts extends to America itself.
>
> —Emilia Sanchez, student

TEACHING TIP

Ask students to read the guidelines for writing a summary on page 119. In small groups, ask students to compare Emilia Sanchez's summary (p. 118) with the original article she is summarizing (Betsy Taylor's "Big Box Stores Are Bad for Main Street," p. 111) and to discuss what makes Sanchez's tone neutral. Then ask students to look in depth at one paragraph in the original article and assess whether Sanchez summarizes effectively.

> ## Guidelines for writing a summary
>
> - In the first sentence, mention the title of the text, the name of the author, and the author's thesis.
> - Maintain a neutral tone; be objective.
> - As you present the author's ideas, use the third-person point of view and the present tense: *Taylor argues.* . . . (If you are writing in APA style, see 60b.)
> - Keep your focus on the text. Don't state the author's ideas as if they were your own.
> - Put all or most of your summary in your own words; if you borrow a phrase or a sentence from the text, put it in quotation marks and give the page number in parentheses.
> - Limit yourself to presenting the text's key points.
> - Be concise; make every word count.

4d Analyze to demonstrate your critical reading.

Whereas a summary most often answers the question of *what* a text says, an analysis looks at *how* a text conveys its main idea. As you read and reread a text—previewing, annotating, and conversing—you are forming a judgment of it. When you analyze that text, you say to readers: "Here's my reading of this text. This is what the text means and why it matters." Assignments calling for an analysis of a text vary

> **MAKING THE MOST OF YOUR HANDBOOK**
>
> Writing about a text often requires you to quote directly from the text.
>
> ▶ Guidelines for using quotation marks: 51c

widely, but they usually ask you to look at how the text's parts contribute to its central argument or purpose, often with the aim of judging its evidence or overall effect.

Balancing summary with analysis

If you have written a summary of a text, you may find it useful to refer to the main points of the summary as you write your analysis. Your readers may or may not be familiar with

---

SCHOLARS ON ACADEMIC THINKING AND WRITING

Critical Thinking Project. Washington State U, 2004. Web. This Web site offers detailed information and advice on how to assess students' higher-order thinking skills during college along with a rubric consisting of seven important dimensions of critical thinking as they can be identified in student writing. The project was begun when an assessment of junior writing portfolios at WSU revealed that students were demonstrating satisfactory proficiency in writing but were scoring low in critical thinking abilities.

the text you are analyzing, so you need to summarize the text briefly to help readers understand the basis of your analysis. The following strategies will help you balance summary with analysis.

- Remember that readers are interested in your ideas about a text.

- Pose questions that lead to an interpretation or a judgment of a text rather than to a summary. The questions on pages 114–15 can help steer you away from summary and toward analysis.

- Focus your analysis on the text's thesis and main ideas or some prominent feature of the reading.

- Pay attention to your topic sentences to make sure they signal analysis.

- Ask reviewers to give you feedback: Do you summarize too much and need to analyze more?

Here is an example of how student writer Emilia Sanchez balances summary with analysis in her essay about Betsy Taylor's article (see p. 111). Before stating her thesis, Sanchez summarizes the article's purpose and central idea.

Summary

[In her essay "Big Box Stores Are Bad for Main Street," Betsy Taylor focuses not on the economic effects of large chain stores but on the effects these stores have on the "soul" of America. She argues that stores like Home Depot, Target, and Wal-Mart are bad for America because they draw people out of downtown shopping districts and cause them to focus on consumption. In contrast, she believes that small businesses are good for America because they provide personal attention, encourage community interaction, and make each city and town unique.] [But Taylor's argument is unconvincing because it is based on sentimentality—on idealized images of a quaint Main Street—rather than on the roles that businesses play in consumers' lives and communities.]

Analysis

TEACHING TIP

Analyzing a text is one of the most important skills for college students to learn and yet one of the most difficult because of the need to balance summary with analysis. Find a piece of analytical writing that you think is well done and shows both summary and analysis. For instance, you could use a former student's essay or a review of a film in the local paper. Ask students to highlight summary sentences in one color highlighter and analytical sentences in a second color. As a class, talk about the proportion of summary to analysis. What role do the summary sentences play?

Drafting an analytical thesis statement

An effective thesis statement for analytical writing responds to a question about a text or tries to resolve a problem in the text. Remember that your thesis shouldn't state what the reading is *about*. Your thesis presents your judgment of the text's argument.

If Emilia Sanchez had started her analysis of "Big Box Stores Are Bad for Main Street" (p. 111) with the following thesis statement, she merely would have repeated the main idea of the article.

> **MAKING THE MOST OF YOUR HANDBOOK**
>
> When you analyze a text, you weave words and ideas from the source into your own writing.
>
> ► Quoting or paraphrasing: 55a (MLA), 60a (APA), 63c *(Chicago)*
>
> ► Using signal phrases: 55b (MLA), 60b (APA), 63c *(Chicago)*

INEFFECTIVE THESIS STATEMENT: Big-box stores such as Wal-Mart and Home Depot promote consumerism by offering endless goods at low prices, but they do nothing to promote community.

Sanchez wrote the following thesis statement, which offers her judgment of Taylor's argument.

EFFECTIVE THESIS STATEMENT: By ignoring the complex economic relationship between large chain stores and their communities, Taylor incorrectly assumes that simply getting rid of big-box stores would have a positive effect on America's communities.

As you draft your thesis, try asking *what*, *why*, and *how* questions to form a judgment about a text you are reading.

- What has the text's author overlooked or failed to consider? Why does this matter?

- Why might a reasonable person draw a different set of conclusions about the subject matter?

- How does the text complicate or clarify something else you've been thinking about or reading about?

hackerhandbooks.com/bedhandbook

e Academic reading and writing > As you write: Drafting and revising an analytical thesis

---

TEACHING TIP

Ask students to take a look at their own drafts and to identify summary sentences in one color and analytical sentences in another (see the teaching tip on p. 120). Doing so will help them see the balance or imbalance between summary and analysis in their own drafts.

TEACHING TIP

If you assign your students to write rhetorical analysis essays, you may find that they get caught up in responding to the topic of a reading instead of analyzing how the writer makes his or her point. Keep focusing your students with a simple heuristic: What is the author's point? How is he or she making the point? Is the author doing it well? Why or why not?

Writing Guide
Analytical Essay

An **analysis** of a text allows you to examine the parts of a text to understand *what* it means and *how* it makes its meaning. Your goal is to offer your judgment of the text and to persuade readers to see it through your analytical perspective. A sample analytical essay begins on page 125.

Key features

- **A careful and critical reading** of a text reveals what the text says, how it works, and what it means. In an analytical essay, you pay attention to the details of the text, especially its thesis and evidence.

- **A thesis that offers a clear judgment** of a text anchors your analysis. Your thesis might be the answer to a question you have posed about a text or the resolution of a problem you have identified in the text.

- **Support for the thesis** comes from evidence in the text. You summarize, paraphrase, and quote passages that support the claims you make about the text.

- **A balance of summary and analysis** helps readers who may not be familiar with the text you are analyzing. Summary answers the question of *what* a text says; an analysis looks at *how* a text makes its point.

Thinking ahead: Presenting and publishing

You may have the opportunity to present or publish your analysis in the form of a multimodal text such as a slide show presentation.
Consider how adding images or sound might strengthen your analysis or help you to better reach your audience. (See section 5.)

Writing your analytical essay

Explore

Generate ideas for your analysis by brainstorming responses to questions such as the following:

- What is the text about?
- What do you find most interesting, surprising, or puzzling about this text?
- What is the author's thesis or central idea? Put the author's thesis to the "So what?" test. (See p. 115.)
- What do your annotations of the text reveal about your response to it?

Draft

- Draft a working thesis to focus your analysis. Remember that your thesis is not the same as the author's thesis. Your thesis presents *your* judgment of the text.
- Draft a plan to organize your paragraphs. Your introductory paragraph will briefly summarize the text and offer your thesis. Your body paragraphs will support your thesis with evidence from the text. Your conclusion will pull together the major points and show the significance of your analysis. (See 1d.)
- Identify specific words, phrases, and sentences as evidence to support your thesis.

Revise

Ask your reviewers to give you specific comments. You can use the following questions to guide their feedback.

- Is the introduction effective and engaging?
- Is summary balanced with analysis?
- Does the thesis offer a clear judgment of the text?
- What objections might other writers pose to your analysis?
- Is the analysis well organized? Are there clear topic sentences and transitions?
- Is there sufficient evidence? Is the evidence analyzed?
- Have you cited words, phrases, or sentences that are summarized or quoted?

Guidelines for analyzing a text

Instructors who ask you to analyze an essay or an article often expect you to address some of the following questions:

- What questions (stated or unstated) does the author address? Or what problem does the author attempt to solve?
- What is the author's thesis, or central idea?
- How does the author structure the text? What are the key parts, and how do they relate to one another and to the thesis?
- Who is the intended audience? What strategies has the author used to generate interest in the argument and to persuade readers of its merit?
- What evidence does the author use to support the thesis? How persuasive is the evidence? (See 6b.)
- Does the author anticipate objections and counter opposing views? (See 6c.)
- Does the author use any faulty reasoning? (See 6a.)

4e Sample student writing: Analysis of an article

Following is Emilia Sanchez's complete essay. Sanchez used MLA (Modern Language Association) style to format her paper and cite the source. A guide to writing an analytical essay appears on pages 122–23.

---

hackerhandbooks.com/bedhandbook

e Academic reading and writing > As you write: Analyzing a text
e Academic reading and writing > As you write: Developing an analysis
e Academic reading and writing > Sample student writing > Sanchez, "Rethinking Big-Box Stores" (analysis of an article)

TEACHING TIP

Consider assigning the "As you write" writing prompts, found in the handbook's Integrated Media at hackerhandbooks.com/bedhandbook. These activities, referenced at the bottoms of many pages in the handbook, help students to apply the handbook's lessons to the writing they are doing for the course.

Sanchez 1

Emilia Sanchez

Professor Goodwin

English 10

23 October 2013

Rethinking Big-Box Stores

In her essay "Big Box Stores Are Bad for Main Street," Betsy
Taylor focuses not on the economic effects of large chain stores but
on the effects these stores have on the "soul" of America. She argues
that stores like Home Depot, Target, and Wal-Mart are bad for America
because they draw people out of downtown shopping districts and
cause them to focus on consumption. In contrast, she believes that
small businesses are good for America because they provide personal
attention, encourage community interaction, and make each city
and town unique. But Taylor's argument is unconvincing because it
is based on sentimentality—on idealized images of a quaint Main
Street—rather than on the roles that businesses play in consumers'
lives and communities. By ignoring the complex economic relationship
between large chain stores and their communities, Taylor incorrectly
assumes that simply getting rid of big-box stores would have a
positive effect on America's communities.

Taylor's use of colorful language reveals that she has a sentimental
view of American society and does not understand economic realities.
In her first paragraph, Taylor refers to a big-box store as a "25-acre slab
of concrete with a 100,000 square foot box of stuff" that "land[s] on
a town," evoking images of a powerful monster crushing the American
way of life (1011). But she oversimplifies a complex issue. Taylor does
not consider that many downtown business districts failed long before
chain stores moved in, when factories and mills closed and workers
lost their jobs. In cities with struggling economies, big-box stores

Opening briefly summarizes the article's purpose and thesis.

Sanchez begins to analyze Taylor's argument.

Thesis expresses Sanchez's judgment of Taylor's article.

Signal phrase introduces quotations from the source; Sanchez uses an MLA in-text citation.

Marginal annotations indicate MLA-style formatting and effective writing.

SCHOLARS ON ACADEMIC THINKING AND THE WEB

Browne, M. Neil, Kari E. Freeman, and Carrie L. Williamson. "The
Importance of Critical Thinking for Student Use of the Internet." *College
Student Journal* 34.3 (2000): 391–98. Print. The authors offer strategies
for helping students become more critical of what they find on the Web.
They argue that if students are not equipped to evaluate the information
and the multiple perspectives they find online, they can become passive
consumers instead of active, critical users of information.

Sanchez 2

can actually provide much-needed jobs. Similarly, while Taylor blames big-box stores for harming local economies by asking for tax breaks, free roads, and other perks, she doesn't acknowledge that these stores also enter into economic partnerships with the surrounding communities by offering financial benefits to schools and hospitals.

Taylor's assumption that shopping in small businesses is always better for the customer also seems driven by nostalgia for an old-fashioned Main Street rather than by the facts. While she may be right that many small businesses offer personal service and are responsive to customer complaints, she does not consider that many customers

appreciate the service at big-box stores. Just as customer service is better at some small businesses than at others, it is impossible to generalize about service at all big-box stores. For example, customers depend on the lenient return policies and the wide variety of products at stores like Target and Home Depot.

Taylor blames big-box stores for encouraging American "hyper-consumerism," but she oversimplifies by equating big-box stores with bad values and small businesses with good values. Like her other points, this claim ignores the economic and social realities of American society today. Big-box stores do not force Americans to buy more. By offering lower prices in a convenient setting, however, they allow consumers to save time and purchase goods they might not be able to afford from small businesses. The existence of more small businesses would not change what most Americans can afford, nor would it reduce their desire to buy affordable merchandise.

Taylor may be right that some big-box stores have a negative impact on communities and that small businesses offer certain advantages. But she ignores the economic conditions that support big-box stores as well as the fact that Main Street was in decline before

Sanchez 3

the big-box store arrived. Getting rid of big-box stores will not bring back a simpler America populated by thriving, unique Main Streets; in reality, Main Street will not survive if consumers cannot afford to shop there.

Conclusion returns to the thesis and shows the wider significance of Sanchez's analysis.

Sanchez 4

Work Cited

Taylor, Betsy. "Big Box Stores Are Bad for Main Street." *CQ Researcher* 9.44 (1999): 1011. Print.

Work cited page is in MLA style.

5 Reading and writing about images and multimodal texts

In many of your college classes, you'll have the opportunity to read and write about images, such as photographs or paintings, as well as multimodal texts, such as advertisements, maps, videos, or Web sites. Multimodal texts are those that combine one or more of the following modes: words, static images, moving images, and sound. You might, for instance, be asked to analyze an advertisement for a composition course, a map for a geology course, or a YouTube video for a sociology course.

Writing about images or multimodal texts differs from writing about written texts — a photograph is a different kind of text from a poem, of course — but there are also similarities. All texts

TEACHING TIP

As a way to introduce section 5, ask students to study the World Wildlife Fund advertisement on page 129. As a writing prompt for a low-stakes (ungraded) response, ask students to write a brief paragraph: How do the words and the image work together to communicate a message? Follow the fifteen-minute writing period with a discussion centered on this question: What are the challenges of reading and analyzing images or advertisements?

can be approached in a critical way. You can engage with them by studying how they work to communicate their message and by discovering within them something that is surprising, interesting, and worthy of interpretation. To analyze an image or a multimodal text, first you need to read it carefully and critically.

5a Read actively.

Any image or multimodal text can be read — that is, carefully approached and examined to understand *what* it says and *how* it communicates its purpose and reaches its audience. Like written texts, images and multimodal texts don't speak for themselves; they don't reveal their meaning with a quick glance or a casual scan. Rather, you need to read and reread, questioning and conversing with them with an open, critical mind.

When you read a multimodal text in particular, you are often reading more than words; you might also be reading a text's design and composition — and perhaps even its pace and volume. Your work involves understanding the modes — words, images, and sound — separately and then analyzing how the modes work together — the interaction among words, images, and sound. As you read a multimodal text, pay attention to the details that make up the entire composition.

When you read images or multimodal texts, it's helpful to preview, annotate, and converse with the text — just as with print texts.

> **MAKING THE MOST OF YOUR HANDBOOK**
>
> Integrating visuals (images and some multimodal texts) can strengthen your writing.
>
> ▸ Adding visuals to your draft: page 43
>
> ▸ Choosing visuals to suit your purpose: pages 44-45

Previewing an image or a multimodal text

Previewing starts by looking at the basic details of an image or a multimodal text and paying attention to first impressions.

TEACHING TIP

Students might be unfamiliar with the word *multimodal*. This chapter provides a good introduction. Ask students to think about a time when they composed a multimodal text. Go around the room and have students share examples.

wwf.org

What will it take before we respect the planet?

Multimodal texts, such as this World Wildlife Fund (WWF) ad, combine modes. Here, words and an image work together to communicate an idea.

You begin to ask questions about the text's subject matter and design, its context and composer or creator, and its purpose and intended audience. The more you can gather from a first look, the easier it will be to dig deeper into the meaning of a text. The following questions will help you as you preview.

FIRST IMPRESSIONS. What strikes you right away? What do you notice that surprises, intrigues, or puzzles you about the text? What is the overall effect of the text?

GENRE. What kind of text is it: Advertisement? Photograph? Video? Podcast?

PURPOSE. What is the text's purpose: To persuade? To inform? To entertain? If the text is an advertisement, what product or idea is it selling?

TEACHING TIP

As a class, take a look at the Equal Exchange advertisement on page 131, along with the student annotations in the margin. Ask your students to consider this question: How is the student writer in the handbook "talking back" to the ad? Distribute magazines and let each student rip out an ad that he or she finds engaging, interesting, or puzzling. Give students ten minutes to write notes that talk back to the ad they have chosen. Conclude the class by asking five or six students to show their ad and share one question or observation from their notes.

AUDIENCE. Who is the target audience? What assumptions are made about the audience?

CONTEXT. Where was the text originally published or viewed?

DESIGN. What seems most prominent in the text's design?

Annotating an image or a multimodal text

Annotating a text—jotting down observations and questions—helps you read actively to answer the basic question "What is this text about?" In annotating, you pay close attention to details—what they imply and how they relate to one another and to the whole image or multimodal text.

When you annotate a text, you are starting to write about it. Often, you are beginning to figure out what *you* want to say about the composer's choices. You'll often find yourself annotating, rereading, and moving back and forth between reading and writing to fully understand and analyze an image or a multimodal text. A second or third reading will raise new questions and reveal details or contradictions that you didn't notice in an earlier reading. The following techniques will help you annotate an image or a multimodal text.

- For a still image, download, copy and paste, or scan the image into a word processing document or a PowerPoint slide so that you can use the space of the page or slide to take notes. Most word processing applications will allow you to copy and paste images and text from a Web page into a word processing page.

- For a video or sound file, create a separate note-taking document in a word processing file or in a traditional notebook. Use the time stamp, if there is one, as you take notes: *04:21 The music stops abruptly, and a single word, "Care," appears on-screen.*

The following example shows how one student, Ren Yoshida, annotated an advertisement.

AN ADDITIONAL RESOURCE ON MULTIMODAL ANALYSIS AND COMPOSING

DeVoss, Dànielle Nicole. *Understanding and Composing Multimodal Projects.* Boston: Bedford, 2013. Print. This brief resource helps students who are assigned to compose or look critically at multimodal texts such as Web sites, video essays, public service announcements, ads, collages, and slide show presentations. The author pays close attention to the project management, copyright, and delivery issues associated with multimodal work.

When you choose Equal Exchange fairly traded coffee, tea or chocolate, you join a network that empowers farmers in Latin America, Africa, and Asia to:
- **Stay on their land**
- **Care for the environment**
- **Farm organically**
- **Support their family**
- **Plan for the future**

www.equalexchange.coop

Photo: Jesus Choqueheranca de Quevero,
Coffee farmer & CEPICAFE Cooperative member, Peru

ANNOTATED ADVERTISEMENT

What is being exchanged?

Why is "fairly traded" so difficult to read?

"Empowering" — why in an elegant font? Who is empowering farmers?

"Farmers" in all capital letters. Sturdy font contrasts with the elegant font.

Straightforward design and not much text.

Outstretched hands. Is she giving a gift? Inviting a partnership?

Hands: heart-shaped, oversized.

Raw coffee is red, earthy, natural.

Positive verbs: consumers choose, join, empower; farmers stay, care, farm, support, plan.

What does it mean to join a network?

How do consumers know their money helps farmers stay on their land?

Source: Equal Exchange.

Conversing with an image or a multimodal text

Conversing with a text — or talking back to a text and its author — helps you move beyond your early notes to form judgments about what you've read. At this stage, you dig a little deeper into the text, perhaps posing more questions, pointing out something that is puzzling or provocative and why, or explaining a disagreement you have with the text. Conversing takes your notes to the next level — and is especially helpful when you have to write about a text. In his annotations to the Equal Exchange ad, notice that Ren Yoshida asks why two words, *empowering* and *farmers,* are in different fonts (see p. 131). And he further questions the purpose and meaning of the difference.

Many writers use a double-entry notebook to converse with a text and generate ideas for writing (see pp. 112–13 for guidelines on creating a double-entry notebook and sample entries). A double-entry notebook allows you to separate what a text says and does from what a text means. As you record details and features of an image or a multimodal text on the left side of the notebook page and your own responses on the right side, you can visualize the conversation as it develops.

5b Outline to identify main ideas.

Writing an outline is one way of getting started on a draft. Outlining can also be a useful tool in understanding a text that you've been assigned to read. When you outline a text, you identify its main idea or purpose and its major parts. One way to outline an image or a multimodal text is to try to define its main idea or purpose and sketch a list of its key elements. Because ads, Web sites, and videos may not explicitly state a purpose, you may have to puzzle it out from the details in the work.

hackerhandbooks.com/bedhandbook

Ⓔ Academic reading and writing > As you write: Reading visual texts actively

TEACHING TIP

Your students may be used to outlining (finding major and minor ideas in) traditional print texts. But what about multimodal texts such as videos or podcasts? Give students practice in outlining audio or video texts by doing one together in class — especially if you assign students to write about multimodal texts.

Here is the informal outline Ren Yoshida developed as he prepared to write an analysis of the advertisement printed on page 131. Notice that Yoshida makes an attempt to state the ad's purpose and sum up its message.

OUTLINE OF EQUAL EXCHANGE ADVERTISEMENT

Purpose: To persuade consumers that they can improve the lives of organic farmers and their families by purchasing Equal Exchange coffee.

Key features:

- The farmer's heart-shaped hands are outstretched, offering the viewer partnership and the product of her hard work.
- The raw coffee is surprisingly fruitlike and fresh—natural and healthy looking.
- A variety of fonts are used for emphasis, such as the elegant font for "empowering."
- Consumer support leads to a higher quality of life for the farmers and for all people, since these farmers care for the environment and plan for the future.
- The simplicity of the design reflects the simplicity of the exchange. The consumer only has to buy a cup of coffee to make a difference.

Conclusion: Equal Exchange is selling more than a product—coffee. It is selling the message that together farmers and consumers hold the future of land, environment, farms, and families in their hands.

5c Summarize to deepen your understanding.

Your goal in summarizing an image or a multimodal text is to state the work's central idea and key points simply, objectively, and accurately, in your own words, and usually in paragraph form. Writing a summary does not require you to judge the text's ideas; it requires you to understand the text's ideas. If you have sketched a brief outline of the text (see 5b), refer to it as you draft your summary.

To summarize an image or a multimodal text, begin with essential information such as who composed the text and why, who

Guidelines for writing a summary of an image or a multimodal text

- In the first two sentences, mention the title of the text and the name of the composer (or the sponsoring organization or company if you cannot identify a composer), and provide some brief information about the context — when, why, and for whom the text was composed and where it appeared.
- State the text's central idea or message.
- Maintain a neutral tone; be objective.
- As you present the text's ideas, use the third-person point of view and the present tense: *The focus of the Zipcar advertisement is. . . . Devaney's slide presentation argues. . . .* (If you are writing in APA style, see 60b.)
- Keep your focus on the text. Don't state the text's or composer's ideas as if they were your own.
- Put your summary in your own words; if you borrow a phrase or a sentence from the text, put it in quotation marks and cite the text (see 51c).
- Limit yourself to presenting the text's key points.

the intended audience is, and when and where the work appeared. Briefly explain the text's main idea or message and identify its key features. Divide the summary into a few major and perhaps minor ideas. Since a summary must be fairly short, you must make judgments about what is most important.

MAKING THE MOST OF YOUR HANDBOOK

Knowing how to summarize is a key research skill.

▸ Summarizing written texts: 4c
▸ Summarizing researched sources: 51c

TEACHING TIP

If you have assigned students to write analytically about an image or a multimodal work, ask them to share their draft with a classmate and to discuss each other's thesis statement. Does it merely state what the image or multimodal text is *about*? Or is the student writer making a *judgment* about the text? Offer suggestions for revising.

> ## Guidelines for analyzing an image or a multimodal text
>
> - What is your first impression of the text? What details in the text create this response?
> - When and why was the text created? Where did the text appear?
> - What clues suggest the text's intended audience? What assumptions are being made about the audience?
> - What is the thesis, central idea, or message of the text? Do you find it persuasive?
> - Does this text tell a story? How would you sum up the story?
> - If the text is multimodal, what modes are used, and why? How do the modes work together?
> - How do the arrangement of sounds or design details — images, illustrations, colors, fonts, perspective — help convey the text's meaning or serve its purpose?

5d Analyze to demonstrate your critical reading.

Whereas a summary most often answers the question of *what* a text says, an analysis looks at *how* a text conveys its main idea or message. As you read and reread an image or a multimodal text—previewing, annotating, and conversing—you are forming a judgment of it. Your analysis says to readers: "Here's my reading of this text. This is what the text means and why it matters." When you are assigned to analyze a text such as a painting, a podcast, or a PowerPoint slide, you will usually be expected to look at how the different parts of the image (color, perspective, composition) or multimodal work (use of words, sounds, images) contribute to its central purpose, often with the aim of judging how effective the text is in achieving its purpose.

hackerhandbooks.com/bedhandbook

🄴 Academic reading and writing > As you write: Analyzing an image or a multimodal text

Balancing summary with analysis

If you have written a summary of a text, you may find it useful to refer to the main points of the summary as you write your analysis. Your readers may or may not be familiar with the visual or multimodal text you are analyzing and will need at least some summary to ground your analysis. For example, student writer Ren Yoshida summarized the Equal Exchange advertisement on page 131 by describing part of the text first, allowing readers to get their bearings, and then moving to an analytical statement about that particular part of the text.

Summary

Analysis

[A farmer, her hardworking hands full of coffee beans, reaches out from an Equal Exchange advertisement. The hands, in the shape of a heart, offer to consumers the fruit of the farmer's labor. The ad's message is straightforward: in choosing Equal Exchange, consumers become global citizens, partnering with farmers to help save the planet.] [Suddenly, a cup of coffee is more than just a morning ritual; a cup of coffee is a moral choice that empowers both consumers and farmers.]

The following strategies will help you balance summary with analysis.

- Remember that readers are interested in your ideas about a text.

- Pose questions that lead to an interpretation or a judgment of a text rather than to a summary. The questions on page 135 can help steer you away from summary and toward analysis.

- Focus your analysis on a few significant details (fonts, use of color, sounds, images) rather than presenting a list of every detail.

- As you draft, pay attention to your topic sentences to make sure they signal analysis.

- Ask reviewers to give you feedback: Do you summarize too much and need to analyze more? (See p. 55.)

ADDITIONAL RESOURCE ON VISUAL RHETORIC

Handa, Carolyn, ed. *Visual Rhetoric in a Digital World: A Critical Sourcebook.* Boston: Bedford, 2004. Print. This collection brings together current scholarship in this emerging field. Part 1, "Toward a Pedagogy of the Visual," includes essays that discuss how teachers can balance the verbal and the visual in their composition classrooms. Parts 2 and 3, "The Rhetoric of the Image" and "The Rhetoric of Design," focus on the persuasive power of illustrations and typography in written texts. The essays in Parts 4 and 5, "Visual Rhetoric and Argument" and "Visual Rhetoric and Culture," address the logic of visual arguments and the pervasiveness of the visual in shaping cultural perceptions.

Drafting an analytical thesis statement

An effective thesis statement for analytical writing about an image or multimodal text responds to a question about the text or tries to resolve a problem in the text. Remember that your thesis isn't the same as the text's thesis or main idea and shouldn't simply restate what the text is *about*. Your thesis presents your judgment of the text's argument. If you find that your thesis is restating the text's message, turn to your notes to see if the questions you asked earlier in the process can help you revise.

> **INEFFECTIVE THESIS STATEMENT**: Consumers who purchase coffee from farmers in the Equal Exchange network are helping farmers stay on their land.

The thesis is ineffective because it summarizes the ad; it doesn't present an analysis. Ren Yoshida focused the thesis by questioning a single detail in the work.

> **QUESTIONS**: The ad promises an equal exchange, but is the exchange equal between consumers and farmers? Do the words *equal exchange* and *empowering farmers* appeal to consumers' emotions?

> **EFFECTIVE THESIS STATEMENT**: Although the ad works successfully on an emotional level, it is less successful on a logical level because of its promise for an equal exchange between consumers and farmers.

5e   Sample student writing: Analysis of an advertisement

On the following pages is Ren Yoshida's analysis of the Equal Exchange advertisement that appears on page 131.

hackerhandbooks.com/bedhandbook

🄴 Academic reading and writing > As you write: Drafting and revising an analytical thesis (for an image or a multimodal text)

🄴 Academic reading and writing > Sample student writing > Yoshida, "Sometimes a Cup of Coffee Is Just a Cup of Coffee" (analysis of an advertisement)

Yoshida 1

Ren Yoshida

Professor Marcotte

English 101

4 November 2012

Sometimes a Cup of Coffee Is Just a Cup of Coffee

A farmer, her hardworking hands full of coffee beans, reaches out from an Equal Exchange advertisement (Equal Exchange). The hands, in the shape of a heart, offer to consumers the fruit of the farmer's labor. The ad's message is straightforward: in choosing Equal Exchange, consumers become global citizens, partnering with farmers to help save the planet. Suddenly, a cup of coffee is more than just a morning ritual; a cup of coffee is a moral choice that empowers both consumers and farmers. This simple exchange appeals to a consumer's desire to be a good person—to protect the environment and do the right thing. Yet the ad is more complicated than it first seems, and its design raises some logical questions about such an exchange. Although the ad works successfully on an emotional level, it is less successful on a logical level because of its promise for an equal exchange between consumers and farmers.

The focus of the ad is a farmer, Jesus Choqueheranca de Quevero, and, more specifically, her outstretched, cupped hands. Her hands are full of red, raw coffee, her life's work. The ad successfully appeals to consumers' emotions, assuming they will find the farmer's welcoming face and hands, caked with dirt, more appealing than startling statistics about the state of the environment or the number of farmers who lose their land each year. It seems almost rude not to accept the farmer's generous offering since we know her name and, as the ad implies, have the choice to "empower" her. In fact, how can a consumer resist helping the farmer "[c]are for the environment" and

Marginal annotations:

The source is cited in the text. No page number is available for the online source.

Yoshida summarizes the content of the ad.

Thesis expresses Yoshida's analysis of the ad.

Details show how the ad appeals to consumers' emotions.

Yoshida interprets details such as the farmer's hands.

Marginal annotations indicate MLA-style formatting and effective writing.

Yoshida 2

"[p]lan for the future," when it is a simple matter of choosing the right coffee? The ad sends the message that our future is a global future in which producers and consumers are bound together.

First impressions play a major role in the success of an advertisement. Consumers are pulled toward a product, or pushed away, by an ad's initial visual and emotional appeal. Here, the intended audience is busy people, so the ad tries to catch viewers' attention and make a strong impression immediately. Yet with a second or third viewing, consumers might start to ask some logical questions about Equal Exchange before buying their morning coffee. Although the farmer extends her heart-shaped hands to consumers, they are not actually buying a cup of coffee or the raw coffee directly from her. In reality, consumers are buying from Equal Exchange, even if the ad substitutes the more positive word *choose* for *buy*. Furthermore, consumers aren't actually empowering the farmer; they are joining "a network that empowers farmers." The idea of a network makes a simple transaction more complicated. How do consumers know their money helps farmers "[s]tay on their land" and "[p]lan for the future" as the ad promises? They don't.

The ad's design elements raise questions about the use of the key terms *equal exchange* and *empowering farmers*. The Equal Exchange logo suggests symmetry and equality, with two red arrows facing each other, but the words of the logo appear almost like an eye exam poster, with each line decreasing in font size and clarity. The words *fairly traded* are tiny. Below the logo, the words *empowering farmers* are presented in contradictory fonts. *Empowering* is written in a flowing, cursive font, almost the opposite of what might be considered empowering, whereas *farmers* is written in a plain, sturdy font.

Yoshida begins to challenge the logic of the ad.

Words from the ad serve as evidence.

Clear topic sentence announces a shift.

Summary of the ad's key features serves Yoshida's analysis.

Yoshida 3

The ad's varying fonts communicate differently and make it hard to know exactly what is being exchanged and who is becoming empowered.

What is being exchanged? The logic of the ad suggests that consumers will improve the future by choosing Equal Exchange. The first exchange is economic: consumers give one thing—dollars—and receive something in return—a cup of coffee—and the farmer stays on her land. The second exchange is more complicated because it involves a moral exchange. The ad suggests that if consumers don't choose "fairly traded" products, farmers will be forced off their land and the environment destroyed. This exchange, when put into motion by consumers choosing to purchase products not "fairly traded," has negative consequences for both consumers and farmers. The message of the ad is that the actual exchange taking place is not economic but moral; after all, nothing is being bought, only chosen. Yet the logic of this exchange quickly falls apart. Consumers aren't empowered to become global citizens simply by choosing Equal Exchange, and farmers aren't empowered to plan for the future by consumers' choices. And even if all this empowerment magically happened, there is nothing equal about such an exchange.

Advertisements are themselves about empowerment—encouraging viewers to believe they can become someone or do something by identifying, emotionally or logically, with a product. In the Equal Exchange ad, consumers are emotionally persuaded to identify with a farmer whose face is not easily forgotten and whose heart-shaped hands hold a collective future. On a logical level, though, the ad raises questions because empowerment, although a good concept to choose, is not easily or equally exchanged. Sometimes a cup of coffee is just a cup of coffee.

Yoshida shows why his thesis matters.

Conclusion includes a detail from the introduction.

Conclusion returns to Yoshida's thesis.

Yoshida 4

Work Cited

Equal Exchange. Advertisement. *Equal Exchange*. Equal Exchange, n.d. Web. 14 Oct. 2012.

6 Reading and writing arguments

Many of your college assignments will ask you to read and write arguments about debatable issues. The questions being debated might be matters of public policy (*Should corporations be allowed to advertise on public school property?* or *What is the least dangerous way to dispose of hazardous waste?*), or they might be scholarly issues (*What role do genes play in determining behavior?* or *What were the causes of the Civil War?*). On such questions, reasonable people may disagree.

As you read arguments across the disciplines and enter into academic or public policy debates, pay attention to the questions being asked, the evidence being presented, and the various positions being argued. It's helpful to approach all arguments with an open, curious mind. You'll find the critical reading strategies introduced in section 4—previewing, annotating, and conversing with texts—to be useful as you ask questions about an argument's logic, evidence, and use of appeals. Many arguments can stand up to critical scrutiny. Sometimes, however, a line of argument that at first seems reasonable turns out to be illogical, unfair, or both.

TEACHING TIP

As you begin your unit on argument, spark a class discussion by presenting or projecting these quotations:

"For example" is not proof.   — Yiddish proverb

The truth is rarely pure and never simple.   — Oscar Wilde

Becoming a College Writer

Consider counterarguments

"Understand the argument you want to make, but also figure out why readers might disagree with your position. At the heart of a good argument is disagreement."

— **Geily Gonzalez**, student, Miami Dade College

Many college writing assignments invite you to take a position in a debate. It isn't enough simply to offer your opinion and assume readers won't have their own. You want to approach arguments, those you read and write, with an open mind — one that sees "disagreement" as useful.

Reasonable people disagree on topics worth debating. Becoming a college writer requires that you take time to reflect on the disagreements in debates that you enter — to think through your own point of view *and* other points of view.

You might worry that if you include counterarguments in your writing, you will contradict yourself. In fact, you will show your understanding of the complexity of the debate and the importance of fairness.

- We are surrounded by disagreements — those that we can follow in the media and those that we follow or engage in personally. Reflect on this question: Why is fairness important in arguing a position?

MORE
Handling opposing views, 6c
Countering opposing arguments, 6i
Sample argument paper, 6k

142

As you write for various college courses, you'll be asked to take positions in academic debates, propose solutions to problems, and persuade readers to accept your arguments. Just as you evaluate arguments with openness, you'll want to construct arguments with the same openness—acknowledging disagreements and opposing views and presenting your arguments fully and fairly to your readers.

See sections 6a–6c for advice about reading arguments. Sections 6d–6k address writing arguments.

6a Distinguish between reasonable and fallacious argumentative tactics.

When you evaluate an argument, look closely at the reasoning and evidence behind it. Some unreasonable argumentative tactics are known as *logical fallacies*. Most of the fallacies—such as hasty generalizations and false analogies—are misguided or dishonest uses of legitimate strategies. The examples in this section suggest when such strategies are reasonable and when they are not.

Generalizing (inductive reasoning)

Writers and thinkers generalize all the time. We look at a sample of data and conclude that data we have not observed will most likely conform to what we have seen. From a spoonful of soup, we conclude just how salty the whole bowl will be. After numerous unpleasant experiences with an airline, we decide to book future flights with a competitor.

When we draw a conclusion from an array of facts, we are engaged in inductive reasoning. Such reasoning deals in probability, not certainty. For a conclusion to be highly probable, it must be based on evidence that is sufficient, representative, and relevant. (See the chart on p. 145.)

hackerhandbooks.com/bedhandbook

[e] Academic reading and writing > As you write: Evaluating ads for logic and fairness

SCHOLARS ON ARGUMENT

Bizzell, Patricia. "The 4th of July and the 22nd of December: The Function of Cultural Archives in Persuasion, as Shown by Frederick Douglass and William Apess." *College Composition and Communication* 48.1 (1997): 44–60. Print. Bizzell observes that when judging the effectiveness of student writing, teachers usually talk about what writers do, ignoring what they know. Using Douglass and Apess as examples, she shows that a broad display of knowledge can be rhetorically effective and can help build common ground to bring about social change.

Academic English

Many hasty generalizations contain words such as *all*, *ever*, *always*, and *never*, when qualifiers such as *most*, *many*, *usually*, and *seldom* would be more accurate.

The fallacy known as *hasty generalization* is a conclusion based on insufficient or unrepresentative evidence.

HASTY GENERALIZATION

In a single year, scores on standardized tests in California's public schools rose by ten points. Therefore, more children than ever are succeeding in America's public school systems.

Data from one state do not justify a conclusion about the whole United States.

A *stereotype* is a hasty generalization about a group. Here are a few examples.

STEREOTYPES

Women are bad bosses.
Politicians are corrupt.
Children are always curious.

Stereotyping is common because of our human tendency to perceive selectively. We tend to see what we want to see; we notice evidence confirming our already formed opinions and fail to notice evidence to the contrary. For example, if you have concluded that politicians are corrupt, your stereotype will be confirmed by news reports of legislators being indicted—even though every day the media describe conscientious officials serving the public honestly and well.

Drawing analogies

An analogy points out a similarity between two things that are otherwise different. Analogies can be an effective means of

TEACHING TIP

Present or project a number of advertisements. They can be commercial ads found in print or online—or public service announcements (PSAs). As a class, talk about how ads make arguments. For each ad, identify the argument being made and any assumptions or stereotypes the ad seems to rely on. Then ask students to identify any logical fallacies. Give students practice in naming the reasonable and unreasonable argumentative tactics.

Testing inductive reasoning

Though inductive reasoning leads to probable and not absolute truth, you can assess a conclusion's likely probability by asking three questions. This chart shows how to apply those questions to a sample conclusion based on a survey.

CONCLUSION   The majority of students on our campus would volunteer at least five hours a week in a community organization if the school provided a placement service for volunteers.

EVIDENCE   In a recent survey, 723 of 1,215 students questioned said they would volunteer at least five hours a week in a community organization if the school provided a placement service for volunteers.

1. Is the evidence sufficient?

That depends. On a small campus (say, 3,000 students), the pool of students surveyed would be sufficient for market research, but on a large campus (say, 30,000), 1,215 students are only 4 percent of the population. If those 4 percent were known to be truly representative of the other 96 percent, however, even such a small sample would be sufficient (see question 2).

2. Is the evidence representative?

Only if those responding to the survey reflect the characteristics of the entire student population: age, sex, race, field of study, number of extracurricular commitments, and so on. If most of those surveyed are majors in a field like social work, the researchers should question the survey's conclusion.

3. Is the evidence relevant?

Yes. The survey results are directly linked to the conclusion. A survey about the number of hours students work for pay would not be relevant because it would not be about *choosing to volunteer.*

TEACHING TIP

As part of a lesson on identifying stereotypes and thinking about bias, ask students to keep a log for a week. Students should make note of stereotypes they notice in media such as ads, TV commercials, TV shows, news coverage, and films. For each entry, students should record the date; the name of the show, film, or broadcast or the product being advertised; the group being stereotyped; whether they detect any bias (evidence that a stereotype is hindering judgment) in the media they're viewing; and their own reflections about the experience. In small groups, ask each student to share just one entry from his or her completed log.

arguing a point. It is not always easy to draw the line between a reasonable and an unreasonable analogy. At times, however, an analogy is clearly off base, in which case it is called a *false analogy*.

FALSE ANALOGY

If we can send a spacecraft to Pluto, we should be able to find a cure for the common cold.

How are these ideas related? The writer has falsely assumed that because two things are alike in one respect, they must be alike in others. Exploring the outer reaches of the solar system and finding a cure for the common cold are both scientific challenges, but the problems confronting medical researchers are quite different from those solved by space scientists.

Tracing causes and effects

Demonstrating a connection between causes and effects is rarely simple. For example, to explain why a chemistry course has a high failure rate, you would begin by listing possible causes: inadequate preparation of students, poor teaching, lack of qualified tutors, and so on. Next you would investigate each possible cause. Only after investigating the possible causes would you be able to weigh the relative impact of each cause and suggest appropriate remedies.

Because cause-and-effect reasoning is so complex, it is not surprising that writers frequently oversimplify it. In particular, writers sometimes assume that because one event follows another, the first is the cause of the second. This common fallacy is known as *post hoc*, from the Latin *post hoc, ergo propter hoc*, meaning "after this, therefore because of this."

POST HOC FALLACY

Since Governor Cho took office, unemployment among minorities in the state has decreased by 7 percent. Governor Cho should be applauded for reducing unemployment among minorities.

SCHOLARS ON ARGUMENT

Lynch, Dennis A., Diana George, and Marilyn M. Cooper. "Moments of Argument: Agonistic Inquiry and Confrontational Cooperation." *College Composition and Communication* 48.1 (1997): 61–85. Print. Instead of viewing arguments as "for or against" stances, the authors see arguments as having "moments of conflict and agonistic positioning as well as moments of understanding and communication." They describe two courses in which they applied their methods.

Is the governor solely responsible for the decrease? Are there other reasons? It is not enough to show that the decrease in unemployment followed the governor's taking office.

Weighing options

Especially when reasoning about problems and solutions, writers must weigh options. To be fair, a writer should mention the full range of options, showing why one is superior to the others or might work well in combination with others.

It is unfair to suggest that there are only two alternatives when in fact there are more. Writers who set up a false choice between their preferred option and one that is clearly unsatisfactory are guilty of the *either . . . or* fallacy.

> **EITHER . . . OR FALLACY**
>
> Our current war against drugs has not worked. Either we should legalize drugs or we should turn the drug war over to our armed forces and let them fight it.

Are these the only solutions—legalizing drugs and calling out the army? Other options, such as funding for drug abuse prevention programs, are possible.

Making assumptions

An assumption is a claim that is taken to be true—without the need of proof. Most arguments are based to some extent on assumptions since writers rarely have the time and space to prove all of the conceivable claims on which their argument is based. For example, someone arguing about the best means of limiting population growth in developing countries might assume that the goal of limiting population growth is worthwhile. For most audiences, there would be no need to articulate this assumption or to defend it.

There is a danger, however, in failing to spell out and prove a claim that is clearly controversial. Consider the following short argument, in which a key claim is missing.

ARGUMENT WITH MISSING CLAIM

Violent crime is increasing. Therefore, we should vigorously enforce the death penalty.

The writer seems to be assuming both that the death penalty deters violent criminals and that it is a fair punishment—and that most readers will agree. These are not reasonable assumptions; the writer will need to state and support both claims.

When a missing claim is an assertion that few would agree with, we say that a writer is guilty of a *non sequitur* (Latin for "does not follow").

NON SEQUITUR

Christopher gets plenty of sleep; therefore, he will be a successful student in the university's pre-med program.

Does it take more than sleep to be a successful student? The missing claim—that people with good sleep habits always make successful students—would be hard to prove.

Deducing conclusions (deductive reasoning)

When we deduce a conclusion, we put things together, like any good detective. We establish that a general principle is true, that a specific case is an example of that principle, and that therefore a particular conclusion about that case is a certainty.

Deductive reasoning can often be structured in a three-step argument called a *syllogism*. The three steps are the major premise, the minor premise, and the conclusion.

1. Anything that increases radiation in the environment is dangerous to public health. (Major premise)

2. Nuclear reactors increase radiation in the environment. (Minor premise)

3. Therefore, nuclear reactors are dangerous to public health. (Conclusion)

The major premise is a generalization. The minor premise is a specific case. The conclusion follows from applying the generalization to the specific case.

Deductive arguments break down if one of the premises is not true or if the conclusion does not follow logically from the premises. In the following short argument, the major premise is very likely untrue.

UNTRUE PREMISE

The police do not give speeding tickets to people driving less than five miles per hour over the limit. Dominic is driving fifty-nine miles per hour in a fifty-five-mile-per-hour zone. Therefore, the police will not give Dominic a speeding ticket.

The conclusion is true only if the premises are true. If the police sometimes give tickets for driving less than five miles per hour over the limit, Dominic cannot safely conclude that he will avoid a ticket.

In the following argument, both premises might be true, but the conclusion does not follow logically from them.

CONCLUSION DOES NOT FOLLOW

All members of our club ran in this year's Boston Marathon. Jay ran in this year's Boston Marathon. Therefore, Jay is a member of our club.

The fact that Jay ran the race is no guarantee that he is a member of the club. Presumably, many runners are nonmembers.

Assuming that both premises are true, the following argument holds up.

CONCLUSION FOLLOWS

All members of our club ran in this year's Boston Marathon. Jay is a member of our club. Therefore, Jay ran in this year's Boston Marathon.

6b Distinguish between legitimate and unfair emotional appeals.

There is nothing wrong with appealing to readers' emotions. After all, many issues worth arguing about have an emotional as well as a logical dimension. Even the Greek logician Aristotle lists *pathos* (emotion) as a legitimate argumentative tactic. For example, in an essay criticizing big-box stores (see p. 111), writer Betsy Taylor has a good reason for tugging at readers' emotions: Her subject is the decline of city and town life. In her conclusion, Taylor appeals to readers' emotions by invoking their national pride.

LEGITIMATE EMOTIONAL APPEAL

Is it anti-American to be against having a retail giant set up shop in one's community? Some people would say so. On the other hand, if you board up Main Street, what's left of America?

Emotional appeals, however, are frequently misused. Many of the arguments we see in the media, for instance, strive to win our sympathy rather than our intelligent agreement. A TV commercial suggesting that you will be thin and attractive if you drink a certain diet beverage is making a pitch to emotions. So is a political speech that recommends electing a candidate because he is a devoted husband and father who serves as a volunteer firefighter.

The following passage illustrates several types of unfair emotional appeals.

UNFAIR EMOTIONAL APPEALS

This progressive proposal to build a ski resort in the state park has been carefully researched by Western Trust, the largest bank in the state; furthermore, it is favored by a majority of the local merchants. The only opposition comes from tree huggers who care more about trees than they do about people. One of their leaders was actually arrested for disturbing the peace several years ago.

hackerhandbooks.com/bedhandbook

e Academic reading and writing > As you write: Identifying appeals

---

TEACHING TIP

Ask students to read and discuss the chart on evaluating ethical, logical, and emotional appeals as a reader (pp. 152–53). After students are comfortable with the language of *ethos*, *logos*, *pathos*, ask them to use these concepts to identify the argumentative appeals of an assigned reading. As an alternative, ask students to share one of their own drafts with a classmate—either hard copies in class or electronically through e-mail or the course Web site. Ask them to identify the argumentative appeals in their partner's writing—and to suggest which kind of appeal they may need more of or less of.

Advertising makes use of ethical, logical, and emotional appeals to persuade consumers to buy a product or embrace a brand. This Patagonia ad makes an ethical appeal with its copy that invites customers to rethink their purchasing practices.

Words with strong positive or negative connotations, such as *progressive* and *tree hugger*, are examples of *biased language*. Attacking the people who hold a belief (environmentalists) rather than refuting their argument is called *ad hominem*, a Latin term meaning "to the man." Associating a prestigious name (Western Trust) with the writer's side is called *transfer*. Claiming that an idea should be accepted because a large number of people (the majority of merchants) are in favor of it is called the *bandwagon appeal*. Bringing in irrelevant issues (the arrest) is a *red herring*, named after a trick used in fox hunts to mislead the dogs by dragging a smelly fish across the trail.

SCHOLARS ON ARGUMENT

Fulkerson, Richard. *Teaching the Argument in Writing.* Urbana: NCTE, 1996. Print. Drawing on classical and contemporary theories of argument, Fulkerson challenges teachers to rethink some conventional views about reasoning. He asserts that the usual English textbook treatment of inductive and deductive reasoning and the logical fallacies is misguided—worth little classroom time. We should focus instead on the kinds of argumentative strategies used in real life; many of these strategies, such as drawing analogies, can be legitimate in one context, fallacious in another. To Fulkerson, the goal of argument is not to win but to reach intelligent, yet tentative, conclusions after giving all points of view a fair hearing.

Evaluating ethical, logical, and emotional appeals as a reader

Ancient Greek rhetoricians distinguished among three kinds of appeals used to influence readers — ethical, logical, emotional. As you evaluate arguments, identify these appeals and question their effectiveness. Are they appropriate for the audience and the argument? Are they balanced and legitimate or lopsided and misleading?

Ethical appeals (*ethos*)

Ethical arguments call upon a writer's character, knowledge, and authority. Ask questions such as the following when you evaluate the ethical appeal of an argument.

- Is the writer informed and trustworthy? How does the writer establish authority and credibility?
- Is the writer fair-minded and unbiased? How does the writer establish reasonableness and good judgment?
- Does the writer use sources knowledgeably and responsibly?
- How does the writer describe the views of others and deal with opposing views?

Logical appeals (*logos*)

Reasonable arguments appeal to readers' sense of logic, rely on evidence, and use inductive and deductive reasoning. Ask questions such as the following to evaluate the logical appeal of an argument.

- Is the evidence sufficient, representative, and relevant?
- Is the reasoning sound?
- Does the argument contain any logical fallacies or unwarranted assumptions?
- Are there any missing or mistaken premises?

EVALUATING ETHICAL, LOGICAL, AND EMOTIONAL APPEALS AS A READER (cont.)

Emotional appeals (*pathos*)

Emotional arguments appeal to readers' beliefs and values. Ask questions such as the following to evaluate the emotional appeal of an argument.

- What values or beliefs does the writer address, either directly or indirectly?
- Are the emotional appeals legitimate and fair?
- Does the writer oversimplify or dramatize an issue?
- Do the emotional arguments highlight or shift attention away from the evidence?

6c Judge how fairly a writer handles opposing views.

The way in which a writer deals with opposing views is telling. Some writers address the arguments of the opposition fairly, conceding points when necessary and countering others, all in a civil spirit. Other writers will do almost anything to win an argument: either ignoring opposing views altogether or misrepresenting such views and attacking their proponents.

Writers build credibility—*ethos*—by addressing opposing arguments fairly. As you read arguments, assess the credibility of your sources by looking at how they deal with views not in agreement with their own.

Describing the views of others

Some writers and speakers deliberately misrepresent the views of others. One way they do this is by setting up a "straw man," a character so weak that he is easily knocked down. The *straw man* fallacy consists of an oversimplification or outright distortion of opposing views. For example, in a California debate over attempts to control the mountain lion population, pro-lion groups characterized their opponents as trophy hunters bent on shooting harmless animals. In truth, hunters were only one faction of those who saw a need to control the lion population.

TEACHING TIP

In discussing an assigned text, focus students' attention on specific passages to show how the author describes the views of others and quotes opposing views. Ask students to assess: Is the treatment fair?

During the District of Columbia's struggle for voting representation, some politicians set up a straw man, as shown in the following example.

STRAW MAN FALLACY

Washington, DC, residents are lobbying for statehood. Giving a city such as the District of Columbia the status of a state would be unfair.

The argument isn't about statehood. It is about voting rights. The straw man wanted statehood. In fact, most DC citizens lobbied for voting representation in any form, not necessarily through statehood.

Quoting opposing views

Writers often quote the words of writers who hold opposing views. In general, this is a good idea, for it assures some level of fairness and accuracy. At times, though, both the fairness and the accuracy are an illusion.

A source may be misrepresented when it is quoted out of context. All quotations are to some extent taken out of context, but a fair writer will explain the context to readers. To select a provocative sentence from a source and to ignore the more moderate sentences surrounding it is both unfair and misleading. Sometimes a writer deliberately distorts a source through the device of ellipsis dots. Ellipsis dots tell readers that words have been omitted from the original source. When those words are crucial to an author's meaning, omitting them is obviously unfair. (See also 39d.)

ORIGINAL SOURCE

Johnson's *History of the American West* is riddled with inaccuracies and astonishing in its blatantly racist description of the Indian wars.

— B. R., reviewer

SCHOLARS ON ARGUMENT

Trail, George Y. "Teaching Argument and the Rhetoric of Orwell's 'Politics and the English Language.'" *College English* 57.5 (1995): 570–83. Print. Trail recommends that instructors resist ahistorical, decontextualized approaches to teaching argument and instead proposes three principles: (1) Recognize that all arguments are situated in a historical time and place; (2) think of an argument's appeal in psychological as opposed to emotional terms; and (3) view logic as a rhetorical device.

| **Checklist for reading and evaluating arguments** |

- What is the writer's thesis, or central claim?
- Are there any gaps in reasoning? Does the argument contain any logical fallacies (see 6a)?
- What assumptions does the argument rest on? Are there any unstated assumptions?
- What appeals — ethical, logical, or emotional — does the writer make? Are these appeals effective?
- What kind of evidence does the writer use to support his or her claims? Could there be alternative interpretations of the evidence?
- How does the writer handle opposing views?
- If you are not persuaded by the writer's argument, what counterarguments could you make to the writer?

MISLEADING QUOTATION

According to B. R., Johnson's *History of the American West* is "astonishing in its . . . description of the Indian wars."

EXERCISE 6-1 Explain what is illogical in the following brief arguments. It may be helpful to identify the logical fallacy or fallacies by name. Answers appear in the back of the book. *More practice:* e

a. My roommate, who is an engineering major, is taking a course called Structures of Tall Buildings. All engineers have to know how to design tall buildings.

b. If you're old enough to vote, you're old enough to drink. Therefore, the drinking age should be lowered to eighteen.

c. If you're not part of the solution, you're part of the problem.

d. American students could be outperforming students in schools around the globe if it weren't for the outmoded, behind-the-times thinking of many statewide education departments.

hackerhandbooks.com/bedhandbook
e Academic reading and writing > As you write: Evaluating an argument
e Academic reading and writing > Exercises: 6–2

TEACHING TIP

Ask students to work in small groups to evaluate the argument of an assigned text. The checklist for reading and evaluating arguments (see p. 155) will provide a useful framework for their discussion.

EXERCISE 6-1 *Answers:*

a. hasty generalization; b. false analogy; c. *either . . . or* fallacy; d. biased language; e. faulty cause-and-effect reasoning

e. Charging a fee for curbside trash pickup will encourage everyone to recycle more because no one in my town likes to spend extra money.

6d When writing arguments, begin by identifying your purpose and context.

Evaluating the arguments of other writers prepares you to construct your own. When you ask questions about the logic and evidence of the arguments you read, you become more aware of such needs in your own writing. And when you pose objections to arguments, you more readily anticipate and counter objections to your own arguments.

In constructing an argument, you take a stand on a debatable issue. Your purpose is to explain your understanding of the truth about a subject or to propose the best solution to a problem, reasonably and logically, without being combative. Your aim is to persuade your readers to reconsider their positions by offering new reasons to question existing viewpoints.

It's best to start by informing yourself about the debate or conversation around a subject—sometimes called its *context*. If you are planning to write about the subject of offshore drilling, you might want to read sources that shed light on the social context (the concerns of consumers, the ideas of lawmakers, the proposals of environmentalists) and sources that may inform you about the intellectual context (scientific or theoretical responses by geologists, oceanographers, or economists) in which the debate is played out.

> **MAKING THE MOST OF YOUR HANDBOOK**
>
> Supporting your claims with evidence from sources can make your argument more effective.
>
> ▶ Conducting research: 50

hackerhandbooks.com/bedhandbook

e Academic reading and writing > As you write: Joining a conversation

---

TEACHING TIP

Assign students to read Sam Jacobs's argument (essay begins on p. 168) and take notes on the following three questions: What issue is he arguing? Why is this issue debatable? What position does he take on this issue?

Because your readers may be aware of the social and intellectual contexts in which your issue is grounded, you will be at a disadvantage if you are not informed. Conduct some research before preparing your argument. Consulting even a few sources can help to deepen your understanding of the conversation around the issue.

6e View your audience as a panel of jurors.

Do not assume that your audience already agrees with you. Instead, envision skeptical readers who, like a panel of jurors, will make up their minds after listening to all sides of the argument. If you are arguing a public policy issue, you may want to aim your paper at readers who represent a variety of positions. In the case of a debate over offshore drilling, for example, imagine a jury that represents those who have a stake in the matter: consumers, policymakers, and environmentalists.

> **MAKING THE MOST OF YOUR HANDBOOK**
>
> You may need to consider a specific audience for your argument.
>
> ▶ Analyzing your audience: 1a
>
> ▶ Writing in a particular discipline, such as business or psychology: 65

At times, you can deliberately narrow your audience. If you are working within a word limit, for example, you might not have the space in which to address the concerns of all interested parties. Or you might be primarily interested in reaching just a segment of a larger audience, such as consumers. Once you target a specific audience, it's helpful to think about what kinds of arguments and evidence will appeal to that audience.

NOTE: Your assignment may require a specific audience, or you may be free to target a broader group of readers. Check with your instructor before you make your case.

hackerhandbooks.com/bedhandbook

e Academic reading and writing > As you write: Appealing to your readers

---

TEACHING TIP

Ask students to identify and highlight Sam Jacobs's use of ethical, logical, and emotional appeals. How does Jacobs establish his credibility? How does he appeal to his readers' sense of logic and to their values and beliefs?

TEACHING TIP

When students are planning their arguments and thinking about audience, ask them to use a device such as a Venn diagram or even just columns to plan the types of appeals that might be effective for specific audiences. Planning in a visual way may help students see that they have more evidence—or just more strategy—to aim for one audience rather than another.

Using ethical, logical, and emotional appeals as a writer

To construct a convincing argument, you must establish your credibility (*ethos*) and appeal to your readers' sense of logic and reason (*logos*) as well as to their values and beliefs (*pathos*). When using these appeals, make sure they are appropriate for your audience and your argument.

Ethical appeals (*ethos*)

To accept your argument, a reader must perceive you as trustworthy and fair, reliable and reasonable. When you acknowledge alternative positions, you build common ground with readers and gain their trust by showing that you are knowledgeable about the arguments relevant to your subject. And when you use sources responsibly, summarizing, paraphrasing, or quoting the views of others respectfully, you inspire readers' confidence in your judgment.

Logical appeals (*logos*)

To persuade readers, you need to appeal to their sense of logic and sound reasoning. When you provide sufficient evidence, you offer readers logical support for your argument. And when you clarify the assumptions that underlie your arguments and avoid logical fallacies, you appeal to readers' desire for reason.

Emotional appeals (*pathos*)

To establish common ground with readers, you need to appeal to their beliefs and values as well as to their minds. When you offer readers vivid examples and illustrations, startling statistics, or compelling visuals, you engage readers and deepen their interest in your argument. And when you balance emotional appeals with logical appeals, you highlight the human dimension of an issue to show readers why they should care about your argument.

WRITERS ON WRITING

A writer has a facility with words. A good writer can also think.

— Cynthia Ozick

Seeking to know is only too often learning to doubt.

— Antoinette Deshoulières

Academic English

Some cultures value writers who argue with force; other cultures value writers who argue subtly or indirectly. Academic audiences in the United States will expect your writing to be assertive and confident—neither aggressive nor passive. You can create an assertive tone by acknowledging different positions and supporting your ideas with specific evidence.

TOO AGGRESSIVE   Of course only registered organ donors should be eligible for organ transplants. It's selfish and shortsighted to think otherwise.

TOO PASSIVE   I might be wrong, but I think that maybe people should have to register as organ donors if they want to be considered for a transplant.

ASSERTIVE TONE   If only registered organ donors are eligible for transplants, more people will register as donors.

If you are uncertain about the tone of your work, ask for help at your school's writing center.

6f In your introduction, establish credibility and state your position.

When you are constructing an argument, make sure your introduction includes a thesis statement that establishes your position on the issue you have chosen to debate. In the sentences leading up to the thesis, establish your credibility (*ethos*) with readers by showing that you are knowledgeable and fair-minded. If possible, build common ground (*pathos*) with readers who may not at first agree with your views, and show them why they should consider your thesis.

MAKING THE MOST OF YOUR HANDBOOK

When you write an argument, you state your position in a thesis.

▶ Writing effective thesis statements: 1c, 1e

TEACHING TIP

Ask students to present their introductions and working thesis statements to peer reviewers. Peer reviewers should pose counterarguments and help their classmates revise their thesis statements. Student writers should ask their peer reviewers: "Have I established enough ethos?"

In the following introduction, student writer Kevin Smith presents himself as someone worth listening to. Because Smith introduces both sides of the debate, readers are likely to approach his essay with an open mind.

Smith shows that he is familiar with the legal issues surrounding school prayer.

Smith is fair-minded, presenting the views of both sides.

Although the Supreme Court has ruled against prayer in public schools on First Amendment grounds, many people still feel that prayer should be allowed. Such people value prayer as a practice central to their faith and believe that prayer is a way for schools to reinforce moral principles. They also compellingly point out a paradox in the First Amendment itself: at what point does the separation of church and state restrict the freedom of those who wish to practice their religion? What proponents of school prayer fail to realize, however, is that the Supreme Court's decision, although it was made on legal grounds, makes sense on religious grounds as well. Prayer is too important to be trusted to our public schools.

Thesis builds common ground.

—Kevin Smith, student

TIP: A good way to test a thesis while drafting and revising is to imagine a counterargument to your argument (see 6i). If you can't think of an opposing point of view, rethink your thesis and ask a classmate or writing center tutor to respond to your argument.

6g Back up your thesis with persuasive lines of argument.

Arguments of any complexity contain lines of argument that, when taken together, might reasonably persuade readers that the thesis has merit. The following, for example, are the main lines of

---

WRITERS ON WRITING

People are usually more firmly convinced that their opinions are precious than that they are true.   — George Santayana

Opinion is a flitting thing, / But truth outlasts the Sun—/ If then we cannot own them both—/ Possess the oldest one—
                    — Emily Dickinson

A great many people think they are thinking when they are only rearranging their prejudices.   — William James

argument that student writer Sam Jacobs used in his paper about the shift from print to online news (see pp. 168–73).

CENTRAL CLAIM

Thesis: The shift from print to online news provides unprecedented opportunities for readers to become more engaged with the news, to hold journalists accountable, and to participate as producers, not simply as consumers.

SUPPORTING CLAIMS

- Print news has traditionally had a one-sided relationship with its readers, delivering information for passive consumption.
- Online news invites readers to participate in a collaborative process—to question and even contribute to the content.
- Links within news stories provide transparency, allowing readers to move easily from the main story to original sources, related articles, or background materials.
- Technology has made it possible for readers to become news producers—posting text, audio, images, and video of news events.
- Citizen journalists can provide valuable information, sometimes more quickly than traditional journalists can.

If you sum up your main lines of argument, as Jacobs did, you will have a rough outline of your essay. In your paper, you will provide evidence for each of these claims.

6h Support your claims with specific evidence.

You will need to support your central claim and any subordinate claims with evidence: facts, statistics, examples and illustrations, visuals (charts, slides, photos), expert opinion, and so on. Debatable

hackerhandbooks.com/bedhandbook

e Academic reading and writing > As you write: Drafting your central claim and supporting claims

---

TEACHING TIP

Ask students to submit an outline of their argument along with their first draft or even in advance of their first draft. Outlining their draft gives students a chance to highlight their central claim and supporting claims—and perhaps identify gaps in their argument early on.

topics require that you consult some sources. As you read through
or view the sources, you will learn more about the arguments and
counterarguments at the center of your debate.

USING SOURCES RESPONSIBLY: Remember that you must document any sources you use as evidence. Documentation gives
credit to authors and shows readers how to locate a source in
case they want to assess its credibility or explore the issue further.

Using facts and statistics

A fact is something that is known
with certainty because it has been
objectively verified: The capital of
Wyoming is Cheyenne. Carbon has
an atomic weight of 12. John F. Kennedy was assassinated on November
22, 1963. Statistics are collections of
numerical facts: Alcohol abuse is a
factor in nearly 40 percent of traffic
fatalities. More than four in ten businesses in the United States are owned by women.

> **MAKING THE MOST OF
> YOUR HANDBOOK**
>
> Sources, when used
> responsibly, can provide
> evidence to support an
> argument.
>
> ▶ Paraphrasing, summarizing,
>   and quoting sources: 51c
> ▶ Punctuating direct
>   quotations: 37a
> ▶ Citing sources: 54b (MLA),
>   59b (APA), 63b (*Chicago*)

Most arguments are supported at least to some extent by
facts and statistics. For example, in the following passage the
writer uses statistics to show that college students carry unrea-
sonably high credit card debt.

> A 2009 study revealed that undergraduates are carrying record-
> high credit card balances and are relying on credit cards more
> than ever, especially in the economic downturn. The average
> credit card debt per college undergraduate is more than three
> thousand dollars, and three-quarters of undergraduates carry
> balances and incur finance charges each month (Hunter).

Writers often use statistics in selective ways to bolster their
own positions. If you suspect that a writer's handling of statistics
is not fair, track down the original sources for those statistics or

---

TEACHING TIP

Ask students to use the criteria for evaluating evidence (p. 145) to
assess the accuracy, sufficiency, relevance, and representativeness of
their evidence. Then, ask them to identify the role of two specific pieces
of evidence. Students might benefit from reading 53c (MLA) to learn
more about the roles that sources play in an argument.

read authors with opposing views, who may give you a fuller understanding of the numbers.

Using examples and illustrations

Examples and illustrations (extended examples, often in story form) rarely prove a point by themselves, but when used in combination with other forms of evidence, they flesh out an argument with details and specific instances and bring it to life. Because examples are often concrete and sometimes vivid, they can reach readers in ways that statistics and abstract ideas cannot.

In a paper arguing that online news provides opportunities for readers that print does not, Sam Jacobs describes how regular citizens using only cell phones and laptops helped save lives during Hurricane Katrina by sending important updates to the rest of the world.

> Citizen reporting made a difference in the wake of Hurricane Katrina in 2005. Armed with cell phones and laptops, regular citizens relayed critical news updates in a rapidly developing crisis, often before traditional journalists were even on the scene.

Using visuals

Visuals — charts, graphs, diagrams, photographs — can support your argument by providing vivid and detailed evidence and by capturing your readers' attention. Bar or line graphs, for instance, describe and organize complex statistical data; photographs can immediately convey abstract ideas; a map can illustrate geography. (See pp. 44–45.)

As you consider using visual evidence, ask yourself the following questions:

- Is the visual accurate, credible, and relevant?
- How will the visual appeal to readers: Logically? Ethically? Emotionally?

TEACHING TIP

Ask students to find and read an article or essay (in a newspaper, magazine, or blog) that uses visual evidence. What role does the visual evidence play in the argument? Ask students to present their text and its evidence (two minutes per student) in class.

- How will the visual evidence function? Will it provide background information? Present complex numerical information? Lend authority? Refute counterarguments?

Citing expert opinion

Although they are no substitute for careful reasoning of your own, the views of an expert can contribute to the force of your argument. For example, to help make the case that print journalism has a one-sided relationship with its readers, student writer Sam Jacobs integrates an expert's key description.

> With the rise of the Internet, however, this model has been criticized by journalists such as Dan Gillmor, founder of the Center for Citizen Media, who argues that traditional print journalism treats "news as a lecture," whereas online news is "more of a conversation" (xxiv).

When you rely on expert opinion, make sure that your source is an expert in the field you are writing about. In some cases, you may need to provide credentials showing why your source is worth listening to, such as listing the person's position or title alongside his or her name. When including expert testimony in your paper, you can summarize or paraphrase the expert's opinion or you can quote the expert's exact words. You will of course need to document the source, as Jacobs did.

6i Anticipate objections; counter opposing arguments.

Readers who already agree with you need no convincing, but skeptical readers may resist your arguments. To be willing to give

hackerhandbooks.com/bedhandbook

e Academic reading and writing > As you write: Practicing counterargument

---

TEACHING TIP

Ask students to exchange drafts with a classmate to help each other anticipate and counter objections. Encourage them to use the questions on page 165 to guide their discussion.

Anticipating and countering objections

To anticipate a possible objection to your argument, consider the following questions.

- Could a reasonable person draw a different conclusion from your facts or examples?
- Might a reader question any of your assumptions or offer an alternative explanation?
- Is there any evidence that might weaken your position?

The following questions may help you respond to a potential objection.

- Can you concede the point to the opposition but challenge the point's importance or usefulness?
- Can you explain why readers should consider a new perspective or question a piece of evidence?
- Should you explain how your position responds to contradictory evidence?
- Can you suggest a different interpretation of the evidence?

When you write, use phrasing to signal to readers that you're about to present an objection. Often the signal phrase can go in the lead sentence of a paragraph.

Critics of this view argue that . . .

Some readers might point out that . . .

Researchers challenge these claims by . . .

up a position that seems reasonable, readers need to see that another position is even more reasonable. In addition to presenting your own case, therefore, you should consider the opposing arguments and attempt to counter them.

It might seem at first that drawing attention to an opposing point of view or contradictory evidence would weaken your argument. But by anticipating and countering objections to your argument, you show yourself as a reasonable and well-informed writer who has a thorough understanding of the significance of the issue.

There is no best place in an essay to deal with opposing views. Often it is useful to summarize the opposing position early in your essay. After stating your thesis but before developing your own arguments, you might have a paragraph that takes up the most important counterargument. Or you can anticipate objections paragraph by paragraph as you develop your case. Wherever you decide to address opposing arguments, you will enhance your credibility if you explain the arguments of others accurately and fairly.

6j Build common ground.

As you counter opposing arguments, try to seek out one or two assumptions you might share with readers who do not initially agree with your views. If you can show that you share their concerns, your readers will be more likely to accept that your argument is valid. For example, to persuade people opposed to controlling the deer population with a regulated hunting season, a state wildlife commission would have to show that it too cares about preserving deer and does not want them to die needlessly. Having established these values in common, the commission might be able to persuade critics that reducing the total number of deer prevents starvation caused by overpopulation.

People believe that intelligence and decency support their side of an argument. To be persuaded, they must see these qualities in your argument. Otherwise, they will persist in their opposition.

6k Sample student writing: Argument

In the paper that begins on the next page, student writer Sam Jacobs argues that the shift from print to online news benefits readers by providing them with new opportunities to produce news and to think more critically as consumers of news. Notice how he appeals to his readers by presenting opposing views fairly before providing his own arguments.

In writing the paper, Jacobs consulted both print and online sources. When he quotes, summarizes, or paraphrases information from a source, he cites the source with an MLA (Modern Language Association) in-text citation. Citations in the paper refer readers to the list of works cited at the end of the paper. (For more details about citing sources, see 54.)

For a guide to writing an argument essay, see pages 174–75.

TEACHING TIP

Ask students to reread Sam Jacobs's argument (beginning on p. 168) with an eye toward his use of evidence. Ask students to take notes on the following questions: What kind of evidence does Jacobs use? Is it persuasive? What do they learn about constructing an argument from studying Sam Jacobs's argument? If you are teaching an online course, use these questions as prompts on the class discussion board.

Jacobs 1

Sam Jacobs

Professor Alperini

English 101

19 March 2012

From Lecture to Conversation: Redefining What's "Fit to Print"

"All the news that's fit to print," the motto of the *New York Times* since 1896, plays with the word *fit*, asserting that a news story must be newsworthy and must not exceed the limits of the printed page. The increase in online news consumption, however, challenges both meanings of the word *fit*, allowing producers and consumers alike to rethink who decides which topics are worth covering and how extensive that coverage should be. Any cultural shift usually means that something is lost, but in this case there are clear gains. The shift from print to online news provides unprecedented opportunities for readers to become more engaged with the news, to hold journalists accountable, and to participate as producers, not simply as consumers.

Guided by journalism's code of ethics—accuracy, objectivity, and fairness—print news reporters have gathered and delivered stories according to what editors decide is fit for their readers. Except for op-ed pages and letters to the editor, print news has traditionally had a one-sided relationship with its readers. The print news media's reputation for objective reporting has been held up as "a stop sign" for readers, sending a clear message that no further inquiry is necessary (Weinberger). With the rise of the Internet, however, this model has been criticized by journalists such as Dan Gillmor, founder of the Center for Citizen Media, who argues that traditional print journalism treats "news as a lecture," whereas online news is "more of a conversation" (xxiv). Print news arrives on the doorstep

In his opening sentences, Jacobs provides background for his thesis.

Thesis states the main point.

Jacobs does not need a citation for common knowledge.

Marginal annotations indicate MLA-style formatting and effective writing.

SCHOLARS ON EVALUATING ARGUMENTS

Lazere, Donald. "Teaching the Political Conflicts: A Rhetorical Schema." *College Composition and Communication* 43.2 (1992): 194–213. Print. Lazere describes a set of assignments that ask students to think critically about politics by using a rhetorical schema. The assignments focus on interpreting semantics, perceiving bias, seeing through deceptive rhetoric, and evaluating partisan sources.

Jacobs 2

every morning as a fully formed lecture, a product created without participation from its readership. By contrast, online news invites readers to participate in a collaborative process—to question and even help produce the content.

One of the most important advantages online news offers over print news is the presence of built-in hyperlinks, which carry readers from one electronic document to another. If readers are curious about the definition of a term, the roots of a story, or other perspectives on a topic, links provide a path. Links help readers become more critical consumers of information by engaging them in a totally new way. For instance, the link embedded in the story "Window into Fed Debate over a Crucial Program" (Healy) allows readers to find out more about the trends in consumer spending and to check the journalist's handling of an original source (see fig. 1). This kind of link gives readers the opportunity to conduct their own evaluation of the evidence and verify the journalist's claims.

Transition moves from Jacobs's main argument to specific examples.

Links provide a kind of transparency impossible in print because they allow readers to see through online news to the "sources, disagreements, and the personal assumptions and values" that may have influenced a news story (Weinberger). The International Center for Media and the Public Agenda underscores the importance of news organizations letting "customers in on the often tightly held little secrets of journalism." To do so, they suggest, will lead to "accountability and accountability leads to credibility" ("Openness"). These tools alone don't guarantee that news producers will be responsible and trustworthy, but they encourage an open and transparent environment that benefits news consumers.

Jacobs clarifies key terms (transparency and accountability).

Source is cited in MLA style.

Not only has technology allowed readers to become more critical news consumers, but it also has helped some to become news

Jacobs develops the thesis.

SCHOLARS ON ASSESSMENT

Sommers, Nancy. "The Call of Research: A Longitudinal View of Writing Development." *College Composition and Communication* 60.1 (2008): 152–64. Print. Sommers wrestles with the question of whether "students leave college as stronger writers than when they entered" in part by telling the stories of two students from her longitudinal study of undergraduate writing at Harvard University. In general, Sommers argues, college writers gain strength over time when they are encouraged to develop expertise in subject and method and when they take part in ongoing debates within their discipline. Yet Sommers warns us not to become too enamored of outcomes and students' success in achieving them because they overemphasize the written product at the expense of recognizing the writer's process.

Jacobs 3

producers. The Web gives ordinary people the power to report on the day's events. Anyone with an Internet connection can publish on blogs and Web sites, engage in online discussion forums, and contribute

But economists greeted the news with a small cheer because sales excluding automobiles actually grew in September, suggesting that consumer spending was stabilizing.

Over all, retail sales fell 1.5 percent in September from a month earlier, the Commerce Department reported, better than an anticipated decline of 2.1 percent.

Retail sales excluding automobiles and parts grew 0.5 percent, largely because of higher sales at gas stations and grocery stores.

Auto dealers bore the brunt of the month's declines.

Consumers swamped dealerships in late July and August to take advantage of the government's $3 billion cash-for-clunkers program, which offered rebates of up to $4,500 to entice people to swap their older cars for more fuel-efficient models.

Sales at auto dealers surged in August, but fell 11 percent in September.

A version of this article
page B3 of the New Y

INSIDE NYTIMES

Timothy Winters / Ian Thomas
CB09-154
Service Sector Statistics Division
(301) 763-2713

U.S. Census Bureau News
U.S. Department of Commerce · Washington, D.C. 20233

FOR IMMEDIATE RELEASE

WEDNESDAY, OCTOBER 14, 2009 AT 8:30 A.M. EDT

ADVANCE MONTHLY SALES FOR RETAIL TRADE AND FOOD SERVICES

SEPTEMBER 2009

The U.S. Census Bureau announced today that advance estimates of U.S. retail and food services sales for September, adjusted for seasonal variation and holiday and trading-day differences, but not for price changes, were $344.7 billion, a decrease of 1.5 percent (±0.5%) from the previous month and 5.7 percent (±0.7%) below September 2008. Total sales for the July through September 2009 period were down 6.6 percent (±0.3%) from the same period a year ago. The July to

Fig. 1. Links embedded in online news articles allow readers to move from the main story to original sources, related articles, or background materials. The link in this online article (Healy) points to a government report, the original source of the author's data on consumer spending.

SCHOLARS ON ASSESSMENT

Yancey, Kathleen Blake. "Looking for Sources of Coherence in a Fragmented World: Notes toward a New Assessment Design." *Computers and Composition* 21.1 (2004): 89–102. Print. Yancey explores the meaning of coherence, a key feature of effective college writing, in print texts and in digital texts. Further, she questions how to assess coherence in a digital text, where coherence is both verbal and visual — and entirely dependent on context and arrangement. She proposes a new heuristic for digital texts and asks us to think about the "relationships between composers, readers, and texts."

Jacobs 4

video and audio recordings. Citizen journalists with laptops, cell
phones, and digital camcorders have become news producers
alongside large news organizations.

Not everyone embraces the spread of unregulated news
reporting online. Critics point out that citizen journalists are not
necessarily trained to be fair or ethical, for example, nor are they
subject to editorial oversight. Acknowledging that citizen reporting is
more immediate and experimental, critics also question its accuracy
and accountability: "While it has its place . . . it really isn't journalism
at all, and it opens up information flow to the strong probability
of fraud and abuse. . . . Information without journalistic standards
is called gossip," writes David Hazinski in the *Atlanta Journal-
Constitution* (23A). In his book *Losing the News*, media specialist Alex
S. Jones argues that what passes for news today is in fact "pseudo
news" and is "far less reliable" than traditional print news (27). Even
a supporter like Gillmor is willing to agree that citizen journalists are
"nonexperts," but he argues that they are "using technology to make a
profound contribution, and a real difference" (140).

Citizen reporting made a difference in the wake of Hurricane
Katrina in 2005. Armed with cell phones and laptops, regular citizens
relayed critical news updates in a rapidly developing crisis, often
before traditional journalists were even on the scene. In 2006,
the enormous contributions of citizen journalists were recognized when
the New Orleans *Times-Picayune* received the Pulitzer Prize in public
service for its online coverage—largely citizen-generated—of
Hurricane Katrina. In recognizing the paper's "meritorious public
service," the Pulitzer Prize board credited the newspaper's blog for
"heroic, multi-faceted coverage of [the storm] and its aftermath"
("2006 Pulitzer"). Writing for the *Online Journalism Review*, Mark Glaser

*Opposing views
are presented
fairly.*

*Jacobs counters
opposing
arguments.*

*A vivid example
helps Jacobs
make his point.*

*Jacobs uses
specific
evidence for
support.*

SCHOLARS ON ASSESSMENT

Huot, Brian. *(Re)Articulating Writing Assessment for Teaching and Learning.*
Logan: Utah State UP, 2002. Print. Huot defines assessment as the judgments we make about student writing, the form these judgments take,
and the context in which they are made. By looking at each aspect of this
definition, he hopes to neutralize the negative influence of assessment and
emphasize the benefits. He calls for increased attention to the ways in which
writing assessment can enhance teaching and learning, beginning with the
importance of teaching students to assess their own writing and of understanding the impact of our judgments on student writers. In Chapter 5, he
argues for increased attention to how we read and respond to student texts,
which he sees as an integral part of teaching writing. In his final chapters,
Huot focuses on writing assessment as a practical, self-conscious, and
reflective practice that can enrich teaching and program development.

Jacobs 5

emphasizes the role that blog updates played in saving storm victims' lives. Further, he calls the *Times-Picayune*'s partnership with citizen journalists a "watershed for online journalism."

Conclusion echoes the thesis without dully repeating it.

The Internet has enabled consumers to participate in a new way in reading, questioning, interpreting, and reporting the news. Decisions about appropriate content and coverage are no longer exclusively in the hands of news editors. Ordinary citizens now have a meaningful voice in the conversation—a hand in deciding what's "fit to print." Some skeptics worry about the apparent free-for-all and loss of tradition. But the expanding definition of news provides opportunities for consumers to be more engaged with events in their communities, their nations, and the world.

SCHOLARS ON ASSESSMENT

Haswell, Richard, ed. *Beyond Outcomes: Assessment and Instruction within a University Writing Program.* Westport: Ablex, 2001. Print. This collection of articles focuses on Washington State University's successful writing assessment initiative, which integrates instruction and assessment so that each informs the other in productive ways. While the authors describe local problems and solutions, the collection provides guidance for writing program administrators planning a similar assessment approach. For teachers, the value of this collection lies in its thoughtful analysis in Parts 3 and 4, "The Circle of Assessment and Instruction" and "Beyond Outcomes," respectively, both of which include articles related to faculty and student stakeholders.

Jacobs 6

Works Cited

Gillmor, Dan. *We the Media: Grassroots Journalism by the People, for the People*. Sebastopol: O'Reilly, 2006. Print.

Glaser, Mark. "NOLA.com Blogs and Forums Help Save Lives after Katrina." *OJR: The Online Journalism Review*. Knight Digital Media Center, 13 Sept. 2005. Web. 2 Mar. 2012.

Hazinski, David. "Unfettered 'Citizen Journalism' Too Risky." *Atlanta Journal-Constitution* 13 Dec. 2007: 23A. *General OneFile*. Web. 2 Mar. 2012.

Healy, Jack. "Window into Fed Debate over a Crucial Program." *New York Times*. New York Times, 14 Oct. 2009. Web. 4 Mar. 2012.

Jones, Alex S. *Losing the News: The Future of the News That Feeds Democracy*. New York: Oxford UP, 2009. Print.

"Openness and Accountability: A Study of Transparency in Global Media Outlets." *ICMPA: International Center for Media and the Public Agenda*. Intl. Center for Media and the Public Agenda, 2006. Web. 26 Feb. 2012.

"The 2006 Pulitzer Prize Winners: Public Service." *The Pulitzer Prizes*. Columbia U, n.d. Web. 2 Mar. 2012.

Weinberger, David. "Transparency Is the New Objectivity." *Joho the Blog*. David Weinberger, 19 July 2009. Web. 26 Feb. 2012.

Works cited page uses MLA style.

List is alphabetized by authors' last names (or by title when a work has no author).

Abbreviation "n.d." indicates that the online source has no update date.

SCHOLARS ON ASSESSMENT

Smith, Jane Bowman, and Kathleen Blake Yancey, eds. *Self-Assessment and Development in Writing: A Collaborative Inquiry*. Cresskill: Hampton, 2000. Print. The essays in this collection argue for self-assessment as an integral part of a writer's development. Students' reflections on their writing also provide useful data for course and program assessment, as many of the authors explain.

Writing Guide
Argument Essay

Composing an **argument** gives you the opportunity to propose a reasonable solution to a debatable issue. You say to your readers: "Here is my position, here is the evidence that supports the position, and here is my response to other positions on the issue." A sample argument essay begins on page 168.

Key features

- **A thesis, stated as a clear position on a debatable issue,** frames an argument essay. The issue is debatable because reasonable people disagree about it.

- **An examination of the issue's context** indicates why the issue is important, why readers should care about it, or how your position fits into the debates surrounding the topic.

- **Sufficient, representative, and relevant evidence** supports the argument's claims. Evidence needs to be specific and persuasive; quoted, summarized, or paraphrased fairly and accurately; and cited correctly.

- **Opposing positions are summarized and countered.** By anticipating and countering objections to your position, you establish common ground with readers and show yourself as a reasonable and well-informed writer.

Thinking ahead: Presenting or publishing

You may have some flexibility in how you present or publish your argument. If you submit your argument as an audio or video essay, make sure you understand the genre's conventions and think through how your voice or a combination of sounds and images can help you establish your *ethos*. If you are taking a position on a local issue, consider publishing your argument in the form of a newspaper op-ed or letter to the editor. The benefit? A real-world audience.

Writing your argument

Explore

Generate ideas by brainstorming responses to questions such as the following.

- What is the debate around your issue? What sources will help you learn more about your issue?
- What position will you take? Why does your position need to be argued?
- What evidence supports your position? What evidence makes you question your position?
- What types of appeals — *ethos, logos, pathos* — might you use to persuade readers? How will you build common ground with your readers?

Draft

Try to figure out the best way to structure your argument. A typical outline might include the following steps: Capture readers' attention; state your position; give background information; outline your major claims with specific evidence; recognize and respond to opposing points of view; and end by reinforcing your point and why it matters.

As you draft, think about the best order for your claims. You could organize by strength, building to your strongest argument (instead of starting with your strongest), or by concerns your audience might have.

Revise

Ask your reviewers for specific feedback. Here are some questions to guide their comments.

- Is the thesis clear? Is the issue debatable?
- Is the evidence persuasive? Is more needed?
- Is your argument organized logically?
- Are there any flaws in your reasoning or assumptions that weaken the argument?
- Have you presented yourself as a knowledgeable, trustworthy writer?
- Does the conclusion pull together your entire argument? How might the conclusion be more effective?

7 Reading and writing about literature

All good writing about literature attempts to answer a question, spoken or unspoken, about the text.

- How does street language function in Gwendolyn Brooks's "We Real Cool"?
- Why does Margaret Atwood make so many biblical allusions in *The Handmaid's Tale*?
- In what ways does Louise Erdrich's *Love Medicine* draw on oral narrative traditions?

The goal of a literature analysis should be to answer such questions with a meaningful and persuasive interpretation.

7a Be an active reader.

Responding to literature starts with becoming an engaged and active reader. Read the work through once, closely and carefully. Think of it as speaking to you: What is it telling you? Asking you? Trying to make you feel? Then go back and read it a second time. Rereading is a central part of the process of developing an analysis. If the work provides an introduction and footnotes, read them as well. They may provide key information. Use the dictionary to look up words unfamiliar to you or words with connotations that may influence the work's meaning.

As you read and reread, interact with the work by posing questions and looking for possible answers. The chart on pages 180–81 suggests some questions about literature that may help you become a more engaged, active reader.

TEACHING TIP

To initiate a discussion of reading and writing about literature, present or project these two quotations:

The illusion of art is to make one believe that great literature is very close to life, but exactly the opposite is true. Life is amorphous, literature is formal.
— Françoise Sagan

Fiction is like a spider's web, attached ever so slightly perhaps, but still attached to life at all four corners.
— Virginia Woolf

TEACHING TIP

Spend some time in class focusing on the following sentence: "All good writing about literature attempts to answer a question, spoken or unspoken,

Annotating the work

Annotating the work—in other words, interacting with the text by taking notes—is a way to focus your reading, capture your responses, and prepare for a class discussion. The first time you read the work through, you may want to indicate passages you find especially significant or puzzling—with a pencil or highlighter or by taking notes electronically. On a more careful rereading, pay particular attention to those passages, and jot down your ideas and reactions in a notebook or (if you own the text) on the pages. As you annotate, you can try out ideas and develop your questions and perspectives about the work. (See 4a for an annotated article.)

Discussing the work

Understanding literature can be a social experience, and class discussions often lead to interesting insights about a literary work, perhaps by calling attention to details that you took little notice of on a first reading. Discussions don't always occur face-to-face. In many classes, they happen online in discussion forums, chat rooms, blogs, or wikis. On page 178 is a set of blog postings about a character in Joyce Carol Oates's short story "Where Are You Going, Where Have You Been?"

7b Form an interpretation.

After rereading, taking notes, and perhaps discussing the work, you are ready to form an interpretation—your understanding of the meaning of details in the work. At this stage, try to focus on one aspect of the work. Look through your notes and annotations for recurring questions and insights.

Focusing on a central issue

In writing an analysis of literature, you will focus on a central issue. Your job isn't to say everything about the work that can

about the text" (p. 176). Use this sentence to guide the discussion of assigned literary texts. Encourage students to keep track of questions they want to ask about the text they are reading. Keep students' focus on the differences between asking *what* questions versus *why* or *how* questions.

TEACHING TIP

Give students practice with annotation by assigning a brief common work — a poem, a brief short story (three pages) — that they can read in class or in a single sitting. Ask students to annotate the assigned literary work. In class, have students share and compare annotations and build an even larger set of annotations on the work as the thoughts of others spark ideas for them. Ask students to reflect on these questions: What do they learn about the text from their annotations? How do their annotations help them understand the meaning of the text?

CONVERSATION ABOUT A SUBJECT

1 Dr. Connolly's Blog | ENG 101, Section 4

Who is Arnold Friend?

Posted by **Professor Barbara Connolly**, Thu Mar 7, 2013 4:36 PM

At one point during the story Arnold Friend demands, "Don't you know who I am?" Who do you think he is? Does the reader or Connie ever really know?

View comments | Add a comment

---

3 comments on
"Who is Arnold Friend?" Original post

2 Posted by **Zoe Marshall**, Thu Mar 7, 2013 7:23 PM
I think we're not supposed to know who Arnold Friend is. When he first arrives at Connie's house she asks him, "Who the hell do you think you are?" but Arnold ignores her question by changing the subject. He never tells her who he really is, only that he's her friend and her lover.

Posted by **Jon Fietze**, Thu Mar 7, 2013 8:04 PM
I found a lot of parallels between Arnold and the wolf in "Little Red Riding Hood." For example, Connie notices Arnold's hair, his teeth, and his grin. It reminded me of that part in "Little Red Riding Hood" when Little Red says, "Oh, Grandmother, what big teeth you have!"

Posted by **Yuko Yoshikawa**, Thu Mar 7, 2013 11:11 PM
I was thinking the same thing. Plus, Arnold seems like he's dressing up to hide who he is. Connie thinks that his hair is like a wig, and later that his face is a mask. It reminded me of when the wolf puts on the grandmother's clothing to trick Little Red Riding Hood, just like Arnold is trying to trick Connie.

1　Instructor's prompt.
2　A series of student responses to the prompt.

TEACHING TIP

Create a classroom blog to provide opportunities for students to converse about a text. Give students prompts and require them to post responses both to the main question and to peers' posts.

TEACHING TIP

Use the questions to ask about literature (p. 180) to guide a class discussion of an assigned reading. Encourage students to begin to focus on a single aspect of the work in their note taking.

possibly be said. It is to develop a sustained, in-depth interpretation that illuminates the work in some specific way. For
example, you may think that *Huckleberry Finn* is an interesting book because it not only contains humor and brilliant
descriptions of scenery but also tells a serious story of one
boy's development. But to develop this general response into
an interpretation, you will have to find a focus. For example,
you might address the ways in which the runaway slave Jim
uses humor to preserve his dignity. Or you might examine the
ironic contradictions between what Huck says and what his
heart tells him.

Asking questions that lead to an interpretation

Good interpretations generally arise from good questions. What
is it about the work that puzzles or intrigues you? What do you
want to know more about? By asking yourself such questions,
you will push yourself beyond your first impressions to deeper
insights.

In writing an analysis, you might answer questions about
literary techniques, such as the author's handling of plot, setting,
or character. Or you could respond to questions about social
context as well—what a work reveals about the time and culture
in which it was written. Both kinds of questions are included in
the chart on pages 180–81.

Often you will find yourself writing about both technique and
social context. For example, Margaret Peel, a student who wrote
an essay on Langston Hughes's poem "Ballad of the Landlord,"
addressed the following question, which touches on both language
and race:

> How does the poem's language—through its four voices—dramatize the
> experience of a black man in a society dominated by whites?

hackerhandbooks.com/bedhandbook

e Academic reading and writing > As you write: Asking questions about literature

SCHOLARS ON WRITING AND LITERATURE

Cahalan, James M. "Teaching Hometown Literature: A Pedagogy of
Place." *College English* 70.3 (2008): 249–74. Print. Cahalan describes the
pedagogy that drives his literature courses—courses on hometown literature designed to emphasize identity and place and extend the reach of new
literary theories such as bioregionalism, ecocriticism, and place studies. He
discusses his focus on place in the study of such diverse authors as Gloria
Anzaldúa, Robert Lowry, and Mahmoud Darwish and then describes the
eagerness with which students undertake studying authors from their own
home places. Cahalan argues that teaching hometown literature is, at
its core, student-centered classroom work—giving students the rare
opportunity to demonstrate expertise and passion in their academic life.

Questions to ask about literature

Questions about technique

Plot: What central conflicts drive the plot? Are they internal (within a character) or external (between characters or between a character and a force)? How are conflicts resolved?

Setting: Does the setting (time and place) create an atmosphere, give an insight into a character, suggest symbolic meanings, or hint at the theme of the work?

Character: What seems to motivate the central characters? Do any characters change significantly? If so, what have they learned from their experiences? Do contrasts between characters highlight important themes?

Point of view: Does the point of view — the perspective from which the story is narrated or the poem is spoken — influence our understanding of events? Does the narration reveal the character traits of the speaker, or does the speaker merely observe others? Is the narrator innocent, naive, or deceitful?

Theme: Does the work have an overall theme (a central insight about people or a truth about life, for example)? If so, how do details in the work illuminate this theme?

Language: Does language — formal or informal, standard or dialect, ordinary or poetic, cool or passionate — reveal the character of speakers? How do metaphors, similes, and sensory images contribute to the work? How do recurring images enrich the work and hint at its meaning?

Questions about social context

Historical context: What does the work reveal about — or how was it shaped by — the time and place in which it was written? Does the work appear to promote or undermine a philosophy that was popular in its time, such as feminism in the mid-twentieth century?

Class: How does social class shape or influence characters' choices and actions? How does class affect the way characters view or are viewed by others? What economic struggles or power relationships does the work reflect or depict?

SCHOLARS ON WRITING AND LITERATURE

Daemmrich, Ingrid G. "Novices Encounter a Novice Literature: Introducing Digital Literature in a First-Year College Writing Class." *Teaching English in the Two-Year College* 34.4 (2007): 420–33. Print. A professor at "technologically oriented" Drexel University, Daemmrich introduced her first-year writers to digital literature—fragmented narratives including text, hypertext links, animated text and images, music, color, and other multimedia features. She watched her students progress from being uncomfortable, hostile, and skeptical to engaged, critical, and open-minded over a semester. The students, Daemmrich asserts, were empowered by their status as pioneers on the one hand and (in the absence of "expert" critics) critics on the other.

QUESTIONS TO ASK ABOUT LITERATURE (cont.)

Race and culture: Are any characters portrayed as being caught between cultures: between a traditional and an emerging culture, for example? Are any characters engaged in a conflict with society because of their race or ethnic background? Does the work celebrate a specific culture and its traditions?

Gender: Are any characters' choices restricted because of gender? What are the power relationships between the sexes? Do any characters resist the gender roles that society has assigned to them? Do other characters choose to conform to those roles?

Archetypes (or universal types): Does a character, an image, or a plot fit a pattern — a type — that has been repeated in stories throughout history and across cultures? (For example, nearly every culture has stories about heroes, quests, redemption, and revenge.) How is an archetypal character, image, or plot line similar to or different from others like it?

In the introduction of your paper, you will usually announce your interpretation in a one- or two-sentence thesis. The thesis answers the central question that you posed. Here, for example, is Margaret Peel's two-sentence thesis:

> Langston Hughes's "Ballad of the Landlord" is narrated through four voices, each with its own perspective on the poem's action. These opposing voices—of a tenant, a landlord, the police, and the press—dramatize a black man's experience in a society dominated by whites.

7c Draft a working thesis.

A thesis, which often appears in the introduction, announces an essay's main point (see also 1c and 53a). In a literature analysis, your thesis will answer the central question that you have asked

hackerhandbooks.com/bedhandbook

e Academic reading and writing > As you write: Evaluating a working thesis
e Academic reading and writing > Exercises: 7–1

AN ADDITIONAL RESOURCE ON READING AND WRITING ABOUT LITERATURE

Re:Writing for Literature (bedfordstmartins.com/rewritinglit) offers free resources for students who are reading and writing about literary works in a composition course or in a literature course. The site features illustrated tutorials for the close reading of stories, poems, and plays; links to information on literary authors; quizzes on literary works; a glossary of literary terms; MLA-style sample papers; and tools for finding and citing sources.

about the work. Putting your working thesis and notes into an informal outline can help you organize your ideas.

Drafting a thesis

When drafting your thesis, aim for a strong, assertive summary of your interpretation. Here, for example, is a successful thesis taken from a student essay, together with the central question the student had posed.

QUESTION

What is the significance of the explorer Robert Walton in Mary Shelley's novel *Frankenstein*?

THESIS

Through the character of Walton, Shelley suggests that the most profound and useful sort of knowledge is not a knowledge of nature's secrets but a knowledge of the limits of knowledge itself.

As in other college writing, the thesis of a literature paper should not be too factual, too broad, or too vague (see 1e). For an essay on Mark Twain's *Huckleberry Finn*, the first three examples would all make weak thesis statements.

TOO FACTUAL

As a runaway slave, Jim is in danger from the law.

TOO BROAD

In *Huckleberry Finn*, Mark Twain criticizes mid-nineteenth-century American society.

TOO VAGUE

Huckleberry Finn is Twain's most exciting work.

SCHOLARS ON WRITING AND LITERATURE

Harmon, William. *A Handbook to Literature.* 10th ed. Upper Saddle River: Prentice, 2006. Print. Including entries on literary terms, styles, and movements, this indispensable text supplements any classroom discussion of literature and offers students concise descriptions of familiar and problematic features of literature.

The following thesis statement is sharply focused and presents a central idea that requires discussion and support. It connects a general point (that Twain objects to empty piety) to those specific aspects of the novel the paper will address (Huck's status as narrator, Huck's comments on religion).

ACCEPTABLE THESIS

Because Huckleberry Finn is a naive narrator, his comments on conventional religion function ironically at every turn, allowing Twain to poke fun at empty piety.

Sketching an outline

Your thesis may strongly suggest a method of organization, in which case you will have little difficulty jotting down your essay's key points. Consider, for example, the following informal outline, based on a thesis that leads naturally to a three-part organization.

Thesis: In Zora Neale Hurston's novel *Their Eyes Were Watching God*, Janie grows into independence through a series of marriages: first to Logan Killicks, who treats her as a source of farm labor; next to Jody Starks, who sees her as a symbol of his own power; and then to Tea Cake, with whom she shares a passionate and satisfying love that leads her to self-discovery.

- Marriage to Logan Killicks: arranged by grandmother, Janie as labor, runs away
- Marriage to Jody Starks: Eatonville, Jody as mayor, violence, Jody's death
- Marriage to Tea Cake: younger man, love, shooting, return to Eatonville

Whether to use an informal or a formal outline (see 1d) is to some extent a matter of personal preference. For most purposes, you will probably find that an informal outline is sufficient, perhaps even preferable.

SCHOLARS ON WRITING AND LITERATURE

LeJeune, Susan G. "Writing for the Ignorant Reader." *Teaching English in the Two-Year College* 26.2 (1998): 163–67. Print. In her introductory composition and literature class, LeJeune gives advice that helps students write clear, well-supported analyses without losing their voices: Write for the ignorant reader. The ignorant reader, like the student writer's classmates, has questions—the very sorts of questions that lead to an interpretation. An audience of ignorant readers won't sit still for jargon-laden academic prose; these readers expect clear, straightforward answers to their questions. In addition, ignorant readers need proof. Finally, because ignorant readers can be somewhat dense, student writers must supply them with explications and analyses.

Drafting an introduction that announces your interpretation

The introduction to a literature analysis is usually one paragraph long. In most cases, you will want to begin the paragraph with a few sentences that provide context for your thesis and to end it with a thesis that sums up your interpretation. You may also want to note the question or issue that motivated your interpretation. In this way, you will help your readers understand not only what your idea or thesis *is* but also why it *matters*.

The following is an introductory paragraph announcing a student's interpretation of one aspect of the novel *Frankenstein*; the thesis is highlighted.

> In Mary Shelley's novel *Frankenstein*, Walton's ambition as an explorer, to find a passage to the North Pole, mirrors Frankenstein's ambition as a scientist, to discover and master the secret of life. But where Frankenstein is ultimately destroyed by his quest for knowledge, Walton turns back from his quest when he learns of Frankenstein's fate. Walton's story might seem unimportant, but paired with Frankenstein's, it keeps us from missing one of the novel's most important themes. Through the character of Walton, Shelley suggests that the most profound and useful sort of knowledge is not a knowledge of nature's secrets but a knowledge of the limits of knowledge itself.

7d Support your interpretation with evidence from the text; avoid plot summary.

Your thesis and preliminary outline will point you toward details in the text relevant to your interpretation. As you begin drafting the body of your paper, make good use of those details.

Supporting your interpretation

As a rule, each paragraph in the body of your paper should focus on some aspect of your overall interpretation and should include

SCHOLARS ON WRITING AND LITERATURE

Hull, Glynda, and Mike Rose. "'This Wooden Shack Place': The Logic of an Unconventional Reading." *College Composition and Communication* 41.3 (1990): 287–98. Print. Hull and Rose discuss student interpretations of literature that strike teachers as "unusual, a little off, not on the mark." The authors suggest that "our particular orientations and readings might blind us to the logic of a student's interpretation and the ways that interpretation might be sensibly influenced by the student's history."

a topic sentence that states the main idea of the paragraph. The rest of the paragraph should present details and quotations from the work that back up your interpretation. In the following paragraph, which develops part of the organization sketched on page 183, the topic sentence comes first. It sums up the significance of Janie's marriage to Logan Killicks in Zora Neale Hurston's novel *Their Eyes Were Watching God*.

> Janie finds her marriage to Logan Killicks unsatisfying because she did not choose him and cannot love him. The marriage is arranged by Janie's grandmother and caretaker, Nanny, so that Janie will have a secure home after Nanny dies. When Janie objects to the marriage, Nanny tells her, "'Tain't Logan Killicks Ah wants you to have, baby, it's protection" (15). Janie marries Logan even though she does not love him. She "wait[s] for love to begin" (22), but love never comes. At first, Logan dotes on Janie, but as time passes he demands more and more work from her. Although she works hard in the kitchen, he wants her to perform traditionally masculine tasks such as chopping wood, plowing fields, and shoveling manure. When Janie suggests that they each have their roles—"Youse in yo' place and Ah'm in mine"—Logan asserts his authority over her and doesn't seem to relate to her as family: "You ain't got no particular place. It's wherever Ah need yuh" (31). As husband and wife, Janie and Logan are estranged from each other. Janie tells him, "You ain't done me no favor by marryin' me" (31). Janie's leaving the marriage is the first step in her growing independence.

Notice that the writer has quoted dialogue from the novel to lend both flavor and substance to her interpretation (quotations are cited with page numbers). Notice too that the writer is *interpreting* the work: She is not merely summarizing the plot.

Avoiding simple plot summary

In a literature paper, it is tempting to rely heavily on plot summary and avoid interpretation. You can resist this temptation by paying special attention to your topic sentences.

TEACHING TIP

When students have completed a rough draft of their analysis, pair them in class (either face-to-face or online) to examine topic sentences. Students should highlight the topic sentences in their papers, exchange papers, and read through them to see if the topic sentences lend themselves more to summary or to analysis. The topic sentences should be analytical. As a reminder, ask students to consult page 186 to see a sample topic sentence that leads to summary and one that announces an interpretation.

DRAFT: A TOPIC SENTENCE THAT LEADS TO PLOT SUMMARY

As they drift down the river on a raft, Huck and Jim have many philosophical discussions.

REVISED: A TOPIC SENTENCE THAT ANNOUNCES AN INTERPRETATION

The theme of growing moral awareness is reinforced by the many philosophical discussions between Huck and Jim as they drift down the river on a raft.

Remember that readers are interested in your ideas about a work—the questions you are asking and the details you find significant. To avoid simple plot summary, keep the following strategies in mind as you write.

- When you write for an academic audience, you can assume that most readers have read the work. You need to include some summary as background, but the emphasis should be on your ideas and your interpretation of the work.

- Pose questions that lead to an interpretation or judgment of the work rather than to a summary. The questions in the chart on pages 180–81 can help steer you away from summary and toward interpretation.

- Read your essay out loud. If you hear yourself listing events from the work, stop and revise.

- Rather than organizing your paper according to the work's sequence of events, organize it in a way that brings out the relationship among your ideas.

7e Observe the conventions of literature papers.

The academic discipline of English literature has certain conventions, or standard practices, that scholars in the field use when writing about literature. These conventions help scholars

---

SCHOLARS ON WRITING AND LITERATURE

Steinberg, Erwin R., Michael Gamer, Erika Lindemann, Gary Tate, and Jane Peterson. "Symposium: Literature in the Composition Classroom." *College English* 57 (1995): 265–318. Print. The authors debate whether literature has a place in the composition classroom.

Young, Art, and Toby Fulwiler, eds. *When Writing Teachers Teach Literature: Bringing Writing to Reading.* Portsmouth: Boynton, 1995. Print. Drawing on a variety of critical approaches, this book suggests ways to help students learn to write about literature.

contribute their ideas clearly and efficiently. If you follow these conventions, you will enhance your credibility and enable your readers to focus more easily on your ideas.

Referring to authors, titles, and characters

The first time you refer to an author of a literary work or a secondary source, such as a critical essay, use the author's full name: *Virginia Woolf is known for her experimental novels.* In subsequent references, you may use the last name only: *Woolf's early work was largely overlooked.* As a rule, do not use personal titles such as *Mr.* or *Ms.* or *Dr.* when referring to authors.

When you mention the title of a short story, an essay, or a short or medium-length poem, put the title in quotation marks: "The Progress of Love" by Alice Munro (see 37c). Italicize the titles of novels, nonfiction books, plays, and long poems: *The Fourth Hand* by John Irving (see 42a).

Using the present tense to describe fictional events

Perhaps because fictional events have not actually occurred in the past, the literary convention is to describe them in the present tense. Until you become used to this convention, you may find yourself shifting between present and past tense. As you revise your draft, make sure that you have used the present tense consistently.

NOTE: See also pages 188–89 on avoiding shifts in tenses when you integrate quotations into your own text.

7f Integrate quotations from the text.

Integrating quotations from a literary text can lend vivid support to your argument, but keep most quotations fairly short. Excessive use of long quotations may interrupt the flow of your interpretation. (The examples in this section use MLA style for citing sources. See 56a for details.)

Introducing literary quotations

When introducing quotations from a literary work, make sure that you don't confuse the author with the narrator of a story, the speaker of a poem, or a character in a story or play. Instead of naming the author, you can refer to the narrator or speaker—or to the work itself.

INAPPROPRIATE

Poet Andrew Marvell describes his fear of death like this: "But at my back I always hear / Time's wingèd chariot hurrying near" (21-22).

APPROPRIATE

Addressing his beloved, the speaker of the poem argues that death gives them no time to waste: "But at my back I always hear / Time's wingèd chariot hurrying near" (21-22).

APPROPRIATE

The poem "To His Coy Mistress" says as much about fleeting time and death as it does about sexual passion. Its most powerful lines are "But at my back I always hear / Time's wingèd chariot hurrying near" (21-22).

In the last example, you could mention the author as well: *Andrew Marvell's poem "To His Coy Mistress" says as much. . . .* Although the author is mentioned, readers will not confuse him with the speaker of the poem.

Providing context for quotations

When you quote the words of a narrator, speaker, or character in a literary work, you should name who is speaking and provide a context for the quoted words. In the following example, the quoted language is from Shirley Jackson's short story "The Lottery."

When a neighbor suggests that the lottery should be abandoned, Old Man Warner responds, "There's *always* been a lottery" (284).

Avoiding shifts in tense when quoting

Because it is conventional to write about literature in the present tense (see p. 187) and because literary works often use other tenses, you will need to exercise some care when weaving quotations into your own writing. One student's draft of an essay on Nadine Gordimer's short story "Friday's Footprint" included the following awkward sentence, in which the present-tense main verb *sees* is followed by the past-tense verb *blushed* in the quotation.

TENSE SHIFT

When Rita <u>sees</u> Johnny's relaxed attitude, "she <u>blushed</u>, like a wave of illness" (159).

When revising, the writer considered two ways to avoid the shift from present to past tense: to paraphrase the reference to Rita's blushing and reduce the length of the quotation or to change the verb in the quotation to the present tense, using brackets to indicate the change. (For advice on using brackets to indicate changes in a quotation, see 39c.)

REVISION 1

When Rita sees Johnny's relaxed attitude, she is overcome with embarrassment, "like a wave of illness" (159).

REVISION 2

When Rita sees Johnny's relaxed attitude, "she blushe[s], like a wave of illness" (159).

Citing quotations

MLA guidelines for citing quotations differ somewhat for short stories or novels, poems, and plays.

Short stories or novels   To cite a passage from a short story or a novel, use a page number in parentheses after the quoted words.

> The narrator of Madeleine Thien's "Simple Recipes" remembers a conversation in which her mother described guilt as something one could "shrink" and "compress." After a time, according to the mother, "you can blow it off your body like a speck of dirt" (12).

When a quotation is five lines or longer, set it off from the text by indenting one inch from the left margin; when you set a quotation off from the text, do not use quotation marks. Put the parenthetical citation after the final mark of punctuation.

> Sister's tale begins with "I," and she makes every event revolve around herself, even her sister's marriage:
>
>> I was getting along fine with Mama, Papa-Daddy, and Uncle Rondo until my sister Stella-Rondo just separated from her husband and came back home again. Mr. Whitaker! Of course I went with Mr. Whitaker first, when he first appeared here in China Grove, taking "Pose Yourself" photos, and Stella-Rondo broke us up. (46)

Poems   To cite lines from a poem, use line numbers in parentheses at the end of the quotation. For the first reference, use the word "lines": (lines 1-2). Thereafter use just the numbers: (12-13).

> The opening lines of Frost's "Fire and Ice" strike a conversational tone: "Some say the world will end in fire, / Some say in ice" (1-2).

Enclose quotations of three or fewer lines of poetry in quotation marks within your text, and indicate line breaks with a slash, as in the example just given. (See also 39e and item 25 on pp. 594–95.)

When you quote four or more lines of poetry, set the quotation off from the text by indenting one inch and omit the quotation marks. Put the line numbers in parentheses after the final mark of punctuation.

Plays To cite lines from a play, include the act number, scene number, and line numbers (as many of these as are available) in parentheses at the end of the quotation. Separate the numbers with periods, and use arabic numerals (1, 2, 3) unless your instructor prefers roman numerals.

> Two attendants silently watch as the sleepwalking Lady Macbeth subconsciously struggles with her guilt: "Here's the smell of the blood still. All the perfumes of Arabia will not sweeten this little hand" (5.1.50-51).

If no act, scene, or line numbers are available, use a page number.

When a quotation from a play takes up four or fewer typed lines in your paper and is spoken by only one character, put quotation marks around it and run it into the text of your essay, as in the previous example. If the quotation consists of two or three lines from a verse play, use a slash for line breaks, as for poetry (see p. 190). When a dramatic quotation by a single character is five typed lines or longer (or more than three lines in a verse play), treat it like a passage from a short story or a novel (see p. 190): Indent the quotation one inch from the left margin and omit quotation marks. Include the citation in parentheses after the final mark of punctuation.

When quoting dialogue between two or more characters in a play, set the quotation off from the text. Type each character's name in all capital letters at a one-inch indent from the left margin. Indent subsequent lines under the character's name an additional one-quarter inch. (See the example on the next page.)

In the opening act of *Translations*, Friel pointedly contrasts the monolingual Captain Lancey with the multilingual Irish:

> HUGH. . . . [Lancey] then explained that he does not speak Irish. Latin? I asked. None. Greek? Not a syllable. He speaks — on his own admission — only English; and to his credit he seemed suitably verecund — James?
>
> JIMMY. *Verecundus* — humble.
>
> HUGH. Indeed — he voiced some surprise that we did not speak his language. (act 1)

7g Document secondary sources appropriately and avoid plagiarism.

Many times, an analysis of literature relies wholly on the primary source — the literary work under discussion. In addition to relying on primary sources, some analyses draw on secondary sources: essays of literary criticism, a biography or autobiography of the author, or histories of the era in which the work was written. When you use secondary sources, you must document them with MLA in-text citations and a list of works cited as explained in 56. (For an example of a paper that uses secondary sources, see pp. 196–98.)

Keep in mind that even when you use secondary sources, your main goal should be to develop your own understanding and interpretation of the literary work.

Whenever you use secondary sources, you must document them to avoid plagiarism. Plagiarism is unacknowledged borrowing of a source's words or ideas. (See 54b.)

Documenting secondary sources

Most literature papers use the documentation system recommended by the Modern Language Association (MLA). This system of documentation is discussed in detail in 56.

TEACHING TIP

Schedule time with a reference librarian, inviting him or her to visit class or, even better, schedule time when your class can visit the library. If you assign students to read secondary sources about literary authors or their works, your reference librarian can cover search strategies or resources to consult for this kind of work. If you teach your course online, your school's reference librarian might agree to post a series of messages on your course discussion board with relevant topics for your students.

MLA recommends in-text citations that refer readers to a list of works cited. An in-text citation names the author of the source, often in a signal phrase, and gives the page number in parentheses. At the end of the paper, a list of works cited provides publication information about the sources used in the paper.

MLA IN-TEXT CITATION

Finding Butler's science fiction novel *Xenogenesis* more hopeful than *Frankenstein*, Theodora Goss and John Paul Riquelme note that "[h]uman and creature never bridge their differences in Shelley's narrative, but in Butler's they do . . ." (437).

SAMPLE ENTRY IN THE LIST OF WORKS CITED

Goss, Theodora, and John Paul Riquelme. "From Superhuman to Posthuman: The Gothic Technological Imaginary in Mary Shelley's *Frankenstein* and Octavia Butler's *Xenogenesis*." *Modern Fiction Studies* 53.3 (2007): 434-59. Print.

As you document secondary sources with in-text citations and a list of works cited, you will need to consult 56a and 56b.

Avoiding plagiarism; being responsible

The rules about plagiarism are the same for literary papers as for other academic and research writing (see 51c and 54 for important details). To be fair and ethical, you must acknowledge your responsibility to the writers of any sources you use. If another critic's work suggested an interpretation to you or if someone else's research clarified an obscure point, it is your responsibility to cite the source. In addition to citing the source, you must place any borrowed language in quotation marks and credit the author. In the following example, the plagiarized words are highlighted.

ORIGINAL SOURCE

Here again Glaspell's story reflects a larger truth about the lives of rural women. Their isolation induced madness in many. The rate of insanity in rural areas, especially for women, was a much-discussed subject in the second half of the nineteenth century.

> — Elaine Hedges, "Small Things Reconsidered:
> 'A Jury of Her Peers,'" p. 59

PLAGIARISM

Glaspell may or may not want us to believe that Minnie Wright's murder of her husband is an insane act, but Minnie's loneliness and isolation certainly could have driven her mad. As Elaine Hedges notes, the rate of insanity in rural areas, especially for women, was a much-discussed subject in the second half of the nineteenth century (59).

BORROWED LANGUAGE IN QUOTATION MARKS

Glaspell may or may not want us to believe that Minnie Wright's murder of her husband is an insane act, but Minnie's loneliness and isolation certainly could have driven her mad. As Elaine Hedges notes, "The rate of insanity in rural areas, especially for women, was a much-discussed subject in the second half of the nineteenth century" (59).

Sometimes writers plagiarize unintentionally because they have difficulty paraphrasing a source's ideas. In the first paraphrase of the following source, the writer has copied the highlighted words (without quotation marks) and followed the sentence structure of the source too closely, merely plugging in synonyms (*prowess* for *skill*, *respect* for *esteem*, and so on).

ORIGINAL SOURCE

Mothers [in the late nineteenth century] were advised to teach their daughters to make small, exact stitches, not only for durability but as a way of instilling habits of patience, neatness, and diligence. But such stitches also became a badge of one's needlework skill, a source of self-esteem and of status, through the recognition and admiration of other women.

> — Elaine Hedges, "Small Things Reconsidered:
> 'A Jury of Her Peers,'" p. 62

PLAGIARISM: UNACCEPTABLE BORROWING

One of the final clues in the story, the irregular stitching in Minnie's quilt patches, connects immediately with Mrs. Hale and Mrs. Peters. In the late nineteenth century, explains Elaine Hedges, small, exact stitches were valued not only for their durability. They became a badge of one's prowess with the needle, a source of self-respect and of prestige, through the recognition and approval of other women (62).

ACCEPTABLE PARAPHRASE

One of the final clues in the story, the irregular stitching in Minnie's quilt patches, connects immediately with Mrs. Hale and Mrs. Peters. In the late nineteenth century, explains Elaine Hedges, precise needlework was valued for more than its strength. It was a source of pride to women, a way of gaining status in the community of other women (62).

Although the acceptable version uses a few words found in the source, it does not borrow entire phrases without quotation marks or closely mimic the structure of the original. To write an acceptable paraphrase, resist the temptation to look at the source while you write; instead, write from memory. When you write from memory, you will be more likely to use your own words. Ask yourself, "What is the author's meaning?" and then in your own words state your understanding of the author's basic point.

7h Sample student writing: Literary analysis

Following are pages from a sample essay that analyzes a literary work. Dan Larson uses evidence from the primary source, a short story, as well as from secondary sources, essays written by literary critics.

hackerhandbooks.com/bedhandbook

e Academic reading and writing > Sample student writing > Larson, "The Transformation of Mrs. Peters: An Analysis of 'A Jury of Her Peers'" (literary analysis)

Larson 1

Dan Larson

Professor Duncan

English 102

19 April 2013

The Transformation of Mrs. Peters:

An Analysis of "A Jury of Her Peers"

In Susan Glaspell's 1917 short story "A Jury of Her Peers,"
two women accompany their husbands and a county attorney to an
isolated house where a farmer named John Wright has been choked
to death in his bed with a rope. The chief suspect is Wright's wife,
Minnie, who is in jail awaiting trial. The sheriff's wife, Mrs. Peters, has
come along to gather some personal items for Minnie, and Mrs. Hale
has joined her. Early in the story, Mrs. Hale sympathizes with Minnie
and objects to the way the male investigators are "snoopin' round and
criticizin'" her kitchen (249). In contrast, Mrs. Peters shows respect
for the law, saying that the men are doing "no more than their duty"
(249). By the end of the story, however, Mrs. Peters has joined
Mrs. Hale in a conspiracy of silence, lied to the men, and committed
a crime—hiding key evidence. What causes this dramatic change?

One critic, Leonard Mustazza, argues that Mrs. Hale recruits
Mrs. Peters "as a fellow 'juror' in the case, moving the sheriff's wife
away from her sympathy for her husband's position and towards
identification with the accused wom[a]n" (494). While this is true,
Mrs. Peters also reaches insights on her own. Her observations in the
kitchen lead her to understand Minnie's grim and lonely plight as the
wife of an abusive farmer, and her identification with both Minnie and
Mrs. Hale is strengthened as the men conducting the investigation
trivialize the lives of women.

The opening lines name the story and establish context.

Present tense is used to describe details from the story.

Quotations from the story are cited with page numbers in parentheses.

The opening paragraph ends with Larson's research question.

The thesis asserts Larson's main point.

Marginal annotations indicate MLA-style formatting and effective writing.

Larson 2

The first evidence that Mrs. Peters reaches understanding on her own surfaces in the following passage:

> The sheriff's wife had looked from the stove to the sink—
> to the pail of water which had been carried in from
> outside. . . . That look of seeing into things, of seeing
> through a thing to something else, was in the eyes of
> the sheriff's wife now. (251-52)

Something about the stove, the sink, and the pail of water connects with her own experience, giving Mrs. Peters a glimpse into the life of Minnie Wright. The details resonate with meaning.

Social historian Elaine Hedges argues that such details, which evoke the drudgery of a farm woman's work, would not have been lost upon Glaspell's readers in 1917. Hedges tells us what the pail and the stove, along with another detail from the story—a dirty towel on a roller—would have meant to women of the time. Laundry was a dreaded all-day affair. Water had to be pumped, hauled, and boiled; then the wash was rubbed, rinsed, wrung through a wringer, carried outside, and hung on a line to dry. "What the women see, beyond the pail and the stove," writes Hedges, "are the hours of work it took Minnie to produce that one clean towel" (56).

On her own, Mrs. Peters discovers clues about the motive for the murder. Her curiosity leads her to pick up a sewing basket filled with quilt pieces and then to notice something strange: a sudden row of badly sewn stitches. "What do you suppose she was so—nervous about?" asks Mrs. Peters (252). A short time later, Mrs. Peters spots another clue, an empty birdcage. Again she observes details on her own, in this case a broken door and hinge, suggesting that the cage has been roughly handled.

A long quotation is set off by indenting; no quotation marks are needed; ellipsis dots indicate a sentence omitted from the source.

Larson summarizes ideas from a secondary source and then quotes from that source; he names the author in a signal phrase and gives a page number in parentheses.

Topic sentences present Larson's interpretation.

Larson 7

Works Cited

Ben-Zvi, Linda. "'Murder, She Wrote': The Genesis of Susan Glaspell's *Trifles*." *Theatre Journal* 44.2 (1992): 141-62. Rpt. in *Susan Glaspell: Essays on Her Theater and Fiction*. Ed. Ben-Zvi. Ann Arbor: U of Michigan P, 1995. 19-48. Print.

Glaspell, Susan. "A Jury of Her Peers." *Literature and Its Writers: A Compact Introduction to Fiction, Poetry, and Drama*. Ed. Ann Charters and Samuel Charters. 6th ed. Boston: Bedford, 2013. 243-58. Print.

Hedges, Elaine. "Small Things Reconsidered: 'A Jury of Her Peers.'" *Women's Studies* 12.1 (1986): 89-110. Rpt. in *Susan Glaspell: Essays on Her Theater and Fiction*. Ed. Linda Ben-Zvi. Ann Arbor: U of Michigan P, 1995. 49-69. Print.

Mustazza, Leonard. "Generic Translation and Thematic Shift in Susan Glaspell's *Trifles* and 'A Jury of Her Peers.'" *Studies in Short Fiction* 26.4 (1989): 489-96. Print.

The works cited page lists the primary source (Glaspell's story) and secondary sources.

PART III

Clear
Sentences

8   Prefer active verbs.

As a rule, choose an active verb and pair it with a subject that names the person or thing doing the action. Active verbs express meaning more emphatically and vigorously than their weaker counterparts—verbs in the passive voice and forms of the verb *be*.

PASSIVE	The pumps *were destroyed* by a surge of power.
***BE* VERB**	A surge of power *was* responsible for the destruction of the pumps.
ACTIVE	A surge of power *destroyed* the pumps.

Verbs in the passive voice lack strength because their subjects receive the action instead of doing it. Forms of the verb *be* (*be, am, is, are, was, were, being, been*) lack vigor because they convey no action.

Although passive verbs and the forms of *be* have legitimate uses, choose an active verb whenever possible.

Even among active verbs, some are more vigorous and colorful than others. Carefully selected verbs can energize a piece of writing.

▶ The goalie crouched low, ~~reached~~ swept out his stick, and ~~sent~~ hooked the rebound away from the mouth of the net.

Academic English

Although you may be tempted to avoid the passive voice completely, keep in mind that some writing situations call for it, especially scientific writing. For appropriate uses of the passive voice, see page 201; for advice about forming the passive voice, see 28b and 47c.

SCHOLARS ON ACTIVE AND PASSIVE VOICE

Robinson, William S. "Sentence Focus, Cohesion, and the Active and Passive Voices." *Teaching English in the Two-Year College* 27.4 (2000): 440–45. Print. Robinson argues that even skilled writers don't consciously choose the active or the passive voice. Instead, they select subjects that name what they are talking about, a technique that produces a cohesive text. Both the active and passive voices can play a role in cohesion, as topic-comment theorists have pointed out. Robinson suggests that when students produce texts lacking cohesion, they may be mimicking academic style. The cure, says Robinson, is to advise students to make their subjects personal rather than abstract.

8a Use the active voice unless you have a good reason for choosing the passive.

In the active voice, the subject does the action; in the passive voice, the subject receives the action (see also 47c). Although both voices are grammatically correct, the active voice is usually more effective because it is clearer and more direct.

ACTIVE   Hernando *caught* the fly ball.

PASSIVE   The fly ball *was caught* by Hernando.

Passive sentences often identify the actor in a *by* phrase, as in the preceding example. Sometimes, however, that phrase is omitted, and who or what is responsible for the action becomes unclear: *The fly ball was caught.*

Most of the time, you will want to emphasize the actor, so you should use the active voice. To replace a passive verb with an active one, make the actor the subject of the sentence.

> The settlers stripped the land of timber before realizing
> ~~The land was stripped of timber before the settlers realized~~
> ∧
> the consequences of their actions.

The revision emphasizes the actors (*settlers*) by naming them in the subject.

Appropriate uses of the passive

The passive voice is appropriate to emphasize the receiver of the action or to minimize the importance of the actor.

APPROPRIATE PASSIVE   Many Hawaiians *were forced* to leave their homes after the earthquake.

APPROPRIATE PASSIVE   Near harvest time, the tobacco plants *are sprayed* with a chemical to slow the growth of suckers.

SCHOLARS ON ACTIVE AND PASSIVE VOICE

Frischkorn, Craig. "Style in Advanced Composition: Active Students and Passive Voice." *Teaching English in the Two-Year College* 26.4 (1999): 415–18. Print. Partly because most grammar checkers blindly condemn the passive voice, Frischkorn thinks we need to teach students to make their own decisions. By using newspaper articles from financial, sports, and even self-help columns, Frischkorn engages his students in rich and lively discussions of the rhetoric of the passive voice.

The writer of the first sentence wished to emphasize the receiver of the action, *Hawaiians*. The writer of the second sentence wished to focus on the tobacco plants, not on the people spraying them.

In much scientific writing, the passive voice properly emphasizes the experiment or process being described, not the researcher. Check with your instructor for the preference in your discipline.

8b Replace *be* verbs that result in dull or wordy sentences.

Not every *be* verb needs replacing. The forms of *be* (*be, am, is, are, was, were, being, been*) work well when you want to link a subject to a noun that clearly renames it or to an adjective that describes it: *Orchard House was the home of Louisa May Alcott. The harvest will be bountiful after the summer rains.*

Be verbs also are essential as helping verbs before present participles (*is flying, are disappearing*) to express ongoing action: *Derrick was fighting the fire when his wife went into labor.* (See 27f.)

If using a *be* verb makes a sentence needlessly dull and wordy, however, consider replacing it. Often a phrase following the verb contains a noun or an adjective (such as *violation, resistant*) that suggests a more vigorous, active verb (*violate, resist*).

▶ Burying nuclear waste in Antarctica would ~~be in violation of~~ violate an international treaty.

Violate is less wordy and more vigorous than *be in violation of*.

▶ When Rosa Parks ~~was resistant to~~ resisted giving up her seat on the bus, she became a civil rights hero.

Resisted is stronger than *was resistant to*.

SCHOLARS ON ACTIVE AND PASSIVE VOICE

Scriven, Karen. "Actively Teaching the Passive Voice." *Teaching English in the Two-Year College* 16.2 (1989): 89–93. Print. Scriven argues that passive constructions "are not the mark of flawed writing . . . but are instead frequent and effective stylistic variants." She suggests that instead of condemning the passive voice, we should show students when it might be effective. For example, at times the passive voice allows the writer to put old information in the subject position, thus preserving what has been called the "given-new contract." Readers usually expect to hear old information in the subject and new information later.

8c As a rule, choose a subject that names the person or thing doing the action.

In weak, unemphatic prose, both the actor and the action may be buried in sentence elements other than the subject and the verb. In the following weak sentence, for example, both the actor and the action appear in prepositional phrases, word groups that do not receive much attention from readers.

WEAK	The institution of the New Deal had the effect of reversing some of the economic inequalities of the Great Depression.
EMPHATIC	The New Deal reversed some of the economic inequalities of the Great Depression.

Consider the subjects and verbs of the two versions — *institution had* versus *New Deal reversed*. The latter expresses the writer's point more emphatically.

▶ ~~The use of~~ p̌ure oxygen can ~~cause~~ healing ~~in~~ wounds that

are otherwise untreatable.

In the original sentence, the subject and verb — *use can cause* — express the point blandly. *Oxygen can heal* makes the point more emphatically and directly.

EXERCISE 8-1 Revise any weak, unemphatic sentences (p. 204) by replacing passive verbs or *be* verbs with active alternatives. You may need to name in the subject the person or thing doing the action. If a sentence is emphatic, do not change it. Possible revisions appear in the back of the book. *More practice:* e ✔

The ranger doused the campfire before giving us
~~The campfire was doused by the ranger before we were given~~
a ticket for unauthorized use of a campsite.

hackerhandbooks.com/bedhandbook

e Clear sentences > Exercises: 8–2 to 8–6
✔ Clear sentences > LearningCurve: Active and passive voice

EXERCISE 8-1 *Possible revisions:*

a. The Prussians defeated the Saxons in 1745.
b. Ahmed, the producer, manages the entire operation.
c. The tour guides expertly paddled the sea kayaks.
d. Emphatic and active; no change
e. Protesters were shouting on the courthouse steps.

a. The Prussians were victorious over the Saxons in 1745.
b. The entire operation is managed by Ahmed, the producer.
c. The sea kayaks were expertly paddled by the tour guides.
d. At the crack of rocket and mortar blasts, I jumped from the top bunk and landed on my buddy below, who was crawling on the floor looking for his boots.
e. There were shouting protesters on the courthouse steps.

9 Balance parallel ideas.

If two or more ideas are parallel, they are easier to grasp when expressed in parallel grammatical form. Single words should be balanced with single words, phrases with phrases, clauses with clauses.

A kiss can be a comma, a question mark, or an exclamation point. — Mistinguett

This novel is not to be tossed lightly aside, but to be hurled with great force. — Dorothy Parker

In matters of principle, stand like a rock; in matters of taste, swim with the current. — Thomas Jefferson

Writers often use parallelism to create emphasis. (See p. 244.)

9a Balance parallel ideas in a series.

Readers expect items in a series to appear in parallel grammatical form. When one or more of the items violate readers' expectations, a sentence will be needlessly awkward.

> Children who study music also learn confidence,
>
> discipline, and ~~they are creative.~~ *creativity.*

The revision presents all the items in the series as nouns: *confidence*, *discipline*, and *creativity*.

> Impressionist painters believed in focusing on ordinary
>
> subjects, capturing the effects of light on those subjects,
>
> and ~~to use~~ *using* short brushstrokes.

The revision uses *-ing* forms for all the items in the series: *focusing*, *capturing*, and *using*.

> Racing to get to work on time, Sam drove down the middle
>
> of the road, ran one red light, and *ignored* two stop signs.

The revision adds a verb to make the three items parallel: *drove*, *ran*, and *ignored*.

In headings and lists, aim for as much parallelism as the content allows.

Headings

Headings on the same level of organization should be written in parallel form—as single words, phrases, or clauses. The following examples show parallel headings from an environmental report and a nursing manual, respectively.

PHRASES AS HEADINGS

Safeguarding Earth's atmosphere

Charting the path to sustainable energy

Conserving global forests

INDEPENDENT CLAUSES AS HEADINGS

Ask the patient to describe current symptoms.

Take a detailed medical history.

Record the patient's vital signs.

Lists

Lists are usually introduced with an independent clause followed by a colon. Lists are most readable when they are presented in parallel grammatical form. Like headings, lists might consist of words, phrases, or clauses. The following list consists of parallel noun phrases.

> Renewable energy technologies include the following: hydroelectric power, solar power, wind energy, and geothermal energy.

9b Balance parallel ideas presented as pairs.

When pairing ideas, underscore their connection by expressing them in similar grammatical form. Paired ideas are usually connected in one of these ways:

- with a coordinating conjunction such as *and, but,* or *or*
- with a pair of correlative conjunctions such as *either . . . or* or *not only . . . but also*
- with a word introducing a comparison, usually *than* or *as*

Parallel ideas linked with coordinating conjunctions

Coordinating conjunctions (*and, but, or, nor, for, so,* and *yet*) link ideas of equal importance. When those ideas are closely

SCHOLARS ON PARALLELISM

Corbett, Edward P. J. *Classical Rhetoric for the Modern Student.* 4th ed. New York: Oxford UP, 1998. 354–58. Print. In his discussion of the "composition of the sentence," Corbett identifies parallelism as a significant feature of effective style.

Graves, Richard L. "Symmetrical Form and the Rhetoric of the Sentence." *Rhetoric and Composition: A Sourcebook for Teachers and Writers.* Ed. Richard L. Graves. Upper Montclair: Boynton, 1984. 119–27. Print. Graves asserts that symmetrical form is essential for effective writing and offers convincing empirical evidence. He argues that we should teach

parallel in content, they should be expressed in parallel grammatical form.

▶ Emily Dickinson's poetry features the use of dashes and the capitalization of ~~capitalizing~~ common words.

The revision balances the nouns *use* and *capitalization*.

▶ Many states are reducing property taxes for home owners and extending ~~extend~~ tax credits to renters.

The revision balances the verb *reducing* with the verb *extending*.

Parallel ideas linked with correlative conjunctions

Correlative conjunctions come in pairs: *either . . . or, neither . . . nor, not only . . . but also, both . . . and, whether . . . or.* Make sure that the grammatical structure following the second half of the pair is the same as that following the first half.

▶ Thomas Edison was not only a prolific inventor but also ~~was~~

a successful entrepreneur.

The words *a prolific inventor* follow *not only*, so *a successful entrepreneur* should follow *but also*. Repeating *was* creates an unbalanced effect.

▶ The clerk told me either to change my flight or to take the train.

To change my flight, which follows *either*, should be balanced with *to take the train*, which follows *or*.

Comparisons linked with than or as

In comparisons linked with *than* or *as*, the elements being compared should be expressed in parallel grammatical structure.

---

parallelism as more than a mechanical skill and should also recognize it as a "major means through which we perceive and structure reality."

TEACHING TIP

It is often helpful to allow students to take charge of teaching a few style and grammar concepts. Assign students in groups to tackle concepts like parallelism or active voice and to prepare a ten-minute mini-lesson in which they show examples and discuss revision strategies. If the class is online, the students can prepare a few slides that they upload to the course Web site.

▶ It is easier to speak in abstractions than ~~grounding~~ one's *to ground*

thoughts in reality.

To speak is balanced with *to ground*.

▶ In Pueblo culture, according to Silko, ~~to write~~ down the *writing*

stories of a tribe is not the same as "keeping track of all the

stories" (290).

When you are quoting from a source, parallel grammatical
structure—such as *writing . . . keeping*—helps create continuity
between your sentence and the words from the source. (See 56a on
citing sources in MLA style.)

Comparisons should also be logical and complete. (See 10c.)

9c Repeat function words to clarify parallels.

Function words such as prepositions (*by, to*) and subordinating
conjunctions (*that, because*) signal the grammatical nature of
the word groups to follow. Although you can sometimes omit
them, be sure to include them whenever they signal parallel
structures that readers might otherwise miss.

▶ Our study revealed that left-handed students were more likely
to have trouble with classroom desks and rearranging *that*

desks for exam periods was useful.

A second subordinating conjunction helps readers sort out the two
parallel ideas: *that* left-handed students have trouble with classroom desks and *that* rearranging desks was useful.

EXERCISE 9-1 Edit the following sentences to correct faulty parallelism. Possible revisions appear in the back of the book. *More practice:* 🄴 ✅

> Rowena began her workday by pouring a cup of coffee and
> checking
> ~~checked~~ her e-mail.
>   ∧

a. Police dogs are used for finding lost children, tracking criminals, and the detection of bombs and illegal drugs.

b. Hannah told her rock-climbing partner that she bought a new harness and of her desire to climb Otter Cliffs.

c. It is more difficult to sustain an exercise program than starting one.

d. During basic training, I was not only told what to do but also what to think.

e. Jan wanted to drive to the wine country or at least Sausalito.

10 Add needed words.

Sometimes writers leave out words intentionally, and the meaning of the sentence is not affected. But leaving out words can occasionally cause confusion for readers or make the sentence ungrammatical. Readers need to see at a glance how the parts of a sentence are connected.

> ### Multilingual
>
> Languages sometimes differ in the need for certain words. In particular, be alert for missing articles, verbs, subjects, or expletives. See 29, 30a, and 30b.

hackerhandbooks.com/bedhandbook

🄴 Clear sentences > Exercises: 9–2 to 9–6
✅ Clear sentences > LearningCurve: Parallelism

EXERCISE 9-1 *Possible revisions:*

a. Police dogs are used for finding lost children, tracking criminals, and detecting bombs and illegal drugs.

b. Hannah told her rock-climbing partner that she bought a new harness and that she wanted to climb Otter Cliffs.

c. It is more difficult to sustain an exercise program than to start one.

d. During basic training, I was told not only what to do but also what to think.

e. Jan wanted to drive to the wine country or at least to Sausalito.

10a Add words needed to complete compound structures.

In compound structures, words are often left out for economy: *Tom is a man who means what he says and [who] says what he means.* Such omissions are acceptable as long as the omitted words are common to both parts of the compound structure.

If a sentence defies grammar or idiom because an omitted word is not common to both parts of the compound structure, the simplest solution is to put the word back in.

▶ Advertisers target customers whom they identify
                                        who
  through demographic research orˆ have purchased their

  product in the past.

> The word *who* must be included because *whom . . . have purchased* is not grammatically correct.

                        accepted
▶ Mayor Davis never has andˆ never will accept a bribe.

> *Has . . . accept* is not grammatically correct.

                                               in
▶ Many South Pacific islanders still believe andˆ live by ancient

  laws.

> *Believe . . . by* is not idiomatic in English. (For a list of common idioms, see 18d.)

NOTE: Even when the omitted word is common to both parts of the compound structure, occasionally it must be inserted to avoid ambiguity.

> *My* favorite *professor* and *mentor* influenced my choice of a career. [Professor and mentor are the same person.]

WRITERS ON WRITING

Easy writing makes hard reading. — Ernest Hemingway

Most people won't realize that writing is a craft. You have to take your apprenticeship in it like anything else. — Katherine Anne Porter

I have rewritten — often several times — every word I have ever published. My pencils outlast their erasers. — Vladimir Nabokov

My favorite *professor* and *my mentor* influenced my choice of a career. [Professor and mentor are two different people; *my* must be repeated.]

10b Add the word *that* if there is any danger of misreading without it.

If there is no danger of misreading, the word *that* may be omitted when it introduces a subordinate clause. *The value of a principle is the number of things [that] it will explain.* When a sentence might be misread without *that*, however, it is necessary to include the word.

▶ In his famous obedience experiments, psychologist Stanley
Milgram discovered ^that ordinary people were willing to inflict

physical pain on strangers.

Milgram didn't discover ordinary people; he discovered that ordinary people were willing to inflict pain on strangers. The word *that* tells readers to expect a clause, not just *ordinary people*, as the direct object of *discovered*.

10c Add words needed to make comparisons logical and complete.

Comparisons should be made between items that are alike. To compare unlike items is illogical and distracting.

▶ The forests of North America are much more extensive
than ^those of Europe.

Forests must be compared with forests, not with all of Europe.

▶ Some say that Ella Fitzgerald's renditions of Cole Porter's

songs are better than any other ~~singer.~~ singer's.

Ella Fitzgerald's renditions cannot logically be compared with a
singer. The revision uses the possessive form *singer's*, with the word
renditions being implied.

Sometimes the word *other* must be inserted to make a comparison logical.

▶ Jupiter is larger than any *other* planet in our solar system.

Jupiter is a planet, and it cannot be larger than itself.

Sometimes the word *as* must be inserted to make a comparison grammatically complete.

▶ The city of Lowell is as old, *as* if not older than, the neighboring

city of Lawrence.

The construction *as old* is not complete without a second *as*: *as old
as . . . the neighboring city of Lawrence.*

Comparisons should be complete enough to ensure clarity.
The reader should understand what is being compared.

INCOMPLETE   Brand X is less salty.

COMPLETE   Brand X is less salty than Brand Y.

Finally, comparisons should leave no ambiguity for readers.
If a sentence lends itself to more than one interpretation, revise
the sentence to state clearly which interpretation you intend.
In the following ambiguous sentence, two interpretations are
possible.

WRITERS ON WRITING

What is written without effort in general is read without pleasure.
— Samuel Johnson

I don't write easily or rapidly. My first draft usually has only a few
elements worth keeping. I have to find what those are and build from
them and throw out what doesn't work, or what simply is not alive.
— Susan Sontag

No one should ever have to read a sentence twice because of the way it
is put together.   — Wilson Follett

AMBIGUOUS	Ken helped me more than my roommate.
CLEAR	Ken helped me more than *he helped* my roommate.
CLEAR	Ken helped me more than my roommate *did*.

10d Add the articles *a*, *an*, and *the* where necessary for grammatical completeness.

It is not always necessary to repeat articles with paired items: *We bought a computer and printer.* However, if one of the items requires *a* and the other requires *an*, both articles must be included.

> We bought a computer and ^an^ antivirus program.

Articles are sometimes omitted in recipes and other instructions that are meant to be followed while they are being read. In nearly all other forms of writing, whether formal or informal, such omissions are inappropriate.

> ### Multilingual
>
> Choosing and using articles can be challenging for multilingual writers. See 29.

EXERCISE 10–1 Add any words needed for grammatical or logical completeness in the following sentences. Possible revisions appear in the back of the book. *More practice:* 🅔

The officer feared ^that^ the prisoner would escape.

a. A grapefruit or orange is a good source of vitamin C.
b. The women entering the military academy can expect haircuts as short as the male cadets.

hackerhandbooks.com/bedhandbook
🅔 Clear sentences > Exercises: 10–2 to 10–5

EXERCISE 10–1 *Possible revisions:*

a. A grapefruit or an orange is a good source of vitamin C.
b. The women entering the military academy can expect haircuts as short as those of the male cadets.
c. Looking out the family room window, Sarah saw that her favorite tree, which she had climbed as a child, was gone.
d. The graphic designers are interested in and knowledgeable about producing posters for the balloon race.
e. The Great Barrier Reef is larger than any other coral reef in the world.

c. Looking out the family room window, Sarah saw her favorite tree, which she had climbed as a child, was gone.

d. The graphic designers are interested and knowledgeable about producing posters for the balloon race.

e. The Great Barrier Reef is larger than any coral reef in the world.

11 Untangle mixed constructions.

A mixed construction contains sentence parts that do not sensibly fit together. The mismatch may be a matter of grammar or of logic.

11a Untangle the grammatical structure.

Once you begin a sentence, your choices are limited by the range of grammatical patterns in English. (See 47 and 48.) You cannot begin with one grammatical plan and switch without warning to another. Often you must rethink the purpose of the sentence and revise.

MIXED   For most drivers who have a blood alcohol content of .05 percent double their risk of causing an accident.

The writer begins the sentence with a long prepositional phrase and makes it the subject of the verb *double*. But a prepositional phrase can serve only as a modifier; it cannot be the subject of a sentence.

REVISED   For most drivers who have a blood alcohol content of .05 percent, the risk of causing an accident is doubled.

REVISED   Most drivers who have a blood alcohol content of .05 percent double their risk of causing an accident.

SCHOLARS ON MIXED CONSTRUCTIONS

Freeman, Donald C. "Linguistics and Error Analysis: On Agency." *The Territory of Language*. Ed. Donald A. McQuade. Carbondale: Southern Illinois UP, 1986. 165–73. Print. In discussing the use of linguistics to help students write grammatical sentences, Freeman offers several examples of tangled syntax. He argues that instead of attempting to apply rules to the problem, instructors should draw the students' attention to the question of "agency" (who is doing what) in the sentence. Thinking about agency often can help students sense what is wrong and see how to fix the problem.

In the first revision, the writer begins with the prepositional phrase and finishes the sentence with a proper subject and verb (*risk . . . is doubled*). In the second revision, the writer stays with the original verb (*double*) and begins the sentence another way, making *drivers* the subject of *double*.

▶ ~~When the country elects~~ Electing a president is the most important
∧
responsibility in a democracy.

The adverb clause *When the country elects a president* cannot serve as the subject of the verb *is*. The revision replaces the adverb clause with a gerund phrase, a word group that can function as a subject. (See 48e and 48b.)

▶ Although the United States is a wealthy nation, ~~but~~ more

than 20 percent of our children live in poverty.

The coordinating conjunction *but* cannot link a subordinate clause (*Although the United States . . .*) with an independent clause (*more than 20 percent of our children live in poverty*).

Occasionally a mixed construction is so tangled that it defies grammatical analysis. When this happens, back away from the sentence, rethink what you want to say, and then rewrite the sentence.

MIXED   In the whole-word method, children learn to recognize entire words rather than by the phonics method in which they learn to sound out letters and groups of letters.

REVISED   The whole-word method teaches children to recognize entire words; the phonics method teaches them to sound out letters and groups of letters.

> **Multilingual**
>
> English does not allow double subjects, nor does it allow an object or an adverb to be repeated in an adjective clause. Unlike some other languages, English does not allow a noun and a pronoun to be repeated in a sentence if they have the same grammatical function. See 30c and 30d.
>
> ► My father ~~he~~ moved to Peru before he met my mother.

11b Straighten out the logical connections.

The subject and the predicate (the verb and its modifiers) should make sense together; when they don't, the error is known as *faulty predication.*

> ► The court decided that ~~Tiffany's welfare~~ Tiffany would not be safe
>
> living with her abusive parents.
>
> Tiffany, not her welfare, may not be safe.

> ► Under the revised plan, the elderly, ~~who now receive a double~~ double personal exemption for the ~~personal exemption,~~ will be abolished.
>
> The exemption, not the elderly, will be abolished.

An appositive is a noun that renames a nearby noun. When an appositive and the noun it renames are not logically equivalent, the error is known as *faulty apposition.* (See 48c.)

> ► ~~The tax accountant,~~ Tax accounting, a very lucrative profession, requires
>
> intelligence, patience, and attention to mathematical detail.
>
> The tax accountant is a person, not a profession.

SCHOLARS ON MIXED CONSTRUCTIONS

Shaughnessy, Mina P. *Errors and Expectations: A Guide for the Teacher of Basic Writing.* New York: Oxford UP, 1979. 44–89. Print. Shaughnessy suggests several causes of tangled syntax, which she calls "blurred constructions."

TEACHING TIP

Consider assigning students to keep an editing log for the semester. When they receive comments on a draft, they should pay special attention to comments related to sentence-level matters. In their editing log, students should record (1) the incorrect sentence, (2) the handbook section (11b, for example) that provides help for editing that sentence, and (3) the corrected sentence. Invite students to add any tips that might help them proofread for that particular error in the future.

11c Avoid *is when, is where,* and *reason . . . is because* constructions.

In formal English, many readers object to *is when, is where,* and *reason . . . is because* constructions on either grammatical or logical grounds. Grammatically, the verb *is* (as well as *are, was,* and *were*) should be followed by a noun that renames the subject or by an adjective that describes the subject, not by an adverb clause beginning with *when, where,* or *because.* (See 47b and 48e.) Logically, the words *when, where,* and *because* suggest relations of time, place, and cause—relations that do not always make sense with *is, are, was,* or *were.*

▶ Anorexia nervosa is ~~where people~~ think they are too
    a disorder suffered by people who
    ^

    fat and diet to the point of starvation.

> *Where* refers to places. Anorexia nervosa is a disorder, not a place.

▶ The ~~reason the~~ experiment failed ~~is~~ because conditions in

    the lab were not sterile.

> The writer might have changed *because* to *that* (*The reason the experiment failed is that conditions in the lab were not sterile*), but the preceding revision is more concise.

EXERCISE 11–1 Edit the following sentences to untangle mixed constructions. Possible revisions appear in the back of the book. *More practice:* e

Taking
~~By taking~~ the oath of allegiance made Ling a US citizen.
^

a. Using surgical gloves is a precaution now worn by dentists to prevent contact with patients' blood and saliva.

b. A physician, the career my brother is pursuing, requires at least ten years of challenging work.

hackerhandbooks.com/bedhandbook

e Clear sentences > Exercises: 11–2 to 11–5

EXERCISE 11–1 *Possible revisions:*

a. Using surgical gloves is a precaution now taken by dentists to prevent contact with patients' blood and saliva.

b. A career in medicine, which my brother is pursuing, requires at least ten years of challenging work.

c. The pharaohs had bad teeth because tiny particles of sand found their way into Egyptian bread.

d. Recurring bouts of flu caused the team to forfeit a record number of games.

e. This box contains the key to your future.

c.   The reason the pharaohs had bad teeth was because tiny particles of sand found their way into Egyptian bread.

d.   Recurring bouts of flu among team members set a record for number of games forfeited.

e.   In this box contains the key to your future.

---

12 Repair misplaced and dangling modifiers.

Modifiers, whether they are single words, phrases, or clauses, should point clearly to the words they modify. As a rule, related words should be kept together.

12a Put limiting modifiers in front of the words they modify.

Limiting modifiers such as *only*, *even*, *almost*, *nearly*, and *just* should appear in front of a verb only if they modify the verb: *At first, I couldn't even touch my toes, much less grasp them.* If they limit the meaning of some other word in the sentence, they should be placed in front of that word.

▶   The literature reveals that students ~~only~~ learn new vocabulary

only

words when they are encouraged to read.

∧

Only limits the meaning of the *when* clause.

just

▶   If you ~~just~~ interview chemistry majors, your picture of the

∧

student body's response to the new grading policies will

be incomplete.

The adverb *just* limits the meaning of *chemistry majors*, not *interview*.

When the limiting modifier *not* is misplaced, the sentence usually suggests a meaning the writer did not intend.

▶ In the United States in 1860, all black southerners were ~~not~~ ^not^

slaves.

The original sentence says that no black southerners were slaves. The revision makes the writer's real meaning clear: Some (but not all) black southerners were slaves.

12b Place phrases and clauses so that readers can see at a glance what they modify.

Although phrases and clauses can appear at some distance from the words they modify, make sure your meaning is clear. When phrases or clauses are oddly placed, absurd misreadings can result.

MISPLACED   The soccer player returned to the clinic where he had undergone emergency surgery in 2004 in a limousine sent by Adidas.

REVISED   Traveling in a limousine sent by Adidas, the soccer player returned to the clinic where he had undergone emergency surgery in 2004.

The revision corrects the false impression that the soccer player underwent emergency surgery in a limousine.

▶ ~~There~~ ^On the walls^ are many pictures of comedians who have performed

at Gavin's. ~~on the walls.~~ ^

The comedians weren't performing on the walls; the pictures were on the walls.

Occasionally the placement of a modifier leads to an ambiguity—a squinting modifier. In such a case, two revisions will be possible, depending on the writer's intended meaning.

AMBIGUOUS   The exchange students we met for coffee occasionally questioned us about our latest slang.

CLEAR   The exchange students we occasionally met for coffee questioned us about our latest slang.

CLEAR   The exchange students we met for coffee questioned us occasionally about our latest slang.

In the original version, it was not clear whether the meeting or the questioning happened occasionally. Both revisions eliminate the ambiguity.

12c Move awkwardly placed modifiers.

As a rule, a sentence should flow from subject to verb to object, without lengthy detours along the way. When a long adverbial word group separates a subject from its verb, a verb from its object, or a helping verb from its main verb, the result is often awkward.

▶ ~~Hong Kong,~~ after more than 150 years of British rule, was Hong Kong transferred back to Chinese control in 1997.

> There is no reason to separate the subject, *Hong Kong*, from the verb, *was transferred*, with a long phrase.

EXCEPTION: Occasionally a writer may choose to delay a verb or an object to create suspense. In the following passage, for example, Robert Mueller inserts the *after* phrase between the subject *women* and the verb *walk* to heighten the dramatic effect.

> I asked a Burmese why women, after centuries of following their men, now walk ahead. He said there were many unexploded land mines since the war.   — Robert Mueller

---

Multilingual

English does not allow an adverb to appear between a verb and its object. See 30f.

>   *easily*
> ▶ Yolanda lifted ~~easily~~ the fifty-pound weight.
>   ^

12d Avoid split infinitives when they are awkward.

An infinitive consists of *to* plus the base form of a verb: *to think, to breathe, to dance.* When a modifier appears between *to* and the verb, an infinitive is said to be "split": *to carefully balance, to completely understand.*

When a long word or a phrase appears between the parts of the infinitive, the result is usually awkward.

>   *If possible, the*
> ▶ ~~The~~ patient should try to ~~if possible~~ avoid going up and
>   ^
>
> down stairs.

Attempts to avoid split infinitives can result in equally awkward sentences. When alternative phrasing sounds unnatural, most experts allow—and even encourage—splitting the infinitive.

AWKWARD   We decided actually to enforce the law.

BETTER   We decided to actually enforce the law.

At times, neither the split infinitive nor its alternative sounds particularly awkward. In such situations, it is usually better not to split the infinitive, especially in formal writing.

> ▶ Nursing students learn to ~~accurately~~ record a patient's vital
>   *accurately.*
>   signs./
>   ^

EXERCISE 12–1 Edit the following sentences to correct misplaced or awkwardly placed modifiers. Possible revisions appear in the back of the book. *More practice:* e

in a telephone survey
Answering questions can be annoying. ~~in a telephone survey.~~

a. More research is needed to effectively evaluate the risks posed by volcanoes in the Pacific Northwest.
b. Many students graduate with debt from college totaling more than fifty thousand dollars.
c. It is a myth that humans only use 10 percent of their brains.
d. A coolhunter is a person who can find in the unnoticed corners of modern society the next wave of fashion.
e. All geese do not fly beyond Narragansett for the winter.

12e Repair dangling modifiers.

A dangling modifier fails to refer logically to any word in the sentence. Dangling modifiers are easy to repair, but they can be hard to recognize, especially in your own writing.

Recognizing dangling modifiers

Dangling modifiers are usually word groups (such as verbal phrases) that suggest but do not name an actor. When a sentence opens with such a modifier, readers expect the subject of the next clause to name the actor. If it doesn't, the modifier dangles.

▶ Understanding the need to create checks and balances on
the framers of
power, the Constitution divided the government into three branches.

hackerhandbooks.com/bedhandbook
e Clear sentences > Exercises: 12–2 to 12–5

EXERCISE 12–1 *Possible revisions:*

a. More research is needed to evaluate effectively the risks posed by volcanoes in the Pacific Northwest.
b. Many students graduate from college with debt totaling more than fifty thousand dollars.
c. It is a myth that humans use only 10 percent of their brains.
d. A coolhunter is a person who can find the next wave of fashion in the unnoticed corners of modern society.
e. Not all geese fly beyond Narragansett for the winter.

The framers of the Constitution (not the document itself) understood the need for checks and balances.

▶ After completing seminary training, ~~women's~~ *women were often denied* access to the priesthood. ~~has often been denied.~~

Women (not their access to the priesthood) complete the training.

The following sentences illustrate four common kinds of dangling modifiers.

DANGLING   *Deciding to join the navy,* the recruiter enthusiastically pumped Joe's hand. [Participial phrase]

DANGLING   *Upon entering the doctor's office,* a skeleton caught my attention. [Preposition followed by a gerund phrase]

DANGLING   *To satisfy her mother,* the piano had to be practiced every day. [Infinitive phrase]

DANGLING   *Though not eligible for the clinical trial,* the doctor prescribed the drug for Ethan on compassionate grounds. [Elliptical clause with an understood subject and verb]

These dangling modifiers falsely suggest that the recruiter decided to join the navy, that the skeleton entered the doctor's office, that the piano intended to satisfy the mother, and that the doctor was not eligible for the clinical trial.

Although most readers will understand the writer's intended meaning in such sentences, the inadvertent humor can be distracting.

SCHOLARS ON DANGLING MODIFIERS

Williams, Joseph. *Style: Ten Lessons in Clarity and Grace.* 8th ed. New York: Longman, 2005. Print. In his chapter on managing long sentences, Williams discusses the dangers of dangling modifiers.

Jordan, Michael P. "Unattached Clauses in Technical Writing." *Journal of Technical Communication* 29.1 (1999): 65–93. Print. Jordan argues that not all dangling (or "unattached") clauses affect meaning in negative ways. In technical writing, unattached clauses are sometimes acceptable, since the name of the agent (actor) may be irrelevant. Jordan suggests that there may be cultural differences "between humanistic teachers and task-oriented engineers."

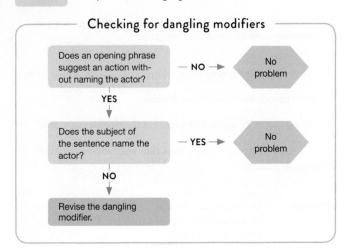

── Checking for dangling modifiers ──

Does an opening phrase suggest an action without naming the actor? — **NO** → No problem

YES ↓

Does the subject of the sentence name the actor? — **YES** → No problem

NO ↓

Revise the dangling modifier.

Repairing dangling modifiers

To repair a dangling modifier, you can revise the sentence in one of two ways:

- Name the actor in the subject of the sentence.
- Name the actor in the modifier.

Depending on your sentence, one of these revision strategies may be more appropriate than the other.

ACTOR NAMED IN SUBJECT

                        I noticed

▶ Upon entering the doctor's office, a skeleton. ~~caught my~~
                                ^   ^

~~attention.~~

                    Jing-mei had to practice

▶ To satisfy her mother, the piano ~~had to be practiced~~
                              ^

every day.

SCHOLARS ON DANGLING MODIFIERS

Noguchi, Rei R. *Grammar and the Teaching of Writing: Limits and Possibilities*. Urbana: NCTE, 1991. 38–58. Print. In his chapter on teaching a "writer's grammar," Noguchi recommends having students form "tag questions" and "yes and no questions" from original declarative sentences. He shows how this method is useful in identifying and clarifying "presentence modifiers."

ACTOR NAMED IN MODIFIER

▶ ~~Deciding~~ *When Joe decided* to join the navy, the recruiter enthusiastically
pumped ~~Joe's~~ *his* hand.

▶ Though *Ethan was* not eligible for the clinical trial, the doctor
prescribed the drug for ~~Ethan~~ *him* on compassionate grounds.

NOTE: You cannot repair a dangling modifier just by moving it. Consider, for example, the sentence about the skeleton. If you put the modifier at the end of the sentence (*A skeleton caught my attention upon entering the doctor's office*), you are still suggesting—absurdly, of course—that the skeleton entered the office. The only way to avoid the problem is to put the word *I* in the sentence, either as the subject or in the modifier.

▶ Upon entering the doctor's office, a skeleton *I noticed*. ~~caught my attention.~~

▶ ~~Upon entering~~ *As I entered* the doctor's office, a skeleton caught my attention.

EXERCISE 12-6 Edit the following sentences to correct dangling modifiers. Most sentences can be revised in more than one way. Possible revisions appear in the back of the book. *More practice:* **e**

To acquire a degree in almost any field, *a student must complete* two science courses. ~~must be completed.~~

a. To complete an online purchase with a credit card, the expiration date and the security code must be entered.

hackerhandbooks.com/bedhandbook

e Clear sentences > Exercises: 12–7 to 12–10

EXERCISE 12-6 *Possible revisions:*

a. To complete an online purchase with a credit card, you must enter the expiration date and the security code.

b. Though Martha was only sixteen, UCLA accepted her application.

c. As I settled in the cockpit, the pounding of the engine was muffled only slightly by my helmet.

d. After studying polymer chemistry, Phuong found computer games less complex.

e. When I was a young man, my mother enrolled me in tap dance classes.

b. Though only sixteen, UCLA accepted Martha's application.

c. Settled in the cockpit, the pounding of the engine was muffled only slightly by my helmet.

d. After studying polymer chemistry, computer games seemed less complex to Phuong.

e. When a young man, my mother enrolled me in tap dance classes.

13 Eliminate distracting shifts.

This section can help you avoid unnecessary shifts that might distract or confuse your readers: shifts in point of view, in verb tense, in mood or voice, or from indirect to direct questions or quotations.

13a Make the point of view consistent in person and number.

The point of view of a piece of writing is the perspective from which it is written: first person (*I* or *we*), second person (*you*), or third person (*he, she, it, one, they*, or any noun).

The *I* (or *we*) point of view, which emphasizes the writer, is a good choice for informal letters and writing based primarily on personal experience. The *you* point of view, which emphasizes the reader, works well for giving advice or explaining how to do something. The third-person point of view, which emphasizes the subject, is appropriate in formal academic and professional writing.

Writers who have trouble settling on an appropriate point of view sometimes shift confusingly from one to another. The solution is to choose a suitable perspective and stay with it.

EXERCISE 13–1 *Possible revisions:*

When online dating first became available, many people thought that it would simplify romance. Hopeful singles believed that they could type in a list of criteria — sense of humor, college education, green eyes, good job — and a database would select the perfect mate. Thousands of people signed up for services and filled out their profiles, confident that true love was only a few mouse clicks away. As it turns out, however, virtual dating is no easier than traditional dating. Online daters still have to contact the people they find, exchange e-mails and phone calls, and meet in the real world. Although a database might produce a list of possibilities and screen out obviously undesirable people, it can't predict chemistry. More often than not, people who seem perfect online just

▶ Our class practiced rescuing a victim trapped in a wrecked

car. We learned to dismantle the car with the essential

tools. ~~You~~ We were graded on ~~your~~ our speed and ~~your~~ our skill in

freeing the victim.

The writer should have stayed with the *we* point of view. *You* is inappropriate because the writer is not addressing readers directly. *You* should not be used in a vague sense meaning "anyone." (See 23d.)

▶ ~~One needs~~ You need a password and a credit card number to access

the database. You will be billed at an hourly rate.

You is an appropriate choice because the writer is giving advice directly to readers.

EXERCISE 13–1   Edit the following paragraph to eliminate distracting shifts in point of view (person and number). *More practice:* e

> When online dating first became available, many people thought that it would simplify romance. We believed that you could type in a list of criteria — sense of humor, college education, green eyes, good job — and a database would select the perfect mate. Thousands of people signed up for services and filled out their profiles, confident that true love was only a few mouse clicks away. As it turns out, however, virtual dating is no easier than traditional dating. I still have to contact the people I find, exchange e-mails and phone calls, and meet him in the real world. Although a database might produce a list of possibilities and screen out obviously undesirable people, you can't predict chemistry. More often than not, people who seem perfect online just don't click in person. Electronic services do help a single person expand their pool of potential dates, but it's no substitute for the hard work of romance.

hackerhandbooks.com/bedhandbook

e Clear sentences > Exercises: 13–2, 13–9 to 13–11 (all shifts)

EXERCISE 13–1   *Possible revisions (continued):*

don't click in person. Electronic services do help single people expand their pool of potential dates, but they're no substitute for the hard work of romance.

13b Maintain consistent verb tenses.

Consistent verb tenses clearly establish the time of the actions being described. When a passage begins in one tense and then shifts without warning and for no reason to another, readers are distracted and confused.

▶ There was no way I could fight the current and win. Just as I

     jumped

  was losing hope, a stranger ~~jumps~~ off a passing boat and

  swam

  ~~swims~~ toward me.

The writer thought that the present tense (*jumps, swims*) would convey immediacy and drama. But having begun in the past tense (*could fight, was losing*), the writer should follow through in the past tense.

Writers often encounter difficulty with verb tenses when writing about literature. Because fictional events occur outside the time frames of real life, the past tense and the present tense may seem equally appropriate. The literary convention, however, is to describe fictional events consistently in the present tense. (See 7e.)

▶ The scarlet letter is a punishment sternly placed on Hester's

     is

  breast by the community, and yet it ~~was~~ a fanciful and

  imaginative product of Hester's own needlework.

EXERCISE 13-3   Edit the following paragraphs to eliminate distracting shifts in tense. *More practice:* e ✔

    The English colonists who settled in Massachusetts received assistance at first from the local Indian tribes, but by 1675 there had been friction between the two groups for

hackerhandbooks.com/bedhandbook

e Clear sentences > Exercises: 13–4, 13–9 to 13–11 (all shifts)
✔ Clear sentences > LearningCurve: Verbs

EXERCISE 13-3 *Possible revisions:*

    The English colonists who settled in Massachusetts received assistance at first from the local Indian tribes, but by 1675 there had been friction between the two groups for many years. In that year, Metacomet, whom the colonists called Philip, led the Wampanoag tribe in the first of a series of attacks on the colonial settlements. The war, known as King Philip's War, raged on for more than a year and left three thousand Indians and six hundred colonists dead. Metacomet's attempt to retain his power failed. He too was killed, and the victorious colonists sold his wife and children into slavery.

many years. In that year, Metacomet, whom the colonists called Philip, leads the Wampanoag tribe in the first of a series of attacks on the colonial settlements. The war, known as King Philip's War, rages on for more than a year and leaves three thousand Indians and six hundred colonists dead. Metacomet's attempt to retain his power failed. He too is killed, and the colonists sell his wife and children into slavery.

The Indians did not leave records of their encounters with the English, but the settlers recorded some of their experiences. One of the few accounts to survive was written by a captured colonist, Mary Rowlandson. She is a minister's wife who is kidnapped by Indians and held captive in 1676. Her history, *A Narrative of the Captivity and Restoration of Mrs. Mary Rowlandson*, tells the story of her experiences with the Wampanoags. Although it did not paint a completely balanced picture of the Indians, Rowlandson's story, which is considered a classic early American text, showed its author to be a keen observer of life in an Indian camp.

13c Make verbs consistent in mood and voice.

Unnecessary shifts in the mood of a verb can be distracting and confusing to readers. There are three moods in English: the *indicative*, used for facts, opinions, and questions; the *imperative*, used for orders or advice; and the *subjunctive*, used in certain contexts to express wishes or conditions contrary to fact (see 27g).

The following passage shifts confusingly from the indicative to the imperative mood.

▶ The counselor advised us to spread out our core requirements
over two or three semesters. ~~Also,~~ pay attention to pre-
    She also suggested that we
    ∧
requisites for elective courses.

The writer began by reporting the counselor's advice in the indicative mood (*counselor advised*) and switched to the imperative mood (*pay attention*); the revision puts both sentences in the indicative.

EXERCISE 13-3 *Possible revisions (continued):*

The Indians did not leave records of their encounters with the English, but the settlers recorded some of their experiences. One of the few accounts to survive was written by a captured colonist, Mary Rowlandson. She was a minister's wife who was kidnapped by Indians and held captive in 1676. Her history, *A Narrative of the Captivity and Restoration of Mrs. Mary Rowlandson*, tells the story of her experiences with the Wampanoags. Although it does not paint a completely balanced picture of the Indians, Rowlandson's story, which is considered a classic early American text, shows its author to be a keen observer of life in an Indian camp.

A verb may be in either the active voice (with the subject doing the action) or the passive voice (with the subject receiving the action). (See 8a.) If a writer shifts without warning from one to the other, readers may be left wondering why.

▶ Each student completes a self-assessment, ~~The self-assessment~~ *gives it*

~~is then given~~ to the teacher, and a copy ~~is exchanged~~ with *exchanges*

a classmate.

> Because the passage began in the active voice (*student completes*) and then switched to the passive (*self-assessment is given, copy is exchanged*), readers are left wondering who gives the self-assessment to the teacher and the classmate. The active voice, which is clearer and more direct, leaves no ambiguity.

13d Avoid sudden shifts from indirect to direct questions or quotations.

An indirect question reports a question without asking it: *We asked whether we could visit Miriam.* A direct question asks directly: *Can we visit Miriam?* Sudden shifts from indirect to direct questions are awkward. In addition, sentences containing such shifts are impossible to punctuate because indirect questions must end with a period and direct questions must end with a question mark. (See 38b.)

▶ I wonder whether Karla knew of the theft and, if so, ~~did~~
whether she reported
~~she report~~ it to the police~~?~~.

> The revision poses both questions indirectly. The writer could also ask both questions directly: *Did Karla know of the theft, and, if so, did she report it to the police?*

An indirect quotation reports someone's words without quoting word-for-word: *Annabelle said that she is a Virgo.* A direct

EXERCISE 13–5 *Possible revisions:*

a. An incredibly talented musician, Ray Charles mastered R&B, soul, and gospel styles. He even performed country music well.

b. Environmentalists point out that shrimp farming in Southeast Asia is polluting water and making farmlands useless. They warn that governments must act before it is too late.

c. We observed the samples for five days before we detected any growth. *Or* The samples were observed for five days before any growth was detected.

d. In his famous soliloquy, Hamlet contemplates whether death would be preferable to his difficult life and, if so, whether he is capable of committing suicide.

quotation presents the exact words of a speaker or writer, set off with quotation marks: *Annabelle said, "I am a Virgo."* Unannounced shifts from indirect to direct quotations are distracting and confusing, especially when the writer fails to insert the necessary quotation marks, as in the following example.

▶ The patient said she had been experiencing heart palpitations
   asked me to
   and ~~please~~ run as many tests as possible to find out the
            ∧
   problem.

The revision reports the patient's words indirectly. The writer also could quote the words directly: *The patient said, "I have been experiencing heart palpitations. Please run as many tests as possible to find out the problem."*

EXERCISE 13-5   Edit the following sentences to make the verbs consistent in mood and voice and to eliminate distracting shifts from indirect to direct questions or quotations. Possible revisions appear in the back of the book. *More practice:* e

As a public relations intern, I wrote press releases, managed
                    fielded all phone calls.
the Web site, and ~~all phone calls were fielded by me.~~
                  ∧

a.   An incredibly talented musician, Ray Charles mastered R&B, soul, and gospel styles. Even country music was performed well by him.

b.   Environmentalists point out that shrimp farming in Southeast Asia is polluting water and making farmlands useless. They warn that action must be taken by governments before it is too late.

c.   The samples were observed for five days before we detected any growth.

d.   In his famous soliloquy, Hamlet contemplates whether death would be preferable to his difficult life and, if so, is he capable of committing suicide?

e.   The lawyer told the judge that Miranda Hale was innocent and allow her to prove the allegations false.

hackerhandbooks.com/bedhandbook
e Clear sentences > Exercises: 13–7, 13–9 to 13–11 (all shifts)

EXERCISE 13-5   *Possible revisions (continued):*

e.   The lawyer told the judge that Miranda Hale was innocent and asked that she be allowed to prove the allegations false. *Or* The lawyer told the judge, "Miranda Hale is innocent. Please allow her to prove the allegations false."

EXERCISE 13-6 Edit the following sentences to eliminate distracting shifts. Possible revisions appear in the back of the book. *More practice:* e

> For many first-year engineering students, adjusting to a
> rigorous course load can be so challenging that ~~you~~ they
> sometimes feel overwhelmed.

a. A courtroom lawyer needs to have more than a touch of theater in their blood.
b. The interviewer asked if we had brought our proof of citizenship and did we bring our passports?
c. The experienced reconnaissance scout knows how to make fast decisions and use sophisticated equipment to keep their team from being detected.
d. After the animators finish their scenes, the production designer arranges the clips according to the storyboard. Synchronization notes must also be made for the sound editor and the composer.
e. Madame Defarge is a sinister figure in Dickens's *A Tale of Two Cities*. On a symbolic level, she represents fate; like the Greek Fates, she knitted the fabric of individual destiny.

14 Emphasize key ideas.

Within each sentence, emphasize your point by expressing it in the subject and verb of an independent clause, the words that receive the most attention from readers (see 14a–14e).

Within longer stretches of prose, you can draw attention to ideas deserving special emphasis by using a variety of techniques, often involving an unusual twist or some element of surprise (see 14f).

hackerhandbooks.com/bedhandbook

e Clear sentences > Exercises: 13–9 to 13–11 (all shifts)

EXERCISE 13-6 *Possible revisions:*
a. Courtroom lawyers need to have more than a touch of theater in their blood.
b. The interviewer asked if we had brought our proof of citizenship and our passports.
c. Experienced reconnaissance scouts know how to make fast decisions and use sophisticated equipment to keep their teams from being detected.
d. After the animators finish their scenes, the production designer arranges the clips according to the storyboard and makes synchronization notes for the sound editor and the composer.
e. Madame Defarge is a sinister figure in Dickens's *A Tale of Two Cities*. On a symbolic level, she represents fate; like the Greek Fates, she knits the fabric of individual destiny.

14a Coordinate equal ideas; subordinate minor ideas.

When combining two or more ideas in one sentence, you have two choices: coordination or subordination. Choose coordination to indicate that the ideas are equal or nearly equal in importance. Choose subordination to indicate that one idea is less important than another.

Coordination

Coordination draws attention equally to two or more ideas. To coordinate single words or phrases, join them with a coordinating conjunction or with a pair of correlative conjunctions: *bananas and strawberries; not only a lackluster plot but also inferior acting* (see 46g).

To coordinate independent clauses—word groups that express a complete thought and that can stand alone as a sentence—join them with a comma and a coordinating conjunction or with a semicolon:

, and	, for
, but	, so
, or	, yet
, nor	;

The semicolon is often accompanied by a conjunctive adverb such as *moreover, furthermore, therefore,* or *however* or by a transitional phrase such as *for example, in other words,* or *as a matter of fact.* (For a longer list, see p. 236.)

Assume, for example, that your intention is to draw equal attention to the following two ideas.

> Social networking Web sites offer ways for people to connect in the virtual world. They do not replace face-to-face forms of social interaction.

To coordinate these ideas, you can join them with a comma and the coordinating conjunction *but* or with a semicolon and the conjunctive adverb *however.*

> Social networking Web sites offer ways for people to connect in the virtual world, but they do not replace face-to-face forms of social interaction.

> Social networking Web sites offer ways for people to connect in the virtual world; however, they do not replace face-to-face forms of social interaction.

It is important to choose a coordinating conjunction or conjunctive adverb appropriate to your meaning. In the preceding example, the two ideas contrast with each other, calling for *but* or *however.* (For specific coordination strategies, see the chart on p. 236.)

Subordination

To give unequal emphasis to two or more ideas, express the major idea in an independent clause and place any minor ideas in subordinate clauses or phrases. (For specific subordination strategies, see the chart on p. 237.)

Let your intended meaning determine which idea you emphasize. Consider the two ideas about social networking Web sites.

> Social networking Web sites offer ways for people to connect in the virtual world. They do not replace face-to-face forms of social interaction.

If your purpose is to stress the ways that people can connect in the virtual world rather than the limitations of these connections, subordinate the idea about the limitations.

> Although they do not replace face-to-face forms of social interaction, social networking Web sites offer ways for people to connect in the virtual world.

SCHOLARS ON SENTENCE RHETORIC

Myers, Sharon A. "ReMembering the Sentence." *College Composition and Communication* 54.4 (2003): 610–28. Print. Drawing on linguistics research and her background with ESL writers, Myers argues that composition teachers should place more emphasis on sentence-combining and imitation exercises to help students acquire a "feel" for written language. With systematic practice in manipulating words and phrasing at the sentence level, students will become more aware of the grammar and syntax options available to them. The article describes several strategies teachers can use to help students vary their sentences.

To focus on the limitations of the virtual world, subordinate the idea about the ways people connect on these Web sites.

> Although social networking Web sites offer ways for people to connect in the virtual world, they do not replace face-to-face forms of social interaction.

14b Combine choppy sentences.

Short sentences demand attention, so you should use them primarily for emphasis. Too many short sentences, one after the other, make for a choppy style.

If an idea is not important enough to deserve its own sentence, try combining it with a sentence close by. Put any minor ideas in subordinate structures such as phrases or subordinate clauses. (See 48.)

> ► The Parks Department keeps the use of insecticides to a
> *because the*
> minimum/ ~~The~~ city is concerned about the environment.
>   ^

The writer wanted to emphasize that the Parks Department minimizes its use of chemicals, so she put the reason in a subordinate clause beginning with *because*.

> ► The Chesapeake and Ohio Canal, ~~is~~ a 184-mile waterway
>   ^
> constructed in the 1800s/, ~~It~~ was a major source of
>   ^
> transportation for goods during the Civil War.

A minor idea is now expressed in an appositive phrase (*a 184-mile waterway constructed in the 1800s*).

Although subordination is ordinarily the most effective technique for combining short, choppy sentences, coordination is appropriate when the ideas are equal in importance.

SCHOLARS ON SENTENCE RHETORIC

Lindemann, Erika. *A Rhetoric for Writing Teachers.* 4th ed. New York: Oxford UP, 2001. 163–74. Print. In the chapter "Teaching about Sentences," Lindemann suggests that our teaching goal "should be to enlarge the student's repertoire of sentence options and rhetorical choices." She offers three approaches to helping students. First, we can help students consider the various expectations that readers bring to sentences. Second, we can encourage students to experiment with combining and decombining sentences, primarily in their own drafts. Third, we can use Christensen's "generative rhetoric" to help students explore alternative sentence constructions and understand how those constructions express relationships among ideas.

Using coordination to combine sentences of equal importance

1. Consider using a comma and a coordinating conjunction. (See 32a.)

   , and , but , or , nor
   , for , so , yet

   ▶ In Orthodox Jewish funeral ceremonies, the shroud is
   and the
   a simple linen vestment, ~~The~~ coffin is plain wood.

2. Consider using a semicolon with a conjunctive adverb or transitional phrase. (See 34b.)

also	however	next
as a result	in addition	now
besides	in fact	of course
consequently	in other words	otherwise
finally	in the first place	still
for example	meanwhile	then
for instance	moreover	therefore
furthermore	nevertheless	thus

   in addition, she
   ▶ Alicia scored well on the SAT. ~~; She also~~ had excellent

   grades and a record of community service.

3. Consider using a semicolon alone. (See 34a.)

   in
   ▶ In youth we learn. ~~; In~~ age we understand.

SCHOLARS ON SENTENCE RHETORIC

Connors, Robert J. "The Erasure of the Sentence." *College Composition and Communication* 52.1 (2000): 96–128. Print. Connors describes sentence-based instruction that was scientifically tested in the 1960s and 1970s — generative rhetoric, imitation exercises, and sentence combining — and suggests why such instruction fell out of favor in the 1980s. "The usefulness of these sentence-based rhetorics was never disproved," writes Connors, "but a growing wave of anti-formalism, anti-behaviorism, and anti-empiricism . . . doomed them to . . . marginality. . . ." In Connors's view, trends in English studies have marginalized not just the rhetoric of the sentence but also the whole notion that instructional effectiveness can be measured at all.

Using subordination to combine sentences of unequal importance

1. Consider putting the less important idea in a subordinate clause beginning with one of the following words. (See 48e.)

after	before	that	which
although	even though	unless	while
as	if	until	who
as if	since	when	whom
because	so that	where	whose

   ►   *When*
   Elizabeth Cady Stanton proposed a convention to discuss the ∧

   status of women in America√, Lucretia Mott agreed.
   ∧

   ►   *that she*
   My sister owes much of her recovery to a yoga program.√ ~~She~~
   ∧

   began ~~the program~~ three years ago.

2. Consider putting the less important idea in an appositive phrase. (See 48c.)

   ►   Karate, is a discipline based on the philosophy of nonviolence√,
   ∧   ∧
   ~~It~~ teaches the art of self-defense.

3. Consider putting the less important idea in a participial phrase. (See 48b.)

   ►   ~~American essayist Cheryl Peck was~~ *E*ncouraged by friends to
   ∧
   American essayist Cheryl Peck
   write about her life,√ ~~She~~ began combining humor and irony
   ∧

   in her essays about being overweight.

Multilingual

Unlike some other languages, English does not repeat objects or adverbs in adjective clauses. The relative pronoun (*that, which, whom*) or relative adverb (*where*) in the adjective clause represents the object or adverb. See 30d.

▶ The apartment that we rented ~~it~~ needed repairs.

The pronoun *it* cannot repeat the relative pronoun *that*.

---

                  and

▶ At 3:30 p.m., Forrest displayed a flag of truce,/~~Forrest~~ sent

in a demand for unconditional surrender.

Combining two short sentences by joining their predicates (*displayed . . . sent*) is an effective coordination technique.

EXERCISE 14-1 Use the coordination or subordination technique in brackets to combine each pair of independent clauses. Possible revisions appear in the back of the book. *More practice:* e

Ted Williams was one of the best hitters in the history of

    baseball, but he

baseball. ~~He~~ never won a World Series ring. [*Use a comma*

and a coordinating conjunction.]

a. Williams played for the Boston Red Sox from 1939 to 1960. He managed the Washington Senators and Texas Rangers for several years after retiring as a player. [*Use a comma and a coordinating conjunction.*]

b. In 1941, Williams finished the season with a batting average of .406. No player has hit over .400 for a season since then. [*Use a semicolon.*]

hackerhandbooks.com/bedhandbook

e Clear sentences > Exercises: 14–3 to 14–7

EXERCISE 14-1 *Possible revisions:*

a. Williams played for the Boston Red Sox from 1939 to 1960, and he managed the Washington Senators and Texas Rangers for several years after retiring as a player.

b. In 1941, Williams finished the season with a batting average of .406; no player has hit over .400 for a season since then.

c. Although he acknowledged that Joe DiMaggio was a better all-around player, Williams felt that he was a better hitter than DiMaggio.

d. Williams was a stubborn man; for example, he always refused to tip his cap to the crowd after a home run because he claimed that fans were fickle.

c. Williams acknowledged that Joe DiMaggio was a better all-around player. Williams felt that he was a better hitter than DiMaggio. [*Use the subordinating conjunction* although.]

d. Williams was a stubborn man. He always refused to tip his cap to the crowd after a home run because he claimed that fans were fickle. [*Use a semicolon and the transitional phrase* for example.]

e. Williams's relationship with the media was unfriendly at best. He sarcastically called baseball writers the "knights of the keyboard" in his memoir. [*Use a semicolon.*]

EXERCISE 14–2 Combine the following sentences by subordinating minor ideas or by coordinating ideas of equal importance. You must decide which ideas are minor because the sentences are given out of context. Possible revisions appear in the back of the book. *More practice:* **e**

Agnes, ~~was~~ a girl I worked with/, ~~She~~ was a hyperactive child.

a. The X-Men comic books and Japanese woodcuts of kabuki dancers were part of Marlena's research project on popular culture. They covered the tabletop and the chairs.

b. Our waitress was costumed in a kimono. She had painted her face white. She had arranged her hair in a lacquered beehive.

c. Students can apply for a spot in the leadership program. The program teaches thinking and communication skills.

d. Shore houses were flooded up to the first floor. Beaches were washed away. Brant's Lighthouse was swallowed by the sea.

e. Laura Thackray was an engineer at Volvo Car Corporation. She addressed women's safety needs. She designed a pregnant crash-test dummy.

14c Avoid ineffective or excessive coordination.

Coordinate structures are appropriate only when you intend to draw readers' attention equally to two or more ideas: *Professor Sakellarios praises loudly, and she criticizes softly.* If one idea is more important than another—or if a coordinating conjunction does not clearly signal the relationship between the ideas—you should subordinate the less important idea.

EXERCISE 14–1 *Possible revisions (continued):*

e. Williams's relationship with the media was unfriendly at best; he sarcastically called baseball writers the "knights of the keyboard" in his memoir.

EXERCISE 14–2 *Possible revisions:*

a. The X-Men comic books and Japanese woodcuts of kabuki dancers, all part of Marlena's research project on popular culture, covered the tabletop and the chairs.

b. Our waitress, costumed in a kimono, had painted her face white and arranged her hair in a lacquered beehive.

| INEFFECTIVE COORDINATION | Closets were taxed as rooms, and most colonists stored their clothes in chests or clothespresses. |
| IMPROVED WITH SUBORDINATION | Because closets were taxed as rooms, most colonists stored their clothes in chests or clothespresses. |

The revision subordinates the less important idea (*closets were taxed as rooms*) by putting it in a subordinate clause. Notice that the subordinating conjunction *Because* signals the relation between the ideas more clearly than the coordinating conjunction *and*.

Because it is so easy to string ideas together with *and*, writers often rely too heavily on coordination in their rough drafts. The cure for excessive coordination is simple: Look for opportunities to tuck minor ideas into subordinate clauses or phrases.

▶ ~~Shareholders~~ When shareholders exchanged investment tips at the company's
    ∧
annual meeting, ~~and~~ they learned that different approaches

can yield similar results.

The minor idea has become a subordinate clause beginning with *When.*

▶ ~~Four hours went by, and~~ After four hours, a rescue truck finally arrived, but
    ∧
by that time we had been evacuated in a helicopter.

Three independent clauses were excessive. The least important idea has become a prepositional phrase.

EXERCISE 14–8 The following sentences (p. 241) show coordinated ideas (ideas joined with a coordinating conjunction or a semicolon). Restructure the sentences by subordinating minor ideas. You must decide which ideas are minor because the sentences are given out of context. Possible revisions appear in the back of the book. *More practice:* e

hackerhandbooks.com/bedhandbook
e Clear sentences > Exercises: 14–9

EXERCISE 14–2 *Possible revisions (continued):*

c. Students can apply for a spot in the leadership program, which teaches thinking and communication skills.

d. Shore houses were flooded up to the first floor, beaches were washed away, and Brant's Lighthouse was swallowed by the sea.

e. Laura Thackray, an engineer at Volvo Car Corporation, addressed women's safety needs by designing a pregnant crash-test dummy.

EXERCISE 14–8 *Possible revisions:*

a. These particles, known as "stealth liposomes," can hide in the body for a long time without detection.

The rowers returned to shore~~, and~~ ^*where they*^ had a party on the beach ^*to celebrate*^ ~~and celebrated~~ the start of the season.
^

a. These particles are known as "stealth liposomes," and they can hide in the body for a long time without detection.

b. Irena is a competitive gymnast and majors in biochemistry; her goal is to apply her athletic experience and her science degree to a career in sports medicine.

c. Students, textile workers, and labor unions have loudly protested sweatshop abuses, so apparel makers have been forced to examine their labor practices.

d. IRC (Internet relay chat) was developed in a European university; it was created as a way for a group of graduate students to talk about projects from their dorm rooms.

e. The cafeteria's new menu has an international flavor, and it includes everything from enchiladas and pizza to pad thai and sauerbraten.

14d Do not subordinate major ideas.

If a sentence buries its major idea in a subordinate construction, readers may not give the idea enough attention. Make sure to express your major idea in an independent clause and to subordinate any minor ideas.

▶ Harry S. Truman, who was the unexpected winner of the ^*defeated Thomas E. Dewey,*^
^

1948 presidential election~~, defeated Thomas E. Dewey.~~
^

The writer wanted to focus on Truman's unexpected victory, but the original sentence buried this information in an adjective clause. The revision puts the more important idea in an independent clause and tucks the less important idea into an adjective clause (*who defeated Thomas E. Dewey*).

EXERCISE 14–8   *Possible revisions (continued):*

b. Irena, a competitive gymnast majoring in biochemistry, intends to apply her athletic experience and her science degree to a career in sports medicine.

c. Because students, textile workers, and labor unions have loudly protested sweatshop abuses, apparel makers have been forced to examine their labor practices.

d. Developed in a European university, IRC (Internet relay chat) was created as a way for a group of graduate students to talk about projects from their dorm rooms.

e. The cafeteria's new menu, which has an international flavor, includes everything from enchiladas and pizza to pad thai and sauerbraten.

> *As*
> ~~I~~ was driving home from my new job, heading down
> ⋀
> Ranchitos Road, ~~when~~ my car suddenly overheated.

The writer wanted to emphasize that the car overheated, not the fact of driving home. The revision expresses the major idea in an independent clause and places the less important idea in an adverb clause (*As I was driving home from my new job*).

14e Do not subordinate excessively.

In attempting to avoid short, choppy sentences, writers some-times go to the opposite extreme, putting more subordinate ideas into a sentence than its structure can bear. If a sentence collapses of its own weight, occasionally it can be restructured. More often, however, such sentences must be divided.

> In *Animal Liberation*, Peter Singer argues that animals possess
>   *H*
> nervous systems and can feel pain . ~~and that~~ ⅂e believes that
>   ⋀   ⋀
> "the ethical principle on which human equality rests
>
> requires us to extend equal consideration to animals" (1).

Excessive subordination makes it difficult for the reader to focus on the quoted passage. By splitting the original sentence into two sep-arate sentences, the writer draws attention to Peter Singer's main claim, that humans should give "equal consideration to animals." (See 56a on citing sources in MLA style.)

EXERCISE 14–10   In each of the following sentences (p. 243), the idea that the writer wished to emphasize is buried in a subordinate construction. Restructure each sentence so that the independent clause expresses the major idea, as indicated in brackets, and lesser ideas are subordinated. Possible revisions appear in the back of the book. *More practice:* 🄴

hackerhandbooks.com/bedhandbook

🄴 Clear sentences > Exercises: 14–11 and 14–12

EXERCISE 14-10   *Possible revisions:*

a.   Working as an aide for the relief agency, Gina distributed food and medical supplies.

b.   Janbir, who spent every Saturday learning tabla drumming, noticed with each hour of practice that his memory for complex patterns was growing stronger.

c.   When the rotor hit, it gouged a hole about an eighth of an inch deep in my helmet.

d.   My grandfather, who was born eighty years ago in Puerto Rico, raised his daughters the old-fashioned way.

e.   By reversing the depressive effect of the drug, the Narcan saved the patient's life.

Although
Catherine has weathered many hardships, ~~although~~ she has
∧
rarely become discouraged. [*Emphasize that Catherine has*
rarely become discouraged.]

a. Gina worked as an aide for the relief agency, distributing food and medical supplies. [*Emphasize distributing food and medical supplies.*]

b. Janbir spent every Saturday learning tabla drumming, noticing with each hour of practice that his memory for complex patterns was growing stronger. [*Emphasize Janbir's memory.*]

c. The rotor hit, gouging a hole about an eighth of an inch deep in my helmet. [*Emphasize that the rotor gouged a hole in the helmet.*]

d. My grandfather, who raised his daughters the old-fashioned way, was born eighty years ago in Puerto Rico. [*Emphasize how the grandfather raised his daughters.*]

e. The Narcan reversed the depressive effect of the drug, saving the patient's life. [*Emphasize that the patient's life was saved.*]

14f Experiment with techniques for gaining emphasis.

By experimenting with certain techniques, usually involving some element of surprise, you can draw attention to ideas
that deserve special emphasis. Use such techniques sparingly,
however, or they will lose their punch. The writer who tries to
emphasize everything ends up emphasizing nothing.

Using sentence endings for emphasis

You can highlight an idea simply by withholding it until the end
of a sentence. The technique works something like a punch line.
In the following example, the sentence's meaning is not revealed
until its very last word.

> The only completely consistent people are the dead.
> — Aldous Huxley

TEACHING TIP

If you find strings of particularly choppy sentences in your students'
drafts, pull them out and project them (with the names removed) to the
whole class as the foundation for a sentence-combining exercise. Talk
about the ideas of *intent* and *emphasis* and how the "correct" revision
depends on what idea the writer is trying to highlight.

Two types of sentences that withhold information until the end are the inversion and the periodic sentence. The *inversion* reverses the normal subject-verb order, placing the subject at the end, where it receives unusual emphasis. (Also see 15c.)

> In golden pots are hidden the most deadly poisons.
> —Thomas Draxe

The *periodic* sentence opens with a pile-up of modifiers and withholds the subject and verb until the end. A *cumulative* sentence begins with the subject and verb and adds modifying elements at the end.

PERIODIC

Twenty-five years ago, at the age of thirteen, while hiking in the mountains near my hometown of Vancouver, Washington, I came face-to-face with a legend.   — Tom Weitzel, student

CUMULATIVE

A metaphysician is one who goes into a dark cellar at midnight without a light, looking for a black cat that is not there.
— Baron Bowan of Colwood

Using parallel structure for emphasis

Parallel grammatical structure draws special attention to paired ideas or to items in a series. (See 9.) When parallel ideas are paired, the emphasis falls on words that underscore comparisons or contrasts, especially when they occur at the end of a phrase or clause.

> We must *stop talking* about the *American dream* and *start listening* to the *dreams of Americans*.   — Reubin Askew

In a parallel series, the emphasis falls at the end, so it is generally best to end with the most dramatic or climactic item in the series.

SCHOLARS ON SENTENCE COMBINING

Killgallon, Don. "Sentence Composing: Notes on a New Rhetoric." *Lessons to Share: On Teaching Grammar in Context.* Ed. Constance Weaver. Portsmouth: Boynton, 1998. Print. Killgallon offers detailed descriptions of four kinds of sentence-composing activities — unscrambling, imitating, combining, and expanding — all of which are designed to help students learn to write sentences that approximate the mature and stylistically varied sentences of professional writers.

> Sister Charity enjoyed passing out writing punishments: translate the Ten Commandments into Latin, type a thousand-word essay on good manners, copy the New Testament with a quill pen. — Marie Visosky, student

Using punctuation for emphasis

Obviously the exclamation point can add emphasis, but you should not overuse it. As a rule, the exclamation point is more appropriate in dialogue than in ordinary prose.

A dash or a colon may be used to draw attention to word groups worthy of special attention. (See 35a, 35b, and 39a.)

> The middle of the road is where the white line is — and that's the worst place to drive. — Robert Frost

> I turned to see what the anemometer read: The needle had pegged out at 106 knots. — Jonathan Shilk, student

Occasionally, a pair of dashes may be used to highlight a word or an idea.

> They carried the land itself—Vietnam, the place, the soil—a powdery orange-red dust that covered their boots and fatigues and faces. —Tim O'Brien

15 Provide some variety.

When a rough draft is filled with too many sentences that begin the same way or have the same structure, try injecting some variety—as long as you can do so without sacrificing clarity or ease of reading.

15a Vary your sentence openings.

Most sentences in English begin with the subject, move to the verb, and continue to the object, with modifiers tucked in along the way or put at the end. For the most part, such sentences are fine. Put too many of them in a row, however, and they become monotonous.

Adverbial modifiers are easily movable when they modify verbs; they can often be inserted ahead of the subject. Such modifiers might be single words, phrases, or clauses.

> ▶ *Eventually a*
> A few drops of sap ~~eventually~~ began to trickle into the
> aluminum bucket.

Like most adverbs, *eventually* does not need to appear close to the verb it modifies (*began*).

> ▶ *Just as the sun was coming up, a*
> A pair of black ducks flew over the pond. ~~just as the sun was coming up.~~

The adverb clause, which modifies the verb *flew*, is as clear at the beginning of the sentence as it is at the end.

Adjectives and participial phrases can frequently be moved to the beginning of a sentence without loss of clarity.

> ▶ *Dejected and withdrawn,*
> Edward, ~~dejected and withdrawn,~~ nearly gave up his search for a job.

TIP: When beginning a sentence with an adjective or a participial phrase, make sure that the subject of the sentence names the person or thing described in the introductory phrase. If it doesn't, the phrase will dangle. (See 12e.)

WRITERS ON WRITING

To shift the structure of a sentence alters the meaning of that sentence, as definitely and inflexibly as the position of a camera alters the meaning of the object photographed.   — Joan Didion

A fluent writer always seems more talented than he [or she] is. To write well, one needs a natural facility and an acquired difficulty.

— Joseph Joubert

15b Use a variety of sentence structures.

A writer should not rely too heavily on simple sentences and compound sentences, for the effect tends to be both monotonous and choppy. (See 14b and 14c.) Too many complex or compound-complex sentences, however, can be equally monotonous. If your style tends to one or the other extreme, try to achieve a better mix of sentence types.

The major sentence types are illustrated in the following sentences, all taken from Flannery O'Connor's "The King of the Birds," an essay describing the author's pet peafowl.

SIMPLE	Frequently the cock combines the lifting of his tail with the raising of his voice.
COMPOUND	Any chicken's dusting hole is out of place in a flower bed, but the peafowl's hole, being the size of a small crater, is more so.
COMPLEX	The peacock does most of his serious strutting in the spring and summer when he has a full tail to do it with.
COMPOUND-COMPLEX	The cock's plumage requires two years to attain its pattern, and for the rest of his life, this chicken will act as though he designed it himself.

For a fuller discussion of sentence types, see 49a.

15c Try inverting sentences occasionally.

A sentence is inverted if it does not follow the normal subject-verb-object pattern (see 47c). Many inversions sound artificial and should be avoided except in the most formal contexts. But if an inversion sounds natural, it can provide a welcome touch of variety.

SCHOLARS ON SENTENCE VARIETY

Williams, James D. *Preparing to Teach Writing*. 3rd ed. Mahwah: Erlbaum, 2003. Print. Williams discusses common myths about sentence openings, closings, and length.

Laib, Nevin. "Conciseness and Amplification." *College Composition and Communication* 41.4 (1990): 443–59. Print. Asserting that "conciseness is not an unqualified good," Laib argues that we should teach amplification as well as conciseness. Though much of his essay focuses on paragraph-level concerns, his suggestions for teaching amplification illustrate fifteen sentence types.

▶ Set at the top two corners of the stage were huge

~~Huge~~ lavender hearts outlined in bright white lights . ~~were~~
    ∧   ∧

~~set at the top two corners of the stage.~~

In the revision, the subject, *hearts*, appears after the verb, *were set*.
Notice that the two parts of the verb are also inverted—and separated from each other (*Set . . . were*)—without any awkwardness or
loss of meaning.

Inverted sentences are used for emphasis as well as for
variety (see 14f).

15d Consider adding an occasional question or quotation.

An occasional question can provide a change of pace, especially
at the beginning of a paragraph, where it engages the reader's
interest.

> Virginia Woolf, in her book *A Room of One's Own*, wrote
> that in order for a woman to write fiction she must have two
> things, certainly: a room of her own (with key and lock) and
> enough money to support herself.
> *What then are we to make of Phillis Wheatley, a slave,
> who owned not even herself?* This sickly, frail black girl who
> required a servant of her own at times—her health was so
> precarious—and who, had she been white, would have been
> easily considered the intellectual superior of all the women and
> most of the men in the society of her day. [Italics added.]
> — Alice Walker

Quotations can also provide variety by adding the voices of
others to your own. These other voices might be bits of dialogue.

> When we got back upstairs, Dr. Haney and Captain
> Shiller, the head nurse, were waiting for us by the elevator. As

the nurse hurried off, pushing Todd, the doctor explained to us what would happen next.

    "Mrs. Barrus," he began, "this last test is one we do only when absolutely necessary. It is very painful and hard on the patient, but we have no other choice." Apologetically, he went on. "I cannot give him an anesthetic." He waited for the statement to sink in.   — Celeste L. Barrus, student

Or they might be quotations from written sources.

    Even when she enters the hospital on the brink of death, the anorexic will refuse help from anyone and will continue to deny needing help, especially from a doctor. At this point, reports Dr. Steven Levenkron, the anorexic is most likely "a frightened, cold, lonely, starved, and physically tortured, exhausted person—not unlike an actual concentration camp inmate" (29). In this condition she is ultimately force-fed through a tube inserted in the chest.   — Jim Drew, student

Notice that the quotation from a written source is documented with a citation in parentheses. (See 56a.)

EXERCISE 15-1 Improve sentence variety in each of the following sentences by using the technique suggested in brackets. Possible revisions appear in the back of the book. *More practice:* e

> To protect endangered marine turtles, fishing
> ~~Fishing~~ crews place turtle excluder devices in fishing nets.
> ^
> ~~to protect endangered marine turtles.~~ [*Begin the sentence*
>
> *with the adverbial infinitive phrase.*]

a. The exhibits for insects and spiders are across the hall from the fossils exhibit. [*Invert the sentence.*]

b. Sayuri becomes a successful geisha after growing up desperately poor in Japan. [*Move the adverb phrase to the beginning of the sentence.*]

hackerhandbooks.com/bedhandbook
e Clear sentences > Exercises: 15–3

EXERCISE 15-1 *Possible revisions:*

a. Across the hall from the fossils exhibit are the exhibits for insects and spiders.

b. After growing up desperately poor in Japan, Sayuri becomes a successful geisha.

c. Researchers who have been studying Mount St. Helens for years believe that a series of earthquakes in the area may have caused the 1980 eruption.

d. Ice cream typically contains 10 percent milk fat, but premium ice cream may contain up to 16 percent milk fat and has considerably less air in the product.

e. If home values climb, the economy may recover more quickly than expected.

c. Researchers have been studying Mount St. Helens for years. They believe that a series of earthquakes in the area may have caused the 1980 eruption. [*Combine the sentences into a complex sentence. See also 49a.*]

d. Ice cream typically contains 10 percent milk fat. Premium ice cream may contain up to 16 percent milk fat and has considerably less air in the product. [*Combine the two sentences as a compound sentence.*]

e. The economy may recover more quickly than expected if home values climb. [*Move the adverb clause to the beginning of the sentence.*]

EXERCISE 15–2 Edit the following paragraph to increase sentence variety. *More practice:* e

Making architectural models is a skill that requires patience and precision. It is an art that illuminates a design. Architects come up with a grand and intricate vision. Draftspersons convert that vision into blueprints. The model maker follows the blueprints. The model maker builds a miniature version of the structure. Modelers can work in traditional materials like wood and clay and paint. Modelers can work in newer materials like Styrofoam and liquid polymers. Some modelers still use cardboard, paper, and glue. Other modelers prefer glue guns, deformable plastic, and thin aluminum and brass wire. The modeler may seem to be making a small mess in the early stages of model building. In the end the modeler has completed a small-scale structure. Architect Rem Koolhaas has insisted that plans reveal the logic of a design. He has argued that models expose the architect's vision. The model maker's art makes this vision real.

hackerhandbooks.com/bedhandbook

e Clear sentences > Exercises: 15–3

EXERCISE 15–2 *Possible revisions:*

Making architectural models is a skill that requires patience and precision and is an art that illuminates a design. Architects come up with a grand and intricate vision, and then draftspersons convert that vision into blueprints. The model maker follows the blueprints to build a miniature version of the structure. Modelers can work in traditional materials like wood and clay and paint or in newer materials like Styrofoam and liquid polymers. Some modelers still use cardboard, paper, and glue; other modelers prefer glue guns, deformable plastic, and thin aluminum and brass wire. Although the modeler may seem to be making a small mess in the early stages of model building, in the end the modeler has completed a small-scale structure. Architect Rem Koolhaas has insisted that plans reveal the logic of a design and that models expose the architect's vision. The model maker's art makes this vision real.

PART IV

Word Choice

16   Tighten wordy sentences.

Long sentences are not necessarily wordy, nor are short sentences always concise. A sentence is wordy if it can be tightened without loss of meaning.

16a Eliminate redundancies.

Writers often repeat themselves unnecessarily, thinking that expressions such as *cooperate together*, *yellow in color*, or *basic essentials* add emphasis to their writing. In reality, such redundancies do just the opposite. There is no need to say the same thing twice.

> ▶ Daniel ~~is now employed~~ at a private rehabilitation center ^works

> ~~working~~ as a registered physical therapist.

Though modifiers ordinarily add meaning to the words they modify, occasionally they are redundant.

> ▶ Sylvia ~~very hurriedly~~ scribbled her name, address, and phone

> number on a greasy napkin.

The word *scribbled* already suggests that Sylvia wrote *very hurriedly*.

16b Avoid unnecessary repetition of words.

Though words may be repeated deliberately, for effect, repetitions will seem awkward if they are clearly unnecessary. When a more concise version is possible, choose it.

WRITERS ON WRITING

I apologize for this long letter; I didn't have time to shorten it.   — Pliny

Clutter is the disease of American writing. We are a society strangling in unnecessary words, circular constructions, pompous frills, and meaningless jargon.   — William Zinsser

▶ Our fifth patient, in room six, is a mentally ill. ~~patient.~~

grow
▶ The best teachers help each student ~~become a better~~

~~student~~ both academically and emotionally.

16c Cut empty or inflated phrases.

An empty phrase can be cut with little or no loss of meaning. Common examples are introductory word groups that weaken the writer's authority by apologizing or hedging: *in my opinion, I think that, it seems that, one must admit that,* and so on.

O
▶ ~~In my opinion,~~ our current immigration policy is misguided.

Readers understand without being told that they are hearing the writer's opinion.

Inflated phrases can be reduced to a word or two without loss of meaning.

INFLATED	CONCISE
along the lines of	like
as a matter of fact	in fact
at all times	always
at the present time	now, currently
at this point in time	now, currently
because of the fact that	because
by means of	by
due to the fact that	because
for the purpose of	for
have the ability to	be able to, can
in order to	to
in spite of the fact that	although, though
in the event that	if
in the final analysis	finally
in the neighborhood of	about

TEACHING TIP

It can be difficult to catch unnecessary repetition and redundancy. If you teach in a computer lab, you may want to have students try this proofreading exercise. Ask them to insert returns after each sentence in their drafts, so they have a list of single sentences. Sometimes it is easier to proofread individual sentences methodically than to proofread whole paragraphs.

16d Simplify the structure.

If the structure of a sentence is needlessly indirect, try simplifying it. Look for opportunities to strengthen the verb.

▶ The financial analyst claimed that because of volatile market conditions she could not ~~make an~~ estimate ~~of~~ the company's future profits.

> The verb *estimate* is more vigorous and concise than *make an estimate of.*

The colorless verbs *is, are, was,* and *were* frequently generate excess words.

▶ Investigators ~~were involved in~~ stud_{studied}ing the effect of classical music on unborn babies.

> The revision is more direct and concise. The action (*studying*), originally appearing in a subordinate structure, has become a strong verb, *studied.*

The expletive constructions *there is* and *there are* (or *there was* and *there were*) can also lead to wordy sentences. The same is true of expletive constructions beginning with *it.* (See 47c.)

▶ ~~There is~~ Another module ~~that~~ tells the story of Charles Darwin and introduces the theory of evolution.

Finally, verbs in the passive voice may be needlessly indirect. When the active voice expresses your meaning as effectively, use it. (See 8a.)

WRITERS ON WRITING

Remember the waterfront shack with the sign FRESH FISH SOLD HERE. Of course it's fresh, we're on the ocean. Of course it's for sale, we're not giving it away. Of course it's here, otherwise the sign would be someplace else. The final sign: FISH. — Peggy Noonan

A sentence should contain no unnecessary words, a paragraph no unnecessary sentences, for the same reason that a drawing should have no unnecessary lines and a machine no unnecessary parts.
  — William Strunk Jr. and E. B. White

I might not know how to use thirty-four words where three would do, but that does not mean that I don't know what I'm talking about.
  — Ruth Shays

16e Reduce clauses to phrases, phrases to single words.

Word groups functioning as modifiers can often be made more compact. Look for any opportunities to reduce clauses to phrases or phrases to single words.

▶ We took a side trip to Monticello, ~~which was~~ the home of Thomas Jefferson.

▶ In ~~the~~ essay, ^this^ ~~that follows,~~ I argue against Immanuel Kant's claim that we should not lie under any ^problematic^ circumstances/. ~~which is a problematic claim.~~

EXERCISE 16–1 Edit the following sentences to reduce wordiness. Possible revisions appear in the back of the book. *More practice:* e ✔

The Wilsons moved into the house ~~in spite of the fact that~~ ^even though^ the back door was only ten yards from the train tracks.

a. Martin Luther King Jr. was a man who set a high standard for future leaders to meet.
b. Alice has been deeply in love with cooking since she was little and could first peek over the edge of a big kitchen tabletop.
c. In my opinion, Bloom's race for the governorship is a futile exercise.
d. It is pretty important in being a successful graphic designer to have technical knowledge and at the same time an eye for color and balance.
e. Your task will be the delivery of correspondence to all employees in the company.

hackerhandbooks.com/bedhandbook
e Word choice > Exercises: 16–3 to 16–7
✔ Word choice > LearningCurve: Word choice and appropriate language

---

EXERCISE 16–1 *Possible revisions:*

a. Martin Luther King Jr. set a high standard for future leaders.
b. Alice has loved cooking since she could first peek over a kitchen tabletop.
c. Bloom's race for the governorship is futile.
d. A successful graphic designer must have technical knowledge and an eye for color and balance.
e. You will deliver mail to all employees.

EXERCISE 16–2   Edit the following business memo to reduce wordiness. *More practice:* e ✓

To:	District managers
From:	Margaret Davenport, Vice President
Subject:	Customer database

It has recently been brought to my attention that a percentage of our sales representatives have been failing to log reports of their client calls in our customer database each and every day. I have also learned that some representatives are not checking the database on a routine basis.

Our clients sometimes receive a multiple number of sales calls from us when a sales representative is not cognizant of the fact that the client has been contacted at a previous time. Repeated telephone calls from our representatives annoy our customers. These repeated telephone calls also portray our company as one that is lacking in organization.

Effective as of immediately, direct your representatives to do the following:

- Record each and every customer contact in the customer database at the end of each day, without fail.

- Check the database at the very beginning of each day to ensure that telephone communications will not be initiated with clients who have already been called.

Let me extend my appreciation to you for cooperating in this important matter.

hackerhandbooks.com/bedhandbook

e Word choice > Exercises: 16–3 to 16–7

✓ Word choice > LearningCurve: Word choice and appropriate language

---

EXERCISE 16–2   *Possible revisions:*

To:	District managers
From:	Margaret Davenport, Vice President
Subject:	Customer database

Some of our sales representatives have been failing to log daily reports of their client calls in our customer database. Also, some representatives are not routinely checking the database. Our clients sometimes receive repeated sales calls from us when a sales representative does not realize that the client has already been contacted. Repeated calls annoy our customers and make us appear disorganized.

17 Choose appropriate language.

Language is appropriate when it suits your subject, engages your audience, and blends naturally with your own voice.

To some extent, your choice of language will be governed by the conventions of the genre in which you are writing. When in doubt about the conventions of a particular genre — lab reports, informal essays, business memos, and so on — consult your instructor or look at models written by experts in the field.

17a Stay away from jargon.

Jargon is special language used among members of a trade, profession, or group. Use jargon only when readers will be familiar with it and when plain English will not do as well.

JARGON   We outsourced the work to an outfit in Ohio because we didn't have the bandwidth to tackle it in-house.

REVISED   We hired a company in Ohio because we had too few employees to do the work.

Broadly defined, jargon includes puffed-up language designed more to impress readers than to inform them. The following are examples from business, government, higher education, and the military, with plain English alternatives in parentheses.

ameliorate (improve)	indicator (sign)
commence (begin)	optimal (best, most favorable)
components (parts)	parameters (boundaries, limits)
endeavor (try)	peruse (read, look over)
exit (leave)	prior to (before)
facilitate (help)	utilize (use)
impact (v.) (affect)	viable (workable)

EXERCISE 16-2 *Possible revisions (continued):*

Effective immediately, direct your representatives to do the following:

- Record each customer contact in the customer database at the end of each day.
- Check the database at the beginning of each day to avoid repeated calls.

Thank you for your cooperation in this important matter.

Sentences filled with jargon are hard to read, and they are often wordy as well.

> The CEO should ~~dialogue~~ *talk* with investors about ~~partnering~~ *working* with clients to ~~purchase~~ *buy* land in ~~economically deprived zones.~~ *poor neighborhoods.*

17b Avoid pretentious language, most euphemisms, and "doublespeak."

Hoping to sound profound or poetic, some writers embroider their thoughts with large words and flowery phrases. Such pretentious language is so ornate and wordy that it obscures the writer's meaning.

> Taylor's ~~employment of multihued means of expression draws~~ *use of colorful language reveals that she has a* ~~back the curtains and lets slip the~~ nostalgic ~~vantage point~~ *view of* ~~from which she observes~~ American society ~~as well as her lack~~ *and does not* ~~of comprehension of~~ *understand* economic realities.

The writer of the original sentence had turned to a thesaurus (a dictionary of synonyms and antonyms) in an attempt to sound authoritative. When such a writer gains enough confidence to speak in his or her own voice, pretentious language disappears.

Euphemisms — nice-sounding words or phrases substituted for words thought to sound harsh or ugly — are sometimes appropriate. Many cultures, for example, accept euphemisms when speaking or writing about excretion (*I have to go to the bathroom*), sexual intercourse (*They did not sleep together*), and the like. We may also use euphemisms out of concern for someone's feelings. Telling parents, for example, that their daughter

---

SCHOLARS ON JARGON AND DOUBLESPEAK

Lutz, William. *The New Doublespeak: Why No One Knows What Anyone's Saying Anymore*. New York: Harper, 1996. Print. The longtime editor of the *Quarterly Review of Doublespeak* continues his campaign to expose misleading language. He offers myriad examples from a wide range of public texts.

is "unmotivated" is more sensitive than saying she's lazy. Tact or politeness, then, can justify an occasional euphemism.

Most euphemisms, however, are needlessly evasive or even deceitful. Like pretentious language, they obscure the intended meaning.

EUPHEMISM	PLAIN ENGLISH
adult entertainment	pornography
preowned automobile	used car
economically deprived	poor
negative savings	debts
strategic withdrawal	retreat, defeat
revenue enhancers	taxes
chemical dependency	drug addiction
downsize	lay off, fire
correctional facility	prison

The term *doublespeak* applies to any deliberately evasive or deceptive language, including euphemisms. Doublespeak is especially common in politics and business. A military retreat is described as *tactical redeployment*; *enhanced interrogation* is a euphemism for "torture"; and *downsizing* really means "firing employees."

EXERCISE 17–1 Edit the following sentences (p. 260) to eliminate jargon, pretentious or flowery language, euphemisms, and doublespeak. You may need to make substantial changes in some sentences. Possible revisions appear in the back of the book. *More practice:* e ✔

After two weeks in the legal department, Sue has ~~worked~~ mastered into the routine, ~~of the office,~~ and her ~~functional and self-management skills have~~ office performance has exceeded all expectations.

hackerhandbooks.com/bedhandbook

e Word choice > Exercises: 17–3 and 17–4

✔ Word choice > LearningCurve: Word choice and appropriate language

EXERCISE 17–1 *Possible revisions:*

a. When I was young, my family was poor.

b. This conference will help me serve my clients better.

c. The meteorologist warned the public about the possible dangers of the coming storm.

d. Government studies show a need for after-school programs.

e. Passengers should try to complete the customs declaration form before leaving the plane.

a. In my youth, my family was under the constraints of difficult financial circumstances.

b. In order that I may increase my expertise in the area of delivery of services to clients, I feel that participation in this conference will be beneficial.

c. The prophetic meteorologist cautioned the general populace regarding the possible deleterious effects of the impending tempest.

d. Governmentally sanctioned investigations into the continued value of after-school programs indicate a perceived need in the public realm at large.

e. Passengers should endeavor to finalize the customs declaration form prior to exiting the aircraft.

EXERCISE 17–2   Edit the following e-mail message to eliminate jargon. *More practice:* e ✓

Dear Ms. Jackson:

We members of the Nakamura Reyes team value our external partnering arrangements with Creative Software, and I look forward to seeing you next week at the trade show in Fresno. Per Mr. Reyes, please let me know when you'll have some downtime there so that he and I can conduct a strategizing session with you concerning our production schedule. It's crucial that we all be on the same page re our 2013–2014 product release dates.

Before we have some face time, however, I have some findings to share. Our customer-centric approach to the new products will necessitate that user testing periods trend upward. The enclosed data should help you effectuate any adjustments to your timeline; let me know ASAP if you require any additional information to facilitate the above.

Before we convene in Fresno, Mr. Reyes and I will agendize any further talking points. Thanks for your help.

Sincerely,

Sylvia Nakamura

hackerhandbooks.com/bedhandbook

e Word choice > Exercises: 17–3 and 17–4

✓ Word choice > LearningCurve: Word choice and appropriate language

---

EXERCISE 17–2   *Possible revisions:*

Dear Ms. Jackson:

We at Nakamura Reyes value our relationship with Creative Software, and I look forward to seeing you next week at the trade show in Fresno. Please let me know when you will have time to meet with Mr. Reyes and me to discuss our production schedule. It's crucial that we all agree on our 2013–2014 product release dates.

Before we meet, however, I have some new information. Our user-friendly approach to the new products will make longer user testing periods necessary. The enclosed data should help you adjust your

17c Avoid obsolete and invented words.

Although dictionaries list obsolete words such as *recomfort* and *reechy*, these words are not appropriate for current use. Invented words or expressions (called *neologisms*) are too recently created to be part of Standard English. Many fade out of use without becoming standard. *YOLO* and *MOOC* are neologisms that may not last. *Prequel* and *e-mail* are no longer neologisms; they have become Standard English. Avoid using invented words in formal writing unless they are given in the dictionary as standard or unless no other word expresses your meaning.

17d In most contexts, avoid slang, regional expressions, and nonstandard English.

Slang is an informal and sometimes private vocabulary that expresses the solidarity of a group such as teenagers, rap musicians, or sports fans; it is subject to more rapid change than Standard English. For example, the slang teenagers use to express approval changes every few years; *cool, groovy, neat, awesome, phat,* and *sick* have replaced one another within the last three decades. Sometimes slang becomes so widespread that it is accepted as standard vocabulary. *Jazz,* for example, started out as slang but is now a standard term for a style of music.

Although slang has a certain vitality, it is a code that not everyone understands, and it is very informal. Therefore, it is inappropriate in most written work.

► When the server crashed unexpectedly, three hours of unsaved data. ~~went down the tubes.~~ *we lost*

► The government's "filth" guidelines for food will ~~gross you out.~~ *disgust you.*

EXERCISE 17-2 *Possible revisions (continued):*

timeline; let me know right away if you require any additional information before making these adjustments.

Before we meet in Fresno, Mr. Reyes and I will outline any other topics for discussion. Thanks for your help.

Sincerely,

Sylvia Nakamura

TEACHING TIP

It often helps to have small groups of students take charge of teaching a few style and grammar concepts. Assign students in groups to tackle

Regional expressions are common to a group in a geographic area. *Let's talk with the bark off* (for *Let's speak frankly*)
is an expression in the southern United States, for example.
Regional expressions have the same limitations as slang and are
therefore inappropriate in most writing.

▶ John was four blocks from the house before he remembered

    turn on

to ~~cut~~ the headlights. ~~on.~~
    ∧   ∧

▶ Seamus wasn't ~~for~~ sure, but he thought the whales might

be migrating during his visit to Oregon.

Standard English is the language used in all academic, business, and professional fields. Nonstandard English is spoken by
people with a common regional or social heritage. Although nonstandard English may be appropriate when spoken within a close
group, it is out of place in most formal and informal writing.

                  doesn't

▶ The governor said he ~~don't~~ know if he will approve the
                    ∧

budget without the clean air provision.

If you speak a nonstandard dialect, try to identify the ways
in which your dialect differs from Standard English. Look especially for the following features of nonstandard English, which
commonly cause problems in writing.

Misusing verb forms such as *began* and *begun* (See 27a.)

Leaving *-s* endings off verbs (See 27c.)

Leaving *-ed* endings off verbs (See 27d.)

Leaving out necessary verbs (See 27e.)

Using double negatives (See 26e.)

---

concepts like avoiding clichés and jargon and to prepare a ten-minute
mini-lesson in which they show examples and discuss revision strategies.
If the class is online, the students can prepare a few slides that they
upload to the course Web site.

WRITERS ON WRITING

There is still no substitute for radical sincerity.   — Gish Jen

"Are you excavating a subterranean channel?" asked the scholar. "No
sir," replied the farmer. "I am only digging a ditch."   — An old joke

I know there are professors in this country who "ligate" arteries. Other
surgeons only tie them, and it stops bleeding just as well.
                                 — Oliver Wendell Holmes Sr.

17e Choose an appropriate level of formality.

In deciding on a level of formality, consider both your subject and your audience. Does the subject demand a dignified treatment, or is a relaxed tone more suitable? Will readers be put off if you assume too close a relationship with them, or might you alienate them by seeming too distant?

For most college and professional writing, some degree of formality is appropriate. In a job application letter, for example, it is a mistake to sound too breezy and informal.

TOO INFORMAL I'd like to get that sales job you've got in the paper.

MORE FORMAL I would like to apply for the position of sales associate advertised in the *Peoria Journal Star*.

Informal writing is appropriate for private letters, personal e-mail and text messages, and business correspondence between close associates. Like spoken conversation, informal writing allows contractions (*don't, I'll*) and colloquial words (*kids, kinda*). Vocabulary and sentence structure are rarely complex.

In choosing a level of formality, above all be consistent. When a writer's voice shifts from one level of formality to another, readers receive mixed messages.

▶ Once a pitcher for the Blue Jays, Jorge shared with me

the secrets of his trade. His lesson ~~commenced~~ began with his

famous curveball, ~~implemented~~ thrown by tucking the little finger

behind the ball. Next he ~~elucidated~~ revealed the mysteries of the

sucker pitch, a slow ball coming behind a fast windup.

Words such as *commenced* and *elucidated* are inappropriate for the subject matter, and they clash with informal terms such as *sucker pitch* and *fast windup*.

SCHOLARS ON NONSTANDARD ENGLISH

Monseau, Virginia R., ed. *And Language for All*. Issue of *English Journal* 90.4 (2001). Print. This issue of the journal for the secondary section of NCTE includes several articles on nonstandard English, including "Standard English and the Migrant Community" by Gregory Shafer, "What's a (White) Teacher to Do about Black English?" by Sara Dalmas Jonsberg, and "Acknowledging the Language of African American Students: Instructional Strategies" by Sharroky Hollie.

EXERCISE 17-5 Revise the following passage so that the level of formality is appropriate for a letter to the editor of a major newspaper.

> In pop culture, college grads who return home to live with the folks are seen as good-for-nothing losers who mooch off their families. And many older adults seem to feel that the trend of moving back home after school, which was rare in their day, is becoming too commonplace today. But society must realize that times have changed. Most young adults want to live on their own ASAP, but they graduate with heaps of debt and need some time to get back on their feet. College tuition and the cost of housing have increased way more than salary increases in the past fifty years. Also, the job market is tighter and more jobs require advanced degrees than in the past. So before people go off on college graduates who move back into their parents' house for a spell, they'd better consider all the facts.

17f Avoid sexist language.

Sexist language is language that stereotypes or demeans women or men. Using nonsexist language is a matter of courtesy—of respect for and sensitivity to the feelings of others.

Recognizing sexist language

Some sexist language is easy to recognize because it reflects genuine contempt for women: referring to a woman as a "chick," for example, or calling a lawyer a "lady lawyer."

Other forms of sexist language are less blatant. The following practices, while they may not result from conscious sexism, reflect stereotypical thinking: referring to members of one profession as exclusively male or exclusively female (teachers as women or computer engineers as men, for instance) or using different conventions when naming or identifying women and men.

EXERCISE 17-5 *Possible revisions:*

In popular culture, college graduates who return home to live with their parents are seen as irresponsible freeloaders. And many older adults seem to feel that the trend of moving back home after school, which was rare in their day, is becoming too commonplace today. But society must realize that times have changed. Most young adults want to live on their own right away, but they graduate with large amounts of debt and need some time to become financially stable. College tuition and the cost of housing have increased far beyond the pace of salary increases in the past fifty years. Also, the job market is tighter and more jobs require advanced degrees than in the past. So before people criticize college graduates who temporarily move back into their parents' house, they should be sure to consider all the facts.

STEREOTYPICAL LANGUAGE

After a nursing student graduates, *she* must face a difficult state board examination. [Not all nursing students are women.]

Running for city council are Boris Stotsky, an attorney, and *Mrs.* Cynthia Jones, a professor of English and *mother of three*. [The title *Mrs.* and the phrase *mother of three* are irrelevant.]

All executives' *wives* are invited to the welcome dinner. [Not all executives are men.]

Still other forms of sexist language result from outdated traditions. The pronouns *he, him,* and *his,* for instance, were traditionally used to refer generically to persons of either sex. Nowadays, to avoid that sexist usage, some writers use *she, her,* and *hers* generically or substitute the female pronouns alternately with the male pronouns.

GENERIC PRONOUNS

A journalist is motivated by *his* deadline.

A good interior designer treats *her* clients' ideas respectfully.

But both forms are sexist—for excluding one sex entirely and for making assumptions about the members of particular professions.

Similarly, the nouns *man* and *men* were once used to refer generically to persons of either sex. Current usage demands gender-neutral terms for references to both men and women.

INAPPROPRIATE	APPROPRIATE
chairman	chairperson, moderator, chair, head
clergyman	member of the clergy, minister, rabbi, imam
congressman	member of Congress, representative, legislator
fireman	firefighter
foreman	supervisor

SCHOLARS ON NONSTANDARD ENGLISH

Williams, James D. "Nonstandard English." *Preparing to Teach Writing.* 3rd ed. Mahwah: Erlbaum, 2003. Print. Williams draws on several decades of sociolinguistic research to define "dialect," to discuss the characteristics of black English and Chicano English, and to explore how these forms of English affect writing performance. His bibliography is extensive.

INAPPROPRIATE	APPROPRIATE
mailman	mail carrier, postal worker, letter carrier
to man	to operate, to staff
mankind	people, humans
manpower	personnel, staff
policeman	police officer
salesman	salesperson, sales associate, salesclerk
weatherman	forecaster, meteorologist

Revising sexist language

When revising sexist language, you may be tempted to substitute *he or she* and *his or her*. These terms are inclusive but wordy; fine in small doses, they can become awkward when repeated throughout an essay. A better revision strategy is to write in the plural; yet another strategy is to recast the sentence so that the problem does not arise.

SEXIST

A journalist is motivated by *his* deadline.

A good interior designer treats *her* clients' ideas respectfully.

ACCEPTABLE BUT WORDY

A journalist is motivated by *his or her* deadline.

A good interior designer treats *his or her* clients' ideas respectfully.

BETTER: USING THE PLURAL

Journalists are motivated by *their* deadlines.

Good interior designers treat *their* clients' ideas respectfully.

BETTER: RECASTING THE SENTENCE

A journalist is motivated by *a* deadline.

A good interior designer treats clients' ideas respectfully.

For more examples of these revision strategies, see 22.

EXERCISE 17–6 *Possible revisions:*

a. Dr. Geralyn Farmer is the chief surgeon at University Hospital. Dr. Paul Green is her assistant.
b. All applicants want to know how much they will earn.
c. Elementary school teachers should understand the concept of nurturing if they intend to be effective.
d. Obstetricians need to be available to their patients at all hours.
e. If we do not stop polluting our environment, we will perish.

EXERCISE 17–7 *Possible revisions:*

We are looking for qualified candidates for the position of elementary school teacher. The ideal candidate should have a bachelor's degree, a

EXERCISE 17-6 Edit the following sentences to eliminate sexist language or sexist assumptions. Possible revisions appear in the back of the book. *More practice:* e ✓

> ~~A scholarship athlete~~ must be as concerned about ~~his~~
> ^{Scholarship athletes}   ^{their}
>
> academic performance as ~~he is~~ about ~~his~~ athletic
>   ^{they are}   ^{their}
>
> performance.

a. Mrs. Geralyn Farmer, who is the mayor's wife, is the chief surgeon at University Hospital. Dr. Paul Green is her assistant.

b. Every applicant wants to know how much he will earn.

c. An elementary school teacher should understand the concept of nurturing if she intends to be effective.

d. An obstetrician needs to be available to his patients at all hours.

e. If man does not stop polluting his environment, mankind will perish.

EXERCISE 17-7 Eliminate sexist language or sexist assumptions in the following job posting for an elementary school teacher. *More practice:* e ✓

> We are looking for qualified women for the position of elementary school teacher. The ideal candidate should have a bachelor's degree, a state teaching certificate, and one year of student teaching. She should be knowledgeable in all elementary subject areas, including science and math. While we want our new teacher to have a commanding presence in the classroom, we are also looking for motherly characteristics such as patience and trustworthiness. She must be able to both motivate an entire classroom and work with each student one-on-one to assess his individual needs. She must also be comfortable communicating with the parents of her students. For salary and benefits

hackerhandbooks.com/bedhandbook

e Word choice > Exercises: 17–8 to 17–10
✓ Word choice > LearningCurve: Word choice and appropriate language

---

EXERCISE 17-7 *Possible revisions (continued):*

state teaching certificate, and one year of student teaching. Candidates should be knowledgeable in all elementary subject areas. We want our new teacher to have a commanding presence in the classroom as well as a patient and trustworthy demeanor. The teacher must be able to both motivate an entire classroom and work with students one-on-one to assess their individual needs. The teacher must also be comfortable communicating with the students' parents. For salary and benefits information, please contact the Martin County School Board. Qualified applicants should submit their résumés by March 15.

information, including maternity leave policy, please contact the Martin County School Board. Any qualified applicant should submit her résumé by March 15.

17g Revise language that may offend groups of people.

Your writing should be respectful and free of stereotypical, biased, or other offensive language. Be especially careful when describing or labeling people. Labels can become dated, and it is important to recognize when their continued use is not acceptable. When naming groups of people, choose labels that the groups currently use to describe themselves. For example, *Negro* is not an acceptable label for African Americans; instead of *Eskimo*, use *Inuit*; for other native peoples, name the specific group when possible.

▶ North Dakota takes its name from the ~~Indian~~ Lakota word meaning "friend" or "ally."

▶ Many ~~Oriental~~ Asian immigrants have recently settled in our town.

Negative stereotypes (such as "drives like a teenager" or "sour as a spinster") are of course offensive. But you should avoid stereotyping a person or a group even if you believe your generalization to be positive.

▶ It was no surprise that Greer, ~~a Chinese American,~~ an excellent math and science student, was selected for the honors chemistry program in her sophomore year.

SCHOLARS ON NONSTANDARD ENGLISH

Balester, Valerie M. *Cultural Divide: A Study of African-American College-Level Writers*. Portsmouth: Boynton, 1993. 77–151. Print. In her study of eight African American college students, Balester explores how these writers draw on language strategies embedded in an African American rhetorical tradition, strategies that are often at odds with expectations for academic prose.

Giannasi, Jenefer M. "Language Varieties and Composition." *Teaching Composition*. Ed. Gary Tate. Rev. ed. Fort Worth: Texas Christian UP, 1987. Print. Giannasi reviews sociolinguistic studies of variations in language and addresses issues that arise in the composition classroom because of differences among dialects.

18 Find the exact words.

Two reference works (or their online equivalents) will help you find words to express your meaning exactly: a good dictionary, such as *The American Heritage Dictionary* or *Merriam-Webster* online, and a collection of synonyms and antonyms, such as *Roget's International Thesaurus.*

TIP: Do not turn to a thesaurus in search of flowery or impressive words. Look instead for words that exactly express your meaning.

18a Select words with appropriate connotations.

In addition to their strict dictionary meanings (or *denotations*), words have *connotations,* emotional colorings that affect how readers respond to them. The word *steel* denotes "commercial iron that contains carbon," but it also calls up a cluster of images associated with steel. These associations give the word its connotations—cold, hard, smooth, unbending.

If the connotation of a word does not seem appropriate for your purpose, your audience, or your subject matter, you should change the word. When a more appropriate synonym does not come quickly to mind, consult a dictionary or a thesaurus.

▶ When American soldiers returned home after World War II,
    left
  many women ~~abandoned~~ their jobs in favor of marriage.
        ∧

  The word *abandoned* is too negative for the context.

TEACHING TIP

Consider assigning students to keep an editing log for the semester. When they receive comments on a draft, they should pay special attention to comments related to sentence-level matters. In their editing log, students should record (1) the incorrect sentence, (2) the handbook section (17b, for example) that provides help for editing that sentence, and (3) the corrected sentence. Invite students to add any tips that might help them proofread for that particular error in the future.

▶ As I covered the boats with marsh grass, the ~~perspiration~~ I

sweat

had worked up evaporated in the wind, and the cold

morning air seemed even colder.

The term *perspiration* is too dainty for the context, which suggests vigorous exercise.

EXERCISE 18–1 Use a dictionary and a thesaurus to find at least four synonyms for each of the following words. Be prepared to explain any slight differences in meaning.

1. decay (verb)   3. hurry (verb)   5. secret (adjective)
2. difficult (adjective) 4. pleasure (noun)   6. talent (noun)

18b Prefer specific, concrete nouns.

Unlike general nouns, which refer to broad classes of things, specific nouns point to particular items. *Film*, for example, names a general class, *fantasy film* names a narrower class, and *The Golden Compass* is more specific still. Other examples: *team, football team, Denver Broncos*; *music, symphony, Beethoven's Ninth*.

Unlike abstract nouns, which refer to qualities and ideas (*justice, beauty, realism, dignity*), concrete nouns point to immediate, often sensory experience and to physical objects (*steeple, asphalt, lilac, stone, garlic*).

Specific, concrete nouns express meaning more vividly than general or abstract ones. Although general and abstract language is sometimes necessary to convey your meaning, use specific, concrete words whenever possible.

▶ The senator spoke about the challenges of the future:

pollution, dwindling resources, and terrorism.

~~the environment and world peace.~~

EXERCISE 18–1 *Possible answers:*

1. decay (verb): decompose, disintegrate, break up, corrode, rot, putrefy, fester, molder; 2. difficult (adjective): hard, tough, rigorous, formidable, arduous, tricky, demanding, complex; 3. hurry (verb): rush, accelerate, bustle, speed, scamper, scramble, quicken, hasten, dash, dart;
4. pleasure (noun): enjoyment, contentment, euphoria, gratification, satisfaction, relish, gusto, fun, entertainment, amusement; 5. secret (adjective): concealed, covert, cryptic, hidden, arcane, clandestine, undercover, furtive, stealthy, mysterious, unknown; 6. talent (noun): ability, genius, skill, faculty, flair, gift, power, forte

Nouns such as *thing, area, aspect, factor,* and *individual* are especially dull and imprecise.

> Toni Morrison's *Beloved* is about slavery, ~~among other things.~~
>
> motherhood, and memory.

18c Do not misuse words.

If a word is not in your active vocabulary, you may find yourself misusing it, sometimes with embarrassing consequences. When in doubt, check the dictionary.

> climbing
> The fans were ~~migrating~~ up the bleachers in search of seats.

> permeated
> The Internet has so ~~diffused~~ our culture that it touches all
>
> segments of society.

Also be alert for misused word forms — using a noun such as *absence* or *significance,* for example, when your meaning requires the adjective *absent* or *significant.*

> persistent
> Most dieters are not ~~persistence~~ enough to make a
>
> permanent change in their eating habits.

EXERCISE 18–2 Edit the following sentences to correct misused words. Possible revisions appear in the back of the book. *More practice:* e ✓

> These days the training required for a ballet dancer is
> all-absorbing.
> ~~all-absorbent.~~

a. We regret this delay; thank you for your patients.

hackerhandbooks.com/bedhandbook

e Word choice > Exercises: 18–3 and 18–4

✓ Word choice > LearningCurve: Word choice and appropriate language

EXERCISE 18–2 *Possible revisions:*

a. We regret this delay; thank you for your patience.

b. Ada's plan is to acquire education and experience to prepare herself for a position as property manager.

c. Serena Williams, the ultimate competitor, has earned millions of dollars just in endorsements.

d. Many people take for granted that public libraries have up-to-date computer systems.

e. The effect of Gao Xingjian's novels on other Chinese exiles is hard to gauge.

b. Ada's plan is to require education and experience to prepare herself for a position as property manager.

c. Serena Williams, the penultimate competitor, has earned millions of dollars just in endorsements.

d. Many people take for granite that public libraries have up-to-date computer systems.

e. The affect of Gao Xingjian's novels on other Chinese exiles is hard to gauge.

18d Use standard idioms.

Idioms are speech forms that follow no easily specified rules. The English say "Bernice went *to hospital*," an idiom strange to American ears, which are accustomed to hearing *the* in front of *hospital*. Native speakers of a language seldom have problems with idioms, but prepositions (such as *with*, *to*, *at*, and *of*) sometimes cause trouble, especially when they follow certain verbs and adjectives. When in doubt, consult a dictionary.

UNIDIOMATIC	IDIOMATIC
abide with (a decision)	abide by (a decision)
according with	according to
agree to (an idea)	agree with (an idea)
angry at (a person)	angry with (a person)
capable to	capable of
comply to	comply with
desirous to	desirous of
different than (a person or thing)	different from (a person or thing)
intend on doing	intend to do
off of	off
plan on doing	plan to do
preferable than	preferable to
prior than	prior to
superior than	superior to
sure and	sure to

WRITERS ON WRITING

Do not be grand. Try to get the ordinary into your writing — breakfast tables rather than the solar system; Middletown today, not Mankind through the ages.   — Darcy O'Brien

It is a good deal easier for most people to state an abstract idea than to describe and thus re-create some object they actually see.

— Flannery O'Connor

An abstract style is always bad. Your sentences should be full of stones, metals, chairs, tables, animals, men, and women.   — Alain de Lille

UNIDIOMATIC	IDIOMATIC
think on	think of, about
try and	try to
type of a	type of

> **Multilingual**
>
> Because idioms follow no particular rules, you must learn them individually. You may find it helpful to keep a list of idioms that you frequently encounter in conversation and in reading.

EXERCISE 18–5 Edit the following sentences to eliminate errors in the use of idiomatic expressions. If a sentence is correct, write "correct" after it. Possible revisions appear in the back of the book. *More practice:* e ✓

> by
> We agreed to abide ~~with~~ the decision of the judge.
> ∧

a. Queen Anne was so angry at Sarah Churchill that she refused to see her again.

b. Jean-Pierre's ambitious travel plans made it impossible for him to comply with the residency requirement for in-state tuition.

c. The parade moved off of the street and onto the beach.

d. The frightened refugees intend on making the dangerous trek across the mountains.

e. What type of a wedding are you planning?

18e Do not rely heavily on clichés.

The pioneer who first announced that he had "slept like a log" no doubt amused his companions with a fresh, unlikely comparison. Today, however, that comparison is a cliché, a saying that can no longer add emphasis or surprise.

hackerhandbooks.com/bedhandbook

e Word choice > Exercises: 18–6 and 18–7

✓ Word choice > LearningCurve: Word choice and appropriate language

EXERCISE 18–5 *Possible revisions:*

a. Queen Anne was so angry with Sarah Churchill that she refused to see her again.

b. Correct

c. The parade moved off the street and onto the beach.

d. The frightened refugees intend to make the dangerous trek across the mountains.

e. What type of wedding are you planning?

To see just how dully predictable clichés are, put your hand over the right-hand column in the following list and then finish the phrases on the left.

cool as a	cucumber
beat around	the bush
blind as a	bat
busy as a	bee, beaver
crystal	clear
dead as a	doornail
out of the frying pan and	into the fire
light as a	feather
like a bull	in a china shop
playing with	fire
selling like	hotcakes
starting out at the bottom	of the ladder
water under the	bridge
white as a	sheet, ghost
avoid clichés like the	plague

The solution for clichés is simple: Just delete them or rewrite them.

▶ When I received a full scholarship from my second-choice
     ~~felt pressured to settle for second best.~~
school, I ~~found myself between a rock and a hard place.~~
                     ᴧ

Sometimes you can write around a cliché by adding an element of surprise. One student revised a cliché about butterflies in her stomach like this:

If all of the action in my stomach is caused by butterflies, there must be a horde of them, with horseshoes on.

The image of butterflies wearing horseshoes is fresh and unlikely, not predictable like the original cliché.

18f Use figures of speech with care.

A figure of speech is an expression that uses words imaginatively (rather than literally) to make abstract ideas concrete. Most often, figures of speech compare two seemingly unlike things to reveal surprising similarities.

In a *simile*, the writer makes the comparison explicitly, usually by introducing it with *like* or *as: By the time cotton had to be picked, Grandfather's neck was as red as the clay he plowed.* In a *metaphor*, the *like* or *as* is omitted, and the comparison is implied. For example, in the Old Testament Song of Solomon, a young woman compares the man she loves to a fruit tree: *With great delight I sat in his shadow, and his fruit was sweet to my taste.*

Although figures of speech are useful devices, writers sometimes use them without thinking through the images they evoke. The result is sometimes a *mixed metaphor*, the combination of two or more images that don't make sense together.

> ► Crossing Utah's salt flats in his new convertible, my father flew
> at jet speed.
> ~~under a full head of steam.~~
>   ∧

Flew suggests an airplane, whereas *under a full head of steam* suggests a steamboat or a train. To clarify the image, the writer should stick with one comparison or the other.

> ► Our manager decided to put all controversial issues
>
> ~~in a holding pattern~~ on a back burner until after the
>
> annual meeting.

Here the writer is mixing airplanes and stoves. Simply deleting one of the images corrects the problem.

EXERCISE 18–8 Edit the following sentences to replace worn-out expressions and clarify mixed figures of speech. Possible revisions appear in the back of the book. *More practice:* e ✓

> the color drained from his face.
> When he heard about the accident, ~~he turned white as a~~
> ^
> ~~sheet.~~

a. John stormed into the room like a bull in a china shop.

b. Some people insist that they'll always be there for you, even when they haven't been before.

c. The Cubs easily beat the Mets, who were in the soup early in the game today at Wrigley Field.

d. We ironed out the sticky spots in our relationship.

e. My mother accused me of beating around the bush when in fact I was just talking off the top of my head.

hackerhandbooks.com/bedhandbook

e Word choice > Exercises: 18–9 and 18–10

✓ Word choice > LearningCurve: Word choice and appropriate language

EXERCISE 18–8 *Possible revisions:*

a. John stormed into the room like a hurricane.

b. Some people insist that they'll always be available to help, even when they haven't been before.

c. The Cubs easily beat the Mets, who were in trouble early in the game today at Wrigley Field.

d. We worked out the problems in our relationship.

e. My mother accused me of evading her questions when in fact I was just saying the first thing that came to mind.

PART V

Grammatical Sentences

19 Repair sentence fragments.

A sentence fragment is a word group that pretends to be a sentence. Sentence fragments are easy to recognize when they appear out of context, like these:

> When the cat leaped onto the table.

> Running for the bus.

When fragments appear next to related sentences, however, they are harder to spot.

> We had just sat down to dinner. When the cat leaped onto the table.

> I tripped and twisted my ankle. Running for the bus.

Recognizing sentence fragments

To be a sentence, a word group must consist of at least one full independent clause. An independent clause includes a subject and a verb, and it either stands alone or could stand alone.

To test whether a word group is a complete sentence or a fragment, use the flowchart on page 279. By using the flowchart, you can see exactly why *When the cat leaped onto the table* is a fragment: It has a subject (*cat*) and a verb (*leaped*), but it begins with a subordinating word (*When*). *Running for the bus* is a fragment because it lacks a subject and a verb (*Running* is a verbal, not a verb). (See also 48b and 48e.)

TEACHING TIP

Use grammar and punctuation exercises, such as those in the handbook's print pages or e-Pages, as a first step in teaching a pattern.

ADDITIONAL RESOURCE ON TEACHING BASIC WRITING

Adler-Kassner, Linda, and Gregory R. Glau. *The Bedford Bibliography for Teachers of Basic Writing*. 2nd ed. Boston: Bedford, 2005. Print. Compiled by members of the Conference on Basic Writing, this text provides an annotated list of hundreds of books, articles, and periodicals selected specifically for their value to teachers of basic writing. Topics include history and theory, pedagogical issues, curriculum development, and administration of basic writing programs. The complete text is available online at bedfordstmartins.com/basicbib.

Test for fragments

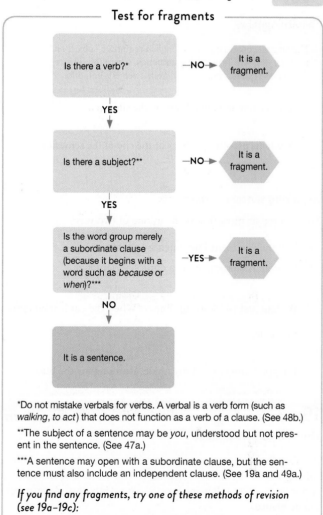

Is there a verb?* —NO→ It is a fragment.

↓ YES

Is there a subject?** —NO→ It is a fragment.

↓ YES

Is the word group merely a subordinate clause (because it begins with a word such as *because* or *when*)?*** —YES→ It is a fragment.

↓ NO

It is a sentence.

*Do not mistake verbals for verbs. A verbal is a verb form (such as *walking, to act*) that does not function as a verb of a clause. (See 48b.)

**The subject of a sentence may be *you*, understood but not present in the sentence. (See 47a.)

***A sentence may open with a subordinate clause, but the sentence must also include an independent clause. (See 19a and 49a.)

If you find any fragments, try one of these methods of revision (see 19a–19c):

1. Attach the fragment to a nearby sentence.
2. Rewrite the fragment as a complete sentence.

SCHOLARS ON ERROR

Lunsford, Andrea A., and Karen J. Lunsford. "'Mistakes Are a Fact of Life': A National Comparative Study." *College Composition and Communication* 59.4 (2008): 781–806. Print. The authors recall previous studies of error as they ask anew the question "What errors are college students making as they write?" From their reading and coding of 877 student papers, the study authors conclude that word processing technology and an emphasis on research writing have led to two of the new top errors: wrong word and incomplete or missing documentation. The authors compare their findings with the findings in Andrea A. Lunsford and Robert J. Connors's 1986 study.

> **Multilingual**

Unlike some other languages, English requires a subject and a verb in every sentence (except in commands, where the subject *you* is understood but not present: *Sit down*). See 30a and 30b.

▶ ~~Is~~ often hot and humid during the summer.
   _It is_ ∧

▶ Students usually very busy at the end of the semester.
   are ∧

Repairing sentence fragments

You can repair most fragments in one of two ways:

- Pull the fragment into a nearby sentence.
- Rewrite the fragment as a complete sentence.

▶ We had just sat down to dinner. ~~When~~ the cat leaped onto the table.
   when ∧

▶ I tripped and twisted my ankle. ~~Running for the bus.~~
   Running for the bus, ∧

19a Attach fragmented subordinate clauses or turn them into sentences.

A subordinate clause is patterned like a sentence, with both a subject and a verb, but it begins with a word that marks it as subordinate. The following words commonly introduce subordinate clauses.

after	as	because	even though	if
although	as if	before	how	since

SCHOLARS ON ERROR

Beason, Larry. "Ethos and Error: How Business People React to Errors." *College Composition and Communication* 53.1 (2001): 33–64. Print. To understand the impact of error on nonacademic readers, Beason examined the responses of fourteen business professionals to a variety of error types. He concludes that readers in business judge the seriousness of errors in part by how much they think readers inside and outside the organization will be bothered by the errors. Teachers cannot assume, he argues, that some types of errors are more serious than others; nor can students assume that teachers are just being picky when they mark seemingly nonserious errors. Rather, teachers and students need to appreciate the larger ways that errors affect and "endanger" a writer's ethos and can reflect on the writer's overall capabilities.

so that	though	when	which	whom
than	unless	where	while	whose
that	until	whether	who	why

Subordinate clauses function within sentences as adjectives, as adverbs, or as nouns. They cannot stand alone. (See 48e.)

Most fragmented clauses beg to be pulled into a sentence nearby.

▶ Americans have come to fear the West Nile virus. ~~Because~~ *because*

  it is transmitted by the common mosquito.

  Because introduces a subordinate clause, so it cannot stand alone. (For punctuation of subordinate clauses appearing at the end of a sentence, see 33f.)

▶ Although psychiatrist Peter Kramer expresses concerns

  about Prozac. ~~Many~~ *many* other doctors believe that the

  benefits of antidepressants outweigh the risks.

  Although introduces a subordinate clause, so it cannot stand alone. (For punctuation of subordinate clauses at the beginning of a sentence, see 32b.)

If a fragmented clause cannot be attached to a nearby sentence or if you feel that attaching it would be awkward, try turning the clause into a sentence. The simplest way to do this is to delete the opening word or words that mark it as subordinate.

▶ Population increases and uncontrolled development are

  Across
  taking a deadly toll on the environment. ~~So that across~~ the

  globe, fragile ecosystems are collapsing.

19b Attach fragmented phrases or turn them into sentences.

Like subordinate clauses, phrases function within sentences as adjectives, as adverbs, or as nouns. They cannot stand alone. Fragmented phrases are often prepositional or verbal phrases; sometimes they are appositives, words or word groups that rename nouns or pronouns. (See 48a, 48b, and 48c.)

Often a fragmented phrase may simply be pulled into a nearby sentence.

▶ The archaeologists worked slowly./~~,~~ ~~Examining~~ ^examining and

labeling every pottery shard they uncovered.

The word group beginning with *Examining* is a verbal phrase.

▶ The patient displayed symptoms of ALS./~~,~~ ^a ~~A~~ neuro-

degenerative disease.

A neurodegenerative disease is an appositive renaming the noun *ALS*. (For punctuation of appositives, see 32e.)

If a fragmented phrase cannot be pulled into a nearby sentence effectively, turn the phrase into a sentence. You may need to add a subject, a verb, or both.

▶ In the training session, Jamie explained how to access our

new database. ^She also taught us ~~Also~~ how to submit expense reports and

request vendor payments.

The revision turns the fragmented phrase into a sentence by adding a subject and a verb.

SCHOLARS ON ERROR

Connors, Robert J. *Composition-Rhetoric: Backgrounds, Theory, and Pedagogy*. Ithaca: Cornell UP, 1997. 112–70. Print. Connors traces American attitudes toward grammar over the past two centuries. At times, class structures have contributed to an obsessive concern for correctness, with elites condemning "vulgarities" and the lower classes looking to improve themselves through language. In colleges, instructors over the years have tried to focus on rhetoric, but underprepared students and heavy workloads have often led them to focus on correctness (it's easier to mark errors than to comment on rhetoric). Connors writes that we will no doubt continue to investigate "how the balance between rhetoric and mechanics can best be struck."

19c Attach other fragmented word groups or turn them into sentences.

Other word groups that are commonly fragmented include parts of compound predicates, lists, and examples introduced by *for example*, *in addition*, or similar expressions.

Parts of compound predicates

A predicate consists of a verb and its objects, complements, and modifiers (see 47b). A compound predicate includes two or more predicates joined with a coordinating conjunction such as *and*, *but*, or *or*. Because the parts of a compound predicate have the same subject, they should appear in the same sentence.

▶ The woodpecker finch of the Galápagos Islands carefully
  selects a twig of a certain size and shape. ~~And~~ and then uses this
  tool to pry out grubs from trees.

  The subject is *finch*, and the compound predicate is *selects . . . and . . .
  uses*. (For punctuation of compound predicates, see 33a.)

Lists

To correct a fragmented list, often you can attach it to a nearby sentence with a colon or a dash. (See 35a and 39a.)

▶ It has been said that there are only three indigenous
  American art forms. ~~Musical~~ : musical comedy, jazz, and soap opera.

  Sometimes terms like *especially*, *namely*, *like*, and *such as* introduce fragmented lists. Such fragments can usually be attached to the preceding sentence.

► In the twentieth century, the South produced some great American writers. ~~Such~~ *such* as Flannery O'Connor, William Faulkner, Alice Walker, Tennessee Williams, and Thomas Wolfe.

Examples introduced by for example, in addition, *or similar expressions*

Other expressions that introduce examples or explanations can lead to unintentional fragments. Although you may begin a sentence with some of the following words or phrases, make sure that what follows has a subject and a verb.

also	for example	mainly
and	for instance	or
but	in addition	that is

Often the easiest solution is to turn the fragment into a sentence.

► In his memoir, Primo Levi describes the horrors of living in a concentration camp. For example, ~~working~~ *he worked* without food and ~~suffering~~ *suffered* emotional abuse.

The writer corrected this fragment by adding a subject —*he*— and substituting verbs for the verbals *working* and *suffering*.

19d Exception: A fragment may be used for effect.

Writers occasionally use sentence fragments for special purposes.

FOR EMPHASIS   Following the dramatic Americanization of their children, even my parents grew more publicly confident. *Especially my mother.*

— Richard Rodriguez

TO ANSWER A QUESTION	Are these new drug tests 100 percent reliable? *Not in the opinion of most experts.*
TRANSITIONS	*And now the opposing arguments.*
EXCLAMATIONS	*Not again!*
IN ADVERTISING	*Fewer carbs. Improved taste.*

Although fragments are sometimes appropriate, writers and readers do not always agree on when they are appropriate. That's why you will find it safer to write in complete sentences.

EXERCISE 19–1 Repair any fragment by attaching it to a nearby sentence or by rewriting it as a complete sentence. If a word group is correct, write "correct" after it. Possible revisions appear in the back of the book. *More practice:* e ✓

One Greek island that should not be missed is Mykonos. A

vacation spot for Europeans and a playground for the rich

and famous.

a.   Listening to the CD her sister had sent, Mia was overcome with a mix of emotions. Happiness, homesickness, and nostalgia.

b.   Cortés and his soldiers were astonished when they looked down from the mountains and saw Tenochtitlán. The magnificent capital of the Aztecs.

c.   Although my spoken Spanish is not very good. I can read the language with ease.

d.   There are several reasons for not eating meat. One reason being that dangerous chemicals are used throughout the various stages of meat production.

e.   To learn how to sculpt beauty from everyday life. This is my intention in studying art and archaeology.

hackerhandbooks.com/bedhandbook

e Grammatical sentences > Exercises: 19–3 to 19–7

✓ Grammatical sentences > LearningCurve: Sentence fragments

EXERCISE 19–1   *Possible revisions:*

a.   Listening to the CD her sister had sent, Mia was overcome with a mix of emotions: happiness, homesickness, and nostalgia.

b.   Cortés and his soldiers were astonished when they looked down from the mountains and saw Tenochtitlán, the magnificent capital of the Aztecs.

c.   Although my spoken Spanish is not very good, I can read the language with ease.

d.   There are several reasons for not eating meat. One reason is that dangerous chemicals are used throughout the various stages of meat production.

e.   To learn how to sculpt beauty from everyday life is my intention in studying art and archaeology.

EXERCISE 19–2 Repair each fragment in the following passage by attaching it to a sentence nearby or by rewriting it as a complete sentence. *More practice:* e ✓

Digital technology has revolutionized information delivery. Forever blurring the lines between information and entertainment. Yesterday's readers of books and newspapers are today's readers of e-books and blogs. Countless readers have moved on from print information entirely. Choosing instead to point, click, and scroll their way through a text online or on an e-reader. Once a nation of people spoon-fed television commercials and the six o'clock evening news. We are now seemingly addicted to YouTube and social media. Remember the family trip when Dad or Mom wrestled with a road map? On the way to St. Louis or Seattle? No wrestling is required with a GPS device. Unless it's Mom and Dad wrestling over who gets to program the address. Accessing information now seems to be America's favorite pastime. John Horrigan, associate director for research at the Pew Internet and American Life Project, reports that nearly half of American adults are "elite" users of technology. Who are "highly engaged" with digital content. As a country, we embrace information and communication technologies. Which now include iPods, smartphones, and tablets. Among children and adolescents, social media and other technology use are well established. For activities like socializing, gaming, and information gathering.

20 Revise run-on sentences.

Run-on sentences are independent clauses that have not been joined correctly. An independent clause is a word group that can stand alone as a sentence. (See 49a.) When two independent clauses appear in one sentence, they must be joined in one of these ways:

hackerhandbooks.com/bedhandbook

e Grammatical sentences > Exercises: 19–3 to 19–7
✓ Grammatical sentences > LearningCurve: Sentence fragments

EXERCISE 19–2 *Possible revisions:*

Digital technology has revolutionized information delivery, forever blurring the lines between information and entertainment. Yesterday's readers of books and newspapers are today's readers of e-books and blogs. Countless readers have moved on from print information entirely, choosing instead to point, click, and scroll their way through a text online or on an e-reader. Once a nation of people spoon-fed television commercials and the six o'clock evening news, we are now seemingly addicted to YouTube and social media. Remember the family trip when Dad or Mom wrestled with a road map on the way to St. Louis or Seattle? No wrestling is required with a GPS device — unless it's Mom and Dad wrestling over who gets to program the address. Accessing

- with a comma and a coordinating conjunction (*and, but, or, nor, for, so, yet*)
- with a semicolon (or occasionally with a colon or a dash)

Recognizing run-on sentences

There are two types of run-on sentences. When a writer puts no mark of punctuation and no coordinating conjunction between independent clauses, the result is called a *fused sentence*.

      — INDEPENDENT CLAUSE ——⌐ ⌐———

FUSED   Air pollution poses risks to all humans it can be

— INDEPENDENT CLAUSE —⌐

deadly for asthma sufferers.

A far more common type of run-on sentence is the *comma splice*—two or more independent clauses joined with a comma but without a coordinating conjunction. In some comma splices, the comma appears alone.

COMMA   Air pollution poses risks to all humans, it can be
SPLICE   deadly for asthma sufferers.

In other comma splices, the comma is accompanied by a joining word that is *not* a coordinating conjunction. There are only seven coordinating conjunctions in English: *and, but, or, nor, for, so,* and *yet.*

COMMA   Air pollution poses risks to all humans, however, it can
SPLICE   be deadly for asthma sufferers.

However is a transitional expression, not a coordinating conjunction, and cannot be used with only a comma to join two independent clauses (see 20b).

Revising run-on sentences

To revise a run-on sentence, you have four choices (see pp. 288–89).

EXERCISE 19–2   *Possible revisions (continued):*

information now seems to be America's favorite pastime. John Horrigan, associate director for research at the Pew Internet and American Life Project, reports that nearly half of American adults are "elite" users of technology who are "highly engaged" with digital content. As a country, we embrace information and communication technologies, which now include iPods, smartphones, and tablets. Among children and adolescents, social media and other technology use are well established for activities like socializing, gaming, and information gathering.

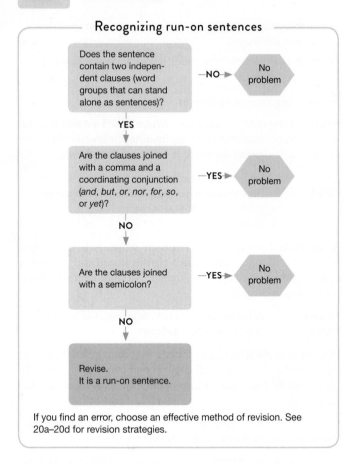

Recognizing run-on sentences

Does the sentence contain two independent clauses (word groups that can stand alone as sentences)? —NO→ No problem

YES ↓

Are the clauses joined with a comma and a coordinating conjunction (*and, but, or, nor, for, so,* or *yet*)? —YES→ No problem

NO ↓

Are the clauses joined with a semicolon? —YES→ No problem

NO ↓

Revise.
It is a run-on sentence.

If you find an error, choose an effective method of revision. See 20a–20d for revision strategies.

1. Use a comma and a coordinating conjunction (*and, but, or, nor, for, so, yet*).

▶ Air pollution poses risks to all humans, but it can be deadly for people with asthma.

TEACHING TIP

It often helps to have small groups of students take charge of teaching a few grammar concepts. Assign students to tackle concepts such as fragments and run-ons and to prepare a ten-minute mini-lesson in which they show examples and discuss revision strategies. If the class is online, the students can prepare a few slides that they upload to the course Web site.

2. Use a semicolon (or, if appropriate, a colon or a dash). A semicolon may be used alone; it can also be accompanied by a transitional expression.

▶ Air pollution poses risks to all humans⁄; it can be deadly for people with asthma.

▶ Air pollution poses risks to all humans⁄; however, it can be deadly for people with asthma.

3. Make the clauses into separate sentences.

▶ Air pollution poses risks to all humans⁄. It can be deadly for people with asthma.

4. Restructure the sentence; try subordinating a clause.

▶ Although air ~~Air~~ pollution poses risks to all humans, it can be deadly for people with asthma.

One of these revision techniques usually works better than the others for a particular sentence. The fourth technique, the one requiring the most extensive revision, is often the most effective.

20a Consider separating the clauses with a comma and a coordinating conjunction.

There are seven coordinating conjunctions in English: *and, but, or, nor, for, so,* and *yet*. When a coordinating conjunction joins independent clauses, it is usually preceded by a comma. (See 32a.)

▶ Some lesson plans include exercises, but completing them should not be the focus of all class periods.

▶ Many government officials privately admit that the poly-

graph is unreliable, ~~however,~~ *yet* they continue to use it as a

security measure.

However is a transitional expression, not a coordinating conjunction, so it cannot be used with only a comma to join independent
clauses. (See also 20b.)

20b Consider separating the clauses with a semicolon, a colon, or a dash.

When the independent clauses are closely related and their relation is clear without a coordinating conjunction, a semicolon is
an acceptable method of revision. (See 34a.)

▶ Tragedy depicts the individual confronted with the fact

of death/; comedy depicts the adaptability of human nature.

A semicolon is required between independent clauses that
have been linked with a transitional expression (such as *however,*
therefore, moreover, in fact, or *for example*). For a longer list, see 34b.

▶ The timber wolf looks like a German shepherd/; however,

the wolf has longer legs, larger feet, and a wider head.

▶ In his film adaptation of the short story "Killings," director

Todd Field changed key details of the plot/; in fact, he

added whole scenes that do not appear in the story.

A colon or a dash may be more appropriate if the first independent clause introduces the second or if the second clause

summarizes or explains the first. (See 35a and 39a.) In formal writing, the colon is usually preferred to the dash.

▶ Nuclear waste is hazardous: ~~this~~ **This** is an indisputable fact.

▶ The female black widow spider is often a widow of her own making, ~~—~~ she has been known to eat her partner after mating.

A colon is an appropriate method of revision if the first independent clause introduces a quoted sentence.

▶ Nobel Peace Prize winner Al Gore had this to say about climate change: "The truth is that our circumstances are not only new; they are completely different than they have ever been in all of human history."

20c Consider making the clauses into separate sentences.

▶ Why should we spend money on space exploration? ~~/~~ **We** ~~we~~ have enough underfunded programs here on Earth.

A question and a statement should be separate sentences.

▶ Some studies have suggested that sexual relationships set bonobos apart from common chimpanzees. **According** ~~according~~ to Stanford (1998), these differences have been exaggerated.

Using a comma alone to join two independent clauses creates a comma splice. (See also 61a on citing sources in APA style.)

NOTE: When two quoted independent clauses are divided by explanatory words, make each clause its own sentence.

▶ "It's always smart to learn from your mistakes," quipped my
                 "It's
supervisor,/ "it's even smarter to learn from the mistakes of
            ∧

others."

20d Consider restructuring the sentence, perhaps by subordinating one of the clauses.

If one of the independent clauses is less important than the other, turn the less important clause into a subordinate clause or phrase. (For more about subordination, see 14, especially the chart on p. 237.)

▶ One of the most famous advertising slogans is Wheaties
                               which
cereal's "Breakfast of Champions," ~~it~~ associated the cereal
                                   ∧

with famous athletes.

   Although many
▶ ~~Many~~ scholars dismiss the abominable snowman of the
  ∧
Himalayas as a myth, some scientists claim it may be a

kind of ape.

▶ Mary McLeod Bethune ,was the seventeenth child of former
                       ∧

slaves, ~~she~~ founded the National Council of Negro Women

in 1935.

Minor ideas in these sentences are now expressed in subordinate clauses or phrases.

EXERCISE 20–1   *Possible revisions:*

a. The city had one public swimming pool that stayed packed with children all summer long.

b. The building is being renovated, so at times we have no heat, water, or electricity.

c. The view was not what the travel agent had described. Where were the rolling hills and the shimmering rivers?

d. Walker's coming-of-age novel is set against a gloomy scientific backdrop; the Earth's rotation has begun to slow down.

e. City officials had good reason to fear a major earthquake: Most [*or* most] of the business district was built on landfill.

EXERCISE 20–1 Revise the following run-on sentences using the method of revision suggested in brackets. Possible revisions appear in the back of the book. *More practice:* e ✓

> *Because*
> Orville had been obsessed with his weight as a teenager, he
> ^
> rarely ate anything sweet. [*Restructure the sentence.*]

a. The city had one public swimming pool, it stayed packed with children all summer long. [*Restructure the sentence.*]

b. The building is being renovated, therefore at times we have no heat, water, or electricity. [*Use a comma and a coordinating conjunction.*]

c. The view was not what the travel agent had described, where were the rolling hills and the shimmering rivers? [*Make two sentences.*]

d. Walker's coming-of-age novel is set against a gloomy scientific backdrop, the Earth's rotation has begun to slow down. [*Use a semicolon.*]

e. City officials had good reason to fear a major earthquake, most of the business district was built on landfill. [*Use a colon.*]

EXERCISE 20–2 Revise any run-on sentences using a technique that you find effective. If a sentence is correct, write "correct" after it. Possible revisions appear in the back of the book. *More practice:* e ✓

> Crossing so many time zones on an eight-hour flight, I knew
> *but*
> I would be tired when I arrived, ~~however,~~ I was too excited
> ^
> to sleep on the plane.

a. Wind power for the home is a supplementary source of energy, it can be combined with electricity, gas, or solar energy.

b. Aidan viewed Sofia Coppola's *Lost in Translation* three times and then wrote a paper describing the film as the work of a mysterious modern painter.

hackerhandbooks.com/bedhandbook

e Grammatical sentences > Exercises: 20–4 to 20–9
✓ Grammatical sentences > LearningCurve: Run-on sentences

EXERCISE 20–2 *Possible revisions:*

a. Wind power for the home is a supplementary source of energy that can be combined with electricity, gas, or solar energy.

b. Correct

c. In the Middle Ages, when the streets of London were dangerous places, it was safer to travel by boat along the Thames.

d. "He's not drunk," I said. "He's in a state of diabetic shock."

e. Are you able to endure extreme angle turns, high speeds, frequent jumps, and occasional crashes? Then supermoto racing may be a sport for you.

c. In the Middle Ages, the streets of London were dangerous places, it was safer to travel by boat along the Thames.

d. "He's not drunk," I said, "he's in a state of diabetic shock."

e. Are you able to endure extreme angle turns, high speeds, frequent jumps, and occasional crashes, then supermoto racing may be a sport for you.

EXERCISE 20-3   In the following rough draft, revise any run-on sentences. *More practice:* e ✓

Some parents and educators argue that requiring uniforms in public schools would improve student behavior and performance. They think that uniforms give students a more professional attitude toward school, moreover, they believe that uniforms help create a sense of community among students from diverse backgrounds. But parents and educators should consider the drawbacks to requiring uniforms in public schools.

Uniforms do create a sense of community, they do this, however, by stamping out individuality. Youth is a time to express originality, it is a time to develop a sense of self. One important way young people express their identities is through the clothes they wear. The self-patrolled dress code of high school students may be stricter than any school-imposed code, nevertheless, trying to control dress habits from above will only lead to resentment or to mindless conformity.

If children are going to act like adults, they need to be treated like adults, they need to be allowed to make their own choices. Telling young people what to wear to school merely prolongs their childhood. Requiring uniforms undermines the educational purpose of public schools, which is not just to teach facts and figures but to help young people grow into adults who are responsible for making their own choices.

hackerhandbooks.com/bedhandbook

e Grammatical sentences > Exercises: 20–4 to 20–9
✓ Grammatical sentences > LearningCurve: Run-on sentences

EXERCISE 20-3   *Possible revisions:*

Some parents and educators argue that requiring uniforms in public schools would improve student behavior and performance. They think that uniforms give students a more professional attitude toward school; moreover, they believe that uniforms help create a sense of community among students from diverse backgrounds. But parents and educators should consider the drawbacks to requiring uniforms in public schools.

Although uniforms do create a sense of community, they do this by stamping out individuality. Youth is a time to express originality, a time to develop a sense of self. One important way young people express their identities is through the clothes they wear. The self-patrolled dress code of high school students may be stricter than any school-imposed code.

21 Make subjects and verbs agree.

In the present tense, verbs agree with their subjects in number (singular or plural) and in person (first, second, third): *I sing, you sing, she sings, we sing, they sing.* Even if your ear recognizes the standard subject-verb combinations in 21a, you will no doubt encounter tricky situations such as those described in 21b–21k.

21a Learn to recognize standard subject-verb combinations.

This section describes the basic guidelines for making present-tense verbs agree with their subjects. The present-tense ending *-s* (or *-es*) is used on a verb if its subject is third-person singular (*he, she, it,* and singular nouns); otherwise the verb takes no ending. Consider, for example, the present-tense forms of the verbs *love* and *try,* given at the beginning of the chart on page 296.

The verb *be* varies from this pattern; it has special forms in *both* the present and the past tense (see the end of the chart).

If you aren't sure of the standard forms, use the charts on pages 296 and 297 as you proofread your work. See also 27c on *-s* endings of regular and irregular verbs.

21b Make the verb agree with its subject, not with a word that comes between.

Word groups often come between the subject and the verb. Such word groups, usually modifying the subject, may contain a noun that at first appears to be the subject. By mentally stripping away such modifiers, you can isolate the noun that is in fact the subject.

EXERCISE 20-3 *Possible revisions (continued):*

Nevertheless, trying to control dress habits from above will only lead to resentment or to mindless conformity.

If children are going to act like adults, they need to be treated like adults and to be allowed to make their own choices. Telling young people what to wear to school merely prolongs their childhood. Requiring uniforms undermines the educational purpose of public schools, which is not just to teach facts and figures but to help young people grow into adults who are responsible for making their own choices.

Subject-verb agreement at a glance

Present-tense forms of *love* and *try* (typical verbs)

	SINGULAR		PLURAL	
FIRST PERSON	I	love	we	love
SECOND PERSON	you	love	you	love
THIRD PERSON	he/she/it*	loves	they**	love

	SINGULAR		PLURAL	
FIRST PERSON	I	try	we	try
SECOND PERSON	you	try	you	try
THIRD PERSON	he/she/it*	tries	they**	try

Present-tense forms of *have*

	SINGULAR		PLURAL	
FIRST PERSON	I	have	we	have
SECOND PERSON	you	have	you	have
THIRD PERSON	he/she/it*	has	they**	have

Present-tense forms of *do* (including negative forms)

	SINGULAR		PLURAL	
FIRST PERSON	I	do/don't	we	do/don't
SECOND PERSON	you	do/don't	you	do/don't
THIRD PERSON	he/she/it*	does/doesn't	they**	do/don't

Present-tense and past-tense forms of *be*

	SINGULAR		PLURAL	
FIRST PERSON	I	am/was	we	are/were
SECOND PERSON	you	are/were	you	are/were
THIRD PERSON	he/she/it*	is/was	they**	are/were

*And singular nouns (*child*, *Roger*)

**And plural nouns (*children*, *the Mannings*)

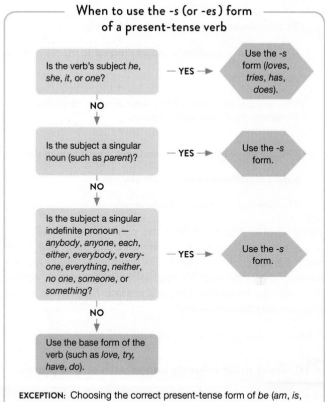

When to use the -s (or -es) form of a present-tense verb

Is the verb's subject *he, she, it,* or *one*? — YES → Use the -s form (*loves, tries, has, does*).

NO ↓

Is the subject a singular noun (such as *parent*)? — YES → Use the -s form.

NO ↓

Is the subject a singular indefinite pronoun — *anybody, anyone, each, either, everybody, everyone, everything, neither, no one, someone,* or *something*? — YES → Use the -s form.

NO ↓

Use the base form of the verb (such as *love, try, have, do*).

EXCEPTION: Choosing the correct present-tense form of *be* (*am, is,* or *are*) is not quite so simple. See the chart on the previous page for both present- and past-tense forms of *be*.

ESL TIP: Do not use the -s form of a verb if it follows a modal verb such as *can, must,* or *should* or another helping verb. (See 28c.)

TEACHING TIP

Require students to maintain editing logs (lists of their own errors, with examples and with corrections). For more on maintaining an editing log, see "Teaching Grammar and Punctuation" in the free Bedford/ St. Martin's instructor resource *Teaching with Hacker Handbooks* (hackerhandbooks.com/teaching).

The *samples* on the tray in the lab *need* testing.

▶ High levels of air pollution causes damage to the respiratory

tract.

> The subject is *levels*, not *pollution*. Strip away the phrase *of air pollu-tion* to hear the correct verb: *levels cause*.

▶ The slaughter of pandas for their pelts ~~have~~ has caused the

panda population to decline drastically.

> The subject is *slaughter*, not *pandas* or *pelts*.

NOTE: Phrases beginning with the prepositions *as well as, in addition to, accompanied by, together with,* and *along with* do not make a singular subject plural. *The governor as well as his press secretary was on the plane.* To emphasize that two people were on the plane, the writer could use *and* instead: *The governor and his press secretary were on the plane.*

21c Treat most subjects joined with *and* as plural.

A subject with two or more parts is said to be compound. If the parts are connected with *and*, the subject is nearly always plural.

Leon and Jan often *jog* together.

▶ The Supreme Court's willingness to hear the case and

its affirmation of the original decision ~~has~~ have set a new

precedent.

SCHOLARS ON SUBJECT-VERB AGREEMENT

Shaughnessy, Mina P. *Errors and Expectations: A Guide for the Teacher of Basic Writing.* New York: Oxford UP, 1979. 16–43. Print. Shaughnessy points out that students who are confused about the inflectional system in Standard English will make far more errors in subject-verb agreement than other students will. She argues that such students need direct instruction in the use of the *-s* verb form.

EXCEPTIONS: When the parts of the subject form a single unit or when they refer to the same person or thing, treat the subject as singular.

> Fish and chips was a last-minute addition to the menu.

> Sue's friend and adviser was surprised by her decision.

When a compound subject is preceded by *each* or *every*, treat it as singular.

> Each tree, shrub, and vine needs to be sprayed.

> Every car, truck, and van is required to pass inspection.

This exception does not apply when a compound subject is followed by *each*: *Alan and Marcia each have different ideas.*

21d With subjects joined with *or* or *nor* (or with *either . . . or* or *neither . . . nor*), make the verb agree with the part of the subject nearer to the verb.

> A driver's *license* or credit *card is* required.

> A driver's *license* or two credit *cards are* required.

▶ If an infant or a child ~~have~~ has a high fever, call a doctor.

▶ Neither the chief financial officer nor the marketing
    managers ~~was~~ were able to convince the client to reconsider.

> The verb must be matched with the part of the subject closer to it: *child has* in the first sentence, *managers were* in the second.

NOTE: If one part of the subject is singular and the other is plural, put the plural one last to avoid awkwardness.

WRITERS ON WRITING

When I say writing, O believe me, it is rewriting that I have chiefly in mind.   — Robert Louis Stevenson

21e Treat most indefinite pronouns as singular.

Indefinite pronouns are pronouns that do not refer to specific persons or things. The following commonly used indefinite pronouns are singular.

anybody	each	everyone	nobody	somebody
anyone	either	everything	no one	someone
anything	everybody	neither	nothing	something

Many of these words appear to have plural meanings, and they are often treated as such in casual speech. In formal written English, however, they are nearly always treated as singular.

Everyone on the team *supports* the coach.

▶ Each of the essays ~~have~~ been graded.
  has

▶ Nobody who participated in the clinical trials ~~were~~ given a
  was

placebo.

> The subjects of these sentences are *Each* and *Nobody*. These indefinite pronouns are third-person singular, so the verbs must be *has* and *was*.

A few indefinite pronouns (*all, any, none, some*) may be singular or plural depending on the noun or pronoun they refer to.

SINGULAR *Some* of our *luggage was* lost.

None of his *advice makes* sense.

PLURAL *Some* of the *rocks are* slippery.

None of the *eggs were* broken.

NOTE: When the meaning of *none* is emphatically "not one," *none* may be treated as singular: *None* [meaning "Not one"] *of the eggs was broken.* Using *not one* is sometimes clearer: *Not one of the eggs was broken.*

21f Treat collective nouns as singular unless the meaning is clearly plural.

Collective nouns such as *jury, committee, audience, crowd, troop, family,* and *couple* name a class or a group. In American English, collective nouns are nearly always treated as singular: They emphasize the group as a unit. Occasionally, when there is some reason to draw attention to the individual members of the group, a collective noun may be treated as plural. (See also 22b.)

SINGULAR   The *class respects* the teacher.

PLURAL   The *class are* debating among themselves.

To underscore the notion of individuality in the second sentence, many writers would add a clearly plural noun.

PLURAL   The class *members are* debating among themselves.

▶ The board of trustees ~~meet~~ meets in Denver twice a year.

  The board as a whole meets; there is no reason to draw attention to its individual members.

▶ A young couple ~~was~~ were arguing about politics while holding hands.

  The meaning is clearly plural. Only separate individuals can argue and hold hands.

NOTE: The phrase *the number* is treated as singular, *a number* as plural.

SINGULAR   *The number* of school-age children *is* declining.

PLURAL   *A number* of children *are* attending the wedding.

NOTE: In general, when fractions or units of measurement are used with a singular noun, treat them as singular; when they are used with a plural noun, treat them as plural.

SINGULAR   *Three-fourths* of the salad *has* been eaten.

SINGULAR   Twenty *inches* of wallboard *was* covered with mud.

PLURAL   *One-fourth* of the drivers *were* texting.

PLURAL   Two *pounds* of blueberries *were* used to make the pie.

21g Make the verb agree with its subject even when the subject follows the verb.

Verbs ordinarily follow subjects. When this normal order is reversed, it is easy to become confused. Sentences beginning with *there is* or *there are* (or *there was* or *there were*) are inverted; the subject follows the verb.

There *are* surprisingly few *honeybees* left in southern China.

                    were
▶ There ~~was~~ a social worker and a journalist at the meeting.
           ∧

The subject, *worker and journalist*, is plural, so the verb must be *were*.

Occasionally you may decide to invert a sentence for variety or effect. When you do so, check to make sure that your subject and verb agree.

▶ Of particular concern ~~is~~ ^are^ penicillin and tetracycline, antibiotics used to make animals more resistant to disease.

> The subject, *penicillin and tetracycline*, is plural, so the verb must be *are*.

21h Make the verb agree with its subject, not with a subject complement.

One basic sentence pattern in English consists of a subject, a linking verb, and a subject complement: *Jack is a lawyer.* Because the subject complement (*lawyer*) names or describes the subject (*Jack*), it is sometimes mistaken for the subject. (See 47b on subject complements.)

These *exercises are* a way to test your ability to perform under pressure.

▶ A tent and a sleeping bag ~~is~~ ^are^ the required equipment.

> *Tent and bag* is the subject, not *equipment*.

▶ A major force in today's economy ~~are~~ ^is^ children—as consumers, decision makers, and trend spotters.

> *Force* is the subject, not *children*. If the corrected version seems too awkward, make *children* the subject: *Children are a major force in today's economy—as consumers, decision makers, and trend spotters.*

21i *Who, which,* and *that* take verbs that agree with their antecedents.

Like most pronouns, the relative pronouns *who, which,* and *that* have antecedents, nouns or pronouns to which they refer. Relative pronouns used as subjects of subordinate clauses take verbs that agree with their antecedents.

ANT   PN   V

Take a *course that prepares* you for classroom management.

One of the

Constructions such as *one of the students who* [or *one of the things that*] cause problems for writers. Do not assume that the antecedent must be *one*. Instead, consider the logic of the sentence.

▶ Our ability to use language is one of the things that sets us

apart from animals.

The antecedent of *that* is *things*, not *one*. Several things set us apart from animals.

Only one of the

When the word *only* comes before *one*, you are safe in assuming that *one* is the antecedent of the relative pronoun.

▶ Veronica was the only one of the first-year Spanish

                was
students who ~~were~~ fluent enough to apply for the exchange
               ^

program.

The antecedent of *who* is *one*, not *students*. Only one student was fluent enough.

21j Words such as *athletics, economics, mathematics, physics, politics, statistics, measles,* and *news* are usually singular, despite their plural form.

>   is
> ▶ Politics ~~are~~ among my mother's favorite pastimes.
>   ^

EXCEPTIONS: Occasionally some of these words, especially *mathematics, economics, politics,* and *statistics,* have plural meanings: *Office politics often sway decisions about hiring and promotion. The economics of the building plan are prohibitive.*

21k Titles of works, company names, words mentioned as words, and gerund phrases are singular.

>   describes
> ▶ *Lost Cities* ~~describe~~ the discoveries of fifty ancient
>   ^
>
> civilizations.

>   specializes
> ▶ Delmonico Brothers ~~specialize~~ in organic produce and
>   ^
>
> additive-free meats.

>   is
> ▶ *Controlled substances* ~~are~~ a euphemism for illegal drugs.
>   ^

A gerund phrase consists of an *-ing* verb form followed by any objects, complements, or modifiers (see 48b). Treat gerund phrases as singular.

>   makes
> ▶ Encountering long hold times ~~make~~ customers impatient
>   ^
>
> with telephone tech support.

EXERCISE 21-1   Edit the following sentences to eliminate problems with subject-verb agreement. If a sentence is correct, write "correct" after it. Answers appear in the back of the book. *More practice:* e ✓

were
Jack's first days in the infantry ~~was~~ grueling.
^

a.   One of the main reasons for elephant poaching are the profits received from selling the ivory tusks.

b.   Not until my interview with Dr. Hwang were other possibilities opened to me.

c.   A number of students in the seminar was aware of the importance of joining the discussion.

d.   Batik cloth from Bali, blue and white ceramics from Delft, and a bocce ball from Turin has made Angelie's room the talk of the dorm.

e.   The board of directors, ignoring the wishes of the neighborhood, has voted to allow further development.

EXERCISE 21-2   For each sentence in the following passage, underline the subject (or compound subject) and then select the verb that agrees with it. (If you have trouble identifying the subject, consult 47a.) *More practice:* e ✓

    Loggerhead sea turtles (migrate / migrates) thousands of miles before returning to their nesting location every two to three years. The nesting season for loggerhead turtles (span / spans) the hottest months of the summer. Although the habitat of Atlantic loggerheads (range / ranges) from Newfoundland to Argentina, nesting for these turtles (take / takes) place primarily along the southeastern coast of the United States. Female turtles that have reached sexual maturity (crawl / crawls) ashore at night to lay their eggs. The cavity that serves as a nest for the eggs (is / are) dug out with the female's strong flippers. Deposited into each nest (is / are) anywhere from fifty to two hundred spherical eggs, also known as a *clutch*. After a two-month incubation period, all eggs in the clutch (begin / begins) to hatch, and within a few days the young turtles attempt to make their way

hackerhandbooks.com/bedhandbook

e Grammatical sentences > Exercises: 21–3 to 21–6

✓ Grammatical sentences > LearningCurve: Subject-verb agreement

EXERCISE 21-1   *Answers:*

a.   One of the main reasons for elephant poaching is the profits received from selling the ivory tusks.

b.   Correct

c.   A number of students in the seminar were aware of the importance of joining the discussion.

d.   Batik cloth from Bali, blue and white ceramics from Delft, and a bocce ball from Turin have made Angelie's room the talk of the dorm.

e.   Correct

into the ocean. A major cause of the loggerhead's decreasing numbers (is / are) natural predators such as raccoons, birds, and crabs. Beach erosion and coastal development also (threaten / threatens) the turtles' survival. For example, a crowd of curious humans or lights from beachfront residences (is / are) enough to make the female abandon her nesting plans and return to the ocean. Since only one in one thousand loggerheads survives to adulthood, special care should be taken to protect this threatened species.

22 Make pronouns and antecedents agree.

A pronoun is a word that substitutes for a noun. (See 46b.) Many pronouns have antecedents, nouns or pronouns to which they refer. A pronoun and its antecedent agree when they are both singular or both plural.

SINGULAR   *Dr. Ava Berto* finished *her* rounds.

PLURAL   The hospital *interns* finished *their* rounds.

Multilingual

The pronouns *he*, *his*, *she*, *her*, *it*, and *its* must agree in gender (masculine, feminine, or neuter) with their antecedents, not with the words they modify.

Steve visited *his* [not *her*] sister in Seattle.

EXERCISE 21–2 *Answers:*

Subject: turtles; verb: migrate; Subject: season; verb: spans; Subject: habitat; verb: ranges; Subject: nesting; verb: takes; Subject: turtles; verb: crawl; Subject: cavity; verb: is; Subject: eggs; verb: are; Subject: eggs; verb: begin; Subject: cause; verb: is; Subject: erosion and development; verb: threaten; Subject: crowd or lights; verb: are

22a Do not use plural pronouns to refer to singular antecedents.

Writers are frequently tempted to use plural pronouns to refer to two kinds of singular antecedents: indefinite pronouns and generic nouns.

Indefinite pronouns

Indefinite pronouns refer to nonspecific persons or things. Even though some of the following indefinite pronouns may seem to have plural meanings, treat them as singular in formal English.

anybody	each	everyone	nobody	somebody
anyone	either	everything	no one	someone
anything	everybody	neither	nothing	something

Everyone performs at *his or her* [not *their*] own fitness level.

When a plural pronoun refers mistakenly to a singular indefinite pronoun, you can usually choose one of three options for revision:

1. Replace the plural pronoun with *he or she* (or *his or her*).

2. Make the antecedent plural.

3. Rewrite the sentence so that no problem of agreement exists.

▶ When someone travels outside the United States for the
first time, ~~they need~~ he or she needs to apply for a passport.

▶ When ~~someone travels~~ people travel outside the United States for the
first time, they need to apply for a passport.

SCHOLARS ON PRONOUN-ANTECEDENT AGREEMENT

Nilsen, Aileen Pace. "Why Keep Searching When It's Already *Their*? Reconsidering *Everybody's* Pronoun Problem." *English Journal* 90.4 (2001): 68–73. Print. Nilsen describes the problems caused by the use of dual pronouns to avoid sexist language and analyzes the real-world use of *they* as a singular, nonsexist pronoun. She categorizes examples of such errors according to speakers' or writers' reasons for their choices: including and persuading, avoiding accusations, moving from general to specific and vice versa, and choosing efficiency. Nilsen concludes with a list of reasons why it might be counterproductive to battle the gradual change from *he/she* to *they*.

> ~~When someone~~ travels outside the United States for the
> *Anyone who*
>   *needs*
> first time,/~~they need~~ to apply for a passport.

Because the *he or she* construction is wordy, often the second or third revision strategy is more effective. Using *he* (or *his*) to refer to persons of either sex, while less wordy, is considered sexist, as is using *she* (or *her*) for all persons. Some writers alternate male and female pronouns throughout a text, but the result is often awkward. See 17f and the chart on page 311 for strategies that avoid sexist usage.

NOTE: If you change a pronoun from singular to plural (or vice versa), check to be sure that the verb agrees with the new pronoun (see 21e).

Generic nouns

A generic noun represents a typical member of a group, such as a typical student, or any member of a group, such as any lawyer. Although generic nouns may seem to have plural meanings, they are singular.

> Every *runner* must train rigorously if *he or she wants* [not *they want*] to excel.

When a plural pronoun refers mistakenly to a generic noun, you will usually have the same three revision options as mentioned on page 308 for indefinite pronouns.

>   *he or she wants*
> ▶ A medical student must study hard if ~~they want~~ to succeed.

>   *Medical students*
> ▶ ~~A medical student~~ must study hard if they want to succeed.

> ▶ A medical student must study hard ~~if they want~~ to succeed.

TEACHING TIP

Bring seven or eight short newspaper articles to class. Pair or group students and ask them to examine a single article. Give each pair or group ten minutes to go through its assigned article, circling all pronouns and drawing an arrow to the antecedent for each pronoun. When students have finished, discuss any sentences they may have found that included faulty agreement. Then ask students to complete exercises 22–1 and 22–2 in *The Bedford Handbook*.

22b Treat collective nouns as singular unless the meaning is clearly plural.

Collective nouns such as *jury, committee, audience, crowd, class, troop, family, team,* and *couple* name a group. Ordinarily the group functions as a unit, so the noun should be treated as singular; if the members of the group function as individuals, however, the noun should be treated as plural. (See also 21f.)

AS A UNIT   The *committee* granted *its* permission to build.

AS INDIVIDUALS   The *committee* put *their* signatures on the document.

When treating a collective noun as plural, many writers prefer to add a clearly plural antecedent such as *members* to the sentence: *The members of the committee put their signatures on the document.*

▶ Defense attorney Clarence Darrow surprisingly urged the

   jury to find his client, John Scopes, guilty so that he could

   appeal the case to a higher court. The jury complied,

   returning ~~their~~ *its* verdict in only nine minutes.

   There is no reason to draw attention to the individual members of the jury, so *jury* should be treated as singular.

22c Treat most compound antecedents joined with *and* as plural.

In 1987, *Reagan and Gorbachev* held a summit where *they* signed the Intermediate-Range Nuclear Forces Treaty.

Choosing a revision strategy that avoids sexist language

Because many readers object to sexist language, avoid using *he*, *him*, and *his* (or *she*, *her*, and *hers*) to refer to both men and women. Also try to avoid the wordy expressions *he or she* and *his or her*. More graceful alternatives are usually possible.

Use an occasional *he or she* (or *his or her*).

> In our office, everyone works at ~~their~~ his or her own pace.

Make the antecedent plural.

> ~~An employee~~ Employees on extended disability leave may continue their life insurance.

Recast the sentence.

> The amount of vacation time a federal worker may accrue depends on ~~their~~ length of service.

> ~~If~~ A child ~~is~~ born to parents who are both tall, ~~they have~~ has a high chance of being tall.

> A year later someone finally admitted ~~that they were~~ to being involved in the kidnapping.

> In his autobiography, Benjamin Franklin suggests that anyone can achieve success ~~as long as they live~~ by living a virtuous life and ~~work~~ working hard.

22d With compound antecedents joined with *or* or *nor* (or with *either . . . or* or *neither . . . nor*), make the pronoun agree with the nearer antecedent.

Either *Bruce* or *Tom* should receive first prize for *his* poem.

Neither the *mouse* nor the *rats* could find *their* way through the maze.

NOTE: If one of the antecedents is singular and the other plural, as in the second example, put the plural one last to avoid awkwardness.

EXCEPTION: If one antecedent is male and the other female, do not follow the traditional rule. The sentence *Either Bruce or Elizabeth should receive first prize for her short story* makes no sense. The best solution is to recast the sentence: *The prize for best short story should go to either Bruce or Elizabeth.*

EXERCISE 22–1 Edit the following sentences to eliminate problems with pronoun-antecedent agreement. Most of the sentences can be revised in more than one way, so experiment before choosing a solution. If a sentence is correct, write "correct" after it. Possible revisions appear in the back of the book. *More practice:* e ✓

> Recruiters
> ~~The recruiter~~ may tell the truth, but there is much that they
> ∧
> choose not to tell.

a. Every presidential candidate must appeal to a wide variety of ethnic and social groups if they want to win the election.

b. David lent his motorcycle to someone who allowed their friend to use it.

hackerhandbooks.com/bedhandbook

e Grammatical sentences > Exercises: 22–3 to 22–6

✓ Grammatical sentences > LearningCurve: Pronoun agreement and reference

---

EXERCISE 22–1 *Possible revisions:*

a. Every presidential candidate must appeal to a wide variety of ethnic and social groups to win the election.

b. David lent his motorcycle to someone who allowed a friend to use it.

c. The aerobics teacher motioned for all the students to move their arms in wide, slow circles.

d. Correct

e. Applicants should be bilingual if they want to qualify for this position.

c. The aerobics teacher motioned for everyone to move their arms in wide, slow circles.

d. The parade committee was unanimous in its decision to allow all groups and organizations to join the festivities.

e. The applicant should be bilingual if they want to qualify for this position.

EXERCISE 22–2 Edit the following paragraph to eliminate problems with pronoun-antecedent agreement or sexist language. *More practice:* e ✓

A common practice in businesses is to put each employee in their own cubicle. A typical cubicle resembles an office, but their walls don't reach the ceiling. Many office managers feel that a cubicle floor plan has its advantages. Cubicles make a large area feel spacious. In addition, they can be moved around so that each new employee can be accommodated in his own work area. Of course, the cubicle model also has problems. Typically, an employee is not as happy with a cubicle as they would be with a traditional office. Also, productivity can suffer. Neither a manager nor a frontline worker can ordinarily do their best work in a cubicle because of noise and lack of privacy. Each worker can hear his neighbors tapping on computer keyboards, making telephone calls, and muttering under their breath.

23 Make pronoun references clear.

Pronouns substitute for nouns; they are a kind of shorthand. In a sentence like *After Andrew intercepted the ball, he kicked it as hard as he could,* the pronouns *he* and *it* substitute for the nouns *Andrew* and *ball.* The word a pronoun refers to is called its *antecedent.*

EXERCISE 22–2 *Possible revisions:*

A common practice in businesses is to put each employee in a cubicle. A typical cubicle resembles an office, but its walls don't reach the ceiling. Many office managers feel that a cubicle floor plan has its advantages. Cubicles make a large area feel spacious. In addition, they can be moved around so that new employees can be accommodated in their own work area. Of course, the cubicle model also has problems. Typically, employees are not as happy with a cubicle as they would be with a traditional office. Also, productivity can suffer. Neither a manager nor a frontline worker can ordinarily do his or her best work in a cubicle because of noise and lack of privacy. Workers can hear their neighbors tapping on computer keyboards, making telephone calls, and muttering under their breath.

23a Avoid ambiguous or remote pronoun reference.

Ambiguous pronoun reference occurs when a pronoun could refer to two possible antecedents.

> The pitcher broke when Gloria set it
> ▶ ~~When Gloria set the pitcher~~ on the glass-topped table~~, it~~
>   ^   ^
>   ~~broke.~~

> "You have
> ▶ Tom told James, ~~that he had~~ won the lottery."
>   ^   ^

What broke—the pitcher or the table? Who won the lottery—Tom or James? The revisions eliminate the ambiguity.

Remote pronoun reference occurs when a pronoun is too far away from its antecedent for easy reading.

> ▶ After the court ordered my ex-husband to pay child support,
>   he refused. Eight months later, the judge ordered him to make
>   payments directly to the court, which would in turn pay me.
>   my ex-husband
>   After six months, payments stopped. Again he was
>   ^
>   summoned to appear in court.

The pronoun *he* was too distant from its antecedent, *ex-husband*, which appeared several sentences earlier.

23b Generally, avoid broad reference of *this, that, which,* and *it.*

For clarity, the pronouns *this, that, which,* and *it* should ordinarily refer to specific antecedents rather than to whole ideas or sentences. When a pronoun's reference is needlessly broad,

---

SCHOLARS ON PRONOUN REFERENCE

Mathews, Alison, and Martin S. Chodorow. "Pronoun Resolution in Two-Clause Sentences: Effects of Ambiguity, Antecedent Location, and Depth of Imbedding." *Journal of Memory and Language* 27 (1988): 245–60. Print. This empirical study focuses on students' comprehension when reading a two-clause sentence. The authors discovered that students resolve any ambiguity if the antecedent is located early in the first clause.

either replace the pronoun with a noun or supply an antecedent to which the pronoun clearly refers.

▶ By advertising on television, pharmaceutical companies

gain exposure for their prescription drugs. Patients
respond to ~~this~~ *the ads* by requesting drugs they might not need.

The writer substituted the noun *ads* for the pronoun *this*, which referred broadly to the idea expressed in the preceding sentence.

▶ Romeo and Juliet were both too young to have acquired
much wisdom, ~~and~~ *a fact* that accounts for their rash actions.

The writer added an antecedent (*fact*) that the pronoun *that* clearly refers to.

23c Do not use a pronoun to refer to an implied antecedent.

A pronoun should refer to a specific antecedent, not to a word that is implied but not present in the sentence.

▶ After braiding Ann's hair, Sue decorated ~~them~~ *the braids* with

ribbons.

The pronoun *them* referred to Ann's braids (implied by the term *braiding*), but the word *braids* did not appear in the sentence.

Modifiers, such as possessives, cannot serve as antecedents. A modifier may strongly imply the noun that a pronoun might logically refer to, but it is not itself that noun.

▶ In ~~Jamaica Kincaid's~~ "Girl," ~~she~~ describes the advice a
      ^Jamaica Kincaid
    ^

mother gives her daughter, including the mysterious

warning not to be "the kind of woman who the baker won't

let near the bread" (454).

Using the possessive form of an author's name to introduce a
source leads to a problem later in this sentence: The pronoun *she*
cannot refer logically to a possessive modifier (*Jamaica Kincaid's*).
The revision substitutes the noun *Jamaica Kincaid* for the pronoun
she, thereby eliminating the problem. (For more on writing with
sources in MLA style, see 55.)

23d Avoid the indefinite use of *they*, *it*, and *you*.

Do not use the pronoun *they* to refer indefinitely to persons who
have not been specifically mentioned. *They* should always refer to
a specific antecedent.

                  the school board
▶ In June, ~~they~~ voted to charge a fee for students to
            ^

participate in sports and music programs.

The word *it* should not be used indefinitely in constructions
such as *It is said on television . . .* or *In the article, it says that. . . .*

    The
▶ ~~In the~~ encyclopedia *it* states that male moths can smell
   ^

female moths from several miles away.

The pronoun *you* is appropriate only when the writer is
addressing the reader directly: *Once you have kneaded the dough,
let it rise in a warm place.* Except in informal contexts, however,
you should not be used to mean "anyone in general." Use a noun
instead.

▶ Ms. Pickersgill's *Guide to Etiquette* stipulates that ~~you~~ ^{a guest}

should not arrive at a party too early or leave too late.

23e To refer to persons, use *who, whom,* or *whose,* not *which* or *that.*

In most contexts, use *who, whom,* or *whose* to refer to persons, and use *which* or *that* to refer to animals or things. *Which* is reserved only for animals or things, so it is impolite to use it to refer to persons.

▶ All thirty-two women in the study, half of ~~which~~ ^{whom} were

unemployed for more than six months, reported higher

self-esteem after job training.

Although *that* is sometimes used to refer to persons, many readers will find such references dehumanizing. It is more polite to use a form of *who*—a word reserved for people.

▶ During the two-day festival El Día de los Muertos (Day of

the Dead), Mexican families celebrate loved ones ~~that~~ ^{who} have

died.

NOTE: Occasionally *whose* may be used to refer to animals and things to avoid the awkward *of which* construction.

▶ A local school, ~~the~~ name ~~of which~~ ^{whose} will be in tomorrow's

paper, has received the Governor's Gold Medal for

outstanding community service.

EXERCISE 23–1 Edit the following sentences to correct errors in pronoun reference. In some cases, you will need to decide on an antecedent that the pronoun might logically refer to. Possible revisions appear in the back of the book. *More practice:* e ✓

> Although Apple makes the most widely recognized MP3
>
> player, other companies have gained a share of the market.
> ~~The competition~~
> ~~This~~ has kept prices from skyrocketing.
> ∧

a. They say that engineering students should have hands-on experience with dismantling and reassembling machines.

b. She had decorated her living room with posters from chamber music festivals. This led her date to believe that she was interested in classical music. Actually she preferred rock.

c. In my high school, you didn't need to get all A's to be considered a success; you just needed to work to your ability.

d. Marianne told Jenny that she was worried about her mother's illness.

e. Though Lewis cried for several minutes after scraping his knee, eventually it subsided.

EXERCISE 23–2 Edit the following passage to correct errors in pronoun reference. In some cases, you will need to decide on an antecedent that the pronoun might logically refer to. *More practice:* e

> Since its launch in the 1980s, the Internet has grown to be one of the largest communications forums in the world. The Internet was created by a team of academics who were building on a platform that government scientists had started developing in the 1950s. They initially viewed it as a noncommercial enterprise that would serve only the needs of the academic and technical communities. But with the introduction of user-friendly browser technology in the 1990s, it expanded tremendously. By the late 1990s, many businesses were connecting to the Internet with high-speed broadband and fiber-optic connections, which is

hackerhandbooks.com/bedhandbook

e Grammatical sentences > Exercises: 23–3 to 23–6

✓ Grammatical sentences > LearningCurve: Pronoun agreement and reference

EXERCISE 23–1 *Possible revisions:*

a. Some professors say that engineering students should have hands-on experience with dismantling and reassembling machines.

b. Because she had decorated her living room with posters from chamber music festivals, her date thought that she was interested in classical music. Actually she preferred rock.

c. In my high school, students didn't need to get all A's to be considered a success; they just needed to work to their ability.

d. Marianne told Jenny, "I am worried about your mother's illness." [*or* ". . . about my mother's illness."]

e. Though Lewis cried for several minutes after scraping his knee, eventually his crying subsided.

also true of home users today. Accessing information, shopping, gaming, and communicating are easier than ever before. This, however, can lead to some possible drawbacks. You forfeit privacy when you search, shop, game, and communicate. They say that avoiding disclosure of personal information and routinely adjusting your privacy settings on social media sites are the best ways to protect yourself on the Internet.

24 Distinguish between pronouns such as *I* and *me*.

The personal pronouns in the following chart change what is known as *case form* according to their grammatical function in a sentence. Pronouns functioning as subjects or subject complements appear in the *subjective* case; those functioning as objects appear in the *objective* case; and those showing ownership appear in the *possessive* case.

	SUBJECTIVE CASE	OBJECTIVE CASE	POSSESSIVE CASE
SINGULAR	I	me	my
	you	you	your
	he/she/it	him/her/it	his/her/its
PLURAL	we	us	our
	you	you	your
	they	them	their

Pronouns in the subjective and objective cases are frequently confused. Most of the rules in this section specify when to use one or the other of these cases (*I* or *me*, *he* or *him*, and so on). Section 24g explains a special use of pronouns and nouns in the possessive case.

EXERCISE 23-2 *Possible revisions:*

Since its launch in the 1980s, the Internet has grown to be one of the largest communications forums in the world. The Internet was created by a team of academics who were building on a platform that government scientists had started developing in the 1950s. The creators initially viewed the Internet as a noncommercial enterprise that would serve only the needs of the academic and technical communities. But with the introduction of user-friendly browser technology in the 1990s, personal and commercial Internet use expanded tremendously. By the late 1990s, many businesses were connecting to the Internet with high-speed broadband and fiber-optic connections, technology available to

24a Use the subjective case (*I, you, he, she, it, we, they*) for subjects and subject complements.

When personal pronouns are used as subjects, ordinarily your ear will tell you the correct pronoun. Problems sometimes arise, however, with compound word groups containing a pronoun, so it is not always safe to trust your ear.

▶ Joel ran away because his stepfather and ~~him~~ had quarreled.
     ^he^

> *His stepfather and he* is the subject of the verb *had quarreled.*
> If we strip away the words *his stepfather and,* the correct pronoun
> becomes clear: *he had quarreled* (not *him had quarreled*).

When a pronoun is used as a subject complement (a word following a linking verb), your ear may mislead you, since the incorrect form is frequently heard in casual speech. (See "subject complement," 47b.)

▶ **During the Lindbergh trial, Bruno Hauptmann repeatedly**
     ^he.^
   denied that the kidnapper was ~~him.~~

> If *kidnapper was he* seems too stilted, rewrite the sentence: *During
> the Lindbergh trial, Bruno Hauptmann repeatedly denied that he was
> the kidnapper.*

24b Use the objective case (*me, you, him, her, it, us, them*) for all objects.

When a personal pronoun is used as a direct object, an indirect object, or the object of a preposition, ordinarily your ear will lead you to the correct pronoun. When an object is compound, however, you may occasionally become confused.

▶ **Janice was indignant when she realized that the salesclerk**
     ^her.^
   was insulting her mother and ~~she.~~

EXERCISE 23–2   *Possible revisions (continued):*

many home users today. Accessing information, shopping, gaming, and communicating are easier than ever before. These conveniences, however, can lead to some possible drawbacks. Computer users forfeit privacy when they search, shop, game, and communicate. Computer experts advise that avoiding disclosure of personal information and routinely adjusting privacy settings on social media sites are the best ways for users to protect themselves on the Internet.

Her mother and her is the direct object of the verb *was insulting*. Strip away the words *her mother and* to hear the correct pronoun: *was insulting her* (not *was insulting she*).

me
▶ The most traumatic experience for her father and I̶ occurred
   ∧

long after her operation.

Her father and me is the object of the preposition *for*. Strip away the words *her father and* to test for the correct pronoun: *for me* (not *for I*).

When in doubt about the correct pronoun, some writers try to avoid making the choice by using a reflexive pronoun such as *myself*. Using a reflexive pronoun in such situations is nonstandard.

me
▶ Nidra gave my cousin and ~~myself~~ some good tips on
   ∧

traveling in New Delhi.

My cousin and me is the indirect object of the verb *gave*. For correct uses of *myself*, see the glossary of usage at the back of the book.

24c Put an appositive and the word to which it refers in the same case.

Appositives are noun phrases that rename nouns or pronouns. A pronoun used as an appositive has the same function (usually subject or object) as the word(s) it renames.

I,
▶ The managers, Dr. Bell and ~~me,~~ could not agree on a plan.
   ∧

The appositive *Dr. Bell and I* renames the subject, *managers*. Test: *I could not agree* (not *me could not agree*).

me.
▶ The reporter found only two witnesses, the bicyclist and I̶.
   ∧

The appositive *the bicyclist and me* renames the direct object, *witnesses*. Test: *found me* (not *found I*).

TEACHING TIP

When you respond to drafts and see surface errors such as problems with pronoun case, don't spend time teaching the lesson in the margin of a student's draft. Instead, refer the writer to a specific section in the handbook (24a, for example). You can also suggest that students complete the book's exercises or the online exercises for strengthening skills.

24d Following *than* or *as*, choose the pronoun that expresses your meaning.

When a comparison begins with *than* or *as*, your choice of a pronoun will depend on your intended meaning. To test for the correct pronoun, mentally complete the sentence: *My roommate likes football more than I [do]*.

▶ In our report on nationalized health care in the United
States, we argued that Canadians are better off than ~~us~~. we.

We is the subject of the verb *are*, which is understood: *Canadians are better off than we [are]*. If the correct English seems too formal, you can always add the verb.

▶ We respected no other candidate as much as ~~she~~. her.

This sentence means that we respected no other candidate as much as *we respected her*. *Her* is the direct object of the understood verb *respected*.

24e For *we* or *us* before a noun, choose the pronoun that would be appropriate if the noun were omitted.

▶ ~~Us~~ We tenants would rather fight than move.

▶ Management is shortchanging ~~we~~ us tenants.

No one would say *Us would rather fight than move* or *Management is shortchanging we*.

24f Use the objective case for subjects and objects of infinitives.

An infinitive is the word *to* followed by the base form of a verb. (See 48b.) Subjects of infinitives are an exception to the rule that

---

WRITERS ON WRITING

If you want to be a writer, you must do two things above all others: read a lot and write a lot. There's no way around these two things that I'm aware of, no shortcut.
　　　　　　　　　　　　　　　　　　　　　　　　— Stephen King

subjects must be in the subjective case. Whenever an infinitive has a subject, it must be in the objective case. Objects of infinitives also are in the objective case.

► Sue asked John and ~~I~~ to drive the mayor and ~~she~~ to the
                 me   *her*

airport.

John and me is the subject of the infinitive *to drive*; *mayor and her* is the direct object of the infinitive.

24g Use the possessive case to modify a gerund.

A pronoun that modifies a gerund or a gerund phrase should be in the possessive case (*my, our, your, his, her, its, their*). A gerund is a verb form ending in *-ing* that functions as a noun. Gerunds frequently appear in phrases; when they do, the whole gerund phrase functions as a noun. (See 48b.)

► The chances of ~~you~~ being hit by lightning are about two
                   your

million to one.

Your modifies the gerund phrase *being hit by lightning*.

Nouns as well as pronouns may modify gerunds. To form the possessive case of a noun, use an apostrophe and an *-s* (*victim's*) or just an apostrophe (*victims'*). (See 36a.)

► The old order in France paid a high price for the ~~aristocracy~~
                                            aristocracy's

exploiting the lower classes.

The possessive noun *aristocracy's* modifies the gerund phrase *exploiting the lower classes*.

Gerund phrases should not be confused with participial phrases, which function as adjectives, not as nouns: *We saw him driving a yellow convertible.* Here *driving a yellow convertible* is a participial phrase modifying the pronoun *him.* (See 48b.)

The choice between the objective case and the possessive case depends on the meaning you intend; sometimes the distinction is subtle.

> We watched *them* dancing.

> We watched *their* dancing.

In the first sentence, the emphasis is on the people; we watched *them,* and they happened to be dancing. In the second sentence, the emphasis is on the dancing; we watched the *dancing*—a noun form modified by the possessive *their.*

NOTE: Do not use the possessive if it creates an awkward effect. Try to reword the sentence instead.

AWKWARD	The president agreed to the applications' being reviewed by a faculty committee.
REVISED	The president agreed that the applications could be reviewed by a faculty committee.
REVISED	The president agreed that a faculty committee could review the applications.

EXERCISE 24–1 Edit the following sentences (p. 325) to eliminate errors in pronoun case. If a sentence is correct, write "correct" after it. Answers appear in the back of the book. *More practice:* e

> Grandfather cuts down trees for neighbors much younger
> ⌃he.
> than ~~him.~~
> ⌃

hackerhandbooks.com/bedhandbook

e Grammatical sentences > Exercises: 24–3 to 24–5, 24/25–6 and 24/25–7
(pronoun case review)

EXERCISE 24–1 *Answers:*

a. Correct [But the writer could change the end of the sentence: . . . *than he was.*]

b. Correct [But the writer could change the end of the sentence: . . . *that she was the coach.*]

c. She appreciated his telling the truth in such a difficult situation.

d. The director has asked you and me to draft a proposal for a new recycling plan.

e. Five close friends and I rented a station wagon, packed it with food, and drove two hundred miles to Mardi Gras.

a. Rick applied for the job even though he heard that other candidates were more experienced than he.

b. The volleyball team could not believe that the coach was she.

c. She appreciated him telling the truth in such a difficult situation.

d. The director has asked you and I to draft a proposal for a new recycling plan.

e. Five close friends and myself rented a station wagon, packed it with food, and drove two hundred miles to Mardi Gras.

EXERCISE 24-2 In the following paragraph, choose the correct pronoun in each set of parentheses. *More practice:* e

We may blame television for the number of products based on characters in children's TV shows — from Big Bird to SpongeBob — but in fact merchandising that capitalizes on a character's popularity started long before television. Raggedy Ann began as a child's rag doll, and a few years later books about (she / her) and her brother, Raggedy Andy, were published. A cartoonist named Johnny Gruelle painted a cloth face on a family doll and applied for a patent in 1915. Later Gruelle began writing and illustrating stories about Raggedy Ann, and in 1918 (he / him) and a publisher teamed up to publish the books and sell the dolls. He was not the only one to try to sell products linked to children's stories. Beatrix Potter published the first of many Peter Rabbit picture books in 1902, and no one was better than (she / her) at making a living from spin-offs. After Peter Rabbit and Benjamin Bunny became popular, Potter began putting pictures of (they / them) and their little animal friends on merchandise. Potter had fans all over the world, and she understood (them / their) wanting to see Peter Rabbit not only in books but also on teapots and plates and lamps and other furnishings for the nursery. Potter and Gruelle, like countless others before and since, knew that entertaining children could be a profitable business.

EXERCISE 24-2 *Answers:*

her, he, she, them, their

25 Distinguish between *who* and *whom*.

The choice between *who* and *whom* (or *whoever* and *whomever*) occurs primarily in subordinate clauses and in questions. *Who* and *whoever*, subjective-case pronouns, are used for subjects and subject complements. *Whom* and *whomever*, objective-case pronouns, are used for objects. (See 25a and 25b.)

An exception to this general rule occurs when the pronoun functions as the subject of an infinitive (see 25c). See also 24f.

Consult the chart on page 329 for a summary of the trouble spots with *who* and *whom*.

25a Use *who* and *whom* correctly in subordinate clauses.

When *who* and *whom* (or *whoever* and *whomever*) introduce subordinate clauses, their case is determined by their function *within the clause they introduce*.

In the following two examples, the pronouns *who* and *whoever* function as the subjects of the clauses they introduce.

▶ First prize goes to the runner ~~whom~~ who earns the most points.

The subordinate clause is *who earns the most points*. The verb of the clause is *earns*, and its subject is *who*.

▶ Maya Angelou's *I Know Why the Caged Bird Sings* should be read by ~~whomever~~ whoever is interested in the effects of racial prejudice on children.

The writer selected the pronoun *whomever*, thinking that it was the object of the preposition *by*. However, the object of the preposition is the entire subordinate clause *whoever is interested in the effects of racial prejudice on children*. The verb of the clause is *is*, and the subject of the verb is *whoever*.

When functioning as an object in a subordinate clause, *whom* (or *whomever*) also appears out of order, before the subject and verb. To choose the correct pronoun, you can mentally restructure the clause.

> whom
> ▸ You will work with our senior traders, ~~who~~ you will meet
>   ∧
>
> later.

The subordinate clause is *whom you will meet later*. The subject of the clause is *you*, and the verb is *will meet*. *Whom* is the direct object of the verb. The correct choice becomes clear if you mentally restructure the clause: *you will meet whom*.

When functioning as the object of a preposition in a subordinate clause, *whom* is often separated from its preposition.

> whom
> ▸ The tutor ~~who~~ I was assigned to was very supportive.
>   ∧

Whom is the object of the preposition *to*. In this sentence, the writer might choose to drop *whom*: *The tutor I was assigned to was very supportive*.

NOTE: Inserted expressions such as *they know*, *I think*, and *she says* should be ignored in determining whether to use *who* or *whom*.

> ▸ The speech pathologist reported a particularly difficult
>   who
>   session with a stroke patient ~~whom~~ she knew was suffering
>   ∧
>
>   from aphasia.

Who is the subject of *was suffering*, not the object of *knew*.

25b Use *who* and *whom* correctly in questions.

When *who* and *whom* (or *whoever* and *whomever*) are used to open questions, their case is determined by their function within the question.

>   Who
> ► ~~Whom~~ was responsible for creating that computer virus?
>   ^
>
> *Who* is the subject of the verb *was*.

When *whom* functions as the object of a verb or the object of a preposition in a question, it appears out of normal order. To choose the correct pronoun, mentally restructure the question.

>   Whom
> ► ~~Who~~ did the Democratic Party nominate in 1952?
>   ^
>
> *Whom* is the direct object of the verb *did nominate*. This becomes clear if you restructure the question: *The Democratic Party did nominate whom in 1952?*

25c Use *whom* for subjects or objects of infinitives.

An infinitive is the word *to* followed by the base form of a verb. (See 48b.) Subjects of infinitives are an exception to the rule that subjects must be in the subjective case. The subject of an infinitive must be in the objective case. Objects of infinitives also are in the objective case.

>   whom
> ► When it comes to money, I know ~~who~~ to believe.
>   ^
>
> The infinitive phrase *whom to believe* is the direct object of the verb *know*, and *whom* is the subject of the infinitive *to believe*.

NOTE: In spoken English, *who* is often used when the correct *whom* sounds too stuffy. Although some readers will accept constructions like *Who* [not *Whom*] *did Senator Boxer replace?* in informal written English, it is safer to use *whom* in formal English.

Checking for problems with *who* and *whom*

In subordinate clauses (25a)

Isolate the subordinate clause. Then read its subject, verb, and any objects, restructuring the clause if necessary. Some writers find it helpful to substitute *he* for *who* and *him* for *whom*.

> Samuels hoped to become the business partner of (whoever/whomever) found the treasure.
>
> **TEST**: . . . *whoever* found the treasure. [. . . *he* found the treasure.]
>
> Ada always seemed to be bestowing a favor on (whoever/whomever) she worked for.
>
> **TEST**: . . . she worked for *whomever*. [. . . she worked for *him*.]

In questions (25b)

Read the subject, verb, and any objects, rearranging the sentence structure if necessary.

> (Who/Whom) conferred with Roosevelt and Stalin at Yalta in 1945?
>
> **TEST**: *Who* conferred . . . ?
>
> (Who/Whom) did the committee nominate?
>
> **TEST**: The committee did nominate *whom*?

EXERCISE 25–1 Edit the following sentences to eliminate errors in the use of *who* and *whom* (or *whoever* and *whomever*). If a sentence is correct, write "correct" after it. Answers appear in the back of the book. *More practice:* e

>   whom
> **What is the address of the artist ~~who~~ Antonio hired?**
>   ∧

a.   Arriving late for rehearsal, we had no idea who was supposed to dance with whom.

hackerhandbooks.com/bedhandbook
e Grammatical sentences > Exercises: 25–2 and 25–3, 24/25–6 and 24/25–7 (pronoun case review)

EXERCISE 25–1 *Answers:*

a.   Correct
b.   The environmental policy conference featured scholars whom I had never heard of. [*or* . . . scholars I had never heard of.]
c.   Correct
d.   Daniel always gives a holiday donation to whoever needs it.
e.   So many singers came to the audition that Natalia had trouble deciding whom to select for the choir.

b.   The environmental policy conference featured scholars who I had never heard of.

c.   Whom did you support in last month's election for student government president?

d.   Daniel always gives a holiday donation to whomever needs it.

e.   So many singers came to the audition that Natalia had trouble deciding who to select for the choir.

26 Choose adjectives and adverbs with care.

Adjectives modify nouns or pronouns. They usually come before the word they modify; occasionally they function as complements following the word they modify. Adverbs modify verbs, adjectives, or other adverbs. (See 46d and 46e.)

Many adverbs are formed by adding -*ly* to adjectives (*normal, normally; smooth, smoothly*). But don't assume that all words ending in -*ly* are adverbs or that all adverbs end in -*ly*. Some adjectives end in -*ly* (*lovely, friendly*), and some adverbs don't (*always, here, there*). When in doubt, consult a dictionary.

> **Multilingual**
>
> Placement of adjectives and adverbs can be a tricky matter for multilingual writers. See 30f and 30h.

26a Use adjectives to modify nouns.

Adjectives ordinarily precede the nouns they modify. But they can also function as subject complements or object complements, following the nouns they modify.

WRITERS ON WRITING

One of the problems we have as writers is we don't take ourselves seriously while writing; being serious is setting aside a time and saying if it comes, good; if it doesn't come, good, I'll just sit here.   — Maya Angelou

I just sit at my typewriter and curse a bit.   — P. G. Wodehouse

Subject complements

A subject complement follows a linking verb and completes the meaning of the subject. (See 47b.) When an adjective functions as a subject complement, it describes the subject.

Justice is *blind*.

Problems can arise with verbs such as *smell*, *taste*, *look*, and *feel*, which sometimes, but not always, function as linking verbs. If the word following one of these verbs describes the subject, use an adjective; if the word following the verb modifies the verb, use an adverb.

ADJECTIVE   The detective looked *cautious*.

ADVERB   The detective looked *cautiously* for fingerprints.

The adjective *cautious* describes the detective; the adverb *cautiously* modifies the verb *looked*.

Linking verbs suggest states of being, not actions. Notice, for example, the different meanings of *looked* in the preceding examples. To look cautious suggests the state of being cautious; to look cautiously is to perform an action in a cautious way.

> sweet
> ▶ The lilacs in our backyard smell especially ~~sweetly~~ this
> ∧
> year.

> The verb *smell* suggests a state of being, not an action. Therefore, it should be followed by an adjective, not an adverb.

WRITERS ON WRITING

Writing, when properly managed (as you may be sure I think mine is), is but a different name for conversation.   — Laurence Sterne

I don't wait to be struck by lightning and I don't need certain slants of light in order to be able to write.   — Toni Morrison

> The drawings looked ~~well~~ ^{good} after the architect made changes.

The verb *looked* is a linking verb suggesting a state of being, not an action. The adjective *good* is appropriate following the linking verb to describe *drawings*. (See also 26c.)

Object complements

An object complement follows a direct object and completes its meaning. (See 47b.) When an adjective functions as an object complement, it describes the direct object.

Sorrow makes *us wise*.

Object complements occur with verbs such as *call*, *consider*, *create*, *find*, *keep*, and *make*. When a modifier follows the direct object of one of these verbs, use an adjective to describe the direct object; use an adverb to modify the verb.

ADJECTIVE   The referee called the plays *perfect*.

ADVERB   The referee called the plays *perfectly*.

The first sentence means that the referee considered the plays to be perfect; the second means that the referee did an excellent job of calling the plays.

26b Use adverbs to modify verbs, adjectives, and other adverbs.

When adverbs modify verbs (or verbals), they nearly always answer the question When? Where? How? Why? Under what conditions? How often? or To what degree? When adverbs modify adjectives or other adverbs, they usually qualify or intensify the meaning of the word they modify. (See 46e.)

Adjectives are often used incorrectly in place of adverbs in casual or nonstandard speech.

> ▶ The travel arrangement worked out ~~perfect~~ for everyone.
>   ^*perfectly**

> ▶ The manager must see that the office runs ~~smooth~~ and
>   ^*smoothly**
>   *efficiently.*
>   ~~efficient.~~
>   ^

The adverb *perfectly* modifies the verb *worked out*; the adverbs *smoothly* and *efficiently* modify the verb *runs*.

> ▶ The chance of recovering lost property looks ~~real~~ slim.
>   ^*really**

Only adverbs can modify adjectives or other adverbs. *Really* intensifies the meaning of the adjective *slim*.

26c Distinguish between *good* and *well, bad* and *badly.*

Good is an adjective (*good performance*). *Well* is an adverb when it modifies a verb (*speak well*). The use of the adjective *good* in place of the adverb *well* to modify a verb is nonstandard and especially common in casual speech.

> ▶ We were glad that Sanya had done ~~good~~ on the CPA exam.
>   ^*well*

The adverb *well* modifies the verb *had done*.

Confusion can arise because *well* is an adjective when it modifies a noun or pronoun and means "healthy" or "satisfactory" (*The babies were well and warm*).

> ▶ Adrienne did not feel ~~good,~~ but she performed anyway.
>   ^*well,*

As an adjective following the linking verb *did feel*, *well* describes Adrienne's health.

TEACHING TIP

Ask students to keep an editing log for the semester. When they receive comments on a draft, they should pay special attention to comments related to sentence-level matters. In their editing log, students should record (1) the incorrect sentence, (2) the handbook section (26b, for example) that provides help for editing that sentence, and (3) the corrected sentence. Invite students to add any tips that might help them proofread for that particular error in the future.

Bad is always an adjective and should be used to describe a noun; *badly* is always an adverb and should be used to modify a verb. The adverb *badly* is often used inappropriately to describe a noun, especially following a linking verb.

▶ The sisters felt ~~badly~~ bad when they realized they had left their

brother out of the planning.

> The adjective *bad* is used after the linking verb *felt* to describe the noun *sisters*.

26d Use comparatives and superlatives with care.

Most adjectives and adverbs have three forms: the positive, the comparative, and the superlative.

POSITIVE	COMPARATIVE	SUPERLATIVE
soft	softer	softest
fast	faster	fastest
friendly	friendlier	friendliest
carefully	more carefully	most carefully
bad	worse	worst
good	better	best

Comparative versus superlative

Use the comparative to compare two things, the superlative to compare three or more.

▶ Which of these two low-carb drinks is ~~best?~~ better?

▶ Though Shaw and Jackson are impressive, Zhao is the
~~more~~ most qualified of the three candidates running for state
senator.

Forming comparatives and superlatives

To form comparatives and superlatives of most one- and two-syllable adjectives, use the endings *-er* and *-est*: *smooth, smoother, smoothest; easy, easier, easiest.* With longer adjectives, use *more* and *most* (or *less* and *least* for downward comparisons): *exciting, more exciting, most exciting; helpful, less helpful, least helpful.*

Some one-syllable adverbs take the endings *-er* and *-est* (*fast, faster, fastest*), but longer adverbs and all of those ending in *-ly* form the comparative and superlative with *more* and *most* (or *less* and *least*).

The comparative and superlative forms of some adjectives and adverbs are irregular: *good, better, best; well, better, best; bad, worse, worst; badly, worse, worst.*

▶ The Kirov is the ~~talentedest~~ ballet company we have seen.
        ^ most talented

▶ According to our projections, sales at local businesses will

  be ~~worser~~ than those at the chain stores this winter.
     ^ worse

Double comparatives or superlatives

Do not use double comparatives or superlatives. When you have added *-er* or *-est* to an adjective or adverb, do not also use *more* or *most* (or *less* or *least*).

▶ Of all her family, Julia is the ~~most~~ happiest about the move.

▶ All the polls indicated that Gore was more ~~likelier~~ to win
                                              ^ likely

  than Bush.

Absolute concepts

Avoid expressions such as *more straight, less perfect, very round,* and *most unique.* Either something is unique or it isn't. It is illogical to suggest that absolute concepts come in degrees.

> That is the most ~~unique~~ *unusual* wedding gown I have ever seen.

> The painting is ~~priceless~~ *valuable* because it is signed.

26e Avoid double negatives.

Standard English allows two negatives only if a positive meaning is intended: *The orchestra was not unhappy with its performance* (meaning that the orchestra was happy). Using a double negative to emphasize a negative meaning is nonstandard.

Negative modifiers such as *never*, *no*, and *not* should not be paired with other negative modifiers or with negative words such as *neither*, *none*, *no one*, *nobody*, and *nothing*.

> The city is not doing ~~nothing~~ *anything* to see that the trash is

collected during the strike.

The double negative *not . . . nothing* is nonstandard.

The modifiers *hardly*, *barely*, and *scarcely* are considered negatives in Standard English, so they should not be used with negatives such as *not*, *no one*, or *never*.

> Maxine is so weak that she ~~can't~~ *can* hardly climb stairs.

EXERCISE 26–1 Edit the following sentences (p. 337) to eliminate errors in the use of adjectives and adverbs. If a sentence is correct, write "correct" after it. Answers appear in the back of the book. *More practice:* e

We weren't surprised by how ~~good~~ *well* the sidecar racing team

flowed through the tricky course.

hackerhandbooks.com/bedhandbook

e Grammatical sentences > Exercises: 26–3 to 26–5

EXERCISE 26–1 *Possible revisions:*

a. Do you expect to perform well on the nursing board exam next week?

b. With the budget deadline approaching, our office has hardly had time to handle routine correspondence.

c. Correct

d. The customer complained that he hadn't been treated nicely by the agent on the phone.

e. Of all the smart people in my family, Uncle Roberto is the cleverest [or most clever].

a. Do you expect to perform good on the nursing board exam next week?

b. With the budget deadline approaching, our office hasn't hardly had time to handle routine correspondence.

c. When I worked in a flower shop, I learned that some flowers smell surprisingly bad.

d. The customer complained that he hadn't been treated nice by the agent on the phone.

e. Of all the smart people in my family, Uncle Roberto is the most cleverest.

EXERCISE 26–2 Edit the following passage to eliminate errors in the use of adjectives and adverbs. *More practice:* ⓔ

Doctors recommend that to give skin the most fullest protection from ultraviolet rays, people should use plenty of sunscreen, limit sun exposure, and wear protective clothing. The commonest sunscreens today are known as "broad spectrum" because they block out both UVA and UVB rays. These lotions don't feel any differently on the skin from the old UVA-only types, but they work best at preventing premature aging and skin cancer.

Many sunscreens claim to be waterproof, but they won't hardly provide adequate coverage after extended periods of swimming or perspiring. To protect good, even waterproof sunscreens should be reapplied liberal and often. All areas of exposed skin, including ears, backs of hands, and tops of feet, need to be coated good to avoid burning or damage. Some people's skin reacts bad to PABA, or para-aminobenzoic acid, so PABA-free (hypoallergenic) sunscreens are widely available. In addition to recommending sunscreen, doctors almost unanimously agree that people should stay out of the sun when rays are the most strongest — between 10:00 a.m. and 3:00 p.m. — and should limit time in the sun. They also suggest that people wear long-sleeved shirts, broad-brimmed hats, and long pants whenever possible.

EXERCISE 26–2 *Possible revisions:*

Doctors recommend that to give skin the fullest protection from ultraviolet rays, people should use plenty of sunscreen, limit sun exposure, and wear protective clothing. The most common sunscreens today are known as "broad spectrum" because they block out both UVA and UVB rays. These lotions don't feel any different on the skin from the old UVA-only types, but they work better at preventing premature aging and skin cancer.

Many sunscreens claim to be waterproof, but they won't provide adequate coverage after extended periods of swimming or perspiring. To protect well, even waterproof sunscreens should be reapplied liberally and often. All areas of exposed skin, including ears, backs of hands, and tops of feet, need to be coated well to avoid burning or damage. Some people's skin reacts badly to PABA, or para-aminobenzoic acid, so

27 Choose appropriate verb forms, tenses, and moods in Standard English.

In speech, some people use verb forms and tenses that match a home dialect or variety of English. In writing, use Standard English verb forms unless you are quoting nonstandard speech or using alternative forms for literary effect. (See 17d.)

Except for the verb *be*, all verbs in English have five forms. The following list shows the five forms and provides a sample sentence in which each might appear.

BASE FORM	Usually I (*walk, ride*).
PAST TENSE	Yesterday I (*walked, rode*).
PAST PARTICIPLE	I have (*walked, ridden*) many times before.
PRESENT PARTICIPLE	I am (*walking, riding*) right now.
-S FORM	He/she/it (*walks, rides*) regularly.

The verb *be* has eight forms instead of the usual five: *be, am, is, are, was, were, being, been.*

27a Choose Standard English forms of irregular verbs.

For all regular verbs, the past-tense and past-participle forms are the same (ending in *-ed* or *-d*), so there is no danger of confusion. This is not true, however, for irregular verbs, such as the following.

BASE FORM	PAST TENSE	PAST PARTICIPLE
go	went	gone
break	broke	broken
fly	flew	flown

EXERCISE 26-2 *Possible revisions (continued):*

PABA-free (hypoallergenic) sunscreens are widely available. In addition to recommending sunscreen, most doctors agree that people should stay out of the sun when rays are the strongest — between 10:00 a.m. and 3:00 p.m. — and should limit time in the sun. They also suggest that people wear long-sleeved shirts, broad-brimmed hats, and long pants whenever possible.

The past-tense form always occurs alone, without a help-ing verb. It expresses action that occurred entirely in the past: *I rode to work yesterday. I walked to work last Tuesday.* The past participle is used with a helping verb. It forms the perfect tenses with *has, have,* or *had*; it forms the passive voice with *be, am, is, are, was, were, being,* or *been.* (See 46c for a complete list of helping verbs and 27f for a survey of tenses.)

PAST TENSE　　　　　　　　　Last July, we *went* to Seoul.

HELPING VERB + PAST PARTICIPLE　　We *have gone* to Seoul twice.

The list of common irregular verbs beginning on the next page will help you distinguish between the past tense and the past participle. Choose the past-participle form if the verb in your sentence requires a helping verb; choose the past-tense form if the verb does not require a helping verb. (See verb tenses in 27f.)

▶　Yesterday we ~~seen~~ *saw* a documentary about Isabel Allende.

The past-tense *saw* is required because there is no helping verb.

▶　The pickup truck was apparently ~~stole~~ *stolen* while the driver ate lunch.

▶　By Friday, the stock market had ~~fell~~ *fallen* two hundred points.

Because of the helping verbs *was* and *had,* the past-participle forms are required: *was stolen, had fallen.*

When in doubt about the Standard English forms of irregu-lar verbs, consult the list on pages 340–42 or look up the base form of the verb in the dictionary, which also lists any irregular forms. (If no additional forms are listed in the dictionary, the verb is regular, not irregular.)

SCHOLARS ON STANDARD ENGLISH VERB FORMS

Epes, Mary. "Tracing Errors to Their Sources." *Journal of Basic Writing* 4.4 (1985): 4–33. Print. In a study of basic writers, Epes discovered that phonological and grammatical features of nonstandard English significantly affected students' ability to "encode" a dictated text. Epes concludes that speakers of nonstandard English need "direct instruction in the grammar of Standard written English," with special focus on whole-word verb forms, hypercorrections, and omitted suffixes.

Common irregular verbs

BASE FORM	PAST TENSE	PAST PARTICIPLE
arise	arose	arisen
awake	awoke, awaked	awaked, awoke, awoken
be	was, were	been
beat	beat	beaten, beat
become	became	become
begin	began	begun
bend	bent	bent
bite	bit	bitten, bit
blow	blew	blown
break	broke	broken
bring	brought	brought
build	built	built
burst	burst	burst
buy	bought	bought
catch	caught	caught
choose	chose	chosen
cling	clung	clung
come	came	come
cost	cost	cost
deal	dealt	dealt
dig	dug	dug
dive	dived, dove	dived
do	did	done
draw	drew	drawn
dream	dreamed, dreamt	dreamed, dreamt
drink	drank	drunk
drive	drove	driven
eat	ate	eaten
fall	fell	fallen
fight	fought	fought
find	found	found
fly	flew	flown
forget	forgot	forgotten, forgot
freeze	froze	frozen
get	got	gotten, got

BASE FORM	PAST TENSE	PAST PARTICIPLE
give	gave	given
go	went	gone
grow	grew	grown
hang (execute)	hanged	hanged
hang (suspend)	hung	hung
have	had	had
hear	heard	heard
hide	hid	hidden
hurt	hurt	hurt
keep	kept	kept
know	knew	known
lay (put)	laid	laid
lead	led	led
lend	lent	lent
let (allow)	let	let
lie (recline)	lay	lain
lose	lost	lost
make	made	made
prove	proved	proved, proven
read	read	read
ride	rode	ridden
ring	rang	rung
rise (get up)	rose	risen
run	ran	run
say	said	said
see	saw	seen
send	sent	sent
set (place)	set	set
shake	shook	shaken
shoot	shot	shot
shrink	shrank	shrunk
sing	sang	sung
sink	sank	sunk
sit (be seated)	sat	sat
slay	slew	slain
sleep	slept	slept
speak	spoke	spoken

BASE FORM	PAST TENSE	PAST PARTICIPLE
spin	spun	spun
spring	sprang	sprung
stand	stood	stood
steal	stole	stolen
sting	stung	stung
strike	struck	struck, stricken
swear	swore	sworn
swim	swam	swum
swing	swung	swung
take	took	taken
teach	taught	taught
throw	threw	thrown
wake	woke, waked	waked, woken
wear	wore	worn
win	won	won
wring	wrung	wrung
write	wrote	written

27b Distinguish among the forms of *lie* and *lay*.

Writers and speakers frequently confuse the various forms of *lie* (meaning "to recline or rest on a surface") and *lay* (meaning "to put or place something"). *Lie* is an intransitive verb; it does not take a direct object: *The tax forms lie on the table.* The verb *lay* is transitive; it takes a direct object: *Please lay the tax forms on the table.* (See 47b.)

In addition to confusing the meaning of *lie* and *lay*, writers and speakers are often unfamiliar with the Standard English forms of these verbs.

BASE FORM	PAST TENSE	PAST PARTICIPLE	PRESENT PARTICIPLE
lie ("recline")	lay	lain	lying
lay ("put")	laid	laid	laying

▶ Sue was so exhausted that she ~~laid~~ down for a nap.
                                  lay ∧

The past-tense form of *lie* ("to recline") is *lay.*

▶ The patient had ~~laid~~ in an uncomfortable position all night.
                    lain ∧

The past-participle form of *lie* ("to recline") is *lain.* If the correct English seems too stilted, recast the sentence: *The patient had been lying in an uncomfortable position all night.*

▶ The prosecutor ~~lay~~ the pistol on a table close to the jurors.
                  laid ∧

The past-tense form of *lay* ("to place") is *laid.*

▶ Letters dating from 1915 were ~~laying~~ in a corner of the chest.
                                lying ∧

The present participle of *lie* ("to rest on a surface") is *lying.*

EXERCISE 27–1 Edit the following sentences to eliminate problems with irregular verbs. If a sentence is correct, write "correct" after it. Answers appear in the back of the book. *More practice:* e ✓

               saw
The ranger ~~seen~~ the forest fire ten miles away.
           ∧

a. When I get the urge to exercise, I lay down until it passes.
b. Grandmother had drove our new hybrid to the sunrise church service, so we were left with the station wagon.
c. A pile of dirty rags was laying at the bottom of the stairs.
d. How did the game know that the player had went from the room with the blue ogre to the hall where the gold was heaped?
e. Abraham Lincoln took good care of his legal clients; the contracts he drew for the Illinois Central Railroad could never be broke.

hackerhandbooks.com/bedhandbook

e Grammatical sentences > Exercises: 27–2 to 27–4
✓ Grammatical sentences > LearningCurve: Verbs

EXERCISE 27–1 *Answers:*

a. When I get the urge to exercise, I lie down until it passes.
b. Grandmother had driven our new hybrid to the sunrise church service, so we were left with the station wagon.
c. A pile of dirty rags was lying at the bottom of the stairs.
d. How did the game know that the player had gone from the room with the blue ogre to the hall where the gold was heaped?
e. Abraham Lincoln took good care of his legal clients; the contracts he drew for the Illinois Central Railroad could never be broken.

27c Use -s (or -es) endings on present-tense verbs that have third-person singular subjects.

All singular nouns (*child, tree*) and the pronouns *he, she,* and *it* are third-person singular; indefinite pronouns such as *everyone* and *neither* are also third-person singular. When the subject of a sentence is third-person singular, its verb takes an *-s* or *-es* ending in the present tense. (See also 21.)

	SINGULAR		PLURAL	
FIRST PERSON	I	know	we	know
SECOND PERSON	you	know	you	know
THIRD PERSON	he/she/it	knows	they	know
	child	knows	parents	know
	everyone	knows		

> drives
> My neighbor ~~drive~~ to Marco Island every weekend in the
> ∧
> summer.

> turns   dissolves   eats
> Sulfur dioxide ~~turn~~ leaves yellow, ~~dissolve~~ marble, and ~~eat~~
> ∧   ∧   ∧
> away iron and steel.

The subjects *neighbor* and *sulfur dioxide* are third-person singular, so the verbs must end in *-s*.

TIP: Do not add the *-s* ending to the verb if the subject is not third-person singular. The writers of the following sentences, knowing they sometimes dropped *-s* endings from verbs, over-corrected by adding the endings where they don't belong.

> I prepares system specifications for every installation.

The writer mistakenly concluded that the *-s* ending belongs on present-tense verbs used with *all* singular subjects, not just *third-person* singular subjects. The pronoun *I* is first-person singular, so its verb does not require the *-s*.

▶ The wood floors requires continual sweeping.

The writer mistakenly thought that the verb needed an -*s* ending because of the plural subject. But the -*s* ending is used only on present-tense verbs with third-person *singular* subjects.

Has *versus* have

In the present tense, use *has* with third-person singular subjects; all other subjects require *have*.

	SINGULAR		PLURAL	
FIRST PERSON	I	have	we	have
SECOND PERSON	you	have	you	have
THIRD PERSON	he/she/it	has	they	have

                                                     has

▶ This respected musician almost always ~~have~~ a message to
                                               ^

convey in his work.

The subject, *musician*, is third-person singular, so the verb should be *has*.

                   have

▶ My law classes ~~has~~ helped me understand contracts.
                    ^

The subject, *classes*, is third-person plural, so Standard English requires the verb *have*. *Has* is used only with third-person singular subjects.

Does *versus* do *and* doesn't *versus* don't

In the present tense, use *does* and *doesn't* with third-person singular subjects; all other subjects require *do* and *don't*.

	SINGULAR		PLURAL	
FIRST PERSON	I	do/don't	we	do/don't
SECOND PERSON	you	do/don't	you	do/don't
THIRD PERSON	he/she/it	does/doesn't	they	do/don't

▶ Grandfather really ~~don't~~ doesn't have a place to call home.

Grandfather is third-person singular, so the verb should be *doesn't*.

Am, is, and are; was and were

The verb *be* has three forms in the present tense (*am, is, are*) and two in the past tense (*was, were*).

	SINGULAR		PLURAL	
FIRST PERSON	I	am/was	we	are/were
SECOND PERSON	you	are/were	you	are/were
THIRD PERSON	he/she/it	is/was	they	are/were

▶ Did you think you ~~was~~ were going to drown?

The subject *you* is second-person singular, so the verb should be *were*.

27d Do not omit *-ed* endings on verbs.

Speakers who do not fully pronounce *-ed* endings sometimes omit them unintentionally in writing. Failure to pronounce *-ed* endings is common in many dialects and in informal speech even in Standard English. In the following frequently used words and phrases, for example, the *-ed* ending is not always fully pronounced.

advised	developed	prejudiced	supposed to
asked	fixed	pronounced	used to
concerned	frightened	stereotyped	

When a verb is regular, both the past tense and the past participle are formed by adding *-ed* (or *-d*) to the base form of the verb.

Past tense

Use the ending *-ed* or *-d* to express the past tense of regular verbs. The past tense is used when the action occurred entirely in the past.

vb

▶ Over the weekend, Ed ~~fix~~ his brother's skateboard and tuned
  fixed
  up his mother's 1991 Fiat.

▶ Last summer, my counselor ~~advise~~ me to ask my graphic
  advised
  arts instructor for help.

Past participles

Past participles are used in three ways: (1) following *have, has,* or *had* to form one of the perfect tenses; (2) following *be, am, is, are, was, were, being,* or *been* to form the passive voice; and (3) as adjectives modifying nouns or pronouns. The perfect tenses are listed on page 350, and the passive voice is discussed in 8a. For a discussion of participles as adjectives, see 48b.

▶ Robin has ~~ask~~ the Office of Student Affairs for more
  asked
  housing staff for next year.

Has asked is present perfect tense (*have* or *has* followed by a past participle).

▶ Though it is not a new phenomenon, domestic violence is
  publicized
  now ~~publicize~~ more than ever.

Is publicized is a verb in the passive voice (a form of *be* followed by a past participle).

▶ All kickboxing classes end in a cool-down period to stretch
  tightened
  ~~tighten~~ muscles.

The past participle *tightened* functions as an adjective modifying the noun *muscles.*

27e Do not omit needed verbs.

Although Standard English allows some linking verbs and helping verbs to be contracted in informal contexts, it does not allow them to be omitted.

Linking verbs, used to link subjects to subject complements, are frequently a form of *be*: *be, am, is, are, was, were, being, been.* (See 47b.) Some of these forms may be contracted (*I'm, she's, we're, you're, they're*), but they should not be omitted altogether.

▶ When we ^{are} quiet in the evening, we can hear the crickets.

▶ Sherman Alexie ^{is} a Native American author whose stories

have been made into a film.

Helping verbs, used with main verbs, include forms of *be, do,* and *have* and the modal verbs *can, will, shall, could, would, should, may, might,* and *must.* (See 46c.) Some helping verbs may be contracted (*he's leaving, we'll celebrate, they've been told*), but they should not be omitted altogether.

▶ We ^{have} been in Chicago since last Thursday.

▶ Do you know someone who ^{would} be good for the job?

Multilingual

Some languages do not require a linking verb between a subject and its complement. English, however, requires a verb in every sentence. See 30a.

▶ Every night, I read a short book to my daughter. When I ^{am}

too busy, my husband reads to her.

EXERCISE 27–5 Edit the following sentences to eliminate problems with -s and -ed verb forms and with omitted verbs. If a sentence is correct, write "correct" after it. Answers appear in the back of the book. *More practice:* 🄴 ✅

> covers
> The Pell Grant sometimes ~~cover~~ the student's full tuition.
> ∧

a. The glass sculptures of the Swan Boats was prominent in the brightly lit lobby.
b. Visitors to the glass museum were not suppose to touch the exhibits.
c. Our church has all the latest technology, even a close-circuit television.
d. Christos didn't know about Marlo's promotion because he never listens. He always talking.
e. Most psychologists agree that no one performs well under stress.

27f Choose the appropriate verb tense.

Tenses indicate the time of an action in relation to the time of the speaking or writing about that action.

The most common problem with tenses—shifting confusingly from one tense to another—is discussed in section 13. Other problems with tenses are detailed in this section, after the following survey of tenses.

Survey of tenses

Tenses are classified as present, past, and future, with simple, perfect, and progressive forms for each.

Simple tenses The simple tenses indicate relatively simple time relations. The *simple present* tense is used primarily for

hackerhandbooks.com/bedhandbook
🄴 Grammatical sentences > Exercises: 27–6 to 27–8
✅ Grammatical sentences > LearningCurve: Verbs

EXERCISE 27–5 *Answers:*

a. The glass sculptures of the Swan Boats were prominent in the brightly lit lobby.
b. Visitors to the glass museum were not supposed to touch the exhibits.
c. Our church has all the latest technology, even a closed-circuit television.
d. Christos didn't know about Marlo's promotion because he never listens. He is [*or* He's] always talking.
e. Correct

actions occurring at the same time they are being discussed
or for actions occurring regularly. The *simple past* tense is used
for actions completed in the past. The *simple future* tense is used
for actions that will occur in the future. In the following table, the
simple tenses are given for the regular verb *walk*, the irregular
verb *ride*, and the highly irregular verb *be*.

SIMPLE PRESENT

SINGULAR		PLURAL	
I	walk, ride, am	we	walk, ride, are
you	walk, ride, are	you	walk, ride, are
he/she/it	walks, rides, is	they	walk, ride, are

SIMPLE PAST

SINGULAR		PLURAL	
I	walked, rode, was	we	walked, rode, were
you	walked, rode, were	you	walked, rode, were
he/she/it	walked, rode, was	they	walked, rode, were

SIMPLE FUTURE

I, you, he/she/it, we, they   will walk, ride, be

Perfect tenses   More complex time relations are indicated by
the perfect tenses. A verb in one of the perfect tenses (a form of
have plus the past participle) expresses an action that was or will
be completed at the time of another action.

PRESENT PERFECT

I, you, we, they	have walked, ridden, been
he/she/it	has walked, ridden, been

PAST PERFECT

I, you, he/she/it, we, they   had walked, ridden, been

FUTURE PERFECT

I, you, he/she/it, we, they   will have walked, ridden, been

TEACHING TIP

If you teach ESL or ELL sections of composition, consider assigning
students to read daily — even if it's just the campus newspaper. Assign
points to those students who keep a reading log. Research shows that
multilingual speakers find it easier to write in English as they read more
English.

Progressive forms The simple and perfect tenses have progressive forms that describe actions in progress. A progressive verb consists of a form of *be* followed by a present participle. The progressive forms are not normally used with certain verbs, such as *believe, know, hear,* and *seem*.

PRESENT PROGRESSIVE

I	am walking, riding, being
he/she/it	is walking, riding, being
you, we, they	are walking, riding, being

PAST PROGRESSIVE

I, he/she/it	was walking, riding, being
you, we, they	were walking, riding, being

FUTURE PROGRESSIVE

I, you, he/she/it, we, they	will be walking, riding, being

PRESENT PERFECT PROGRESSIVE

I, you, we, they	have been walking, riding, being
he/she/it	has been walking, riding, being

PAST PERFECT PROGRESSIVE

I, you, he/she/it, we, they	had been walking, riding, being

FUTURE PERFECT PROGRESSIVE

I, you, he/she/it, we, they	will have been walking, riding, being

---

Multilingual

See 28a for more specific examples of verb tenses that can be challenging for multilingual writers.

Special uses of the present tense

Use the present tense when expressing general truths, when writing about literature, and when quoting, summarizing, or paraphrasing an author's views.

General truths or scientific principles should appear in the present tense unless such principles have been disproved.

> *revolves*
> ► Galileo taught that the earth ~~revolved~~ around the sun.
> ^

Because Galileo's teaching has not been discredited, the verb should be in the present tense. The following sentence, however, is acceptable: *Ptolemy taught that the sun revolved around the earth.*

When writing about a work of literature, you may be tempted to use the past tense. The convention in the humanities, however, is to describe fictional events in the present tense.

> *reaches*
> ► In Masuji Ibuse's *Black Rain*, a child ~~reached~~ for a
> ^
> pomegranate in his mother's garden, and a moment later
> *is*
> he ~~was~~ dead, killed by the blast of the atomic bomb.
> ^

When you are quoting, summarizing, or paraphrasing the author of a nonliterary work, use present-tense verbs such as *writes, reports, asserts,* and so on to introduce the source. This convention is usually followed even when the author is dead (unless a date or the context specifies the time of writing).

> *argues*
> ► Dr. Jerome Groopman ~~argued~~ that doctors are
> ^
> "susceptible to the subtle and not so subtle efforts of the
> pharmaceutical industry to sculpt our thinking" (9).

In MLA style, signal phrases are written in the present tense, not the past tense. (See also 55b.)

APA NOTE: When you are documenting a paper with the APA (American Psychological Association) style of in-text citations, use past tense verbs such as *reported* or *demonstrated* or present perfect verbs such as *has reported* or *has demonstrated* to introduce the source. (See 60b.)

The past perfect tense

The past perfect tense consists of a past participle preceded by *had* (*had worked, had gone*). This tense is used for an action already completed by the time of another past action or for an action already completed at some specific past time.

> Everyone *had spoken* by the time I arrived.

> I pleaded my case, but Paula *had made up* her mind.

Writers sometimes use the simple past tense when they should use the past perfect.

> By the time dinner was served, the guest of honor ^had^ left.

The past perfect tense is needed because the action of leaving was already completed at a specific past time (when dinner was served).

Some writers tend to overuse the past perfect tense. Do not use the past perfect if two past actions occurred at the same time.

> When Ernest Hemingway lived in Cuba, he ~~had written~~ ^wrote^

> *For Whom the Bell Tolls.*

Sequence of tenses with infinitives and participles

An infinitive is the base form of a verb preceded by *to*. (See 48b.) Use the present infinitive to show action at the same time as or later than the action of the verb in the sentence.

> Barb had hoped to ~~have paid~~ the bill by May 1.

pay (written above "have paid")

The action expressed in the infinitive (*to pay*) occurred later than the action of the sentence's verb (*had hoped*).

Use the perfect form of an infinitive (*to have* followed by the past participle) for an action occurring earlier than that of the verb in the sentence.

> Dan would like to ~~join~~ the navy, but he could not swim.

have joined (written above "join")

The liking occurs in the present; the joining would have occurred in the past.

Like the tense of an infinitive, the tense of a participle is governed by the tense of the sentence's verb. Use the present participle (ending in *-ing*) for an action occurring at the same time as that of the sentence's verb.

Hiking the Appalachian Trail, we spotted many wildflowers.

Use the past participle (such as *given* or *helped*) or the present perfect participle (*having* plus the past participle) for an action occurring before that of the verb.

Discovered off the coast of Florida, the Spanish galleon yielded many treasures.

Having worked her way through college, Lee graduated debt-free.

27g Use the subjunctive mood in the few contexts that require it.

There are three moods in English: the *indicative*, used for facts, opinions, and questions; the *imperative*, used for orders or advice; and the *subjunctive*, used in certain contexts to express wishes, requests, or conditions contrary to fact. For many writers, the subjunctive causes the most problems.

Forms of the subjunctive

In the subjunctive mood, present-tense verbs do not change form to indicate the number and person of the subject (see 21). Instead, the subjunctive uses the base form of the verb (*be*, *drive*, *employ*) with all subjects. Also, in the subjunctive mood, there is only one past-tense form of *be*: *were* (never *was*).

> It is important that you *be* [not *are*] prepared for the interview.

> We asked that she *drive* [not *drives*] more slowly.

> If I *were* [not *was*] you, I'd try a new strategy.

Uses of the subjunctive

The subjunctive mood appears only in a few contexts: in contrary-to-fact clauses beginning with *if* or expressing a wish; in *that* clauses following verbs such as *ask*, *insist*, *recommend*, *request*, and *suggest*; and in certain set expressions.

In contrary-to-fact clauses beginning with *if* When a subordinate clause beginning with *if* expresses a condition contrary to fact, use the subjunctive *were* in place of *was*.

>   were
> ► If I ~~was~~ a member of Congress, I would vote for that bill.
>   ^

> ► The astronomers would be able to see the moons of Jupiter
>   were
> tonight if the weather ~~was~~ clearer.
>   ^

> The writer is not a member of Congress, and the weather is not clear.

Do not use the subjunctive mood in *if* clauses expressing conditions that exist or may exist.

> If Dana *wins* the contest, she will leave for Barcelona in June.

In contrary-to-fact clauses expressing a wish   In formal English, use the subjunctive *were* in clauses expressing a wish or desire.

INFORMAL	I wish that Dr. Vaughn *was* my professor.
FORMAL	I wish that Dr. Vaughn *were* my professor.

In *that* clauses following verbs such as *ask*, *insist*, *request*, and *suggest*   Because requests have not yet become reality, they are expressed in the subjunctive mood.

> be
> ▶ Professor Moore insists that her students ~~are~~ on time.
>   ∧

> file
> ▶ We recommend that Lambert ~~files~~ form 1050 soon.
>   ∧

In certain set expressions   The subjunctive mood, once more widely used, remains in certain set expressions: *Be that as it may*, *as it were*, *far be it from me*, and so on.

EXERCISE 27–9   Edit the following sentences to eliminate errors in verb tense or mood. If a sentence is correct, write "correct" after it. Answers appear in the back of the book. *More practice:* e ☑

> had been
> After the path ~~was~~ plowed, we were able to walk in the park.
>   ∧

a. The palace of Knossos in Crete is believed to have been destroyed by fire around 1375 BCE.

b. Watson and Crick discovered the mechanism that controlled inheritance in all life: the workings of the DNA molecule.

c. When city planners proposed rezoning the waterfront, did they know that the mayor promised to curb development in that neighborhood?

d. Tonight's concert begins at 9:30. If it was earlier, I'd consider going.

e. The math position was filled by the woman who had been running the tutoring center.

hackerhandbooks.com/bedhandbook

e Grammatical sentences > Exercises: 27–10 to 27–12
☑ Grammatical sentences > LearningCurve: Verbs

EXERCISE 27-9   *Possible revisions:*

a. Correct

b. Watson and Crick discovered the mechanism that controls inheritance in all life: the workings of the DNA molecule.

c. When city planners proposed rezoning the waterfront, did they know that the mayor had promised to curb development in that neighborhood?

d. Tonight's concert begins at 9:30. If it were earlier, I'd consider going.

e. Correct

PART VI

Multilingual Writers and ESL Challenges

This part of *The Bedford Handbook* is primarily for multilingual writers. You may find this section helpful if you learned English as a second language (ESL) or if you speak a language other than English with your friends and family.

Besides concentrating on specific points of grammar and usage, you can strengthen your English-language skills by reading, writing, listening to, and speaking English in a variety of settings.

- **Reading:** To familiarize yourself with the ways in which other writers use the language, you can read textbooks, with a focus on vocabulary and sentence patterns, or read fiction or nonfiction books, newspapers, magazines, and Web sites to absorb popular uses of language.

- **Writing:** You will write in your college courses, but you also can practice your skills by writing e-mail messages or blog posts for various audiences or by keeping a personal journal.

- **Listening:** Paying attention to and following directions in class can help you focus on academic conversation. Listening to speakers on campus, to friends, or to TV or radio programs can help you understand colloquial usage.

- **Speaking:** Conversing with English-speaking friends privately or in class discussions can help you develop an "ear" for pronunciation and appropriate usage in various situations.

28   Verbs

Both native and nonnative speakers of English encounter challenges with verbs. Section 28 focuses on specific challenges that

---

SCHOLARS ON TEACHING MULTILINGUAL WRITERS

Leki, Ilona, and Tony Silva, eds. *Journal of Second Language Writing.* <http://www.jslw.org>. This refereed quarterly journal includes current scholarship on the characteristics, attitudes, and composing processes of second-language (L2) writers; features of L2 writers' texts and readers' responses to those texts; the assessment and evaluation of L2 writing; and analyses of the social, cultural, political, and situational contexts for L2 writing. In addition, each issue includes an annotated bibliography of recent L2 books and articles.

multilingual writers sometimes face. You can find more help with verbs in other sections in the book:

> making subjects and verbs agree (21)
>
> using irregular verb forms (27a, 27b)
>
> leaving off verb endings (27c, 27d)
>
> choosing the correct verb tense (27f)
>
> avoiding inappropriate uses of the passive voice (8a)

28a Use the appropriate verb form and tense.

This section offers a brief review of English verb forms and tenses. For additional help, see 27 and 46c.

Basic verb forms

Every main verb in English has five forms, which are used to create all of the verb tenses in Standard English. The following chart shows these forms for the regular verb *help* and the irregular verbs *give* and *be*. See 27a for a list of other common irregular verbs.

Basic verb forms			
	REGULAR VERB *HELP*	IRREGULAR VERB *GIVE*	IRREGULAR VERB *BE**
BASE FORM	help	give	be
PAST TENSE	helped	gave	was, were
PAST PARTICIPLE	helped	given	been
PRESENT PARTICIPLE	helping	giving	being
-S FORM	helps	gives	is

*Be also has the forms *am* and *are*, which are used in the present tense.

SCHOLARS ON TEACHING MULTILINGUAL WRITERS

Bean, Janet, et al. "Should We Invite Students to Write in Home Languages? Complicating the Yes/No Debate." *Composition Studies* 31.1 (2003): 25–42. Print. The authors ask a series of questions in their examination of this central question: Is there a place for multilingual writers' home languages in the academy? They ask practitioners to consider in what contexts and under what circumstances students should be invited to compose in their native language rather than in Standard English. The invitation, the authors conclude, must be issued with respect, help, and awareness.

Verb tenses commonly used in the active voice

For descriptions and examples of all verb tenses, see 27f. For verb tenses commonly used in the passive voice, see the chart beginning on page 363.

Simple tenses
For general facts, states of being, habitual actions

Simple present	**Base form or -s form**
• general facts	College students often *study* late at night.
• states of being	Water *becomes* steam at 100 degrees centigrade.
• habitual, repetitive actions	We *donate* to a different charity each year.
• scheduled future events	The train *arrives* tomorrow at 6:30 p.m.

NOTE: For uses of the present tense in writing about literature, see page 352.

Simple past	**Base form + -ed or -d or irregular form**
• completed actions at a specific time in the past	The storm *destroyed* their property. She *drove* to Montana three years ago.
• facts or states of being in the past	When I *was* young, I usually *walked* to school with my sister.

Simple future	***will* + base form**
• future actions, promises, or predictions	I *will exercise* tomorrow. The snowfall *will begin* around midnight.

Simple progressive forms
For continuing actions

Present progressive	***am, is, are* + present participle**
• actions in progress at the present time, not continuing indefinitely	The students *are taking* an exam in Room 105. The valet *is parking* the car.
• future actions (with *leave, go, come, move,* etc.)	I *am leaving* tomorrow morning.

TEACHING TIP

When you respond to drafts and see surface errors such as problems with pronoun case, don't spend time teaching the lesson in the margin of a student's draft. Instead, refer the writer to a specific section in the handbook (28a, for example). You can also suggest that students complete the book's exercises or the online exercises for strengthening skills.

WRITERS ON WRITING

I heard an old Negro street singer last week, Reverend Pearly Brown, singing, "God don't never change!" This is a precise thing he is singing. He does not mean "God does not ever change!" He means "God don't never change." — Imamu Amiri Baraka

VERB TENSES COMMONLY USED IN THE ACTIVE VOICE *(cont.)*	

Past progressive | *was*, *were* + present participle

- actions in progress at a specific time in the past | They *were swimming* when the storm struck.

- *was going to*, *were going to* for past plans that did not happen | We *were going to* drive to Florida for spring break, but the car broke down.

NOTE: Some verbs are not normally used in the progressive: *appear*, *believe*, *belong*, *contain*, *have*, *hear*, *know*, *like*, *need*, *see*, *seem*, *taste*, *understand*, and *want*.

> ▶ I ~~am wanting~~ to see August Wilson's *Radio Golf*.
>   want
>   ∧

Perfect tenses
For actions that happened before another present or past time

Present perfect | *has*, *have* + past participle

- repetitive or constant actions that began in the past and continue to the present | I *have loved* cats since I was a child. Alicia *has worked* in Kenya for ten years.

- actions that happened at an unknown or unspecific time in the past | Stephen *has visited* Wales three times.

Past perfect | *had* + past participle

- actions that began or occurred before another time in the past | She *had* just *crossed* the street when the runaway car crashed into the building.

NOTE: For more on the past perfect, see 27f. For uses of the past perfect in conditional sentences, see 28e.   →

SCHOLARS ON TEACHING MULTILINGUAL WRITERS

Reynolds, Nedra, Jay Dolmage, Bruce Herzberg, and Patricia Bizzell. "Teaching English as a Second Language and Language Policy." *The Bedford Bibliography for Teachers of Writing.* 7th ed. Boston: Bedford, 2012. 278–93. Print. The authors address a wide range of teachers' and administrators' concerns. Their annotations are extensive and helpful.

VERB TENSES COMMONLY USED IN THE ACTIVE VOICE (cont.)	
Perfect progressive forms *For continuous past actions before another present or past time*	
Present perfect progressive	*has, have + been + present participle*
• continuous actions that began in the past and continue to the present	Yolanda *has been trying* to get a job in Boston for five years.
Past perfect progressive	*had + been + present participle*
• actions that began and continued in the past until another past action	By the time I moved to Georgia, I *had been supporting* myself for five years.

Verb tenses

Section 27f describes all the verb tenses in English, showing the forms of a regular verb, an irregular verb, and the verb *be* in each tense. The chart beginning on page 360 provides more details about the tenses commonly used in the active voice in writing; the chart beginning on page 363 gives details about tenses commonly used in the passive voice.

28b To write a verb in the passive voice, use a form of *be* with the past participle.

When a sentence is written in the passive voice, the subject receives the action instead of doing it. (See 47c.)

The solution *was measured* by the lab assistant.

Melissa *was taken* to the theater.

To form the passive voice, use a form of *be*—*am, is, are, was, were, being, be,* or *been*—followed by the past participle of the

Verb tenses commonly used in the passive voice

For details about verb tenses in the active voice, see pages 360–62.

Simple tenses (passive voice)

Simple present	*am*, *is*, *are* + past participle
• general facts	Breakfast *is served* daily.
• habitual, repetitive actions	The receipts *are counted* every night.
Simple past	*was*, *were* + past participle
• completed past actions	He *was punished* for being late.
Simple future	*will be* + past participle
• future actions, promises, or predictions	The decision *will be made* by the committee next week.

Simple progressive forms (passive voice)

Present progressive	*am*, *is*, *are* + *being* + past participle
• actions in progress at the present time	The new stadium *is being built* with private money.
• future actions (with *leave*, *go*, *come*, *move*, etc.)	Jo *is being moved* to a new class next month.
Past progressive	*was*, *were* + *being* + past participle
• actions in progress at a specific time in the past	We thought we *were being followed*.

Perfect tenses (passive voice)

Present perfect	*has*, *have* + *been* + past participle
• actions that began in the past and continue to the present	The flight *has been delayed* because of storms in the Midwest.
• actions that happened at an unknown or un-specific time in the past	Wars *have been fought* throughout history.

VERB TENSES COMMONLY USED IN THE PASSIVE VOICE *(cont.)*

Past perfect	*had* + *been* + past participle
• actions that began or occurred before another time in the past	He *had been given* all the hints he needed to complete the puzzle.

NOTE: Future progressive, future perfect, and perfect progressive forms are not used in the passive voice.

---

main verb: *was chosen, are remembered.* (Sometimes a form of *be* follows another helping verb: *will be considered, could have been broken.*)

> written
> ▶ *Dreaming in Cuban* was ~~writing~~ by Cristina García.
>   ∧

In the passive voice, the past participle *written*, not the present participle *writing*, must follow *was* (the past tense of *be*).

> tested.
> ▶ The child is being ~~test.~~
>   ∧

The past participle *tested*, not the base form *test*, must be used with *is being* to form the passive voice.

For details on forming the passive in various tenses, consult the chart on pages 363–64. (The active voice is generally stronger and more direct than the passive voice. The passive voice does have appropriate uses; see 8a and 47c.)

NOTE: Only transitive verbs, those that take direct objects, may be used in the passive voice. Intransitive verbs such as *occur, happen, sleep, die, become,* and *fall* are not used in the passive. (See 47b.)

> ▶ The accident ~~was~~ happened suddenly.

EXERCISE 28–1 Revise the following sentences to correct errors in verb forms and tenses in the active and the passive voice. You may need to look at 27a for the correct form of some irregular verbs and at 27f for help with tenses. Answers appear in the back of the book. *More practice:* e ✓

> *begins*
> The meeting ~~begin~~ tonight at 7:30.
> ∧

a. In the past, tobacco companies deny any connection between smoking and health problems.

b. The volunteer's compassion has touch many lives.

c. I am wanting to register for a summer tutoring session.

d. By the end of the year, the state will have test 139 birds for avian flu.

e. The golfers were prepare for all weather conditions.

28c Use the base form of the verb after a modal.

The modal verbs are *can, could, may, might, must, shall, should, will,* and *would.* (*Ought to* is also considered a modal verb.) The modals are used with the base form of a verb to show ability, certainty, necessity, permission, obligation, or possibility.

Modals and the verbs that follow them do not change form to indicate tense. For a summary of modals and their meanings, see the chart on pages 366–67. (See also 27e.)

> *launch*
> ▶ The art museum will ~~launches~~ its fundraising campaign
>   ∧
> next month.

The modal *will* must be followed by the base form *launch,* not the present tense *launches.*

hackerhandbooks.com/bedhandbook

e Multilingual/ESL > Exercises: 28–2 and 28–3

✓ Multilingual/ESL > LearningCurve: Verbs for multilingual writers

EXERCISE 28–1 *Answers:*

a. In the past, tobacco companies denied any connection between smoking and health problems.

b. The volunteer's compassion has touched many lives.

c. I want to register for a summer tutoring session.

d. By the end of the year, the state will have tested 139 birds for avian flu.

e. The golfers were prepared for all weather conditions.

Modals and their meanings

can

• general ability (present)	Ants *can survive* anywhere, even in space. Jorge *can run* a marathon faster than his brother.
• informal requests or permission	*Can* you *tell* me where the light is? Sandy *can borrow* my calculator.

could

• general ability (past)	Lea *could read* when she was only three years old.
• polite, informal requests or permission	*Could* you *give* me that pen?

may

• formal requests or permission	*May* I *see* the report? Students *may park* only in the yellow zone.
• possibility	I *may try* to finish my homework tonight, or I *may wake up* early and *finish* it tomorrow.

might

• possibility	Funding for the language lab *might double* by 2017.

NOTE: *Might* usually expresses a stronger possibility than *may*.

must

• necessity (present or future)	To be effective, welfare-to-work programs *must provide* access to job training.
• strong probability	Amy *must be* nervous. [She is probably nervous.]
• near certainty (present or past)	I *must have left* my wallet at home. [I almost certainly left my wallet at home.]

SCHOLARS ON TEACHING MULTILINGUAL WRITERS

Cooper, Charles R., and Lee Odell, eds. *Evaluating Writing: The Role of Teachers' Knowledge about Text, Learning, and Culture*. Urbana: NCTE, 1999. Print. Two chapters in this useful collection focus on the writing of multilingual students: Guadalupe Valdes and Patricia Anloff Sanders's "Latino ESL Students and the Development of Writing Abilities" and Guanjun Cai's "Texts in Contexts: Understanding Chinese Students' English Compositions." Both chapters synthesize previous research and offer teachers fresh perspectives for teaching multilingual students and evaluating their writing.

MODALS AND THEIR MEANINGS (cont.)

should

• suggestions or advice	Diabetics *should drink* plenty of water every day.
• obligations or duties	The government *should protect* citizens' rights.
• expectations	The books *should arrive* soon. [We expect the books to arrive soon.]

will

• certainty	If you don't leave now, you *will be* late for your rehearsal.
• requests	*Will* you *help* me study for my psychology exam?
• promises and offers	Jonah *will arrange* the carpool.

would

• polite requests	*Would* you *help* me carry these books? I *would like* some coffee. [*Would like* is more polite than *want*.]
• habitual or repeated actions (in the past)	Whenever Elena needed help with sewing, she *would call* her aunt.

▶ The translator could ~~spoke~~ ^speak^ many languages, so the ambassador hired her for the European tour.

The modal *could* must be followed by the base form *speak*, not the past tense *spoke*.

TIP: Do not use *to* before a main verb that follows a modal.

▶ Gina can ~~to~~ drive us home if we miss the last train.

For the use of modals in conditional sentences, see 28e.

TEACHING TIP

Ask students to read brief articles taken from newspapers or popular magazines. Ask them to circle modal + base form combinations. Assign students in pairs or groups to classify what they find. What does each combination show (ability, certainty, permission, necessity, and so forth)?

EXERCISE 28–4   Edit the following sentences to correct errors in the use of verb forms with modals. You may find it helpful to consult the chart on pages 366–67. If a sentence is correct, write "correct" after it. Answers appear in the back of the book. *More practice:* e ✓

> **We should ~~to~~ order pizza for dinner.**

a. A major league pitcher can to throw a baseball more than ninety-five miles per hour.

b. The writing center tutor will helps you revise your essay.

c. A reptile must adjusted its body temperature to its environment.

d. In some states, individuals may renew a driver's license online.

e. My uncle, a cartoonist, could sketched a face in less than a minute.

28d To make negative verb forms, add *not* in the appropriate place.

If the verb is the simple present or past tense of *be* (*am, is, are, was, were*), add *not* after the verb.

> Gianna is *not* a member of the club.

For simple present-tense verbs other than *be*, use *do* or *does* plus *not* before the base form of the verb. (For the correct forms of *do* and *does*, see the chart on p. 378.)

> does
> ▶ **Mariko not want more dessert.**
> ʌ

> ▶ **Mariko does not want~~s~~ more dessert.**

For simple past-tense verbs other than *be*, use *did* plus *not* before the base form of the verb.

> plant
> ▶ **They did not ~~planted~~ corn this year.**
> ʌ

hackerhandbooks.com/bedhandbook

e Multilingual/ESL > Exercises: 28–5, 28–6, and 28–13
✓ Multilingual/ESL > LearningCurve: Verbs for multilingual writers

---

EXERCISE 28–4   *Answers:*

a. A major league pitcher can throw a baseball more than ninety-five miles per hour.

b. The writing center tutor will help you revise your essay.

c. A reptile must adjust its body temperature to its environment.

d. Correct

e. My uncle, a cartoonist, could sketch a face in less than a minute.

In a verb phrase consisting of one or more helping verbs and a present or past participle (*is watching*, *were living*, *has played*, *could have been driven*), use the word *not* after the first helping verb.

▶ Inna should have ~~not~~ *not* gone dancing last night.

▶ Bonnie is ~~no~~ *not* singing this weekend.

NOTE: English allows only one negative in an independent clause to express a negative idea; using more than one is an error known as a *double negative* (see 26e for more on double negatives to express a positive idea).

▶ We could not find ~~no~~ *any* books about the history of our school.

28e In a conditional sentence, choose verb tenses according to the type of condition expressed in the sentence.

Conditional sentences contain two clauses: a subordinate clause (usually starting with *if*, *when*, or *unless*) and an independent clause. The subordinate clause (sometimes called the *if* or *unless* clause) states the condition or cause; the independent clause states the result or effect. In each example in this section, the subordinate clause (*if* clause) is marked SUB, and the independent clause is marked IND. (See 48e on subordinate clauses.)

Factual

Factual conditional sentences express relationships based on facts. If the relationship is a scientific truth, use the present tense in both clauses.

```
┌───────────── SUB ─────────────┐ ┌─ IND ─┐
```
If water *cools* to 32 degrees Fahrenheit, it *freezes*.

SCHOLARS ON TEACHING MULTILINGUAL WRITERS

Celce-Murcia, Marianne, and Diane Larsen-Freeman. *The Grammar Book: An ESL/EFL Teacher's Course.* 2nd ed. Boston: Heinle, 1999. Print. This book, written for ESL and EFL teachers, is a thorough description of English grammar. The authors provide practical teaching suggestions.

If the sentence describes a condition that is (or was) habitually true, use the same tense in both clauses.

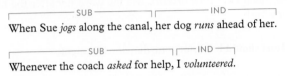

When Sue *jogs* along the canal, her dog *runs* ahead of her.

Whenever the coach *asked* for help, I *volunteered*.

Predictive

Predictive conditional sentences are used to predict the future or to express future plans or possibilities. To form a predictive sentence, use a present-tense verb in the subordinate clause; in the independent clause, use the modal *will, can, may, should,* or *might* plus the base form of the verb.

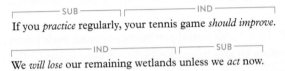

If you *practice* regularly, your tennis game *should improve*.

We *will lose* our remaining wetlands unless we *act* now.

TIP: In all types of conditional sentences (factual, predictive, and speculative), *if* or *unless* clauses do not use the modal verb *will*.

▶ If Liv ~~will pass~~ her history test, she will graduate this year.
  passes

Speculative

Speculative conditional sentences express unlikely, contrary-to-fact, or impossible conditions. English uses the past or past perfect tense in the *if* clause, even for conditions in the present or the future.

Unlikely possibilities   If the condition is possible but unlikely in the present or the future, use the past tense in the subordinate clause; in the independent clause, use *would, could,* or *might* plus the base form of the verb.

SCHOLARS ON TEACHING MULTILINGUAL WRITERS

Zamel, Vivian. "Strangers in Academia: The Experiences of Faculty and ESL Students across the Curriculum." *College Composition and Communication* 46.4 (1995): 506–21. Print. Reporting on surveys of ESL students and of faculty across the disciplines, Zamel contrasts two groups of faculty: those who value multilingual students' knowledge and abilities, in spite of their struggles with language, and those who equate language difficulties with lack of intellect. She argues that when we build on students' strengths we are not compromising our standards.

```
    ┌──── SUB ────┐┌──── IND ────┐
```
If I *won* the lottery, I *would travel* to Egypt.

The writer does not expect to win the lottery. Because this is a possible but unlikely present or future situation, the past tense is used in the subordinate clause.

Conditions contrary to fact   In conditions that are currently unreal or contrary to fact, use the past-tense verb *were* (not *was*) in the *if* clause for all subjects. (See also 27g, on the subjunctive mood.)

>   were
> ▶ If I ~~was~~ president, I would make children's issues a priority.
>   ∧

The writer is not president, so *were* is correct in the *if* clause.

Events that did not happen   In a conditional sentence that speculates about an event that did not happen or was impossible in the past, use the past perfect tense in the *if* clause; in the independent clause, use *would have*, *could have*, or *might have* with the past participle. (See also past perfect tense, p. 361.)

```
    ┌─────── SUB ───────┐┌─────────── IND ───────────┐
```
If I *had saved* more money, I *would have visited* Laos last year.

The writer did not save more money and did not travel to Laos. This sentence shows a possibility that did not happen.

EXERCISE 28-7   Edit the following sentences (p. 372) to correct problems with verbs. In some cases, more than one revision is possible. Possible revisions appear in the back of the book. *More practice:* e ✓

>   had
> If I ~~have~~ time, I would study both French and Russian next
>   ∧
> semester.

e Multilingual/ESL > Exercises: 28–8, 28–9, and 28–13
✓ Multilingual/ESL > LearningCurve: Verbs for multilingual writers

a. The electrician might have discovered the broken circuit if she went through the modules one at a time.

b. If Verena wins a scholarship, she would go to graduate school.

c. Whenever a rainbow appears after a storm, everybody came out to see it.

d. Sarah did not understood the terms of her internship.

e. If I live in Budapest with my cousin Szusza, she would teach me Hungarian cooking.

28f Become familiar with verbs that may be followed by gerunds or infinitives.

A gerund is a verb form that ends in -*ing* and is used as a noun: *sleeping, dreaming.* An infinitive is the word *to* plus the base form of the verb: *to sleep, to dream.* The word *to* is an infinitive marker, not a preposition, in this use. (See 48b.)

A few verbs may be followed by either a gerund or an infinitive; others may be followed by a gerund but not by an infinitive; still others may be followed by an infinitive but not by a gerund.

Verb + gerund or infinitive (no change in meaning)

The following commonly used verbs may be followed by a gerund or an infinitive, with little or no difference in meaning:

begin	hate	love
continue	like	start

I love *skiing.* I love *to ski.*

Verb + gerund or infinitive (change in meaning)

With a few verbs, the choice of a gerund or an infinitive changes the meaning dramatically:

forget	remember	stop	try

EXERCISE 28-7 *Possible revisions:*

a. The electrician might have discovered the broken circuit if she had gone through the modules one at a time.

b. If Verena wins a scholarship, she will go to graduate school.

c. Whenever a rainbow appears after a storm, everybody comes out to see it.

d. Sarah did not understand the terms of her internship.

e. If I lived in Budapest with my cousin Szusza, she would teach me Hungarian cooking.

She stopped *speaking* to Lucia. [She no longer spoke to Lucia.]

She stopped *to speak* to Lucia. [She paused so that she could speak to Lucia.]

Verb + gerund

These verbs may be followed by a gerund but not by an infinitive:

admit	discuss	imagine	put off	risk
appreciate	enjoy	miss	quit	suggest
avoid	escape	postpone	recall	tolerate
deny	finish	practice	resist	

Bill enjoys *playing* [not *to play*] the piano.

Jamie quit *smoking*.

Verb + infinitive

These verbs may be followed by an infinitive but not by a gerund:

agree	decide	manage	plan	wait
ask	expect	mean	pretend	want
beg	help	need	promise	wish
claim	hope	offer	refuse	would like

Jill has offered *to water* [not *watering*] the plants while we are away.

Joe finally managed *to find* a parking space.

A few of these verbs may be followed either by an infinitive directly or by a noun or pronoun plus an infinitive:

ask	help	promise	would like
expect	need	want	

We asked *to speak* to the congregation.

We asked *Rabbi Abrams to speak* to our congregation.

SCHOLARS ON TEACHING MULTILINGUAL WRITERS

Fox, Helen. *Listening to the World: Cultural Issues in Academic Writing.* Urbana: NCTE, 1994. Print. Fox argues that the communication style promoted in US academic settings — favoring argument, analysis, and critical thinking — is "shared by only a tiny fraction of the world's peoples." She urges us to be respectful of other communication styles.

Verb + noun or pronoun + infinitive

With certain verbs in the active voice, a noun or pronoun must come between the verb and the infinitive that follows it. The noun or pronoun usually names a person who is affected by the action of the verb.

advise	convince	order	tell
allow	encourage	persuade	urge
cause	have ("own")	remind	warn
command	instruct	require	

        V   N ⌐INF⌐

The class encouraged Luis to tell the story of his escape.

The counselor *advised Haley to take* four courses instead of five.

Verb + noun or pronoun + unmarked infinitive

An unmarked infinitive is an infinitive without *to*. A few verbs (often called *causative verbs*) may be followed by a noun or pronoun and an unmarked infinitive.

have ("cause")	let ("allow")
help	make ("force")

▶ Rose had the attendant ~~to~~ wash the windshield.

▶ Frank made me ~~to~~ carry his book for him.

Help can be followed by a noun or pronoun and either an unmarked or a marked infinitive.

Emma *helped Brian wash* the dishes.

Emma *helped Brian to wash* the dishes.

NOTE: The infinitive is used in some typical constructions with *too* and *enough*.

TOO + ADJECTIVE + INFINITIVE

The gift is *too large to wrap*.

ENOUGH + NOUN + INFINITIVE

Our emergency pack has *enough bottled water to last* a week.

ADJECTIVE + ENOUGH + INFINITIVE

Some of the hikers felt *strong enough to climb* another thousand feet.

EXERCISE 28-10   Form sentences by adding gerund or infinitive constructions to the following sentence openings. In some cases, more than one kind of construction is possible. Possible answers appear in the back of the book. *More practice:* e ✓

> **Please remind** your sister to call me.
>   ∧

a.   I enjoy

b.   The tutor told Samantha

c.   The team hopes

d.   Ricardo and his brothers miss

e.   Jon remembered

29 Articles (*a, an, the*)

Articles (*a, an, the*) are part of a category of words known as *noun markers* or *determiners*.

29a Be familiar with articles and other noun markers.

Standard English uses noun markers to help identify the nouns that follow. In addition to articles (*a, an,* and *the*), noun markers include the following:

hackerhandbooks.com/bedhandbook

e Multilingual/ESL > Exercises: 28–11 to 28–13

✓ Multilingual/ESL > LearningCurve: Verbs for multilingual writers

EXERCISE 28-10   *Possible answers:*

a.   I enjoy riding my motorcycle.

b.   The tutor told Samantha to come to the writing center.

c.   The team hopes to work hard and win the championship.

d.   Ricardo and his brothers miss surfing during the winter.

e.   Jon remembered to lock the door. *Or* Jon remembered seeing that movie years ago.

- possessive nouns, such as *Elena's* (See 36a.)
- possessive pronoun/adjectives: *my, your, his, her, its, our, their* (See 46b.)
- demonstrative pronoun/adjectives: *this, that, these, those* (See 46b.)
- quantifiers: *all, any, each, either, every, few, many, more, most, much, neither, several, some,* and so on (See 29d.)
- numbers: *one, twenty-three,* and so on

Using articles and other noun markers

Articles and other noun markers always appear before nouns; sometimes other modifiers, such as adjectives and adverbs, come between a noun marker and a noun.

> ART N
> Felix is reading a book about mythology.

> ART ADJ N
> We took an exciting trip to Alaska last summer.

> NOUN
> MARKER ADV ADJ N
> That very delicious meal was expensive.

In most cases, do not use an article with another noun marker.

> ▸ ~~The~~ Natalie's older brother lives in Wisconsin.

Expressions like *a few, the most,* and *all the* are exceptions: *a few potatoes, all the rain.* See also 29d.

Types of articles and types of nouns

To choose an appropriate article for a noun, you must first determine whether the noun is *common* or *proper, count* or

ADDITIONAL RESOURCE ON TUTORING MULTILINGUAL WRITERS

Ryan, Leigh, and Lisa Zimmerelli. *The Bedford Guide for Writing Tutors.* 5th ed. Boston: Bedford, 2010. Print. In this concise introduction to tutoring in the writing center, Ryan and Zimmerelli offer practical suggestions and strategies for working with the variety of writers, assignments, and situations that tutors are apt to encounter. Ideal for tutor training courses, the fifth edition pays special attention to the challenges and opportunities of online tutoring.

noncount, *singular* or *plural*, and *specific* or *general*. The chart on pages 378–79 describes the types of nouns.

Articles are classified as *indefinite* and *definite*. The indefinite articles, *a* and *an*, are used with general nouns. The definite article, *the*, is used with specific nouns. (The last section of the chart on p. 379 explains general and specific nouns.)

A and *an* both mean "one" or "one among many." Use *a* before a consonant sound: *a banana, a vacation, a happy child, a united family.* Use *an* before a vowel sound: *an eggplant, an uncle, an honorable person.* (See also *a, an* in the glossary of usage.)

The shows that a noun is specific; use *the* with one or more than one specific thing: *the newspaper, the soldiers.*

29b Use *the* with most specific common nouns.

The definite article, *the*, is used with most nouns—both count and noncount—that the reader can identify specifically. Usually the identity will be clear to the reader for one of the following reasons. (See the chart on pp. 378–79.)

1. The noun has been previously mentioned.

> the
> ▶ A truck cut in front of our van. When ⌃ truck skidded a few
>
> seconds later, we almost crashed into it.

> The article *A* is used before *truck* when the noun is first mentioned. When the noun is mentioned again, it needs the article *the* because readers can now identify which truck skidded—the one that cut in front of the van.

2. A phrase or clause following the noun restricts its identity.

> the
> ▶ Bryce warned me that ⌃ GPS in his car was not working.

> The phrase *in his car* identifies the specific GPS.

SCHOLARS ON TUTORING MULTILINGUAL WRITERS

Bruce, Shanti, and Ben Rafoth, eds. *ESL Writers: A Guide for Writing Center Tutors*. 2nd ed. Portsmouth: Boynton, 2009. Print. This is the first book to focus on the theory and practice of tutoring ESL writers. The articles in Parts 1 and 3 provide a theoretical context for the issues addressed in Part 2 on the tutoring session itself. The twelve articles in Part 2 offer practical suggestions for conducting tutoring sessions with ESL writers, including how to avoid appropriating the writer's text, how and when to pay attention to global and local concerns, how to deal with plagiarism, and how to address needs that go beyond writing, such as interpreting syllabi, assigned readings, and teachers' assignments.

Types of nouns

Common or proper

Common nouns	Examples	
• name general persons, places, things, or ideas	religion	beauty
	knowledge	student
• begin with lowercase	rain	country

Proper nouns	Examples	
• name specific persons, places, things, or ideas	Hinduism	President Adams
	Philip	Washington Monument
• begin with capital letter	New Jersey	Supreme Court
	Vietnam	Renaissance

Count or noncount (common nouns only)

Count nouns	Examples
• name persons, places, things, or ideas that can be counted	girl, girls
	city, cities
	goose, geese
• have plural forms	philosophy, philosophies

Noncount nouns	Examples	
• name things or abstract ideas that cannot be counted	water	patience
	silver	knowledge
• cannot be made plural	furniture	air

NOTE: See the chart on page 383 for lists of commonly used noncount nouns.

SCHOLARS ON TUTORING MULTILINGUAL WRITERS

Rafoth, Ben. "Responding Online." *ESL Writers: A Guide for Writing Center Tutors.* Ed. Shanti Bruce and Ben Rafoth. 2nd ed. Portsmouth: Boynton, 2009. 149–60. Print. Rafoth describes the lessons he and his tutors learned about the kinds of online responses that are most useful to both multilingual and native-speaking writers. He concludes with the following advice to online tutors: Rather than making lots of comments on a paper, focus on a few changes that need to be made; separate comments on rhetorical matters involving key points from comments on items that do not interfere with comprehension; state advice plainly and directly instead of couching it with qualifiers about what readers might think; offer a clear and consistent message and reinforce it throughout the paper.

TYPES OF NOUNS (cont.)

Singular or plural (both common and proper)

Singular nouns (count and noncount)

- represent one person, place, thing, or idea

Examples

backpack	rain
country	beauty
woman	Nile River
achievement	Block Island

Plural nouns (count only)

- represent more than one person, place, thing, or idea
- must be count nouns

Examples

backpacks	Ural Mountains
countries	Falkland Islands
women	achievements

Specific (definite) or general (indefinite) (count and noncount)

Specific nouns

- name persons, places, things, or ideas that can be identified within a group of the same type

Examples

The students in Professor Martin's *class* should study.

The airplane carrying *the senator* was late.

The furniture in *the truck* was damaged.

General nouns

- name categories of persons, places, things, or ideas (often plural)

Examples

Students should study.

Books bridge *gaps* between *cultures*.

The airplane has made commuting between *cities* easy.

SCHOLARS ON TUTORING MULTILINGUAL WRITERS

Severino, Carol. "Avoiding Appropriation." *ESL Writers: A Guide for Writing Center Tutors.* Ed. Shanti Bruce and Ben Rafoth. 2nd ed. Portsmouth: Boynton, 2009. 51–65. Print. Drawing on her experience of learning to write in Italian, Severino explains the loss of voice and ownership multilingual writers often feel when their writing has been reformulated by teachers or tutors. Severino offers ten specific recommendations for honoring the writer's voice, with an emphasis on addressing the student's expressed needs in a session and on metatutoring, that is, explaining how and why one is using particular tutoring techniques.

NOTE: Descriptive adjectives do not necessarily make a noun specific. A specific noun is one that readers can identify within a group of nouns of the same type.

▶ If I win the lottery, I will buy ~~the~~ brand-new bright red sports car.

a (above "the")

> The reader cannot identify which specific brand-new bright red sports car the writer will buy. Even though *car* has many adjectives in front of it, it is a general noun in this sentence.

3. A superlative adjective such as *best* or *most intelligent* makes the noun's identity specific. (See also 26d.)

▶ Our petite daughter dated tallest boy in her class.

the (inserted before "tallest")

> The superlative *tallest* makes the noun *boy* specific. Although there might be several tall boys, only one boy can be the tallest.

4. The noun describes a unique person, place, or thing.

▶ During an eclipse, one should not look directly at sun.

the (inserted before "sun")

> There is only one sun in our solar system, so its identity is clear.

5. The context or situation makes the noun's identity clear.

▶ Please don't slam door when you leave.

the (inserted before "door")

> Both the speaker and the listener know which door is meant.

6. The noun is singular and refers to a scientific class or category of items (most often animals, musical instruments, and inventions).

▶ ~~Tin~~ whistle is common in traditional Irish music.

The tin (above "Tin")

> The writer is referring to the tin whistle as a class of musical instruments.

29c Use *a* (or *an*) with common singular count nouns that refer to "one" or "any."

If a count noun refers to one unspecific item (not a whole category), use the indefinite article, *a* or *an*. *A* and *an* usually mean "one among many" but can also mean "any one." (See the chart on p. 382.)

> ▶ My English professor asked me to bring ^a dictionary to class.
>
> The noun *dictionary* refers to "one unspecific dictionary" or "any dictionary."

> ▶ We want to rent ^an apartment close to the lake.
>
> The noun *apartment* refers to "any apartment close to the lake," not a specific apartment.

29d Use a quantifier such as *some* or *more*, not *a* or *an*, with a noncount noun to express an approximate amount.

Do not use *a* or *an* with noncount nouns. Also do not use numbers or words such as *several* or *many*; they must be used with plural nouns, and noncount nouns do not have plural forms. (See the chart on p. 383 for lists of commonly used noncount nouns.)

> ▶ Dr. Snyder gave us ~~an~~ information about the Peace Corps.

> ▶ Do you have ~~many~~ money with you?

You can use quantifiers such as *enough, less,* and *some* to suggest approximate amounts or nonspecific quantities of noncount nouns: *a little salt, any homework, enough wood, less information, much pollution.*

SCHOLARS ON TEACHING ENGLISH ARTICLES

Master, Peter. "Teaching the English Articles as a Binary System." *TESOL Quarterly* 24.3 (1990): 461–78. Print. Master argues that English articles can be taught as a "binary division between classification (*a*) and identification (*the*). All the other elements of article usage can be understood within this framework, allowing a one form/one function correspondence for *a* and *the*."

Choosing articles for common nouns

Use *the*

• if the reader has enough information to identify the noun specifically	COUNT: Please turn on *the lights*. We're going to *the zoo* tomorrow.
	NONCOUNT: *The food* throughout Italy is excellent.

Use *a* or *an*

• if the noun refers to one item *and* if the item is singular but not specific	COUNT: Bring *a pencil* to class. Charles wrote *an essay* about his first job.

NOTE: Do not use *a* or *an* with plural or noncount nouns.

Use a quantifier (*enough, many, some,* etc.)

• if the noun represents an unspecified amount of something	COUNT (PLURAL): Amir showed us *some photos* of India. *Many turtles* return to the same nesting site each year.
• if the amount is more than one but not all items in a category	NONCOUNT: We didn't get *enough rain* this summer.

NOTE: Sometimes no article conveys an unspecified amount: *Amir showed us photos of India.*

Use no article

• if the noun represents all items in a category	COUNT (PLURAL): *Students* can attend the show for free.
• if the noun represents a category in general	NONCOUNT: *Coal* is a natural resource.

NOTE: *The* is occasionally used when a singular count noun refers to all items in a class or a specific category: *The bald eagle is no longer endangered in the United States.*

TEACHING TIP

It is often helpful to allow students to take charge of teaching a few grammar concepts. Assign students in pairs or groups to tackle concepts such as articles or verb tense and to prepare a ten-minute mini-lesson in which they show examples and discuss revision strategies. If the class is online, the students can prepare a few slides that they upload to the course Web site.

Commonly used noncount nouns
Food and drink
beef, bread, butter, candy, cereal, cheese, cream, meat, milk, pasta, rice, salt, sugar, water, wine
Nonfood substances
air, cement, coal, dirt, gasoline, gold, paper, petroleum, plastic, rain, silver, snow, soap, steel, wood, wool
Abstract nouns
advice, anger, beauty, confidence, courage, employment, fun, happiness, health, honesty, information, intelligence, knowledge, love, poverty, satisfaction, wealth
Other
biology (and other areas of study), clothing, equipment, furniture, homework, jewelry, luggage, machinery, mail, money, news, poetry, pollution, research, scenery, traffic, transportation, violence, weather, work
NOTE: A few noncount nouns (such as *love*) can also be used as count nouns: *He had two loves: music and archery.*

29e Do not use articles with nouns that refer to all of something or something in general.

When a noncount noun refers to all of its type or to a concept in general, it is not marked with an article.

      Kindness
▶ ~~The kindness~~ is a virtue.
      ∧

    The noun represents kindness in general; it does not represent a specific type of kindness, such as *the kindness he showed me after my mother's death.*

▶ In some places, ~~the~~ rice is preferred to all other grains.

The noun *rice* represents rice in general. To refer to a specific type or serving of rice, the definite article is appropriate: *The rice my husband served last night is the best I've ever tasted.*

In most cases, when you use a count noun to represent a general category, make the noun plural. Do not use unmarked singular count nouns to represent whole categories.

　　　　　　Fountains are
▶ ~~Fountain is~~ an expensive element of landscape design.
　　∧

Fountains is a count noun that represents fountains in general.

EXCEPTION: In some cases, *the* can be used with singular count nouns to represent a class or specific category: *The Chinese alligator is smaller than the American alligator.* See also number 6 in 29b.

29f Do not use articles with most singular proper nouns. Use *the* with most plural proper nouns.

Since singular proper nouns are already specific, they typically do not need an article: *Prime Minister Cameron, Jamaica, Lake Huron, Mount Etna.*

There are, however, many exceptions. In most cases, if the proper noun consists of a common noun with modifiers (adjectives or an *of* phrase), use *the* with the proper noun.

　　　　　　the
▶ We visited Great Wall of China last year.
　　　　　∧

　　　　　　　　　　　　the
▶ Rob wants to be a translator for Central Intelligence Agency.
　　　　　　　　　　　∧

The is used with most plural proper nouns: *the McGregors, the Bahamas, the Finger Lakes, the United States.*

Geographic names create problems because there are so many exceptions to the rules. When in doubt, consult the chart on page 385, check a dictionary, or ask a native speaker.

SCHOLARS ON TEACHING MULTILINGUAL WRITERS

Dean, Terry. "Multicultural Classrooms, Monocultural Teachers." *College Composition and Communication* 40.1 (1989): 23–37. Print. Dean offers a number of teaching strategies for multicultural classes, including the use of culturally oriented topics, peer response groups, and class newsletters. Dean believes that "in helping students make cultural transitions, we learn from them how to make transitions ourselves."

Using *the* with geographic nouns

When to omit *the*

streets, squares, parks	Ivy Street, Union Square, Denali National Park
cities, states, counties	Miami, New Mexico, Bee County
most countries, continents	Italy, China, South America, Africa
bays, single lakes	Tampa Bay, Lake Geneva
single mountains, islands	Mount Everest, Crete

When to use *the*

country names with *of* phrase	the United States (of America), the People's Republic of China
large regions, deserts	the East Coast, the Sahara
peninsulas	the Baja Peninsula, the Sinai Peninsula
oceans, seas, gulfs	the Pacific Ocean, the Dead Sea, the Persian Gulf
canals and rivers	the Panama Canal, the Amazon
mountain ranges	the Rocky Mountains, the Alps
groups of islands	the Solomon Islands

EXERCISE 29–1 Edit the following sentences for proper use of articles and nouns. If a sentence is correct, write "correct" after it. Answers appear in the back of the book. *More practice:* 🄴 ✅

~~The~~ Josefina's dance routine was flawless.

a. Doing volunteer work often brings a satisfaction.
b. As I looked out the window of the plane, I could see the Cape Cod.
c. Melina likes to drink her coffees with lots of cream.
d. Recovering from abdominal surgery requires patience.
e. I completed the my homework assignment quickly.

hackerhandbooks.com/bedhandbook

🄴 Multilingual/ESL > Exercises: 29–3 to 29–6
✅ Multilingual/ESL > LearningCurve: Articles and nouns for multilingual writers

---

EXERCISE 29–1 *Answers:*

a. Doing volunteer work often brings satisfaction.
b. As I looked out the window of the plane, I could see Cape Cod.
c. Melina likes to drink her coffee with lots of cream.
d. Correct
e. I completed my homework assignment quickly. *Or* I completed the homework assignment quickly.

EXERCISE 29–2   Articles have been omitted from the following description of winter weather. Insert the articles *a*, *an*, and *the* where English requires them and be prepared to explain the reasons for your choices. *More practice:* e ✔

> Many people confuse terms *hail*, *sleet*, and *freezing rain*. Hail normally occurs in thunderstorm and is caused by strong updrafts that lift growing chunks of ice into clouds. When chunks of ice, called hailstones, become too heavy to be carried by updrafts, they fall to ground. Hailstones can cause damage to crops, windshields, and people. Sleet occurs during winter storms and is caused by snowflakes falling from layer of cold air into warm layer, where they become raindrops, and then into another cold layer. As they fall through last layer of cold air, raindrops freeze and become small ice pellets, forming sleet. When it hits car windshield or windows of house, sleet can make annoying racket. Driving and walking can be hazardous when sleet accumulates on roads and sidewalks. Freezing rain is basically rain that falls onto ground and then freezes after it hits ground. It causes icy glaze on trees and any surface that is below freezing.

30   Sentence structure

Although their structure can vary widely, sentences in English generally flow from subject to verb to object or complement: *Bears eat fish.* This section focuses on the major challenges that multilingual students face when writing sentences in English. For more details on the parts of speech and the elements of sentences, consult sections 46–49.

hackerhandbooks.com/bedhandbook

e Multilingual/ESL > Exercises: 29–3 to 29–6
✔ Multilingual/ESL > LearningCurve: Articles and nouns for multilingual writers

EXERCISE 29–2   *Answers:*

> Many people confuse the terms *hail*, *sleet*, and *freezing rain*. Hail normally occurs in a thunderstorm and is caused by strong updrafts that lift growing chunks of ice into the clouds. When the chunks of ice, called hailstones, become too heavy to be carried by the updrafts, they fall to the ground. Hailstones can cause damage to crops, windshields, and people. Sleet occurs during winter storms and is caused by snowflakes falling from a layer of cold air into a warm layer, where they become raindrops, and then into another cold layer. As they fall through the last layer of cold air, the raindrops freeze and become small ice pellets, forming sleet. When it hits a car windshield or the windows of a house, sleet can make an annoying racket. Driving and walking can be

30a Use a linking verb between a subject and its complement.

Some languages, such as Russian and Turkish, do not use linking verbs (*is*, *are*, *was*, *were*) between subjects and complements (nouns or adjectives that rename or describe the subject). Every English sentence, however, must include a verb. For more on linking verbs, see 27e.

> is
> ► Jim intelligent.
>   ∧

> are
> ► Many streets in San Francisco very steep.
>   ∧

30b Include a subject in every sentence.

Some languages, such as Spanish and Japanese, do not require a subject in every sentence. Every English sentence, however, needs a subject. Commands are an exception: The subject *you* is understood but not present in the sentence ([*You*] *Give me the book*).

> She seems
> ► Your aunt is very energetic. ~~Seems~~ young for her age.
>   ∧

The word *it* is used as the subject of a sentence describing the weather or temperature, stating the time, indicating distance, or suggesting an environmental fact.

> It is
> ► ~~Is~~ raining in the valley and snowing in the mountains.
>   ∧

> It is
> ► ~~Is~~ 9:15 a.m.
>   ∧

In most English sentences, the subject appears before the verb. Some sentences, however, are inverted: The subject comes after the verb. In these sentences, a placeholder called an *expletive* (*there* or *it*) often comes before the verb.

EXERCISE 29-2 *Answers (continued):*

hazardous when sleet accumulates on roads and sidewalks. Freezing rain is basically rain that falls onto the ground and then freezes after it hits the ground. It causes an icy glaze on trees and any surface that is below freezing.

EXP   V   ┌───S───┐   ┌───S───┐   V
There are many people here today. (Many people are here today.)

> ~~There is~~
> ~~Is~~ an apple pie in the refrigerator.
>   ∧

>   *there are*
> As you know, many religious sects in India.
>   ∧

Notice that the verb agrees with the subject that follows it: *apple pie is*, *sects are*. (See 21g.)

Sometimes an inverted sentence has an infinitive (*to work*) or a noun clause (*that she is intelligent*) as the subject. In such sentences, the placeholder *it* is needed before the verb. (Also see 48b and 48e.)

EXP V   ┌─S─┐   ┌─S─┐   V
It is important to study daily. (To study daily is important.)

>   *it*
> Because the road is flooded, is necessary to change our route.
>   ∧

TIP: The words *here* and *there* are not used as subjects. When they mean "in this place" (*here*) or "in that place" (*there*), they are adverbs, which are never subjects.

>   *It*   *there.*
> I just returned from Japan. ~~There~~ is very beautiful/
>   ∧   ∧

> *This school*   *that school*
> ~~Here~~ offers a master's degree in physical therapy; ~~there~~ has
> ∧   ∧
>
> only a bachelor's program.

30c Do not use both a noun and a pronoun to perform the same grammatical function in a sentence.

English does not allow a subject to be repeated in its own clause.

> The doctor ~~she~~ advised me to cut down on salt.

The pronoun *she* cannot repeat the subject, *doctor*.

SCHOLARS ON MULTILINGUAL WRITERS AND PEER GROUPS

Nelson, Gayle L., and John M. Murphy. "Peer Response Groups: Do L2 Writers Use Peer Comments in Revising Their Drafts?" *TESOL Quarterly* 27.1 (1993): 135–41. Print. According to several studies, peer response groups have been successful in L1 writing classes, but "findings of L1 studies do not necessarily apply to L2 students." L2 writers may not trust responses from a peer who is struggling as they are trying to learn English; and in some cases, cultural differences may lead writers to devalue the comments of peers and view the teacher as the sole authority in the class. Nelson and Murphy's study suggests that students are more likely to use peer comments when writing groups promote cooperation and negotiation.

Do not add a pronoun even when a word group comes between the subject and the verb.

▶ The watch that I lost on vacation ~~it~~ was in my backpack.

The pronoun *it* cannot repeat the subject, *watch*.

Some languages allow "topic fronting," placing a word or phrase (a "topic") at the beginning of a sentence and following it with an independent clause that explains something about the topic. This form is not allowed in English because the sentence seems to start with one subject but then introduces a new subject in an independent clause.

┌TOPIC┐ ┌──────IND CLAUSE──────┐
INCORRECT   The seeds I planted them last fall.

The sentence can be corrected by bringing the topic (*seeds*) into the independent clause.

the seeds
▶ ~~The seeds~~ I planted ~~them~~ last fall.
            ∧

30d Do not repeat a subject, an object, or an adverb in an adjective clause.

Adjective clauses begin with relative pronouns (*who, whom, whose, which, that*) or relative adverbs (*when, where*). Relative pronouns usually serve as subjects or objects in the clauses they introduce; another word in the clause cannot serve the same function. Relative adverbs should not be repeated by other adverbs later in the clause.

┌─────── ADJ CLAUSE ───────┐
The cat ran under the car that was parked on the street.

▶ The cat ran under the car that ~~it~~ was parked on the street.

The relative pronoun *that* is the subject of the adjective clause, so the pronoun *it* cannot be added as a subject.

TEACHING TIP

Require students to maintain editing logs (lists of their own errors, with examples and with corrections). For more on maintaining an editing log, see "Teaching Grammar and Punctuation" in the free Bedford/St. Martin's instructor resource *Teaching with Hacker Handbooks* (hackerhandbooks.com/teaching).

▶ Myrna enjoyed the investment seminars that she attended

~~them~~ last week.

The relative pronoun *that* is the object of the verb *attended*. The pronoun *them* cannot also serve as an object.

Sometimes the relative pronoun is understood but not present in the sentence. In such cases, do not add another word with the same function as the omitted pronoun.

▶ Myrna enjoyed the investment seminars she attended ~~them~~

last week.

The relative pronoun *that* is understood after *seminars* even though it is not present in the sentence.

If the clause begins with a relative adverb, do not use another adverb with the same meaning later in the clause.

▶ The office where I work ~~there~~ is one hour from the city.

The adverb *there* cannot repeat the relative adverb *where*.

EXERCISE 30-1 In the following sentences, add needed subjects or expletives and delete any repeated subjects, objects, or adverbs. Answers appear in the back of the book. *More practice:* 🄴 ☑

The new geology professor is the one whom we saw ~~him~~ on TV.

a.   Are some cartons of ice cream in the freezer.
b.   I don't use the subway because am afraid.
c.   The prime minister she is the most popular leader in my country.
d.   We tried to get in touch with the same manager whom we spoke to him earlier.
e.   Recently have been a number of earthquakes in Turkey.

hackerhandbooks.com/bedhandbook
🄴 Multilingual/ESL > Exercises: 30–2 and 30–3
☑ Multilingual/ESL > LearningCurve: Sentence structure for multilingual writers

EXERCISE 30-1 *Answers:*

a.   There are some cartons of ice cream in the freezer.
b.   I don't use the subway because I am afraid.
c.   The prime minister is the most popular leader in my country.
d.   We tried to get in touch with the same manager whom we spoke to earlier.
e.   Recently there have been a number of earthquakes in Turkey.

30e Avoid mixed constructions beginning with *although* or *because.*

A word group that begins with *although* cannot be linked to a word group that begins with *but* or *however.* The result is an error called a *mixed construction* (see also 11a). Similarly, a word group that begins with *because* cannot be linked to a word group that begins with *so* or *therefore.*

If you want to keep *although* or *because,* drop the other linking word.

▶ Although Nikki Giovanni is best known for her poetry for

adults, ~~but~~ she has written several books for children.

▶ Because German and Dutch are related languages, ~~therefore~~

tourists from Berlin can usually read a few signs in

Amsterdam.

If you want to keep the other linking word, omit *although* or *because.*

▶ ~~Although~~ Nikki Giovanni is best known for her poetry for

adults, but she has written several books for children.

▶ ~~Because~~ German and Dutch are related languages,/;

therefore, tourists from Berlin can usually read a few

signs in Amsterdam.

For advice about using commas and semicolons with linking words, see 32a and 34b.

SCHOLARS ON RESPONDING TO MULTILINGUAL WRITERS

Cai, Guanjun. "Texts in Contexts: Understanding Students' English Compositions." *Evaluating Writing: The Role of Teachers' Knowledge about Text, Learning, and Culture.* Ed. Charles R. Cooper and Lee Odell. Urbana: NCTE, 1999. 279–97. Print. Cai writes that expectations of what constitutes an academic essay depend on rhetorical conventions — conventions that are connected to ideological and cultural values. Cai argues that instructors can better respond to multilingual students' writing if they are familiar with typical rhetorical strategies of other cultures. Using a case study of a Chinese student writer, he demonstrates ways to analyze compositions by multilingual writers and to help students revise their academic writing with an understanding of audience.

30f Do not place an adverb between a verb and its direct object.

Adverbs modifying verbs can appear in various positions: at the beginning or end of a sentence, before or after a verb, or between a helping verb and its main verb.

Slowly, we drove along the rain-slick road.

Mia handled the teapot *very carefully*.

Martin *always* wins our tennis matches.

Christina is *rarely* late for our lunch dates.

My daughter has *often* spoken of you.

The election results were being *closely* followed by analysts.

However, an adverb cannot appear between a verb and its direct object.

▶ Mother wrapped ~~carefully~~ the gift.
  carefully
  ∧

The adverb *carefully* cannot appear between the verb, *wrapped*, and its direct object, *the gift*.

EXERCISE 30-4 Edit the following sentences for proper sentence structure. If a sentence is correct, write "correct" after it. Possible revisions appear in the back of the book. *More practice:* e ✓

She peeled ~~slowly~~ the banana. slowly.
                            ∧

a. Although freshwater freezes at 32 degrees Fahrenheit, however ocean water freezes at 28 degrees Fahrenheit.

b. Because we switched cable packages, so our channel lineup has changed.

hackerhandbooks.com/bedhandbook

e Multilingual/ESL > Exercises: 30–5 and 30–6

✓ Multilingual/ESL > LearningCurve: Sentence structure for multilingual writers

---

EXERCISE 30-4 *Possible revisions:*

a. Although freshwater freezes at 32 degrees Fahrenheit, ocean water freezes at 28 degrees Fahrenheit.

b. Because we switched cable packages, our channel lineup has changed.

c. The competitor confidently mounted his skateboard.

d. My sister performs the *legong*, a Balinese dance, well.

e. Correct

c. The competitor mounted confidently his skateboard.

d. My sister performs well the *legong*, a Balinese dance.

e. Because product development is behind schedule, we will have to launch the product next spring.

30g Distinguish between present participles and past participles used as adjectives.

Both present and past participles may be used as adjectives. The present participle always ends in *-ing*. Past participles usually end in *-ed, -d, -en, -n,* or *-t.* (See 27a.)

PRESENT PARTICIPLES   confusing, speaking, boring

PAST PARTICIPLES   confused, spoken, bored

Like all other adjectives, participles can come before nouns; they also can follow linking verbs, in which case they describe the subject of the sentence. (See 47b.)

Use a present participle to describe a person or thing *causing or stimulating an experience.*

The *boring lecture* put us to sleep. [The lecture caused boredom.]

Use a past participle to describe a person or thing *undergoing an experience.*

The *audience* was *bored and restless.* [The audience experienced boredom.]

Participles that describe emotions or mental states often cause the most confusion.

annoying/annoyed	exhausting/exhausted
boring/bored	fascinating/fascinated
confusing/confused	frightening/frightened
depressing/depressed	satisfying/satisfied
exciting/excited	surprising/surprised

SCHOLARS ON RESPONDING TO MULTILINGUAL WRITERS

Leki, Ilona. "Coaching from the Margins: Issues in Written Response." *Second Language Writing: Research Insights for the Classroom.* Ed. Barbara Kroll. Cambridge: Cambridge UP, 1990. 57–68. Print. Though there is little evidence that thorough annotation of papers helps students improve their writing, a survey of multilingual students showed that "these students wanted to have every error marked." Leki offers suggestions for responding to papers by multilingual students, including dialogues with writers (written or oral) about works in progress or about comments they have received on their work.

WRITERS ON WRITING

Who does not know another language, does not know his own. — Goethe

EXERCISE 30-7 Edit the following sentences for proper use of present and past participles. If a sentence is correct, write "correct" after it. Answers appear in the back of the book. *More practice:* e ✓

> excited
> Danielle and Monica were very ~~exciting~~ to be going to a
>   ^
> Broadway show for the first time.

a. Listening to everyone's complaints all day was irritated.

b. The long flight to Singapore was exhausted.

c. His skill at chess is amazing.

d. After a great deal of research, the scientist made a fascinated discovery.

e. Surviving that tornado was one of the most frightened experiences I've ever had.

30h Place cumulative adjectives in an appropriate order.

Adjectives usually come before the nouns they modify and may also come after linking verbs. (See 46d and 47b.)

>   ADJ   N   V ADJ
> Janine wore a new necklace. Janine's necklace was new.

Cumulative adjectives, which cannot be joined by the word *and* or separated by commas, must come in a particular order. If you use cumulative adjectives before a noun, see the chart on page 395. The chart is only a guide; don't be surprised if you encounter exceptions. (See also 33d.)

>   stained red plastic
> ▶ My dorm room has only a desk and a ~~plastic red stained~~ chair.
>   ^

hackerhandbooks.com/bedhandbook

e Multilingual/ESL > Exercises: 30–8 and 30–9

✓ Multilingual/ESL > LearningCurve: Sentence structure for multilingual writers

---

EXERCISE 30-7 *Answers:*

a. Listening to everyone's complaints all day was irritating.

b. The long flight to Singapore was exhausting.

c. Correct

d. After a great deal of research, the scientist made a fascinating discovery.

e. Surviving that tornado was one of the most frightening experiences I've ever had.

Order of cumulative adjectives

FIRST   **ARTICLE OR OTHER NOUN MARKER** a, an, the, her, Joe's, two, many, some

        EVALUATIVE WORD attractive, dedicated, delicious, ugly, disgusting

        SIZE large, enormous, small, little

        LENGTH OR SHAPE long, short, round, square

        AGE new, old, young, antique

        COLOR yellow, blue, crimson

        NATIONALITY French, Peruvian, Vietnamese

        RELIGION Catholic, Protestant, Jewish, Muslim

        MATERIAL silver, walnut, wool, marble

LAST   **NOUN/ADJECTIVE** tree (as in *tree* house), kitchen (as in *kitchen* table)

THE NOUN MODIFIED house, coat, bicycle, bread, woman, coin

    My large blue wool coat is in the attic.

EXERCISE 30–10   Using the chart on this page as necessary, arrange the following modifiers and nouns in their proper order. Answers appear in the back of the book. *More practice:* e ✔

    ~~two new French racing bicycles~~
    new, French, two, bicycles, racing

a.   sculptor, young, an, Vietnamese, intelligent
b.   dedicated, a, priest, Catholic
c.   old, her, sweater, blue, wool
d.   delicious, Joe's, Scandinavian, bread
e.   many, boxes, jewelry, antique, beautiful

hackerhandbooks.com/bedhandbook

e Multilingual/ESL > Exercises: 30–11 and 30–12
✔ Multilingual/ESL > LearningCurve: Sentence structure for multilingual writers

---

EXERCISE 30–10   *Answers:*

a.   an intelligent young Vietnamese sculptor
b.   a dedicated Catholic priest
c.   her old blue wool sweater
d.   Joe's delicious Scandinavian bread
e.   many beautiful antique jewelry boxes

31 Prepositions and idiomatic expressions

31a Become familiar with prepositions that show time and place.

The most frequently used prepositions in English are *at*, *by*, *for*, *from*, *in*, *of*, *on*, *to*, and *with*. Prepositions can be difficult to master because the differences among them are subtle and idiomatic. The chart on page 398 is limited to three troublesome prepositions that show time and place: *at*, *on*, and *in*.

Not every possible use is listed in the chart, so don't be surprised when you encounter exceptions and idiomatic uses that you must learn one at a time. For example, in English a person rides *in* a car but *on* a bus, plane, train, or subway.

▶ My first class starts ~~on~~ at 8:00 a.m.

▶ The farmers go to market ~~in~~ on Wednesday.

EXERCISE 31-1 In the following sentences, replace prepositions that are not used correctly. You may need to refer to the chart on page 398. If a sentence is correct, write "correct" after it. Answers appear in the back of the book. *More practice:* e

The play begins ~~on~~ at 7:20 p.m.

a. Whenever we eat at the Centerville Café, we sit at a small table on the corner of the room.

b. In the 1990s, entrepreneurs created new online businesses in record numbers.

hackerhandbooks.com/bedhandbook

e Multilingual/ESL > Exercises: 31–2 and 31–3

EXERCISE 31-1 *Answers:*

a. Whenever we eat at the Centerville Café, we sit at a small table in the corner of the room.

b. Correct

c. On Thursday, Nancy will attend her first home repair class at the community center.

d. Correct

e. We decided to go to a restaurant because there was no fresh food in the refrigerator.

c. In Thursday, Nancy will attend her first home repair class at the community center.

d. Alex began looking for her lost mitten in another location.

e. We decided to go to a restaurant because there was no fresh food on the refrigerator.

31b Use nouns (including -*ing* forms) after prepositions.

In a prepositional phrase, use a noun (not a verb) after the preposition. Sometimes the noun will be a gerund, the -*ing* verb form that functions as a noun (see 48b).

▶ Our student government is good at ~~save~~ saving money.

Distinguish between the preposition *to* and the infinitive marker *to*. If *to* is a preposition, it should be followed by a noun or a gerund.

▶ We are dedicated to ~~help~~ helping the poor.

If *to* is an infinitive marker, it should be followed by the base form of the verb.

▶ We want to ~~helping~~ help the poor.

To test whether *to* is a preposition or an infinitive marker, insert a word that you know is a noun after the word *to*. If the noun makes sense in that position, *to* is a preposition. If the noun does not make sense after *to*, then *to* is an infinitive marker.

Zoe is addicted *to* _____.
They are planning *to* _____.

In the first sentence, a noun (such as *magazines*) makes sense after *to*, so *to* is a preposition and should be followed by a noun or a gerund: Zoe is addicted *to magazines*. Zoe is addicted *to running*.

TEACHING TIP

If you teach composition, consider assigning students to read daily — even if it's just the campus newspaper. Assign points to those students who keep a reading log. You might even ask them to hunt for idiomatic expressions. Research shows that multilingual speakers find it easier to write in English as they read more English.

At, on, and in to show time and place

Showing time

AT   at a specific time: *at* 7:20, *at* dawn, *at* dinner

ON   on a specific day or date: *on* Tuesday, *on* June 4

IN   in a part of a 24-hour period: *in* the afternoon, *in* the daytime [but *at* night]

in a year or month: *in* 2008, *in* July

in a period of time: finished *in* three hours

Showing place

AT   at a meeting place or location: *at* home, *at* the club

at the edge of something: sitting *at* the desk

at the corner of something: turning *at* the intersection

at a target: throwing the snowball *at* Lucy

ON   on a surface: placed *on* the table, hanging *on* the wall

on a street: the house *on* Spring Street

on an electronic medium: *on* television, *on* the Internet

IN   in an enclosed space: *in* the garage, *in* an envelope

in a geographic location: *in* San Diego, *in* Texas

in a print medium: *in* a book, *in* a magazine

In the second sentence, a noun (such as *magazines*) does not make sense after *to*, so *to* is an infinitive marker and must be followed by the base form of the verb: They are planning *to build* a new school.

31c Become familiar with common adjective + preposition combinations.

Some adjectives appear only with certain prepositions. These expressions are idiomatic and may be different from the combinations used in your native language.

▶ Paula is married ~~with~~ ^{to} Jon.

Check an ESL dictionary for combinations that are not listed in the chart at the bottom of this page.

31d Become familiar with common verb + preposition combinations.

Many verbs and prepositions appear together in idiomatic phrases. Pay special attention to the combinations that are different from the combinations used in your native language.

▶ Your success depends ~~of~~ ^{on} your effort.

Check an ESL dictionary for combinations that are not listed in the chart on page 400.

Adjective + preposition combinations

accustomed to	connected to	guilty of	preferable to
addicted to	covered with	interested in	proud of
afraid of	dedicated to	involved in	responsible for
angry with	devoted to	involved with	
ashamed of	different from	known as	satisfied with
aware of	engaged in	known for	scared of
committed to	engaged to	made of (or	similar to
concerned about	excited about	made from)	tired of
	familiar with	married to	worried about
concerned with	full of	opposed to	

Verb + preposition combinations

agree with	compare with	forget about	speak to (*or* speak with)
apply to	concentrate on	happen to	stare at
approve of	consist of	hope for	succeed at
arrive at	count on	insist on	succeed in
arrive in	decide on	listen to	take advantage of
ask for	depend on	participate in	take care of
believe in	differ from	rely on	think about
belong to	disagree with	reply to	think of
care about	dream about	respond to	wait for
care for	dream of	result in	wait on
compare to	feel like	search for	

Punctuation

32　The comma

The comma was invented to help readers. Without it, sentence parts can collide into one another unexpectedly, causing misreadings.

CONFUSING　　If you cook Elmer will do the dishes.

CONFUSING　　While we were eating a rattlesnake approached our campsite.

Add commas in the logical places (after *cook* and *eating*), and suddenly all is clear. No longer is Elmer being cooked, the rattlesnake being eaten.

Various rules have evolved to prevent such misreadings and to speed readers along through complex grammatical structures. Those rules are detailed in this section. (Section 33 explains when not to use commas.)

32a Use a comma before a coordinating conjunction joining independent clauses.

When a coordinating conjunction connects two or more independent clauses—word groups that could stand alone as separate sentences—a comma must precede the conjunction. There are seven coordinating conjunctions in English: *and, but, or, nor, for, so,* and *yet.*

A comma tells readers that one independent clause has come to a close and that another is about to begin.

▶ The department sponsored a seminar on college survival skills, and it also hosted a barbecue for new students.

SCHOLARS ON PUNCTUATION

Hassett, Michael. "Toward a Broader Understanding of the Rhetoric of Punctuation." *College Composition and Communication* 47.3 (1996): 419–21. Print. Although he agrees with Dawkins that punctuation is a rhetorical tool, Hassett criticizes Dawkins's 1995 article on four grounds. First, because Dawkins used literary essayists in his study, his conclusions may not apply to other genres, such as technical writing. Second, professional essayists can break the rules in ways that job applicants and college students cannot. Third, writers and readers may interpret the emphasis of marks of punctuation in different ways. And finally, weak student writers may be tempted to mimic literary writers by using punctuation not for their own purposes but to make their writing "*look* like the work of those valued writers."

EXCEPTION: If the two independent clauses are short and there is no danger of misreading, the comma may be omitted.

The plane took off and we were on our way.

TIP: As a rule, do *not* use a comma with a coordinating conjunction that joins only two words, phrases, or subordinate clauses. (See 33a. See also 32c for commas with coordinating conjunctions joining three or more elements.)

▶ A good money manager controls expenses/and invests

surplus dollars to meet future needs.

The word group following *and* is not an independent clause; it is the second half of a compound predicate (*controls . . . and invests*).

32b Use a comma after an introductory clause or phrase.

The most common introductory word groups are clauses and phrases functioning as adverbs. Such word groups usually tell when, where, how, why, or under what conditions the main action of the sentence occurred. (See 48a, 48b, and 48e.)

A comma tells readers that the introductory clause or phrase has come to a close and that the main part of the sentence is about to begin.

▶ When Irwin was ready to iron, his cat tripped on the cord.

Without the comma, readers may think that Irwin is ironing his cat. The comma signals that *his cat* is the subject of a new clause, not part of the introductory one.

EXCEPTION: The comma may be omitted after a short adverb clause or phrase if there is no danger of misreading. *In no time we were at 2,800 feet.*

SCHOLARS ON PUNCTUATION

Dawkins, John. "Teaching Punctuation as a Rhetorical Tool." *College Composition and Communication* 46.4 (1995): 533–48. Print. Dawkins argues that the rules approach to punctuation used in handbooks is wrongheaded because good writers often break the rules for rhetorical reasons. Believing that handbook rules are both oversimplified and too complicated, Dawkins proposes a new system based on rhetoric. He classifies punctuation marks according to the degree of separation they signal and claims that good writers choose a maximum or minimum separation to raise or lower the emphasis. Dawkins uses a patterns approach to show students which choices are allowed in sentences with one or multiple independent clauses.

Sentences also frequently begin with participial phrases that function as adjectives, describing the noun or pronoun immediately following them. The comma tells readers that they are about to learn the identity of the person or thing described; therefore, the comma is usually required even when the phrase is short. (See 48b.)

▶ Buried under layers of younger rocks, the earth's oldest

rocks contain no fossils.

NOTE: Other introductory word groups include transitional expressions and absolute phrases (see 32f).

EXERCISE 32–1 Add or delete commas where necessary in the following sentences. If a sentence is correct, write "correct" after it. Answers appear in the back of the book. *More practice:* e ✓

Because we had been saving molding for a few weeks, we had

enough wood to frame all thirty paintings.

a. Alisa brought the injured bird home, and fashioned a splint out of Popsicle sticks for its wing.
b. Considered a classic of early animation *The Adventures of Prince Achmed* used hand-cut silhouettes against colored backgrounds.
c. If you complete the evaluation form and return it within two weeks you will receive a free breakfast during your next stay.
d. After retiring from the New York City Ballet in 1965, legendary dancer Maria Tallchief went on to found the Chicago City Ballet.
e. Roger had always wanted a handmade violin but he couldn't afford one.

EXERCISE 32–2 Add or delete commas where necessary in the following sentences (p. 405). If a sentence is correct, write "correct" after it. Answers appear in the back of the book. *More practice:* e ✓

hackerhandbooks.com/bedhandbook

e Punctuation > Exercises: 32–3, 32–4, 32–13 to 32–17 (comma review)
✓ Punctuation > LearningCurve: Commas

EXERCISE 32–1 *Answers:*

a. Alisa brought the injured bird home and fashioned a splint out of Popsicle sticks for its wing.
b. Considered a classic of early animation, *The Adventures of Prince Achmed* used hand-cut silhouettes against colored backgrounds.
c. If you complete the evaluation form and return it within two weeks, you will receive a free breakfast during your next stay.
d. Correct
e. Roger had always wanted a handmade violin, but he couldn't afford one.

The car had been sitting idle for a month, so the battery was

completely dead.

a. J. R. R. Tolkien finished writing his draft of *The Lord of the Rings* trilogy in 1949 but the first book in the series wasn't published until 1954.

b. In the first two minutes of its ascent the space shuttle had broken the sound barrier and reached a height of over twenty-five miles.

c. German shepherds can be gentle guide dogs or they can be fierce attack dogs.

d. Some former professional cyclists admit that the use of performance-enhancing drugs is widespread in cycling but they argue that no rider can be competitive without doping.

e. As an intern, I learned most aspects of the broadcasting industry but I never learned about fundraising.

32c Use a comma between all items in a series.

When three or more items are presented in a series, those items should be separated from one another with commas. Items in a series may be single words, phrases, or clauses.

▶ Langston Hughes's poetry is concerned with racial pride,

social justice, and the diversity of the African American

experience.

Although some writers view the last comma in a series as optional, most experts advise using the comma because its omission can result in ambiguity or misreading.

▶ My uncle willed me all of his property, houses, and boats.

Did the uncle will his property *and* houses *and* boats — or simply his property, consisting of houses and boats? If the former meaning is intended, a comma is necessary to prevent ambiguity.

EXERCISE 32-2 *Answers:*

a. J. R. R. Tolkien finished writing his draft of *The Lord of the Rings* trilogy in 1949, but the first book in the series wasn't published until 1954.

b. In the first two minutes of its ascent, the space shuttle had broken the sound barrier and reached a height of over twenty-five miles.

c. German shepherds can be gentle guide dogs, or they can be fierce attack dogs.

d. Some former professional cyclists admit that the use of performance-enhancing drugs is widespread in cycling, but they argue that no rider can be competitive without doping.

e. As an intern, I learned most aspects of the broadcasting industry, but I never learned about fundraising.

32d Use a comma between coordinate adjectives not joined with *and*. Do not use a comma between cumulative adjectives.

When two or more adjectives each modify a noun separately, they are coordinate.

> Roberto is a *warm, gentle, affectionate* father.

If the adjectives can be joined with *and*, the adjectives are coordinate, so you should use commas: *warm* and *gentle* and *affectionate* (*warm, gentle, affectionate*).

Adjectives that do not modify the noun separately are cumulative.

> *Three large gray* shapes moved slowly toward us.

Beginning with the adjective closest to the noun *shapes*, these modifiers lean on one another, piggyback style, with each modifying a larger word group. *Gray* modifies *shapes*, *large* modifies *gray shapes*, and *three* modifies *large gray shapes*. Cumulative adjectives cannot be joined with *and* (not *three* and *large* and *gray shapes*).

COORDINATE ADJECTIVES

▶ Should patients with severe⌃ irreversible brain damage be put on life support systems?

Adjectives are coordinate if they can be connected with *and*: *severe and irreversible*.

CUMULATIVE ADJECTIVES

▶ Ira ordered a rich⁄ chocolate⁄ layer cake.

Ira didn't order a cake that was rich and chocolate and layer. He ordered a *layer cake* that was *chocolate*, a *chocolate layer cake* that was *rich*.

EXERCISE 32–5 *Answers:*

a. The cold, impersonal atmosphere of the university was unbearable.
b. An ambulance threaded its way through police cars, fire trucks, and irate citizens.
c. Correct
d. After two broken arms, three cracked ribs, and one concussion, Ken quit the varsity football team.
e. Correct

EXERCISE 32-5 Add or delete commas where necessary in the following sentences. If a sentence is correct, write "correct" after it. Answers appear in the back of the book. *More practice:* e ✓

We gathered our essentials, took off for the great outdoors⌄

and ignored the fact that it was Friday the 13th.

a. The cold impersonal atmosphere of the university was unbearable.

b. An ambulance threaded its way through police cars, fire trucks and irate citizens.

c. The *1812 Overture* is a stirring, magnificent piece of music.

d. After two broken arms, three cracked ribs and one concussion, Ken quit the varsity football team.

e. My cat's pupils had constricted to small black shining slits.

EXERCISE 32-6 Add or delete commas where necessary in the following sentences. If a sentence is correct, write "correct" after it. Answers appear in the back of the book. *More practice:* e ✓

Good social workers excel in patience, diplomacy⌄ and

positive thinking.

a. NASA's rovers on Mars are equipped with special cameras that can take close-up high-resolution pictures of the terrain.

b. A baseball player achieves the triple crown by having the highest batting average, the most home runs, and the most runs batted in during the regular season.

c. If it does not get enough sunlight, a healthy green lawn can turn into a shriveled brown mess within a matter of days.

d. Love, vengeance, greed and betrayal are common themes in Western literature.

e. Many experts believe that shark attacks on surfers are a result of the sharks' mistaking surfboards for small, injured seals.

hackerhandbooks.com/bedhandbook

e Punctuation > Exercises: 32-7, 32-8, 32-13 to 32-17 (comma review)
✓ Punctuation > LearningCurve: Commas

EXERCISE 32-6 *Answers:*

a. NASA's rovers on Mars are equipped with special cameras that can take close-up, high-resolution pictures of the terrain.

b. Correct

c. Correct

d. Love, vengeance, greed, and betrayal are common themes in Western literature.

e. Many experts believe that shark attacks on surfers are a result of the sharks' mistaking surfboards for small injured seals.

32e Use commas to set off nonrestrictive (nonessential) elements. Do not use commas to set off restrictive (essential) elements.

Certain word groups that modify nouns or pronouns can be restrictive or nonrestrictive—that is, essential or not essential to the meaning of a sentence. These word groups are usually adjective clauses, adjective phrases, or appositives.

Restrictive elements

A restrictive element defines or limits the meaning of the word it modifies; it is therefore essential to the meaning of the sentence and is not set off with commas. If you remove a restrictive modifier from a sentence, the meaning changes significantly, becoming more general than you intended.

RESTRICTIVE (NO COMMAS)

The campers need clothes *that are durable.*

Scientists *who study the earth's structure* are called geologists.

The first sentence does not mean that the campers need clothes in general. The intended meaning is more limited: The campers need durable clothes. The second sentence does not mean that scientists in general are called geologists; only those scientists who specifically study the earth's structure are called geologists. The italicized word groups are essential and are therefore not set off with commas.

Nonrestrictive elements

A nonrestrictive modifier describes a noun or pronoun whose meaning has already been clearly defined or limited. Because the modifier contains nonessential or parenthetical information, it is set off with commas. If you remove a nonrestrictive element from a sentence, the meaning does not change dramatically. Some meaning may be lost, but the defining characteristics of the person or thing described remain the same.

TEACHING TIP

Ask students to keep an editing log for the semester. When they receive comments on a draft, they should pay special attention to comments related to sentence-level matters. In their editing log, students should record (1) the incorrect sentence, (2) the handbook section (32a, for example) that provides help for editing that sentence, and (3) the corrected sentence. Invite students to add any tips that might help them proofread for that particular error in the future.

NONRESTRICTIVE (WITH COMMAS)

The campers need sturdy shoes, *which are expensive.*

The scientists, *who represented eight different universities,* met to review applications for the prestigious Advancements in Science Award.

In the first sentence, the campers need sturdy shoes, and the shoes happen to be expensive. In the second sentence, the scientists met to review applications for the award; that they represented eight different universities is informative but not critical to the meaning of the sentence. The nonessential information in both sentences is set off with commas.

NOTE: Often it is difficult to tell whether a word group is restrictive or nonrestrictive without seeing it in context and considering the writer's meaning. Both of the following sentences are grammatically correct, but their meaning is slightly different.

The dessert made with fresh raspberries was delicious.

The dessert, made with fresh raspberries, was delicious.

In the first example, the phrase *made with fresh raspberries* tells readers which of two or more desserts the writer is referring to. In the example with commas, the phrase merely adds information about one dessert.

Adjective clauses

Adjective clauses are patterned like sentences, containing subjects and verbs, but they function within sentences as modifiers of nouns or pronouns. They always follow the word they modify, usually immediately. Adjective clauses begin with a relative pronoun (*who, whom, whose, which, that*) or with a relative adverb (*where, when*). (See also 48e.)

Nonrestrictive adjective clauses are set off with commas; restrictive adjective clauses are not.

NONRESTRICTIVE CLAUSE (WITH COMMAS)

▶ Ed's house, which is located on thirteen acres, was

completely furnished with bats in the rafters and mice in

the kitchen.

The adjective clause *which is located on thirteen acres* does not restrict the meaning of *Ed's house*; the information is nonessential
and is therefore set off with commas.

RESTRICTIVE CLAUSE (NO COMMAS)

▶ The giant panda/ that was born at the San Diego Zoo in

2003/ was sent to China in 2007.

Because the adjective clause *that was born at the San Diego Zoo in
2003* identifies one particular panda out of many, the information
is essential and is therefore not set off with commas.

NOTE: Use *that* only with restrictive (essential) clauses. Many
writers prefer to use *which* only with nonrestrictive (nonessential)
clauses, but usage varies.

Adjective phrases

Prepositional or verbal phrases functioning as adjectives may be
restrictive or nonrestrictive. Nonrestrictive phrases are set off
with commas; restrictive phrases are not.

NONRESTRICTIVE PHRASE (WITH COMMAS)

▶ The helicopter, with its million-candlepower spotlight

illuminating the area, circled above.

The *with* phrase is nonessential because its purpose is not to
specify which of two or more helicopters is being discussed. The
phrase is not required for readers to understand the meaning of
the sentence.

RESTRICTIVE PHRASE (NO COMMAS)

▶ One corner of the attic was filled with newspapers/ dating

from the early 1900s.

Dating from the early 1900s restricts the meaning of *newspapers*, so the comma should be omitted.

Appositives

An appositive is a noun or noun phrase that renames a nearby noun. Nonrestrictive appositives are set off with commas; restrictive appositives are not.

NONRESTRICTIVE APPOSITIVE (WITH COMMAS)

▶ Darwin's most important book, *On the Origin of Species,*

was the result of many years of research.

Most important restricts the meaning to one book, so the appositive *On the Origin of Species* is nonrestrictive and should be set off with commas.

RESTRICTIVE APPOSITIVE (NO COMMAS)

▶ The song/ "Viva la Vida/" was blasted out of huge

amplifiers at the concert.

Once they've read *song*, readers still don't know precisely which song the writer means. The appositive following *song* restricts its meaning, so the appositive should not be set off with commas.

EXERCISE 32–9 Add or delete commas where necessary in the following sentences (p. 412). If a sentence is correct, write "correct" after it. Answers appear in the back of the book. *More practice:* e ✓

hackerhandbooks.com/bedhandbook

e Punctuation > Exercises: 32–10, 32–13 to 32–17 (comma review)
✓ Punctuation > LearningCurve: Commas

My sister, who plays center on the Sparks, now lives at

The Sands, a beach house near Los Angeles.

a. Choreographer Alvin Ailey's best-known work *Revelations* is more than just a crowd-pleaser.

b. Twyla Tharp's contemporary ballet *Push Comes to Shove* was made famous by the Russian dancer Baryshnikov. [*Tharp has written more than one contemporary ballet.*]

c. The glass sculptor sifting through hot red sand explained her technique to the other glassmakers. [*There is more than one glass sculptor.*]

d. A member of an organization, that provides job training for teens, was also appointed to the education commission.

e. Brian Eno who began his career as a rock musician turned to meditative compositions in the late 1970s.

32f Use commas to set off transitional and parenthetical expressions, absolute phrases, and word groups expressing contrast.

Transitional expressions

Transitional expressions serve as bridges between sentences or parts of sentences. They include conjunctive adverbs such as *however, therefore,* and *moreover* and transitional phrases such as *for example, as a matter of fact,* and *in other words.* (For complete lists of these expressions, see 34b.)

When a transitional expression appears between independent clauses in a compound sentence, it is preceded by a semicolon and is usually followed by a comma. (See 34b.)

▶ Minh did not understand our language; moreover, he was

unfamiliar with our customs.

EXERCISE 32-9 *Answers:*

a. Choreographer Alvin Ailey's best-known work, *Revelations,* is more than just a crowd-pleaser.

b. Correct

c. Correct

d. A member of an organization that provides job training for teens was also appointed to the education commission.

e. Brian Eno, who began his career as a rock musician, turned to meditative compositions in the late 1970s.

When a transitional expression appears at the beginning of a sentence or in the middle of an independent clause, it is usually set off with commas.

▶ Natural foods are not always salt free; celery, for example, contains more sodium than most people think.

EXCEPTION: If a transitional expression blends smoothly with the rest of the sentence, calling for little or no pause in reading, it does not need to be set off with a comma. Expressions such as *also, at least, certainly, consequently, indeed, of course, moreover, no doubt, perhaps, then,* and *therefore* do not always call for a pause.

Alice's bicycle is broken; *therefore* you will need to borrow Sue's.

Parenthetical expressions

Expressions that are distinctly parenthetical, providing only supplemental information, should be set off with commas. They interrupt the flow of a sentence or appear at the end as afterthoughts.

▶ Evolution, as far as we know, doesn't work this way.

Absolute phrases

An absolute phrase, which modifies the whole sentence, usually consists of a noun followed by a participle or participial phrase. (See 48d.) Absolute phrases may appear at the beginning or at the end of a sentence and should be set off with commas.

```
┌──────── ABSOLUTE PHRASE ────────┐
│ N    PARTICIPLE                 │
```

The sun appearing for the first time in a week, we were at last able to begin the archaeological dig.

▶ Elvis Presley made music industry history in the 1950s, his records having sold more than ten million copies.

SCHOLARS ON PUNCTUATION

Meyer, Charles F. *A Linguistic Study of American Punctuation.* New York: Lang, 1987. Print. Meyer introduces a hierarchy for punctuation marks based on syntax, semantics, and prosody. The period, question mark, and exclamation point are level one, setting off sentences. The colon, parentheses, and the dash are level two, setting off sentences, clauses, and phrases. The semicolon is level three, setting off clauses or clauses and phrases in a series. The comma is level four, setting off clauses and phrases.

NOTE: Do not insert a comma between the noun and the participle in an absolute construction.

▶ The next contestant,/ being five years old, the host adjusted the height of the microphone.

Word groups expressing contrast

Sharp contrasts beginning with words such as *not*, *never*, and *unlike* are set off with commas.

▶ Unlike Robert, Celia loved dance contests.

32g Use commas to set off nouns of direct address, the words *yes* and *no*, interrogative tags, and mild interjections.

▶ Forgive me, Angela, for forgetting your birthday.

▶ The film was faithful to the book, wasn't it?

32h Use commas with expressions such as *he said* to set off direct quotations.

▶ In his "Letter from Birmingham Jail," Martin Luther King Jr. wrote, "We know through painful experience that freedom is never voluntarily given by the oppressor; it must be demanded by the oppressed" (225).

See 37 on the use of quotation marks and pages 594–95 on citing literary sources in MLA style.

32i Use commas with dates, addresses, titles, and numbers.

Dates

In dates, set off the year with a pair of commas.

> ► On December 12, 1890, orders were sent out for the arrest
>
> of Sitting Bull.

EXCEPTIONS: Commas are not needed if the date is inverted or if only the month and year are given: 15 April 2009; January 2008.

Addresses

The elements of an address or a place name are separated with commas. A zip code, however, is not preceded by a comma.

> ► Please send the package to Greg Tarvin at 708 Spring
>
> Street, Washington, IL 61571.

Titles

If a title follows a name, set off the title with a pair of commas.

> ► Ann Hall, MD, has been appointed to the board of trustees.

Numbers

In numbers more than four digits long, use commas to separate the numbers into groups of three, starting from the right. In numbers four digits long, a comma is optional.

> 3,500 [*or* 3500]   100,000   5,000,000

EXCEPTIONS: Do not use commas in street numbers, zip codes, telephone numbers, or years with four or fewer digits.

SCHOLARS ON PUNCTUATION

Meyer, Charles F. "Teaching Punctuation to Advanced Writers." *Journal of Advanced Composition* 6.1 (1985–86): 117–29. Print. Meyer discusses how the deliberate violation of punctuation norms affects meaning. He recommends that writers not violate punctuation norms if the violation confuses the reader, creates a stylistically awkward construction, or goes against the tone of a formal piece of writing. Meyer lists numerous examples of how norms can be violated to create an effect, including the use of semicolons instead of commas to punctuate coordinated clauses.

EXERCISE 32–11 This exercise covers the major uses of the comma described in 32a–32e. Add or delete commas where necessary. If a sentence is correct, write "correct" after it. Answers appear in the back of the book. *More practice:* e ✅

> Even though our brains actually can't focus on two tasks
>
> at a time, many people believe they can multitask.

a. Cricket which originated in England is also popular in Australia, South Africa and India.
b. At the sound of the starting pistol the horses surged forward toward the first obstacle, a sharp incline three feet high.
c. After seeing an exhibition of Western art Gerhard Richter escaped from East Berlin, and smuggled out many of his notebooks.
d. Corrie's new wet suit has an intricate, blue pattern.
e. We replaced the rickety, old, spiral staircase with a sturdy, new ladder.

EXERCISE 32–12 This exercise covers all uses of the comma. Add or delete commas where necessary in the following sentences. If a sentence is correct, write "correct" after it. Answers appear in the back of the book. *More practice:* e ✅

> "Yes, dear, you can have dessert," my mother said.

a. On January 15, 2012 our office moved to 29 Commonwealth Avenue, Mechanicsville VA 23111.
b. The coach having bawled us out thoroughly, we left the locker room with his harsh words ringing in our ears.
c. Ms. Carlson you are a valued customer whose satisfaction is very important to us.
d. Mr. Mundy was born on July 22, 1939 in Arkansas, where his family had lived for four generations.
e. Her board poised at the edge of the half-pipe, Nina waited her turn to drop in.

hackerhandbooks.com/bedhandbook

e Punctuation > Exercises: 32–13 to 32–17 (comma review)
✅ Punctuation > LearningCurve: Commas

EXERCISE 32–11 *Answers:*

a. Cricket, which originated in England, is also popular in Australia, South Africa, and India.
b. At the sound of the starting pistol, the horses surged forward toward the first obstacle, a sharp incline three feet high.
c. After seeing an exhibition of Western art, Gerhard Richter escaped from East Berlin and smuggled out many of his notebooks.
d. Corrie's new wet suit has an intricate blue pattern.
e. We replaced the rickety old spiral staircase with a sturdy new ladder.

33 Unnecessary commas

Many common misuses of the comma result from a misunderstanding of the major comma rules presented in 32.

33a Do not use a comma with a coordinating conjunction that joins only two words, phrases, or subordinate clauses.

Though a comma should be used before a coordinating conjunction joining independent clauses (see 32a) or with a series of three or more elements (see 32c), these rules should not be extended to other compound word groups.

▶ Ron discovered a leak,/ and came back to fix it.

> The coordinating conjunction *and* links two verbs in a compound predicate: *discovered* and *came.*

▶ We knew that she had won,/ but that the election was close.

> The coordinating conjunction *but* links two subordinate clauses, each beginning with *that.*

33b Do not use a comma to separate a verb from its subject or object.

A sentence should flow from subject to verb to object without unnecessary pauses. Commas may appear between these major sentence elements only when a specific rule calls for them.

EXERCISE 32-12   *Answers:*

a. On January 15, 2012, our office moved to 29 Commonwealth Avenue, Mechanicsville, VA 23111.

b. Correct

c. Ms. Carlson, you are a valued customer whose satisfaction is very important to us.

d. Mr. Mundy was born on July 22, 1939, in Arkansas, where his family had lived for four generations.

e. Correct

▶ Zoos large enough to give the animals freedom to roam⁄

are becoming more popular.

> The comma should not separate the subject, *Zoos*, from the verb,
> *are becoming*.

33c Do not use a comma before the first or after the last item in a series.

Though commas are required between items in a series (32c), do not place them either before or after the whole series.

▶ Other causes of asthmatic attacks are⁄ stress, change in

temperature, and cold air.

▶ Ironically, even novels that focus on horror, evil, and

alienation⁄often have themes of spiritual renewal and

redemption as well.

33d Do not use a comma between cumulative adjectives, between an adjective and a noun, or between an adverb and an adjective.

Commas are required between coordinate adjectives (those that can be joined with *and*), but they do not belong between cumulative adjectives (those that cannot be joined with *and*). (For a full discussion, see 32d.)

▶ In the corner of the closet, we found an old⁄ maroon hatbox.

A comma should never be used between an adjective and the noun that follows it.

▶ It was a senseless, dangerous⁄ mission.

TEACHING TIP

Use punctuation exercises, such as those in the handbook's print pages or e-Pages, as a first step in teaching a pattern.

Nor should a comma be used between an adverb and an adjective that follows it.

▶ The Hillside is a good home for severely/ disturbed youths.

33e Do not use commas to set off restrictive elements.

Restrictive elements are modifiers or appositives that restrict the meaning of the nouns they follow. Because they are essential to the meaning of the sentence, they are not set off with commas. (For a full discussion of restrictive and nonrestrictive elements, see 32e.)

▶ Drivers/ who think they own the road/ make cycling a

dangerous sport.

> The modifier *who think they own the road* restricts the meaning of *Drivers* and is essential to the meaning of the sentence. Putting commas around the *who* clause falsely suggests that all drivers think they own the road.

▶ Margaret Mead's book/ *Coming of Age in Samoa/* stirred up

considerable controversy when it was published in 1928.

> Since Mead wrote more than one book, the appositive contains information essential to the meaning of the sentence.

33f Do not use a comma to set off a concluding adverb clause that is essential for meaning.

When adverb clauses introduce a sentence, they are nearly always followed by a comma (see 32b). When they conclude a sentence, however, they are not set off by commas if their content is essential to the meaning of the earlier part of the sentence. Adverb clauses beginning with *after, as soon as, because, before, if, since, unless, until,* and *when* are usually essential.

WRITERS ON WRITING

This morning I took out a comma and this afternoon I put it back again.
— Oscar Wilde

Punctuation, whether we call it a science that contains touches of art or an art reared on underpinnings of science, is a graphic device for showing how sentences are constructed. — Wilson Follett

Many writers profess great exactness of punctuation, who never yet made a point. — George Dennison Prentice

no ,

▶ Don't visit Paris at the height of the tourist season,/ unless

you have booked hotel reservations.

Without the *unless* clause, the meaning of the sentence might at first seem broader than the writer intended.

When a concluding adverb clause is nonessential, it should be preceded by a comma. Clauses beginning with *although*, *even though*, *though*, and *whereas* are usually nonessential.

▶ The lecture seemed to last only a short time, although the
    ∧
clock said it had gone on for more than an hour.

33g Do not use a comma after a phrase that begins an inverted sentence.

Though a comma belongs after most introductory phrases (see 32b), it does not belong after phrases that begin an inverted sentence. In an inverted sentence, the subject follows the verb, and a phrase that ordinarily would follow the verb is moved to the beginning (see 47c).

▶ At the bottom of the hill,/ sat the stubborn mule.

33h Avoid other common misuses of the comma.

Do not use a comma in the following situations.

AFTER A COORDINATING CONJUNCTION (*AND*, *BUT*, *OR*, *NOR*, *FOR*, *SO*, *YET*)

▶ Occasionally TV talk shows are performed live, but,/ more

often they are taped.

WRITERS ON WRITING

The most important fact about a comma is that there are places where it must not be used.   — Bergen Evans and Cornelia Evans

I like to use as few commas as possible so that sentences will go down in one swallow without touching the sides.   — Pamela Frankau

AFTER *SUCH AS* OR *LIKE*

▶ Shade-loving plants such as,/begonias, impatiens, and coleus can add color to a shady garden.

AFTER *ALTHOUGH*

▶ Although,/ the air was balmy, the water was cold.

BEFORE A PARENTHESIS

▶ Though Sylvia's ACT score was low,/(only 15), her admissions essay was superior.

TO SET OFF AN INDIRECT (REPORTED) QUOTATION

▶ Samuel Goldwyn once said,/ that a verbal contract isn't worth the paper it's written on.

WITH A QUESTION MARK OR AN EXCLAMATION POINT

▶ "Why don't you try it?,/" she coaxed. "You can't do any worse than the rest of us."

EXERCISE 33–1 Delete any unnecessary commas in the following sentences. If a sentence is correct, write "correct" after it. Answers appear in the back of the book. *More practice:* e

In his Silk Road Project, Yo-Yo Ma incorporates work by musicians such as,/ Kayhan Kahlor and Richard Danielpour.

a. After the morning rains cease, the swimmers emerge from their cottages.

hackerhandbooks.com/bedhandbook

e Punctuation > Exercises: 33–3 to 33–5

EXERCISE 33–1 *Answers:*

a. Correct
b. Tricia's first artwork was a bright blue clay dolphin.
c. Some modern musicians (trumpeter John Hassell is an example) blend several cultural traditions into a unique sound.
d. Myra liked hot, spicy foods such as chili, kung pao chicken, and buffalo wings.
e. On the display screen was a soothing pattern of light and shadow.

b.   Tricia's first artwork was a bright, blue, clay dolphin.

c.   Some modern musicians, (trumpeter John Hassell is an example) blend several cultural traditions into a unique sound.

d.   Myra liked hot, spicy foods such as, chili, kung pao chicken, and buffalo wings.

e.   On the display screen, was a soothing pattern of light and shadow.

EXERCISE 33–2   Delete unnecessary commas in the following passage. *More practice:* 📧

Each spring since 1970, New Orleans has hosted the Jazz and Heritage Festival, an event that celebrates the music, food, and culture, of the region. Although, it is often referred to as "Jazz Fest," the festival typically includes a wide variety of musical styles such as, gospel, Cajun, blues, zydeco, and, rock and roll. Famous musicians who have appeared regularly at Jazz Fest, include Dr. John, B. B. King, and Aretha Franklin. Large stages are set up throughout the fairgrounds in a way, that allows up to ten bands to play simultaneously without any sound overlap. Food tents are located throughout the festival, and offer popular, local dishes like crawfish Monica, jambalaya, and fried, green tomatoes. Following Hurricane Katrina in 2005, Jazz Fest revived quickly, and attendance has steadily increased each year. Fans, who cannot attend the festival, still enjoy the music by downloading MP3 files, and watching performances online.

34   The semicolon

The semicolon is used to connect major sentence elements of equal grammatical rank.

hackerhandbooks.com/bedhandbook

📧 Punctuation > Exercises: 33–3 to 33–5

EXERCISE 33–2   *Answers:*

Each spring since 1970, New Orleans has hosted the Jazz and Heritage Festival, an event that celebrates the music, food, and culture of the region. Although it is often referred to as "Jazz Fest," the festival typically includes a wide variety of musical styles such as gospel, Cajun, blues, zydeco, and rock and roll. Famous musicians who have appeared regularly at Jazz Fest include Dr. John, B. B. King, and Aretha Franklin. Large stages are set up throughout the fairgrounds in a way that allows up to ten bands to play simultaneously without any sound overlap. Food tents are located throughout the festival and offer popular local

34a Use a semicolon between closely related independent clauses not joined with a coordinating conjunction.

When two independent clauses appear in one sentence, they are usually linked with a comma and a coordinating conjunction (*and, but, or, nor, for, so, yet*). If the clauses are closely related and the relation is clear without a conjunction, they may be linked with a semicolon instead.

> In film, a low-angle shot makes the subject look powerful; a high-angle shot does just the opposite.

A semicolon must be used whenever a coordinating conjunction has been omitted between independent clauses. To use merely a comma creates a type of run-on sentence known as a *comma splice*. (See 20.)

> ▶ In 1800, a traveler needed six weeks to get from New York
>
> to Chicago/; in 1860, the trip by train took only two days.
>   ∧

34b Use a semicolon between independent clauses linked with a transitional expression.

Transitional expressions include conjunctive adverbs and transitional phrases.

CONJUNCTIVE ADVERBS

accordingly	furthermore	moreover	still
also	hence	nevertheless	subsequently
anyway	however	next	then
besides	incidentally	nonetheless	therefore
certainly	indeed	now	thus
consequently	instead	otherwise	
conversely	likewise	similarly	
finally	meanwhile	specifically	

EXERCISE 33–2 *Answers (continued):*

dishes like crawfish Monica, jambalaya, and fried green tomatoes. Following Hurricane Katrina in 2005, Jazz Fest revived quickly, and attendance has steadily increased each year. Fans who cannot attend the festival still enjoy the music by downloading MP3 files and watching performances online.

TRANSITIONAL PHRASES

after all	even so	in fact
as a matter of fact	for example	in other words
as a result	for instance	in the first place
at any rate	in addition	on the contrary
at the same time	in conclusion	on the other hand

When a transitional expression appears between independent clauses, it is preceded by a semicolon and usually followed by a comma.

▶ Many corals grow very gradually/; in fact, the creation of

a coral reef can take centuries.

When a transitional expression appears in the middle or at the end of the second independent clause, the semicolon goes *between the clauses*.

▶ Biologists have observed laughter in primates other than

humans/; chimpanzees, however, sound more like they

are panting than laughing.

Transitional expressions should not be confused with the coordinating conjunctions *and, but, or, nor, for, so,* and *yet,* which are preceded by a comma when they link independent clauses. (See 32a.)

34c Use a semicolon between items in a series containing internal punctuation.

▶ Classic science fiction sagas are *Star Trek*, with Mr. Spock/;

Battlestar Galactica, with its Cylons/; and *Star Wars*, with

Han Solo, Luke Skywalker, and Darth Vader.

WRITERS ON WRITING

It is almost always a greater pleasure to come across a semicolon than a period. The period tells you that that is that; if you didn't get all the meaning you wanted or expected, anyway you got all the writer intended to parcel out and now you have to move along. But with a semicolon there you get a pleasant little feeling of expectancy; there is more to come; read on; it will get clearer. — Lewis Thomas

Semicolons . . . signal, rather than shout, a relationship. . . . A semicolon is a compliment from the writer to the reader. It says: "I don't have to draw you a picture; a hint will do." — George Will

Without the semicolons, the reader would have to sort out the major groupings, distinguishing between important and less important pauses according to the logic of the sentence. By inserting semicolons at the major breaks, the writer does this work for the reader.

34d Avoid common misuses of the semicolon.

Do not use a semicolon in the following situations.

BETWEEN A SUBORDINATE CLAUSE AND THE REST OF THE SENTENCE

▶ Although children's literature was added to the National Book Awards in 1969⨍, it has had its own award, the Newbery Medal, since 1922.

BETWEEN AN APPOSITIVE AND THE WORD IT REFERS TO

▶ The scientists were fascinated by the species *Argyroneta aquatica⨍,* a spider that lives underwater.

TO INTRODUCE A LIST

▶ Some of my favorite celebrities have their own blogs⨍: Ashton Kutcher, Beyoncé, and Zach Braff.

BETWEEN INDEPENDENT CLAUSES JOINED BY *AND, BUT, OR, NOR, FOR, SO, OR YET*

▶ Five of the applicants had worked with spreadsheets⨍, but only one was familiar with database management.

EXCEPTION: If one or both of the independent clauses contains a comma, you may use a semicolon with a coordinating conjunction between the clauses.

SCHOLARS ON THE SEMICOLON

Bruthiaux, Paul. "The Rise and Fall of the Semicolon: English Punctuation Theory and English Teaching Practice." *Applied Linguistics* 16.1 (1995): 1–14. Print. Exploring semicolon use from the mid-sixteenth century, compared with the use of colons and dashes, Bruthiaux concludes that the semicolon may have become a marginal part of our punctuation system.

EXERCISE 34-1   Add commas or semicolons where needed in the following well-known quotations. If a sentence is correct, write "correct" after it. Answers appear in the back of the book. *More practice:* e

> If an animal does something *,* we call it instinct *;* if we do
>
> the same thing *,* we call it intelligence.   — Will Cuppy

a.   Do not ask me to be kind just ask me to act as though I were.
                                                — Jules Renard

b.   When men talk about defense they always claim to be protecting women and children but they never ask the women and children what they think.   — Pat Schroeder

c.   When I get a little money I buy books if any is left I buy food and clothes.   — Desiderius Erasmus

d.   America is a country that doesn't know where it is going but is determined to set a speed record getting there.
                                                — Lawrence J. Peter

e.   Wit has truth in it wisecracking is simply calisthenics with words.
                                                — Dorothy Parker

EXERCISE 34-2   Edit the following sentences to correct errors in the use of the comma and the semicolon. If a sentence is correct, write "correct" after it. Answers appear in the back of the book. *More practice:* e

> Love is blind *;* envy has its eyes wide open.

a.   Strong black coffee will not sober you up, the truth is that time is the only way to get alcohol out of your system.

b.   Margaret was not surprised to see hail and vivid lightning, conditions had been right for violent weather all day.

c.   There is often a fine line between right and wrong; good and bad; truth and deception.

d.   My mother always says that you can't learn common sense; either you're born with it or you're not.

e.   Severe, unremitting pain is a ravaging force; especially when the patient tries to hide it from others.

hackerhandbooks.com/bedhandbook

e Punctuation > Exercises: 34–3 to 34–6

EXERCISE 34-1   *Answers:*

a.   Do not ask me to be kind; just ask me to act as though I were.

b.   When men talk about defense, they always claim to be protecting women and children, but they never ask the women and children what they think.

c.   When I get a little money, I buy books; if any is left, I buy food and clothes.

d.   Correct

e.   Wit has truth in it; wisecracking is simply calisthenics with words.

35 The colon

The colon is used primarily to call attention to the words that follow it. In addition, the colon has some conventional uses.

35a Use a colon after an independent clause to direct attention to a list, an appositive, a quotation, or a summary or an explanation.

A LIST

The daily exercise routine should include at least the following: twenty knee bends, fifty sit-ups, and five minutes of running in place.

AN APPOSITIVE

My roommate is guilty of two of the seven deadly sins: gluttony and sloth.

A QUOTATION

Consider the words of Benjamin Franklin: "There never was a good war or a bad peace."

A SUMMARY OR AN EXPLANATION

Faith is like love: It cannot be forced.

The novel is clearly autobiographical: The author even gives his own name to the main character.

NOTE: For other ways of introducing quotations, see "Introducing quoted material" on pages 438–40. When an independent clause

---

EXERCISE 34-2 *Answers:*

a. Strong black coffee will not sober you up; the truth is that time is the only way to get alcohol out of your system.

b. Margaret was not surprised to see hail and vivid lightning; conditions had been right for violent weather all day.

c. There is often a fine line between right and wrong, good and bad, truth and deception.

d. Correct

e. Severe, unremitting pain is a ravaging force, especially when the patient tries to hide it from others.

follows a colon, begin with a capital letter. Some disciplines use a lowercase letter instead. See 45f for variations.

35b Use a colon according to convention.

SALUTATION IN A LETTER　Dear Editor:

HOURS AND MINUTES　5:30 p.m.

PROPORTIONS　The ratio of women to men was 2:1.

TITLE AND SUBTITLE　*The Glory of Hera: Greek Mythology and the Greek Family*

BIBLIOGRAPHIC ENTRIES　Boston: Bedford, 2012

CHAPTER AND VERSE IN SACRED TEXT　Luke 2:14, Qur'an 67:3

35c Avoid common misuses of the colon.

A colon must be preceded by a full independent clause. Therefore, avoid using it in the following situations.

BETWEEN A VERB AND ITS OBJECT OR COMPLEMENT

▶ Some important vitamins found in vegetables are: vitamin A, thiamine, niacin, and vitamin C.

BETWEEN A PREPOSITION AND ITS OBJECT

▶ The heart's two pumps each consist of: an upper chamber, or atrium, and a lower chamber, or ventricle.

AFTER *SUCH AS*, *INCLUDING*, OR *FOR EXAMPLE*

▶ The NCAA regulates college athletic teams, including: basketball, baseball, softball, and football.

EXERCISE 35-1 Edit the following sentences to correct errors in the use of the comma, the semicolon, or the colon. If a sentence is correct, write "correct" after it. Answers appear in the back of the book. *More practice:* e

> Lifting the cover gently, Luca found the source of the odd
>
> sound ̷;̷: a marble in the gears.
>   ∧

a. We always looked forward to Thanksgiving in Vermont: It was our only chance to see our Grady cousins.

b. If we have come to fight, we are far too few, if we have come to die, we are far too many.

c. The travel package includes: a round-trip ticket to Athens, a cruise through the Cyclades, and all hotel accommodations.

d. The news article portrays the land use proposal as reckless; although 62 percent of the town's residents support it.

e. Psychologists Kindlon and Thompson (2000) offer parents a simple starting point for raising male children, "Teach boys that there are many ways to be a man" (p. 256).

36 The apostrophe

36a Use an apostrophe to indicate that a noun is possessive.

Possessive nouns usually indicate ownership, as in *Tim's hat* or *the lawyer's desk.* Frequently, however, ownership is only loosely implied: *the tree's roots, a day's work.* If you are not sure whether a noun is possessive, try turning it into an *of* phrase: *the roots of the tree, the work of a day.* (Pronouns also have possessive forms. See 36b and 36e.)

hackerhandbooks.com/bedhandbook

e Punctuation > Exercises: 35–2 and 35–3

When to add -'s

1. If the noun does not end in -s, add -'s.

    Luck often propels a rock musician's career.

    The Children's Defense Fund is a nonprofit organization that supports programs for poor and minority children.

2. If the noun is singular and ends in -s or an s sound, add -'s to indicate possession.

    Lois's sister spent last year in India.

    Her article presents an overview of Marx's teachings.

NOTE: To avoid potentially awkward pronunciation, some writers use only the apostrophe with a singular noun ending in -s: *Sophocles'*.

When to add only an apostrophe

If the noun is plural and ends in -s, add only an apostrophe.

Both diplomats' briefcases were searched by guards.

Joint possession

To show joint possession, use -'s or (-s') with the last noun only; to show individual possession, make all nouns possessive.

Have you seen Joyce and Greg's new camper?

John's and Marie's expectations of marriage couldn't have been more different.

Joyce and Greg jointly own one camper. John and Marie individually have different expectations.

Compound nouns

If a noun is compound, use -'s (or -s') with the last element.

My father-in-law's memoir about his childhood in Sri Lanka was published in October.

TEACHING TIP

It is often helpful to allow students to take charge of teaching a few punctuation concepts. Assign students in groups to tackle concepts such as apostrophes and commas and to prepare a ten-minute mini-lesson in which they show examples and discuss editing strategies. If the class is online, the students can prepare a few slides that they upload to the course Web site.

36b Use an apostrophe and -s to indicate that an indefinite pronoun is possessive.

Indefinite pronouns refer to no specific person or thing: *everyone, someone, no one, something.* (See 46b.)

> Someone's raincoat has been left behind.

36c Use an apostrophe to mark omissions in contractions and numbers.

In a contraction, the apostrophe takes the place of one or more missing letters. *It's* stands for *it is, can't* for *cannot.*

> It's a shame that Frank can't go on the tour.

The apostrophe is also used to mark the omission of the first two digits of a year (*the class of '12*) or years (*the '60s generation*).

36d Do not use an apostrophe in certain situations.

An apostrophe typically is not used to pluralize numbers, letters, abbreviations, and words mentioned as words. Note the few exceptions and be consistent throughout your paper.

Plural of numbers

Do not use an apostrophe in the plural of any numbers.

> Oksana skated nearly perfect figure 8s.

> The 1920s are known as the Jazz Age.

Plural of letters

Italicize the letter and use roman (regular) font style for the *-s* ending. (Do not italicize academic grades.)

> Two large *P*s were painted on the door.

> He received two Ds for the first time in his life.

WRITERS ON WRITING

Lately, I've been trying to be a lot more calm about apostrophes. I still mark a fair number of them in the margin and try to help students to learn how to write "it's" for "it is" and how to recognize simple problems like the "dogs bone" and "Hashimotos brain." But I'm slowly learning how difficult such ideas are for some students in a world where apostrophes are not so important, where life goes on with or without punctuation. — Irvin Hashimoto

EXCEPTIONS: To avoid misreading, use an apostrophe to form the plural of lowercase letters and the capital letters *A* and *I*.

> Beginning readers often confuse *b*'s and *d*'s.

> Students with straight A's earn high honors.

MLA NOTE: MLA recommends using an apostrophe for the plural of single capital and lowercase letters: *H's, p's*.

Plural of abbreviations

Do not use an apostrophe to pluralize an abbreviation.

> Harriet has thirty DVDs on her desk.

> Marco earned two PhDs before his thirtieth birthday.

Plural of words mentioned as words

Generally, omit the apostrophe to form the plural of words mentioned as words. If the word is italicized, the *-s* ending appears in roman (regular) type.

> We've heard enough *maybe*s.

Words mentioned as words may also appear in quotation marks. When you choose this option, use the apostrophe.

> We've heard enough "maybe's."

36e Avoid common misuses of the apostrophe.

Do not use an apostrophe with nouns that are not possessive or with the possessive pronouns *its, whose, his, hers, ours, yours,* and *theirs*.

> outpatients
> ▶ Some ~~outpatient's~~ have special parking permits.
>   ∧

EXERCISE 36–1   *Answers:*

a.   Correct
b.   The innovative shoe fastener was inspired by the designer's young son.
c.   Each day's menu features a different European country's dish.
d.   Sue worked overtime to increase her family's earnings.
e.   Ms. Jacobs is unwilling to listen to students' complaints about computer failures.

▶ Each area has ~~it's~~ *its* own conference room.

It's means "it is." The possessive pronoun *its* contains no apostrophe despite the fact that it is possessive.

▶ We attended a reading by Junot Díaz, ~~who's~~ *whose* work focuses on the Dominican immigration experience.

Who's means "who is." The possessive pronoun is *whose*.

EXERCISE 36–1   Edit the following sentences to correct errors in the use of the apostrophe. If a sentence is correct, write "correct" after it. Answers appear in the back of the book. *More practice:* e ✓

Our favorite barbecue restaurant is Poor ~~Richards~~ *Richard's* Ribs.

a.   This diet will improve almost anyone's health.

b.   The innovative shoe fastener was inspired by the designers young son.

c.   Each days menu features a different European country's dish.

d.   Sue worked overtime to increase her families earnings.

e.   Ms. Jacobs is unwilling to listen to students complaints about computer failures.

EXERCISE 36–2   Edit the following passage to correct errors in the use of the apostrophe. *More practice:* e ✓

Its never too soon to start holiday shopping. In fact, some people choose to start shopping as early as January, when last seasons leftover's are priced at their lowest. Many stores try to lure customers in with promise's of savings up to 90 percent. Their main objective, of course, is to make way for next years inventory. The big problem with postholiday shopping, though, is that there isn't much left to choose from. Store's shelves have

hackerhandbooks.com/bedhandbook

e Punctuation > Exercises: 36–3 to 36–5

✓ Punctuation > LearningCurve: Apostrophes

EXERCISE 36–2   *Answers:*

It's never too soon to start holiday shopping. In fact, some people choose to start shopping as early as January, when last season's leftovers are priced at their lowest. Many stores try to lure customers in with promises of savings up to 90 percent. Their main objective, of course, is to make way for next year's inventory. The big problem with postholiday shopping, though, is that there isn't much left to choose from. Stores' shelves have been picked over by last-minute shoppers desperately searching for gifts. The other problem is that it's hard to know what to buy so far in advance. Next year's hot items are anyone's guess. But proper timing, mixed with lots of luck and determination, can lead to good purchases at great prices.

been picked over by last-minute shoppers desperately searching for gifts. The other problem is that its hard to know what to buy so far in advance. Next year's hot items are anyones guess. But proper timing, mixed with lot's of luck and determination, can lead to good purchases at great price's.

37 Quotation marks

Writers use quotation marks primarily to enclose direct quotations of another person's spoken or written words. You will also find these other uses and exceptions:

- for quotations within quotations (single quotation marks: 37b)
- for titles of short works (37c)
- for words used as words (37d)
- with other marks of punctuation (37e)
- with brackets and ellipsis marks (39c–39d)
- no quotation marks for indirect quotations, paraphrases, and summaries (p. 435)
- no quotation marks for long quotations (p. 435)

37a Use quotation marks to enclose direct quotations.

Direct quotations of a person's words, whether spoken or written, must be in quotation marks.

> "Twitter," according to social media researcher Jameson Brown, "is the best social network for brand to customer engagement."

In dialogue, begin a new paragraph to mark a change in speaker.

> "Mom, his name is Willie, not William. A thousand times I've told you, it's *Willie*."
>
> "Willie is a derivative of William, Lester. Surely his birth certificate doesn't have Willie on it, and I like calling people by their proper names."
>
> "Yes, it does, ma'am. My mother named me Willie K. Mason."
>
> — Gloria Naylor

If a single speaker utters more than one paragraph, introduce each paragraph with a quotation mark, but do not use a closing quotation mark until the end of the speech.

Exception: indirect quotations

Do not use quotation marks around indirect quotations. An indirect quotation reports someone's ideas without using that person's exact words. In academic writing, indirect quotation is called *paraphrase* or *summary*. (See 51c.)

> Social media researcher Jameson Brown finds Twitter the best social media tool for companies that want to reach their consumers.

Exception: long quotations

Long quotations of prose or poetry are generally set off from the text by indenting. Quotation marks are not used because the indented format tells readers that the quotation is taken word-for-word from the source.

> After making an exhaustive study of the historical record, James Horan evaluates Billy the Kid like this:
>
> > The portrait that emerges of [the Kid] from the thousands of pages of affidavits, reports, trial transcripts, his letters, and his testimony is neither the mythical Robin Hood nor the

---

TEACHING TIP

If you ask your students to write from sources, spend a class period discussing the punctuation involved in quoting directly from sources. Review the handbook section on direct quotations, do the exercises as a class or in pairs or small groups, and look at examples of quoted material in a few sources, asking students to highlight or circle the punctuation.

> stereotyped adenoidal moron and pathological killer. Rather
> Billy appears as a disturbed, lonely young man, honest, loyal
> to his friends, dedicated to his beliefs, and betrayed by our
> institutions and the corrupt, ambitious, and compromising
> politicians in his time. (158)

The number in parentheses is a citation handled according to
MLA style (see 56a). (For details about citing long quotations
from poetry, see "Citing quotations" in 7f.)

MLA, APA, and *Chicago* have specific guidelines for what
constitutes a long quotation and how it should be indented (see
pp. 573, 673, and 749, respectively).

37b Use single quotation marks to enclose a quotation within a quotation.

> Megan Marshall notes that Elizabeth Peabody's school focused
> on "not merely 'teaching' but 'educating children morally and
> spiritually as well as intellectually from the first'" (107).

37c Use quotation marks around the titles of short works.

Short works include newspaper and magazine articles, poems,
short stories, songs, episodes of television and radio programs,
and chapters or subdivisions of books.

> James Baldwin's story "Sonny's Blues" tells the story of two
> brothers who come to understand each other's suffering.

NOTE: Titles of long works such as books, plays, television and
radio programs, films, magazines, and so on are put in italics.
(See 42a.)

WRITERS ON WRITING

I quote others in order to better express my own self.   — Montaigne

37d Quotation marks may be used to set off words used as words.

Although words used as words are ordinarily italicized (see 42d), quotation marks are also acceptable. Be consistent throughout your paper.

> The words "accept" and "except" are frequently confused.

> The words *accept* and *except* are frequently confused.

37e Use punctuation with quotation marks according to convention.

This section describes the conventions American publishers use in placing various marks of punctuation inside or outside quotation marks. It also explains how to punctuate when introducing quoted material. (For the use of quotation marks in MLA, APA, and *Chicago* styles, see 56a, 61a, and 63d, respectively. The examples in this section show MLA style.)

Periods and commas

Place periods and commas inside quotation marks.

> "I'm here as part of my service-learning project," I told the classroom teacher. "I'm hoping to become a reading specialist."

This rule applies to single quotation marks as well as double quotation marks. (See 37b.) It also applies to all uses of quotation marks: for quoted material, for titles of works, and for words used as words.

EXCEPTION: In the MLA and APA styles of parenthetical in-text citations, the period follows the citation in parentheses.

James M. McPherson comments, approvingly, that the Whigs "were not averse to extending the blessings of American liberty, even to Mexicans and Indians" (48).

Colons and semicolons

Put colons and semicolons outside quotation marks.

Harold wrote, "I regret that I am unable to attend the fund-raiser for AIDS research"; his letter, however, came with a substantial contribution.

Question marks and exclamation points

Put question marks and exclamation points inside quotation marks unless they apply to the whole sentence.

Dr. Abram's first question on the first day of class was "What three goals do you have for the course?"

Have you heard the old proverb "Do not climb the hill until you reach it"?

In the first sentence, the question mark applies only to the quoted question. In the second sentence, the question mark applies to the whole sentence.

NOTE: In MLA and APA styles for a quotation that ends with a question mark or an exclamation point, the parenthetical citation and a period should follow the entire quotation.

Rosie Thomas asks, "Is nothing in life ever straight and clear, the way children see it?" (77).

Introducing quoted material

After a word group introducing a quotation, choose a colon, a comma, or no punctuation at all, whichever is appropriate in context.

Formal introduction If a quotation is formally introduced, a colon is appropriate. A formal introduction is a full independent clause, not just an expression such as *he writes* or *she remarked*.

> Thomas Friedman provides a challenging yet optimistic view of the future: "We need to get back to work on our country and on our planet. The hour is late, the stakes couldn't be higher, the project couldn't be harder, the payoff couldn't be greater" (25).

Expression such as *he writes* If a quotation is introduced with an expression such as *he writes* or *she remarked*—or if it is followed by such an expression—a comma is needed.

> "With regard to air travel," Stephen Ambrose notes, "Jefferson was a full century ahead of the curve" (53).

> "Unless another war is prevented it is likely to bring destruction on a scale never before held possible and even now hardly conceived," Albert Einstein wrote in the aftermath of the atomic bomb (29).

Blended quotation When a quotation is blended into the writer's own sentence, either a comma or no punctuation is appropriate, depending on the way in which the quotation fits into the sentence structure.

> The future champion could, as he put it, "float like a butterfly and sting like a bee."

> Virginia Woolf wrote in 1928 that "a woman must have money and a room of her own if she is to write fiction" (4).

Beginning of sentence If a quotation appears at the beginning of a sentence, use a comma after it unless the quotation ends with a question mark or an exclamation point.

> "I've always thought of myself as a reporter," American poet Gwendolyn Brooks has stated (162).

> "What is it?" she asked, bracing herself.

Interrupted quotation   If a quoted sentence is interrupted by explanatory words, use commas to set off the explanatory words. If two successive quoted sentences from the same source are interrupted by explanatory words, use a comma before the explanatory words and a period after them.

> "Everyone agrees journalists must tell the truth," Bill Kovach and Tom Rosenstiel write. "Yet people are befuddled about what 'the truth' means" (37).

37f Avoid common misuses of quotation marks.

Do not use quotation marks to draw attention to familiar slang, to disown trite expressions, or to justify an attempt at humor.

▶ The economist estimated that single-family home prices

would decline another 5 percent by the end of the year,

emphasizing that this was only a ⸝ballpark figure.⸍

Do not use quotation marks around the title of your own essay.

EXERCISE 37–1   Add or delete quotation marks as needed and make any other necessary changes in punctuation in the following sentences. If a sentence is correct, write "correct" after it. Answers appear in the back of the book. *More practice:* e

Gandhi once said, "An eye for an eye only ends up making
                  ∧
the whole world blind."
                     ∧

a.   As for the advertisement "Sailors have more fun", if you consider chipping paint and swabbing decks fun, then you will have plenty of it.
b.   Even after forty minutes of discussion, our class could not agree on an interpretation of Robert Frost's poem "The Road Not Taken."

hackerhandbooks.com/bedhandbook
e Punctuation > Exercises: 37–3 to 37–5

EXERCISE 37–1   *Answers:*

a.   As for the advertisement "Sailors have more fun," if you consider chipping paint and swabbing decks fun, then you will have plenty of it.
b.   Correct
c.   After winning the lottery, Juanita said that she would give half the money to charity.
d.   After the movie, Vicki said, "The reviewer called this flick 'trash of the first order.' I guess you can't believe everything you read."
e.   Correct

c. After winning the lottery, Juanita said that “she would give half the money to charity.”

d. After the movie, Vicki said, “The reviewer called this flick “trash of the first order.” I guess you can’t believe everything you read.”

e. “Cleaning your house while your kids are still growing,” said Phyllis Diller, “is like shoveling the walk before it stops snowing.”

EXERCISE 37–2 Add or delete quotation marks as needed and make any other necessary changes in punctuation in the following passage. Citations should conform to MLA style (see 56a). *More practice:* e

In his article The Moment of Truth, former vice president Al Gore argues that global warming is a genuine threat to life on Earth and that we must act now to avoid catastrophe. Gore calls our situation a “true *planetary emergency*” and cites scientific evidence of the greenhouse effect and its consequences (170-71). “What is at stake, Gore insists, is the survival of our civilization and the habitability of the Earth (197).” With such a grim predicament at hand, Gore questions why so many political and economic leaders are reluctant to act. “Is it simply more convenient to ignore the warnings,” he asks (171)?

The crisis, of course, will not go away if we just pretend it isn’t there. Gore points out that in Chinese two symbols form the character for the word crisis. The first of those symbols means “danger”, and the second means “opportunity.” The danger we face, he claims, is accompanied by “unprecedented opportunity.” (172) Gore contends that throughout history we have won battles against seemingly unbeatable evils such as slavery and fascism and that we did so by facing the truth and choosing the moral high ground. Gore’s final appeal is to our humanity:

> “Ultimately, [the fight to end global warming] is not about any scientific discussion or political dialogue; it is about who we are as human beings. It is about our capacity to transcend our limitations, to rise to this new occasion. To see with our hearts, as well as our heads, the response that is now called for.” (244)

Gore feels that the fate of our world rests in our own hands, and his hope is that we will make the choice to save the planet.

Source of quotations: Al Gore; “The Moment of Truth”; *Vanity Fair* May 2006: 170+; print.

EXERCISE 37–2 *Answers:*

In his article “The Moment of Truth,” former vice president Al Gore argues that global warming is a genuine threat to life on Earth and that we must act now to avoid catastrophe. Gore calls our situation a “true *planetary emergency*” and cites scientific evidence of the greenhouse effect and its consequences (170-71). “What is at stake,” Gore insists, “is the survival of our civilization and the habitability of the Earth” (197). With such a grim predicament at hand, Gore questions why so many political and economic leaders are reluctant to act. “Is it simply more convenient to ignore the warnings?” he asks (171).

The crisis, of course, will not go away if we just pretend it isn’t there. Gore points out that in Chinese two symbols form the character for the word “crisis.” [*or crisis.*] The first of those symbols means “danger,” and

38 End punctuation

38a The period

Use a period to end all sentences except direct questions or genuine exclamations. Also use periods in abbreviations according to convention.

To end sentences

Most sentences should end with a period. A sentence that reports a question instead of asking it directly (an indirect question) should end with a period, not a question mark.

▶ **The professor asked whether talk therapy was more**

beneficial than antidepressants?̶.
                                  ∧

If a sentence is not a genuine exclamation, it should end with a period, not an exclamation point. (See also 38c.)

▶ **After years of working her way through school, Geeta**

finally graduated with high honors!̶.
                              ∧

In abbreviations

A period is conventionally used in abbreviations of titles and Latin words or phrases, including the time designations for morning and afternoon.

Mr.	i.e.	a.m. (or AM)
Ms.	e.g.	p.m. (or PM)
Dr.	etc.	

EXERCISE 37-2 *Answers (continued):*

the second means "opportunity." The danger we face, he claims, is accompanied by "unprecedented opportunity" (172). Gore contends that throughout history we have won battles against seemingly unbeatable evils such as slavery and fascism and that we did so by facing the truth and choosing the moral high ground. Gore's final appeal is to our humanity:

> Ultimately, [the fight to end global warming] is not about any scientific discussion or political dialogue; it is about who we are as human beings. It is about our capacity to transcend our limitations, to rise to this new occasion. To see with our hearts, as well as our heads, the response that is now called for. (244)

Gore feels that the fate of our world rests in our own hands, and his hope is that we will make the choice to save the planet.

NOTE: If a sentence ends with a period marking an abbreviation, do not add a second period.

Do not use a period with US Postal Service abbreviations for states: MD, TX, CA.

Current usage is to omit the period in abbreviations of organization names, academic degrees, and designations for eras.

NATO	UNESCO	UCLA	BS	BC
IRS	AFL-CIO	NIH	PhD	BCE

38b The question mark

A direct question should be followed by a question mark.

What is the horsepower of a 777 engine?

TIP: Do not use a question mark after an indirect question, one that is reported rather than asked directly. Use a period instead.

▶ He asked me who was teaching the math course this year?̣.
   ∧

38c The exclamation point

Use an exclamation point after a word group or sentence to express exceptional feeling or to provide special emphasis. The exclamation point is rarely appropriate in academic writing.

When Gloria entered the room, I switched on the lights, and we all yelled, "Surprise!"

TIP: Do not overuse the exclamation point.

▶ In the fisherman's memory, the fish lives on, increasing in

length and weight with each passing year, until at last it is

big enough to shade a fishing boat!̣.
                                 ∧

This sentence doesn't need to be pumped up with an exclamation point. It is emphatic enough without it.

WRITERS ON WRITING

My attitude toward punctuation is that it ought to be as conventional as *possible*. The game of golf would lose a great deal if croquet mallets and billiard cues were allowed on the putting green. You ought to be able to show that you can do it a good deal better than anyone else with the regular tools before you have a license to bring in your own improvements.
— Ernest Hemingway

There's not much to be said about the period except that most writers don't reach it soon enough.
— William Zinsser

EXERCISE 38-1   Add appropriate end punctuation in the following paragraph. *More practice:* <kbd>e</kbd>

Although I am generally rational, I am superstitious I never walk under ladders or put shoes on the table If I spill the salt, I go into frenzied calisthenics picking up the grains and tossing them over my left shoulder As a result of these curious activities, I've always wondered whether knowing the roots of superstitions would quell my irrational responses Superstition has it, for example, that one should never place a hat on the bed This superstition arises from a time when head lice were common and placing a guest's hat on the bed stood a good chance of spreading lice through the host's bed Doesn't this make good sense And doesn't it stand to reason that, if I know that my guests don't have lice, I shouldn't care where their hats go Of course it does It is fair to ask, then, whether I have changed my ways and place hats on beds Are you kidding I wouldn't put a hat on a bed if my life depended on it

39   Other punctuation marks

39a   The dash

When typing, use two hyphens to form a dash (--). Do not put spaces before or after the dash. If your word processing program has what is known as an "em-dash" (—), you may use it instead, with no space before or after it.

Use a dash to set off parenthetical material that deserves emphasis.

> Everything that went wrong—from the peeping Tom at her window last night to my head-on collision today—we blamed on our move.

hackerhandbooks.com/bedhandbook

<kbd>e</kbd> Punctuation > Exercises: 38–2

EXERCISE 38-1   *Answers:*

Although I am generally rational, I am superstitious. I never walk under ladders or put shoes on the table. If I spill the salt, I go into frenzied calisthenics picking up the grains and tossing them over my left shoulder. As a result of these curious activities, I've always wondered whether knowing the roots of superstitions would quell my irrational responses. Superstition has it, for example, that one should never place a hat on the bed. This superstition arises from a time when head lice were common and placing a guest's hat on the bed stood a good chance of spreading lice through the host's bed. Doesn't this make good sense? And doesn't it stand to reason that, if I know that my guests don't have lice, I shouldn't care where their hats go? Of course it does. It is fair to

Use a dash to set off appositives that contain commas. An appositive is a noun or noun phrase that renames a nearby noun. Ordinarily most appositives are set off with commas (32e), but when the appositive itself contains commas, a pair of dashes helps readers see the relative importance of all the pauses.

> In my hometown, people's basic needs—food, clothing, and shelter—are less costly than in a big city like Los Angeles.

A dash can also be used to introduce a list, a restatement, an amplification, or a dramatic shift in tone or thought.

> Along the wall are the bulk liquids—sesame seed oil, honey, safflower oil, and that half-liquid "peanuts only" peanut butter.

> In his last semester, Peter tried to pay more attention to his priorities—applying to graduate school and getting financial aid.

> Everywhere we looked there were little kids—a bag of Skittles in one hand and their mommy or daddy's sleeve in the other.

> Kiere took a few steps back, came running full speed, kicked a mighty kick—and missed the ball.

In the first two examples, the writer could also use a colon. (See 35a.) The colon is more formal than the dash and not quite as dramatic.

TIP: Unless there is a specific reason for using the dash, avoid it. Unnecessary dashes create a choppy effect.

39b Parentheses

Use parentheses to enclose supplemental material, minor digressions, and afterthoughts.

> Nurses record patients' vital signs (temperature, pulse, and blood pressure) several times a day.

Use parentheses to enclose letters or numbers labeling items in a series.

EXERCISE 38–1   *Answers (continued):*

ask, then, whether I have changed my ways and place hats on beds. Are you kidding? I wouldn't put a hat on a bed if my life depended on it! [*or . . . on it.*]

WRITERS ON WRITING

The most frequent use of the dash is in pairs, to interrupt and set off a thought, long or short, which does not form an integral part of the sentence. In this capacity it serves somewhat the same purpose as the parentheses, though writers who like distinctions tend to think of the latter as slipping in a thought under the breath, perhaps for explanation, whereas the paired dashes throw in a fresh, not easily assimilable thought.

— Wilson Follett

Regulations stipulated that only the following equipment could be used on the survival mission: (1) a knife, (2) thirty feet of parachute line, (3) a book of matches, (4) two ponchos, (5) an E tool, and (6) a signal flare.

TIP: Rough drafts are likely to contain unnecessary parentheses. As writers head into a sentence, they often think of additional details, using parentheses to work them in as best they can. Such sentences usually can be revised to add the details without parentheses.

▶ Researchers have said that seventeen million ~~(estimates run~~ *from*

~~as high as~~ twenty-three million*)* Americans have diabetes. *to*

39c Brackets

Use brackets to enclose any words or phrases that you have inserted into an otherwise word-for-word quotation.

> *Audubon* reports that "if there are not enough young to balance deaths, the end of the species [California condor] is inevitable" (4).

The sentence quoted from the *Audubon* article did not contain the words *California condor* (since the context of the full article made clear what species was meant), so the writer needed to add the name in brackets.

The Latin word "sic" in brackets indicates that an error in a quoted sentence appears in the original source.

> According to the review, Nelly Furtado's performance was brilliant, "exceding [sic] the expectations of even her most loyal fans."

Do not overuse "sic," however, since calling attention to others' mistakes can appear snobbish. The preceding quotation, for example, might have been paraphrased instead: *According to the review, even Nelly Furtado's most loyal fans were surprised by the brilliance of her performance.*

NOTE: For advice on using "sic" in MLA, APA, and Chicago styles, see 55a, 60a, and 63c, respectively.

WRITERS ON WRITING

Its overuse is [the dash's] greatest danger, and the writer who can't resist dashes may be suspected of uncoordinated thinking.

— Bergen Evans and Cornelia Evans

One has to dismount from an idea, and get into the saddle again, at every parenthesis.

— Oliver Wendell Holmes Sr.

39d The ellipsis mark

The ellipsis mark consists of three spaced periods. Use an ellipsis mark to indicate that you have deleted words from an otherwise word-for-word quotation.

> Shute acknowledges that treatment for autism can be expensive: "Sensory integration therapy . . . can cost up to $200 an hour" (82).

If you delete a full sentence or more in the middle of a quoted passage, use a period before the three ellipsis dots.

> "If we don't properly train, teach, or treat our growing prison population," says Luis Rodríguez, "somebody else will. . . . This may well be the safety issue of the new century" (16).

TIP: Ordinarily, do not use the ellipsis mark at the beginning or at the end of a quotation. Readers will understand that the quoted material is taken from a longer passage. (If you have cut some words from the end of the final quoted sentence, however, MLA requires an ellipsis mark.)

In quoted poetry, use a full line of ellipsis dots to indicate that you have dropped a line or more from the poem, as in this example from "To His Coy Mistress" by Andrew Marvell:

> Had we but world enough, and time,
> This coyness, lady, were no crime.
> . . . .
> But at my back I always hear
> Time's wingèd chariot hurrying near; (1-2, 21-22)

39e The slash

Use the slash to separate two or three lines of poetry that have been run into your text. Add a space both before and after the slash.

> In the opening lines of "Jordan," George Herbert pokes gentle fun at popular poems of his time: "Who says that fictions only and false hair / Become a verse? Is there in truth no beauty?" (1-2).

WRITERS ON WRITING

Exclamation marks, also called "notes of admiration," should be sparingly used. Queen Victoria used so many of them in her letters that a sentence by her that ends with a mere full-stop seems hardly worth reading.   — Robert Graves and Alan Hodge

Cut out all these exclamation points. An exclamation point is like laughing at your own joke.   — F. Scott Fitzgerald

Four or more lines of poetry should be handled as an indented quotation. (See p. 191.)

The slash may occasionally be used to separate paired terms such as *pass/fail* and *producer/director.* Do not use a space before or after the slash. Be sparing in this use of the slash. In particular, avoid the use of *and/or, he/she,* and *his/her.* Instead of using *he/she* and *his/her* to solve sexist language problems, you can usually find more graceful alternatives. (See 17f and 22a.)

EXERCISE 39-1 Edit the following sentences to correct errors in punctuation, focusing especially on appropriate use of the dash, parentheses, brackets, the ellipsis mark, and the slash. If a sentence is correct, write "correct" after it. Answers appear in the back of the book. *More practice:* e

Social insects/—bees, for example/—are able to
        ∧   ∧
communicate complicated messages to one another.

a. A client left his/her cell phone in our conference room after the meeting.

b. The films we made of Kilauea — on our trip to Hawaii Volcanoes National Park — illustrate a typical spatter cone eruption.

c. Although he was confident in his course selections, Greg chose the pass/fail option for Chemistry 101.

d. Of three engineering fields, chemical, mechanical, and materials, Keegan chose materials engineering for its application to toy manufacturing.

e. The writer Chitra Divakaruni explained her work with other Indian American immigrants: "Many women who came to Maitri [a women's support group in San Francisco] needed to know simple things like opening a bank account or getting citizenship. . . . Many women in Maitri spoke English, but their English was functional rather than emotional. They needed someone who understands their problems and speaks their language."

hackerhandbooks.com/bedhandbook

e Punctuation > Exercises: 39–2 and 39–3

EXERCISE 39-1 *Answers:*

a. A client left his or her [*or* a] cell phone in our conference room after the meeting.

b. The films we made of Kilauea on our trip to Hawaii Volcanoes National Park illustrate a typical spatter cone eruption.

c. Correct

d. Of three engineering fields — chemical, mechanical, and materials — Keegan chose materials engineering for its application to toy manufacturing.

e. Correct

Mechanics

40   Abbreviations

In the text of a paper, use abbreviations only when they are clearly appropriate and universally understood (such as *Dr.*, *a.m.*, *PhD*, and so on). This section provides details about common abbreviations and about how to handle abbreviations that might not be familiar to your readers.

40a Use standard abbreviations for titles immediately before and after proper names.

TITLES BEFORE PROPER NAMES	TITLES AFTER PROPER NAMES
Mr. Rafael Zabala	William Albert Sr.
Ms. Nancy Linehan	Thomas Hines Jr.
Dr. Margaret Simmons	Robert Simkowski, MD
Rev. John Stone	Mia Chin, LLD

Do not abbreviate a title if it is not used with a proper name. *My history professor* (not *prof.*) *is an expert on race relations in South Africa.*

Avoid redundant titles such as *Dr. Amy Day, MD.* Choose one title or the other: *Dr. Amy Day* or *Amy Day, MD.*

40b Use abbreviations only when you are sure your readers will understand them.

Familiar abbreviations for the names of organizations, companies, countries, academic degrees, and common terms, written without periods, are generally acceptable.

SCHOLARS ON ABBREVIATIONS

Kemp, Nenagh, and Catherine Bushnell. "Children's Text Messaging: Abbreviations, Input Methods, and Links with Literacy." *Journal of Computer-Assisted Learning* 27.1 (2011): 18–27. Kemp and Bushnell's findings show that today's youngest writers, though constantly using abbreviations in text messages, are not experiencing any adverse effects on their overall literacy or writing skill because of the practice.

CIA	FBI	MD	NAACP
NBA	CEO	PhD	DVD

Talk show host Conan O'Brien is a Harvard graduate with a BA in history.

When using an unfamiliar abbreviation (such as *NASW* for National Association of Social Workers) or a potentially ambiguous abbreviation (such as *AMA*, which can refer to either the American Medical Association or the American Management Association), write the full name followed by the abbreviation in parentheses at the first mention of the name. Then use just the abbreviation throughout the rest of the paper.

NOTE: An abbreviation that can be pronounced as a word is called an *acronym*: *NATO, MADD, OPEC*.

40c Use *BC, AD, a.m., p.m., No.,* and *$* only with specific dates, times, numbers, and amounts.

The abbreviation *BC* ("before Christ") follows a date, and *AD* ("*anno Domini*") precedes a date. Acceptable alternatives are *BCE* ("before the common era") and *CE* ("common era"), both of which follow a date.

40 BC (or 40 BCE)	4:00 a.m. (or AM)	No. 12 (or no. 12)
AD 44 (or 44 CE)	6:00 p.m. (or PM)	$150

Avoid using *a.m.*, *p.m.*, *No.*, or *$* when not accompanied by a specific numeral: *in the morning* (not *in the a.m.*).

40d Units of measurement

The following are typical abbreviations for units of measurement. Most social sciences and related fields use metric units (*km, mg*), but in other fields and in everyday use, US standard units (*mi, lb*)

WRITERS ON WRITING

There is no royal path to good writing; and such paths as exist do not lead through neat critical gardens, various as they are, but through the jungles of self, the world, and of craft.   — Jessamyn West

Having imagination, it takes you an hour to write a paragraph that, if you were unimaginative, would take you only a minute. Or you might not write the paragraph at all.   — Franklin P. Adams

You don't write because you want to say something; you write because you've got something to say.   — F. Scott Fitzgerald

are typical. Generally, use abbreviations for units when they appear with numerals; spell out the units when they are used alone or when they are used with spelled-out numbers (see also 41a).

METRIC UNITS	US STANDARD UNITS
m, cm, mm	yd, ft, in.
km, kph	mi, mph
kg, g, mg	lb, oz

Results were measured in pounds.

Runners in the 5-km race had to contend with a stiff headwind.

Use no periods after abbreviations for units of measurement, except the abbreviation for "inch" (*in.*), to distinguish it from the preposition *in*.

40e Be sparing in your use of Latin abbreviations.

Latin abbreviations are acceptable in notes and bibliographies.

cf. (Latin *confer*, "compare")

e.g. (Latin *exempli gratia*, "for example")

et al. (Latin *et alia*, "and others")

etc. (Latin *et cetera*, "and so forth")

i.e. (Latin *id est*, "that is")

N.B. (Latin *nota bene*, "note well")

In the text of a paper in most academic fields, use the appropriate English phrases.

40f Plural of abbreviations

To form the plural of most abbreviations, add -*s*, without an apostrophe: *PhDs*, *DVDs*. Do not add -*s* to indicate the plural of units of measurement: *mm* (not *mms*), *lb* (not *lbs*), *in.* (not *ins.*).

40g Avoid inappropriate abbreviations.

In academic writing, abbreviations for the following are not commonly accepted.

PERSONAL NAMES Charles (not Chas.)

DAYS OF THE WEEK Monday (not Mon.)

HOLIDAYS Christmas (not Xmas)

MONTHS January, February, March (not Jan., Feb., Mar.)

COURSES OF STUDY political science (not poli. sci.)

DIVISIONS OF WRITTEN WORKS chapter, page (not ch., p.)

STATES AND COUNTRIES Massachusetts (not MA or Mass.)

PARTS OF A BUSINESS NAME Adams Lighting Company (not Adams Lighting Co.); Kim and Brothers (not Kim and Bros.)

NOTE: Use abbreviations for units of measurement when they are preceded by numerals (*13 cm*). Do not abbreviate them when they are used alone. See 40d.

EXCEPTION: Abbreviate states and provinces in complete addresses, and always abbreviate *DC* when used with *Washington*.

EXERCISE 40–1   Edit the following sentences to correct errors in abbreviations. If a sentence is correct, write "correct" after it. Answers appear in the back of the book. *More practice:* e

This year ~~Xmas~~ will fall on a ~~Tues.~~
               ^Christmas   ^Tuesday.

a.   Since its inception, the BBC has maintained a consistently high standard of radio and television broadcasting.

b.   Some combat soldiers are trained by govt. diplomats to be sensitive to issues of culture, history, and religion.

hackerhandbooks.com/bedhandbook

e Mechanics > Exercises: 40–2 and 40–3

EXERCISE 40–1   *Answers:*

a.   Correct

b.   Some combat soldiers are trained by government diplomats to be sensitive to issues of culture, history, and religion.

c.   Correct

d.   How many pounds have you lost since you began running four miles a day?

e.   Denzil spent all night studying for his psychology exam.

c. Mahatma Gandhi has inspired many modern leaders, including Martin Luther King Jr.

d. How many lb have you lost since you began running four miles a day?

e. Denzil spent all night studying for his psych. exam.

41 Numbers

41a Follow the conventions in your discipline for spelling out or using numerals to express numbers.

In the humanities, which generally follow Modern Language Association (MLA) style, use numerals only for specific numbers larger than one hundred: *353; 1,020.* Spell out numbers one hundred and below and large round numbers: *eleven, thirty-five, fifteen million.* Treat related numbers in a passage consistently: *The survey found that 9 of the 157 students had not taken a course on alcohol use.*

The social sciences and other disciplines that follow American Psychological Association (APA) style use numerals for all but the numbers one through nine. Spell out numbers from one to nine even when they are used with related numerals in a passage: *The survey found that nine of the 157 respondents had not taken a course on alcohol use.* (An exception is the abstract of a paper, where numerals are used for all numbers. See 62a.)

If a sentence begins with a number, spell out the number or rewrite the sentence.

▶ ~~150~~ One hundred fifty children in our program need expensive dental treatment.

Rewriting the sentence may be less awkward if the number is long: *In our program, 150 children need expensive dental treatment.*

WRITERS ON WRITING

Don't fake enthusiasms. Say what you think, not what you think you ought to think.
— Darcy O'Brien

41b Use numerals according to convention in dates, addresses, and so on.

DATES July 4, 1776; 56 BC; AD 30

ADDRESSES 77 Latches Lane, 519 West 42nd Street

PERCENTAGES 55 percent (or 55%)

FRACTIONS, DECIMALS ⅞, 0.047

SCORES 7 to 3, 21–18

STATISTICS average age 37, average weight 180

SURVEYS 4 out of 5

EXACT AMOUNTS OF MONEY $105.37, $106,000

DIVISIONS OF BOOKS volume 3, chapter 4, page 189

DIVISIONS OF PLAYS act 3, scene 3 (or act III, scene iii)

TIME OF DAY 4:00 p.m., 1:30 a.m.

NOTE: When not using *a.m.* or *p.m.*, write out the time in words (*two o'clock in the afternoon, twelve noon, seven in the morning*).

EXERCISE 41–1 Edit the following sentences to correct errors in the use of numbers. If a sentence is correct, write "correct" after it. Answers appear in the back of the book. *More practice:* e

By the end of the evening, Ashanti had only ~~three dollars~~ $3.06
~~and six cents~~ left.

a. The carpenters located 3 maple timbers, 21 sheets of cherry, and 10 oblongs of polished ebony for the theater set.

b. The program's cost is well over one billion dollars.

c. The score was tied at 5–5 when the momentum shifted and carried the Standards to a decisive 12–5 win.

d. 8 students in the class had been labeled "learning disabled."

hackerhandbooks.com/bedhandbook
e Mechanics > Exercises: 41–2 and 41–3

EXERCISE 41–1 *Answers:*

a. *MLA style:* The carpenters located three maple timbers, twenty-one sheets of cherry, and ten oblongs of polished ebony for the theater set. *APA style:* The carpenters located three maple timbers, 21 sheets of cherry, and 10 oblongs of polished ebony for the theater set.

b. Correct

c. Correct

d. Eight students in the class had been labeled "learning disabled."

e. The Vietnam Veterans Memorial in Washington, DC, had 58,132 names inscribed on it when it was dedicated in 1982.

e. The Vietnam Veterans Memorial in Washington, DC, had fifty-eight thousand one hundred thirty-two names inscribed on it when it was dedicated in 1982.

42 Italics

This section describes conventional uses for italics. (If your instructor prefers underlining, simply substitute underlining for italics in the examples in this section.)

Some computer and online applications do not allow for italics. To indicate words that should be italicized, you can use underscore marks or asterisks before and after the words.

> I am planning to write my senior thesis on _The Hunger Games_.

NOTE: Excessive use of italics to emphasize words or ideas, especially in academic writing, is distracting and should be avoided.

42a Italicize the titles of works according to convention.

Titles of the following types of works should be italicized.

    TITLES OF BOOKS *The Color Purple, The Round House*

    MAGAZINES *Time, Scientific American, Slate*

    NEWSPAPERS the *Baltimore Sun,* the *Orlando Sentinel*

    PAMPHLETS *Common Sense, Facts about Marijuana*

    LONG POEMS *The Waste Land, Paradise Lost*

    PLAYS *'Night Mother, Wicked*

    FILMS *Casablanca, Argo*

TELEVISION PROGRAMS *The Voice, Frontline*

RADIO PROGRAMS *All Things Considered*

MUSICAL COMPOSITIONS *Porgy and Bess*

CHOREOGRAPHIC WORKS *Brief Fling*

WORKS OF VISUAL ART *American Gothic*

VIDEO GAMES *Everquest, Call of Duty*

DATABASES [MLA] *ProQuest*

WEB SITES [MLA] *Salon, Google*

COMPUTER SOFTWARE OR APPS [MLA] *Photoshop, Instagram*

The titles of other works—including short stories, essays, episodes of radio and television programs, songs, and short poems — are enclosed in quotation marks. (See 37c.)

NOTE: Do not use italics when referring to the Bible, titles of books in the Bible (Genesis, not *Genesis*), or titles of legal documents (the Constitution, not the *Constitution*).

42b Italicize the names of specific ships, spacecraft, and aircraft.

Queen Mary 2, Endeavour, Wright Flyer

The success of the Soviets' *Sputnik* energized the US space program.

42c Italicize foreign words used in an English sentence.

Shakespeare's Falstaff is a comic character known for both his excessive drinking and his general *joie de vivre*.

EXCEPTION: Do not italicize foreign words that have become a standard part of the English language—"laissez-faire," "fait accompli," "modus operandi," and "per diem," for example.

WRITERS ON WRITING

The ancients wrote at a time when the great art of writing badly had not yet been invented. In those days to write at all meant to write well.
— G. C. Lichtenberg

Writing doesn't get easier with experience. The more you know, the harder it is to write. — Tim O'Brien

When I stepped from hard manual work to writing, I just stepped from one kind of hard work to another. — Sean O'Casey

42d Italicize words mentioned as words, letters mentioned as letters, and numbers mentioned as numbers.

Tomás assured us that the chemicals could probably be safely mixed, but his *probably* stuck in our minds.

Some toddlers have trouble pronouncing the letters *f* and *s*.

A big *3* was painted on the stage door.

NOTE: Quotation marks may be used instead of italics to set off words mentioned as words. (See 37d.)

EXERCISE 42–1 Edit the following sentences to correct errors in the use of italics. If a sentence is correct, write "correct" after it. Answers appear in the back of the book. *More practice:* e

We had a lively discussion about Gini Alhadeff's memoir

The Sun at Midday. Correct

a. Howard Hughes commissioned the Spruce Goose, a beautifully built but thoroughly impractical wooden aircraft.

b. The old man *screamed* his anger, *shouting* to all of us, "I will not leave my money to you worthless layabouts!"

c. I learned the Latin term ad infinitum from an old nursery rhyme about fleas: "Great fleas have little fleas upon their back to bite 'em, / Little fleas have lesser fleas and so on ad infinitum."

d. Cinema audiences once gasped at hearing the word *damn* in *Gone with the Wind*.

e. Neve Campbell's lifelong interest in ballet inspired her involvement in the film "The Company," which portrays a season with the Joffrey Ballet.

hackerhandbooks.com/bedhandbook

e Mechanics > Exercises: 42–2 and 42–3

EXERCISE 42–1 *Answers:*

a. Howard Hughes commissioned the *Spruce Goose*, a beautifully built but thoroughly impractical wooden aircraft.

b. The old man screamed his anger, shouting to all of us, "I will not leave my money to you worthless layabouts!"

c. I learned the Latin term *ad infinitum* from an old nursery rhyme about fleas: "Great fleas have little fleas upon their back to bite 'em, / Little fleas have lesser fleas and so on *ad infinitum*."

d. Correct

e. Neve Campbell's lifelong interest in ballet inspired her involvement in the film *The Company*, which portrays a season with the Joffrey Ballet.

43 Spelling

You learned to spell from repeated experience with words in both reading and writing. As you proofread, you can probably tell if a word doesn't look quite right. In such cases, the solution is simple: Look up the word in the dictionary. (See 43b.)

43a Become familiar with the major spelling rules.

i *before* e *except after* c

In general, use *i* before *e* except after *c* and except when sounded like *ay*, as in *neighbor* and *weigh*.

I BEFORE E	relieve, believe, sieve, niece, fierce, frieze
E BEFORE I	receive, deceive, sleigh, freight, eight
EXCEPTIONS	seize, either, weird, height, foreign, leisure

Suffixes

Final silent -e Generally, drop a final silent *-e* when adding a suffix that begins with a vowel. Keep the final *-e* if the suffix begins with a consonant.

combine, combination	achieve, achievement
desire, desiring	care, careful
prude, prudish	entire, entirety
remove, removable	gentle, gentleness

Words such as *changeable*, *judgment*, *argument*, and *truly* are exceptions.

Final -y When adding -*s* or -*d* to words ending in -*y,* ordinarily change -*y* to -*ie* when the -*y* is preceded by a consonant but not when it is preceded by a vowel.

comedy, comedies | monkey, monkeys
dry, dried | play, played

With proper names ending in -*y*, however, do not change the -*y* to -*ie* even if it is preceded by a consonant: *the Doughertys.*

Final consonants If a final consonant is preceded by a single vowel *and* the consonant ends a one-syllable word or a stressed syllable, double the consonant when adding a suffix beginning with a vowel.

bet, betting | occur, occurrence
commit, committed

Plurals

-s or -es Add -*s* to form the plural of most nouns; add -*es* to singular nouns ending in -*s*, -*sh*, -*ch*, and -*x*.

table, tables | church, churches
paper, papers | dish, dishes

Ordinarily add -*s* to nouns ending in -*o* when the -*o* is preceded by a vowel. Add -*es* when it is preceded by a consonant.

radio, radios | hero, heroes
video, videos | tomato, tomatoes

Other plurals To form the plural of a hyphenated compound word, add -*s* to the chief word even if it does not appear at the end.

mother-in-law, mothers-in-law

WRITERS ON WRITING

Writing is easy; all you do is sit staring at a blank sheet of paper until the drops of blood form on your forehead. — Gene Fowler

Wearing down seven number two pencils is a good day's work.
— Ernest Hemingway

I knew I couldn't spell but I knew I could write. — Stephen J. Cannell

English words derived from other languages such as Latin, Greek, or French sometimes form the plural as they would in their original language.

medium, media   chateau, chateaux
criterion, criteria

Multilingual

Spelling varies slightly among English-speaking countries. Variations can be confusing for some multilingual students in the United States. Following is a list of some common words with different American and British spellings. Consult a dictionary for others.

AMERICAN	BRITISH
canceled, traveled	cancelled, travelled
color, humor	colour, humour
judgment	judgement
check	cheque
realize, apologize	realise, apologise
defense	defence
anemia, anesthetic	anaemia, anaesthetic
theater, center	theatre, centre
fetus	foetus
mold, smolder	mould, smoulder
civilization	civilisation
connection, inflection	connexion, inflexion
licorice	liquorice

43b Become familiar with your dictionary.

A good dictionary, whether print or online—such as *The Random House College Dictionary* or *Merriam-Webster* online—is an indispensable writer's aid.

A sample print dictionary entry, taken from *The American Heritage Dictionary of the English Language*, appears on this page. A sample online dictionary entry, taken from *Merriam-Webster* online, appears on page 463.

PRINT DICTIONARY ENTRY

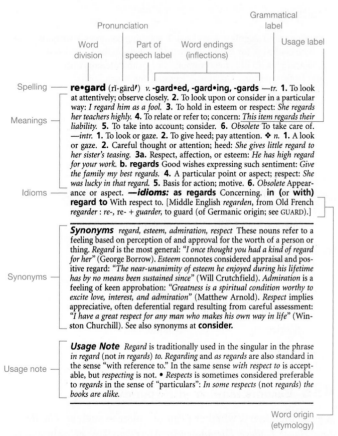

Source: *The American Heritage Dictionary of the English Language*, 4th ed. (Boston: Houghton, 2010).

SCHOLARS ON SPELLING

Wood, Clare, et al. "The Effect of Text Messaging on Nine- and Ten-Year-Old Children's Reading, Spelling, and Phonological Processing Skills." *Journal of Computer-Assisted Learning* 27.1 (2011): 28–36. Print. After studying 114 nine- and ten-year-olds over a ten-week period, the authors found links between text messaging frequency and improvement in spelling.

"Vygotsky and the Bad Speller's Nightmare." *English Journal* 80.8 (1991): 65–70. Print. The anonymous author of this article is a high school English teacher who never could, and still cannot, spell. He describes his experiences writing doctoral comprehensive exams in

ONLINE DICTIONARY ENTRY

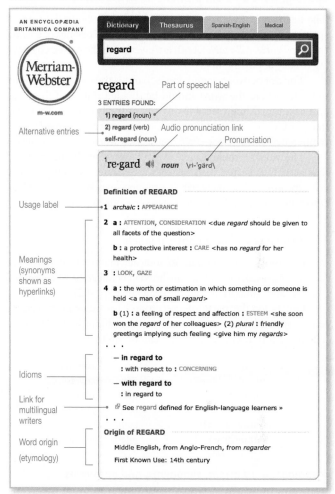

Source: Merriam-Webster, www.Merriam-Webster.com (2010).

English education, arguing that spelling problems are not an "error in thinking." Instead, following Vygotsky, the author suggests that bad spellers are merely "displaying a faulty translation of perfectly sensible inner speech." The writer proposes that students with spelling problems need more effective editing strategies, familiarity with spelling aids, and opportunities for multiple revisions.

Spelling, word division, pronunciation

The main entry (*re·gard* in the sample entries) shows the correct spelling of the word. When there are two correct spellings of a word (as in *collectible, collectable*), both are given, with the preferred spelling usually appearing first.

The dot between *re* and *gard* separates the two syllables and indicates where the word should be divided if it can't fit at the end of a typed line (see 44f). When a word is compound, the main entry shows how to write it: as one word (*crossroad*), as a hyphenated word (*cross-stitch*), or as two words (*cross section*).

The word's pronunciation is given just after the main entry. The accents indicate which syllables are stressed; the other marks are explained in the dictionary's pronunciation key. Many online entries include an audio link to a voice pronouncing the word.

Word endings and grammatical labels

When a word takes endings to indicate grammatical functions (called *inflections*), the endings are listed in boldface, as with *-garded*, *-garding*, and *-gards* in the sample print entry (p. 462).

Labels for the parts of speech and for other grammatical terms are sometimes abbreviated, as they are in the print entry. The most commonly used abbreviations are these:

n.	noun	adj.	adjective
pl.	plural	adv.	adverb
sing.	singular	pron.	pronoun
v.	verb	prep.	preposition
tr.	transitive verb	conj.	conjunction
intr.	intransitive verb	interj.	interjection

Meanings, word origin, synonyms, and antonyms

Sometimes a word can be used as more than one part of speech (*regard*, for instance, can be used as either a verb or a noun). In such

---

SCHOLARS ON SPELLING

White, Linda F. "Spelling Instruction in the Writing Center." *Writing Center Journal* 12.1 (1991): 34–47. Print. White describes a four-lesson sequence to help students improve their spelling. Beginning with a lesson that has students explore their feelings about being labeled bad spellers, the sequence moves to a lesson on self-assessment in which students identify error patterns and tailor proofreading strategies. Following these lessons, students learn how to use tools such as dictionaries and spell checkers. The sequence ends with a lesson on the rules of spelling. White suggests that students can learn to spell, but not by memorizing or by having instructors or tutors mark every spelling error.

a case, all the meanings for one part of speech are given before all the meanings for another, as in the sample entries.

The origin of the word, called its *etymology*, appears in brackets after all the meanings in the print and online versions.

Synonyms, words similar in meaning to the main entry, are frequently listed. In the sample print entry, the dictionary draws distinctions in meaning among the various synonyms. In the online entry, synonyms appear as hyperlinks. Antonyms, which do not appear in the sample entries, are words having a meaning opposite from that of the main entry.

Usage

Usage labels indicate when, where, or under what conditions a particular meaning for a word is appropriately used. Common labels are *informal* (or *colloquial*), *slang*, *archaic*, *poetic*, *nonstandard*, *dialect*, *obsolete*, and *British*. In the sample print entry, two meanings of *regard* are labeled *obsolete* because they are no longer in use. The sample online entry (p. 463) has one meaning labeled *archaic*.

Dictionaries sometimes include usage notes as well. Advice in the notes is based on the opinions of many experts and on actual usage in current publications.

43c Discriminate between words that sound alike but have different meanings.

Words that sound alike or nearly alike but have different meanings and spellings are called *homophones*. The following sets of words are commonly confused. A careful writer will double-check their every use. (See also the glossary of usage at the back of the book.)

> affect (verb: to exert an influence)
> effect (verb: to accomplish; noun: result)
>
> its (possessive pronoun: of or belonging to it)
> it's (contraction of *it is* or *it has*)

SCHOLARS ON SPELLING

Martin, Charles L., and Dorothy E. Ranson. "Spelling Skills of Business Students: An Empirical Investigation." *Journal of Business Communication* 27.4 (1990): 377–400. Print. Recognizing the importance of spelling skills in business settings, Martin and Ranson seek answers to three questions: How widespread are spelling problems? How concerned are business educators and professionals about spelling skills? How can educators identify and help problem spellers? The authors point to numerous studies that document the increased concern with written communication skills of business students, but they point out that most studies do not address the importance of spelling. Martin and Ranson propose that spelling problems are serious, affecting readability and conveying negative impressions.

loose (adjective: free, not securely attached)
lose (verb: to fail to keep, to be deprived of)

principal (adjective: most important; noun: head of a school)
principle (noun: a fundamental guideline or truth)

their (possessive pronoun: belonging to them)
they're (contraction of *they are*)
there (adverb: that place or position)

who's (contraction of *who is* or *who has*)
whose (possessive form of *who*)

your (possessive pronoun: belonging to you)
you're (contraction of *you are*)

43d Be alert to commonly misspelled words.

absence	ascend	conceivable	exaggerated
accidentally	athlete	conscience	exercise
accommodate	attendance	conscientious	exhaust
achievement	basically	conscious	existence
acknowledge	beautiful	criticism	extraordinary
acquaintance	beginning	criticize	familiar
acquire	believe	decision	fascinate
address	benefited	definitely	February
all right	bureau	descendant	foreign
amateur	business	desperate	forty
analyze	calendar	different	fourth
answer	cemetery	disastrous	friend
apparently	changeable	eighth	government
appearance	column	eligible	grammar
arctic	commitment	embarrass	harass
argument	committed	emphasize	height
arithmetic	committee	environment	humorous
arrangement	competitive	especially	incidentally

WRITERS ON WRITING

Avoid theatrical flourishes — the phrases that sound so damned good
that they stand up and beg to be recognized as "good writing," and
therefore must be struck from the text.   — Donald Spoto

incredible	occasion	privilege	similar
independence	occurred	proceed	sincerely
indispensable	occurrence	pronunciation	sophomore
inevitable	pamphlet	publicly	strictly
intelligence	parallel	quiet	subtly
irrelevant	particularly	quite	succeed
irresistible	pastime	quizzes	surprise
knowledge	permanent	receive	thorough
library	permissible	recognize	tomorrow
license	perseverance	referred	tragedy
lightning	phenomenon	restaurant	transferred
loneliness	physically	rhythm	truly
maintenance	practically	roommate	unnecessarily
maneuver	precede	sandwich	usually
marriage	preference	schedule	vacuum
mathematics	preferred	seize	villain
mischievous	prejudice	separate	weird
necessary	presence	sergeant	whether
noticeable	prevalent	siege	writing

EXERCISE 43-1 The following memo has been run through a spell checker. Proofread it carefully, editing the spelling and typographical errors that remain. *More practice:* e

November 2, 2012

To: Patricia Wise
From: Constance Mayhew
Subject: Express Tours annual report

Thank you for agreeing to draft the annual report for Express Tours. Before you begin you're work, let me outline the initial steps.

First, its essential for you to include brief profiles of top management. Early next week, I'll provide profiles for all manages accept Samuel Heath, who's biographical information

hackerhandbooks.com/bedhandbook
e Mechanics > Exercises: 43–2

EXERCISE 43-1 *Answers:*

November 2, 2012

To: Patricia Wise
From: Constance Mayhew
Subject: Express Tours annual report

Thank you for agreeing to draft the annual report for Express Tours. Before you begin your work, let me outline the initial steps.

First, it's essential for you to include brief profiles of top management. Early next week, I'll provide profiles for all managers except Samuel Heath, whose biographical information is being revised. You should edit these profiles carefully and then format them according to the enclosed instructions. We may ask you to include other employees' profiles at some point.

is being revised. You should edit these profiles carefully and than format them according to the enclosed instructions. We may ask you to include other employee's profiles at some point.

Second, you should arrange to get complete financial information for fiscal year 2012 from our comptroller, Richard Chang. (Helen Boyes, to, can provide the necessary figures.) When you get this information, precede according tot he plans we discuss in yesterday's meeting. By the way, you will notice from the figures that the sale of our Charterhouse division did not significantly effect net profits.

Third, you should e-mail first draft of the report by December 14. Of coarse, you should proofread you writing.

I am quiet pleased that you can take on this project. If I can answers questions, don't hesitate to call.

44 The hyphen

In addition to the guidelines in this section, a dictionary will help you make decisions about hyphenation.

44a Consult the dictionary to determine how to treat a compound word.

The dictionary indicates whether to treat a compound word as hyphenated (*water-repellent*), as one word (*waterproof*), or as two words (*water table*). If the compound word is not in the dictionary, treat it as two words.

▶   **The prosecutor chose not to cross–examine any witnesses.**
                                          ∧

EXERCISE 43-1   *Answers (continued):*

Second, you should arrange to get complete financial information for fiscal year 2012 from our comptroller, Richard Chang. (Helen Boyes, too, can provide the necessary figures.) When you get this information, proceed according to the plans we discussed in yesterday's meeting. By the way, you will notice from the figures that the sale of our Charterhouse division did not significantly affect net profits.

Third, you should e-mail a [*or* the] first draft of the report by December 14. Of course, you should proofread your writing.

I am quite pleased that you can take on this project. If I can answer questions, don't hesitate to call.

▶ All students are expected to record their data in a small note‿book.

▶ Alice walked through the looking⁄glass into a backward world.

44b Hyphenate two or more words used together as an adjective before a noun.

▶ Today's teachers depend on both traditional textbook material and Web‑delivered content.

▶ Richa Gupta is not yet a well‑known candidate.

Generally, do not use a hyphen when such compounds follow the noun.

▶ After our television campaign, Richa Gupta will be well⁄known.

Do not use a hyphen to connect -*ly* adverbs to the words they modify.

▶ A slowly⁄moving truck tied up traffic.

44c Hyphenate fractions and certain numbers when they are spelled out.

For numbers written as words, use a hyphen in all fractions (*two-thirds*) and in all forms of compound numbers from twenty-one to ninety-nine (*thirty-five, sixty-seventh*).

WRITERS ON WRITING

One writes to find words' meanings.   — Joy Williams

Words have basic inalienable meanings, departure from which is either conscious metaphor or inexcusable vulgarity.   — Evelyn Waugh

Words are weapons.   — George Santayana

44d Use a hyphen with the prefixes *all-*, *ex-* (meaning "former"), and *self-* and with the suffix *-elect*.

▶ The private foundation is funneling more money into

self-help projects.
    ∧

▶ The Student Senate bylaws require the president-elect to
    ∧

attend all senate meetings before the transfer of office.

44e Use a hyphen in certain words to avoid ambiguity.

Without the hyphen, there would be no way to distinguish between words such as *re-creation* and *recreation*.

> Bicycling in the city has always been my favorite form of recreation.

> The film was praised for its astonishing re-creation of nineteenth-century London.

Hyphens are sometimes used to separate awkward double or triple letters in compound words (*anti-intellectual, cross-stitch*).

44f Check for correct word breaks when words must be divided at the end of a line.

Some word processing programs and other computer applications automatically generate word breaks at the ends of lines. In academic writing, it's best to set your computer application not to hyphenate automatically. This setting will ensure that only words already containing a hyphen (such as *long-distance, pre-Roman*) will be hyphenated at the ends of lines.

E-mail addresses and URLs need special attention when they occur at the end of a line of text or in bibliographic citations. You must make a decision about hyphenation in each case.

Do not insert a hyphen to divide electronic addresses. Instead, break an e-mail address after the @ symbol or before a period. It is common practice to break a URL before most marks of punctuation. (For variations in MLA, APA, and *Chicago* styles, see 57a, 62a, and 63e, respectively.)

> I repeatedly e-mailed Janine at janine.r.rose@dunbaracademy .org before I gave up and called her cell phone.

> To avoid standing in line, I now order stamps online at http://www .usps.com.

EXERCISE 44–1 Edit the following sentences to correct errors in hyphenation. If a sentence is correct, write "correct" after it. Answers appear in the back of the book. *More practice:* 🄴

> Émile Zola's first readers were scandalized by his slice‑of‑life novels.
> ∧ ∧

a. Gold is the seventy-ninth element in the periodic table.

b. The swiftly-moving tugboat pulled alongside the barge and directed it away from the oil spill in the harbor.

c. The Moche were a pre-Columbian people who established a sophisticated culture in ancient Peru.

d. Your dog is well-known in our neighborhood.

e. Road-blocks were set up along all the major highways leading out of the city.

hackerhandbooks.com/bedhandbook

🄴 Mechanics > Exercises: 44–2 and 44–3

EXERCISE 44–1 *Answers:*

a. Correct

b. The swiftly moving tugboat pulled alongside the barge and directed it away from the oil spill in the harbor.

c. Correct

d. Your dog is well known in our neighborhood.

e. Roadblocks were set up along all the major highways leading out of the city.

45 Capitalization

In addition to the rules in this section, a good dictionary can tell you when to use capital letters.

45a Capitalize proper nouns and words derived from them; do not capitalize common nouns.

Proper nouns are the names of specific persons, places, and things. All other nouns are common nouns. The following types of words are usually capitalized: names of deities, religions, religious followers, sacred books; words of family relationship used as names; particular places; nationalities and their languages, races, tribes; educational institutions, departments, particular courses; government departments, organizations, political parties; historical movements, periods, events, documents; and trade names.

PROPER NOUNS	COMMON NOUNS
God (used as a name)	a god
Book of Common Prayer	a sacred book
Uncle Pedro	my uncle
Father (used as a name)	my father
Lake Superior	a picturesque lake
the Capital Center	a center for advanced studies
the South	a southern state
Wrigley Field	a baseball stadium
University of Wisconsin	a state university
Geology 101	geology
the Democratic Party	a political party
the Enlightenment	the eighteenth century
Advil	a painkiller

WRITERS ON WRITING

The words! I collected them in all shapes and sizes and hung them like bangles in my mind.
— Hortense Calisher

The secret of good writing is to say an old thing a new way or to say a new thing an old way.
— Richard Harding Davis

Months, holidays, and days of the week are treated as proper nouns; the seasons and numbers of the days of the month are not.

> Our academic year begins on a Tuesday in early September, right after Labor Day.

> Graduation is in late spring, on the second of June.

EXCEPTION: Capitalize Fourth of July (or July Fourth) when referring to the holiday.

Names of school subjects are capitalized only if they are names of languages. Names of particular courses are capitalized.

> This semester Lee is taking math, physics, French, and English.

> Professor Obembe offers Modern American Fiction 501 to graduate students.

The terms *Web* and *Internet* are typically capitalized, but related common nouns are not: *home page, operating system.* Usage varies widely, however, so check with your instructor about whether you should follow the guidelines for MLA, APA, or *Chicago* style (57a, 62a, or 63e, respectively).

CAUTION: Do not capitalize common nouns to make them seem important.

45b Capitalize titles of persons when used as part of a proper name but usually not when used alone.

> Professor Margaret Barnes; Dr. Sinyee Sein; John Scott Williams Jr.

> District Attorney Marshall was reprimanded for badgering the witness.

> The district attorney was elected for a two-year term.

Usage varies when the title of an important public figure is used alone: *The president* [or *President*] *vetoed the bill.*

45c Capitalize titles according to convention.

In both titles and subtitles of works mentioned in the text of a paper, major words such as nouns, pronouns, verbs, adjectives, and adverbs should be capitalized. Minor words such as articles, prepositions, and coordinating conjunctions are not capitalized unless they are the first or last word of a title or subtitle. (In APA style, also capitalize all words of four or more letters. See 62a.)

Capitalize the second part of a hyphenated term in a title if it is a major word but not if it is a minor word. Capitalize chapter titles and the titles of other major divisions of a work following the same guidelines used for titles of complete works.

> *Seizing the Enigma: The Race to Break the German U-Boat Codes*
> *A River Runs through It*
> "I Want to Hold Your Hand"
> *The Canadian Green Page*

To see why some of the titles in the list are italicized and some are put in quotation marks, see 42a and 37c.

Titles of works are handled differently in the APA reference list. See "Preparing the list of references" in 62a.

45d Capitalize the first word of a sentence.

The first word of a sentence should be capitalized. When a sentence appears within parentheses, capitalize its first word unless the parentheses appear within another sentence.

> Early detection of breast cancer significantly increases survival rates. (See table 2.)

> Early detection of breast cancer significantly increases survival rates (see table 2).

45e Capitalize the first word of a quoted sentence but not a quoted word or phrase.

Loveless writes, "If failing schools are ever to be turned around, much more must be learned about how schools age as institutions" (25).

Russell Baker has written that in this country, sports are "the opiate of the masses" (46).

If a quoted sentence is interrupted by explanatory words, do not capitalize the first word after the interruption. (See also 37e.)

"If you want to go out," he said, "tell me now."

When quoting poetry, copy the poet's capitalization exactly. Many poets capitalize the first word of every line of poetry; a few contemporary poets dismiss capitalization altogether.

it was the week   that
i felt the city's narrow breezes rush about
me   — Don L. Lee

45f Capitalize the first word after a colon if it begins an independent clause.

If a group of words following a colon could stand on its own as a complete sentence, capitalize the first word.

Clinical trials called into question the safety profile of the drug: A high percentage of participants reported hypertension and kidney problems.

Preferences vary among academic disciplines. See 57a, 62a, and 63e.

Always use lowercase for a list or an appositive that follows a colon (see 35a).

Students were divided into two groups: residents and commuters.

EXERCISE 45–1 Edit the following sentences to correct errors in capitalization. If a sentence is correct, write "correct" after it. Answers appear in the back of the book. *More practice:* e ✓

On our trip to the West, we visited the g̶rand c̶anyon and the
g̶reat s̶alt d̶esert.

a. Assistant dean Shirin Ahmadi recommended offering more world language courses.

b. We went to the Mark Taper Forum to see a production of *Angels in America*.

c. Kalindi has an ambitious semester, studying differential calculus, classical hebrew, brochure design, and greek literature.

d. Lydia's Aunt and Uncle make modular houses as beautiful as modernist works of art.

e. We amused ourselves on the long flight by discussing how Spring in Kyoto stacks up against Summer in London.

hackerhandbooks.com/bedhandbook

e Mechanics > Exercises: 45–2 and 45–3
✓ Mechanics > LearningCurve: Capitalization

EXERCISE 45–1 *Answers:*

a. Assistant Dean Shirin Ahmadi recommended offering more world language courses.

b. Correct

c. Kalindi has an ambitious semester, studying differential calculus, classical Hebrew, brochure design, and Greek literature.

d. Lydia's aunt and uncle make modular houses as beautiful as modernist works of art.

e. We amused ourselves on the long flight by discussing how spring in Kyoto stacks up against summer in London.

PART IX

Grammar Basics

46 Parts of speech

Traditional grammar recognizes eight parts of speech: noun, pronoun, verb, adjective, adverb, preposition, conjunction, and interjection. Many words can function as more than one part of speech. For example, depending on its use in a sentence, the word *paint* can be a noun (*The paint is wet*) or a verb (*Please paint the ceiling next*).

46a Nouns

A noun is the name of a person, place, thing, or concept.

> N   N   N
> The *lion* in the *cage* growled at the *zookeeper*.

Nouns sometimes function as adjectives modifying other nouns. Because of their dual roles, nouns used in this manner may be called *noun/adjectives*.

> N/ADJ   N/ADJ
> The *leather* notebook was tucked in the *student's* backpack.

Nouns are classified in a variety of ways. *Proper* nouns are capitalized, but *common* nouns are not (see 45a). For clarity, writers choose between *concrete* and *abstract* nouns (see 18b). The distinction between *count* nouns and *noncount* nouns can be especially helpful to multilingual writers (see 29a). Most nouns have singular and plural forms; *collective* nouns may be either singular or plural, depending on how they are used (see 21f and 22b). *Possessive* nouns require an apostrophe (see 36a).

TEACHING TIP

Use grammar exercises, such as those in the handbook's print pages or e-Pages as a first step in teaching a part of speech. You can ask students to complete the exercises by themselves as classwork or homework, in pairs or small groups, or together in a whole-class setting.

EXERCISE 46-1 Underline the nouns (and noun/adjectives) in the following sentences. Answers appear in the back of the book. *More practice:* 🄴 ☑

> The best <u>part</u> of <u>dinner</u> was the <u>chef's</u> newest <u>dessert</u>.

a. The stage was set for a confrontation of biblical proportions.

b. The courage of the mountain climber was an inspiration to the rescuers.

c. The need to arrive before the guest of honor motivated us to navigate the thick fog.

d. The defense attorney made a final appeal to the jury.

e. A national museum dedicated to women artists opened in 1987.

46b Pronouns

A pronoun is a word used in place of a noun. Usually the pronoun substitutes for a specific noun, known as its *antecedent*.

ANT   PN
When the <i>battery</i> wears down, we recharge <i>it</i>.

Although most pronouns function as substitutes for nouns, some can function as adjectives modifying nouns. Such pronouns may be called *pronoun/adjectives*.

PN/ADJ

That bird was at the same window yesterday morning.

Pronouns are classified in the following ways.

Personal pronouns   Personal pronouns refer to specific persons or things. They always function as substitutes for nouns.

> *Singular:* I, me, you, she, her, he, him, it
>
> *Plural:* we, us, you, they, them

hackerhandbooks.com/bedhandbook

🄴 Grammar basics > Exercises: 46–2 to 46–4, 46–19 and 46–20 (all parts of speech)

☑ Grammar basics > LearningCurve: Nouns and pronouns

EXERCISE 46-1 *Answers:*

a. stage, confrontation, proportions; b. courage, mountain (noun/adjective), climber, inspiration, rescuers; c. need, guest, honor, fog; d. defense (noun/adjective), attorney, appeal, jury; e. museum, women (noun/adjective), artists, 1987

Possessive pronouns   Possessive pronouns indicate ownership.

> *Singular:* my, mine, your, yours, her, hers, his, its
>
> *Plural:* our, ours, your, yours, their, theirs

Some of these possessive pronouns function as adjectives modifying nouns: *my, your, his, her, its, our, their.*

Intensive and reflexive pronouns   Intensive pronouns emphasize a noun or another pronoun (The senator *herself* met us at the door). Reflexive pronouns name a receiver of an action identical with the doer of the action (Paula cut *herself*).

> *Singular:* myself, yourself, himself, herself, itself
>
> *Plural:* ourselves, yourselves, themselves

Relative pronouns   Relative pronouns introduce subordinate clauses functioning as adjectives (The writer *who won the award* refused to accept it). The relative pronoun, in this case *who*, also points back to a noun or pronoun that the clause modifies (*writer*). (See 48e.)

> who, whom, whose, which, that

The pronouns *whichever, whoever, whomever, what,* and *whatever* are sometimes considered relative pronouns, but they introduce noun clauses and do not point back to a noun or pronoun. (See "Noun clauses" in 48e.)

Interrogative pronouns   Interrogative pronouns introduce questions (*Who* is expected to win the election?).

> who, whom, whose, which, what

Demonstrative pronouns   Demonstrative pronouns identify or point to nouns. Frequently they function as adjectives (*This*

SCHOLARS ON GRAMMAR BASICS

Fearn, Leif, and Nancy Farnan. "When Is a Verb? Using Functional Grammar to Teach Writing." *Journal of Basic Writing* 26.1 (2007): 63–87. Print. Fearn and Farnan address whether writing instructors can teach grammar in a way that prepares students for standardized tests and helps them improve their writing. They measured the effect of replacing traditional grammar instruction, which emphasizes definition and identification, with practice that emphasizes the "roles and function" grammatical elements play in writing and that focuses "students' attention . . . on using grammar to think about writing." After a five-week period with four groups of tenth graders, the authors concluded that the functional grammar group wrote better than the traditional grammar group and that grammar test scores between the two groups were equal.

chair is my favorite), but they may also function as substitutes for nouns (*This* is my favorite chair).

> this, that, these, those

Indefinite pronouns   Indefinite pronouns refer to nonspecific persons or things. Most are always singular (*everyone, each*); some are always plural (*both, many*); a few may be singular or plural (see 21e). Most indefinite pronouns function as substitutes for nouns (*Something* is burning), but some can also function as adjectives (*All* campers must check in at the lodge).

all	anything	everyone	nobody	several
another	both	everything	none	some
any	each	few	no one	somebody
anybody	either	many	nothing	someone
anyone	everybody	neither	one	something

Reciprocal pronouns   Reciprocal pronouns refer to individual parts of a plural antecedent (By turns, the penguins fed *one another*).

> each other, one another

NOTE: See also pronoun-antecedent agreement (22), pronoun reference (23), distinguishing between pronouns such as *I* and *me* (24), and distinguishing between *who* and *whom* (25).

EXERCISE 46–5   Underline the pronouns (and pronoun/adjectives) in the following sentences. Answers appear in the back of the book. *More practice:* e ✔

> <u>We</u> were intrigued by the video <u>that</u> the fifth graders produced as <u>their</u> final project.

a.   The governor's loyalty was his most appealing trait.

hackerhandbooks.com/bedhandbook
e Grammar basics > Exercises: 46–6 to 46–8, 46–19 and 46–20 (all parts of speech)
✔ Grammar basics > LearningCurve: Nouns and pronouns

EXERCISE 46–5   *Answers:*

a. his; b. that, our (pronoun/adjective); c. he, himself, some, his (pronoun/adjective); d. I, my (pronoun/adjective), you, one; e. no one, her

TEACHING TIP

It is often helpful to allow students to take charge of teaching a few basic grammar concepts. Assign students in groups to tackle parts of speech or types of sentences and to prepare a ten-minute mini-lesson in which they show examples and discuss editing strategies. If the class is online, the students can prepare a few slides that they upload to the course Web site.

b.   In the fall, the geese that fly south for the winter pass through our town in huge numbers.

c.   As Carl Sandburg once said, even he himself did not understand some of his poetry.

d.   I appealed my parking ticket, but you did not get one.

e.   Angela did not mind gossip as long as no one gossiped about her.

46c Verbs

The verb of a sentence usually expresses action (*jump*, *think*) or being (*is*, *become*). It is composed of a main verb possibly preceded by one or more helping verbs.

> MV
> The horses *exercise* every day.

>   HV   MV
> The task force report *was* not *completed* on schedule.

>   HV HV   MV
> No one *has been defended* with more passion than our pastor.

Notice that words, usually adverbs, can intervene between the helping verb and the main verb (was *not* completed). (See 46e.)

Helping verbs

There are twenty-three helping verbs in English: forms of *have*, *do*, and *be*, which may also function as main verbs; and nine modals, which function only as helping verbs. *Have*, *do*, and *be* change form to indicate tense; the nine modals do not.

FORMS OF *HAVE*, *DO*, AND *BE*

have, has, had

do, does, did

be, am, is, are, was, were, being, been

SCHOLARS ON GRAMMAR BASICS

Lindemann, Erika. *A Rhetoric for Writing Teachers*. 4th ed. New York: Oxford UP, 2001. 60–85. Print. Lindemann examines several different approaches to grammar and provides brief overviews of structural and generative-transformational grammars.

Weaver, Constance. *Teaching Grammar in Context*. Portsmouth: Boynton, 1996. Print. Weaver includes an analysis of the meanings of "grammar," an overview of the history of grammar instruction, a summary of the arguments for and against teaching grammar, a discussion of error, and an exploration of the relation between learning theory and grammar instruction. An appendix includes mini-lessons on teaching grammar in context.

MODALS

can, could, may, might, must, shall, should, will, would

The verb phrase *ought to* is often classified as a modal as well.

Main verbs

The main verb of a sentence is always the kind of word that would change form if put into these test sentences:

BASE FORM	Usually I (*walk*, *ride*).
PAST TENSE	Yesterday I (*walked*, *rode*).
PAST PARTICIPLE	I have (*walked*, *ridden*) many times before.
PRESENT PARTICIPLE	I am (*walking*, *riding*) right now.
-S FORM	Usually he/she/it (*walks*, *rides*).

If a word doesn't change form when slipped into the test sentences, you can be certain that it is not a main verb. For example, the noun *revolution*, though it may seem to suggest an action, can never function as a main verb. Just try to make it behave like one (*Today I revolution . . . Yesterday I revolutioned . . .*) and you'll see why.

When both the past-tense and the past-participle forms of a verb end in -ed, the verb is regular (*walked*, *walked*). Otherwise, the verb is irregular (*rode*, *ridden*). (See 27a.)

The verb *be* is highly irregular, having eight forms instead of the usual five: the base form *be*; the present-tense forms *am*, *is*, and *are*; the past-tense forms *was* and *were*; the present participle *being*; and the past participle *been*. Helping verbs combine with main verbs to create tenses. See 28a.

NOTE: Some verbs are followed by words that look like prepositions but are so closely associated with the verb that they are a part of its meaning. These words are known as *particles*. Common

SCHOLARS ON GRAMMAR BASICS

Parker, Frank, and Kim Sydow Campbell. "Linguistics and Writing: A Reassessment." *College Composition and Communication* 44.3 (1993): 295–314. Print. Responding to arguments that linguistics has not contributed significantly to composition studies, Parker and Campbell reevaluate the relevance of linguistics to writing instruction. They point to recent approaches to linguistics that move beyond the sentence level and focus on language in its fuller discourse contexts. Such approaches, the authors suggest, can provide a theoretical foundation for composition pedagogy.

verb-particle combinations include *bring up, call off, drop off, give in, look up, run into*, and *take off*.

TIP: For more information about using verbs, see these sections of the handbook: active verbs (8), subject-verb agreement (21), Standard English verb forms (27), verb tense and mood (27f and 27g), and multilingual/ESL challenges with verbs (28).

EXERCISE 46–9 Underline the verbs in the following sentences, including helping verbs and particles. If a verb is part of a contraction (such as *is* in *isn't* or *would* in *I'd*), underline only the letters that represent the verb. Answers appear in the back of the book. *More practice:* 🄴 ✅

The ground under the pine trees <u>wasn't</u> wet from the rain.

a. My grandmother always told me a soothing story before bed.
b. There were fifty apples on the tree before the frost killed them.
c. Morton brought down the box of letters from the attic.
d. Stay on the main road and you'll arrive at the base camp before us.
e. The fish struggled vigorously but was trapped in the net.

46d Adjectives

An adjective is a word used to modify, or describe, a noun or pronoun. An adjective usually answers one of these questions: Which one? What kind of? How many?

ADJ
the *frisky* horse [Which horse?]

ADJ ADJ
cracked old plates [What kind of plates?]

---

hackerhandbooks.com/bedhandbook

🄴 Grammar basics > Exercises: 46–10 to 46–12, 46–19 and 46–20 (all parts of speech)
✅ Grammar basics > LearningCurve: Verbs, adjectives, and adverbs

---

EXERCISE 46–9 *Answers:*

a. told; b. were, killed; c. brought down; d. Stay, 'll [will] arrive;
e. struggled, was trapped

SCHOLARS ON GRAMMAR BASICS

Sedgwick, Ellery. "Alternatives to Teaching Formal, Analytical Grammar." *Journal of Developmental Education* 12.3 (1989): 8+. Print. Sedgwick suggests techniques such as sentence combining, imitation exercises, and inductive grammar in place of formal grammatical instruction. He discusses a variety of ways to teach editing and proofreading skills, including peer editing, student-teacher conferences, and selective marking of errors.

ADJ

nine months [How many months?]

ADJ

qualified applicants [What kind of applicants?]

Adjectives usually precede the words they modify. They may also follow linking verbs, in which case they describe the subject. (See 47b.)

ADJ

The decision was *unpopular*.

The definite article *the* and the indefinite articles *a* and *an* are also classified as adjectives.

ART   ART   ART

A defendant should be judged on *the* evidence provided to *the* jury, not on hearsay.

Some possessive, demonstrative, and indefinite pronouns can function as adjectives: *their, its, this, all* (see 46b). And nouns can function as adjectives when they modify other nouns: *apple pie* (the noun *apple* modifies the noun *pie*; see 46a).

TIP: You can find more details about using adjectives in 26. If you are a multilingual writer, you may find help with articles and specific uses of adjectives in 29, 30g, and 30h.

46e Adverbs

An adverb is a word used to modify, or qualify, a verb (or verbal), an adjective, or another adverb. It usually answers one of these questions: When? Where? How? Why? Under what conditions? To what degree?

Pull *firmly* on the emergency handle. [Pull how?]

SCHOLARS ON GRAMMAR BASICS

Noguchi, Rei R. *Grammar and the Teaching of Writing: Limits and Possibilities.* Urbana: NCTE, 1991. Print. Though grammar instruction has a place in writing classes, the role of such instruction "will need to be a much more selective and efficient one than that currently played," Noguchi argues. He recommends that instructors introduce only basic categories such as subjects, verbs, and modifiers. "Ultimately," he says, "the choice and number of categories and principles will be determined by their utility in treating the most frequent and most socially consequential writing errors."

Read the text *first* and *then* complete the exercises. [Read when? Complete when?]

Place the flowers *here*. [Place where?]

Adverbs modifying adjectives or other adverbs usually intensify or limit the intensity of the word they modify.

ADV

Be *extremely* kind, and you will have many friends.

ADV

We proceeded *very* cautiously in the dark house.

The words *not* and *never* are classified as adverbs. A word such as *cannot* contains the helping verb *can* and the adverb *not*. The word *can't* contains the helping verb *can* and a contracted form of *not* (see 36c).

TIP: You can find more details about using adverbs in 26b–26d. Multilingual writers can find more about the placement of adverbs in 30f.

EXERCISE 46–13 Underline the adjectives and circle the adverbs in the following sentences. If a word is a noun or pronoun functioning as an adjective, underline it and mark it as a noun/adjective or pronoun/ adjective. Also treat the articles *a*, *an*, and *the* as adjectives. Answers appear in the back of the book. *More practice:* e ✓

Finding <u>an</u> <u>available</u> room during <u>the</u> convention was (not) <u>easy</u>.

a. Generalizations lead to weak, unfocused essays.
b. The Spanish language is wonderfully flexible.
c. The wildflowers smelled especially fragrant after the steady rain.
d. I'd rather be slightly hot than bitterly cold.
e. The cat slept soundly in its wicker basket.

hackerhandbooks.com/bedhandbook
e Grammar basics > Exercises: 46–14 to 46–18, 46–19 and 46–20 (all parts of speech)
✓ Grammar basics > LearningCurve: Verbs, adjectives, and adverbs

EXERCISE 46–13 *Answers:*

a. Adjectives: weak, unfocused; b. Adjectives: The (article), Spanish, flexible; adverb: wonderfully; c. Adjectives: The (article), fragrant, the (article), steady; adverb: especially; d. Adjectives: hot, cold; adverbs: rather, slightly, bitterly; e. Adjectives: The (article), its (pronoun/ adjective), wicker (noun/adjective); adverb: soundly

46f Prepositions

A preposition is a word placed before a noun or a pronoun to form a phrase that modifies another word in the sentence. The prepositional phrase functions as an adjective or an adverb.

> P   P   P
>
> The winding road *to* the summit travels *past* craters *from* an extinct volcano.

To the summit functions as an adjective modifying the noun *road*; *past craters* functions as an adverb modifying the verb *travels*; *from an extinct volcano* functions as an adjective modifying the noun *craters*. (For more on prepositional phrases, see 48a.)

English has a limited number of prepositions. The most common are included in the following list.

about	beside	from	outside	toward
above	besides	in	over	under
across	between	inside	past	underneath
after	beyond	into	plus	unlike
against	but	like	regarding	until
along	by	near	respecting	unto
among	concerning	next	round	up
around	considering	of	since	upon
as	despite	off	than	with
at	down	on	through	within
before	during	onto	throughout	without
behind	except	opposite	till	
below	for	out	to	

Some prepositions are more than one word long. *Along with*, *as well as*, *in addition to*, *next to*, and *rather than* are examples.

TIP: Prepositions are used in idioms such as *capable of* and *dig up* (see 18d). For specific issues for multilingual writers, see 31.

SCHOLARS ON GRAMMAR BASICS

Connors, Robert J. "Grammar in American College Composition: An Historical Overview." *The Territory of Language: Linguistics, Stylistics, and the Teaching of Composition.* Ed. Donald A. McQuade. Carbondale: Southern Illinois UP, 1986. 3–22. Print. Connors surveys how grammar has affected the teaching of writing from the mid-nineteenth century and finds that a "great deal of the history of composition in America seems to be a clumsy shuffle-dance of grammar with rhetoric, with first one and then another leading."

46g Conjunctions

Conjunctions join words, phrases, or clauses, and they indicate the relation between the elements joined.

Coordinating conjunctions A coordinating conjunction is used to connect grammatically equal elements. (See 9b and 14a.) The coordinating conjunctions are *and, but, or, nor, for, so,* and *yet.*

> The sociologist interviewed children *but* not their parents.

> Write clearly, *and* your readers will appreciate your efforts.

In the first sentence, *but* connects two noun phrases; in the second, *and* connects two independent clauses.

Correlative conjunctions Correlative conjunctions come in pairs; they connect grammatically equal elements.

> either . . . or
> neither . . . nor
> not only . . . but also
> whether . . . or
> both . . . and

> *Either* the painting was brilliant *or* it was a forgery.

Subordinating conjunctions A subordinating conjunction introduces a subordinate clause and indicates the relation of the clause to the rest of the sentence. (See 48e.) The most common subordinating conjunctions are *after, although, as, as if, because, before, if, in order that, once, since, so that, than, that, though,*

hackerhandbooks.com/bedhandbook

e Grammar basics > Exercises: 46–19 and 46–20 (all parts of speech)

☑ Grammar basics > LearningCurve: Prepositions and conjunctions

WRITERS ON WRITING

As to the adjective, when in doubt, strike it out.   — Mark Twain

The adjective is the banana peel of the parts of speech.

— Clifton Fadiman

If the noun is good and the verb is strong, you almost never need an adjective.   — J. Anthony Lukas

Don't say it "was delightful"; make us say "delightful" when we've read the description. You see, all those words (horrifying, wonderful, hideous, exquisite) are only like saying to your readers "Please will you do my job for me?"   — C. S. Lewis

unless, until, when, where, whether, and *while.* (For a complete list, see p. 507.)

> *When* the fundraiser ends, we expect to have raised more than half a million dollars.

Conjunctive adverbs Conjunctive adverbs connect independent clauses and indicate the relation between the clauses. They can be used with a semicolon to join two independent clauses in one sentence, or they can be used alone with an independent clause. The most common conjunctive adverbs are *finally, furthermore, however, moreover, nevertheless, similarly, then, therefore,* and *thus.* (For a complete list, see p. 423.)

> The photographer failed to take a light reading; *therefore,* all the pictures were underexposed.

> During the day, the kitten sleeps peacefully. *However,* when night falls, the kitten is wide awake and ready to play.

Conjunctive adverbs can appear at the beginning or in the middle of a clause.

> When night falls, *however,* the kitten is wide awake and ready to play.

TIP: The ability to distinguish between conjunctive adverbs and coordinating conjunctions will help you avoid run-on sentences and make punctuation decisions (see 20, 32a, and 32f). The ability to recognize subordinating conjunctions will help you avoid sentence fragments (see 19).

46h Interjections

An interjection is a word used to express surprise or emotion (*Oh! Hey! Wow!*).

SCHOLARS ON GRAMMAR BASICS

Hartwell, Patrick. "Grammar, Grammars, and the Teaching of Grammar." *College English* 47.2 (1985): 105–27. Print. As part of his attempt to move beyond disputes about the value of teaching formal grammar in composition courses, Hartwell carefully defines the term *grammar* and offers five meanings. These meanings range from Grammar 1, "the grammar in our heads," or the internal system of rules that native speakers of a language share, to Grammar 5, stylistic grammar, which consists of "grammatical terms used in the interest of teaching prose style."

47   Sentence patterns

The vast majority of English sentences conform to one of these five patterns:

> subject/verb/subject complement
> subject/verb/direct object
> subject/verb/indirect object/direct object
> subject/verb/direct object/object complement
> subject/verb

Adverbial modifiers (single words, phrases, or clauses) may be added to any of these patterns, and they may appear nearly anywhere—at the beginning, in the middle, or at the end.

Predicate is the grammatical term given to the verb plus its objects, complements, and adverbial modifiers.

47a Subjects

The subject of a sentence names whom or what the sentence is about. The simple subject is always a noun or pronoun; the complete subject consists of the simple subject and any words or word groups modifying the simple subject.

The complete subject

To find the complete subject, ask Who? or What?, insert the verb, and finish the question. The answer is the complete subject.

    ┌────── COMPLETE SUBJECT ──────┐
The devastating effects of famine can last for many years.

WRITERS ON WRITING

Grammar is to a writer what anatomy is to a sculptor, or the scales to a musician. You may loathe it, it may bore you, but nothing will replace it, and once mastered it will support you like a rock.　　— B. J. Chute

Who or what can last for many years? *The devastating effects of famine.*

┌──────────── COMPLETE SUBJECT ────────────┐
Adventure novels that contain multiple subplots are often made into successful movies.

Who or what are often made into movies? *Adventure novels that contain multiple subplots.*

                 COMPLETE
         ┌── SUBJECT ──┐
In our program, student teachers work full-time for ten months.

Who or what works full-time for ten months? *Student teachers.* Notice that *In our program, student teachers* is not a sensible answer to the question. (It is not safe to assume that the subject must always appear first in a sentence.)

The simple subject

To find the simple subject, strip away all modifiers in the complete subject. This includes single-word modifiers such as *the* and *devastating*, phrases such as *of famine*, and subordinate clauses such as *that contain multiple subplots.*

                ┌ SS ┐
The devastating effects of famine can last for many years.

          ┌ SS ┐
Adventure novels that contain multiple subplots are often made into successful movies.

A sentence may have a compound subject containing two or more simple subjects joined with a coordinating conjunction such as *and, but,* or *or.*

       ┌─── SS ───┐   ┌ SS ┐
Great commitment and a little luck make a successful actor.

WRITERS ON WRITING

Where strictness of grammar does not weaken expression, it should be attended to. . . . But where, by small grammatical negligences, the energy of an idea is condensed, or a word stands for a sentence, I hold grammatical rigor in contempt.   — Thomas Jefferson

Looking back at homework in Taft Junior High School, I suppose I found no more pleasure in diagramming a dozen sentences than I found in running twelve arpeggios. Of what use, I wondered, are subjects, predicates, prepositional phrases, and subordinate clauses? In time I would discover that they are the raw material of a writer's life.   — James J. Kilpatrick

Understood subjects

In imperative sentences, which give advice or issue commands, the subject is understood but not actually present in the sentence. The subject of an imperative sentence is understood to be *you*.

[*You*] Put your hands on the steering wheel.

Subject after the verb

Although the subject ordinarily comes before the verb (*The planes took off*), occasionally it does not. When a sentence begins with *There is* or *There are* (or *There was* or *There were*), the subject follows the verb. In such inverted constructions, the word *There* is an expletive, an empty word serving merely to get the sentence started.

           ⌐ SS ¬
There are *eight planes waiting to take off.*

Occasionally a writer will invert a sentence for effect.

         ⌐ SS ¬
Joyful is *the child whose school closes for snow.*

Joyful is an adjective, so it cannot be the subject. Turn this sentence around and its structure becomes obvious.

The *child* whose school closes for snow is joyful.

In questions, the subject frequently appears between the helping verb and the main verb.

HV   ⌐——— SS ———¬ MV
Do *Kenyan marathoners* train year-round?

TIP: The ability to recognize the subject of a sentence will help you edit for fragments (19), subject-verb agreement (21), pronouns such as *I* and *me* (24), missing subjects (30b), and repeated subjects (30c).

WRITERS ON WRITING

A dependent clause is like a dependent child: incapable of standing on its own but able to cause a lot of trouble.   — William Safire

EXERCISE 47-1 In the following sentences, underline the complete subject and write *SS* above the simple subject(s). If the subject is an understood *you*, insert *you* in parentheses. Answers appear in the back of the book. *More practice:* e

⌐SS⌐   ⌐SS⌐
<u>Parents and their children</u> often look alike.

a. The hills and mountains seemed endless, and the snow atop them glistened.

b. In foil fencing, points are scored by hitting an electronic target.

c. Do not stand in the aisles or sit on the stairs.

d. There were hundreds of fireflies in the open field.

e. The evidence against the defendant was staggering.

47b Verbs, objects, and complements

Section 46c explains how to find the verb of a sentence. A sentence's verb is classified as linking, transitive, or intransitive, depending on the kinds of objects or complements the verb can (or cannot) take.

Linking verbs and subject complements

Linking verbs connect the subject to a subject complement, a word or word group that completes the meaning of the subject by renaming or describing it.

If the subject complement renames the subject, it is a noun or noun equivalent (sometimes called a *predicate noun*).

⌐————————————— S —————————————⌐ ⌐ V ⌐
A phone call requesting personal information may be
⌐ SC ⌐
a scam.

EXERCISE 47-1 *Answers:*

a. Complete subjects: The hills and mountains, the snow atop them; simple subjects: hills, mountains, snow; b. Complete subject: points; simple subject: points; c. Complete subject: (You); d. Complete subject: hundreds of fireflies; simple subject: hundreds; e. Complete subject: The evidence against the defendant; simple subject: evidence

If the subject complement describes the subject, it is an adjective or adjective equivalent (sometimes called a *predicate adjective*).

```
         ———————— S ———————  V    SC
```
Last month's temperatures were mild.

Whenever they appear as main verbs (rather than helping verbs), the forms of *be—be, am, is, are, was, were, being, been—* usually function as linking verbs. In the preceding examples, for instance, the main verbs are *be* and *were.*

Verbs such as *appear, become, feel, grow, look, make, seem, smell, sound,* and *taste* are linking when they are followed by a word or word group that renames or describes the subject.

```
         ——— S ———— — V —     SC
```
As it thickens, the sauce will look unappealing.

Transitive verbs and direct objects

A transitive verb takes a direct object, a word or word group that names a receiver of the action.

```
     ———— S ———   V   ———— DO ————
```
The hungry cat clawed the bag of dry food.

The simple direct object is always a noun or pronoun, in this case *bag.* To find it, simply strip away all modifiers.

Transitive verbs usually appear in the active voice, with the subject doing the action and a direct object receiving the action. Active-voice sentences can be transformed into passive, with the subject receiving the action. (See 47c.)

Transitive verbs, indirect objects, and direct objects

The direct object of a transitive verb is sometimes preceded by an indirect object, a noun or pronoun telling to whom or for whom the action of the sentence is done.

```
   S   V   IO ——DO——     S  —V—  IO  —DO—
```
You give her some yarn, and she will knit you a scarf.

The simple indirect object is always a noun or pronoun. To test for an indirect object, insert the word *to* or *for* before the word or word group in question. If the sentence makes sense, the word or word group is an indirect object.

You give [to] *her* some yarn, and she will knit [for] *you* a scarf.

An indirect object may be turned into a prepositional phrase using *to* or *for*: *You give some yarn to her, and she will knit a scarf for you.*

Only certain transitive verbs take indirect objects. Some examples are *ask, bring, find, get, give, hand, lend, make, offer, pay, promise, read, send, show, teach, tell, throw,* and *write*.

Transitive verbs, direct objects, and object complements

The direct object of a transitive verb is sometimes followed by an object complement, a word or word group that renames or describes the object.

> S   V   DO ┌──── OC ────┐
> People often consider chivalry a thing of the past.

> ┌─ S ─┐   V   DO ┌──── OC ────┐
> The kiln makes clay firm and strong.

When the object complement renames the direct object, it is a noun or pronoun (such as *thing*). When it describes the direct object, it is an adjective (such as *firm* and *strong*).

Intransitive verbs

Intransitive verbs take no objects or complements.

> ┌──── S ────┐   V
> The audience laughed.

> ┌──── S ────┐   V
> The driver accelerated in the straightaway.

Nothing receives the actions of laughing and accelerating in these sentences, so the verbs are intransitive. Notice that such verbs may or may not be followed by adverbial modifiers. In the second sentence, *in the straightaway* is an adverbial prepositional phrase modifying *accelerated*.

NOTE: The dictionary will tell you whether a verb is transitive or intransitive. Some verbs can be both transitive and intransitive.

TRANSITIVE   Sandra *flew* her small plane over the canyon.

INTRANSITIVE   A flock of migrating geese *flew* overhead.

In the first example, *flew* has a direct object that receives the action: *her small plane*. In the second example, the verb is followed by an adverb (*overhead*), not by a direct object.

EXERCISE 47–5   Label the subject complements and direct objects in the following sentences, using the labels *SC* and *DO*. If a subject complement or a direct object consists of more than one word, bracket and label all of it. Answers appear in the back of the book. *More practice:* e

$$\overset{\overline{\qquad DO \qquad}}{}$$
The sharp right turn confused most drivers.

a.   Textbooks are expensive.

b.   Samurai warriors never fear death.

c.   Successful coaches always praise their players' efforts.

d.   St. Petersburg was the capital of the Russian Empire for two centuries.

e.   The medicine tasted bitter.

EXERCISE 47–6   Each of the following sentences (p. 497) has either an indirect object followed by a direct object or a direct object followed by an object complement. Label the objects and complements, using the labels *IO*, *DO*, and *OC*. If an object or a complement consists of more than one word, bracket and label all of it. Answers appear in the back of the book. *More practice:* e

hackerhandbooks.com/bedhandbook
e Grammar basics > Exercises: 47–7 to 47–12

EXERCISE 47–5   *Answers:*

a. Subject complement: expensive; b. Direct object: death; c. Direct object: their players' efforts; d. Subject complement: the capital of the Russian Empire; e. Subject complement: bitter

```
                    ┌────── DO ──────┐ ┌─ OC ─┐
Most people consider their own experience normal.
```

a. Stress can make adults and children weary.
b. The dining hall offered students healthy meal choices.
c. Consider the work finished.
d. We showed the agent our tickets, and she gave us boarding passes.
e. Zita has made community service her priority this year.

47c Pattern variations

Although most sentences follow one of the five patterns listed on page 490, variations of these patterns commonly occur in questions, commands, sentences with delayed subjects, and passive transformations.

Questions and commands

Questions are sometimes patterned in normal word order, with the subject preceding the verb.

```
    S   ┌─ V ─┐
Who will have the most hits this season?
```

Often, the pattern of a question is inverted, with the subject appearing between the helping verb and the main verb or after the verb.

```
HV  S  MV
Will he have the most hits this season?
```

```
    V ┌──────── S ────────┐
Why is the number of hits an important statistic?
```

In commands, the subject of the sentence is an understood *you*.

```
    S      V
[You] Pay attention to the road.
```

EXERCISE 47–6 *Answers:*

a. Direct objects: adults and children; object complement: weary;
b. Indirect object: students; direct object: healthy meal choices; c. Direct object: the work; object complement: finished; d. Indirect objects: agent, us; direct objects: our tickets, boarding passes; e. Direct object: community service; object complement: her priority

Sentences with delayed subjects

Writers sometimes choose to delay the subject of a sentence to achieve a special effect such as suspense or humor.

> V ⌐——— S ———⌐
> Behind the phony tinsel of Hollywood lies the real tinsel.

The subject of the sentence is also delayed in sentences opening with the expletive *There* or *It*. When used as expletives, the words *There* and *It* have no strict grammatical function; they serve merely to get the sentence started.

> V ⌐——————— S ———————⌐
> There are thirty thousand spectators in the stadium.

> V ⌐——— S ———⌐
> It is best to avoid trans fats.

The subject in the second example is an infinitive phrase. (See 48b.)

Passive transformations

Transitive verbs, those that can take direct objects, usually appear in the active voice. In the active voice, the subject does the action, and a direct object receives the action.

> ⌐——— S ———⌐   V   ⌐——— DO ———
> **ACTIVE**   The fireworks display dazzled the viewers on the
>
> ⌐———⌐
> Esplanade.

Sentences in the active voice may be transformed into the passive voice, with the subject receiving the action instead.

> ⌐——————— S ———————⌐   HV   MV
> **PASSIVE**   The viewers on the Esplanade were dazzled by the
> fireworks display.

What was once the direct object (*the viewers on the Esplanade*) has become the subject in the passive-voice transformation, and the original subject appears in a prepositional phrase beginning with *by*. The *by* phrase is frequently omitted in passive-voice constructions.

PASSIVE   The viewers on the Esplanade were dazzled.

Verbs in the passive voice can be identified by their form alone. The main verb is always a past participle, such as *dazzled* (see 46c), preceded by a form of *be* (*be, am, is, are, was, were, being, been*): *were dazzled*. Sometimes adverbs intervene (*were usually dazzled*).

TIP: Avoid using the passive voice when the active voice would be more appropriate (see 8a).

48 Subordinate word groups

Subordinate word groups include phrases and clauses. Phrases are subordinate because they lack a subject and a verb; they are classified as prepositional, verbal, appositive, and absolute (see 48a–48d). Subordinate clauses have a subject and a verb, but they begin with a word (such as *although, that,* or *when*) that marks them as subordinate (see 48e).

48a Prepositional phrases

A prepositional phrase begins with a preposition such as *at, by, for, from, in, of, on, to,* or *with* (see 46f) and usually ends with a noun or noun equivalent: *on the table, for him, by sleeping late.* The noun or noun equivalent is known as the *object of the preposition.*

Prepositional phrases function as adjectives or as adverbs. As an adjective, a prepositional phrase nearly always appears immediately following the noun or pronoun it modifies.

The hut had *walls of mud.*

Adjective phrases usually answer one or both of the questions Which one? and What kind of? If we ask Which walls? or What kind of walls? we get a sensible answer: *walls of mud.*

Adverbial prepositional phrases usually modify the verb, but they can also modify adjectives or other adverbs. When a prepositional phrase modifies the verb, it can appear nearly anywhere in a sentence.

James *walked* his dog *on a leash.*

Sabrina *will in time adjust* to life in Ecuador.

During a mudslide, the terrain *can change* drastically.

If a prepositional phrase is movable, you can be certain that it is adverbial.

> *In the cave,* the explorers found well-preserved prehistoric drawings.

> The explorers found well-preserved prehistoric drawings *in the cave.*

Adverbial word groups usually answer one of these questions: When? Where? How? Why? Under what conditions? To what degree?

> James walked his dog *how? On a leash.*

> Sabrina will adjust to life in Ecuador *when? In time.*

The terrain can change drastically *under what conditions?*
During a mudslide.

In questions and subordinate clauses, a preposition may appear after its object.

What are you afraid *of*?

We avoided the bike trail *that* John had warned us *about*.

EXERCISE 48–1 Underline the prepositional phrases in the following sentences. Tell whether each one is an adjective phrase or an adverb phrase and what it modifies in the sentence. Answers appear in the back of the book. *More practice:* e

> Flecks of mica glittered in the new granite floor. (Adjective phrase
> modifying "Flecks"; adverb phrase modifying "glittered")

a. In northern Italy, we met many people who speak German as their first language.

b. William completed the three-mile hike through the thick forest with ease.

c. To my boss's dismay, I was late for work again.

d. The traveling exhibit of Mayan artifacts gave viewers new insight into pre-Columbian culture.

e. In 2002, the euro became the official currency in twelve European countries.

48b Verbal phrases

A verbal is a verb form that does not function as the verb of a clause. Verbals include infinitives (the word *to* plus the base form of the verb), present participles (the *-ing* form of the verb), and past participles (the verb form usually ending in *-d*, *-ed*, *-n*, *-en*, or *-t*). (See 27a and 46c.)

hackerhandbooks.com/bedhandbook

e Grammar basics > Exercises: 48–2 to 48–5

EXERCISE 48–1 *Answers:*

a. In northern Italy (adverb phrase modifying *met*); as their first language (adverb phrase modifying *speak*); b. through the thick forest (adjective phrase modifying *hike*); with ease (adverb phrase modifying *completed*); c. To my boss's dismay (adverb phrase modifying *was*); for work (adverb phrase modifying *late*); d. of Mayan artifacts (adjective phrase modifying *exhibit*); into pre-Columbian culture (adjective phrase modifying *insight*); e. In 2002, in twelve European countries (adverb phrases modifying *became*)

INFINITIVE	PRESENT PARTICIPLE	PAST PARTICIPLE
to dream	dreaming	dreamed
to choose	choosing	chosen
to build	building	built
to grow	growing	grown

Instead of functioning as the verb of a clause, a verbal functions as an adjective, a noun, or an adverb.

ADJECTIVE	*Broken* promises cannot be fixed.
NOUN	Constant *complaining* becomes wearisome.
ADVERB	Can you wait *to celebrate*?

Verbals with objects, complements, or modifiers form verbal phrases.

In my family, *singing loudly* is more appreciated than *singing well*.

Governments exist *to protect the rights of minorities*.

Like verbals, verbal phrases function as adjectives, nouns, or adverbs. Verbal phrases are ordinarily classified as participial, gerund, and infinitive.

Participial phrases

Participial phrases always function as adjectives. Their verbals are either present participles (such as *dreaming, asking*) or past participles (such as *stolen, reached*).

Participial phrases frequently appear immediately following the noun or pronoun they modify.

Congress shall make no *law abridging the freedom of speech or of the press*.

Participial phrases are often movable. They can precede the word they modify.

TEACHING TIP

Ask students to keep an editing log for the semester. When they receive comments on a draft, they should pay special attention to comments related to sentence-level matters. In their editing log, students should record (1) the incorrect sentence, (2) the handbook section (48b, for example) that provides help for editing that sentence, and (3) the corrected sentence. Invite students to add any tips that might help them proofread for that particular error in the future.

Being a weight-bearing joint, the *knee* is among the most frequently injured.

They may also appear at some distance from the word they modify.

Last night we saw a *play* that affected us deeply, *written with profound insight into the lives of immigrants.*

Gerund phrases

Gerund phrases are built around present participles (verb forms that end in *-ing*), and they always function as nouns: usually as subjects, subject complements, direct objects, or objects of a preposition.

— S —
Rationalizing a fear can eliminate it.

— SC —
The key to good sauce is browning the mushrooms.

— DO —
Lizards usually enjoy sunning themselves.

The American Heart Association has documented the benefits
— OBJ OF PREP —
of diet and exercise in reducing the risk of heart attack.

Infinitive phrases

Infinitive phrases, usually constructed around *to* plus the base form of the verb (*to call, to drink*), can function as nouns, as adjectives, or as adverbs. When functioning as a noun, an infinitive phrase may appear in almost any noun slot in a sentence, usually as a subject, subject complement, or direct object.

─── S ───
To live without health insurance is risky.

─── DO ───
The orchestra wanted to make its premier season memorable.

Infinitive phrases functioning as adjectives usually appear immediately following the noun or pronoun they modify.

The Nineteenth Amendment gave women the *right to vote*.

The infinitive phrase modifies the noun *right*. Which right? *The right to vote*.

Adverbial infinitive phrases usually qualify the meaning of the verb, telling when, where, how, why, under what conditions, or to what degree an action occurred.

Volunteers *rolled up* their pants *to wade through the flood waters*.

NOTE: In some constructions, the infinitive is unmarked; that is, the *to* does not appear. (See 28f.)

Graphs and charts can help researchers [*to*] *present complex data*.

EXERCISE 48–6 Underline the verbal phrases in the following sentences. Tell whether each phrase is participial, gerund, or infinitive and how each is used in the sentence. Answers appear in the back of the book. *More practice:* e

Do you want <u>to watch that documentary</u>? (Infinitive phrase used as direct object of "Do want")

a. Updating your software will fix the computer glitch.

b. The challenge in decreasing the town budget is identifying non-essential services.

hackerhandbooks.com/bedhandbook
e Grammar basics > Exercises: 48–7 to 48–9

EXERCISE 48–6 *Answers:*

a. Updating your software (gerund phrase used as subject); b. decreasing the town budget (gerund phrase used as object of the preposition *in*); identifying nonessential services (gerund phrase used as subject complement); c. to help her mother by raking the lawn (infinitive phrase used as direct object); raking the lawn (gerund phrase used as object of the preposition *by*); d. Understanding little (participial phrase modifying *I*); passing my biology final (gerund phrase used as object of the preposition *of*); e. Working with animals (gerund phrase used as subject)

c. Cathleen tried to help her mother by raking the lawn.
d. Understanding little, I had no hope of passing my biology final.
e. Working with animals gave Steve a sense of satisfaction.

48c Appositive phrases

Appositive phrases describe nouns or pronouns. Instead of modifying nouns or pronouns, however, appositive phrases rename them. In form they are nouns or noun equivalents.

> Bloggers, *conversationalists at heart,* are the online equivalent of radio talk show hosts.

Appositives are said to be "in apposition to" the nouns or pronouns they rename. *Conversationalists at heart* is in apposition to the noun *Bloggers.*

48d Absolute phrases

An absolute phrase modifies a whole clause or sentence, not just one word. It consists of a noun or noun equivalent usually followed by a participial phrase.

> *Her words reverberating in the hushed arena,* the senator urged the crowd to support her former opponent.

48e Subordinate clauses

Subordinate clauses are patterned like sentences, having subjects and verbs and sometimes objects or complements. But they function within sentences as adjectives, adverbs, or nouns. They cannot stand alone as complete sentences.

A subordinate clause usually begins with a subordinating conjunction or a relative pronoun. The chart on page 507 classifies these words according to the kinds of clauses (adjective, adverb, or noun) they introduce.

Adjective clauses

Adjective clauses modify nouns or pronouns, usually answering the question Which one? or What kind of? Most adjective clauses begin with a relative pronoun (*who, whom, whose, which,* or *that*). In addition to introducing the clause, the relative pronoun points back to the noun that the clause modifies.

The coach chose *players who would benefit from intense drills.*

A *book that goes unread* is a writer's worst nightmare.

Relative pronouns are sometimes "understood."

The things [*that*] *we cherish most* are the things [*that*] *we might lose.*

Occasionally an adjective clause is introduced by a relative adverb, usually *when, where,* or *why.*

The aging actor returned to the *stage where he had made his debut as Hamlet half a century earlier.*

The parts of an adjective clause are often arranged as in sentences (subject/verb/object or complement).

　　　　　　　　　　　　　　　　　　S　　V　　DO
Sometimes it is our closest friends who disappoint us.

Frequently, however, the object or complement appears first, out of the normal order of subject/verb/object.

　　　　　　　　　　　　　　　DO　S　　V
They can be the very friends whom we disappoint.

TIP: For punctuation of adjective clauses, see 32e and 33e. For advice about avoiding repeated words in adjective clauses, see 30d.

Words that introduce subordinate clauses
Words introducing adjective clauses
Relative pronouns: that, which, who, whom, whose   **Relative adverbs:** when, where, why
Words introducing adverb clauses
Subordinating conjunctions: after, although, as, as if, because, before, even though, if, in order that, since, so that, than, that, though, unless, until, when, where, whether, while
Words introducing noun clauses
Relative pronouns: which, who, whom, whose   **Other pronouns:** what, whatever, whichever, whoever, whomever   **Other subordinating words:** how, if, that, when, whenever, where, wherever, whether, why

Adverb clauses

Adverb clauses modify verbs, adjectives, or other adverbs, usually answering one of these questions: When? Where? Why? How? Under what conditions? To what degree? They always begin with a subordinating conjunction (such as *after*, *although*, *because*, *that*, *though*, *unless*, or *when*). (For a complete list, see the chart on this page.)

When the sun went down, the hikers *prepared* their camp.

Kate *would have made* the team *if she hadn't broken her ankle.*

Adverb clauses are usually movable when they modify a verb. In the preceding examples, for instance, the adverb clauses can be moved without affecting the meaning of the sentences.

The hikers prepared their camp *when the sun went down.*

If she hadn't broken her ankle, Kate would have made the team.

When an adverb clause modifies an adjective or an adverb, it is not movable; it must appear next to the word it modifies. In the following examples, the *when* clause modifies the adjective *Uncertain,* and the *than* clause modifies the adverb *better.*

Uncertain *when the baby would be born,* Ray and Leah stayed close to home.

Jackie can dance better *than I can walk.*

Adverb clauses are sometimes elliptical, with some of their words being understood but not appearing in the sentence.

When [it is] renovated, the dorm will hold six hundred students.

Noun clauses

A noun clause functions just like a single-word noun, usually as a subject, a subject complement, a direct object, or an object of a preposition. It usually begins with one of the following words: *how, if, that, what, whatever, when, where, whether, which, who, whoever, whom, whomever, whose, why.* (For a complete list, see the chart on p. 507.)

$$\overline{\qquad\qquad S \qquad\qquad}$$
Whoever leaves the house last must double-lock the door.

$$\overline{\qquad\qquad DO \qquad\qquad}$$
Copernicus argued that the sun is the center of the universe.

The subordinating word introducing the clause may or may not play a significant role in the clause. In the preceding examples, *Whoever* is the subject of its clause, but *that* does not perform a function in its clause.

As with adjective clauses, the parts of a noun clause may appear in normal order (subject/verb/object or complement) or out of their normal order.

S   V   ┌── DO ──┐
Loyalty is what keeps a friendship strong.

DO   S   V
New Mexico is where we live.

EXERCISE 48-10   Underline the subordinate clauses in the following sentences. Tell whether each clause is an adjective clause, an adverb clause, or a noun clause and how it is used in the sentence. Answers appear in the back of the book. *More practice:* e

Show the committee the latest draft before you print the

final report. (Adverb clause modifying "Show")

a. The city's electoral commission adjusted the voting process so that every vote would count.

b. A marketing campaign that targets baby boomers may not appeal to young professionals.

c. After the Tambora volcano erupted in the southern Pacific in 1815, no one realized that it would contribute to the "year without a summer" in Europe and North America.

d. The concept of peak oil implies that at a certain point there will be no more oil to extract from the earth.

e. Details are easily overlooked when you are rushing.

49   Sentence types

Sentences are classified in two ways: according to their structure (simple, compound, complex, and compound-complex) and according to their purpose (declarative, imperative, interrogative, and exclamatory).

hackerhandbooks.com/bedhandbook

e Grammar basics > Exercises: 48–11 to 48–15

EXERCISE 48-10   *Answers:*

a. so that every vote would count (adverb clause modifying *adjusted*); b. that targets baby boomers (adjective clause modifying *campaign*); c. After the Tambora volcano erupted in the southern Pacific in 1815 (adverb clause modifying *realized*); that it would contribute to the "year without a summer" in Europe and North America (noun clause used as direct object of *realized*); d. that at a certain point there will be no more oil to extract from the earth (noun clause used as direct object of *implies*); e. when you are rushing (adverb clause modifying *are overlooked*)

49a Sentence structures

Depending on the number and the types of clauses they contain, sentences are classified as simple, compound, complex, or compound-complex.

Clauses come in two varieties: independent and subordinate. An independent clause contains a subject and a predicate, and it either stands alone or could stand alone as a sentence. A subordinate clause also contains a subject and a predicate, but it functions within a sentence as an adjective, an adverb, or a noun; it cannot stand alone. (See 48e.)

Simple sentences

A simple sentence is one independent clause with no subordinate clauses.

──────── INDEPENDENT CLAUSE ────────
Without a passport, Eva could not visit her grandparents in

Hungary.

A simple sentence may contain compound elements—a compound subject, verb, or object, for example—but it does not contain more than one full sentence pattern. The following sentence is simple because its two verbs (*comes in* and *goes out*) share a subject (*Spring*).

──────── INDEPENDENT CLAUSE ────────
Spring comes in like a lion and goes out like a lamb.

Compound sentences

A compound sentence is composed of two or more independent clauses with no subordinate clauses. The independent clauses are usually joined with a comma and a coordinating conjunction (*and, but, or, nor, for, so, yet*) or with a semicolon. (See 14a.)

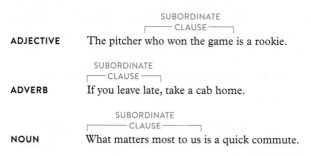

INDEPENDENT CLAUSE   INDEPENDENT CLAUSE

The car broke down, but a rescue van arrived within minutes.

INDEPENDENT CLAUSE   INDEPENDENT CLAUSE

A shark was spotted near shore; people left immediately.

Complex sentences

A complex sentence is composed of one independent clause with one or more subordinate clauses. (See 48e.)

SUBORDINATE CLAUSE

ADJECTIVE   The pitcher who won the game is a rookie.

SUBORDINATE CLAUSE

ADVERB   If you leave late, take a cab home.

SUBORDINATE CLAUSE

NOUN   What matters most to us is a quick commute.

Compound-complex sentences

A compound-complex sentence contains at least two independent clauses and at least one subordinate clause. The following sentence contains two independent clauses, each of which contains a subordinate clause.

INDEPENDENT CLAUSE   INDEPENDENT CLAUSE
SUB CL

Tell the doctor how you feel, and she will decide whether

SUB CL

you can go home.

49b Sentence purposes

Writers use declarative sentences to make statements, imperative sentences to issue requests or commands, interrogative sentences to ask questions, and exclamatory sentences to make exclamations.

DECLARATIVE	The echo sounded in our ears.
IMPERATIVE	Love your neighbor.
INTERROGATIVE	Did the better team win tonight?
EXCLAMATORY	We're here to save you!

EXERCISE 49-1 Identify the following sentences as simple, compound, complex, or compound-complex. Identify the subordinate clauses and classify them according to their function: adjective, adverb, or noun. (See 48e.) Answers appear in the back of the book. *More practice:*

> The deli in Courthouse Square was crowded with lawyers
>
> at lunchtime. (Simple)

a. Fires that are ignited in dry areas spread especially quickly.
b. The early Incas were advanced; they used a calendar and developed a decimal system.
c. Elaine's jacket was too thin to block the wintry air.
d. Before we leave for the station, we always check the Amtrak Web site.
e. Decide when you want to leave, and I will be there to pick you up.

hackerhandbooks.com/bedhandbook

e Grammar basics > Exercises: 49–2 and 49–3

EXERCISE 49-1 *Answers:*

a. Complex; that are ignited in dry areas (adjective clause); b. Compound; c. Simple; d. Complex; Before we leave for the station (adverb clause); e. Compound-complex; when you want to leave (noun clause)

Researched Writing

Becoming a College Writer

curiosity   engagement   responsibility   reflection

Join a research conversation

"Pursue your research with passion and energy. Find out what has been written about your topic, but also what's missing from the conversation."   — **Stephen Thacker**, University of Alabama

You probably have conducted research in the past—perhaps to seek information or report what others have said about a topic. For college research, you'll be asked to go beyond reporting the views of others; you'll develop your own authority by stating your positions and *contributing* your ideas to ongoing conversations. Becoming a college writer requires you to engage with, learn from, and question the ideas of experts in order to shape your own ideas.

One approach is to start with your own curiosity: What problems interest you? What topics do you want to learn more about? Read and view a wide range of sources, and try to understand not only what has been written about an issue but also, as Thacker suggests, "what's missing from the conversation." Asking such questions can help you find entry points in a debate.

- Think about issues you care about—either because you have strong opinions about them or because they affect you, your family, or your community. Write briefly about one issue: What new angle might you bring? What's "missing from the conversation"?

MORE
Assessing the writing situation, 1a
Asking a research question, 50b

TEACHING TIP

Ask students to respond to the "Becoming a College Writer" page with questions and comments. Many students will be surprised by Stephen Thacker's advice to find "what's missing from the conversation," especially if their previous research experiences focused more on hunting for and gathering facts than on joining a conversation. Use students' comments and questions to start a conversation about what makes a good, meaningful research project.

50 Thinking like a researcher; gathering sources

A college research assignment asks you to pose questions worth exploring, read widely in search of possible answers, interpret what you read, draw reasoned conclusions, and support those conclusions with evidence. In short, it asks you to enter a research conversation by being *in* conversation with other writers and thinkers who have explored and studied your topic. As you listen to and learn from the voices already in the conversation—paying attention to the evidence presented and countered—you may begin to realize what hasn't been said and needs to be said, and you'll find entry points where you can add your own insights and ideas.

Becoming a confident researcher means figuring out how to respond to and engage with ideas, find your own voice, and present your ideas alongside other people's thoughts. It also requires embracing the idea that writing with sources is a process that takes time. As your ideas evolve, you may find that the process leads you in unexpected directions—perhaps new questions in the conversation require you to create a new search strategy, find additional sources, and challenge your initial assumptions. Keep an open mind throughout the process, be curious, and enjoy the work of finding answers to questions that matter to you.

50a Manage the project.

When you get started on a research project, you need to understand the assignment, choose what direction to head in, and quickly get the big picture for the topic you choose. You then have to fit all of these tasks into an already crowded schedule. The following tips will help you manage the beginning phase of research.

TEACHING TIP

Some teachers like to introduce the metaphor of conversation by using a specific topic, often a heated one, to help students identify various positions and counterpositions in the conversation. Have students ask "What's missing from the conversation?" as a way to practice finding entry points in a conversation.

SCHOLARS ON THE TEACHING OF RESEARCH

Kenneth Burke's parlor metaphor, which he detailed in his 1941 book *The Philosophy of Literary Form*, is often paraphrased:

> Imagine that you enter a parlor. You come late. When you arrive, others have long preceded you, and they are engaged in a heated discussion, a discussion too heated for them to pause and

Managing time

When you receive your assignment, set a realistic schedule of dead-lines. Think about how much time you might need for each step on the way to your final draft. One student created a calendar to map out her tasks for a research paper assigned on October 3 and due October 31, keeping in mind that some tasks might overlap or need to be repeated. Notice that at the beginning of her project she started a research log to keep accurate records of the sources she read and her ideas about them. Notice, too, that she has budgeted more than a week for drafting and revising the paper.

Getting the big picture

As you consider a possible research topic, set aside some time to learn what people are saying about it by skimming sources on the Web or in library databases recommended by an instructor or a librarian. Ask yourself what aspects of the topic are generating the most debate. Why and how are people disagreeing? Which approaches seem the most intriguing? Think of this process as taking an aerial view of the topic. Once you have a sense of the landscape of the topic, you can zoom in closer to examine subtopics that look interesting. You may have to zoom in and out several times before you decide where to focus. If you zoom in too close, you may have difficulty finding sources or identifying the debate. You may have to zoom out to get a slightly broader view.

50b Pose questions worth exploring.

Working within the guidelines of your assignment, come up with a few preliminary questions that seem worth researching—questions that you are interested in exploring, that you feel would engage your audience, and about which there is substantial debate. You'll find the research process more rewarding and meaningful if you choose questions that you care about.

tell you exactly what it is about. In fact, the discussion had already begun long before any of them got there, so that no one present is qualified to retrace for you all the steps that had gone before. You listen for a while, until you decide that you have caught the tenor of the argument; then you put in your oar. Someone answers; you answer him; another comes to your defense; another aligns himself against you, to either the embarrassment or gratification of your opponent, depending upon the quality of your ally's assistance. However, the discussion is interminable. The hour grows late, you must depart. And you do depart, with the discussion still vigorously in progress. (110–11)

Source: Burke, Kenneth. *The Philosophy of Literary Form*. 1941. 3rd ed. Berkeley: U of California P, 1973. Print.

SAMPLE CALENDAR FOR A RESEARCH ASSIGNMENT

2	3	4	5	6	7	8
	Receive and analyze the assignment.	Pose questions you might explore.	Talk with a reference librarian; plan a search strategy. →	Start research log.	Settle on a topic; narrow the focus. →	Revise research questions. Locate sources. →

9	10	11	12	13	14	15
Read, take notes, and compile a working bibliography. →				Draft a working thesis and an outline.	Draft the paper. →	

16	17	18	19	20	21	22
→ Draft the paper. →			Visit the writing center for feedback.	Do additional research if needed. →		

23	24	25	26	27	28	29
Ask peers for feedback. Revise the paper; if necessary, revise the thesis. →				Prepare a list of works cited. →		Proofread the final draft. →

30	31					
Proofread the final draft.	Submit the final draft.					

TEACHING TIP

The sample calendar illustrates that tasks in a research project often overlap and gives students a realistic view of how much time they need to devote to the project. If you feel it would be useful for your students to keep a calendar for the project you assign, set aside some class time to do so, or assign it as homework.

TEACHING TIP

Give students a topic and ask them to do some research to figure out what aspects of the topic are generating the most debate. As a class, zoom in and out of the topic to find which subtopics are the most intriguing and fruitful as subjects of research.

Thinking like a researcher

To develop your authority as a researcher, you need to think like a researcher — asking interesting questions, becoming well informed through reading and evaluating sources, and citing sources to acknowledge other researchers.

Be curious. What makes you angry, concerned, or perplexed? What topics and debates do you care about? What problems do you want to help solve? Explore your topic from multiple perspectives, and let your curiosity drive your project.

Be engaged. Talk with a librarian and learn how to use your library's research tools and resources. Once you find promising sources, let one source lead you to another; follow bibliographic clues to learn who else has written about your topic. Listen to the key voices in the research conversation you've joined — and then respond.

Be responsible. Use sources to develop and support your ideas rather than patching them together to let them speak for you. From the start of your research project, keep careful track of sources you read or view (see 51), place quotation marks around words copied from sources, and maintain accurate records for all bibliographic information.

Be reflective. Keep a research log, and use your log to explore various points you are developing and to pose counterarguments to your research argument. Research is never a straightforward path, so use your log to reflect on the evolution of your project as well as your evolution as a researcher.

Here, for example, are some preliminary questions jotted down by students enrolled in a variety of college courses.

- Why are boys diagnosed with attention deficit disorder more often than girls are?

- Do nutritional food labels inform consumers or confuse them?

- Should states require public schools to adopt antibullying policies?

- Why was amateur archaeologist Heinrich Schliemann such a controversial figure in his own time?

SCHOLARS ON RESEARCH ASSIGNMENTS

Houdyshell, Mara L. "Navigating the Library: What Students (and Faculty) Need to Know." *College Teaching* 51.2 (2003): 76–78. Print. Houdyshell, a reference librarian, offers practical tips for designing effective library research assignments.

Melzer, Daniel, and Pavel Zemliansky. "Research Writing in First-Year Composition and across Disciplines: Assignments, Attitudes, and Student Performance." *Kairos* 8.1 (2003). Web. <http://english.ttu.edu/Kairos/8.1/index.html>. The authors report on two studies. The first explores first-year composition students' reactions to nontraditional research assignments — "ethnographic, multi-genre, hypertext, and

As you think about possible questions, choose those that are focused (not too broad), challenging (not just factual), and grounded (not too speculative) as possible entry points in a conversation.

Choosing a focused question

If your initial question is too broad, given the length of the paper you plan to write, look for ways to restrict your focus (see also "Subject" on p. 14). Here, for example, is how two students refined their initial questions.

TOO BROAD	FOCUSED
What are the benefits of stricter auto emissions standards?	How will stricter auto emissions standards create new auto industry jobs and make US carmakers more competitive in the world market?
What causes depression?	How has the widespread of antidepressant drugs affected teenage suicide rates?

Choosing a challenging question

Your research paper will be more interesting to both you and your audience if you base it on an intellectually challenging line of inquiry. Avoid factual questions that fail to provoke thought or engage readers in a debate; such questions lead to reports or lists of facts, not to researched arguments.

TOO FACTUAL	CHALLENGING
Is autism on the rise?	Why is autism so difficult to treat?
Where is wind energy being used?	What makes wind farms economically viable?

You will need to address a factual question in the course of answering a more challenging one. For example, if you were writing about promising treatments for autism, you would no

other 'alternative' types of research projects." The second study examines the kinds of research assignments students are asked to do in other disciplines.

TEACHING TIP

Students' research projects often succeed or fail because of the questions they ask. Take time in class to show students how to ask effective research questions and to give them practice doing so.

doubt answer the question "What is autism?" at some point in your paper and even analyze competing definitions of autism to help support your arguments about the challenges of treating the condition. It would be unproductive, however, to use the factual question as the focus for the entire paper.

Choosing a grounded question

Make sure that your research question is grounded, not too speculative. Although speculative questions—such as those that address morality or beliefs—are worth asking in a research paper, they are unsuitable central questions. For most college courses, the central argument of a research paper should be grounded in facts and should not be based entirely on beliefs.

TOO SPECULATIVE	GROUNDED
Is it wrong to share pornographic personal photos by cell phone?	What role should the US government play in regulating mobile content?
Do medical scientists have the right to experiment on animals?	How have technical breakthroughs made medical experiments on animals increasingly unnecessary?

Finding an entry point in a research conversation

As you pose preliminary research questions, you may wonder where and how to step into a research conversation. You may need to ask Who are the major writers or thinkers in the debate? What are the major arguments? What are the background and the scope of the problem? As you orient yourself, the following statements may help you find points of entry in a research conversation.

> On one side of the debate is position X, on the other side is Y, but there is a middle position, Z.

hackerhandbooks.com/bedhandbook

e Researched writing > Exercise: Research: 50–1

e Researched writing > As you write: Asking a research question

---

TEACHING TIP

Students benefit from keeping a research log to help them plan and organize their research. Many of the "As you write" exercises in the e-Pages ask students to use their research log to advance their thinking and to reflect on their evolution as a researcher.

TEACHING TIP

It can be useful for students to work in peer groups to practice posing and revising preliminary research questions.

The conventional view about the problem or issue needs to be challenged because . . .

Key details in this debate that have been overlooked are . . .

Researchers have drawn conclusion X from the evidence, but one could also draw conclusion Y.

50c Map out a search strategy.

A search strategy is a systematic plan for locating sources. To create a search strategy appropriate for your research question, it may help to consult a librarian and take a look at your library's Web site, which will give you an overview of available resources.

Keep in mind that no single search strategy works for every topic. For some topics, it may be useful to search for information in popular newspapers, magazines, and Web sites. For others, the best sources might be found in scholarly journals and books. Still other topics might be enhanced by field research—interviews, surveys, or direct observation.

With the help of a librarian, each of the students whose research essays can be found in this handbook constructed a search strategy appropriate for his or her research question.

Anna Orlov (see her full paper in 57b). Anna Orlov's topic, Internet surveillance in the workplace, was current and influenced by technological changes, so she relied heavily on recent sources, especially those online. To find information on her topic, Orlov decided to

- search the Web to locate current news, government publications, and information from organizations that focus on the issues surrounding technology and privacy
- check a library database for current research articles
- use the library catalog to search for a recently published book mentioned on several Web sites

WRITERS ON WRITING

The way to do research is to attack the facts at the point of greatest astonishment. — Celia Green

TEACHING TIP

When your students begin to work with sources, you may find it useful to create a scavenger hunt to get students inside the library (sample question: On what floor is the reference librarian's desk?) or to familiarize them with the library's home page (sample question: What databases does the library offer?). Work with a librarian to design something that meshes with your goals for the assignment or for the course.

Luisa Mirano (see her full paper in 62b). Luisa Mirano's topic, the limitations of medication for childhood obesity, is the subject of psychological studies as well as articles in newspapers and magazines aimed at the general public. Thinking that both scholarly and popular sources would be appropriate, Mirano decided to

- search the Web to see what issues about childhood obesity might be interesting
- refine her search to focus on medications reported in newspaper and magazine articles, advocacy Web sites, and government sites
- search specialized databases related to psychology and medicine for recent scholarly and scientific articles
- track down an article that several of her sources cited as an influential study

Ned Bishop (see pages from his paper in 63f). Ned Bishop's topic, Nathan Bedford Forrest's role in the Fort Pillow massacre during the Civil War, has been investigated and debated by historians. Given the nature of his historical topic, Bishop consulted a reference librarian and decided to

- locate books through the library's online catalog
- locate scholarly articles by searching a database specializing in history sources
- locate newspaper articles from 1864 by searching a historical newspaper database
- use the Web to track down additional primary documents mentioned in his sources

See 52a for more on assessing how different sources might contribute to your paper.

hackerhandbooks.com/bedhandbook

e Researched writing > As you write: Mapping out a search strategy

---

TEACHING TIP

Students benefit from understanding that an effective search strategy is at the heart of an effective research project. Ask students to use their research log to draft notes about their preliminary search strategy before they meet with a reference librarian.

SCHOLARS ON THE RESEARCH PROCESS

McClure, Randall. "WritingResearchWriting: The Semantic Web and the Future of the Research Project." *Computers and Composition* 28.4 (2011): 315–26. Print. According to McClure, conducting research and writing the researched essay are too often taught as separate tasks having separate processes. Research and writing, however, should be seen as steps in a single process, and this article explores how students'

NOTE FOR DISTANCE LEARNERS: Even if you are unable to visit the library, as an enrolled student you can still use its resources. Most libraries offer chat reference services and access to online databases, though you may have to follow special procedures to use them. Check your library's Web site for information.

50d Search efficiently; master a few shortcuts to finding good sources.

Most students use a combination of library databases and the Web in their research. You can save yourself a lot of time by becoming an efficient searcher.

Using the library

The Web site hosted by your college library is full of useful information. In addition to dozens of databases and links to other references, many libraries offer online subject guides as well as one-on-one help from reference librarians through e-mail or chat. You can save yourself a lot of time if you get advice from your instructor, a librarian, or your library's Web site about the best place to start your search for good sources.

Visiting your library can also be helpful. You can consult personally with reference librarians, who can show you what resources are available, help you refine your keywords for catalog or database searches, or suggest ways to narrow your search.

Savvy searchers cut down on the clutter of a broad search by adding additional search terms, limiting a search to recent publications, or clicking on a database option to look at only one type of source, such as peer-reviewed articles, if that's what is needed. When looking for books, you can broaden a catalog search by asking "What kind of book might contain the information I need?" After you've identified a promising book on the library shelves, looking through the books on nearby shelves can also be valuable.

interactions with semantic Web searching could help change ideas about the relationship between research and writing. McClure also deals with issues related to information overload and researcher anxiety.

SCHOLARS ON THE RESEARCH PROCESS

Profozich, Richard. "Coping with the Research Paper." *Teaching English in the Two-Year College* 24.4 (1997): 304–07. Print. In this brief piece, Profozich shares his methods for engaging students in inquiry and making students more comfortable with the research paper. Throughout his course, Profozich emphasizes process rather than final product, giving students ongoing opportunities to practice research. He places the research assignment early in the semester and provides social context for reading, research, discussion, and writing.

For her paper on Internet surveillance in the workplace, student writer Anna Orlov conducted a keyword search in a library database. She typed *"internet use"* and *employee* and *surveillance.* She also restricted the date of publication to the last five years to keep search results current. This search brought up twenty possible articles, some of which looked promising. Orlov e-mailed several full-text articles to herself and printed citations for others so that she could locate them in the library.

Using the Web

When using a search engine, it's a good idea to use terms that are as specific as possible and to enclose search phrases in quotation marks. You can refine your search by date or domain; for example, *autism site:.gov* will search for information about autism on government Web sites. Use clues in what you find (such as organizations or government agencies that seem particularly informative) to refine your search.

For her paper on Internet surveillance in the workplace, Anna Orlov had difficulty restricting the number of hits. When she typed the words *internet, surveillance, workplace,* and *privacy* into a search engine, she got more than 80,000 matches. After examining the first page of results and viewing some that looked promising, Orlov grouped her search terms into the phrases *"internet surveillance"* and *"workplace privacy"* and added the term *employee* to narrow the focus. The result was 422 matches. To refine her search further, Orlov clicked on Advanced Search and restricted her search to sites with URLs ending in .org and to those updated in the last three months.

As you examine sites, look for "about" links to learn about the site's author or sponsoring agency. Examine URLs for clues. Those that contain .k12 may be intended for young audiences; URLs ending in .gov lead to official information from US government entities. URLs may also offer clues about the country of origin: .au for Australia, .uk for United Kingdom, .in for India, and so on.

TEACHING TIP

Showing students how to be information-savvy will help them become more efficient and effective college researchers. Try the following exercise as a warm-up to individual research essays. Divide students into groups and give each group a topic to search. Ask students to work together to map out a search strategy, limiting and focusing where needed, and to find two to four promising sources. In a brief piece of writing, ask students to detail what search techniques they used and what sources they found.

If you aren't sure where a page originated, erase everything in the URL after the first slash in your address bar; the result should be the root page of the site, which may offer useful information about the site's purpose and audience (see p. 526). Avoid sites that provide information but no explanation of who the authors are or why the site was created. They may simply be advertising platforms attracting visitors with commonly sought information that is not original or substantial. For more on evaluating Web sites, see 52e.

Using bibliographies and citations as shortcuts

Scholarly books and articles list the works the author has cited, usually at the end. These lists are useful shortcuts to additional reliable sources on your topic. For example, most of the scholarly articles that student writer Luisa Mirano consulted contained citations to related research studies, selected by experts in the field. Through these citations, she quickly located other sources related to her topic, treatments for childhood obesity. Even popular sources such as news articles, videos, and interviews may refer to additional relevant sources that may be worth tracking down.

> **MAKING THE MOST OF YOUR HANDBOOK**
>
> Freewriting, listing, and clustering can help you come up with additional search terms.
>
> ▶ Exploring your subject: 1b

Using a variety of online tools and databases

You will probably find that your instructor, your librarian, or your library's Web site can be helpful in pointing you in the right direction once you have a topic and a research question. If you are still seeking some guidance about which Web sites, directories, databases, and other sources might yield useful searches, see the URL at the bottom of the page; follow the path for a list of sources that might provide a jump start.

hackerhandbooks.com/bedhandbook

e Researched writing > Finding research help: Locating sources using online tools and databases

SCHOLARS ON THE RESEARCH PROCESS

McClure, Randall. "Googlepedia: Turning Information Behaviors into Research Skills." In *Writing Spaces: Readings on Writing*. Ed. Charles Lowe and Pavel Zemliansky. Vol. 2. Anderson: Parlor Press, 2011. 221–41. Print. McClure offers case studies of two student researchers to explore the definition of information literacy and the overreliance on sites like Google and Wikipedia for college research. He uses what he learns from "Edward" and "Susan" to offer an "eight step research process to move from relying on instinctive information behaviors to acquiring solid research skills" (237).

CHECK URLS FOR CLUES ABOUT SPONSORSHIP

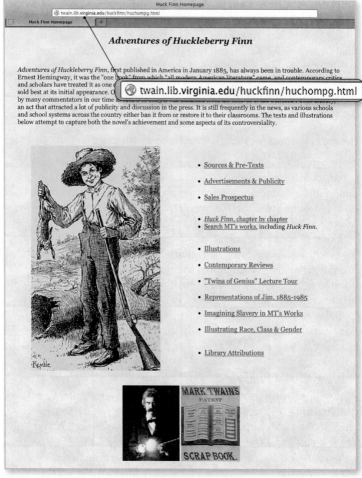

This source, from an internal page of a Web site, provides no indication of an author or a sponsor. Shortening the URL to http://twain.lib.virginia.edu/ leads to a main page that lists a university literature professor as the author and the University of Virginia Library as the sponsor.

TEACHING TIP

Students benefit from seeing how a topic is discussed differently in a popular magazine versus a scholarly journal. Choose a topic that is relevant to your course or your school, and bring in a magazine article and a journal article that cover this topic. As a class, discuss the samples, noting differences in tone, evidence, approach, citations, and use of visuals.

TEACHING TIP

Ask your students to write a research proposal to help them focus their search and to provide an opportunity for feedback. In writing the proposal, they need to identify their preliminary research questions and the research conversation they are entering, detail their search strategy, and provide a working bibliography based on their initial searches.

Tips for smart searching

For currency. If you need current information, news outlets such as the *New York Times* and the BBC, think tanks, government agencies, and advocacy groups may provide appropriate sources for your research. When using Google, you can limit a search to the most recent year, month, week, or day.

For authority. As you search, keep an eye out for any experts being cited in sources you examine. Following the trail of citation may lead you to sources by those experts — or the organizations they represent — that may be even more helpful. You can limit a Google search by type of Web site and type of source. Add *site:.gov* to focus on government sources or *filetype:pdf* to zero in on reports and research papers as PDF files.

For scholarship. When you need scholarly or peer-reviewed articles, use a library database to look for reports of original research written by the people who conducted it. Scholarly articles provide information about where the authors work (such as universities or research centers), use a formal writing style, and include footnotes or a bibliography. Articles that are only one or two pages long are probably not scholarly. In the sciences, peer-reviewed articles can be as short as three or four pages; in other disciplines, articles may be thirty or forty pages long. Don't rule out an article just because it's long. Read the abstract or the introductory paragraphs and the conclusion to see if the source is worth further investigation.

For context. Books are important sources in many fields such as history, philosophy, and sociology, and they often do a better job than scholarly articles of putting ideas in context. Don't be put off by their length. You don't have to read every book cover to cover. You may find a single chapter or even a few pages that are just what you need.

For firsthand authenticity. Some projects can benefit from primary sources; in some fields, primary sources may be required. In historical research, a primary source is one that originated in the historical period under discussion or is a firsthand account from a witness. In the sciences, a primary source (sometimes called a *primary article*) is a published report of research written by the scientist who conducted it. For more information, see page 546.

SCHOLARS ON RESEARCH ASSIGNMENTS

Sutton, Brian. "Writing in the Disciplines, First-Year Composition, and the Research Paper." *Language and Learning across the Disciplines* 2.1 (1997): 46–57. Print. Should the research assignments in first-year courses be designed to prepare students for specific writing assignments and discourse communities they will encounter in other academic disciplines? Or should they provide writers with general research skills that will transfer to a variety of settings? Building on existing scholarly work, Sutton revisits these questions, suggesting that we consider ways to incorporate both goals.

50e Conduct field research, if appropriate.

Your own field research can enhance or be the focus of a writing project. For a composition class, for example, you might want to interview a local politician about a current issue, such as the use of alternative energy sources. For a sociology class, you might decide to conduct a survey regarding campus trends in community service.

NOTE: Colleges and universities often require researchers to submit projects to an institutional review board (IRB) if the research involves human subjects outside a classroom setting. Before administering a survey or conducting other fieldwork, check with your instructor to see if IRB approval is required.

Interviewing

Interviews can often shed new light on a topic. Look for an expert who has firsthand knowledge of the subject, or seek out someone whose personal experience provides a valuable perspective on your topic.

When asking for an interview, be clear about who you are, what the purpose of the interview is, and how you would prefer to conduct it: via e-mail, over the phone, or in person. Plan for the interview by writing down a series of questions. Try to avoid questions with yes or no answers. Instead, ask questions that lead to facts, anecdotes, and opinions that will add a meaningful dimension to your paper.

INEFFECTIVE INTERVIEW QUESTIONS

How many years have you spent studying childhood obesity?

Is your work interesting?

EFFECTIVE INTERVIEW QUESTIONS

What are some current interpretations of the causes of childhood obesity?

What treatments have you found to be most effective? Why do you think they work?

SCHOLARS ON FIELD RESEARCH

Dellinger, Dixie G. "Alternatives to Clip and Stitch: Real Research and Writing in the Classroom." *English Journal* 78.5 (1989): 31–38. Print. Dellinger demonstrates the importance of having students use various tools of inquiry—interviews, surveys, experiments—to create their own research and then write about their discoveries.

When quoting your source (the interviewee) in your paper, be accurate and fair. To ensure accuracy, you might want to ask permission to record the interview or conduct it by e-mail.

Surveying opinion

For some topics, you may find it useful to survey opinions through written questionnaires, telephone or e-mail polls, or questions posted on a social media site. Many people are reluctant to fill out long questionnaires, so for a good response rate, limit your questions with your purpose in mind.

When possible, ask yes/no questions or give multiple-choice options. Surveys with such queries can be completed quickly, and the results are easy to tally. You may also want to ask a few open-ended questions to elicit more individual responses, some of which may be worth quoting in your paper.

SAMPLE YES/NO QUESTION

Do you favor the use of Internet surveillance in the workplace?

SAMPLE OPEN-ENDED QUESTION

What, if any, experiences have you had with Internet surveillance in the workplace?

Other field methods

Your firsthand visits to and observations of significant places, people, or events can enhance a paper in a variety of disciplines. If you aren't able to visit an organization, a company, or a historic site, you may find useful information on an official Web site or a phone number or e-mail address to use to contact a representative.

SCHOLARS ON RESEARCH ASSIGNMENTS

Davis, Robert, and Mark Shadle. "'Building a Mystery': Alternative Research Writing and the Academic Act of Seeking." *College Composition and Communication* 51.3 (2000): 417–41. Print. Davis and Shadle argue that the explosion of and access to information have made the research process more complex and that traditional approaches need to be reconsidered. They argue for four alternatives to the traditional research paper that they believe will help students think of research in terms of "uncertainty, passionate exploration, and mystery." This article offers a brief history of the traditional research paper, a description of the proposed four alternatives, and strategies for teaching them.

51 Managing information; taking notes responsibly

An effective researcher is a good record keeper. Whether you decide to keep records in your research log or in a file on your computer, you will need methods for managing information: maintaining a working bibliography (see 51a), keeping track of source materials (see 51b), and taking notes without plagiarizing your sources (see 51c). (For more on avoiding plagiarism, see 54 for MLA style, 59 for APA style, and 63b for *Chicago* style.)

51a Maintain a working bibliography.

Keep a record of any sources you read or view. This record, called a *working bibliography*, will help you compile the list of sources that will appear at the end of your paper. The format of this list depends on the documentation style you are using (for MLA style, see 56b; for APA style, see 61b; for *Chicago* style, see 63d). Using the proper style in your working bibliography will ensure that you have all the information you need to correctly cite any sources you use. (See 52f for advice on using your working bibliography as the basis for an annotated bibliography.)

Most researchers save bibliographic information from the library's catalog and databases and from the Web. The information you need is given in the chart on pages 532–33. If you download a visual, gather the same information as for a print source.

For Web sources, some bibliographic information may not be available, but spend time looking for it before assuming that it doesn't exist. When information isn't available on the home page, you may have to drill into the site, following links to interior

hackerhandbooks.com/bedhandbook

e Research writing > Choosing a documentation style

SCHOLARS ON PLAGIARISM

Colvin, Benie B. "Another Look at Plagiarism in the Digital Age: Is It Time to Turn in My Badge?" *Teaching English in the Two-Year College* 35.2 (2007): 149–58. Print. Colvin admits to being "torn" about how to respond to plagiarism and plagiarists in the academy. She surveys opinions from the field—from would-be police officers to those who "embrace a less punitive philosophy" about the treatment of student plagiarists. A key factor in incidents of plagiarism is that students don't trust their own voices and don't fully understand the concept of authorship. According to Colvin, too many first-year writers simply aren't

pages. (See also pp. 524 and 549 for more details about finding bibliographic information in online sources.)

51b Keep track of source materials.

The best way to keep track of source materials is to save a copy of each potential source as you conduct your research. Many database services will allow you to e-mail, save, or print citations or full texts of articles, and you can easily download, copy, or take screen shots of information from the Web.

Working with photocopies, printouts, and electronic files—as opposed to relying on memory or hastily written notes—has several benefits. You can highlight key passages, perhaps even color-coding them to reflect topics in your outline. You can get a head start on note taking. Finally, you reduce the chances of unintentional plagiarism since you will be able to compare your use of a source in your paper with the actual source, not just with your notes.

51c As you take notes, avoid unintentional plagiarism.

When you take notes and jot down ideas, be careful not to borrow exact language from your sources. Even if you half-copy the author's sentences—either by mixing the author's phrases with your own without using quotation marks or by plugging your synonyms into the author's sentence structure—you are committing plagiarism, a serious academic offense. (For examples of this kind of plagiarism, sometimes referred to as *patchwriting*, see 54b, 59b, and 63b.)

To take notes responsibly, resist the temptation to look at the source as you take notes—except when you are quoting. Keep the source close by so that you can check for accuracy, but don't try to put ideas in your own words with the source's sentences

confident authors; at the same time, too many teachers of student plagiarists take the easy route, teaching (and policing) through technology. Colvin advocates reworking assignments to avoid opportunities for plagiarism and cultivating an "active student/teacher partnership" to welcome students into the academy.

Information to collect for a working bibliography

For an entire book

- All authors; any editors or translators
- Title and subtitle
- Edition (if not the first)
- Publication information: city, publisher, and date
- Medium: print, Web, and so on
- Date you retrieved the source (for an online source)

For an article

- All authors of the article
- Title and subtitle of the article
- Title of the journal, magazine, or newspaper
- Date; volume, issue, and page numbers
- Medium: print, Web, DVD, and so on
- Date you retrieved the source (for an online source)

For an article retrieved from a database (in addition to preceding information)

- Name of the database
- Accession number or other number assigned by the database
- Digital object identifier (DOI), if there is one
- URL of the journal's home page, if there is no DOI
- Date you retrieved the source

NOTE: Use particular care when printing or saving articles in PDF files. The files themselves may not include some of the elements you need to cite the source properly. You may need to record additional information from the database or Web site where you retrieved the PDF file.

SCHOLARS ON PLAGIARISM

Klausman, Jeffrey. "Teaching Plagiarism in the Age of the Internet." *Teaching English in the Two-Year College* 27.2 (1999): 209–12. Print. Klausman writes that the use of electronic texts as sources, which may be easy to copy and incorporate in student writing, combined with students' attitudes toward text ownership on the Web, may lead to increased instances of unintentional plagiarism. Klausman describes his classroom activities that show students how to avoid plagiarism. He reinforces his discussion of plagiarism by pointing out to students how easily the reader can check electronic sources and how quickly an instructor can track down a suspected plagiarized passage.

INFORMATION TO COLLECT FOR A WORKING BIBLIOGRAPHY *(cont.)*

For a Web source (including visual, audio, and multimedia sources)

- All authors, editors, or composers of the source
- Editor or compiler of the Web source, if there is one
- Title and subtitle of the source
- Title of the longer work, if the source is contained in a longer work
- Title of the Web site
- Print publication information for the source, if available
- Online page or paragraph numbers, if any
- Date of online publication (or latest update)
- Sponsor of the site
- Date you accessed the source
- The site's URL

NOTE: For the exact bibliographic format to use in your working bibliography and in the final paper, see 56b (MLA), 61b (APA), or 63d (*Chicago*).

TIP: Your school may provide citation software, which automatically formats citations in any style using bibliographic information submitted by researchers. Many databases format citations with a mouse click, and some Web sites offer fill-in-the-blank forms for generating formatted citations. You must carefully proofread the results from these programs, however, because the citations sometimes include errors.

WRITING CENTER DIRECTORS ON PLAGIARISM

"Plagiarism often results from a lack of comprehension or impatience with reading; true paraphrasing, for example, depends on true understanding of the original text. Documentation trouble may start at the most global level of writing, when a writer lacks a strong sense of purpose and decides that some other author's purpose will do. The citations may be perfect, but the writing reflects nothing more than somebody else's focus and organization."

— Deanne Gute, writing specialist, University of Northern Iowa

in front of you. When you need to quote the exact words of a source, make sure you copy the words precisely and put quotation marks around them.

For strategies for avoiding plagiarism when using sources from the Web, see pages 536–37.

USING SOURCES RESPONSIBLY: Be especially careful when using copy-and-paste functions in electronic files. Some researchers plagiarize their sources because they lose track of which words came from sources and which are their own. To prevent unintentional plagiarism, put quotation marks around any source text that you copy during your research.

There are three kinds of note taking: summarizing, paraphrasing, and quoting. Be sure to keep track of exact page references for all three types of notes; you will need the page numbers later if you use the information in your paper.

Summarizing without plagiarizing

A summary condenses information, perhaps reducing a chapter to a short paragraph or a paragraph to a single sentence. A summary should be written in your own words; if you use phrases from the source, put them in quotation marks.

Academic English

Even in the early stages of note taking, it is important to keep in mind that in the United States written texts are considered an author's property. (This "property" isn't a physical object, so it is often referred to as *intellectual property*.) The author (or the publisher) owns the language as well as any original ideas contained in the writing, whether the source is published in print, online, or in electronic form. When you use another author's property in your own writing, you are required to follow certain conventions for citing the material, or you risk committing *plagiarism*.

TEACHING TIP

In class, discuss the advice in "Using sources responsibly" to show students the dangers of taking quotations out of context or taking quotations that aren't representative of the work as a whole.

TEACHING TIP

Throughout the research chapters, students will encounter tips that encourage them to think like researchers and to use sources responsibly. Use these tips to spark class discussion in an online discussion board or in a face-to-face setting—or to be the basis of a low-stakes (ungraded) writing opportunity related to conducting research and using a research process.

Here is a passage about marine pollution from a National Oceanic and Atmospheric Administration (NOAA) Web site. Following the passage is the student's summary. (The bibliographic information is recorded in MLA style.)

ORIGINAL SOURCE

A question that is often posed to the NOAA Marine Debris Program (MDP) is "How much debris is actually out there?" The MDP has recognized the need for this answer as well as the growing interest and value of citizen science. To that end, the MDP is developing and testing two types of monitoring and assessment protocols: 1) rigorous scientific survey and 2) volunteer at-sea visual survey. These types of monitoring programs are necessary in order to compare marine debris, composition, abundance, distribution, movement, and impact data on national and global scales.

— NOAA Marine Debris Program. "Efforts and Activities Related to the 'Garbage Patches.'" *Marine Debris*. NOAA Marine Debris Program, 2012. Web. 28 Nov. 2012.

SUMMARY

Source: NOAA Marine Debris Program. "Efforts and Activities Related to the 'Garbage Patches.'" *Marine Debris*. NOAA Marine Debris Program, 2012. Web. 28 Nov. 2012.

Having to field citizens' questions about the size of debris fields in Earth's oceans, the Marine Debris Program, an arm of the US National Oceanic and Atmospheric Administration, is currently implementing methods to monitor and draw conclusions about our oceans' patches of pollution (NOAA Marine Debris Program).

Paraphrasing without plagiarizing

Like a summary, a paraphrase is written in your own words; but whereas a summary reports significant information in fewer words than the source, a paraphrase retells the information in roughly the same number of words. If you retain occasional

SCHOLARS ON INTELLECTUAL PROPERTY

Zwagerman, Sean. "The Scarlet *P*: Plagiarism, Panopticism, and the Rhetoric of Academic Integrity." *College Composition and Communication* 59.4 (2008): 676–710. Print. Zwagerman argues that the "crusade" against plagiarists casts a darker shadow on a university than on its cheating students. He discusses academic anxiety, social pressure, and pragmatism as motivators for cheaters and critiques a new breed of detection technology. Infusing the writing process with trust and fostering engagement and critical thinking throughout a student's process are essential, according to Zwagerman.

choice phrases from the source, use quotation marks so that later you will know which phrases are not your own. If you paraphrase a source, you must still cite the source.

As you read the following paraphrase of the original source (see p. 535), notice that the language is significantly different from that in the original.

PARAPHRASE

Source: NOAA Marine Debris Program. "Efforts and Activities Related
   to the 'Garbage Patches.'" *Marine Debris*. NOAA Marine Debris
   Program, 2012. Web. 28 Nov. 2012.

Citizens concerned and curious about the amount, makeup, and locations
of debris patches in our oceans have been pressing NOAA's Marine Debris
Program for answers. In response, the organization is preparing to
implement plans and standards for expert study and nonexpert observation,
both of which will yield results that will be helpful in determining the
significance of the pollution problem (NOAA Marine Debris Program).

Using quotation marks to avoid plagiarizing

A quotation consists of the exact words from a source. In your notes, put all quoted material in quotation marks; do not assume that you will remember later which words, phrases, and passages you have quoted and which are your own. When you quote, be sure to copy the words of your source exactly, including punctuation and capitalization.

QUOTATION

Source: NOAA Marine Debris Program. "Efforts and Activities Related
   to the 'Garbage Patches.'" *Marine Debris*. NOAA Marine Debris
   Program, 2012. Web. 28 Nov. 2012.

The NOAA Marine Debris Program has noted that, as our oceans become
increasingly polluted, surveillance is "necessary in order to compare
marine debris, composition, abundance, distribution, movement, and
impact data on national and global scales."

Avoiding plagiarism from the Web

Understand what plagiarism is. When you use another author's intellectual property—language, visuals, or ideas—in your own writing without giving proper credit, you commit a kind of academic theft called *plagiarism*.

Treat Web sources the same way you treat print sources. Any language that you find on the Web must be carefully cited, even if the material is in the public domain (which generally includes older works no longer protected by copyright law) or is publicly accessible on free sites. When you use material from Web sites sponsored by federal, state, or municipal governments (.gov sites) or by nonprofit organizations (.org sites), you must acknowledge that material, too, as intellectual property owned by those agencies.

Keep track of which words come from sources and which are your own. To prevent unintentional plagiarism when you copy and paste passages from Web sources to an electronic file, put quotation marks around any text that you have inserted into your own work. During note taking and drafting you might use a different color font or highlighting to draw attention to text taken from sources—so that material from articles, Web sites, and other sources stands out unmistakably as someone else's words.

Avoid Web sites that bill themselves as "research services" and sell essays. When you use Web search engines to research a topic, you will often see links to sites that appear to offer legitimate writing support but that actually sell college essays. Of course, submitting a paper that you have purchased is cheating, but even using material from such a paper is considered plagiarism.

For details on avoiding plagiarism while working with sources, see 54b (MLA), 59b (APA), and 63b (*Chicago*).

52 Evaluating sources

For a college writing assignment in any discipline, you can often locate dozens or even hundreds of potential sources for your topic—far more than you will have time to read. Your challenge will be to determine what kinds of sources you need and to zero in on a reasonable number of quality sources. This kind of decision making is referred to as *evaluating sources*. When you evaluate a source, you make a judgment about how useful the source is to your project. Evaluating requires you to ask critical questions about sources as you plan, as you search, as you read, and as you write—all the while keeping an open mind.

Evaluating sources isn't something you do in one sitting. Being an effective researcher doesn't mean following a formula (*find some sources > evaluate those sources > write the paper*). Rather, it means looking at the process as more dynamic. After you do some planning, searching, and reading, for example, you may reflect on the information you have and conclude that you need to rethink your research question—and so you may return to assessing the kinds of sources you need. Or you may be midway through drafting your paper when you begin to question a particular source's credibility, at which point you return to searching and reading.

52a Think about how sources might contribute to your writing.

How you plan to use sources in your paper will affect how you evaluate them. Not every source must directly support your

---

TEACHING TIP

Encourage students to view the evaluation of sources as an ongoing process and not as an isolated stage. Ask students to use their research logs to judge the usefulness of sources while planning, searching, reading, and writing.

Viewing evaluation as a process

When you use sources in your writing, make a habit of evaluating, or judging the value of, those sources at each stage of your project. The following questions may help.

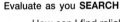

Evaluate as you PLAN

What kinds of sources do I need?

What do I need these sources to help me do: Define? Persuade? Inform?

Evaluate as you SEARCH

How can I find reliable sources that help me answer my research question?

Which sources will help me build my credibility as a researcher?

Evaluate as you READ

What positions do these sources take in the debate on my topic? What are their biases?

How do these sources inform my own understanding of the topic and the position I will take?

Evaluate as you WRITE

How do the sources I've chosen help me make my point?

How do my own ideas fit into the conversation on my research topic?

---

thesis; sources can have a range of functions in a paper. They can do any of the following:

- provide background information or context for your topic
- explain terms or concepts that your readers might not understand
- provide evidence for your argument
- lend authority to your argument
- identify a gap or contradiction in the conversation
- offer counterarguments and alternative interpretations to your argument

As you plan, you will need to think through the kinds of sources that will help you fulfill your purpose. The following are notes that one student took as she planned a paper.

Purpose: to persuade

My argument: that public funding for the arts should be granted on artistic merit alone and not on so-called decency standards

Sources I could use for background/context:

- 1998 Supreme Court decision (*National Endowment for the Arts v. Finley*)
- First Amendment

Sources that support my argument:

- interviews of controversial artists Karen Finley and Tim Miller

Source that represents an alternative viewpoint:

- passages from a profile of conservative North Carolina senator Jesse Helms

With her overall purpose in mind, the student judged each source according to the specific role it would play in her argument. For more examples of how student writers use sources for a variety of purposes, see 53c and 58c.

52b Select sources worth your time and attention.

As you search for sources in databases, the library catalog, and search engines, you're likely to get many more results than you can read or use. This section explains how to scan through the results for the most promising sources, and how to evaluate them as you preview them, to see whether they meet your needs.

Scanning search results

As you scan through a list of search results, watch for clues indicating whether a source might be useful for your purposes or not

hackerhandbooks.com/bedhandbook

e Researched writing > As you write: Planning with sources

TEACHING TIP

Have students examine the range of functions that sources play in Sam Jacobs's research argument (in section 6k) or in Anna Orlov's MLA research paper (in section 57b). You might assign students in small groups to annotate these papers to identify the functions of each source. You can share responses in class.

TEACHING TIP

Consider assigning the "As you write" writing prompts, found in the handbook's Integrated Media at hackerhandbooks.com/bedhandbook. These activities, referenced at the bottoms of many pages in the handbook, help students to apply the handbook's lessons to the writing they are doing for the course.

worth pursuing. You will need to use somewhat different strategies when scanning search results from a database, a library catalog, and a Web search engine.

Databases   Most databases list at least the following information, which can help you decide if a source is relevant, current, and scholarly (see the chart on p. 544).

> Title and brief description (How relevant?)
>
> Date (How current?)
>
> Name of periodical or other publication (How scholarly?)
>
> Length (How extensive in coverage?)

Many databases allow you to sort your list of results by relevance or date; sorting may help you scan the information more efficiently.

Library catalogs   The library's catalog usually lists basic information about books, periodicals, DVDs, and other material—enough to give you a first impression (see also p. 523). As in database search results, the title and date of publication of books and other sources listed in the catalog will often be your first clues about whether the source is worth consulting. If a title looks interesting, you can click on it for information about the subject matter and length. For books or other long sources, such as reports, a table of contents may also be available.

Web search engines   Reliable and unreliable sources live side-by-side online. As you scan through search results, look for the following clues about the probable relevance, currency, and reliability of a Web site.

> The title, keywords, headings, and lead-in text
> (How relevant?)
>
> A date (How current?)

SCHOLARS ON EVALUATING SOURCES

Elder, Linda, and Richard Paul. "Critical Thinking and the Art of Close Reading, Part IV." *Journal of Developmental Education* 28.2 (2004): 36–37. Print. In the last of a series of four columns on the topic of close reading, Elder and Paul outline skills needed for reading at different levels: paraphrasing the text, explicating the thesis, analyzing the author's logic, and evaluating or assessing that logic.

An indication of the site's sponsor or purpose (How reliable?)

The URL, especially the domain name extension: for example, .com, .edu, .gov, or .org (How relevant? How reliable?)

At the bottom of this page are a few of the results that student writer Luisa Mirano retrieved after typing the keywords *childhood obesity* into a search engine; she limited her search to works with those words in the title.

Mirano found the first site, sponsored by a research-based organization, promising enough to explore for her paper. The second and fourth sites held less promise because they seemed to offer popular rather than scholarly information. In addition, the second site was full of distracting advertisements. Mirano rejected the third source not because she doubted its reliability—in fact, research from the National Institutes of Health was what she hoped to find—but because a skim of its contents revealed that the information was too general for her purposes.

EVALUATING SEARCH RESULTS: INTERNET SEARCH ENGINE

Content from a research-based organization. Promising.

> **American Obesity Association - Childhood Obesity**
> **Childhood Obesity. Obesity in children** ... Note: The term "**childhood obesity**" may refer to both **children** and adolescents. In general, we ...
> www.**obesity**.org/subs/**childhood**/ - 17k - Jan 8, 2005 - <u>Cached</u> - <u>Similar pages</u>

Popular rather than scholarly source. Not relevant.

> **Childhood Obesity**
> KS Logo, **Childhood Obesity**. advertisement. Source. ERIC Clearinghouse on Teaching and Teacher Education. Contents. ... Back to the Top Causes of **Childhood Obesity**. ...
> www.kidsource.com/kidsource/content2/**obesity**.html - 18k - <u>Cached</u> - <u>Similar pages</u>

Content too general. Not relevant.

> **Childhood Obesity**, June 2002 Word on Health - National Institutes ...
> **Childhood Obesity** on the Rise, an article in the June 2002 edition of The NIH Word on Health - Consumer Information Based on Research from the National ...
> www.nih.gov/news/WordonHealth/ jun2002/**childhoodobesity**.htm - 22k -
> <u>Cached</u> - <u>Similar pages</u>

Popular and too general. Not relevant.

> MayoClinic.com - **Childhood obesity**: Parenting advice
> ... **Childhood obesity**: Parenting advice By Mayo Clinic staff. ... Here are some other tips to help your **obese child** — and yourself. Be a positive role model. ...
> www.mayoclinic.com/invoke.cfm?id=FL00058 - 42k - Jan 8, 2005 - <u>Cached</u> - <u>Similar pages</u>

SCHOLARS ON EVALUATING SOURCES

Grobman, Laurie. "'Found It on the Web, so Why Can't I Put It in My Paper?' Authorizing Basic Writers." *Journal of Basic Writing* 18.1 (1999): 76–90. Print. Grobman suggests that Web sources—more than traditional library sources—provide students with opportunities to analyze and evaluate information with a greater sense of authority. Grobman writes that when students search the Web, they are making decisions throughout the process that they don't make when they use library sources. And because of the range of information available on the Web, they are also developing a broader understanding of "texts" and the ways they are used.

Previewing sources

Once you have decided that a source looks promising, preview it quickly to see whether it lives up to its promise. If you can evaluate as you search, rejecting irrelevant or unreliable sources before actually reading them, you will save yourself time.

PREVIEWING AN ARTICLE

- Consider the publication in which the article is printed. Is it a scholarly journal (see the chart on p. 545)? A popular magazine? A newspaper with a national reputation?

- For a magazine or journal article, look for an abstract or a statement of purpose at the beginning; also look for a summary at the end.

- For a newspaper article, focus on the headline and the opening paragraphs for relevance.

- Scan any headings and look at any visuals — charts, graphs, diagrams, or illustrations — that might indicate the article's focus and scope.

PREVIEWING A BOOK

- Glance through the table of contents, keeping your research question in mind. Even if the entire book is not relevant, parts of it may prove useful.

- Scan the preface in search of a statement of the author's purposes.

- Use the index to look up a few words related to your topic.

- If a chapter looks useful, read its opening and closing paragraphs and skim any headings.

WRITERS ON WRITING

What is research but a blind date with knowledge? — Anonymous

The beginning of research is curiosity, its essence is discernment, and its goal truth and justice. — Isaac H. Satanov

Research is formalized curiosity. It is poking and prying with a purpose. — Zora Neale Hurston

PREVIEWING A WEB SITE

- Check to see if the sponsor is a reputable organization, a government agency, or a university. Is the group likely to look at only one side of a debatable issue?

- If you have landed on an internal page of a site and no author or sponsor is evident, try navigating to the home page, either through a link or by truncating the URL (see p. 526).

- Try to determine the purpose of the Web site. Is the site trying to sell a product? Promote an idea? Inform the public? Is the purpose consistent with your research?

- If the Web site includes statistical data (tables, graphs, charts), can you tell how and by whom the statistics were compiled? Is research cited?

- Find out when the site was created or last updated. Is it current enough for your purposes?

52c Select appropriate versions of online sources.

An online source may appear as an abstract, an excerpt, or a full-text work. It is important to distinguish among these versions of sources and to use a complete version of a source, preferably one with page numbers, for your research.

Abstracts and excerpts are shortened versions of complete works. An abstract—a summary of a work's contents—might appear in a database record for a source and can give you clues about the usefulness of the source for your paper. Abstracts are brief (usually fewer than five hundred words) and often do not contain enough information to function alone as sources in a research paper. Reading the complete article is the best way to understand the author's argument before referring to it in your own writing. If you cannot access the complete article electronically, ask a librarian if the library has a print copy.

An excerpt is the first few sentences or paragraphs of a newspaper or magazine article and sometimes appears in a

Determining if a source is scholarly

For many college assignments, you will be asked to use scholarly sources. These are written by experts for a knowledgeable audience and usually go into more depth than books and articles written for a general audience. (Scholarly sources are sometimes called *refereed* or *peer-reviewed* because the work is evaluated by experts in the field before publication.) To determine if a source is scholarly, you should look for the following:

- Formal language and presentation
- Authors who are academics or scientists
- Footnotes or a bibliography documenting the works cited by the author in the source
- Original research and interpretation (rather than a summary of other people's work)
- Quotations from and analysis of primary sources (in humanities disciplines such as literature, history, and philosophy)
- A description of research methods or a review of related research (in the sciences and social sciences)

NOTE: In some databases, searches can be limited to refereed or peer-reviewed journals.

list of hits in an online search. From an excerpt, you can often determine whether the complete article would be useful for your paper. Be sure to retrieve and read the full text of any article you might want to cite.

A full-text work may appear online as a PDF file or as an HTML file (sometimes called a *text file*). A PDF file is usually an exact copy of the pages of an article or a book as they appeared in print, including the page numbers. A full-text document that appears as an HTML or a text file is not paginated. If your source is available in both formats, choose the PDF file for your research because you will be able to cite specific page numbers.

52d Read with an open mind and a critical eye.

As you begin reading the sources you have chosen, keep an open mind. Do not let your personal beliefs prevent you from listening to new ideas and opposing viewpoints. Be curious about the wide range of positions in the research conversation you are entering. Your research question should guide you as you engage your sources.

When you read critically, you are not necessarily judging an author's work harshly; you are simply examining its assumptions, assessing its evidence, and weighing its conclusions.

Reading critically means

- reading carefully (*What does the source say?*)
- reading skeptically (*Are any of the author's points or conclusions problematic?*)
- reading evaluatively (*How does this source help me make my argument?*)

To see one student's careful reading of a source text, see 5a.

USING SOURCES RESPONSIBLY: Take time to read the entire source, if possible, to understand an author's arguments, assumptions, and conclusions. Try to avoid taking quotations from the first few pages of a source before you understand if the words and ideas are representative of the work as a whole.

Distinguishing between primary and secondary sources

As you begin assessing evidence in a source, determine whether you are reading a primary or a secondary source. Primary sources include original documents such as letters, diaries, films, legislative bills, laboratory studies, field research reports, and eyewitness accounts. Secondary sources are commentaries on primary sources—another writer's opinions about or interpretation of a primary source.

TEACHING TIP

Students will benefit from either reading or reviewing the key lessons in sections 4 ("Reading and writing critically") and 6 ("Reading and writing arguments"). If you have not assigned these sections, consider consulting key passages as a class or assigning students to read the two sections for homework.

Although a primary source is not necessarily more reliable than a secondary source, it has the advantage of being a firsthand account. You can better evaluate what a secondary source says if you have first read any primary sources it discusses.

Being alert for signs of bias

Bias is a way of thinking, a tendency to be partial, that prevents people and publications from viewing a topic objectively. Both in print and online, some sources are more objective than others. If you are exploring the rights of organizations like WikiLeaks to distribute sensitive government documents over the Internet, for example, you may not find objective, unbiased information in a US State Department report. If you are researching timber harvesting practices, you are likely to encounter bias in publications sponsored by environmental groups. As you read sources, however, you need not reject those that are biased. Publications that are known to be reputable can be editorially biased. As a researcher, you will need to consider any suspected bias as you assess the source. If you are uncertain about a source's special interests, seek the help of a reference librarian.

Like publishers, some authors are more objective than others. If you have reason to believe that a writer is particularly biased, you will want to assess his or her arguments with special care. For a list of questions worth asking, see the chart on page 549.

Assessing the author's argument

In nearly all subjects worth writing about, there is some element of argument, so expect to encounter authors who disagree. In fact, areas of disagreement give you entry points in a research conversation. The questions in the chart on page 155 can help you weigh the strengths and weaknesses of each author's arguments.

> **MAKING THE MOST OF YOUR HANDBOOK**
>
> Good college writers read critically.
>
> ► Judging whether a source is reasonable: 6a
>
> ► Judging whether a source is fair: 6c

Evaluating all sources

Checking for signs of bias

- Does the author or publisher endorse political or religious views that could affect objectivity?

- Is the author or publisher associated with a special-interest group, such as PETA or the National Rifle Association, that might present only one side of an issue?

- Are alternative views presented and addressed? How fairly does the author treat opposing views? (See 6c.)

- Does the author's language show signs of bias? (See 6b.)

Assessing an argument

- What is the author's central claim or thesis?

- How does the author support this claim — with relevant and sufficient evidence or with just a few anecdotes or emotional examples?

- Are statistics consistent with those you encounter in other sources? Have they been used fairly? Does the author explain where the statistics come from?

- Are any of the author's assumptions questionable?

- Does the author consider opposing arguments and refute them persuasively? (See 6c.)

- Does the author use flawed logic? (See 6a.)

52e Assess Web sources with care.

Sources found on the Web can provide valuable information, but verifying their credibility may take time. Before using a Web source in your paper, make sure you know who created the material and for what purpose. Sites with reliable information can stand up to careful scrutiny. For a checklist on evaluating Web sources, see the chart on page 549.

hackerhandbooks.com/bedhandbook

🄴 Researched writing > As you write: Evaluating sources you find on the Web

Evaluating sources you find on the Web

Authorship

- Does the Web site or document have an author? You may need to do some clicking and scrolling to find the author's name. If you have landed directly on an internal page of a site, for example, you may need to navigate to the home page or find an "about this site" link to learn the name of the author.

- If there is an author, can you tell whether he or she is knowledgeable and credible? When the author's qualifications aren't listed on the site itself, look for links to the author's home page, which may provide evidence of his or her interests and expertise.

Sponsorship

- Who, if anyone, sponsors the site? The sponsor of a site is often named and described on the home page.

- What does the URL tell you? The domain name extension often indicates the type of group hosting the site: commercial (.com), educational (.edu), nonprofit (.org), governmental (.gov), military (.mil), or network (.net). URLs may also indicate a country of origin: .uk (United Kingdom) or .jp (Japan), for instance.

Purpose and audience

- Why was the site created: To argue a position? To sell a product? To inform readers?

- Who is the site's intended audience?

Currency

- How current is the site? Check for the date of publication or the latest update, often located at the bottom of the home page or at the beginning or end of an internal page.

- How current are the site's links? If many of the links no longer work, the site may be too dated for your purposes.

EVALUATING A WEB SITE: CHECKING RELIABILITY

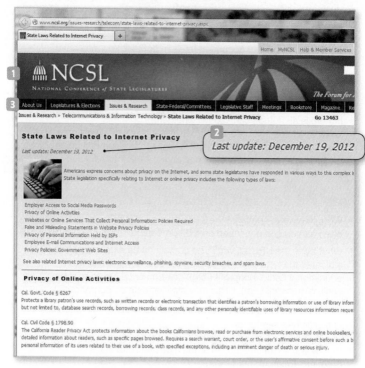

1 This page on Internet monitoring and workplace privacy appears on a Web site sponsored by the National Conference of State Legislatures. The NCSL is a bipartisan group that functions as a clearinghouse of ideas and research of interest to state lawmakers. It is also a lobby for state issues before the US government. The domain ending .org marks this sponsor as a nonprofit organization.

2 A clear date of publication shows currency.

3 An "About Us" page confirms that this is a credible organization whose credentials can be verified.

EVALUATING A WEB SITE: CHECKING PURPOSE

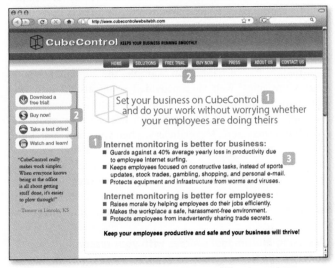

1 The site is sponsored by a company that specializes in employee-monitoring software.

2 Repeated links for trial downloads and purchase suggest the site's intended audience: consumers seeking to purchase software (probably not researchers seeking detailed information about employees' use of the Internet in the workplace).

3 The site appears to provide information and even shows statistics from studies, but ultimately the purpose of the site is to sell a product.

Student writer Ned Bishop came across unreliable Web sources while researching his topic, the Fort Pillow massacre. This topic is of great interest to Civil War buffs, who might not have scholarly backgrounds. One impressive-looking site turned out to have been created by a high school junior—an intelligent young man, no doubt, but not an authority on the subject.

In researching Internet surveillance and workplace privacy, student writer Anna Orlov encountered sites that raised her suspicions. In particular, some sites were authored by surveillance software companies, which have an obvious interest in focusing on the benefits of such software to company management.

Knowing that the creator of a site is an amateur or could be biased is not sufficient reason, however, to reject the site's information out of hand. For example, the surveillance software companies' Web sites provided some insight into why company management would want to monitor employees, and the high school junior had intelligent things to say about the Fort Pillow massacre. Nevertheless, when you know something about the creator of a site and have a sense of a site's purpose, you will be in a good position to evaluate the likely worth of its information. Consider, for example, the two sites pictured on pages 550 and 551. Anna Orlov decided that the first Web site would be more useful for her project than sites like the second.

Assessing multimodal sources with your research question in mind

You may find that, for your topic, the best sources are videos such as public service ads or interviews delivered as podcasts or blog posts that include opinion, data, or graphics. Though these are generally not considered scholarly sources, such sources may be perfectly appropriate given your topic, your purpose, and your audience. When student writer Anna Orlov entered a debate about the rights of employers to monitor employees' time on the Web, she used a CBS video that she found on YouTube. It added the perspective and the evidence she needed: employers discussing the uses of the social Web for corporate benefit.

hackerhandbooks.com/bedhandbook

e Researched writing > As you write: Developing an annotated bibliography
e Researched writing > Sample student writing
 > Orlov, "Online Monitoring: A Threat to Employee Privacy in the Wired Workplace: An Annotated Bibliography" (annotated bibliography)
 > Niemeyer, "Keynesian Policy: Implications for the Current U.S. Economic Crisis" (annotated bibliography)

TEACHING TIP

Ask students to compose an annotated bibliography either as a stand-alone project or as a step in a larger research project. Writing an annotated bibliography as a step in the research process helps students figure out how each source will contribute to their project.

52f Construct an annotated bibliography.

Section 51a describes how to write a working bibliography, a document that helps you keep track of publication information for all of the sources you may be considering for your project. You may be assigned to write an annotated bibliography, a more formal document in which you summarize and evaluate those sources—at least the most promising ones. Writing brief sentences summarizing key points of a source will help you identify how the source relates to your argument and to your other sources and will help you judge whether the source is relevant and appropriate for your project. Clarifying your sources' ideas will help you separate them from your own and from each other, and it will also help you move toward a draft in which you synthesize sources and present your own research thesis. (See 55c and 60c for more on synthesis.) For more help with writing an annotated bibliography, see the Writing Guide on pages 554–55.

SAMPLE ANNOTATED BIBLIOGRAPHY ENTRY (MLA STYLE)

Gonsalves, Chris. "Wasting Away on the Web." *eWeek.com*. Ziff Davis Enterprise Holdings, 8 Aug. 2005. Web. 27 Nov. 2009.

Summarize the source.

In this editorial, Gonsalves considers the implications of several surveys, including one in which 61% of respondents said that their companies have the right to spy on them. The author agrees with this majority, claiming that it's fine if his company chooses to monitor him as long as the company discloses its monitoring practices. He adds that he would prefer not to know the extent of the monitoring. This article, though not entirely objective, offers an employee's perspective on Internet surveillance in the workplace. It also contradicts some of my other sources, which claim that employees want to know and should know all the details of their company's monitoring procedures.

Annotations should be three to seven sentences long.

Evaluate the source for bias and relevance.

Interpret the relationship between this source and others in the bibliography.

Writing Guide
Annotated Bibliography

An **annotated bibliography** gives you an opportunity to summarize, evaluate, and record publication information for your sources before drafting your research paper. You summarize each source to understand its main ideas; you evaluate each source for accuracy, quality, and relevance. Finally, you reflect, asking yourself how the source will contribute to your research project. A sample annotated bibliography entry appears on page 553.

Key features

- **A list of sources arranged in alphabetical order by author** includes complete bibliographic information for each source.

- **A brief entry for each source** is typically one hundred to two hundred words.

- **A summary** of each source states the work's main ideas and key points briefly and accurately. The summary is written in the third person and the present tense. Summarizing helps you test your understanding of a source and convey its meaning responsibly.

- **An evaluation** of the source's role and usefulness in your project includes an assessment of the source's strengths and limitations, the author's qualifications and expertise, and the function of the source in your project. Evaluating a source helps you analyze how the source fits into your project and separate the source's ideas from your own.

Thinking ahead: Presenting or publishing

You may be asked to submit your annotated bibliography electronically. If this is the case, and if any of your sources are from the Web, you may want to format some of the text as hyperlinks to make it easier for your readers to access the sources if they need to do so.

Writing your annotated bibliography

Explore

For each source, begin by brainstorming responses to questions such as the following.

- What is the purpose of the source? Who is its intended audience?
- What is the author's thesis? What evidence supports the thesis?
- Do you agree or disagree with the author's conclusions?
- What qualifications and expertise does the author bring? Does the author have any biases or make any questionable assumptions?
- Why do you think this source is useful for your project?
- How does this source relate to the other sources in your bibliography?

Draft

- Arrange the sources in alphabetical order by author (or by title for works with no author).
- Provide consistent bibliographic information for each source. For the exact bibliographic format, see 56b (MLA), 61b (APA), or 63d (*Chicago*).
- Start your summary by identifying the thesis and purpose of the source as well as the credentials of the source's author.
- Keep your research question in mind. How does this source contribute to your project? How does it help you take your place in the conversation?

Revise

Ask reviewers for specific feedback. Here are some questions to guide their comments.

- Is each source summarized clearly? Have you identified the author's main idea?
- For each source, have you made a clear judgment about how and why the source is useful for your project?
- Have you used quotation marks around exact words from a source?

555

Writing MLA papers

Most English instructors and some humanities instructors will ask you to document your sources with the Modern Language Association (MLA) system of citations described in section 56.

When writing an MLA paper that is based on sources, you face three main challenges: (1) supporting a thesis, (2) citing your sources and avoiding plagiarism, and (3) integrating quotations and other source material.

Examples in sections 53–55 are drawn from a student's research related to online monitoring of employees' computer use. Anna Orlov's research paper, which argues that electronic surveillance in the workplace threatens employees' privacy, appears on pages 656–61.

NOTE: For advice on finding and evaluating sources and on managing information in all your college courses, see sections 50–52.

53   Supporting a thesis

Most research assignments ask you to form a thesis, or main idea, and to support that thesis with well-organized evidence. (See also 1c.) A working thesis will help you focus your project but remain flexible as you draft. Research is an ongoing process; your ideas and your working thesis will evolve as you learn more about your topic.

53a   Form a working thesis.

Once you have read a variety of sources, considered your issue from different perspectives, and chosen an entry point in the research conversation (see 50b), you are ready to form a working thesis: a one-sentence (or occasionally a two-sentence) statement of your central idea. (See also 1c and 53d.) Because it is a working, or tentative, thesis, it is flexible enough to change as your ideas develop. Ultimately, the thesis expresses not your opinion but your informed, reasoned position.

In a research paper, your thesis will answer the central research question that you pose (see 50b). Here, for example, are student writer Anna Orlov's research question and working thesis.

RESEARCH QUESTION

Should employers monitor their employees' online activities in the workplace?

WORKING THESIS

Employers should not monitor their employees' online activities because electronic surveillance can compromise workers' privacy.

hackerhandbooks.com/bedhandbook

e Researched writing > As you write: Writing a working thesis for a research paper
e Researched writing > Exercises: MLA papers: 53–1 and 53–2

TEACHING TIP

Consider building a research proposal into a research paper assignment. One benefit is that writing a research proposal allows students to define their topic as meaningful and relevant. Pitch the proposal as a persuasive piece of writing: Students have to tell you why their topic matters, who the stakeholders are, and what's at stake. A proposal also gives students the opportunity to explore the debate and present different positions in the course of framing their own position.

After you have written a rough draft and perhaps done more reading, you may decide to revise your thesis, as Orlov did. Her revised thesis represents a fuller understanding of the different positions in the debate about workplace monitoring.

REVISED THESIS

Although companies often have legitimate concerns that lead them to monitor employees' Internet usage—from expensive security breaches to reduced productivity—the benefits of electronic surveillance are outweighed by its costs to employees' privacy and autonomy.

The thesis usually appears at the end of the introductory paragraph. To read Anna Orlov's thesis within her introduction, see page 656.

53b Organize ideas with a rough outline.

The body of your paper will consist of evidence in support of your thesis. It will be useful to sketch an informal plan that helps you begin to organize your ideas. Anna Orlov, for example, used this simple plan to outline the structure of her argument:

> **MAKING THE MOST OF YOUR HANDBOOK**
>
> It's helpful to start off with a working thesis and a rough outline — especially when writing from sources.
>
> ▶ Draft a working thesis: 1c
> ▶ Draft a plan: 1d

- Electronic surveillance allows employers to monitor workers more efficiently than they could do with older types of surveillance.
- Some experts argue that companies have important financial and legal reasons to monitor employees' Internet usage.
- But monitoring employees' Internet usage may lower worker productivity if workers feel their privacy is violated and begin to distrust their employer.

- Current laws do little to protect employees' privacy rights, so employees and employers have to negotiate the potential risks and benefits of electronic surveillance.

After you have written a rough draft, a more formal outline can be a useful way to shape the complexities of your argument (see 1d).

53c Use sources to inform and support your argument.

Used thoughtfully, the source materials you have gathered will make your argument more complex and convincing for readers. Sources can play several different roles as you develop your points.

Providing background information or context

You can use facts and statistics to support generalizations or to establish the importance of your topic, as student writer Anna Orlov does in her introduction.

> As the Internet has become an integral tool of businesses, company policies on Internet usage have become as common as policies regarding vacation days or sexual harassment. A 2005 study by the American Management Association and ePolicy Institute found that 76% of companies monitor employees' use of the Web, and the number of companies that block employees' access to certain Web sites has increased 27% since 2001 (1).

Explaining terms or concepts

If readers are unlikely to be familiar with a word or an idea important to your topic, you must explain it for them. Quoting or paraphrasing a source can help you define terms and concepts in accessible language.

TEACHING TIP

Make an appointment with a reference librarian for a session with your class. A reference librarian can help students think about the roles that various sources might play in their college papers and begin to think strategically about their searching.

> One popular monitoring method is keystroke logging, which is done
> by means of an undetectable program on employees' computers. . . .
> As Lane explains, these programs record every key entered into the
> computer in hidden directories that can later be accessed or uploaded
> by supervisors; the programs can even scan for keywords tailored to
> individual companies (128-29).

Supporting your claims

As you draft your argument, make sure to back up your assertions
with facts, examples, and other evidence from your research.
(See also 6h.) Orlov, for example, uses an anecdote from one of
her sources to support her claim that limiting computer access
causes resentment among a company's staff.

> Monitoring online activities can have the unintended effect
> of making employees resentful. . . . Kesan warns that "prohibiting
> personal use can seem extremely arbitrary and can seriously harm
> morale. . . . Imagine a concerned parent who is prohibited from
> checking on a sick child by a draconian company policy" (315-16).
> As this analysis indicates, employees can become disgruntled when
> Internet usage policies are enforced to their full extent.

Lending authority to your argument

Expert opinion can give weight to your argument. (See also 6h.)
But don't rely on experts to make your arguments for you. Construct your argument in your own words and, when appropriate,
cite the judgment of an authority in the field to support your
position.

> Additionally, many experts disagree with employers' assumption
> that online monitoring can increase productivity. Employment law
> attorney Joseph Schmitt argues that, particularly for employees who
> are paid a salary rather than an hourly wage, "a company shouldn't

---

TEACHING TIP

Assign students to work in pairs or small groups to identify the roles
that sources play in a text that you distribute. Choose a text that is fairly
brief (no more than three pages) and uses at least three sources, one of
which might be visual. The text should be short enough so that students
can complete the activity in a single class period or a manageable chat
session online. Ask students to identify the sources the writer has used
as well as the function of each source in the context of the piece of writing. Does the source provide background? Explain a term? Support the
author's claim? Present an objection? Provide an illustration?

care whether employees spend one or 10 hours on the Internet as long as they are getting their jobs done—and provided that they are not accessing inappropriate sites" (qtd. in Verespej).

Anticipating and countering objections

Do not ignore sources that seem contrary to your position or that offer arguments different from your own. Instead, use them to give voice to opposing points of view and to state potential objections to your argument before you counter them (see 6i). Readers often have opposing points of view in mind already, whether or not they agree with you. Anna Orlov, for example, cites conflicting evidence to acknowledge that some readers may feel that unlimited Internet access in the workplace hinders productivity. In doing so, she creates an opportunity to counter that objection and persuade those readers.

> On the one hand, computers and Internet access give employees
> powerful tools to carry out their jobs; on the other hand, the same
> technology offers constant temptations to avoid work. As a 2005 study
> by *Salary.com* and *America Online* indicates, the Internet ranked as the
> top choice among employees for ways of wasting time on the job; it
> beat talking with co-workers—the second most popular method—by a
> margin of nearly two to one (Frauenheim).

53d Draft an introduction for your thesis.

In a research paper, readers are accustomed to seeing the thesis statement—the paper's main point—at the end of the first or second paragraph. The advantage of putting it in the first paragraph is that readers can easily recognize your position. The advantage of delaying the thesis until the second paragraph is that you can provide a fuller context for your point.

TEACHING TIP

The Bedford Handbook includes three samples of MLA-style papers written from sources—an argument essay (pp. 168–73), an analysis of a literary text (pp. 196–98), and a research paper (pp. 656–61). As a class, review the introductions to these papers. If you have a rubric for a current assignment and part of the rubric deals with the introduction, ask students to apply this rubric to each of the sample papers.

As you draft your introduction, you may revise your working thesis, either because you have refined your thinking or because new wording fits more smoothly into the context you have created for it.

In addition to stating your thesis, an introduction should hook readers (see 1c). For example, in your first sentence or two you might introduce readers to the research conversation by connecting your topic to a recent news item or by pointing to emerging trends in an academic discipline. Other strategies are to pose a puzzling problem or to cite a startling statistic. Anna Orlov begins her paper by using results from a recent study to show a significant trend in companies' electronic surveillance of employees (see p. 656).

53e Draft the paper in an appropriate voice.

A chatty, breezy voice is usually not appropriate in a research paper, but neither is a stuffy, pretentious style or a timid, unsure one.

TOO CHATTY

What's up with companies snooping around when their employees are surfing the Net? Employers who constantly spy on their workers' Internet habits are messing with people's rights.

MORE FORMAL

Although companies often have legitimate concerns that lead them to monitor employees' Internet usage, the benefits of electronic surveillance are outweighed by its costs to employees' privacy and autonomy.

TOO STUFFY

It has been concluded that an evident majority of companies undertake the monitoring of employees' utilization of the Internet.

MORE DIRECT

A recent study found that 76% of companies monitor employees' Internet use.

TOO TIMID

I may not be an expert, but it seems to me that monitoring online activities maybe has the unintended effect of making employees resentful.

MORE AUTHORITATIVE

Monitoring online activities can have the unintended effect of making employees resentful.

54 Citing sources; avoiding plagiarism

In a research paper, you will draw on the work of other writers, and you must document their contributions by citing your sources. Sources are cited for two reasons:

1. to tell readers where your information comes from — so that they can assess its reliability and, if interested, find and read the original source
2. to give credit to the writers from whom you have borrowed words and ideas

Borrowing another writer's language, sentence structures, or ideas without proper acknowledgment is a form of dishonesty known as *plagiarism.*

SCHOLARS ON AVOIDING PLAGIARISM

Haviland, Carol P., and Joan A. Mullin. *Who Owns This Text? Plagiarism, Authorship, and Disciplinary Cultures.* Logan: Utah State UP, 2009. Print. The authors address citation practices in different academic disciplines and how definitions of authorship, plagiarism, and intellectual property are constructed in each discipline. Haviland, Mullin, and others spent three years interviewing college faculty from fields such as biology, sociology, computer science, and visual media. They conclude that faculty should model for students discipline-specific practices for collaboration and "knowledge building" (159).

You must include a citation when you quote from a source, when you summarize or paraphrase, and when you borrow facts that are not common knowledge (see also 54b).

54a Understand how the MLA system works.

Most English professors and some humanities professors require the MLA (Modern Language Association) system of in-text citations. Here, briefly, is how the MLA citation system usually works. (See 56 for more details and model citations.)

1. The source is introduced by a signal phrase that names its author.

2. The material being cited is followed by a page number in parentheses.

3. At the end of the paper, a list of works cited (arranged alphabetically by authors' last names) gives complete publication information for the source.

IN-TEXT CITATION

Legal scholar Jay Kesan points out that the law holds employers liable for employees' actions such as violations of copyright laws, the distribution of offensive or graphic sexual material, and illegal disclosure of confidential information (312).

ENTRY IN THE LIST OF WORKS CITED

Kesan, Jay P. "Cyber-Working or Cyber-Shirking? A First Principles Examination of Electronic Privacy in the Workplace." *Florida Law Review* 54.2 (2002): 289-332. Print.

This basic MLA format varies for different types of sources. For a detailed discussion and other models, see 56.

54b Avoid plagiarism when quoting, summarizing, and paraphrasing sources.

Your research paper represents your ideas in conversation with the ideas in your sources. To be fair and responsible, you must acknowledge your debt to the writers of those sources. If you don't, you commit plagiarism, a serious academic offense. (See also 51c.)

In general, these three acts are considered plagiarism: (1) failing to cite quotations and borrowed ideas, (2) failing to enclose borrowed language in quotation marks, and (3) failing to put summaries and paraphrases in your own words. Definitions of plagiarism may vary; it's a good idea to find out how your school defines academic dishonesty.

Citing quotations and borrowed ideas

You must cite all direct quotations. You must also cite any ideas borrowed from a source: summaries and paraphrases; statistics and other specific facts; and visuals such as cartoons, graphs, and diagrams.

The only exception is common knowledge — information your readers could easily find in any number of general sources. For example, most encyclopedias will tell readers that Joel Coen directed *Fargo* in 1996 and that Emily Dickinson published only a handful of her many poems during her lifetime.

As a rule, when you have seen information repeatedly in your reading, you don't need to cite it. However, when information has appeared in only one or two sources, when it is highly specific (as with statistics), or when it is controversial, you should cite the source. If a topic is new to you and you are

SCHOLARS ON RESEARCH WRITING

Shi, Ling. "Rewriting and Paraphrasing Source Texts in Second Language Writing." *Journal of Second Language Writing* 21.2 (2012): 134–48. Print. For most college students, paraphrasing and summarizing texts are difficult skills to master. For multilingual students, such skills are even harder to master, according to the author. Shi concludes that paraphrasing and summarizing are "in fact complex and depend on one's knowledge of the content, the disciplinary nature of citation practices, and the rhetorical purposes of using citations in a specific context of disciplinary writing" (134).

not sure what is considered common knowledge or what is controversial, ask your instructor or someone else with expertise. When in doubt, cite the source. (See 56 for details.)

> **MAKING THE MOST OF YOUR HANDBOOK**
>
> When you use exact language from a source, you need to show that it is a quotation.
>
> ▶ Quotation marks for direct quotations: 37a
> ▶ Setting off long quotations: page 573

Enclosing borrowed language in quotation marks

To indicate that you are using a source's exact phrases or sentences, you must enclose them in quotation marks unless they have been set off from the text by indenting (see 55a). To omit the quotation marks is to claim—falsely—that the language is your own. Such an omission is plagiarism even if you have cited the source.

ORIGINAL SOURCE

Without adequate discipline, the World Wide Web can be a tremendous time sink; no other medium comes close to matching the Internet's depth of materials, interactivity, and sheer distractive potential.

— Frederick Lane, *The Naked Employee*, p. 142

PLAGIARISM

Frederick Lane points out that if people do not have adequate discipline, the World Wide Web can be a tremendous time sink; no other medium comes close to matching the Internet's depth of materials, interactivity, and sheer distractive potential (142).

BORROWED LANGUAGE IN QUOTATION MARKS

Frederick Lane points out that for those not exercising self-control, "the World Wide Web can be a tremendous time sink; no other medium comes close to matching the Internet's depth of materials, interactivity, and sheer distractive potential" (142).

Putting summaries and paraphrases in your own words

Summaries and paraphrases are written in your own words. A summary condenses information from a source; a paraphrase uses roughly the same number of words as the original source to convey the information. When you summarize or paraphrase, it is not enough to name the source; you must restate the source's meaning using your own language. (See also 51c.) You commit plagiarism if you patchwrite—half-copy the author's sentences, either by mixing the author's phrases with your own without using quotation marks or by plugging your synonyms into the author's sentence structure.

The first paraphrase of the following source is plagiarized. Even though the source is cited, too much of its language is borrowed from the original. The highlighted strings of words have been copied exactly (without quotation marks). In addition, the writer has closely echoed the sentence structure of the source, merely substituting some synonyms (*restricted* for *limited*, *modern era* for *computer age*, *monitoring* for *surveillance*, and *inexpensive* for *cheap*).

ORIGINAL SOURCE

In earlier times, surveillance was limited to the information that a supervisor could observe and record firsthand and to primitive counting devices. In the computer age surveillance can be instantaneous, unblinking, cheap, and, maybe most importantly, easy.

 — Carl Botan and Mihaela Vorvoreanu, "What Do Employees Think about Electronic Surveillance at Work?," p. 126

PLAGIARISM: UNACCEPTABLE BORROWING

Scholars Carl Botan and Mihaela Vorvoreanu argue that in earlier times monitoring of employees was restricted to the information that a supervisor could observe and record firsthand. In the modern era, monitoring can be instantaneous, inexpensive, and, most importantly, easy.

To avoid plagiarizing an author's language, resist the temptation to look at the source while you are summarizing or paraphrasing. After you have read the passage you want to paraphrase, set the source aside. Ask yourself, "What is the author's meaning?" In your own words, state your understanding of the author's basic point. Return to the source and check that you haven't used the author's language or sentence structure or misrepresented the author's ideas. Following these steps will help you avoid plagiarizing the source. When you fully understand another writer's meaning, you can more easily and accurately represent those ideas in your own words.

ACCEPTABLE PARAPHRASE

Scholars Carl Botan and Mihaela Vorvoreanu claim that the nature of workplace surveillance has changed over time. Before the arrival of computers, managers could collect only small amounts of information about their employees based on what they saw or heard. Now, because computers are standard workplace technology, employers can monitor employees efficiently (126).

For more discussion of summary and paraphrase, see 51c.

Becoming a College Writer

Provide context for sources

"When you write with sources, don't make quotations stand on their own. You have to support a quotation on either side (leading into it and then analyzing it) and give it a place to stand."

— **Danielle Novotny**, student, Brandeis University

It's an exciting moment when you think you've found the perfect source or the perfect quotation to support a point you're making in a researched essay, something that says exactly what you were trying to say or felt you needed to say. It's tempting to let this quotation make your point for you. However, when you write papers for college courses, papers in which you are expected to make a genuine contribution to the conversation about a subject, it's useful to remember that *you* are in charge of the conversation in your paper. You shape the argument with your words and ideas, making, as Danielle Novotny suggests, "a place" for each source to stand.

Becoming a college writer requires you not only to use evidence, integrating sources into your argument and responsibly acknowledging their contributions to your thinking, but also to put that evidence into a context that will help readers understand your ideas — your stand on the issue.

- Writing a research paper is a common requirement in college courses. What do you find challenging about using sources? What does it mean to you to be a researcher who is "in charge of the conversation" when you write a research essay?

MORE
Putting source materials in context, 55b

569

55   Integrating sources

Quotations, summaries, paraphrases, and facts will help you develop your argument, but they cannot speak for you. You can use several strategies to integrate information from research sources into your paper while maintaining your own voice.

55a   Use quotations appropriately.

In your academic writing, keep the emphasis on your ideas and your language; use your own words to summarize and to paraphrase your sources and to explain your points. Sometimes, however, quotations can be the most effective way to integrate a source's ideas.

WHEN TO USE QUOTATIONS

- When language is especially vivid or expressive

- When exact wording is needed for technical accuracy

- When it is important to let the debaters of an issue explain their positions in their own words

- When the words of an expert lend weight to an argument

- When the language of a source is the topic of your discussion (as in an analysis or interpretation)

Limiting your use of quotations

Although it is tempting to insert many quotations in your paper and to use your own words only for connecting passages, do not

hackerhandbooks.com/bedhandbook

e Researched writing > Exercises: MLA papers: 55–1 to 55–4 quote excessively. It is almost impossible to integrate numerous quotations smoothly into your own text.

It is not always necessary to quote full sentences from a source. To reduce your reliance on the words of others, you can often integrate language from a source into your own sentence structure.

> Kizza and Ssanyu observe that technology in the workplace has been accompanied by "an array of problems that needed quick answers," such as electronic monitoring to prevent security breaches (4).

Using the ellipsis mark and brackets

Two useful marks of punctuation, the ellipsis mark and brackets, allow you to keep quoted material to a minimum and to integrate it smoothly into your text.

The ellipsis mark To condense a quoted passage, you can use the ellipsis mark (three periods, with spaces between) to indicate that you have left words out. What remains must be grammatically complete.

> Lane acknowledges the legitimate reasons that many companies have for monitoring their employees' online activities, particularly management's concern about preventing "the theft of information that can be downloaded to a . . . disk, e-mailed to oneself . . . , or even posted to a Web page for the entire world to see" (12).

The writer has omitted from the source the words *floppy or Zip* before *disk* and *or a confederate* after *oneself.*

On the rare occasions when you want to leave out one or more full sentences, use a period before the three ellipsis dots.

> Charles Lewis, director of the Center for Public Integrity, points out that "by 1987, employers were administering nearly 2,000,000

> polygraph tests a year to job applicants and employees. . . . Millions of workers were required to produce urine samples under observation for drug testing . . ." (22).

Ordinarily, do not use an ellipsis mark at the beginning or at the end of a quotation. Your readers will understand that the quoted material is taken from a longer passage, so such marks are not necessary. The only exception occurs when you have dropped words at the end of the final quoted sentence. In such cases, put three ellipsis dots before the closing quotation mark and parenthetical reference, as in the previous example.

USING SOURCES RESPONSIBLY: Make sure omissions and ellipsis marks do not distort the meaning of your source.

Brackets Brackets allow you to insert your own words into quoted material. You can insert words in brackets to clarify a confusing reference or to keep a sentence grammatical in your context. You also use brackets to indicate that you are changing a letter from capital to lowercase (or vice versa) to fit into your sentence.

> Legal scholar Jay Kesan notes that "[a] decade ago, losses [from employees' computer crimes] were already mounting to five billion dollars annually" (311).

This quotation began *A decade ago* . . . in the source, so the writer indicated the change to lowercase with brackets and inserted words in brackets to clarify the meaning of *losses*.

To indicate an error such as a misspelling in a quotation, insert the word "sic" in brackets right after the error.

> Johnson argues that "while online monitoring is often imagined as harmles [sic], the practice may well threaten employees' rights to privacy" (14).

Do not overuse "sic" to call attention to errors in a source. Sometimes paraphrasing is a better option. (See 39c.)

Setting off long quotations

When you quote more than four typed lines of prose or more than three lines of poetry, set off the quotation by indenting it one inch from the left margin.

Long quotations should be introduced by an informative sentence, usually followed by a colon. Quotation marks are unnecessary because the indented format tells readers that the passage is taken word-for-word from the source.

> Botan and Vorvoreanu examine the role of gender in company practices of electronic surveillance:
>
> > There has never been accurate documentation of the extent of gender differences in surveillance, but by the middle 1990s, estimates of the proportion of surveilled employees that were women ranged from 75% to 85%. . . . Ironically, this gender imbalance in workplace surveillance may be evening out today because advances in surveillance technology are making surveillance of traditionally male dominated fields, such as long-distance truck driving, cheap, easy, and frequently unobtrusive. (127)

Notice that at the end of an indented quotation the parenthetical citation goes outside the final mark of punctuation. (When a quotation is run into your text, the opposite is true. See the sample citations on pp. 571–72.)

55b Use signal phrases to integrate sources.

Whenever you include a paraphrase, summary, or direct quotation of another writer's work in your paper, prepare your readers for it with introductory words called a *signal phrase*. A signal phrase usually names the author of the source and often provides some context for the source material. (See also p. 577 and 55c.)

Using signal phrases in MLA papers

To avoid monotony, try to vary both the language and the place-ment of your signal phrases.

Model signal phrases

In the words of researchers Greenfield and Davis, "..."

As legal scholar Jay Kesan has noted, "..."

The ePolicy Institute, an organization that advises companies about reducing risks from technology, reports that "..."

"...," writes Daniel Tynan, "..."

"...," attorney Schmitt claims.

Kizza and Ssanyu offer a persuasive counterargument: "..."

Verbs in signal phrases

acknowledges	comments	endorses	reasons
adds	compares	grants	refutes
admits	confirms	illustrates	rejects
agrees	contends	implies	reports
argues	declares	insists	responds
asserts	denies	notes	suggests
believes	disputes	observes	thinks
claims	emphasizes	points out	writes

When you write a signal phrase, choose a verb that is appro-priate for the way you are using the source (see 53c). Are you providing background, explaining a concept, supporting a claim, lending authority, or refuting a belief? See the chart above for a list of verbs commonly used in signal phrases.

Note that MLA style calls for verbs in the present or present perfect tense (*argues, has argued*) to introduce source material unless you include a date that specifies the time of the original author's writing.

Marking boundaries

Readers need to move from your words to the words of a source without feeling a jolt. Avoid dropping quotations into the text without warning. Instead, provide clear signal phrases, including at least the author's name, to indicate the boundary between your words and the source's words. (The signal phrase is highlighted in the second example.)

DROPPED QUOTATION

Some experts have argued that a range of legitimate concerns justifies employer monitoring of employee Internet usage. "Employees could accidentally (or deliberately) spill confidential corporate information . . . or allow worms to spread throughout a corporate network" (Tynan).

QUOTATION WITH SIGNAL PHRASE

Some experts have argued that a range of legitimate concerns justifies employer monitoring of employee Internet usage. As *PC World* columnist Daniel Tynan points out, "Employees could accidentally (or deliberately) spill confidential corporate information . . . or allow worms to spread throughout a corporate network."

NOTE: Because this quotation is from an unpaginated Web source, no page number appears in parentheses after the quotation. See item 4 on page 586.

Establishing authority

Good research writers use evidence from reliable sources. The first time you mention a source, include in the signal phrase the author's title, credentials, or experience—anything that would help your readers recognize the source's authority. (Signal phrases are highlighted in the next two examples.)

SOURCE WITH NO CREDENTIALS

Jay Kesan points out that the law holds employers liable for employees' actions such as violations of copyright laws, the distribution of

offensive or graphic sexual material, and illegal disclosure of
confidential information (312).

SOURCE WITH CREDENTIALS

Legal scholar Jay Kesan points out that the law holds employers
liable for employees' actions such as violations of copyright laws,
the distribution of offensive or graphic sexual material, and illegal
disclosure of confidential information (312).

When you establish your source's authority, you also signal to
readers your own credibility as a responsible researcher who has
located reliable sources.

Introducing summaries and paraphrases

Introduce most summaries and paraphrases with a signal phrase
that names the author and places the material in the context of
your argument. (See also 55c.) Readers will then understand
that everything between the signal phrase and the parenthetical
citation summarizes or paraphrases the cited source.

Without the signal phrase (highlighted) in the following
example, readers might think that only the quotation at the end
is being cited, when in fact the whole paragraph is based on the
source.

> Frederick Lane believes that the personal computer has posed
> new challenges for employers worried about workplace productivity.
> Whereas early desktop computers were primitive enough to prevent
> employees from using them to waste time, the machines have become
> so sophisticated that they now make non-work-related computer
> activities easy and inviting. Many employees spend considerable
> company time customizing features and playing games on their
> computers. But perhaps most problematic from the employer's point of
> view, Lane asserts, is giving employees access to the Internet, "roughly
> the equivalent of installing a gazillion-channel television set for each
> employee" (15-16).

There are times when a summary or a paraphrase does not require a signal phrase. When the context makes clear where the cited material begins, you may omit the signal phrase and include the author's last name in parentheses.

Using signal phrases with statistics and other facts

When you cite a statistic or another specific fact, a signal phrase is often not necessary. Readers usually will understand that the citation refers to the statistic or fact (not the whole paragraph).

> Roughly 60% of responding companies reported disciplining employees who had used the Internet in ways the companies deemed inappropriate; 30% had fired their employees for those transgressions (Greenfield and Davis 347).

There is nothing wrong, however, with using a signal phrase to introduce a statistic or fact.

Putting source material in context

Readers should not have to guess why source material appears in your paper. A signal phrase can help you make the connection between your own ideas and those of another writer by clarifying how the source will contribute to your paper (see 52a).

If you use another writer's words, you must explain how they relate to your point. It's a good idea to embed a quotation between sentences of your own. In addition to introducing it with a signal phrase, follow the quotation with interpretive comments that link it to your paper's argument (see also 55c).

QUOTATION WITH EFFECTIVE CONTEXT

The difference, Lane argues, between old methods of data gathering and electronic surveillance involves quantity:

> Technology makes it possible for employers to gather enormous amounts of data about employees, often far

beyond what is necessary to satisfy safety or productivity
concerns. And the trends that drive technology—faster,
smaller, cheaper—make it possible for larger and larger
numbers of employers to gather ever-greater amounts of
personal data. (3-4)

In an age when employers can collect data whenever employees use
their computers—when they send e-mail, surf the Web, or even arrive
at or depart from their workstations—the challenge for both employers
and employees is to determine how much is too much.

55c Synthesize sources.

When you synthesize multiple sources in a research paper, you
create a conversation about your research topic. You show readers that your argument is based on your active analysis and inte-
gration of ideas, not just a series of quotations and paraphrases.
Your synthesis will show how your sources relate to one another;
one source may support, extend, or counter the ideas of another.
Not every source has to "speak" to another in a research paper,
but readers should be able to see how each one functions in your
argument (see 52a).

Considering how sources relate to your argument

Before you integrate sources and show readers how they relate
to one another, consider how each one might contribute to your
own argument. As student writer Anna Orlov became more
informed through her research about Internet surveillance
in the workplace, she asked herself these questions: *What do I
think about monitoring employees online? What have I learned from
my sources? Which sources might support my ideas or illustrate the
points I want to make? What common counterarguments do I need to
address to strengthen my position?* She annotated a passage from

---

TEACHING TIP

The conversation metaphor can be a useful concept when students are
learning how to synthesize sources. To help students understand how
various ideas relate to one another, ask students to imagine that they
and their sources are in a room together. Students should understand
their sources well enough to be able to predict how one source will react
to another. It may be helpful to ask students to role-play or to write a
brief script in which the sources converse about the issue being debated.

an *eWeek* article that challenged the case she was building against Internet surveillance in the workplace.

STUDENT NOTES ON THE ORIGINAL SOURCE

Catchy—
a good
quotation.

Common
examples—
readers can
relate.

While bosses can easily detect and interrupt water-cooler chatter, the employee who is shopping at Lands' End or IMing with fellow fantasy baseball managers may actually appear to be working. Thwarting the activity is a technology challenge, and it's one that more and more enterprises are taking seriously, despite resistance from privacy advocates and some employees themselves.

Strong case for
monitoring,
but I'm not
convinced.
Counter with
useful work-
place Web
surfing?

—Chris Gonsalves, "Wasting Away on the Web"

Because Orlov felt that Gonsalves's article would convince many readers that Internet surveillance was good for workplace productivity, she knew she needed to present and counter his argument. The author's memorable language and clear illustration seemed worth quoting, but she wanted to keep the emphasis on her own argument. So she quoted the passage from Gonsalves and then analyzed it, discussing and countering his view in her own writing. She also found other sources to support and extend her counterargument.

Placing sources in conversation

You can show readers how the ideas of one source relate to those of another by connecting and analyzing the ideas in your own voice. After all, you've done the research and thought through the issues, so you should control the conversation. When you effectively synthesize sources, the emphasis is still on your own writing; the thread of your argument should be easy to identify and to understand, with or without your sources.

SAMPLE SYNTHESIS (DRAFT)

Student writer Anna Orlov begins with a claim that needs support.

> Productivity is not easily measured in the wired workplace. As a result, employers find it difficult to determine how much freedom to allow their employees. On the one hand, computers and Internet access give employees powerful tools to carry out their jobs; on the other hand, the same technology offers constant temptations to avoid work.

Student writer

Signal phrases indicate how sources contribute to Orlov's paper and show that the ideas that follow are not her own.

> As a 2005 study by *Salary.com* and *America Online* indicates, the Internet ranked as the top choice among employees for ways of wasting time on the job (Frauenheim). Chris Gonsalves, an editor for *eWeek.com,* argues that technology has changed the terms between employers and employees: "While bosses can easily detect and interrupt water-cooler chatter," he writes, "the employee who is shopping at Lands' End or IMing with fellow fantasy baseball managers may actually appear to be working."

Source 1

Source 2

> The gap between observable behaviors and actual online activities has motivated some employers to invest in surveillance programs.

Student writer

Orlov presents a counterposition to extend her argument.

> Many experts, however, disagree with employers' assumption that online monitoring can increase productivity. Employment law attorney Joseph Schmitt argues that, particularly for salaried employees, "a company shouldn't care whether employees spend one or 10 hours on the Internet as long as they are getting their jobs done—and provided that they are not accessing inappropriate sites" (qtd. in Verespej).

Source 3

Orlov builds her case—each quoted passage offers a more detailed claim or example in support of her larger claim.

> Other experts even argue that time spent on personal Internet browsing can actually be productive for companies. According to Bill Coleman, an executive at *Salary.com,* "Personal Internet use and casual office conversations often turn into new business ideas or suggestions for gaining operating efficiencies" (qtd. in Frauenheim). Employers, in other words, may benefit from showing more faith in their employees' ability to exercise their autonomy.

Student writer

Source 4

Student writer

Reviewing an MLA paper: Use of sources

Use of quotations

- Is quoted material enclosed in quotation marks (unless it has been set off from the text)? (See 54b and p. 573.)
- Is quoted language word-for-word accurate? If not, do ellipsis marks or brackets indicate the omissions or changes? (See p. 571.)
- Does a clear signal phrase (usually naming the author) prepare readers for each quotation and for the purpose the quotation serves? (See 55b.)
- Does a parenthetical citation follow each quotation? (See 56a.)
- Is each quotation put in context? (See 55c.)

Use of summaries and paraphrases

- Are summaries and paraphrases free of plagiarized wording — not copied or half-copied from the source? (See 54b.)
- Are summaries and paraphrases documented with parenthetical citations? (See 54b and 56a.)
- Do readers know where the cited material begins? In other words, does a signal phrase mark the boundary between your words and the summary or paraphrase? Or does the context alone make clear exactly what you are citing? (See 55b.)
- Does a signal phrase prepare readers for the purpose the summary or paraphrase has in your argument?

Use of statistics and other facts

- Are statistics and facts (other than common knowledge) documented with parenthetical citations? (See 54b and 56a.)
- If there is no signal phrase, will readers understand exactly which facts are being cited? (See 55b.)

In the draft on page 580, Orlov uses her own analyses to shape the conversation among her sources. She does not simply string quotations together or allow them to overwhelm her writing. The final sentence, written in her own voice, gives her an opportunity to explain to readers how the various sources support her argument.

When synthesizing sources in your own writing, ask yourself the following questions:

- Which sources inform, support, or extend your argument?

- Have you varied the functions of sources—to provide background information, to explain terms or concepts, to lend authority, and to anticipate counterarguments?

- Do you explain how your sources support your argument?

- Do you connect and analyze sources in your own voice?

- Is your own argument easy to identify and to understand, with or without your sources?

56 MLA documentation style

In English and other humanities classes, you may be asked to use the MLA (Modern Language Association) system for documenting sources, which is set forth in the *MLA Handbook for Writers of Research Papers*, 7th ed. (New York: MLA, 2009).

MLA recommends in-text citations that refer readers to a list of works cited. A typical in-text citation names the author of the source, often in a signal phrase, and gives a page number

---

SCHOLARS ON CITATION

Shi, Ling. "Common Knowledge, Learning, and Citation Practices in University Writing." *Research in the Teaching of English* 45.3 (2011): 308–34. Print. Shi's work is based on interviews with seventy-five college students and instructors in a variety of disciplines. Participants in the study commented on examples of writing that included unacknowledged uses of sources, but they could not agree on whether the writers were using common knowledge or were committing plagiarism.

in parentheses. At the end of the paper, the list of works cited provides publication information about the source; the list is alphabetized by authors' last names (or by titles for works without authors). There is a direct connection between the in-text citation and the alphabetical listing. In the following example, that connection is highlighted in orange.

> **MAKING THE MOST OF YOUR HANDBOOK**
>
> A works cited list includes all the sources cited in the text of a paper.
>
> ▶ MLA works cited list: 56b
> ▶ Preparing the list of works cited: 57a
> ▶ Sample lists of works cited: pages 198, 661

IN-TEXT CITATION

Jay Kesan notes that even though many companies now routinely monitor employees through electronic means, "there may exist less intrusive safeguards for employers" (293).

ENTRY IN THE LIST OF WORKS CITED

Kesan, Jay P. "Cyber-Working or Cyber-Shirking? A First Principles Examination of Electronic Privacy in the Workplace." *Florida Law Review* 54.2 (2002): 289-332. Print.

For a list of works cited that includes this entry, see page 661.

56a MLA in-text citations

MLA in-text citations are made with a combination of signal phrases and parenthetical references. A signal phrase introduces information taken from a source (a quotation, summary, paraphrase, or fact); usually the signal phrase includes the author's name. The parenthetical reference comes after the cited material, often at the end of the sentence. It includes at least a page number (except for unpaginated sources, such as those found on the Web). In the models in 56a, the elements of the in-text citation are highlighted in orange.

hackerhandbooks.com/bedhandbook

e Researched writing > Exercises: MLA papers: 56–1 to 56–3

IN-TEXT CITATION

Kwon points out that the Fourth Amendment does not give
employees any protections from employers' "unreasonable
searches and seizures" (6).

Readers can look up the author's last name in the alphabetized
list of works cited, where they will learn the work's title and other
publication information. If readers decide to consult the source,
the page number will take them straight to the passage that has
been cited.

General guidelines for signal phrases and page numbers

Items 1–5 explain how the MLA system usually works for all
sources—in print, on the Web, in other media, and with or without authors and page numbers. Items 6–27 give variations on the
basic guidelines.

1. Author named in a signal phrase   Ordinarily, introduce the
material being cited with a signal phrase that includes the author's
name. In addition to preparing readers for the source, the signal
phrase allows you to keep the parenthetical citation brief.

> Frederick Lane reports that employers do not necessarily have to use
> software to monitor how their employees use the Web: employers can
> "use a hidden video camera pointed at an employee's monitor" and
> even position a camera "so that a number of monitors [can] be viewed
> at the same time" (147).

The signal phrase—*Frederick Lane reports*—names the author;
the parenthetical citation gives the page number of the book in
which the quoted words may be found.

Notice that the period follows the parenthetical citation.
When a quotation ends with a question mark or an exclamation

Directory to MLA in-text citation models

point, leave the end punctuation inside the quotation mark and add a period at the end of your sentence.

> O'Connor asks a critical question: "When does Internet surveillance cross the line between corporate responsibility and invasion of privacy?" (16).

2. Author named in parentheses If you do not give the author's name in a signal phrase, put the last name in parentheses along with the page number. Use no punctuation between the name and the page number.

> Companies can monitor employees' every keystroke without legal
> penalty, but they may have to combat low morale as a result
> (Lane 129).

3. Author unknown If a source has no author, the works cited
entry will begin with the title. In your in-text citation, either use
the complete title in a signal phrase or use a short form of the
title in parentheses. Titles of books and other long works are italicized; titles of articles and other short works are put in quotation
marks (see also p. 653).

> A popular keystroke logging program operates invisibly on workers'
> computers yet provides supervisors with details of the workers' online
> activities ("Automatically").

NOTE: The works cited entry may begin with the name of a corporation or a government agency. If it does, use that name as the
author in your in-text citation (see items 8 and 17 on pp. 588 and
591, respectively).

4. Page number unknown Do not include the page number if a
work lacks page numbers, as is the case with many Web sources.
Even if a printout from a Web site shows page numbers, treat
the source as unpaginated in the in-text citation because not all
printouts give the same page numbers. (When the pages of a
Web source are stable, as in PDF files, supply a page number in
your in-text citation.)

> As a 2005 study by *Salary.com* and *America Online* indicates, the
> Internet ranked as the top choice among employees for ways of wasting
> time on the job; it beat talking with co-workers—the second most
> popular method—by a margin of nearly two to one (Frauenheim).

If a source has numbered paragraphs or sections, use "par." (or
"pars.") or "sec." (or "secs.") in the parentheses: (Smith, par.
4). Notice that a comma follows the author's name in this case.

5. **One-page source** If the source is one page long, MLA allows (but does not require) you to omit the page number. It's generally a good idea to include the page number because without it readers may not know where your citation ends or, worse, may not realize that you have provided a citation at all.

NO PAGE NUMBER IN CITATION

Anush Yegyazarian reports that in 2000 the National Labor Relations Board's Office of the General Counsel helped win restitution for two workers who had been dismissed because their employers were displeased by the employees' e-mails about work-related issues. The case points to the ongoing struggle to define what constitutes protected speech in the workplace.

PAGE NUMBER IN CITATION

Anush Yegyazarian reports that in 2000 the National Labor Relations Board's Office of the General Counsel helped win restitution for two workers who had been dismissed because their employers were displeased by the employees' e-mails about work-related issues (62). The case points to the ongoing struggle to define what constitutes protected speech in the workplace.

Variations on the general guidelines

This section describes the MLA guidelines for handling a variety of situations not covered in items 1–5.

6. **Two or three authors** Name the authors in a signal phrase, as in the following example, or include their last names in the parenthetical reference: (Kizza and Ssanyu 2).

Kizza and Ssanyu note that "employee monitoring is a dependable, capable, and very affordable process of electronically or otherwise recording all employee activities at work" and elsewhere (2).

When you name three authors in the parentheses, separate the names with commas: (Alton, Davies, and Rice 56).

7. Four or more authors Name all authors or include only the first author's name followed by "et al." (Latin for "and others"). The format you use should match the format in your works cited entry (see item 3 on p. 597).

> The study was extended for two years, and only after results were reviewed by an independent panel did the researchers publish their findings (Blaine et al. 35).

8. Organization as author When the author is a corporation or an organization, name that author either in the signal phrase or in the parentheses. (For a government agency as author, see item 17 on p. 591.)

> According to a 2001 survey of human resources managers by the American Management Association, more than three-quarters of the responding companies reported disciplining employees for "misuse or personal use of office telecommunications equipment" (2).

In the list of works cited, the American Management Association is treated as the author and alphabetized under *A*. When you give the organization name in parentheses, abbreviate common words in the name: "Assn.," "Dept.," "Natl.," "Soc.," and so on.

> In a 2001 survey of human resources managers, more than three-quarters of the responding companies reported disciplining employees for "misuse or personal use of office telecommunications equipment" (Amer. Management Assn. 2).

9. Authors with the same last name If your list of works cited includes works by two or more authors with the same last name, include the author's first name in the signal phrase or first initial in the parentheses.

Estimates of the frequency with which employers monitor employees'
use of the Internet each day vary widely (A. Jones 15).

10. Two or more works by the same author   Mention the title of
the work in the signal phrase or include a short version of the title
in the parentheses.

The American Management Association and ePolicy Institute have
tracked employers' practices in monitoring employees' e-mail use. The
groups' 2003 survey found that one-third of companies had a policy of
keeping and reviewing employees' e-mail messages ("2003 E-mail" 2);
in 2005, more than 55% of companies engaged in e-mail monitoring
("2005 Electronic" 1).

Titles of articles and other short works are placed in quotation
marks; titles of books are italicized. (See also p. 653.)

In the rare case when both the author's name and a short
title must be given in parentheses, separate them with a comma.

A 2004 survey found that 20% of employers responding had
employees' e-mail "subpoenaed in the course of a lawsuit or regulatory
investigation," up 7% from the previous year (Amer. Management Assn.
and ePolicy Inst., "2004 Workplace" 1).

11. Two or more works in one citation   To cite more than one
source in the parentheses, list the authors (or titles) in alphabetical order and separate them with a semicolon.

The effects of sleep deprivation among college students have been well
documented (Cahill 42; Leduc 114; Vasquez 73).

Multiple citations can be distracting, so you should not overuse
the technique. If you want to alert readers to several sources that
discuss a particular topic, consider using an information note
instead (see 56c).

12. Repeated citations from the same source   When you are writing about a single work, you do not need to include the author's name each time you quote from or paraphrase the work. After you mention the author's name at the beginning of your paper, you may include just the page number in your parenthetical citations. (For specific guidelines for citing novels, plays, and poems, see 7f.)

> In Susan Glaspell's short story "A Jury of Her Peers," two women accompany their husbands and a county attorney to an isolated house where a farmer named John Wright has been choked to death in his bed with a rope. The chief suspect is Wright's wife, Minnie, who is in jail awaiting trial. The sheriff's wife, Mrs. Peters, has come along to gather some personal items for Minnie, and Mrs. Hale has joined her. Early in the story, Mrs. Hale sympathizes with Minnie and objects to the way the male investigators are "snoopin' round and criticizin'" her kitchen (249). In contrast, Mrs. Peters shows respect for the law, saying that the men are doing "no more than their duty" (249).

In a paper with multiple sources, if you are citing a source more than once in a paragraph, you may omit the author's name after the first mention in the paragraph as long as it is clear that you are still referring to the same source.

13. Encyclopedia or dictionary entry   Unless an encyclopedia or a dictionary has an author, it will be alphabetized in the list of works cited under the word or entry that you consulted (see item 28 on p. 620). Either in your text or in your parenthetical citation, mention the word or entry. No page number is required, since readers can easily look up the word or entry.

> The word *crocodile* has a surprisingly complex etymology ("Crocodile").

14. Multivolume work   If your paper cites more than one volume of a multivolume work, indicate in the parentheses the volume you are referring to, followed by a colon and the page number.

> In his studies of gifted children, Terman describes a pattern of
> accelerated language acquisition (2: 279).

If you cite only one volume of a multivolume work, you will
include the volume number in the list of works cited and will
not need to include it in the parentheses. (See the second example in item 38 on p. 628.)

15. Entire work   Use the author's name in a signal phrase or a
parenthetical citation. There is no need to use a page number.

> Lane explores the evolution of surveillance in the workplace.

16. Selection in an anthology   Put the name of the author of the
selection (not the editor of the anthology) in the signal phrase or
the parentheses.

> In "Love Is a Fallacy," the narrator's logical teachings disintegrate
> when Polly declares that she should date Petey because "[h]e's got a
> raccoon coat" (Shulman 391).

In the list of works cited, the work is alphabetized under *Shulman*,
not under the name of the editor of the anthology. (See item 35
on p. 625.)

Shulman, Max. "Love Is a Fallacy." *Current Issues and Enduring Questions.*
   Ed. Sylvan Barnet and Hugo Bedau. 9th ed. Boston: Bedford,
   2011. 383-91. Print.

17. Government document   When a government agency is the
author, you will alphabetize it in the list of works cited under the
name of the government, such as United States or Great Britain
(see item 72 on p. 648). For this reason, you must name the government as well as the agency in your in-text citation.

> Online monitoring by the United States Department of the Interior over
> a one-week period found that employees' use of "sexually explicit and

gambling websites . . . accounted for over 24 hours of Internet use"
and that "computer users spent over 2,004 hours accessing game and
auction sites" during the same period (3).

18. Historical document   For a historical document, such as the
United States Constitution or the Canadian Charter of Rights
and Freedoms, provide the document title, neither italicized nor
in quotation marks, along with relevant article and section numbers. In parenthetical citations, use common abbreviations such
as "art." and "sec." and abbreviations of well-known titles: (US
Const., art. 1, sec. 2).

While the United States Constitution provides for the formation of
new states (art. 4, sec. 3), it does not explicitly allow or prohibit the
secession of states.

Cite other historical documents as you would any other work, by
the first element in the works cited entry (see item 74 on p. 649).

19. Legal source   For a legislative act (law) or court case, name
the act or case either in a signal phrase or in parentheses. Italicize
the names of cases but not the names of acts. (See also items 75
and 76 on p. 649.)

The Jones Act of 1917 granted US citizenship to Puerto Ricans.

In 1857, Chief Justice Roger B. Taney declared in *Dred Scott v. Sandford*
that blacks, whether enslaved or free, could not be citizens of the
United States.

20. Visual such as a table, a chart, or another graphic   To cite a
visual that has a figure number in the source, use the abbreviation "fig." and the number in place of a page number in your
parenthetical citation: (Manning, fig. 4). If you refer to the figure
in your text, spell out the word "figure."

To cite a visual that does not have a figure number in a print source, use the visual's title or a general description in your text and cite the author and page number as for any other source.

For a visual that is not in a print source, identify the visual in your text and then in parentheses use the first element in the works cited entry: the artist's or photographer's name or the title of the work. (See items 65–70 on pp. 644–47.)

> Photographs such as *Woman Aircraft Worker* (Bransby) and *Women Welders* (Parks) demonstrate the US government's attempt to document the contributions of women on the home front during World War II.

21. Personal communication and social media   Cite personal letters, personal interviews, e-mail messages, and social media posts by the name listed in the works cited entry, as you would for any other source. Identify the type of source in your text if you feel it is necessary for clarity. (See items 27d, 29c, and 77–81 in section 56b.)

22. Web source   Your in-text citation for a source from the Web should follow the same guidelines as for other sources. If the source lacks page numbers but has numbered paragraphs, sections, or divisions, use those numbers with the appropriate abbreviation in your in-text citation: "par.," "sec.," "ch.," "pt.," and so on. Do not add such numbers if the source itself does not use them; simply give the author or title in your in-text citation.

> Julian Hawthorne points out profound differences between his father and Ralph Waldo Emerson but concludes that, in their lives and their writing, "together they met the needs of nearly all that is worthy in human nature" (ch. 4).

23. Indirect source (source quoted in another source)   When a writer's or a speaker's quoted words appear in a source written by someone else, begin the parenthetical citation with the abbreviation "qtd. in." (See also item 12 on p. 607.) In the following example, Kizza and Ssanyu are the authors of the source given in the works cited list; the source contains a quotation by Botan and McCreadie.

> Researchers Botan and McCreadie point out that "workers are objects of information collection without participating in the process of exchanging the information . . ." (qtd. in Kizza and Ssanyu 14).

Literary works and sacred texts

Literary works and sacred texts are usually available in a variety of editions. Your list of works cited will specify which edition you are using, and your in-text citation will usually consist of a page number from the edition you consulted (see item 24). When possible, give enough information—such as book parts, play divisions, or line numbers—so that readers can locate the cited passage in any edition of the work (see items 25–27).

24. Literary work without parts or line numbers   Many literary works, such as most short stories and many novels and plays, do not have parts or line numbers. In such cases, simply cite the page number.

> At the end of Kate Chopin's "The Story of an Hour," Mrs. Mallard drops dead upon learning that her husband is alive. In the final irony of the story, doctors report that she has died of a "joy that kills" (25).

25. Verse play or poem   For verse plays, give act, scene, and line numbers that can be located in any edition of the work. Use arabic numerals and separate the numbers with periods.

> In Shakespeare's *King Lear*, Gloucester, blinded for suspected treason, learns a profound lesson from his tragic experience: "A man may see how this world goes / with no eyes" (4.2.148-49).

For a poem, cite the part, stanza, and line numbers, if it has them, separated by periods.

> The Green Knight claims to approach King Arthur's court "because the
> praise of you, prince, is puffed so high, / And your manor and your men
> are considered so magnificent" (1.12.258-59).

For poems that are not divided into numbered parts or stanzas, use line numbers. For a first reference, use the word "lines": (lines 5-8). Thereafter use just the numbers: (12-13).

26. Novel with numbered divisions When a novel has numbered divisions, put the page number first, followed by a semicolon, and then the book, part, or chapter in which the passage may be found. Use abbreviations such as "bk.," "pt.," and "ch."

> One of Kingsolver's narrators, teenager Rachel, pushes her vocabulary
> beyond its limits. For example, Rachel complains that being forced to
> live in the Congo with her missionary family is "a sheer tapestry of
> justice" because her chances of finding a boyfriend are "dull and void"
> (117; bk. 2, ch. 10).

27. Sacred text When citing a sacred text such as the Bible or the Qur'an, name the edition you are using in your works cited entry (see item 39 on p. 628). In your parenthetical citation, give the book, chapter, and verse (or their equivalent), separated with periods. Common abbreviations for books of the Bible are acceptable.

> Consider the words of Solomon: "If your enemy is hungry, give him
> bread to eat; and if he is thirsty, give him water to drink" (*Oxford
> Annotated Bible*, Prov. 25.21).

The title of a sacred work is italicized when it refers to a specific edition of the work, as in the preceding example. If you refer to the book in a general sense in your text, neither italicize it nor put it in quotation marks (see also the note on p. 457 in section 42a).

> The Bible and the Qur'an provide allegories that help readers understand
> how to lead a moral life.

56b MLA list of works cited

The elements you will need for the works cited list at the end of your paper or project will differ slightly for some sources, but the main principles apply to all sources, whether in print or from the Web: You should identify an author, a creator, or a producer whenever possible; give a title; provide the date on which the source was produced; and indicate the medium of delivery. Some sources will require page numbers; some will require a sponsoring person or organization; and some will require other identifying information.

Section 56b provides details for how to cite many of the sources you are likely to encounter. It also provides hints for what you can do when a source does not match one of the models exactly. When you cite sources, your goals are to show that your sources are reliable and relevant, to provide readers with enough information to find sources easily, and to provide that information consistently according to MLA conventions.

▸ Directory to MLA works cited models, page 598
▸ General guidelines for the works cited list, page 601

General guidelines for listing authors

The formatting of authors' names in items 1–12 applies to all sources—books, articles, Web sites—in print, on the Web, or in the media. For more models of specific source types, see items 13–81.

1. Single author

author: last
name first   title (book)   city of
                                                 publication publisher

Bowker, Gordon. *James Joyce: A New Biography*. New York: Farrar,

date medium

2012. Print.

2. Two or three authors

first author: last name first / second author: in normal order / title (book) / city of publication

Gourevitch, Philip, and Errol Morris. *Standard Operating Procedure.* New York:

publisher / date / medium

Penguin, 2008. Print.

first author: last name first / other authors: in normal order / title (newspaper article)

Farmer, John, John Azzarello, and Miles Kara. "Real Heroes, Fake Stories."

newspaper title / date of publication / page / medium

New York Times 14 Sept. 2008: WK10. Print.

3. Four or more authors Either name all the authors or name the first author followed by "et al." (Latin for "and others"). In an in-text citation, use the same form for the authors' names as you use in the works cited entry. See item 7 on page 588.

first author: last name first / other authors: in normal order

Leech, Geoffrey, Marianne Hundt, Christian Mair, and Nicholas Smith.

title (book) / city of publication

Change in Contemporary English: A Grammatical Study. Cambridge:

publisher / year / medium

Cambridge UP, 2009. Print.

4. Organization or company as author

author: organization name, not abbreviated / title (book)

National Geographic. *National Geographic Visual Atlas of the World.*

city of publication / publisher, with common abbreviations / date / medium

Washington: Natl. Geographic Soc., 2008. Print.

Your in-text citation also should treat the organization as the author (see item 8 on p. 588).

(*continued on p. 603*)

Directory to MLA works cited models

Directory to MLA works cited models (cont.)

General guidelines for the works cited list

In the list of works cited, include only sources that you have quoted, summarized, or paraphrased in your paper.

Authors and titles

- Arrange the list alphabetically by authors' last names or by titles for works without authors.

- Invert the first author's name (place the last name first, a comma, and the first name). If the source has other authors, put their names in normal order (first name followed by last name).

- In titles of works, capitalize all words except articles (*a, an, the*), prepositions (*to, from, between, at, under,* and so on), coordinating conjunctions (*and, but, or, nor, for, so, yet*), and the *to* in infinitives — unless the word is first or last in the title or subtitle.

- Use quotation marks around titles of articles and other short works.

- Italicize titles of books and other long works.

Place of publication and publisher

- For sources that require a place of publication, give the city of publication without a state or country name.

- Shorten publishers' names, usually to the first principal word ("Wiley" for "John Wiley and Sons," for instance). Use the abbreviations "U" and "P" for "University" and "Press" in the names of university publishers: UP of Florida.

- If a work has two publishers, give the city and name for both (in the order listed on the title page), separated with a semicolon.

- List a sponsor or a publisher for most sources from the Web, usually immediately after the Web site title.

- If a source has no sponsor or publisher, use the abbreviation "N.p." (for "No publisher").

- Do not give a sponsor for a work found in a database; the title of the database is sufficient.   →

GENERAL GUIDELINES FOR THE WORKS CITED LIST *(cont.)*

Dates

- For a print source, give the most recent date on the title page or the copyright page.
- For a source found on the Web, use the copyright date or the most recent update.
- For books and for most journals, use the year of publication.
- For monthly magazines, use the month and the year. Abbreviate all months except May, June, and July.
- For weekly magazines and newspapers, give the day, month, and year in that order, with no commas (18 Feb. 2013). Abbreviate all months except May, June, and July.
- If there is no date of publication or update, use "n.d." (for "no date").
- For sources found on the Web or in a database, provide the date you accessed the source, usually at the end of the entry.

Page numbers

- For most articles and other short works, give page numbers when they are available.
- If page numbers are not available in the source (as is often the case with sources found on the Web), use the abbreviation "n. pag." (for "no pagination") in place of page numbers.
- Do not use the page numbers from a printout of a source — different printers will paginate the work differently, so the page numbers are not stable.
- For articles in journals, magazines, and newspapers, if the work does not appear on consecutive pages, give the number of the first page followed by a plus sign: 35+.

Medium

- Include the medium in which a work was published, produced, or delivered.
- Capitalize the medium, but do not italicize it or put it in quotation marks.

GENERAL GUIDELINES FOR THE WORKS CITED LIST (*cont.*)

- Typical designations for the medium are "Print," "Web," "Radio," "Television," "CD," "Film," "DVD," "Photograph," "Performance," "Lecture," "MP3 file," and "PDF file."

URLs

- MLA guidelines assume that readers can locate most Web sources by entering the author, title, or other identifying information in a search engine or a database. Consequently, the *MLA Handbook* does not require a URL (Web address) in citations for online sources.

- Some instructors may require a URL; for an example, see the note at the end of item 47.

5. No author listed

a. Article or other short work

article title   label   newspaper title (city in brackets)

"Policing Ohio's Online Courses." Editorial. *Plain Dealer* [Cleveland]

date   page(s)   medium

9 Oct. 2012: A5. Print.

article title   title of long work   title of Web site

"Chapter 2: What Can Be Patented?" *Inventor's Handbook.* Lemelson-MIT.

sponsor   no date   medium   date of access

Massachusetts Inst. of Technology, n.d. Web. 31 Oct. 2012.

b. Television program

episode title   title of TV show   producer   network

"Fast Times at West Philly High." *Frontline.* Prod. Debbie Morton. PBS.

local station, city   date of broadcast   medium

KTWU, Topeka, 4 Dec. 2012. Television.

5. No author listed **(cont.)**

c. Book, entire Web site, or other long work

title (Web site)
─────────────────────────────────────
Women of Protest: Photographs from the Records of the National Woman's Party.

     sponsor   no date   medium   date of access
                 ┌────┐   ┌────┐   ┌────┐
Lib. of Cong., n.d. Web. 29 Sept. 2012.

TIP: Often the author's name is available but is not easy to find. It may appear at the end of the page, in tiny print, or on another page of the site, such as the home page. Also, an organization or a government may be the author (see items 4 and 72).

How to answer the basic question "Who is the author?"

PROBLEM: Sometimes when you need to cite a source, it's not clear who the author is. This is especially true for sources on the Web or other nonprint sources, which may have been created by one person and uploaded by a different person or an organization. Whom do you cite as the author in such a case? How do you determine who *is* the author?

EXAMPLE: The video "Surfing the Web on the Job" (see below) was uploaded to YouTube by CBSNewsOnline. Is the person or organization who uploads the video the author of the video? Not necessarily.

Surfing the Web on The Job

 CBSNewsOnline · 42,491 videos

▶ **Subscribe** 85,736

Uploaded on Nov 12, 2009
As the Internet continues to emerge as a critical facet of everyday life, CBS News' Daniel Sieberg reports that companies are cracking down on employees' personal Web use.

6. Two or more works by the same author   First alphabetize the works by title (ignoring the article *A*, *An*, or *The* at the beginning of a title). Use the author's name for the first entry; for subsequent entries, use three hyphens and a period. The three hyphens must stand for exactly the same name as in the first entry.

García, Cristina. *Dreams of Significant Girls*. New York: Simon, 2011. Print.

---. *The Lady Matador's Hotel*. New York: Scribner, 2010. Print.

7. Two or more works by the same group of authors   To list multiple works by the same group of two or more authors, alphabetize the works by title (ignoring the article *A*, *An*, or *The* at the

STRATEGY: After you view or listen to the source a few times, ask yourself whether you can tell who is chiefly responsible for creating the content in the source. It might be an organization. It might be an identifiable individual. This video consists entirely of reporting by Daniel Sieberg, so in this case the author is Sieberg.

CITATION: To cite the source, you would use the basic MLA guidelines for a video found on the Web (item 56).

author:
last name first   title of video   Web site title   sponsor   update date

Sieberg, Daniel. "Surfing the Web on the Job." *YouTube*. YouTube, 12 Nov. 2009.

medium   date of access

Web. 26 Nov. 2009.

If you want to include the person or organization who uploaded the video, you can add it as supplementary information at the end.

author:
last name first   title of video   Web site title   sponsor   update date

Sieberg, Daniel. "Surfing the Web on the Job." *YouTube*. YouTube, 12 Nov. 2009.

medium   date of access   supplementary information

Web. 26 Nov. 2009. Uploaded by CBSNewsOnline.

beginning of a title). Use all authors' names for the first entry; begin subsequent entries with three hyphens and a period. The three hyphens must stand for all the authors' names.

Agha, Hussein, and Robert Malley. "The Arab Counterrevolution." *New York Review of Books*. NYREV, 29 Sept. 2011. Web. 12 Dec. 2012.

---. "This Is Not a Revolution." *New York Review of Books*. NYREV, 8 Nov. 2012. Web. 12 Dec. 2012.

8. Editor or translator   Begin with the editor's or translator's name followed by the abbreviation "ed." or "trans." for one editor or translator. Use "eds." or "trans." for more than one editor or translator.

first editor:
last name first   other editor(s):
in normal order   title (book)

Jones, Russell M., and John H. Swanson, eds. *Dear Helen: Wartime Letters*

city of
publication   publisher

from a Londoner to Her American Pen Pal. Columbia: U of Missouri P,

year medium

2009. Print.

9. Author with editor or translator   Begin with the name of the author. Place the editor's or translator's name after the title. Here the abbreviation "Ed." or "Trans." means "Edited by" or "Translated by," so it is the same for one or more editors or translators.

author:
last name first   title (book)   translator:
in normal order

Scirocco, Alfonso. *Garibaldi: Citizen of the World*. Trans. Allan Cameron.

city of
publication   publisher   year medium

Princeton: Princeton UP, 2007. Print.

10. Illustrated work   If a work has both an author and an illustrator, the order of elements in your citation will depend on which of those persons you emphasize in your paper.

a. Author first If you emphasize the author's work, begin with the author's name. After the title, use the abbreviation "Illus." (meaning "Illustrated by") followed by the illustrator's name.

Moore, Alan. *V for Vendetta.* Illus. David Lloyd. New York: Vertigo-DC Comics, 2008. Print.

b. Illustrator first If you emphasize the illustrator, begin your citation with the illustrator's name, followed by the abbreviation "illus." (meaning "illustrator"). After the title of the work, put the author's name, preceded by "By."

Weaver, Dustin, illus. *The Tenth Circle.* By Jodi Picoult. New York: Washington Square, 2006. Print.

c. Author and illustrator the same person If the illustrator and the author are the same person, cite the work as you would any other work with one author (not using the label "illus." or "by").

Smith, Lane. *Abe Lincoln's Dream.* New York: Roaring Brook, 2012. Print.

11. Author using a pseudonym (pen name) or screen name　Give the author's name as it appears in the source (the pseudonym), followed by the author's real name in brackets. If you don't know the author's real name, use only the pseudonym. (For screen names in social media, see items 80 and 81 on pp. 650 and 651.)

Grammar Girl [Mignon Fogarty]. "When Are Double Words OK?" *Grammar Girl: Quick and Dirty Tips for Better Writing.* Macmillan, 28 Sept. 2012. Web. 10 Nov. 2012.

Pauline. Comment. "Is This the End?" By James Atlas. *New York Times.* New York Times, 25 Nov. 2012. Web. 29 Nov. 2012.

12. Author quoted by another author (indirect source)　If one of your sources uses a quotation from another source and you'd like to use the quotation, provide a works cited entry for the source in which you found the quotation. In the text of your paper, you

will cite the person quoted and indicate that the quoted words
appear in the source (see item 23 on p. 593). In the following
examples, Belmaker is the source in the works cited list; Townson
is quoted in Belmaker.

SOURCE (BELMAKER) QUOTING ANOTHER SOURCE (TOWNSON)

Peter Townson, a journalist working with the DOHA Center
for Press Freedom in Qatar, says there is one obvious reason
that some countries in the Middle East have embraced social
media so heartily. "It's kind of the preferred way for people
to get news, because they know there's no self-censorship
involved," Townson said in a phone interview.

WORKS CITED ENTRY

Belmaker, Genevieve. "Five Ways Journalists Can Use Social
　　　Media for On-the-Ground Reporting in the Middle East."
　　　Poynter. Poynter Inst., 20 Nov. 2012. Web. 24 Nov. 2012.

IN-TEXT CITATION

In describing the growing popularity and acceptance of social media
tools in the Middle East, Peter Townson points out that social media are
"kind of the preferred way for people to get news, because they know
there's no self-censorship involved" (qtd. in Belmaker).

Articles and other short works

▶ Citation at a glance: Article in a journal, page 610
▶ Citation at a glance: Article from a database, page 612

13. Basic format for an article or other short work

a. Print

author:
last name first
article title

Ferris, William R. "Southern Literature: A Blending of Oral, Visual, and

journal   volume,
title   issue   year   page(s)   medium

　　Musical Voices." *Daedalus* 141.1 (2012): 139-53. Print.

b. Web

author:
last name first | title of short work

Sonderman, Jeff. "Survey: Public Prefers News from Professional Journalists."

title of
Web site | sponsor | update date | medium | date of access

Poynter. Poynter Inst., 29 Aug. 2012. Web. 31 Oct. 2012.

c. Database

author:
last name first | article title | journal title

Emanuel, Lynn Collins. "The Noirs: Collecting the Evidence." *American Poetry Review*

volume, issue | year | page(s) | database title | medium | date of access

41.6 (2012): 6. *General OneFile*. Web. 14 Dec. 2012.

14. Article in a journal

a. Print

author: last
name first | article title

Fuqua, Amy. "'The Furrow of His Brow': Providence and Pragmatism in Toni

journal title | volume, issue | year | page(s) | medium

Morrison's *Paradise*." *Midwest Quarterly* 54.1 (2012): 38-52. Print.

b. Online journal

author:
last name first | article title

Cáceres, Sigfrido Burgos. "Towards Concert in Africa: Seeking Progress and Power

journal title | volume, issue | year

through Cohesion and Unity." *African Studies Quarterly* 12.4 (2011):

page(s) | medium | date of access

59-73. Web. 31 Oct. 2012.

Citation at a glance

Article in a journal MLA

To cite an article in a print journal in MLA style, include the following elements:

1. Author(s) of article
2. Title and subtitle of article
3. Title of journal
4. Volume and issue numbers (if any)
5. Year of publication
6. Page number(s) of article
7. Medium

JOURNAL TABLE OF CONTENTS

RHETORIC REVIEW 3

Volume 31, Number 4, 2012
4 5

Articles

FIRST PAGE OF ARTICLE

Rhetoric Review, Vol. 31, No. 4, 371–388, 2012
Copyright © Taylor & Francis Group, LLC
ISSN: 0735-0198 print / 1532-7981 online
DOI: 10.1080/07350198.2012.711196

R Routledge
Taylor & Francis Group

1 JOSEPH TURNER

University of Delaware

2 *Sir Gawain and the Green Knight* and the History
of Medieval Rhetoric

*During the Middle Ages, rhetoric and literature were thoroughly intertwined,
whereas current notions of disciplinarity, in which literature and rhetoric
are constructed as separate traditions, muddy our understanding of medieval*

WORKS CITED ENTRY FOR AN ARTICLE IN A PRINT JOURNAL

1   2

Turner, Joseph. "*Sir Gawain and the Green Knight* and the History of Medieval

3   4   5   6   7

Rhetoric." *Rhetoric Review* 31.4 (2012): 371-88. Print.

For more on citing articles in MLA style, see items 13–16.

14. Article in a journal (*cont.*)

c. Database

author:
last name first   article title   journal title

Maier, Jessica. "A 'True Likeness': The Renaissance City Portrait." *Renaissance*

volume,
issue   year   page(s)   database title   medium   date of access

Quarterly 65.3 (2012): 711-52. *JSTOR*. Web. 30 Aug. 2012.

15. Article in a magazine

a. Print (monthly)

author:
last name first   article title   magazine title   date   page(s)   medium

Bryan, Christy. "Ivory Worship." *National Geographic* Oct. 2012: 28-61. Print.

Citation at a glance

Article from a database MLA

To cite an article from a database in MLA style, include the following elements:

1. Author(s) of article
2. Title and subtitle of article
3. Title of journal, magazine, or newspaper
4. Volume and issue numbers (for journal)
5. Date or year of publication
6. Page numbers of article ("n. pag." if none)
7. Name of database
8. Medium
9. Date of access

DATABASE RECORD

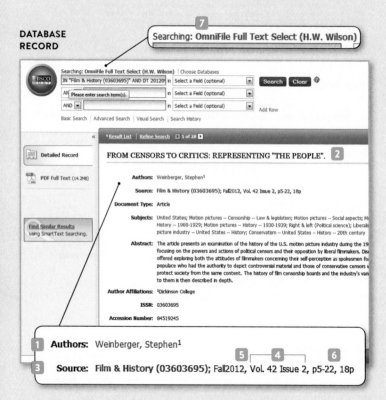

Searching: OmniFile Full Text Select (H.W. Wilson)

Authors: Weinberger, Stephen[1]

Source: Film & History (03603695); Fall2012, Vol. 42 Issue 2, p5-22, 18p

WORKS CITED ENTRY FOR AN ARTICLE FROM A DATABASE

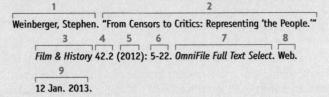

Weinberger, Stephen. "From Censors to Critics: Representing 'the People.'" *Film & History* 42.2 (2012): 5-22. *OmniFile Full Text Select*. Web. 12 Jan. 2013.

For more on citing articles from a database in MLA style, see items 13–16.

15. Article in a magazine *(cont.)*

b. Print (weekly)

Vick, Karl. "The Stateless Statesman." *Time* 15 Oct. 2012: 32-37. Print.

c. Web

Leonard, Andrew. "The Surveillance State High School." *Salon*. Salon Media Group, 27 Nov. 2012. Web. 4 Dec. 2012.

d. Database

Rosenbaum, Ron. "The Last Renaissance Man." *Smithsonian* Nov. 2012: 39-44. *OmniFile Full Text Select*. Web. 12 Jan. 2013.

16. Article in a newspaper   If the city of publication is not obvious from the title of the newspaper, include the city in brackets after the newspaper title (see item 5a).

If sections are identified by letter, include the section letter as part of the page number (see item 16a). If sections are numbered, include the section number between the date and the page number, using the abbreviation "sec.": 14 Sept. 2012, sec. 2: 21. If you accessed an e-reader edition of the newspaper, give page numbers if they are available.

a. Print

author:
last name first   article title

Sherry, Allison. "Volunteers' Personal Touch Turns High-Tech Data into Votes."

newspaper
title   date   page(s) medium

Denver Post 30 Oct. 2012: 1A+. Print.

b. Web

author:
last name first   article title

Amos, Adria. "STEM Teacher Uses 'Flip' Method to Put Classroom Focus on

Web site
title   sponsor

Students, Not Educator." *Knoxnews.com.* Knoxville News Sentinel,

date of
date   medium   access

1 Oct. 2012. Web. 29 Oct. 2012.

c. E-reader

newspaper
article title   title   date   page(s) medium

"Church Votes No on Female Bishops." *Boston Globe* 21 Nov. 2012: A3. E-reader.

d. Database

		newspaper		
article title	label	title	date	page(s)

"The Road toward Peace." Editorial. *New York Times* 15 Feb. 1945: 18.

		date of
database title	medium	access

ProQuest Historical Newspapers: The New York Times. Web. 18 June 2012.

17. Abstract or executive summary   Include the label "Abstract" or "Executive summary," neither italicized nor in quotation marks, after the title of the work.

a. Abstract of an article

Bottomore, Stephen. "The Romance of the Cinematograph." Abstract. *Film
   History* 24.3 (2012): 341-44. *General OneFile.* Web. 25 Oct. 2012.

b. Abstract of a paper

Dixon, Rosemary, Dmitri Iourinski, and Kyle B. Roberts. "The Opportunities
   and Challenges of Virtual Library Systems: A Case Study." Abstract.
   Paper presented at the 2011 Chicago Colloquium on Digital Humanities
   and Computer Science. U of Chicago. 20 Nov. 2011. Web. 28 Nov. 2012.

c. Abstract of a dissertation

Chen, Shu-Ling. "Mothers and Daughters in Morrison, Tan, Marshall, and
   Kincaid." Diss. U of Washington, 2000. *DAI* 61.6 (2000): AAT9975963.
   ProQuest Dissertations and Theses. Web. 22 Feb. 2012.

d. Executive summary

Pintak, Lawrence. *The Murrow Rural Information Initiative: Final Report.*
   Executive summary. Pullman: Murrow Coll. of Communication,
   Washington State U, 25 May 2012. PDF file.

18. Article with a title in its title   Use single quotation marks around a title of a short work or a quoted term that appears in an article title. Italicize a title or term normally italicized.

Silber, Nina. "From 'Great Emancipator' to 'Vampire Hunter': The Many
    Stovepipe Hats of Cinematic Lincoln." *Cognoscenti*. WBUR, 22 Nov.
    2012. Web. 13 Dec. 2012.

19. Editorial   Cite as a source with no author (see item 5) and use the label "Editorial" following the article title.

"New State for the US?" Editorial. *Columbus Dispatch*. Dispatch Printing,
    24 Nov. 2012. Web. 27 Nov. 2012.

20. Unsigned article   Cite as a source with no author (see item 5).

"Public Health Response to a Changing Climate." *Centers for Disease Control
    and Prevention*. Centers for Disease Control and Prevention, 1 Oct.
    2012. Web. 31 Oct. 2012.

"Harper's Index." *Harper's Magazine* Feb. 2012: 11. Print.

21. Letter to the editor   Use the label "Letter" after the title. If the letter has no title, place the label directly after the author's name.

Fahey, John A. "Recalling the Cuban Missile Crisis." Letter. *Washington Post*
    28 Oct. 2012: A16. *LexisNexis Library Express*. Web. 15 Dec. 2012.

22. Comment on an online article   If the writer of the comment uses a screen name, see item 11. After the name, include the label "Comment" followed by the title of the article and the author of the article (preceded by "By"). Continue with publication information for the article.

author:
screen name   label   article title

pablosharkman. Comment. "'We Are All Implicated': Wendell Berry Laments

author of article

a Disconnection from Community and the Land." By Scott Carlson.

Web site title   sponsor   update date

Chronicle of Higher Education. Chronicle of Higher Educ., 23 Apr. 2012.

date of
medium   access

Web. 30 Oct. 2012.

23. Paper or presentation at a conference   If the paper or presentation is included in the proceedings of a conference, cite it as a selection in an anthology (see item 35; see also item 45 for proceedings of a conference). If you viewed the presentation live, cite it as a lecture or public address (see item 62).

first author:
last name first   other contributors: in normal order

Zuckerman, Ethan, with Tim Berners-Lee, Esther Dyson, Jaron Lanier, and

presentation title

Kaitlin Thaney. "Big Data, Big Challenges, and Big Opportunities."

label   conference title

Presentation at Wired for Change: The Power and the Pitfalls of Big Data.

conference   date of
sponsor   location   date   medium   access

Ford Foundation, New York. 15 Oct. 2012. Web. 30 Oct. 2012.

24. Book review   Name the reviewer and the title of the review, if any, followed by "Rev. of" and the title and author of the work reviewed. Add the publication information for the publication in which the review appears. If the review has no author and no title, begin with "Rev. of" and alphabetize the entry by the first principal word in the title of the work reviewed.

24. Book review (cont.)

a. Print

Flannery, Tim. "A Heroine in Defense of Nature." Rev. of *On a Farther Shore: The Life and Legacy of Rachel Carson*, by William Souder. *New York Review of Books* 22 Nov. 2012: 21-23. Print.

b. Web

Telander, Alex C. "In an MMO Far Far Away." Rev. of *Omnitopia Dawn*, by Diane Duane. *San Francisco Book Review*. 1776 Productions, 17 Jan. 2012. Web. 8 Aug. 2012.

c. Database

Petley, Christer. Rev. of *The Atlantic World and Virginia, 1550-1624*, by Peter C. Mancall. *Caribbean Studies* 38.1 (2008): 175-77. *JSTOR*. Web. 14 Oct. 2012.

25. Film review or other review Name the reviewer and the title of the review, if any, followed by "Rev. of" and the title and writer or director of the work reviewed. Add the publication information for the publication in which the review appears. If the review has no author and no title, begin with "Rev. of" and alphabetize the entry by the first principal word in the title of the work reviewed.

a. Print

Lane, Anthony. "Film within a Film." Rev. of *Argo*, dir. Ben Affleck, and *Sinister*, dir. Scott Derrickson. *New Yorker* 15 Oct. 2012: 98-99. Print.

b. Web

Cobbett, Richard. "World of Warcraft: *Mists of Pandaria* Review." Rev. of *Mists of Pandaria*, by Blizzard Entertainment. *PC Gamer*. Future Publishing, 4 Oct. 2012. Web. 13 Oct. 2012.

26. Performance review   Name the reviewer and the title of the review, if any, followed by "Rev. of" and the title and author of the work reviewed. Add the publication information for the publication in which the review appears. If the review has no author and no title, begin with "Rev. of" and alphabetize the entry by the first principal word in the title of the work reviewed.

Matson, Andrew. Rev. of *Until the Quiet Comes*, by Flying Lotus. *Seattle Times.*
    Seattle Times, 31 Oct. 2012. Web. 10 Nov. 2012.

27. Interview   Begin with the person interviewed, followed by the title of the interview (if there is one). If the interview does not have a title, include the word "Interview" after the interviewee's name. If you wish to include the name of the interviewer, put it after the title of the interview (or after the name of the interviewee if there is no title). (See also item 60 for citing transcripts of interviews.)

a. Print

Robert Bellah. "A Conversation with Robert Bellah." Interview by Hans Joas.
    Hedgehog Review 14.2 (2012): n. pag. Web. 27 Nov. 2012.

b. Web

Kapoor, Anil. "Anil Kapoor on Q." Interview by Jian Ghomeshi. *Q.* CBC Radio,
    n.d. *CBC Radio.* Web. 29 Oct. 2012.

c. Television or radio

Buffett, Warren, and Carol Loomis. Interview by Charlie Rose. *Charlie Rose.*
    PBS. WGBH, Boston, 26 Nov. 2012. Television.

d. Personal To cite an interview that you conducted, begin with the name of the person interviewed. Then write "Personal interview" or "Telephone interview," followed by the date of the interview.

Akufo, Dautey. Personal interview. 11 Apr. 2012.

28. Article in a reference work (encyclopedia, dictionary, wiki)   List the author of the entry (if there is one), the title of the entry, the title of the reference work, the edition number (if any), the date of the edition, and the medium. Page numbers are not necessary, even for print sources, because the entries in the source are arranged alphabetically and are therefore easy to locate.

a. Print

Posner, Rebecca. "Romance Languages." *The Encyclopaedia Britannica: Macropaedia*. 15th ed. 1987. Print.

"Sonata." *The American Heritage Dictionary of the English Language*. 5th ed. 2011. Print.

b. Web

"Hip Hop Music." *Wikipedia*. Wikimedia Foundation, 19 Nov. 2012. Web. 18 Dec. 2012.

Durante, Amy M. "Finn Mac Cumhail." *Encyclopedia Mythica*. Encyclopedia Mythica, 17 Apr. 2011. Web. 20 Nov. 2012.

29. Letter

a. Print   Begin with the writer of the letter, the words "Letter to" and the recipient, and the date of the letter (use "N.d." if it is undated). Add the title of the collection, the editor, and publication information. Add the page range before the medium.

Wharton, Edith. Letter to Henry James. 28 Feb. 1915. *Henry James and Edith Wharton: Letters, 1900-1915*. Ed. Lyall H. Powers. New York: Scribner's, 1990. 323-26. Print.

b. Web   After information about the letter writer, recipient, and date (if known), give the location of the document, neither italicized nor in quotation marks; the name of the Web site or archive, italicized; the medium ("Web"); and your date of access.

Oblinger, Maggie. Letter to Charlie Thomas. 31 Mar. 1895. Nebraska State
Hist. Soc. *Prairie Settlement: Nebraska Photographs and Family Letters,*
1862-1912. Web. 3 Sept. 2012.

c. Personal To cite a letter that you received, begin with the writer's name and add the phrase "Letter to the author," followed by the date. Add the medium ("MS" for "manuscript," or a handwritten letter; "TS" for "typescript," or a typed letter).

Primak, Shoshana. Letter to the author. 6 May 2012. TS.

Books and other long works

▸ Citation at a glance: Book, page 622

30. Basic format for a book

a. Print

author: last
name first   book title   city   publisher date medium

Wolfe, Tom. *Back to Blood*. New York: Little, 2012. Print.

b. E-book

author: last
name first   book title   translators: in normal order

Tolstoy, Leo. *War and Peace*. Trans. Richard Pevear and Larissa Volokhonsky.

  city   publisher date   medium

New York: Knopf, 2007. Nook file.

c. Web Give whatever print publication information is available for the work, followed by the title of the Web site, the medium, and your date of access.

Citation at a glance

Book MLA

To cite a print book in MLA style, include the following elements:

1 Author(s)
2 Title and subtitle
3 City of publication
4 Publisher

5 Date of publication (latest date)
6 Medium

TITLE PAGE

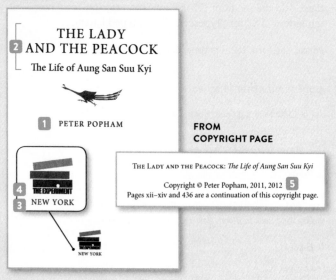

WORKS CITED ENTRY FOR A PRINT BOOK

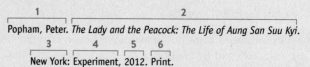

Popham, Peter. *The Lady and the Peacock: The Life of Aung San Suu Kyi.*
New York: Experiment, 2012. Print.

For more on citing books in MLA style, see items 30–42.

30. Basic format for a book, Web (cont.)

author: last
name first   book title   contributor(s):
in normal order

Thoreau, Henry David. *Thoreau's Walden*. Ed. and introd. Raymond MacDonald

                       original   Web site
      city   publisher   date   series   title

Alden. New York: Longmans, 1910. Longmans' English Classics. *Google*

      medium date of access
Books. Web. 31 Oct. 2012.

Saalman, Lora, ed. and trans. *The China-India Nuclear Crossroads*. Washington:

    Carnegie Endowment for Intl. Peace, 2012. *Scribd*. Web. 27 Nov. 2012.

d. Database

author: last
name first   book title

Cullender, Rose. *A Tryal of Witches at the Assizes Held at Bury St. Edmonds for*

                                      city and date
                                      of original

the Count of Suffolk on the Tenth Day of March, 1664. London, 1682.

      database title   medium date of access
Early English Books Online. Web. 29 Apr. 2012.

31. Parts of a book

a. Foreword, introduction, preface, or afterword

author of foreword:
last name first   book part   book title

Bennett, Hal Zina. Foreword. *Shimmering Images: A Handy Little Guide to*

                  author of book:
                  in normal order   city   imprint-publisher

Writing Memoir. By Lisa Dale Norton. New York: Griffin-St. Martin's,

date   page(s) medium
2008. xiii-xvi. Print.

Ozick, Cynthia. "Portrait of the Essay as a Warm Body." Introduction. *The Best*

    American Essays 1998. Ed. Ozick. Boston: Houghton, 1998. xv-xxi. Print.

31. Parts of a book **(cont.)**

b. Chapter in a book

Adams, Henry. "Diplomacy." *The Education of Henry Adams*. Boston: Houghton,
1918. N. pag. *Bartleby.com: Great Books Online*. Web. 8 Dec. 2012.

32. Book with a title in its title   If the book title contains a title normally italicized, neither italicize the internal title nor place it in quotation marks. If the title within the title is normally put in quotation
marks, retain the quotation marks and italicize the entire book title.

Masur, Louis P. *Runaway Dream:* Born to Run *and Bruce Springsteen's American
Vision*. New York: Bloomsbury, 2009. Print.

Millás, Juan José. *"Personality Disorders" and Other Stories*. Trans. Gregory B.
Kaplan. New York: MLA, 2007. Print.

33. Book in a language other than English   If your readers are
not familiar with the language of the book, include a translation
of the title in brackets. Capitalize the title according to the conventions of the book's language.

Vargas Llosa, Mario. *El sueño del celta* [*The Dream of the Celt*]. Madrid:
Alfaguara, 2010. Print.

34. Entire anthology or collection   An anthology is a collection of works on a common theme, often with different
authors for the selections and usually with an editor for the
entire volume. (The abbreviation "eds." is for multiple editors. If the book has only one editor, use the singular "ed.")

first editor: / other editor(s): / title of
last name first / in normal order / anthology

Belasco, Susan, and Linck Johnson, eds. *The Bedford Anthology of American*

volume / city / publisher / date / medium

Literature. Vol. 2. Boston: Bedford, 2008. Print.

35. One selection from an anthology or a collection

► Citation at a glance: Selection from an anthology or a collection, page 626

author of
selection: title of
last name first   selection   title of anthology

Lorde, Audre. "Black Mother Woman." *The Bedford Anthology of American*

                    editor(s) of anthology   volume   city

  Literature. Ed. Susan Belasco and Linck Johnson. Vol. 2. Boston:

publisher date page(s) medium

  Bedford, 2008. 1419. Print.

36. Two or more selections from an anthology or a collection

For two or more works from the same anthology, provide an entry for the entire anthology (see item 34) and a shortened entry for each selection. Use the medium only for the complete anthology. Alphabetize the entries by authors' or editors' last names.

first editor: other editor(s):
last name first   in normal order   title of anthology

Belasco, Susan, and Linck Johnson, eds. *The Bedford Anthology of American*

            volume   city   publisher date medium

  Literature. Vol. 2. Boston: Bedford, 2008. Print.

author of
selection: title of   editor(s)
last name first   selection   of anthology   page(s)

Lorde, Audre. "Black Mother Woman." Belasco and Johnson 1419.

author of selection: title of   editor(s)
last name first   selection   of anthology   page(s)

Silko, Leslie Marmon. "Yellow Woman." Belasco and Johnson 1475-81.

37. Edition other than the first

Include the number of the edition (2nd, 3rd, and so on). If the book has a translator or an

(*continued on p. 628*)

Citation at a glance

Selection from an anthology or a collection MLA

To cite a selection from an anthology in MLA style, include the
following elements:

1   Author(s) of selection
2   Title and subtitle of
    selection
3   Title and subtitle of
    anthology
4   Editor(s) of anthology

5   City of publication
6   Publisher
7   Date of publication
8   Page numbers of
    selection
9   Medium

TITLE PAGE OF ANTHOLOGY

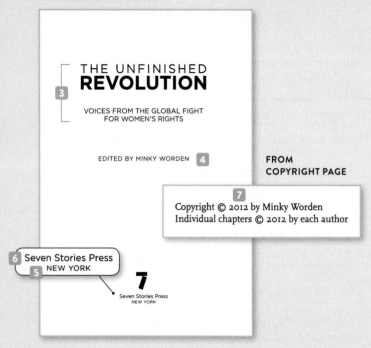

THE UNFINISHED
REVOLUTION

VOICES FROM THE GLOBAL FIGHT
FOR WOMEN'S RIGHTS

EDITED BY MINKY WORDEN 4

**FROM
COPYRIGHT PAGE**

7
Copyright © 2012 by Minky Worden
Individual chapters © 2012 by each author

6 Seven Stories Press
5 NEW YORK

7

Seven Stories Press
NEW YORK

CHAPTER 3

 **Technology's Quiet Revolution
for Women**

Isobel Coleman

On the eve of Egypt's January 2011 revolution, I happened to be in Cairo, having dinner with Gamila Ismail, a longtime Egyptian political activist who had spent decades opposing the Mubarak regime. "What will happen tomorrow?" I asked her, referring to the public demonstration planned for the next day in Tahrir Square. "It will be the huge," she insisted, monitoring Twitter and Facebook feeds on her cell phone. Gamila and a young assistant had spent weeks helping to organize the demonstration through social media. "We think hundreds of thousands of people could join the protest. This could finally be our moment for real change." Indeed.

Much has been made of the role of social media in the Arab uprisings, in particular how it has given voice to youth and women in unprecedented ways. But social media is just the latest in a long line of technologies that have been driving profound changes in civil society for centuries. From the first notions of community developed

Isobel Coleman, a senior fellow at the Council on Foreign Relations, is the Director of the Council's Civil Society, Markets, and Democracy Initiative and CFR's Women and Foreign Policy Program. She is the author of Paradise Beneath Her Feet: How Women Are Transforming the Middle East (Random House, 2010) and a contributing author to Restoring the Balance: A Middle East Strategy for the Next President (Brookings Institution Press, 2008). She has also served as a track leader for the Girls and Women Action Area at the Clinton Global Initiative. In 2011, Newsweek named her as one of "150 Women Who Shake the World."

41 ● ───────── 41 **8**

WORKS CITED ENTRY FOR A SELECTION FROM AN ANTHOLOGY

1   2   3

Coleman, Isobel. "Technology's Quiet Revolution for Women." *The Unfinished*

4

Revolution: Voices from the Global Fight for Women's Rights. Ed. Minky

5   6   7   8   9

Worden. New York: Seven Stories, 2012. 41-49. Print.

For more on citing selections from anthologies in MLA style, see items 34–36.

editor in addition to the author, give the name of the translator or editor before the edition number, using the abbreviation "Trans." for "Translated by" or "Ed." for "Edited by" (see
item 9).

Eagleton, Terry. *Literary Theory: An Introduction*. 3rd ed. Minneapolis: U of
Minnesota P, 2008.

38. Multivolume work Include the total number of volumes
before the city and publisher, using the abbreviation "vols." If
the volumes were published over several years, give the inclusive
dates of publication. (The abbreviation "Ed." means "Edited by,"
so it is the same for one or more editors.)

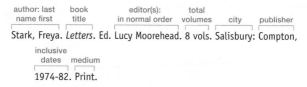

If you cite only one of the volumes in your paper, include
the volume number before the city and publisher and give
the date of publication for that volume. After the date, give
the medium of publication followed by the total number of
volumes.

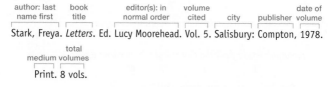

39. Sacred text Give the title of the edition of the sacred text
(taken from the title page), italicized; the editor's or translator's
name (if any); publication information; and the medium. Add the
name of the version, if there is one, after the medium.

The Oxford Annotated Bible with the Apocrypha. Ed. Herbert G. May and Bruce
    M. Metzger. New York: Oxford UP, 1965. Print. Rev. Standard Vers.

The Qur'an: Translation. Trans. Abdullah Yusuf Ali. Elmhurst: Tahrike, 2000.
    Print.

40. Book in a series   After the publication information, give the
medium and then the series name as it appears on the title page,
followed by the series number, if any.

Denham, A. E., ed. *Plato on Art and Beauty*. New York: Palgrave, 2012. Print.
    Philosophers in Depth.

41. Republished book   After the title of the book, give the original year of publication, followed by the current publication information. If the republished book contains new material, such as an
introduction or an afterword, include information about the new
material after the original date.

Trilling, Lionel. *The Liberal Imagination*. 1950. Introd. Louis Menand. New
    York: New York Rev. of Books, 2008. Print.

42. Publisher's imprint   If a book was published by an imprint (a
division) of a publishing company, give the name of the imprint, a
hyphen, and the name of the publisher.

Mantel, Hilary. *Bring Up the Bodies*. New York: Macrae-Holt, 2012. Print.

43. Pamphlet, brochure, or newsletter   Cite as you would a book.

The Legendary Sleepy Hollow Cemetery. Concord: Friends of Sleepy Hollow
    Cemetery, 2008. Print.

44. Dissertation

a. Published   For dissertations that have been published in book
form, italicize the title. After the title and before the book's publication information, give the abbreviation "Diss.," the name of

the institution, and the year the dissertation was accepted. Add the medium of publication at the end.

Damberg, Cheryl L. *Healthcare Reform: Distributional Consequences of an Employer Mandate for Workers in Small Firms*. Diss. Rand Graduate School, 1995. Santa Monica: Rand, 1996. Print.

b. Unpublished Begin with the author's name, followed by the dissertation title in quotation marks; the abbreviation "Diss."; the name of the institution; the year the dissertation was accepted; and the medium of the dissertation.

Jackson, Shelley. "Writing Whiteness: Contemporary Southern Literature in Black and White." Diss. U of Maryland, 2000. Print.

45. Proceedings of a conference Cite as you would a book, adding the name, date, and location of the conference after the title.

Sowards, Stacey K., Kyle Alvarado, Diana Arrieta, and Jacob Barde, eds. *Across Borders and Environments: Communication and Environmental Justice in International Contexts*. Proc. of Eleventh Biennial Conf. on Communication and the Environment, 25-28 June 2011, U of Texas at El Paso. Cincinnati: Intl. Environmental Communication Assn., 2012. PDF file.

46. Manuscript Give the author, a title or a description of the manuscript, and the date of composition. Use the abbreviation "MS" for "manuscript" (handwritten) or "TS" for "typescript." Add the name and location of the institution housing the material. For a manuscript found on the Web, give the preceding information but omit "MS" or "TS." List the title of the Web site, the medium ("Web"), and your date of access.

Arendt, Hannah. *Between Past and Future*. N.d. 1st draft. Hannah Arendt Papers. MS Div., Lib. of Cong. *Manuscript Division, Library of Congress*. Web. 24 Aug. 2012.

Web sites and parts of Web sites

47. An entire Web site

a. Web site with author or editor

author or editor: title of
last name first   Web site   sponsor

Railton, Stephen. *Mark Twain in His Times*. Stephen Railton and U of Virginia Lib.,

     update   date of
     date   medium   access

     2012. Web. 27 Nov. 2012.

Halsall, Paul, ed. *Internet Modern History Sourcebook*. Fordham U, 4 Nov.

     2011. Web. 19 Sept. 2012.

b. Web site with organization as author

                             title of   update
government   department   Web site   sponsor   date

United States. Dept. of Agriculture. *USDA*. US Dept. of Agriculture, 31 Oct. 2012.

               date of
    medium   access

     Web. 30 Nov. 2012.

c. Web site with no author Begin with the title of the site. If the site has no title, begin with a label such as "Home page."

Jacob Leisler Papers Project. Dept. of History, New York U, n.d. Web.

     24 Aug. 2012.

d. Web site with no title Use the label "Home page" or another appropriate description in place of a title.

Gray, Bethany. Home page. Iowa State U, 2012. Web. 22 Sept. 2012.

NOTE: If your instructor requires a URL for Web sources, include the URL, enclosed in angle brackets, at the end of the entry.

Railton, Stephen. *Mark Twain in His Times*. Stephen Railton and U of Virginia

     Lib., 2012. Web. 27 Nov. 2012. <http://twain.lib.virginia.edu/>.

Citation at a glance

Short work from a Web site   MLA

To cite a short work from a Web site in MLA style, include the following elements:

1   Author(s) of short work (if any)
2   Title and subtitle of short work
3   Title and subtitle of Web site
4   Sponsor of Web site ("N.p." if none)
5   Latest update date ("n.d." if none)
6   Medium
7   Date of access

INTERNAL PAGE OF WEB SITE

FOOTER ON PAGE

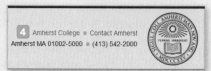

           2   3   4   5

"Losing a Country, Finding a Home." *Amherst College*. Amherst Coll., n.d.

    6   7

    Web. 12 Jan. 2013.

For more on citing sources from Web sites in MLA style, see items 48 and 49.

48. Short work from a Web site

▸ Citation at a glance: Short work from a Web site, page 632

a. Short work with author

author: last
name first   title of short work   title of
                                                                   Web site

Gallagher, Sean. "The Last Nomads of the Tibetan Plateau." *Pulitzer Center on*

                                    update   date of
                    sponsor   date   medium   access

    Crisis Reporting. Pulitzer Center, 25 Oct. 2012. Web. 30 Oct. 2012.

b. Short work with no author

              title of article   title of Web site

"Social and Historical Context: Vitality." *Arapesh Grammar and Digital*

                                            sponsor

    Language Archive Project. Inst. for Advanced Technology in the

          no   date of
          date medium access

    Humanities, n.d. Web. 30 Oct. 2012.

49. Long work from a Web site

author: last   title of   title of
name first   long work   Web site   sponsor

Milton, John. *Paradise Lost: Book I*. *Poetry Foundation*. Poetry Foundation,

    update   date of
    date   medium   access

    2012. Web. 14 Dec. 2012.

50. Entire blog Cite a blog as you would an entire Web site (see item 47).

Kiuchi, Tatsuro. *Tatsuro Kiuchi: News & Blog*. N.p., 19 Oct. 2012. Web.
    29 Oct. 2012.

51. Blog post or comment Cite a blog post or comment (a response to a post) as you would a short work from a Web site (see item 48). If the post or comment has no title, use the label "Blog post" or "Blog comment." Follow with the remaining information as for an entire blog (see item 50). (See item 11 for the use of screen names.)

author: last name first — title of blog post — title of blog — sponsor — update date

Eakin, Emily. "*Cloud Atlas*'s Theory of Everything." *NYR Blog*. NYREV, 2 Nov. 2012.

medium — date of access

    Web. 3 Dec. 2012.

author: screen name — label — title of blog post

mitchellfreedman. Blog comment. "*Cloud Atlas*'s Theory of Everything," by

author of blog post — title of blog — sponsor — date — medium — date of access

    Emily Eakin. *NYR Blog*. NYREV, 3 Nov. 2012. Web. 3 Dec. 2012.

52. Academic course or department home page Cite as a short work from a Web site (see item 48). For a course home page, begin with the name of the instructor and the title of the course or title of the page (use "Course home page" if there is no other title). For a department home page, begin with the name of the department and the label "Dept. home page."

Masiello, Regina. "355:101: Expository Writing." *Rutgers School of Arts and*
    Sciences. Writing Program, Rutgers U, 2012. Web. 19 Aug. 2012.

Comparative Media Studies. Dept. home page. *Massachusetts Institute of Technology*. MIT, n.d. Web. 6 Oct. 2012.

Audio, visual, and multimedia sources

53. Podcast If you view or listen to a podcast on the Web, cite it as you would a short work from a Web site (see item 48). If you download the podcast and view or listen to it on a computer or portable player, give the file type (such as "MP3 file" or "MOV file") as the medium.

a. Web

author:
last name first | podcast title | Web site title | sponsor

Tanner, Laura. "Virtual Reality in 9/11 Fiction." *Literature Lab*. Dept. of

no
date medium | date of access

    English, Brandeis U, n.d. Web. 30 Oct. 2012.

b. Downloaded

author:
last name first | podcast title | Web site title | sponsor

Tanner, Laura. "Virtual Reality in 9/11 Fiction." *Literature Lab*. Dept. of English,

no
date | medium

    Brandeis U, n.d. MP3 file.

54. Film (DVD, BD, or other format) Begin with the title, italicized. Then give the director ("Dir.") and the lead actors ("Perf.") or narrator ("Narr."); the distributor; the year of the film's release; and the medium. For the medium, use "Film" if you viewed the film in a theater or streamed it through a service such as Netflix; use "DVD" or "BD" if you viewed the film on a DVD or Blu-ray Disc; use "Web" if you viewed the film on a Web site on a computer. If you aren't sure of the medium, use "Film."

If your paper emphasizes a person or a category of people involved with the film, you may begin with those names and titles, as in the second example.

Frozen River. Dir. Courtney Hunt. Perf. Melissa Leo, Charlie McDermott, and Misty Upham. Sony, 2008. Film.

[film title] [director] [major performers] [distributor] [release date] [medium]

Forster, Marc, dir. *Finding Neverland.* Perf. Johnny Depp, Kate Winslet, Julie Christie, Radha Mitchell, and Dustin Hoffman. Miramax, 2004. DVD.

[director: last name first] [film title] [major performers] [distributor] [release date] [medium]

55. Supplementary material accompanying a film   Begin with the title of the supplementary material, in quotation marks, and the names of any important contributors, as for a film. End with information about the film, as in item 54.

"Sweeney's London." Prod. Eric Young. *Sweeney Todd: The Demon Barber of Fleet Street.* Dir. Tim Burton. DreamWorks, 2007. DVD. Disc 2.

56. Video or audio from the Web   Cite video or audio that you accessed on the Web as you would a short work from a Web site (see item 48), giving information about the author before other information about the video or audio.

Lewis, Paul. "Citizen Journalism." *YouTube.* YouTube, 14 May 2011. Web. 24 Sept. 2012.

[author: last name first] [title of video] [Web site title] [sponsor] [update date] [medium] [date of access]

author:
last name first
title of video
narrator
(or host or speaker)

Fletcher, Antoine. "The Ancient Art of the Atlatl." Narr. Brenton Bellomy.

Web site title
sponsor
update date
medium

Russell Cave National Monument. Natl. Park Service, 10 Oct. 2011. Web.

date of access
30 Oct. 2012.

author:
last name first
title of video
Web site title

Burstein, Julie. "Four Lessons in Creativity." *TED: Ideas Worth Spreading.*

sponsor
update
date
medium
date of
access

TED Conf., Mar. 2012. Web. 18 Aug. 2012.

57. Video game   List the developer or author of the game (if any); the title, italicized; the version ("Vers."), if there is one; the distributor and date of publication; and the platform or medium. If the game can be played on the Web, add information as for a work from a Web site (see item 48).

Firaxis Games. *Sid Meier's Civilization Revolution.* Take-Two Interactive, 2008. Xbox
360. *Edgeworld.* Atom Entertainment, 1 May 2012. Web. 15 June 2012.

58. Computer software or app   Cite as a video game (see item 57), giving whatever information is available about the version, distributor, date, and platform.

Words with Friends. Vers. 5.84. Zynga, 2013. iOS 4.3.

59. Television or radio episode or program   If you are citing an episode or a segment of a program, begin with the title of the episode or segment, in quotation marks. Then give the title of the program, italicized; relevant information about the program, such as the writer ("By"), director ("Dir."), performers ("Perf."), or narrator or host ("Narr."); the network; the local station and location (not necessary for cable networks, as in the second example on p. 639); the date of broadcast; and the medium ("Television," "Radio").

For a program you accessed on the Web, after the information about the program give the network, the original broadcast date, the title of the Web site, the medium ("Web"), and your date of access. If you are citing an entire program (not an episode or a segment), begin your entry with the title of the program, italicized.

How to cite a source reposted from another source

PROBLEM: Some sources that you find online, particularly on blogs or on video-sharing sites, did not originate with the person who uploaded or published the source online. In such a case, how do you give proper credit for the source?

EXAMPLE: Say you need to cite President John F. Kennedy's inaugural address. You have found a video on YouTube that provides footage of the address (see image). The video was uploaded by PaddyIrishMan2 on October 29, 2006. But clearly, PaddyIrishMan2 is not the author of the video or of the address.

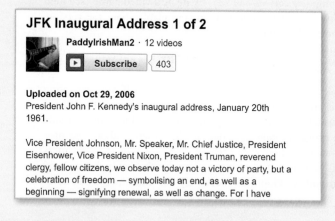

JFK Inaugural Address 1 of 2

PaddyIrishMan2 · 12 videos

▶ Subscribe ❮ 403

Uploaded on Oct 29, 2006
President John F. Kennedy's inaugural address, January 20th 1961.

Vice President Johnson, Mr. Speaker, Mr. Chief Justice, President Eisenhower, Vice President Nixon, President Truman, reverend clergy, fellow citizens, we observe today not a victory of party, but a celebration of freedom — symbolising an end, as well as a beginning — signifying renewal, as well as change. For I have

a. Broadcast

title of episode | program title | narrator (or host or speaker)

"Federal Role in Support of Autism." *Washington Journal.* Narr. Robb Harleston.

network | broadcast date | medium

C-SPAN. 1 Dec. 2012. Television.

The Daily Show with Jon Stewart. Comedy Central. 29 Nov. 2012. Television.

STRATEGY: Start with what you know. The source is a video that you viewed on the Web. For this particular video, John F. Kennedy is the speaker and the author of the inaugural address. PaddyIrishMan2 is identified as the person who uploaded the source to YouTube.

CITATION: To cite the source, you can combine the basic MLA guidelines for a lecture or public address (see item 62) and for a video found on the Web (see item 56).

author/speaker: last name first | title of address | Web site title | sponsor | update date

Kennedy, John F. "JFK Inaugural Address: 1 of 2." *YouTube.* YouTube, 29 Oct. 2006.

medium | date of access

Web. 24 Nov. 2012.

Because Kennedy's inauguration is a well-known historical event, you can be fairly certain that this is not the only version of the inauguration video. It is a good idea, therefore, to include information about which version you viewed as supplementary information at the end of your citation.

author/speaker: last name first | title of address | Web site title | sponsor | update date

Kennedy, John F. "JFK Inaugural Address: 1 of 2." *YouTube.* YouTube, 29 Oct. 2006.

medium | date of access | supplementary information

Web. 24 Nov. 2012. Uploaded by PaddyIrishMan2.

NOTE: If your work calls for a primary source, you should try to find the original source of the video; a reference librarian can help.

59. Television or radio episode or program *(cont.)*

b. Web

<small>title of episode   program title   narrator (or host or speaker)   network</small>

"Back-to-School Cure." *Currently Concordia*. Narr. Melissa Mulligan. CJLO,

<small>date of posting   Web site title   medium   date of access</small>

22 Sept. 2012. *CJLO.com*. Web. 23 Sept. 2012.

c. Podcast

<small>podcast title   episode number (if any)   narrator (or host or sponsor)   Web site title</small>

"NIH Research Radio." Episode 0170. Narr. Joe Balintfy. *NIH Radio*.

<small>sponsor   date of posting   medium</small>

Natl. Inst. of Health, 19 Oct. 2012. MP3 file.

60. Transcript You might find a transcript related to an interview or a program on a radio or television Web site or in a transcript database, such as in the first example. Cite the source as you would an interview (see item 27) or a radio or television program (see item 59). Add the label "Transcript" at the end of the entry.

Cullen, Heidi. "Weather Warnings for a 'Climate Changed Planet.'" Interview
     by Terry Gross. *Fresh Air*. Natl. Public Radio, 25 July 2011. *LexisNexis*
     Library Express. Web. 5 Apr. 2012. Transcript.

"Missing Athletes Join a Long List of Olympic Defectors." Narr. Melissa Block.
     All Things Considered. Natl. Public Radio, 9 Aug. 2012. Web. 28 Aug.
     2012. Transcript.

61. Performance For a live performance of a concert, a play, a ballet, or an opera, begin with the title of the work performed, italicized (unless it is named by form, number, and key). Then give the author or composer of the work ("By"); relevant information such as the director ("Dir."), the choreographer

("Chor."), the conductor ("Cond."), or the major performers ("Perf."); the theater, ballet, or opera company, if any; the theater and location; the date of the performance; and the label "Performance."

Wetu in the City: An Urban Black Indian Tale. By Mwalim [Morgan James Peters]. Dir. Naheem Garcia. Hibernian Hall, Boston. 16 Nov. 2012. Performance.

Symphony no. 4 in G. By Gustav Mahler. Cond. Mark Wigglesworth. Perf. Juliane Banse and Boston Symphony Orch. Symphony Hall, Boston. 17 Apr. 2009. Performance.

62. Lecture or public address   Begin with the speaker's name, followed by the title of the lecture (if any), in quotation marks; the organization sponsoring the lecture; the location; the date; and a label such as "Lecture" or "Address." If you viewed the lecture on the Web, cite as you would a short work from a Web site (see item 48).

a. Live

Berry, Wendell E. "It All Turns on Affection." Natl. Endowment for the Humanities. John F. Kennedy Center for the Performing Arts, Washington. 23 Apr. 2012. Lecture.

b. Web

Clinton, Hillary Rodham. "Remarks on 'Creating an AIDS-Free Generation.'" *US Department of State: Diplomacy in Action.* US Dept. of State, 8 Nov. 2011. Web. 29 Oct. 2012.

63. Musical score   For both print and online versions, begin with the composer's name; the title of the work, italicized (unless it is named by form, number, and key); and the date of composition. For a print source, give the place of publication; the name of the publisher and date of publication; and the medium. For an online source, give the title of the Web site; the publisher or sponsor of the site; the date of Web publication; the medium; and your date of access.

Beethoven, Ludwig van. Symphony no. 5 in C Minor, op. 67. 1807. *Center for Computer Assisted Research in the Humanities.* CCARH, Stanford U, 2000. Web. 23 Aug. 2012.

How to cite course materials

PROBLEM: Sometimes you will be assigned to work with materials that an instructor has uploaded to a course Web site or has handed out in class. Complete publication information may not always be given for such sources. A PDF file or a hard-copy article, for instance, may have a title and an author's name but give no other information. Or a video may not include information about the creator or the date the video was created. When you write a paper using such sources, how should you cite them in your own work?

EXAMPLE: Perhaps your instructor has included a PDF file of an article in a collection of readings on the course Web site (see image at right). You are writing a paper in which you use a passage from the work.

THE IMAGE OF THE RAILROAD IN *ANNA KARENINA*

Gary R. Jahn, University of Minnesota

The motif of the railroad recurs so frequently in Lev Tolstoj's *Anna Karenina* that the conclusion that it is somehow integral to a full understanding of the novel is inescapable. According to a recent study the railroad is mentioned at least thirty-two times in the book,[1] and every reader will remember that Anna and Vronskij first meet at a railway station, that Levin intensely dislikes the railroad, and that Anna commits suicide by leaping under a train.[2]

M. S. Al'tman once asked why Anna, having decided to do away with herself, should have selected such a gruesome method. The question is flippant only in its formulation, and a great deal of scholarly effort has been devoted to answering it. A searching of the extensive biographical data on Tolstoj has amply attested his personal aversion for the railroad. He wrote Turgenev in 1857 that "the railroad is to travel as a whore is to love,"[3] and it is known that he was discomfited to the point of nausea by the swaying of railway carriages. These facts provide a credible physiological basis for the standard, although not unanimous,[4] Soviet view that Levin's dyspeptic attitude toward the railroad is the correlative of Tolstoj's, that the highly autobiographical Levin was expressing Tolstoj's belief that the railroad served only to pander to and further inflame the already monstrous appetite of the idle and privileged for foreign luxuries, and that this belief overlies their mutual resentment of the forces tending to displace the landholding nobility from its position of inherited privilege: forces which the railroad is said to symbolize. The railroad is present in the novel so that it can be attacked, and this is precisely what Levin does in the book which he writes about contemporary Russian life.[5] There is an indubitable measure of truth in this understanding of the railway motif. It does account for Levin's view of the railroad and it is also true that for him the railroad symbolizes forces harmful to the traditional style of life of

64. Sound recording Begin with the name of the person you want to emphasize: the composer, conductor ("Cond."), or performer ("Perf."). For a long work, give the title, italicized (unless it is named by form, number, and key); the names of pertinent artists (such as performers, readers, or musicians); and the orchestra and conductor, if relevant. End with the manufacturer, the date, and the medium ("CD," "Audiocassette"). For a song,

STRATEGY: Look through section 56b for a model that matches the type of source you're working with. Is it an article? A chapter from a book? A photograph? A video? The model or models you find will give you an idea of the information you need to gather about the source. The usual required information is (1) the author or creator, (2) the title, (3) the date the work was published or created, (4) the date you accessed the source (usually only for sources on the Web), and (5) the medium in which the source was presented (see p. 602).

CITATION: For your citation, you can give only as much of the required information as you can find in the source. In this example, you know the source is an article with an author and a title, and you accessed it as a PDF file. So you can combine items 13a (basic format for an article) and 71 (digital file) to create the works cited entry for the source. Since you can't tell when the article was published, you should use "N.d." for "No date." At the end of your citation, it is a good idea to include the description "Course materials" and supplementary information about the course (such as its title or number and the term).

author: last name first	article title	no date	medium

Jahn, Gary R. "The Image of the Railroad in *Anna Karenina*." N.d. PDF file.

supplementary information

Course materials, EN101, Fall 2012.

NOTE: When in doubt about how much information to include or where to find it, consult your instructor.

put the title in quotation marks. If you include the name of the album or CD, italicize it.

a. CD

Bizet, Georges. *Carmen*. Perf. Jennifer Larmore, Thomas Moser, Angela
Gheorghiu, and Samuel Ramey. Bavarian State Orch. and Chorus. Cond.
Giuseppe Sinopoli. Warner, 1996. CD.

Blige, Mary J. "Don't Mind." *Life II: The Journey Continues (Act 1)*. Geffen,
2011. CD.

b. Downloaded

Blige, Mary J. "Don't Mind." *Life II: The Journey Continues (Act 1)*. Geffen,
2011. MP3 file.

65. Work of art   (a) For an original work of art, cite the artist's name; the title of the artwork, italicized; the date of composition; the medium of composition (for instance, "Oil on canvas," "Charcoal on paper"); and the institution and city in which the artwork is located. (b) For artworks found on the Web, omit the medium of composition and include the title of the Web site, the medium ("Web"), and your date of access. (c) If you downloaded a digital file from an archive or other online source, cite as in (a) but include the type of file as the medium ("JPEG file," "TIFF file"). (d) If you viewed the artwork as a reproduction in a print source, omit the medium of composition and add publication information about the print source, including the page number or figure number for the artwork; give the medium of reproduction at the end.

a. Original

Constable, John. *Dedham Vale*. 1802. Oil on canvas. Victoria and Albert
Museum, London.

b. Web

Hessing, Valjean. *Caddo Myth*. 1976. Joslyn Art Museum, Omaha. *Joslyn Art Museum*. Web. 19 Apr. 2012.

c. Digital file

Diebenkorn, Richard. *Ocean Park No. 38*. 1971. Phillips Collection, Washington. JPEG file.

d. Reproduction (print)

O'Keeffe, Georgia. *Black and Purple Petunias*. 1925. Private collection. *Two Lives: A Conversation in Paintings and Photographs*. Ed. Alexandra Arrowsmith and Thomas West. New York: Harper, 1992. 67. Print.

66. Photograph   (a) For an original photograph, cite the photographer's name; the title of the photograph, italicized; the date of composition; the medium ("Photograph"); and the institution and city in which the photograph is located. (b) For photographs found on the Web, omit the medium "Photograph" and include the title of the Web site, the medium "Web," and your date of access. (c) If you downloaded a digital file from an archive or other online source, cite as in (a) but include the type of file as the medium ("JPEG file," "TIFF file"). (d) If you viewed the photograph as a reproduction in a print source, omit the medium of composition and add publication information about the print source, including the page number or figure number for the artwork; give the medium of reproduction at the end.

a. Original

Feinstein, Harold. *Hangin' Out, Sharing a Public Bench, NYC*. 1948. Photograph. Panopticon Gallery, Boston.

66. Photograph (*cont.*)

b. Web

McCurry, Steve. *A World of Prayer*. *Magnum Photos*. Magnum Photos, 29 Oct.
    2012. Web. 31 Oct. 2012.

c. Digital file

Lucy Branham in Occoquan Prison Dress. 1919. Lib. of Cong. JPEG file.

d. Reproduction (print)

Kertész, André. *Meudon*. 1928. *Street Photography: From Atget to Cartier-
    Bresson*. By Clive Scott. London: Tauris, 2011. 61. Print.

67. Cartoon   Give the cartoonist's name; the title of the cartoon, if it has one, in quotation marks; the label "Cartoon" or
"Comic strip"; publication information; and the medium. To cite
an online cartoon, give the title of the Web site, the sponsor or
publisher, the medium, and your date of access.

Zyglis, Adam. "Delta and Denial." Cartoon. *Buffalo News*. Buffalo News,
    11 Jan. 2013. Web. 21 Jan. 2013.

68. Advertisement   Name the product or company being
advertised, followed by the word "Advertisement." Give
publication information for the source in which the advertisement appears.

UnitedHealthcare. Advertisement. *Smithsonian* Dec. 2012: 27. Print.

Corolla. Advertisement. *Root*. Slate Group, 28 Nov. 2012. Web. 28 Nov.
    2012.

69. Visual such as a table, a chart, or another graphic   Cite a
visual as you would a short work within a longer work. Use the

label "Table," "Chart," or "Graphic" following the title. Add the medium and, for an online source, the sponsor or publisher and the date of access. If the visual has a number in the source, give that number immediately before the medium.

"Canada's Energy Flow 2007." Chart. *Economist*. Economist Newspaper, 26 Oct. 2012. Web. 30 Oct. 2012.

"CDC Climate Ready States and Cities Initiative." Graphic. *Centers for Disease Control and Prevention*. Centers for Disease Control and Prevention, 1 Oct. 2012. Web. 31 Oct. 2012.

70. Map   Cite a map as you would a short work within a longer work. Or, if the map is published on its own, cite it as a book or another long work. Use the label "Map" following the title. Add the medium and, for an online source, the sponsor or publisher and the date of access.

"Population Origin Groups in Rural Texas." Map. *Perry-Castañeda Library Map Collection*. U of Texas at Austin, 1976. Web. 17 Mar. 2012.

71. Digital file   A digital file is any document or image that exists in digital form, independent of a Web site. To cite a digital file, begin with information required for the source (such as a photograph, a report, a sound recording, or a radio program), following the guidelines throughout section 56b. Then for the medium, indicate the type of file: "JPEG file," "PDF file," "MP3 file," and so on.

	photographer	photograph title	date of composition	location of photograph

Hine, Lewis W. *Girl in Cherryville Mill*. 1908. Prints and Photographs Div., Lib.

	medium

of Cong. JPEG file.

"Back to School." *This American Life*. Narr. Ira Glass. Episode 474. Chicago Public Media, 14 Sept. 2012. MP3 file.

National Institute of Mental Health. *What Rescue Workers Can Do*.
Washington: US Dept. of Health and Human Services, 2006. PDF file.

Government and legal documents

72. Government document Treat the government agency as
the author, giving the name of the government followed by the
name of the department and the agency, if any. For print sources,
add the medium at the end of the entry. For sources found on
the Web, follow the model for an entire Web site (see item 47) or
for short or long works from a Web site (see items 48 and 49).

government	department	agency (or agencies)

United States. Dept. of Agriculture. Food and Nutrition Service. Child

title (long work)

Nutrition Programs. *Eligibility Manual for School Meals: Determining and*

Web site title · sponsor

Verifying Eligibility. *National School Lunch Program*. US Dept. of

update
date · medium · date of access

Agriculture, Aug. 2012. Web. 30 Oct. 2012.

Canada. Minister of Indian Affairs and Northern Dev. *Gathering Strength:
Canada's Aboriginal Action Plan*. Ottawa: Minister of Public Works and
Govt. Services Can., 2000. Print.

73. Testimony before a legislative body

Carson, Johnnie. "Assessing US Policy on Peacekeeping Operations in
Africa." Testimony before the US House Foreign Affairs Committee,
Subcommittee on Africa, Global Health, and Human Rights.
US Department of State: Diplomacy in Action. US Dept. of State, 13 Sept.
2012. Web. 29 Sept. 2012.

74. Historical document To cite a historical document, such as the US Constitution or the Canadian Charter of Rights and Freedoms, begin with the document author, if it has one, and then give the document title, neither italicized nor in quotation marks, and the document date. For a print version, continue as for a selection in an anthology (see item 35) or for a book (with the title not italicized). For an online version, cite as a short work from a Web site (see item 48).

Jefferson, Thomas. First Inaugural Address. 1801. *The American Reader*. Ed.
   Diane Ravitch. New York: Harper, 1990. 42-44. Print.

Constitution of the United States. 1787. *The Charters of Freedom*. US Natl.
   Archives and Records Administration, n.d. Web. 19 Jan. 2013.

75. Legislative act (law) Begin with the name of the act, neither italicized nor in quotation marks. Then provide the act's Public Law number; its Statutes at Large volume and page numbers; its date of enactment; and the medium of publication.

Electronic Freedom of Information Act Amendments of 1996. Pub. L.
   104-231. 110 Stat. 3048. 2 Oct. 1996. Print.

76. Court case Name the first plaintiff and the first defendant. Then give the volume, name, and page number of the law report; the court name; the year of the decision; and publication information. Do not italicize the name of the case. (In the text of the paper, the name of the case is italicized; see item 19 on p. 592.)

Utah v. Evans. 536 US 452. Supreme Court of the US. 2002. *Supreme Court
   Collection*. Legal Information Inst., Cornell U Law School, n.d. Web.
   30 Apr. 2012.

Personal communication and social media

77. E-mail message   Begin with the writer's name and the subject line. Then write "Message to" followed by the name of the recipient. End with the date of the message and the medium ("E-mail").

Lowe, Walter. "Review Questions." Message to the author. 15 Mar. 2013. E-mail.

78. Text message   Cite like an e-mail message, giving the medium as "Text message."

Wiley, Joanna. Message to the author. 29 Nov. 2012. Text message.

79. Posting to an online discussion list   When possible, cite archived versions of postings. If you cannot locate an archived version, keep a copy of the posting for your records. Begin with the author's name, followed by the title or subject line, in quotation marks (use the label "Online posting" if the posting has no title). Then proceed as for a short work from a Web site (see item 48).

Baker, Frank. "A New Twist on a Classic." *Developing Digital Literacies*. NCTE,
    30 Nov. 2012. Web. 10 Jan. 2013.

80. Facebook post or comment   Cite as a short work from a Web site (see item 48), beginning with the writer's real name followed by the screen name in parentheses, if both are given. Otherwise use whatever name is given in the source. Follow with the title of the post, if any, in quotation marks. If there is no title, use the label "Post."

Bedford/St. Martin's. "Liz Losh Discusses Teaching about Interactive
    Media with Comics: http://ow.ly/imucP." *Facebook*. Facebook,
    5 Mar. 2013. Web. 26 Mar. 2013.

Erin Houlihan. Post. *Facebook*. Facebook, 23 Nov. 2012. Web. 26 Nov. 2012.

81. Twitter post (tweet) Begin with the writer's real name followed by the screen name in parentheses, if both are given. Otherwise use whatever name is given in the source. Give the text of the entire tweet in quotation marks, using the writer's capitalization and punctuation. Follow the text with the date and time noted on the tweet. Use "Tweet" as the medium.

Curiosity Rover. "The journey of 352,000,000 miles begins with a single
    launch. One year ago today, I left Earth for Mars http://twitpic.com
    /bgq1vn." 26 Nov. 2012, 10:10 a.m. Tweet.

56c MLA information notes (optional)

Researchers who use the MLA system of parenthetical documentation may also use information notes for one of two purposes:

1. to provide additional material that is important but might interrupt the flow of the paper
2. to refer to several sources that support a single point or to provide comments on sources

Information notes may be either footnotes or endnotes. Footnotes appear at the foot of the page; endnotes appear on a separate page at the end of the paper, just before the list of works cited. For either style, the notes are numbered consecutively throughout the paper. The text of the paper contains a raised arabic numeral that corresponds to the number of the note.

TEXT

In the past several years, employees have filed a number of lawsuits
against employers because of online monitoring practices.[1]

NOTE

1. For a discussion of federal law applicable to electronic
surveillance in the workplace, see Kesan 293.

57 MLA manuscript format; sample research paper

The following guidelines are consistent with advice given in the *MLA Handbook for Writers of Research Papers*, 7th ed. (New York: MLA, 2009), and with typical requirements for student papers. For a sample MLA research paper, see pages 656–61.

57a MLA manuscript format

Formatting the paper

Papers written in MLA style should be formatted as follows.

Font If your instructor does not require a specific font, choose one that is standard and easy to read (such as Times New Roman).

Title and identification MLA does not require a title page. On the first page of your paper, place your name, your instructor's name, the course title, and the date on separate lines against the left margin. Then center your title. (See p. 656 for a sample first page.)

If your instructor requires a title page, ask for formatting guidelines. A format similar to the one on page 729 may be acceptable.

Page numbers (running head) Put the page number preceded by your last name in the upper right corner of each page, one-half inch below the top edge. Use arabic numerals (1, 2, 3, and so on).

Margins, line spacing, and paragraph indents Leave margins of one inch on all sides of the page. Left-align the text.

Double-space throughout the paper. Do not add extra space above or below the title of the paper or between paragraphs.

Indent the first line of each paragraph one-half inch from the left margin.

Capitalization, italics, and quotation marks In titles of works, capitalize all words except articles (*a, an, the*), prepositions (*to, from, between,* and so on), coordinating conjunctions (*and, but, or, nor, for, so, yet*), and the *to* in infinitives — unless the word is first or last in the title or subtitle. Follow these guidelines in your paper even if the title appears in all capital or all lowercase letters in the source.

In the text of an MLA paper, when a complete sentence follows a colon, lowercase the first word following the colon unless the sentence is a quotation or a well-known expression or principle.

Italicize the titles of books, journals, magazines, and other long works, such as Web sites. Use quotation marks around the titles of articles, short stories, poems, and other short works.

Long quotations When a quotation is longer than four typed lines of prose or three lines of poetry, set it off from the text by indenting the entire quotation one inch from the left margin. Double-space the indented quotation and do not add extra space above or below it.

Do not use quotation marks when a quotation has been set off from the text by indenting. See page 656 for an example.

URLs When you need to break a URL at the end of a line in the text of your paper, break it only after a slash or a double slash and do not insert a hyphen. For MLA rules on dividing URLs in your list of works cited, see page 655.

Headings MLA neither encourages nor discourages the use of headings and provides no guidelines for their use. If you would like to insert headings in a long essay or research paper, check first with your instructor.

Visuals   MLA classifies visuals as tables and figures (figures include graphs, charts, maps, photographs, and drawings). Label each table with an arabic numeral ("Table 1," "Table 2," and so on) and provide a clear caption that identifies the subject. Capitalize the caption as you would a title (see 45c); do not italicize the label and caption or place them in quotation marks. Place the label and caption on separate lines above the table, flush with the left margin.

For a table that you have borrowed or adapted, give the source below the table in a note like the following:

Source: Boris Groysberg and Michael Slind; "Leadership Is a Conversation"; *Harvard Business Review* June 2012: 83; print.

For each figure, place the figure number (using the abbreviation "Fig.") and a caption below the figure, flush left. Capitalize the caption as you would a sentence; include source information following the caption. (When referring to the figure in your paper, use the abbreviation "fig." in parenthetical citations; otherwise spell out the word.) See page 659 for an example of a figure in a paper.

Place visuals in the text, as close as possible to the sentences that relate to them, unless your instructor prefers that visuals appear in an appendix.

Preparing the list of works cited

Begin the list of works cited on a new page at the end of the paper. Center the title "Works Cited" about one inch from the top of the page. Double-space throughout. See pages 198 and 661 for sample lists of works cited.

Alphabetizing the list Alphabetize the list by the last names of the authors (or editors); if a work has no author or editor, alphabetize by the first word of the title other than *A*, *An*, or *The*.

If your list includes two or more works by the same author, use the author's name for the first entry only. For subsequent entries, use three hyphens followed by a period. List the titles in alphabetical order. (See items 6 and 7 on pp. 605–06.)

Indenting Do not indent the first line of each works cited entry, but indent any additional lines one-half inch. This technique highlights the names of the authors, making it easy for readers to scan the alphabetized list. See page 661.

URLs (Web addresses) If you need to include a URL in a works cited entry and it must be divided across lines, break the URL only after a slash or a double slash. Do not insert a hyphen at the end of the line. Insert angle brackets around the URL. (See the note following item 47 on p. 631.) If your word processing program automatically turns URLs into links (by underlining them and changing the color), turn off this feature.

57b Sample MLA research paper

On the following pages is a research paper on the topic of electronic surveillance in the workplace, written by Anna Orlov, a student in a composition class. Orlov's paper is documented with in-text citations and a list of works cited in MLA style. Annotations in the margins of the paper draw your attention to Orlov's use of MLA style and her effective writing.

Orlov 1

Anna Orlov

Professor Willis

English 101

7 December 2009

Title is centered.

Online Monitoring:

A Threat to Employee Privacy in the Wired Workplace

Opening sentences provide background for thesis.

As the Internet has become an integral tool of businesses, company policies on Internet usage have become as common as policies regarding vacation days or sexual harassment. A 2005 study by the American Management Association and ePolicy Institute found that 76% of companies monitor employees' use of the Web, and the number of companies that block employees' access to certain Web sites has increased 27% since 2001 (1). Unlike other company rules, however, Internet usage policies often include language authorizing companies to secretly monitor their employees, a practice that raises questions about rights in the workplace. Although companies often have legitimate concerns that lead them to monitor employees' Internet usage—from expensive security breaches to reduced productivity—the benefits of electronic surveillance are outweighed by its costs to employees' privacy and autonomy.

Thesis asserts Orlov's main point.

While surveillance of employees is not a new phenomenon, electronic surveillance allows employers to monitor workers with unprecedented efficiency. In his book *The Naked Employee*, Frederick Lane describes offline ways in which employers have been permitted to intrude on employees' privacy for decades, such as drug testing, background checks, psychological exams, lie detector tests, and in-store video surveillance. The difference, Lane argues, between these old methods of data gathering and electronic surveillance involves quantity:

Summary and long quotation are introduced with a signal phrase naming the author.

Long quotation is set off from the text; quotation marks are omitted.

> Technology makes it possible for employers
> to gather enormous amounts of data about
> employees, often far beyond what is necessary to

Marginal annotations indicate MLA-style formatting and effective writing.

Orlov 2

satisfy safety or productivity concerns. And the
trends that drive technology—faster, smaller,
cheaper—make it possible for larger and larger
numbers of employers to gather ever-greater amounts
of personal data. (3-4)

In an age when employers can collect data whenever employees use
their computers—when they send e-mail, surf the Web, or even arrive
at or depart from their workstations—the challenge for both employers
and employees is to determine how much is too much.

> Page number
> is given in
> parentheses after
> the final period.

Another key difference between traditional surveillance and
electronic surveillance is that employers can monitor workers' computer
use secretly. One popular monitoring method is keystroke logging, which is
done by means of an undetectable program on employees' computers. The
Web site of a vendor for Spector Pro, a popular keystroke logging program,
explains that the software can be installed to operate in "Stealth" mode so
that it "does not show up as an icon, does not appear in the Windows
system tray, . . . [and] cannot be uninstalled without the Spector Pro
password which YOU specify" ("Automatically"). As Lane explains, these
programs record every key entered into the computer in hidden directories
that can later be accessed or uploaded by supervisors; the programs can
even scan for keywords tailored to individual companies (128-29).

> Clear topic
> sentences, like
> this one, are
> used throughout
> the paper.

> Source with an
> unknown author
> is cited by a
> shortened title.

Some experts have argued that a range of legitimate concerns
justifies employer monitoring of employee Internet usage. As *PC World*
columnist Daniel Tynan points out, companies that don't monitor
network traffic can be penalized for their ignorance: "Employees could
accidentally (or deliberately) spill confidential information . . . or
allow worms to spread throughout a corporate network." The ePolicy
Institute, an organization that advises companies about reducing risks
from technology, reported that breaches in computer security cost
institutions $100 million in 1999 alone (Flynn). Companies also are

> Orlov anticipates
> objections and
> provides sources
> for opposing
> views.

Orlov 3

held legally accountable for many of the transactions conducted on
their networks and with their technology. Legal scholar Jay Kesan
points out that the law holds employers liable for employees' actions
such as violations of copyright laws, the distribution of offensive or
graphic sexual material, and illegal disclosure of confidential
information (312).

Transition helps readers move from one paragraph to the next.

These kinds of concerns should give employers, in certain
instances, the right to monitor employee behavior. But employers
rushing to adopt surveillance programs might not be adequately
weighing the effect such programs can have on employee morale.
Employers must consider the possibility that employees will perceive
surveillance as a breach of trust that can make them feel like
disobedient children, not responsible adults who wish to perform their
jobs professionally and autonomously.

Orlov treats both sides fairly; she provides a transition to her own argument.

Yet determining how much autonomy workers should be given is
complicated by the ambiguous nature of productivity in the wired
workplace. On the one hand, computers and Internet access give
employees powerful tools to carry out their jobs; on the other hand,
the same technology offers constant temptations to avoid work. As a
2005 study by *Salary.com* and *America Online* indicates, the Internet
ranked as the top choice among employees for ways of wasting time
on the job; it beat talking with co-workers—the second most
popular method—by a margin of nearly two to one (Frauenheim). Chris
Gonsalves, an editor for *eWeek.com*, argues that the technology has
changed the terms between employers and employees: "While bosses
can easily detect and interrupt water-cooler chatter," he writes, "the
employee who is shopping at Lands' End or IMing with fellow fantasy
baseball managers may actually appear to be working." The gap
between behaviors that are observable to managers and the
employee's actual activities when sitting behind a computer has

No page number is available for this Web source.

Orlov 4

Fig. 1. This "Dilbert" comic strip suggests that personal Internet usage is widespread in the workplace (Adams 106).

> Illustration has figure number, caption, and source information.

created additional motivations for employers to invest in surveillance programs. "Dilbert," a popular cartoon that spoofs office culture, aptly captures how rampant recreational Internet use has become in the workplace (see fig. 1).

But monitoring online activities can have the unintended effect of making employees resentful. As many workers would be quick to point out, Web surfing and other personal uses of the Internet can provide needed outlets in the stressful work environment; many scholars have argued that limiting and policing these outlets can exacerbate tensions between employees and managers. Kesan warns that "prohibiting personal use can seem extremely arbitrary and can seriously harm morale. . . . Imagine a concerned parent who is prohibited from checking on a sick child by a draconian company policy" (315-16). As this analysis indicates, employees can become disgruntled when Internet usage policies are enforced to their full extent.

> Orlov counters opposing views and provides support for her argument.

> Orlov uses a brief signal phrase to move from her argument to the words of a source.

Additionally, many experts disagree with employers' assumption that online monitoring can increase productivity. Employment law attorney Joseph Schmitt argues that, particularly for employees who are paid a salary rather than an hourly wage, "a company shouldn't care whether employees spend one or 10 hours on the Internet

Orlov 5

as long as they are getting their jobs done—and provided that

Orlov cites an indirect source: words quoted in another source.

they are not accessing inappropriate sites" (qtd. in Verespej). Other experts even argue that time spent on Internet browsing can actually be productive for companies. As a CBS News video reports, some companies have started using the growing popularity of social media to their advantage. Comcast, for example, has hired a small group of employees to "answer customer complaints" via Twitter. Some companies recognize that "socializing online doesn't have to mean a drain on productivity," that it can become a "new way of doing business" (Sieberg). Employers, in other words, may benefit from showing more faith in their employees' ability to exercise their autonomy.

Employees' right to privacy and autonomy in the workplace, however, remains a murky area of the law. Although evaluating where to draw the line between employee rights and employer powers is often a duty that falls to the judicial system, the courts have shown little willingness to intrude on employers' exercise of control over their computer networks. Federal law provides few guidelines related to online monitoring of employees, and only Connecticut and Delaware require companies to disclose this type of surveillance to employees (Tam et al.). "It is unlikely that we will see a legally guaranteed zone of privacy in the American workplace," predicts Kesan (293). This reality leaves employees and employers to sort the potential risks and benefits of technology in contract agreements and terms of employment.

Orlov sums up her argument and suggests a course of action.

With continuing advances in technology, protecting both employers and employees will require greater awareness of these programs, better disclosure to employees, and a more public discussion about what types of protections are necessary to guard individual freedoms in the wired workplace.

Orlov 6

Works Cited

Adams, Scott. *Dilbert and the Way of the Weasel*. New York: Harper, 2002. Print.

American Management Association and ePolicy Institute. "2005 Electronic Monitoring and Surveillance Survey." *American Management Association*. Amer. Management Assn., 2005. Web. 25 Nov. 2009.

"Automatically Record Everything They Do Online! Spector Pro 5.0 FAQ's." *Netbus.org*. Netbus.Org, n.d. Web. 27 Nov. 2009.

Flynn, Nancy. "Internet Policies." *ePolicy Institute*. ePolicy Inst., n.d. Web. 26 Nov. 2009.

Frauenheim, Ed. "Stop Reading This Headline and Get Back to Work." *CNET News.com*. CNET Networks, 11 July 2005. Web. 25 Nov. 2009.

Gonsalves, Chris. "Wasting Away on the Web." *eWeek.com*. Ziff Davis Enterprise Holdings, 8 Aug. 2005. Web. 27 Nov. 2009.

Kesan, Jay P. "Cyber-Working or Cyber-Shirking? A First Principles Examination of Electronic Privacy in the Workplace." *Florida Law Review* 54.2 (2002): 289-332. Print.

Lane, Frederick S., III. *The Naked Employee: How Technology Is Compromising Workplace Privacy*. New York: Amer. Management Assn., 2003. Print.

Sieberg, Daniel. "Surfing the Web on the Job." *YouTube*. YouTube, 12 Nov. 2009. Web. 26 Nov. 2009.

Tam, Pui-Wing, et al. "Snooping E-mail by Software Is Now a Workplace Norm." *Wall Street Journal* 9 Mar. 2005: B1+. Print.

Tynan, Daniel. "Your Boss Is Watching." *PC World*. PC World Communications, 6 Oct. 2004. Web. 27 Nov. 2009.

Verespej, Michael A. "Inappropriate Internet Surfing." *Industry Week*. Penton Media, 7 Feb. 2000. Web. 25 Nov. 2009.

Heading is centered.

List is alphabetized by authors' last names (or by title when a work has no author).

Abbreviation "n.d." indicates that the online source has no update date.

First line of each entry is at the left margin; extra lines are indented ½".

Double-spacing is used throughout.

A work with four authors is listed by the first author's name and the abbreviation "et al." (for "and others").

Writing APA papers

BRIEF DIRECTORY

Most instructors in the social sciences and some instructors in other disciplines will ask you to document your sources with the American Psychological Association (APA) system of in-text citations and references described in section 61. You face three main challenges when writing an APA-style paper that draws on sources: (1) supporting a thesis, (2) citing your sources and avoiding plagiarism, and (3) integrating quotations and other source material.

Examples in this section are drawn from one student's research for a review of the literature on treatments for childhood obesity. Luisa Mirano's paper appears on pages 729–38.

NOTE: For advice on finding and evaluating sources and on managing information in all your college courses, see sections 50–52.

58 Supporting a thesis

Most research assignments ask you to form a thesis, or main idea, and to support that thesis with well-organized evidence. (See also 1c.) In a paper reviewing the literature on a topic, the thesis analyzes the often competing conclusions drawn by a variety of researchers.

58a Form a working thesis.

Once you have read a range of sources, considered your issue from different perspectives, and chosen an entry point in the research conversation (see 50b), you are ready to form a working thesis: a one-sentence (or occasionally a two-sentence) statement of your central idea. (See also 1c.) Because it is a working, or tentative, thesis, you can remain flexible and revise it as your ideas develop. Ultimately, your thesis will express not just your opinion but your informed, reasoned answer to your research question (see 50b). Here, for example, is a research question posed by Luisa Mirano, a student in a psychology class, followed by her thesis in answer to that question.

RESEARCH QUESTION

Is medication the right treatment for the escalating problem of childhood obesity?

WORKING THESIS

Treating cases of childhood obesity with medication alone is too narrow an approach for this growing problem.

hackerhandbooks.com/bedhandbook

e Researched writing > Exercises: APA papers: 58–1 and 58–2

TEACHING TIP

Consider building a research proposal into a research paper assignment. One benefit is that writing a research proposal allows students to define their topic as meaningful and relevant. Pitch the proposal as a persuasive piece of writing: Students have to tell you why their topic matters, who the stakeholders are, and what's at stake. A proposal also gives students the opportunity to explore the debate and present different positions in the course of framing their own position.

The thesis usually appears at the end of the introductory paragraph. To read Luisa Mirano's thesis in the context of her introduction, see page 731.

58b Organize your ideas.

The American Psychological Association (APA) encourages the use of headings to help readers follow the organization of a paper. For an original research report, the major headings often follow a standard model: Method, Results, Discussion. The introduction does not have a heading; it consists of the material between the title of the paper and the first heading.

> **MAKING THE MOST OF YOUR HANDBOOK**
>
> It's helpful to start off with a working thesis and a rough outline — especially when writing from sources.
>
> ▶ Draft a working thesis: 1c
> ▶ Sketch a plan: 1d

For a literature review, headings will vary. The student who wrote about treatments for childhood obesity used four questions to focus her research; the questions then became headings in her paper (see 62b).

58c Use sources to inform and support your argument.

Used thoughtfully, your source materials will make your argument more complex and convincing for readers. Sources can play several different roles as you develop your points.

Providing background information or context

You can use facts and statistics to support generalizations or to establish the importance of your topic, as student writer Luisa Mirano does in her introduction.

> In March 2004, U.S. Surgeon General Richard Carmona called attention to a health problem in the United States that, until recently, has been overlooked: childhood obesity. Carmona said that the "astounding"

TEACHING TIP

Make an appointment with a reference librarian for a session with your class. A reference librarian can help students think about the roles that various sources might play in their college papers.

15% child obesity rate constitutes an "epidemic." Since the early 1980s, that rate has "doubled in children and tripled in adolescents." Now more than nine million children are classified as obese.

Explaining terms or concepts

If readers are unlikely to be familiar with a word, a phrase, or an idea important to your topic, you must explain it for them. Quoting or paraphrasing a source can help you define terms and concepts in accessible language. Luisa Mirano uses a scholarly source to explain how one of the major obesity drugs functions.

> Sibutramine suppresses appetite by blocking the reuptake of the neurotransmitters serotonin and norepinephrine in the brain (Yanovski & Yanovski, 2002, p. 594).

Supporting your claims

As you draft, make sure to back up your assertions with facts, examples, and other evidence from your research (see also 6h). Student writer Luisa Mirano, for example, uses one source's findings to support her central idea that the medical treatment of childhood obesity has limitations.

> As journalist Greg Critser (2003) noted in his book *Fat Land*, use of weight-loss drugs is unlikely to have an effect without the proper "support system"—one that includes doctors, facilities, time, and money (p. 3).

Lending authority to your argument

Expert opinion can add credibility to your argument (see also 6h). But don't rely on experts to make your argument for you. Construct your argument in your own words and, when appropriate, cite the judgment of an authority in the field for support.

> Both medical experts and policymakers recognize that solutions might come not only from a laboratory but also from policy, education, and advocacy. A handbook designed to educate doctors on obesity called

TEACHING TIP

Assign students to work in pairs or small groups to identify the roles that sources play in a text that you distribute. Choose a text that is fairly brief (no more than three pages) and uses at least three sources, one of which might be visual. The text should be short enough so that students can complete the activity in a single class period or a manageable chat session online. Ask students to identify the sources the writer has used as well as the function of each source in the context of the piece of writing. Does the source provide background? Explain a term? Support the author's claim? Present an objection? Provide an illustration?

for "major changes in some aspects of western culture" (Hoppin &
Taveras, 2004, Conclusion section, para. 1).

Anticipating and countering alternative interpretations

Do not ignore sources that seem contrary to your position or that
offer interpretations different from your own. Instead, use them to
give voice to opposing points of view and alternative interpretations before you counter them (see 6i). Readers often have objections in mind already, whether or not they agree with you. Mirano
uses a source to acknowledge value in her opponents' position that
medication alone can successfully treat childhood obesity.

> As researchers Yanovski and Yanovski (2002) have explained, obesity
> was once considered "either a moral failing or evidence of underlying
> psychopathology" (p. 592). But this view has shifted: Many medical
> professionals now consider obesity a biomedical rather than a moral
> condition, influenced by both genetic and environmental factors.
> Yanovski and Yanovski have further noted that the development of
> weight-loss medications in the early 1990s showed that "obesity should
> be treated in the same manner as any other chronic disease . . . through
> the long-term use of medication" (p. 592).

59   Citing sources; avoiding plagiarism

In a research paper, you will draw on the work of other researchers and writers, and you must document their contributions by
citing your sources. Sources are cited for two reasons:

1. to tell readers where your information comes from—so that
   they can assess its reliability and, if interested, find and read
   the original source

SCHOLARS ON AVOIDING PLAGIARISM

Haviland, Carol P., and Joan A. Mullin. *Who Owns This Text? Plagiarism,
Authorship, and Disciplinary Cultures.* Logan: Utah State UP, 2009. Print.
The authors pulled together a collection that addresses citation practices
in different academic disciplines and how definitions of authorship,
plagiarism, and intellectual property are constructed in each discipline.
Haviland, Mullin, and others spent three years interviewing college faculty from fields such as biology, sociology, computer science, and visual
media. They conclude that faculty should model for students discipline-
specific practices for collaboration and "knowledge building" (159).

2. to give credit to the writers from whom you have borrowed words and ideas

You must cite anything you borrow from a source, including direct quotations; statistics and other specific facts; visuals such as tables, graphs, and diagrams; and any ideas you present in a summary or paraphrase. Borrowing without proper acknowledgment is a form of dishonesty known as *plagiarism*.

The only exception is common knowledge—information that your readers may know or could easily locate in any number of reference sources.

59a Use the APA system for citing sources.

The American Psychological Association recommends an author-date system of citations. The following is a brief description of how the author-date system usually works.

1. The source is introduced by a signal phrase that includes the last name of the author followed by the date of publication in parentheses.

2. The material being cited is followed by a page number in parentheses.

3. At the end of the paper, an alphabetized list of references gives complete publication information for the source.

IN-TEXT CITATION

As researchers Yanovski and Yanovski (2002) have explained, obesity was once considered "either a moral failing or evidence of underlying psychopathology" (p. 592).

ENTRY IN THE LIST OF REFERENCES

Yanovski, S. Z., & Yanovski, J. A. (2002). Drug therapy: Obesity. *The New England Journal of Medicine, 346,* 591-602.

This basic APA format varies for different types of sources. For a detailed discussion and other models, see 61.

59b Avoid plagiarism when quoting, summarizing, and paraphrasing sources.

Your research paper represents your ideas in conversation with the ideas in your sources. To be fair and responsible, you must acknowledge your debt to the writers of those sources. When you acknowledge your sources, you avoid plagiarism, a form of academic dishonesty.

Three different acts are considered plagiarism: (1) failing to cite quotations and borrowed ideas, (2) failing to enclose borrowed language in quotation marks, and (3) failing to put summaries and paraphrases in your own words. Definitions of plagiarism may vary; it's a good idea to find out how your school defines and addresses academic dishonesty.

Citing quotations and borrowed ideas

To indicate that you are using a source's exact phrases or sentences, you must enclose them in quotation marks unless they have been set off from the text by indenting (see 60a). To omit the quotation marks is to claim—falsely—that the language is your own. Such an omission is plagiarism even if you have cited the source.

> **MAKING THE MOST OF YOUR HANDBOOK**
>
> When you use exact language from a source, you need to show that it is a quotation.
> - ▶ Quotation marks for direct quotations: 37a
> - ▶ Setting off long quotations: page 673

ORIGINAL SOURCE

In an effort to seek the causes of this disturbing trend, experts have pointed to a range of important potential contributors

SCHOLARS ON RESEARCH WRITING

Shi, Ling. "Rewriting and Paraphrasing Source Texts in Second Language Writing." *Journal of Second Language Writing* 21.2 (2012): 134–48. Print. For most college students, paraphrasing and summarizing texts are difficult skills to master. For multilingual students, such skills are even harder to master, according to the author. Shi concludes that paraphrasing and summarizing are "in fact complex and depend on one's knowledge of the content, the disciplinary nature of citation practices, and the rhetorical purposes of using citations in a specific context of disciplinary writing" (134).

to the rise in childhood obesity that are unrelated to media: a reduction in physical education classes and after-school athletic programs, an increase in the availability of sodas and snacks in public schools, the growth in the number of fast-food outlets across the country, the trend toward "super-sizing" food portions in restaurants, and the increasing number of highly processed high-calorie and high-fat grocery products.

— Henry J. Kaiser Family Foundation, "The Role of Media in Childhood Obesity" (2004), p. 1

PLAGIARISM

According to the Henry J. Kaiser Family Foundation (2004), experts have pointed to a range of important potential contributors to the rise in childhood obesity that are unrelated to media (p. 1).

BORROWED LANGUAGE IN QUOTATION MARKS

According to the Henry J. Kaiser Family Foundation (2004), "experts have pointed to a range of important potential contributors to the rise in childhood obesity that are unrelated to media" (p. 1).

NOTE: Quotation marks are not used when quoted sentences are set off from the text by indenting (see 60a).

Putting summaries and paraphrases in your own words

Summaries and paraphrases are written in your own words. A summary condenses information; a paraphrase conveys the information using roughly the same number of words as in the original source. When you summarize or paraphrase, it is not enough to name the source; you must restate the source's meaning using your own language. (See also 51c.) You commit plagiarism if you patchwrite—half-copy the author's sentences, either by mixing the author's phrases with your own without using quotation marks or by plugging your own synonyms into the author's sentence structure. The following paraphrases are plagiarized—even though the source is cited—because their language and sentence structure are too close to those of the source.

ORIGINAL SOURCE

In an effort to seek the causes of this disturbing trend, experts have pointed to a range of important potential contributors to the rise in childhood obesity that are unrelated to media.

— Henry J. Kaiser Family Foundation, "The Role of Media in Childhood Obesity" (2004), p. 1

UNACCEPTABLE BORROWING OF PHRASES

According to the Henry J. Kaiser Family Foundation (2004), experts have indicated a range of significant potential contributors to the rise in childhood obesity that are not linked to media (p. 1).

UNACCEPTABLE BORROWING OF STRUCTURE

According to the Henry J. Kaiser Family Foundation (2004), experts have identified a variety of key factors causing a rise in childhood obesity, factors that are not tied to media (p. 1).

To avoid plagiarizing an author's language, resist the temptation to look at the source while you are summarizing or paraphrasing. After you have read the passage you want to paraphrase, set the source aside. Ask yourself, "What is the author's meaning?" In your own words, state your understanding of the author's basic point. Return to the source and check that you haven't used the author's language or sentence structure or misrepresented the author's ideas. When you fully understand another writer's meaning, you can more easily and accurately present those ideas in your own words.

ACCEPTABLE PARAPHRASE

A report by the Henry J. Kaiser Family Foundation (2004) described causes other than media for the childhood obesity crisis.

60 Integrating sources

Quotations, summaries, paraphrases, and facts will help you develop your argument, but they cannot speak for you. You can use several strategies to integrate information from sources into your paper while maintaining your own voice.

60a Use quotations appropriately.

In your academic writing, keep the emphasis on your ideas; use your own words to summarize and to paraphrase your sources and to explain your points. Sometimes, however, quotations can be the most effective way to integrate a source.

Limiting your use of quotations

Although it is tempting to insert many quotations in your paper and to use your own words only for connecting passages, do not quote excessively. It is almost impossible to integrate numerous long quotations smoothly into your own text.

WHEN TO USE QUOTATIONS

- When language is especially vivid or expressive
- When exact wording is needed for technical accuracy
- When it is important to let the debaters of an issue explain their positions in their own words
- When the words of an authority lend weight to an argument
- When the language of a source is the topic of your discussion

It is not always necessary to quote full sentences from a source. To reduce your reliance on the words of others, you can often integrate language from a source into your own sentence structure.

> Carmona (2004) advised the subcommittee that the situation constitutes an "epidemic" and that the skyrocketing statistics are "astounding."

> As researchers continue to face a number of unknowns about obesity, it may be helpful to envision treating the disorder, as Yanovski and Yanovski (2002) suggested, "in the same manner as any other chronic disease" (p. 592).

Using the ellipsis mark

To condense a quoted passage, you can use the ellipsis mark (three periods, with spaces between) to indicate that you have omitted words. What remains must be grammatically complete.

> Roman (2003) reported that "social factors are nearly as significant as individual metabolism in the formation of . . . dietary habits of adolescents" (p. 345).

The writer has omitted the words *both healthy and unhealthy* from the source.

When you want to leave out one or more full sentences, use a period before the three ellipsis dots.

> According to Sothern and Gordon (2003), "Environmental factors may contribute as much as 80% to the causes of childhood obesity. . . . Research suggests that obese children demonstrate decreased levels of physical activity and increased psychosocial problems" (p. 104).

Ordinarily, do not use an ellipsis mark at the beginning or at the end of a quotation. Readers will understand that you have taken the quoted material from a longer passage. The only exception occurs when you feel it is necessary, for clarity, to indicate that your quotation begins or ends in the middle of a sentence.

USING SOURCES RESPONSIBLY: Make sure that omissions and ellipsis marks do not distort the meaning of your source.

Using brackets

Brackets allow you to insert your own words into quoted material. You can insert words in brackets to clarify a confusing reference or to keep a sentence grammatical in the context of your own writing.

> The cost of treating obesity currently totals $117 billion per year—a price, according to the surgeon general, "second only to the cost of [treating] tobacco use" (Carmona, 2004).

To indicate an error such as a misspelling in a quotation, insert [*sic*], italicized and with brackets around it, right after the error. (See 39c.)

Setting off long quotations

When you quote forty or more words from a source, set off the quotation by indenting it one-half inch from the left margin. Use the normal right margin and do not single-space the quotation.

Long quotations should be introduced by an informative sentence, usually followed by a colon. Quotation marks are unnecessary because the indented format tells readers that the passage is taken word-for-word from the source.

> Yanovski and Yanovski (2002) have described earlier treatments of obesity that focused on behavior modification:
>
> > With the advent of behavioral treatments for obesity in the 1960s, hope arose that modification of maladaptive eating and

exercise habits would lead to sustained weight loss, and that time-limited programs would produce permanent changes in weight. Medications for the treatment of obesity were proposed as short-term adjuncts for patients, who would presumably then acquire the skills necessary to continue to lose weight, reach "ideal body weight," and maintain a reduced weight indefinitely. (p. 592)

Notice that at the end of an indented quotation the parenthetical citation goes outside the final mark of punctuation. (When a quotation is run into your text, the opposite is true. See the sample citations on p. 672.)

60b Use signal phrases to integrate sources.

Whenever you include a paraphrase, summary, or direct quotation of another writer's work in your paper, prepare your readers for it with a signal phrase. A signal phrase usually names the author of the source, gives the publication year in parentheses, and often provides some context. It is generally acceptable in APA style to call authors by their last name only, even on a first mention. If your paper refers to two authors with the same last name, use initials as well.

When you write a signal phrase, choose a verb that is appropriate for the way you are using the source (see 58c). Are you providing background, explaining a concept, supporting a claim, lending authority, or refuting an argument? See the chart on page 677 for a list of verbs commonly used in signal phrases. Note that APA requires using verbs in the past tense or present perfect tense (*explained* or *has explained*) to introduce source material. Use the present tense only for discussing the applications or effects of your own results (*the data suggest*) or knowledge that has been clearly established (*researchers agree*).

Marking boundaries

Readers need to move from your words to the words of a source without feeling a jolt. Avoid dropping direct quotations into your text without warning. Instead, provide clear signal phrases, including at least the author's name and the year of publication. Signal phrases mark the boundaries between source material and your own words; they can also tell readers why a source is worth quoting. (The signal phrase is highlighted in the second example.)

DROPPED QUOTATION

Obesity was once considered in a very different light. "For many years, obesity was approached as if it were either a moral failing or evidence of underlying psychopathology" (Yanovski & Yanovski, 2002, p. 592).

QUOTATION WITH SIGNAL PHRASE

Obesity was once considered in a very different light. As researchers Yanovski and Yanovski (2002) have explained, obesity was widely thought of as "either a moral failing or evidence of underlying psychopathology" (p. 592).

Using signal phrases with summaries and paraphrases

As with quotations, you should introduce most summaries and paraphrases with a signal phrase that mentions the author and the year and places the material in the context of your own writing. Readers will then understand where the summary or paraphrase begins.

Without the signal phrase (highlighted) in the following example, readers might think that only the last sentence is being cited, when in fact the whole paragraph is based on the source.

Carmona (2004) advised a Senate subcommittee that the problem of childhood obesity is dire and that the skyrocketing statistics—

which put the child obesity rate at 15%—are cause for alarm. More than nine million children, double the number in the early 1980s, are classified as obese. Carmona warned that obesity can cause myriad physical problems that only worsen as children grow older.

There are times, however, when a summary or a paraphrase does not require a signal phrase naming the author. When the context makes clear where the cited material begins, you may omit the signal phrase and include the author's name and the year in parentheses.

Integrating statistics and other facts

When you are citing a statistic or another specific fact, a signal phrase is often not necessary. In most cases, readers will understand that the citation refers to the statistic or fact (not the whole paragraph).

In purely financial terms, the drugs cost more than $3 a day on average (Duenwald, 2004).

There is nothing wrong, however, with using a signal phrase to introduce a statistic or another fact.

Putting source material in context

Readers should not have to guess why source material appears in your paper. If you use another writer's words, you must explain how they relate to your point. In other words, you must put the source in context. It's a good idea to embed a quotation between sentences of your own. In addition to introducing it with a signal phrase, follow the quotation with interpretive comments that link it to your paper's argument. (See also 60c.)

Using signal phrases in APA papers

To avoid monotony, try to vary both the language and the place-ment of your signal phrases.

Model signal phrases

In the words of Carmona (2004), ". . ."

As Yanovski and Yanovski (2002) have noted, ". . ."

Hoppin and Taveras (2004), medical researchers, pointed out that ". . ."

". . . ," claimed Critser (2003).

". . . ," wrote Duenwald (2004), ". . ."

Researchers McDuffie et al. (2003) have offered a compelling argument for this view: ". . ."

Hilts (2002) answered objections with the following analysis: ". . ."

Verbs in signal phrases

admitted	contended	reasoned
agreed	declared	refuted
argued	denied	rejected
asserted	emphasized	reported
believed	insisted	responded
claimed	noted	suggested
compared	observed	thought
confirmed	pointed out	wrote

QUOTATION WITH EFFECTIVE CONTEXT

A report by the Henry J. Kaiser Family Foundation (2004) outlined trends that may have contributed to the childhood obesity crisis, including food advertising for children as well as

> a reduction in physical education classes . . . , an increase in the availability of sodas and snacks in public schools, the growth in the number of fast-food outlets . . . , and the increasing number of highly processed high-calorie and high-fat grocery products. (p. 1)

Addressing each of these areas requires more than a doctor armed with a prescription pad; it requires a broad mobilization not just of doctors and concerned parents but of educators, food industry executives, advertisers, and media representatives.

60c Synthesize sources.

When you synthesize multiple sources in a research paper, you create a conversation about your research topic. You show readers how the ideas of one source relate to those of another by connecting and analyzing the ideas in the context of your argument. Keep the emphasis on your own writing. The thread of your argument should be easy to identify and to understand, with or without your sources.

SAMPLE SYNTHESIS (DRAFT)

Student writer Luisa Mirano begins with a claim that needs support.

Signal phrases indicate how sources contribute to Mirano's paper and show that the ideas that follow are not her own.

> Medical treatments have clear costs for individual patients, including unpleasant side effects, little information about long-term use, and uncertainty that they will yield significant weight loss. The financial burden is heavy as well; the drugs cost more than $3 a day on average (Duenwald, 2004). In each of the clinical trials, use of medication was accompanied by expensive behavioral therapies, including counseling, nutrition education, fitness advising, and monitoring. As Critser (2003) noted in his

Student writer

Source 1

Student writer

TEACHING TIP

The conversation metaphor can be a useful concept when students are learning how to synthesize sources. To help students understand how various ideas relate to one another, ask students to imagine that they and their sources are in a room together. Students should understand their sources well enough to be able to predict how one source will react to another. It may even be helpful to ask students to role-play or to write a brief script in which the sources converse about the issue being debated.

Mirano interprets and connects sources. Each paragraph ⎯⎯➤ ends with her own thoughts.

book *Fat Land*, use of weight-loss drugs is unlikely to have | Source 2
an effect without the proper "support system"—one that
includes doctors, facilities, time, and money (p. 3). For many | Student writer
families, this level of care is prohibitively expensive.

Both medical experts and policymakers recognize that | Student writer
solutions might come not only from a laboratory but also
from policy, education, and advocacy. A handbook designed
to educate doctors on obesity called for "major changes | Source 3
in some aspects of western culture" (Hoppin & Taveras,
2004, Conclusion section, para. 1). Solving the childhood | Student writer
obesity problem will require broad mobilization of doctors
and concerned parents and also of educators, food industry
executives, advertisers, and media representatives.

In this draft, Mirano uses her own analyses to shape the conversation among her sources. She does not simply string quotations and statistics together or allow her sources to overwhelm her writing. The final sentence, written in her own voice, gives her an opportunity to explain to readers how her sources support and extend her argument.

When synthesizing sources, ask yourself these questions:

- Which sources inform, support, or extend your argument?

- Have you varied the functions of sources—to provide background, explain concepts, lend authority, and anticipate counterarguments? Do your signal phrases indicate these functions?

- Do you explain how your sources support your argument?

- Do you connect and analyze sources in your own voice?

- Is your own argument easy to identify and to understand, with or without your sources?

61 APA documentation style

In most social science classes, you will be asked to use the APA system for documenting sources, which is set forth in the *Publication Manual of the American Psychological Association*, 6th ed. (Washington, DC: APA, 2010).

APA recommends in-text citations that refer readers to a list of references. An in-text citation gives the author of the source (often in a signal phrase), the year of publication, and often a page number in parentheses. At the end of the paper, a list of references provides publication information about the source; the list is alphabetized by authors' last names (or by titles for works with no authors). The direct link between the in-text citation and the entry in the reference list is highlighted in the following example.

> **MAKING THE MOST OF YOUR HANDBOOK**
>
> A reference list includes all the sources cited in the text of a paper.
>
> ▶ APA reference list: 61b
> ▶ Preparing the reference list: 62a
> ▶ Sample reference list: page 738

IN-TEXT CITATION

Yanovski and Yanovski (2002) reported that "the current state of the treatment for obesity is similar to the state of the treatment of hypertension several decades ago" (p. 600).

ENTRY IN THE LIST OF REFERENCES

Yanovski, S. Z., & Yanovski, J. A. (2002). Drug therapy: Obesity. *The New England Journal of Medicine, 346,* 591-602.

For a reference list that includes this entry, see page 738.

SCHOLARS ON CITATION

Shi, Ling. "Common Knowledge, Learning, and Citation Practices in University Writing." *Research in the Teaching of English* 45.3 (2011): 308–34. Print. Shi's work is based on interviews with seventy-five college students and instructors in a variety of disciplines. Participants in the study commented on examples of writing that included unacknowledged uses of sources, but they could not agree on whether the writers were using common knowledge or were committing plagiarism.

Directory to APA in-text citation models

61a APA in-text citations

APA's in-text citations provide the author's last name and the year of publication, usually before the cited material, and a page number in parentheses directly after the cited material. In the following models, the elements of the in-text citation are highlighted.

NOTE: APA style requires the use of the past tense or the present perfect tense in signal phrases introducing cited material: *Smith (2012) reported, Smith (2012) has argued.*

1. Basic format for a quotation   Ordinarily, introduce the quotation with a signal phrase that includes the author's last name followed by the year of publication in parentheses. Put the page number (preceded by "p.") in parentheses after the quotation. For sources from the Web without page numbers, see item 12a on page 685.

> Critser (2003) noted that despite growing numbers of overweight Americans, many health care providers still "remain either in ignorance or outright denial about the health danger to the poor and the young" (p. 5).

If the author is not named in the signal phrase, place the author's name, the year, and the page number in parentheses after the quotation: (Critser, 2003, p. 5). (See items 6 and 12 for citing sources that lack authors; item 12 also explains how to handle sources without dates or page numbers.)

NOTE: Do not include a month in an in-text citation, even if the entry in the reference list includes the month.

2. Basic format for a summary or a paraphrase   As for a quotation (see item 1), include the author's last name and the year either in a signal phrase introducing the material or in parentheses following it. Use a page number, if one is available, following the cited material to help your readers find the passage in the work. For sources from the Web without page numbers, see item 12a on page 685.

> Yanovski and Yanovski (2002) explained that sibutramine suppresses appetite by blocking the reuptake of the neurotransmitters serotonin and norepinephrine in the brain (p. 594).

> Sibutramine suppresses appetite by blocking the reuptake of the neurotransmitters serotonin and norepinephrine in the brain (Yanovski & Yanovski, 2002, p. 594).

3. Work with two authors   Name both authors in the signal phrase or in parentheses each time you cite the work. In the parentheses, use "&" between the authors' names; in the signal phrase, use "and."

> According to Sothern and Gordon (2003), "Environmental factors may contribute as much as 80% to the causes of childhood obesity" (p. 104).

Obese children often engage in limited physical activity (Sothern & Gordon, 2003, p. 104).

4. Work with three to five authors Identify all authors in the signal phrase or in parentheses the first time you cite the source.

In 2003, Berkowitz, Wadden, Tershakovec, and Cronquist concluded, "Sibutramine . . . must be carefully monitored in adolescents, as in adults, to control increases in [blood pressure] and pulse rate" (p. 1811).

In subsequent citations, use the first author's name followed by "et al." in either the signal phrase or the parentheses.

As Berkowitz et al. (2003) advised, "Until more extensive safety and efficacy data are available, . . . weight-loss medications should be used only on an experimental basis for adolescents" (p. 1811).

5. Work with six or more authors Use the first author's name followed by "et al." in the signal phrase or in parentheses.

McDuffie et al. (2002) tested 20 adolescents, aged 12-16, over a three-month period and found that orlistat, combined with behavioral therapy, produced an average weight loss of 4.4 kg, or 9.7 pounds (p. 646).

6. Work with unknown author If the author is unknown, mention the work's title in the signal phrase or give the first word or two of the title in the parenthetical citation. Titles of short works such as articles are put in quotation marks; titles of long works such as books and reports are italicized.

Children struggling to control their weight must also struggle with the pressures of television advertising that, on the one hand, encourages the consumption of junk food and, on the other, celebrates thin celebrities ("Television," 2002).

NOTE: In the rare case when "Anonymous" is specified as the author, treat it as if it were a real name: (Anonymous, 2001). In the list of references, also use the name Anonymous as author.

7. Organization as author If the author is an organization or a government agency, name the organization in the signal phrase or in the parentheses the first time you cite the source.

> Obesity puts children at risk for a number of medical complications, including Type 2 diabetes, hypertension, sleep apnea, and orthopedic problems (Henry J. Kaiser Family Foundation, 2004, p. 1).

If the organization has a familiar abbreviation, you may include it in brackets the first time you cite the source and use the abbreviation alone in later citations.

> **FIRST CITATION**   (Centers for Disease Control and Prevention [CDC], 2012)
>
> **LATER CITATIONS**   (CDC, 2012)

8. Authors with the same last name To avoid confusion if your reference list includes two or more authors with the same last name, use initials with the last names in your in-text citations.

> Research by E. Smith (1989) revealed that . . .

> One 2012 study contradicted . . . (R. Smith, p. 234).

9. Two or more works by the same author in the same year When your list of references includes more than one work by the same author in the same year, you will use lowercase letters ("a," "b," and so on) with the year to order the entries in the reference list. (See item 8 on p. 695.) Use those same letters with the year in the in-text citation.

> Research by Durgin (2003b) has yielded new findings about the role of counseling in treating childhood obesity.

10. Two or more works in the same parentheses When your parenthetical citation names two or more works, put them in the same order that they appear in the reference list, separated with semicolons.

Researchers have indicated that studies of pharmacological treatments for childhood obesity are inconclusive (Berkowitz et al., 2003; McDuffie et al., 2002).

11. Multiple citations to the same work in one paragraph If you give the author's name in the text of your paper (not in parentheses) and you mention that source again in the text of the same paragraph, give only the author's name, not the date, in the later citation. If any subsequent reference in the same paragraph is in parentheses, include both the author and the date in the parentheses.

Principal Jean Patrice said, "You have to be able to reach students where they are instead of making them come to you. If you don't, you'll lose them" (personal communication, April 10, 2006). Patrice expressed her desire to see all students get something out of their educational experience. This feeling is common among members of Waverly's faculty. With such a positive view of student potential, it is no wonder that 97% of Waverly High School graduates go on to a four-year university (Patrice, 2006).

12. Web source When possible, cite sources from the Web as you would cite any other source, giving the author and the year.

Atkinson (2001) found that children who spent at least four hours a day watching TV were less likely to engage in adequate physical activity during the week.

Usually a page number is not available; occasionally a Web source will lack an author or a date (see 12a, 12b, and 12c below).

a. No page numbers When a Web source lacks stable numbered pages, include paragraph numbers or headings to help readers locate the passage being cited.

If the source has numbered paragraphs, use the paragraph number preceded by the abbreviation "para.": (Hall, 2012, para. 5). If the source has no numbered paragraphs but contains headings, cite the appropriate heading in parentheses; you may also indicate which paragraph under the heading you are referring to, even if the paragraphs are not numbered.

> Hoppin and Taveras (2004) pointed out that several other medications were classified by the Drug Enforcement Administration as having the "potential for abuse" (Weight-Loss Drugs section, para. 6).

NOTE: For PDF documents that have stable page numbers, give the page number in the parenthetical citation.

b. Unknown author If no author is named in the source, mention the title of the source in a signal phrase or give the first word or two of the title in parentheses (see also item 6). (If an organization serves as the author, see item 7.)

> The body's basal metabolic rate, or BMR, is a measure of its at-rest energy requirement ("Exercise," 2003).

c. Unknown date When the source does not give a date, use the abbreviation "n.d." (for "no date").

> Attempts to establish a definitive link between television programming and children's eating habits have been problematic (Magnus, n.d.).

13. An entire Web site If you are citing an entire Web site, not an internal page or a section, give the URL in the text of your paper but do not include it in the reference list.

> The U.S. Center for Nutrition Policy and Promotion website (http://www.cnpp.usda.gov/) provides useful information about diet and nutrition for children and adults.

14. Multivolume work If you have used more than one volume from a multivolume work, add the volume number in parentheses with the page number.

> Banford (2009) has demonstrated stable weight loss over time from a combination of psychological counseling, exercise, and nutritional planning (Volume 2, p. 135).

15. Personal communication Interviews that you conduct, memos, letters, e-mail messages, social media posts, and similar communications that would be difficult for your readers to retrieve should be cited in the text only, not in the reference list. (Use the first initial with the last name in parentheses.)

> One of Atkinson's colleagues, who has studied the effect of the media on children's eating habits, has contended that advertisers for snack foods will need to design ads responsibly for their younger viewers (F. Johnson, personal communication, October 20, 2013).

16. Course materials Cite lecture notes from your instructor or your own class notes as personal communication (see item 15). If your instructor distributes or posts materials that contain publication information, cite as you would the appropriate source (for instance, an article, a section in a Web document, or a video). See also item 65 on page 721.

17. Part of a source (chapter, figure) To cite a specific part of a source, such as a whole chapter or a figure or table, identify the element in parentheses. Don't abbreviate terms such as "Figure," "Chapter," and "Section"; "page" is always abbreviated "p." (or "pp." for more than one page).

> The data support the finding that weight loss stabilizes with consistent therapy and ongoing monitoring (Hanniman, 2010, Figure 8-3, p. 345).

18. Indirect source When a writer's or a speaker's quoted words appear in a source written by someone else, begin the parenthetical citation with the words "as cited in." In the following example, Critser is the author of the source given in the reference list; that source contains a quotation by Satcher.

> Former surgeon general Dr. David Satcher described "a nation of young people seriously at risk of starting out obese and dooming themselves to the difficult task of overcoming a tough illness" (as cited in Critser, 2003, p. 4).

19. Sacred or classical text   Identify the text, the version or edition you used, and the relevant part (chapter, verse, line). It is not necessary to include the source in the reference list.

> Peace activists have long cited the biblical prophet's vision of a world without war: "And they shall beat their swords into plowshares, and their spears into pruning hooks; nation shall not lift up sword against nation, neither shall they learn war any more" (Isaiah 2:4, Revised Standard Version).

61b APA list of references

As you gather sources for an assignment, you will likely find sources in print, on the Web, and in other places. The information you will need for the reference list at the end of your paper will differ slightly for some sources, but the main principles apply to all sources: You should identify an author, a creator, or a producer whenever possible; give a title; and provide the date on which the source was produced. Some sources will require page numbers; some will require a publisher; and some will require retrieval information.

▶ General guidelines for the reference list, page 692

Directory to APA reference list models

General guidelines for listing authors

hackerhandbooks.com/bedhandbook

e Researched writing > Exercises: APA papers: 61–4 to 61–8

Directory to APA reference list models (*cont.*)

Directory to APA reference list models (*cont.*)

Section 61b provides specific requirements for and examples of many of the sources you are likely to encounter. When you cite sources, your goals are to show that the sources you've used are reliable and relevant to your work, to provide your readers with enough information so that they can find your sources easily, and to provide that information in a consistent way according to APA conventions.

In the list of references, include only sources that you have quoted, summarized, or paraphrased in your paper.

General guidelines for listing authors

The formatting of authors' names in items 1–12 applies to all sources in print and on the Web — books, articles, Web sites, and so on. For more models of specific source types, see items 13–69.

1. Single author

```
author: last        year
name + initial(s)   (book)              title (book)
```
Rosenberg, T. (2011). *Join the club: How peer pressure can transform the world.*
```
        place of
      publication   publisher
```
New York, NY: Norton.

2. Two to seven authors   List up to seven authors by last names followed by initials. Use an ampersand (&) before the name of the last author. (See items 3–5 on pp. 682–83 for citing works with multiple authors in the text of your paper.)

```
    all authors:                 year
  last name + initial(s)        (book)              title (book)
```
Stanford, D. J., & Bradley, B. A. (2012). *Across the Atlantic ice: The origins of*
```
                        place of
                      publication        publisher
```
America's Clovis culture. Berkeley: University of California Press.

```
            all authors:
          last name + initial(s)
```
Ludwig, J., Duncan, G. J., Gennetian, L. A., Katz, L. F., Kessler, R. C., Kling,
```
                                year
                              (journal)         title (article)
```
J. R., & Sanbonmatsu, L. (2012). Neighborhood effects on the long-
```
                                     journal
                                     title    volume  page(s)
```
term well-being of low-income adults. *Science, 337,* 1505-1510.
```
                DOI
```
doi:10.1126/science.1224648

3. Eight or more authors   List the first six authors followed by three ellipsis dots and the last author's name.

Tøttrup, A. P., Klaassen, R. H. G., Kristensen, M. W., Strandberg, R., Vardanis, Y., Lindström, Å., . . . Thorup, K. (2012). Drought in Africa caused delayed arrival of European songbirds. *Science, 338,* 1307. doi:10.1126 /science.1227548

General guidelines for the reference list

In APA style, the alphabetical list of works cited, which appears at the end of the paper, is titled "References."

Authors and dates

- Alphabetize entries in the list of references by authors' last names; if a work has no author, alphabetize it by its title.

- Invert all authors' names—put the last name first, followed by a comma; use initials for the first and middle names.

- With two or more authors, use an ampersand (&) before the last author's name. Separate the names with commas. Include names for the first seven authors; if there are eight or more authors, give the first six authors, three ellipsis dots, and the last author.

- If the author is a company or an organization, give the name in normal order.

- Put the date of publication immediately after the first element of the citation. Enclose the date in parentheses, followed by a period (outside the parentheses).

- For books, give the year of publication. For magazines, newspapers, and newsletters, give the exact date as in the publication (the year plus the month or the year plus the month and the day). For sources on the Web, give the date of posting, if it is available. Use the season if the publication gives only a season and not a month.

Titles

- Italicize the titles and subtitles of books, journals, and other long works.

- Use no italics or quotation marks for the titles of articles.

- For books and articles, capitalize only the first word of the title and subtitle and all proper nouns.

- For the titles of journals, magazines, and newspapers, capitalize all words of four letters or more (and all nouns, pronouns, verbs, adjectives, and adverbs of any length).

GENERAL GUIDELINES FOR THE REFERENCE LIST *(cont.)*

Place of publication and publisher

- Take the information about a book from its title page and copyright page. If more than one place of publication is listed, use only the first.

- Give the city and state for all US cities. Use postal abbreviations for all states.

- Give the city and country for all non-US cities; include the province for Canadian cities. Do not abbreviate the country and province.

- Do not give a state if the publisher's name includes it (Ann Arbor: University of Michigan Press, for example).

- In publishers' names, omit terms such as "Company" (or "Co.") and "Inc." but keep "Books" and "Press." Omit first names or initials (Norton, not W. W. Norton, for example).

- If the publisher is the same as the author, use the word "Author" in the publisher position.

Volume, issue, and page numbers

- For a journal or a magazine, give only the volume number if the publication is paginated continuously through each volume; give the volume and issue numbers if each issue of the volume begins on page 1.

- Italicize the volume number and put the issue number, not italicized, in parentheses.

- For monthly magazines, give the year and the month; for weekly magazines, add the day.

- For daily and weekly newspapers, give the month, day, and year; use "p." or "pp." before page numbers (if any).

- For journals, magazines, and newspapers, when an article appears on consecutive pages, provide the range of pages. When an article does not appear on consecutive pages, give all page numbers: A1, A17. →

URLs, DOIs, and other retrieval information

- For articles and books from the Web, use the DOI (digital object identifier) if the source has one, and do not give a URL. If a source from the Web or a database does not have a DOI, give the URL.

- Use a retrieval date for a Web source only if the content is likely to change. Most of the examples in 61b do not show a retrieval date because the content of the sources is stable. If you are unsure about whether to use a retrieval date, include the date or consult your instructor.

4. Organization as author

author:
organization name   year   title (book)

American Psychiatric Association. (2013). *Diagnostic and statistical manual of*

                              place   organization
                              of publication   as author
             edition   and publisher

   mental disorders (5th ed.). Washington, DC: Author.

5. Unknown author   Begin the entry with the work's title.

                           year + month + day
       title (article)   (weekly publication)   journal title

The rise of the sharing economy. (2013, March 9). *The Economist,*

     volume,
     issue   page(s)

   406(8826), 14.

                          place of
     title (book)   year   publication   publisher

New concise world atlas. (2010). New York, NY: Oxford University Press.

6. Author using a pseudonym (pen name) or screen name   Use the author's real name, if known, and give the pseudonym or screen name in brackets exactly as it appears in the source. If only the screen name is known, begin with that name and do not

use brackets. (See also items 47 and 68 on citing screen names in social media such as Twitter.)

```
           year + month + day
screen name  (daily publication)              title of original article
littlebigman. (2012, December 13). Re: Who's watching? Privacy concerns
                                      label        title of publication
     persist as smart meters roll out [Comment]. National Geographic Daily News.
                        URL for Web publication
     Retrieved from http://news.nationalgeographic.com/
```

7. Two or more works by the same author   Use the author's name for all entries. List the entries by year, the earliest first.

Heinrich, B. (2009). *Summer world: A season of bounty*. New York, NY: Ecco.

Heinrich, B. (2012). *Life everlasting: The animal way of death*. New York, NY: Houghton Mifflin Harcourt.

8. Two or more works by the same author in the same year   List the works alphabetically by title. In the parentheses, following the year add "a," "b," and so on. Use these same letters when giving the year in the in-text citation. (See also p. 727 and item 9 on p. 684.)

Bower, B. (2012a, December 15). Families in flux. *Science News, 182*(12), 16.

Bower, B. (2012b, November 3). Human-Neandertal mating gets a new date. *Science News, 182*(9), 8.

9. Editor   Begin with the name of the editor or editors; place the abbreviation "Ed." (or "Eds." for more than one editor) in parentheses following the name. (See item 10 for a work with both an author and an editor.)

```
          all editors:
          last name + initial(s)              year      title (book)
Carr, S. C., MacLachlan, M., & Furnham, A. (Eds.). (2012). Humanitarian work
                  place of
                  publication   publisher
     psychology. New York, NY: Palgrave.
```

10. Author and editor Begin with the name of the author, followed by the name of the editor and the abbreviation "Ed." For an author with two or more editors, use the abbreviation "Ed." after each editor's name: Gray, W., & Jones, P. (Ed.), & Smith, A. (Ed.).

author · editor · year · title (book)
James, W., & Pelikan, J. (Ed.). (2009). *The varieties of religious experience.*

place of publication · publisher · original publication information
New York, NY: Library of America. (Original work published 1902)

11. Translator Begin with the name of the author. After the title, in parentheses place the name of the translator (in normal order) and the abbreviation "Trans." (for "Translator"). Add the original date of publication at the end of the entry.

author · year · title (book) · translator · place of publication
Scheffer, P. (2011). *Immigrant nations* (L. Waters, Trans.). Cambridge, England:

publisher · original publication information
Polity Press. (Original work published 2007)

12. Editor and translator If the editor and translator are the same person, the same name appears in both the editor position and the translator position.

Girard, R., & Williams, J. G. (Ed.). (2012). *Resurrection from the underground*
(J. G. Williams, Trans.). East Lansing: Michigan State University Press.
(Original work published 1996)

Articles and other short works

▶ Citation at a glance: Article in a journal or magazine, page 698
▶ Citation at a glance: Article from a database, page 700

13. Article in a journal If an article from the Web or a database has no DOI, include the URL for the journal's home page.

a. Print

all authors: last name + initial(s) · year · article title

Bippus, A. M., Dunbar, N. E., & Liu, S.-J. (2012). Humorous responses to

interpersonal complaints: Effects of humor style and nonverbal expression.

journal title · volume · page(s)

The Journal of Psychology, 146, 437-453.

b. Web

all authors: last name + initial(s) · year · article title

Vargas, N., & Schafer, M. H. (2013). Diversity in action: Interpersonal networks

journal title · volume, issue · page(s)

and the distribution of advice. *Social Science Research, 42*(1), 46-58.

DOI

doi:10.1016/j.ssresearch.2012.08.013

author · year · article title

Brenton, S. (2011). When the personal becomes political: Mitigating damage

journal title (no volume available)

following scandals. *Current Research in Social Psychology.* Retrieved from

URL for journal home page

http://www.uiowa.edu/~grpproc/crisp/crisp.html

(continued on p. 701)

Citation at a glance

Article in a journal or magazine   APA

To cite an article in a print journal or magazine in APA style, include the following elements:

1 Author(s)
2 Year of publication for journal; complete date for magazine
3 Title and subtitle of article
4 Name of journal or magazine
5 Volume number; issue number, if required (see p. 693)
6 Page number(s) of article

JOURNAL TABLE OF CONTENTS

TITLE PAGE OF ARTICLE

feature

School Choice
Marches Forward

3

One year ago, the *Wall Street Journal* dubbed 2011 "the year of school choice," opining that "this year is shaping up as the best for reformers in a very long time." Such quotes were bound to circulate among education reformers and give traditional opponents of school choice, such as teachers unions, heartburn. Thirteen states enacted new programs that allow K–12 students to choose a public or private school instead of attending their assigned school, and similar bills were under consideration in more than two dozen states.

With so much activity, school choice moved from the margins of education reform debates and became the headline. In January 2012, *Washington Post* education reporter Michael Alison Chandler said school choice has become "a mantra of 21st-century education reform," citing pol **1** across the country have traditional pa schools competing for students alongside charter schools and private schools.

"It took us 20 years to pass the first 20 private school–choice programs America and in the 21st year we passed new programs," says Scott Jensen with th American Federation for Children (AFC

2011
a year of
new laws
and
new lawsuits

By
JONATHAN BUTCHER

a school-choice advocacy group based in Washington, D.C. "So we went from passing, on average, one each year, to seven in one fell swoop."

Programs enacted in 2011 include
• a tax-credit scholarship program in North Carolina
• Arizona's education savings account system for K–12 students
• Maine's new charter school law, which brings the total number of states, along with the District of Columbia, with charter schoo

2 **4** WINTER 2013 / EDUCATION NEXT

educationnext.org WINTER 2013 / EDUCATION NEXT **21**

REFERENCE LIST ENTRY FOR AN ARTICLE IN A PRINT JOURNAL OR MAGAZINE

1   2   3   4   5

Butcher, J. (2013). School choice marches forward. *Education Next, 13*(1),

6
20-27.

For more on citing articles in APA style, see items 13–15.

Citation at a glance

Article from a database APA

To cite an article from a database in APA style, include the following elements:

1 Author(s)
2 Year of publication for journal; complete date for magazine or newspaper
3 Title and subtitle of article
4 Name of periodical
5 Volume number; issue number, if required (see p. 693)
6 Page number(s)
7 DOI (digital object identifier)
8 URL for periodical's home page (if there is no DOI)

DATABASE RECORD

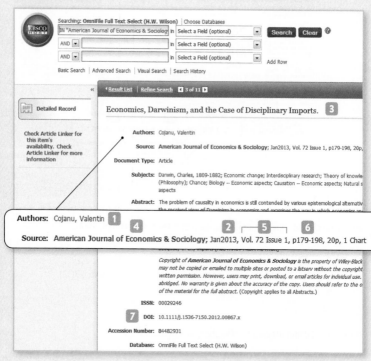

1   2   3

Cojanu, V. (2013). Economics, Darwinism, and the case of disciplinary

                        4   5   6

   imports. *American Journal of Economics & Sociology, 72*, 179-198.

                   7

   doi:10.1111/j.1536-7150.2012.00867.x

For more on citing articles from a database in APA style, see items 13–15.

13. Article in a journal (*cont.*)

c. Database

            year
   author (journal)   article title

Sohn, K. (2012). The social class origins of U.S. teachers, 1860-1920.

                            volume,
          journal title   issue   page(s)   DOI

   Journal of Social History, 45(4), 908-935. doi:10.1093/jsh/shr121

14. Article in a magazine   If an article from the Web or a database has no DOI, include the URL for the journal's home page.

a. Print

             year + month
   author   (monthly magazine)   article title   magazine title

Comstock, J. (2012, December). The underrated sense. *Psychology Today,*

   volume,
    issue   page(s)

   45(6), 46-47.

14. Article in a magazine *(cont.)*

b. *Web*

author | date of posting (when available) | article title | magazine title

Burns, J. (2012, December 3). The measure of all things. *The American Prospect*.

URL for home page

Retrieved from http://prospect.org/

c. *Database*

author | year + month (monthly magazine) | article title | magazine title | volume, issue | page(s)

Tucker, A. (2012, November). Primal instinct. *Smithsonian, 43*(7), 54-63.

URL for magazine home page

Retrieved from http://www.smithsonianmag.com/

15. Article in a newspaper

a. *Print*

author | year + month + day | article title

Swarns, R. L. (2012, December 9). A family, for a few days a year. *The*

newspaper title | page(s)

New York Times, pp. 1, 20.

b. *Web*

author: last name + initial(s) | year + month + day | article title

Villanueva-Whitman, E. (2012, November 27). Working to stimulate

newspaper title

memory function. *Des Moines Register*. Retrieved from http://www

URL for home page

.desmoinesregister.com/

16. Abstract Add the label "Abstract," in brackets, after the title.

a. Abstract of a journal article

Morales, J., Calvo, A., & Bialystok, E. (2013). Working memory development
in monolingual and bilingual children [Abstract]. *Journal of
Experimental Child Psychology, 114*, 187-202. Retrieved from http://
www.sciencedirect.com/

b. Abstract of a paper

Denham, B. (2012). Diffusing deviant behavior: A communication perspective
on the construction of moral panics [Abstract]. Paper presented at the
AEJMC 2012 Conference, Chicago, IL. Retrieved from http://www.aejmc
.org/home/2012/04/ctm-2012-abstracts/

17. Supplemental material Some articles on the Web contain
supplemental materials that are not part of the main article
but that provide supporting data or other information related
to the article. Cite such material as you would an article and
add the label "Supplemental material" in brackets following
the title.

Reis, S., Grennfelt, P., Klimont, Z., Amann, M., ApSimon, H., Hettelingh,
J.-P., . . . Williams, M. (2012). From acid rain to climate change
[Supplemental material]. *Science 338*(6111), 1153-1154. doi:10.1126
/science.1226514

18. Article with a title in its title If an article title contains
another article title or a term usually placed in quotation marks,
use quotation marks around the internal title or the term.

Easterling, D., & Millesen, J. L. (2012, Summer). Diversifying civic
leadership: What it takes to move from "new faces" to adaptive
problem solving. *National Civic Review*, 20-27. doi:10.1002/ncr.21073

19. Letter to the editor   Insert the words "Letter to the editor" in brackets after the title of the letter. If the letter has no title, use the bracketed words as the title (as in the following example).

Lim, C. (2012, November-December). [Letter to the editor]. *Sierra*. Retrieved from http://www.sierraclub.org/sierra/

20. Editorial or other unsigned article

The business case for transit dollars [Editorial]. (2012, December 9). *Star Tribune*. Retrieved from http://www.startribune.com/

21. Newsletter article   Cite as you would an article in a magazine, giving whatever publication information is available (volume, issue, page numbers, and so on).

Scrivener, L. (n.d.). Why is the minimum wage issue important for food justice advocates? *Food Workers — Food Justice, 15*. Retrieved from http://www.thedatabank.com/dpg/199 /pm.asp?nav=1&ID=41429

22. Review   Give the author and title of the review (if any) and, in brackets, the type of work, the title, and the author for a book or the year for a film. If the review has no author or title, use the material in brackets as the title.

author of review	year (journal)		book title

Aviram, R. B. (2012). [Review of the book *What do I say? The therapist's guide*

	book author(s)

to answering client questions, by L. N. Edelstein & C. A. Waehler].

journal title	volume, issue	page(s)	DOI

Psychotherapy, 49(4), 570-571. doi:10.1037/a0029815

author(s)   year (journal)   review title

Bradley, A., & Olufs, E. (2012). Family dynamics and school violence [Review of

film title   year (film)   journal title

the motion picture *We need to talk about Kevin*, 2011]. *PsycCRITIQUES,*

volume, issue   DOI

57(49). doi:10.1037/a0030982

23. Published interview   Begin with the person interviewed, and put the interviewer in brackets following the title (if any).

Githongo, J. (2012, November 20). A conversation with John Githongo
     [Interview by Baobab]. *The Economist.* Retrieved from http://
     www.economist.com/

24. Article in a reference work (encyclopedia, dictionary, wiki)

a. Print   See also item 32 on citing a volume in a multivolume work.

Konijn, E. A. (2008). Affects and media exposure. In W. Donsbach (Ed.), *The
     international encyclopedia of communication* (Vol. 1, pp. 123-129).
     Malden, MA: Blackwell.

b. Web

Ethnomethodology. (2006). In *STS wiki.* Retrieved December 15, 2012, from
     http://www.stswiki.org/index.php?title=Ethnomethodology

25. Comment on an online article   Begin with the writer's real name or screen name. If both are given, put the real name first, followed by the screen name in brackets. Before the title, use "Re" and a colon. Add "Comment" in brackets following the title.

Danboy125. (2012, November 9). Re: No flowers on the psych ward
     [Comment]. *The Atlantic.* Retrieved from http://www.theatlantic.com/

26. Testimony before a legislative body

Carmona, R. H. (2004, March 2). *The growing epidemic of childhood obesity*.
    Testimony before the Subcommittee on Competition, Foreign Commerce,
    and Infrastructure of the U.S. Senate Committee on Commerce, Science,
    and Transportation. Retrieved from http://www.hhs.gov/asl/testify
    /t040302.html

27. Paper presented at a meeting or symposium (unpublished)

Karimi, S., Key, G., & Tat, D. (2011, April 22). *Complex predicates in focus*.
    Paper presented at the West Coast Conference on Formal Linguistics,
    Tucson, AZ.

28. Poster session at a conference

Lacara, N. (2011, April 24). *Predicate which appositives*. Poster session
    presented at the West Coast Conference on Formal Linguistics,
    Tucson, AZ.

Books and other long works

▶ Citation at a glance: Book, page 707

29. Basic format for a book

a. Print

author(s):
last name
+ initial(s)   year   book title

Child, B. J. (2012). *Holding our world together: Ojibwe women and the survival*

                        place of
                        publication   publisher

    of community. New York, NY: Viking.

Citation at a glance

Book [APA]

To cite a print book in APA style, include the following elements:

1. Author(s)
2. Year of publication
3. Title and subtitle
4. Place of publication
5. Publisher

TITLE PAGE

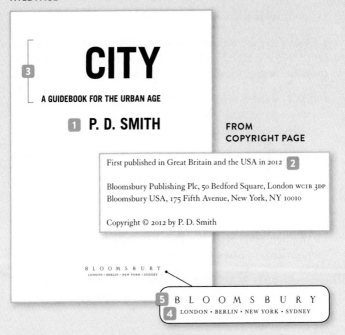

FROM COPYRIGHT PAGE

First published in Great Britain and the USA in 2012 [2]

Bloomsbury Publishing Plc, 50 Bedford Square, London WC1B 3DP
Bloomsbury USA, 175 Fifth Avenue, New York, NY 10010

Copyright © 2012 by P. D. Smith

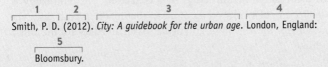

REFERENCE LIST ENTRY FOR A PRINT BOOK

Smith, P. D. (2012). *City: A guidebook for the urban age*. London, England: Bloomsbury.

For more on citing books in APA style, see items 29–37.

29. Basic format for a book (cont.)

b. Web (or online library) Give the URL for the home page of the Web site or the online library after the book title.

author(s)   year   book title

Amponsah, N. A., & Falola, T. (2012). *Women's roles in sub-Saharan Africa.*

URL

Retrieved from http://books.google.com/

c. E-book Give the version in brackets after the title ("Kindle version," "Nook version," and so on). Include the DOI or the URL for the home page of the site from which you downloaded the book.

Wolf, D. A., & Folbre, N. (Eds.). (2012). *Universal coverage of long-term care in the United States* [Adobe Digital Editions version]. Retrieved from https://www.russellsage.org/

d. Database Give the URL for the database after the book title.

Beasley, M. H. (2012). *Women of the Washington press: Politics, prejudice, and persistence.* Retrieved from http://muse.jhu.edu/

30. Edition other than the first
Include the edition number (abbreviated) in parentheses after the title.

Harvey, P. (2013). *An introduction to Buddhism: Teachings, history, and practices* (2nd ed.). Cambridge, England: Cambridge University Press.

31. Selection in an anthology or a collection
An anthology is a collection of works on a common theme, often with different authors for the selections and usually with an editor for the entire volume.

a. Entire anthology

editor(s)   year

Warren, A. E. A., Lerner, R. M., & Phelps, E. (Eds.). (2011). *Thriving and*

title of anthology

spirituality among youth: Research perspectives and future possibilities.

place of
publication   publisher

Hoboken, NJ: Wiley.

b. Selection in an anthology

author of
selection   year   title of selection

Lazar, S. W. (2012). Neural correlates of positive youth development.

editors of anthology

In A. E. A. Warren, R. M. Lerner, & E. Phelps (Eds.), *Thriving and spirituality*

page numbers
of selection

title of anthology

among youth: Research perspectives and future possibilities (pp. 77-90).

place of
publication   publisher

Hoboken, NJ: Wiley.

32. Multivolume work   If the volumes have been published over several years, give the span of years in parentheses. If you have used only one volume of a multivolume work, indicate the volume number after the title of the complete work; if the volume has its own title, add that title after the volume number.

a. All volumes

Khalakdina, M. (2008-2011). *Human development in the Indian context: A socio-cultural focus* (Vols. 1-2). New Delhi, India: Sage.

32. Multivolume work (*cont.*)

b. One volume, with title

Jensen, R. E. (Ed.). (2012). *Voices of the American West: Vol. 1. The Indian interviews of Eli S. Ricker, 1903-1919*. Lincoln: University of Nebraska Press.

33. Introduction, preface, foreword, or afterword

Zachary, L. J. (2012). Foreword. In L. A. Daloz, *Mentor: Guiding the journey of adult learners* (pp. v-vii). San Francisco, CA: Jossey-Bass.

34. Dictionary or other reference work

Leong, F. T. L. (Ed.). (2008). *Encyclopedia of counseling* (Vols. 1-4). Thousand Oaks, CA: Sage.

Nichols, J. D., & Nyholm, E. (2012). *A concise dictionary of Minnesota Ojibwe*. Minneapolis: University of Minnesota Press.

35. Republished book

Mailer, N. (2008). *Miami and the siege of Chicago: An informal history of the Republican and Democratic conventions of 1968*. New York, NY: New York Review Books. (Original work published 1968)

36. Book with a title in its title   If the book title contains another book title or an article title, do not italicize the internal title and do not put quotation marks around it.

Marcus, L. (Ed.). (1999). *Sigmund Freud's* The interpretation of dreams: *New interdisciplinary essays*. Manchester, England: Manchester University Press.

37. Book in a language other than English   Place the English translation, not italicized, in brackets.

Carminati, G. G., & Méndez, A. (2012). *Étapes de vie, étapes de soins* [Stages of life, stages of care]. Chêne-Bourg, Switzerland: Médecine & Hygiène.

38. Dissertation

a. Published

Hymel, K. M. (2009). *Essays in urban economics* (Doctoral dissertation). Available from ProQuest Dissertations and Theses database. (AAT 3355930)

b. Unpublished

Mitchell, R. D. (2007). *The Wesleyan Quadrilateral: Relocating the conversation* (Unpublished doctoral dissertation). Claremont School of Theology, Claremont, CA.

39. Conference proceedings

Yu, F.-Y., Hirashima, T., Supnithi, T., & Biswas, G. (2011). *Proceedings of the 19th International Conference on Computers in Education: ICCE 2011.* Retrieved from http://www.apsce.net:8080/icce2011/program /proceedings/

40. Government document   If the document has a number, place the number in parentheses after the title.

U.S. Transportation Department, Pipeline and Hazardous Materials Safety Administration. (2012). *Emergency response guidebook 2012.* Washington, DC: Author.

U.S. Census Bureau, Bureau of Economic Analysis. (2012, December). *U.S. international trade in goods and services, October 2012* (Report No. CB12-232, BEA12-55, FT-900 [12-10]). Retrieved from http://www .census.gov/foreign-trade/Press-Release/2012pr/10/

41. Report from a private organization   If the publisher and the author are the same, begin with the publisher. For a print source, use "Author" as the publisher at the end of the entry (see item 4 on p. 694); for an online source, give the URL. If the report has a number, put it in parentheses following the title.

Ford Foundation. (2012, November). *Eastern Africa*. Retrieved from http:// www.fordfoundation.org/pdfs/library/Eastern-Africa-brochure-2012.pdf

Atwood, B., Beam, M., Hindman, D. B., Hindman, E. B., Pintak, L., & Shors, B. (2012, May 25). *The Murrow Rural Information Initiative: Final report*. Pullman: Murrow College of Communication, Washington State University.

Wan, G. (2012). *Key indicators for Asia and the Pacific*. Retrieved from http:// www.urban.org/events/Urbanization-in-Asia.cfm

42. Legal source   The title of a court case is italicized in an in-text citation, but it is not italicized in the reference list.

Sweatt v. Painter, 339 U.S. 629 (1950). Retrieved from Cornell University Law School, Legal Information Institute website: http://www.law.cornell .edu/supct/html/historics/USSC_CR_0339_0629_ZS.html

43. Sacred or classical text   It is not necessary to list sacred works such as the Bible or the Qur'an or classical Greek and Roman works (such as the *Odyssey*) in your reference list. See item 19 on page 688 for how to cite these sources in the text of your paper.

Web sites and parts of Web sites

▶ Citation at a glance: Section in a Web document, page 714

NOTE: In an APA paper or an APA reference list entry, the word "website" is spelled all lowercase, as one word.

44. Entire Web site Do not include an entire Web site in the reference list. Give the URL in parentheses when you mention it in the text of your paper. (See item 13 on p. 686.)

45. Document from a Web site List as many of the following elements as are available: author's name, publication date (or "n.d." if there is no date), title (in italics), publisher (if any), and URL. If the publisher is known and is not named as the author, include the publisher in your retrieval statement.

Wagner, D. A., Murphy, K. M., & De Korne, H. (2012, December). *Learning first: A research agenda for improving learning in low-income countries.* Retrieved from Brookings Institution website: http://www.brookings .edu/research/papers/2012/12/learning-first-wagner-murphy-de-korne

Gerber, A. S., & Green, D. P. (2012). *Field experiments: Design, analysis, and interpretation.* Retrieved from Yale Institution for Social and Policy Studies website: http://isps.yale.edu/research/data/d081#.UUy2HFdPL5w

Centers for Disease Control and Prevention. (2012, December 10). *Concussion in winter sports.* Retrieved from http://www.cdc.gov/Features /HockeyConcussions/index.html

46. Section in a Web document Cite as you would a chapter in a book or a selection in an anthology (see item 31b).

Pew Research Center. (2012, December 12). About the 2012 Pew global attitudes survey. In *Social networking popular across globe.* Retrieved from http://www.pewglobal.org/2012/12/12 /social-networking-popular-across-globe

Chang, W.-Y., & Milan, L. M. (2012, October). Relationship between degree field and emigration. In *International mobility and employment characteristics among recent recipients of U.S. doctorates.* Retrieved from National Science Foundation website: http://www.nsf.gov/statistics/infbrief/nsf13300

Citation at a glance

Section in a Web document APA

To cite a section in a Web document in APA style, include the following elements:

1   Author(s)
2   Date of publication or most recent update ("n.d." if there is no date)
3   Title of section
4   Title of document
5   URL of section

WEB DOCUMENT CONTENTS PAGE

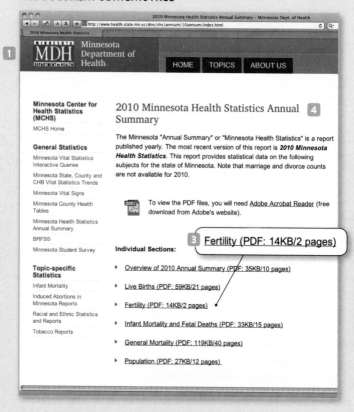

2010 Minnesota Health Statistics Annual Summary – Minnesota Dept. of Health

http://www.health.state.mn.us/divs/chs/annsum/10annsum/index.html

Minnesota MDH Department of Health

HOME   TOPICS   ABOUT US

Minnesota Center for Health Statistics (MCHS)

MCHS Home

General Statistics

Minnesota Vital Statistics Interactive Queries

Minnesota State, County and CHB Vital Statistics Trends

Minnesota Vital Signs

Minnesota County Health Tables

Minnesota Health Statistics Annual Summary

BRFSS

Minnesota Student Survey

Topic-specific Statistics

Infant Mortality

Induced Abortions in Minnesota Reports

Racial and Ethnic Statistics and Reports

Tobacco Reports

2010 Minnesota Health Statistics Annual Summary 4

The Minnesota "Annual Summary" or "Minnesota Health Statistics" is a report published yearly. The most recent version of this report is *2010 Minnesota Health Statistics*. This report provides statistical data on the following subjects for the state of Minnesota. Note that marriage and divorce counts are not available for 2010.

To view the PDF files, you will need Adobe Acrobat Reader (free download from Adobe's website).

3 **Fertility (PDF: 14KB/2 pages)**

Individual Sections:

▸ Overview of 2010 Annual Summary (PDF: 35KB/10 pages)

▸ Live Births (PDF: 59KB/21 pages)

▸ Fertility (PDF: 14KB/2 pages)

▸ Infant Mortality and Fetal Deaths (PDF: 33KB/15 pages)

▸ General Mortality (PDF: 119KB/40 pages)

▸ Population (PDF: 27KB/12 pages)

ON-SCREEN VIEW OF DOCUMENT

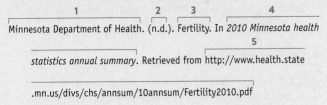

Fertility Table 1
Total Reported Pregnancies by Outcome and Rate
Minnesota Residents, 1981 - 2010

Year	Total Reported Pregnancies*	Live Births	Induced Abortions	Fetal Deaths	Female Population Ages 15-44	Pregnancy Rate**
1981	84,934	68,652	15,821	461	967,087	87.8
1982	84,500	68,512	15,559	429	977,905	86.4
1983	80,530	65,559	14,514	457	981,287	82.1
1984	82,736	66,715	15,556	465	985,608	83.9
1985	83,853	67,412	16,002	439	994,249	84.3
1986	81,882	65,766	15,716	400	997,501	82.1
1987	81,318	65,168	15,746	404	1,004,801	80.9
1988	83,335	66,745	16,124	466	1,020,209	81.7
1989	83,426	67,490	15,506	430	1,024,576	81.4
1990	83,714	67,985	15,280	449	1,025,919	81.6
1991	81,904	67,037	14,441	426	1,036,146	79.0
1992	79,844	65,591	13,846	407	1,049,175	76.1
1993	77,939	64,646	12,955	338	1,060,396	73.5
1994	78,344	64,277	13,702	365	1,073,649	73.0
1995	76,338	63,259	12,715	364	1,053,136	72.5
1996	76,909	63,681	12,876	352	1,066,220	72.1
1997	77,850	64,491	12,997	362	1,050,544	74.1
1998	78,646	65,207	13,050	389	1,054,458	74.6
1999	79,374	65,953	13,037	384	1,054,543	75.3
2000	81,039	67,451	13,200	388	1,082,642	74.9

REFERENCE LIST ENTRY FOR A SECTION IN A WEB DOCUMENT

1   2   3   4

Minnesota Department of Health. (n.d.). Fertility. In *2010 Minnesota health

5

statistics annual summary. Retrieved from http://www.health.state

.mn.us/divs/chs/annsum/10annsum/Fertility2010.pdf

For more on citing documents from Web sites in APA style, see items 45 and 46.

47. Blog post Begin with the writer's real name or screen name. If both are given, put the real name first, followed by the screen name in brackets. Add the date of the post (or "n.d." if the post is undated). Place the label "Blog post" in brackets following the title of the post. If there is no title, use the bracketed material as the title. End with the URL for the post.

Kerssen, T. (2012, October 5). Hunger is political: Food Sovereignty Prize
    honors social movements [Blog post]. Retrieved from http://www
    .foodfirst.org/en/node/4020

48. Blog comment Cite as a blog post, but add "Re" and a colon before the title of the original post and the label "Blog comment" following the title.

Studebakerhawk_14611. (2012, December 5). Re: A people's history of MOOCs
    [Blog comment]. Retrieved from http://www.insidehighered.com/blogs
    /library-babel-fish/people's-history-moocs

Audio, visual, and multimedia sources
49. Podcast

Schulz, K. (2011, March). *Kathryn Schulz: On being wrong* [Video podcast].
    Retrieved from TED on http://itunes.apple.com/

Taylor, A., & Parfitt, G. (2011, January 13). *Physical activity and mental
    health: What's the evidence?* [Audio podcast]. Retrieved from Open
    University on http://itunes.apple.com/

50. Video or audio on the Web

Kurzen, B. (2012, April 5). *Going beyond Muslim-Christian conflict in
    Nigeria* [Video file]. Retrieved from http://www.youtube.com
    /watch?v=JD8MIJOA050

Malone, T. W. *Collective intelligence* [Video file]. Retrieved from http://edge
.org/conversation/collective-intelligence

Bever, T., Piattelli-Palmarini, M., Hammond, M., Barss, A., & Bergesen,
A. (2012, February 2). *A basic introduction to Chomsky's linguistics*
[Audio file]. Retrieved from University of Arizona, College of Social
& Behavioral Sciences, Department of Linguistics website: http://
linguistics.arizona.edu/node/711

51. Transcript of an audio or a video file

Malone, T. W. *Collective intelligence* [Transcript of video file]. Retrieved from
http://edge.org/conversation/collective-intelligence

Glass, I. (2012, September 14). *Back to school* [Transcript of audio file No. 474].
In *This American life*. Retrieved from http://www.thisamericanlife.org/

52. Film (DVD, BD, or other format)   Give the director, producer, and other relevant contributors, followed by the year of the film's release and the title. In brackets, add a description of the medium. Use "Motion picture" if you viewed the film in a theater; use "Video file" if you downloaded the film from the Web or through a streaming service such as Netflix; use "DVD" or "BD" if you viewed the film on DVD or Blu-ray Disc. For a motion picture or a DVD or BD, add the location where the film was made and the studio. If you retrieved the film from the Web or used a streaming service, give the URL for the home page.

Affleck, B. (Director). (2012). *Argo* [Motion picture]. Burbank, CA: Warner
Bros. Pictures.

Ross, G. (Director and Writer), & Collins, S. (Writer). (2012). *The hunger
games* [Video file]. Retrieved from http://netflix.com/

53. Television or radio program

a. Series

Hager, M. (Executive producer), & Schieffer, B. (Moderator). (2012). *Face the nation* [Television series]. Washington, DC: CBS News.

b. Episode on the air

Harleston, R. (Host). (2012, December 1). Federal role in support of autism [Television series episode]. In *Washington journal*. Washington, DC: C-SPAN.

c. Episode on the Web

Morton, D. (Producer). (2012). Fast times at West Philly High [Television series episode]. In M. Hager (Executive producer), *Frontline*. Retrieved from http://www.wgbh.org/

Glass, I. (Host). (2012, November 23). Little war on the prairie (No. 479) [Radio series episode]. In *This American life*. Retrieved from http://www.thisamericanlife.org/

54. Music recording

Chibalonza, A. Jubilee. (2012). On *African voices* [CD]. Merenberg, Germany: ZYX Music.

African voices [CD]. (2012). Merenberg, Germany: ZYX Music.

55. Lecture, speech, or address

Verghese, A. (2012, December 6). *Colonialism and patterns of ethnic conflict in contemporary India*. Address at the Freeman Spogli Institute, Stanford University, Stanford, CA.

Donovan, S. (2012, June 12). *Assisted housing mobility in challenging times* [Video file]. Address at the 5th National Conference on Assisted Housing Mobility, Urban Institute, Washington, DC.

56. Data set or graphic representation of data (graph, chart, table) Give information about the type of source in brackets following the title. If there is no title, give a brief description of the content of the source in brackets in place of the title. If the item is numbered in the source, indicate the number in parentheses after the title. If the graphic appears within a larger document, do not italicize the title of the graphic.

U.S. Department of Agriculture, Economic Research Service. (2011). *Daily intake of nutrients by food source: 2005-08* [Data set]. Retrieved from http://www .ers.usda.gov/data-products/food-consumption-and-nutrient-intakes.aspx

Gallup. (2012, December 5). *In U.S., more cite obesity as most urgent health problem* [Graphs]. Retrieved from http://www.gallup.com/poll/159083 /cite-obesity-urgent-health-problem.aspx

57. Mobile application software (app) Begin with the developer of the app, if known. Add the label "Mobile application software" in brackets after the title of the program.

MindNode Touch 2.3 [Mobile application software]. (2012). Retrieved from http://itunes.apple.com/

Source Tree Solutions. mojoPortal [Mobile application software]. (2012). Retrieved from http://www.microsoft.com/web/gallery/

58. Video game Begin with the creator of the video game, if known. Add the label "Video game" in brackets after the title of the program. If the game can be played on the Web or was downloaded from the Web, give the URL instead of publication information.

Firaxis Games. (2010). Sid Meier's Civilization V [Video game]. New York, NY: Take-Two Interactive. Xbox 360.

Atom Entertainment. (2012). Edgeworld [Video game]. Retrieved from http:// www.addictinggames.com/

59. Map

Ukraine [Map]. (2008). Retrieved from the University of Texas at Austin Perry-Castañeda Library Map Collection website: http://www.lib.utexas .edu/maps/cia08/ukraine_sm_2008.gif

Syrian uprising map [Map]. (2012, October). Retrieved from http://www .polgeonow.com/2012/10/syria-uprising-map-october-2012-7.html

60. Advertisement

VMware [Advertisement]. (2012, September). *Harvard Business Review, 90*(9), 27.

61. Work of art or photograph

Olson, A. (2011). *Short story* [Painting]. Museum of Contemporary Art, Chicago, IL.

Crowner, S. (2012). *Kurtyna fragments* [Painting]. Retrieved from http:// www.walkerart.org/

Weber, J. (1992). *Toward freedom* [Outdoor mural]. Sherman Oaks, CA.

62. Brochure or fact sheet

National Council of State Boards of Nursing. (2011). *A nurse's guide to professional boundaries* [Brochure]. Retrieved from https://www.ncsbn .org/

World Health Organization. (2012, September). *Road traffic injuries* (No. 358) [Fact sheet]. Retrieved from http://www.who.int/mediacentre /factsheets/fs358/en/index.html

Uggen, C. (2012, October). *Crime and the great recession* [Fact sheet]. Retrieved from https://www.stanford.edu/group/recessiontrends /cgi-bin/web/research-areas/crime

63. Press release Generally, list the organization responsible for the press release. Give the exact date.

Urban Institute. (2012, October 11). Two studies address health policy on campaign trail [Press release]. Retrieved from http://www.urban.org /publications/901537.html

64. Presentation slides

Boeninger, C. F. (2008, August). *Web 2.0 tools for reference and instructional services* [Presentation slides]. Retrieved from http://libraryvoice.com /archives/2008/08/04/opal-20-conference-presentation-slides

65. Lecture notes or other course materials Cite materials that your instructor has posted on the Web as you would a Web document or a section in a Web document (see item 45 or 46). If the materials are handouts or printouts, cite whatever information is available in the source. Cite the instructor's personal notes or material that is not posted (such as slides) as personal communication in the text of your paper (see items 15 and 16 on p. 687).

Blum, R. (2011). Neurodevelopment in the first decade of life [Lecture notes and audio file]. In R. Blum & L. M. Blum, *Child health and development*. Retrieved from http://ocw.jhsph.edu/index.cfm/go/viewCourse/course /childhealth/coursePage/lectureNotes/

Personal communication and social media

66. E-mail E-mail messages, letters, and other personal communication are not included in the list of references. (See p. 687 for citing these sources in the text of your paper.)

67. Online posting If an online posting is not archived, cite it as a personal communication in the text of your paper and do not include it in the list of references. If the posting is archived, give the URL and the name of the discussion list if it is not part of the URL.

McKinney, J. (2006, December 19). Adult education-healthcare partnerships [Electronic mailing list message]. Retrieved from http://www.nifl.gov /pipermail/healthliteracy/2006/000524.html

68. Twitter post (tweet)   Use the author's real name, if it is given, and give the screen name in brackets exactly as it appears in the source (including capitalization and punctuation). If only the screen name is known, begin with that name and do not enclose it in brackets. Include the entire text of the tweet as the title, followed by the label "Tweet" in brackets; end with the URL.

CQ Researcher. (2012, December 5). Up to 80 percent of the 600,000 processed foods sold in America have sugar added to their recipes. See http://bit.ly/UmfA4L [Tweet]. Retrieved from https://twitter.com /cqresearcher/status/276449095521038336

69. Facebook post   Use the author's name exactly as it appears in the post. In place of a title, give a few words of the post followed by the label "Facebook post" in brackets. Include the date you retrieved the source and the URL for the poster's Facebook page. If you are citing a personal Facebook page that will not be accessible to your readers, cite it as personal communication in your text, not in the reference list (see item 15 on p. 687).

U.S. Department of Education. (2012, October 9). They are resilient [Facebook post]. Retrieved October 15, 2012, from http://www .facebook.com/ED.gov

62 APA manuscript format; sample research paper

The guidelines in this section are consistent with advice given in the *Publication Manual of the American Psychological Association*, 6th ed. (Washington, DC: APA, 2010), and with typical requirements for undergraduate papers.

62a APA manuscript format

Formatting the paper

Font If your instructor does not require a specific font, choose one that is standard and easy to read (such as Times New Roman).

Title page Begin at the top left, with the words "Running head," followed by a colon and the title of your paper (shortened to no more than fifty characters) in all capital letters. Put the page number 1 flush with the right margin.

About halfway down the page, on separate lines, center the full title of your paper, your name, and your school's name. At the bottom of the page, you may add the heading "Author Note," centered, followed by a brief paragraph that lists specific information about the course or department or provides acknowledgments or contact information. See page 729 for a sample title page.

Page numbers and running head Number all pages with arabic numerals (1, 2, 3, and so on) in the upper right corner one-half inch from the top of the page. Flush with the left margin on the same line as the page number, type a running head consisting of the title of the paper (shortened to no more than fifty characters) in all capital letters. On the title page only, include the words "Running head" followed by a colon before the title. See pages 729–38.

Margins, line spacing, and paragraph indents   Use margins of one inch on all sides of the page. Left-align the text.

Double-space throughout the paper. Indent the first line of each paragraph one-half inch.

Capitalization, italics, and quotation marks   In headings and in titles of works that appear in the text of the paper, capitalize all words of four letters or more (and all nouns, pronouns, verbs, adjectives, and adverbs of any length). Capitalize the first word following a colon if the word begins a complete sentence.

Italicize the titles of books, journals, magazines, and other long works, such as Web sites. Use quotation marks around the titles of articles, short stories, and other short works.

NOTE: APA has different requirements for titles in the reference list. See page 727.

Long quotations   When a quotation is forty or more words, set it off from the text by indenting it one-half inch from the left margin. Double-space the quotation. Do not use quotation marks around it. (See p. 737 for an example. See also pp. 673–74 for more information about integrating long quotations.)

Footnotes   If you insert a footnote number in the text of your paper, place the number, raised above the line, immediately following any mark of punctuation except a dash. At the bottom of the page, begin the note with a one-half-inch indent and the superscript number corresponding to the number in the text. Insert an extra double-spaced line between the last line of text on the page and the footnote. Double-space the footnote. (See p. 731 for an example.)

Abstract and keywords   An abstract is a 150-to-250-word paragraph that provides readers with a quick overview of your essay. It should express your main idea and your key points; it might also briefly suggest any implications or applications of the research you discuss in the paper.

If your paper requires one, include an abstract immediately after the title page. Center the word "Abstract" (in regular font, not boldface) one inch from the top of the page. Double-space the abstract and do not indent the first line.

For a paper prepared for publication, a list of keywords follows the abstract; the keywords help readers search for the paper on the Web or in a database. Leave one line of space after the abstract and begin the next line with the word "Keywords," italicized and indented one-half inch, followed by a colon. Then list important words related to your paper. Check with your instructor for requirements in your course. (See p. 730 for an example of an abstract.)

Headings   Although headings are not always necessary, their use is encouraged in the social sciences. For most undergraduate papers, one level of heading is usually sufficient. (See pp. 729–38.)

First-level headings are centered and boldface. In research papers and laboratory reports, the major headings are "Method," "Results," and "Discussion." In other types of papers, the major headings should be informative and concise, conveying the structure of the paper.

Second-level headings are flush left and boldface. Third-level headings are indented and boldface, followed by a period and the text on the same line.

In first- and second-level headings, capitalize the first and last words and all words of four or more letters (and nouns, pronouns, verbs, adjectives, and adverbs of any length). In third-level headings, capitalize only the first word, any proper nouns, and the first word after a colon.

First-Level Heading Centered

Second-Level Heading Flush Left

   Third-level heading indented. Text immediately follows.

Visuals (tables and figures) APA classifies visuals as tables and figures (figures include graphs, charts, drawings, and photographs).

Label each table with an arabic numeral (Table 1, Table 2, and so on) and provide a clear title. Place the label and title on separate lines above the table, flush left and double-spaced. Type the table number in regular font; italicize the table title.

If you have used data from an outside source or have taken or adapted the table from a source, give the source information in a note below the table. Begin with the word "Note," italicized and followed by a period. If any data in the table require an explanatory footnote, use a superscript lowercase letter in the table and in a footnote following the source note. Double-space source notes and footnotes; do not indent the first line of each note. (See p. 734.)

For each figure, place the figure number and a caption below the figure, flush left and double-spaced. Begin with the word "Figure" and an arabic numeral, both italicized, followed by a period. Place the caption, not italicized, on the same line. If you have taken or adapted the figure from an outside source, give the source information immediately following the caption. Use the term "From" or "Adapted from" before the source information.

In the text of your paper, discuss the most significant features of each visual. Place the visual as close as possible to the sentences that relate to it unless your instructor prefers that visuals appear in an appendix.

Preparing the list of references

Begin your list of references on a new page at the end of the paper. Center the title "References" one inch from the top of the page. Double-space throughout. For a sample reference list, see page 738.

Indenting entries Type the first line of each entry flush left and indent any additional lines one-half inch.

Alphabetizing the list Alphabetize the reference list by the last names of the authors (or editors) or by the first word of an organization name (if the author is an organization). When a work has no author or editor, alphabetize by the first word of the title other than *A*, *An*, or *The*.

If your list includes two or more works by the same author, arrange the entries by year, the earliest first. If your list includes two or more works by the same author in the same year, arrange the works alphabetically by title. Add the letters "a," "b," and so on within the parentheses after the year. For journal articles, use only the year and the letter: (2012a). For articles in magazines and newspapers, use the full date and the letter in the reference list: (2012a, July 7); use only the year and the letter in the in-text citation.

Authors' names Invert all authors' names and use initials instead of first names. Separate the names with commas. For two to seven authors, use an ampersand (&) before the last author's name. For eight or more authors, give the first six authors, three ellipsis dots, and the last author (see item 3 on p. 691).

Titles of books and articles Italicize the titles and subtitles of books. Do not italicize or use quotation marks around the titles of articles. For both books and articles, capitalize only the first word of the title and subtitle (and all proper nouns). Capitalize names of journals, magazines, and newspapers as you would capitalize them normally (see 45c).

Abbreviations for page numbers Abbreviations for "page" and "pages" ("p." and "pp.") are used before page numbers of newspaper articles and selections in anthologies (see item 15 on p. 702 and item 31 on p. 708). Do not use "p." or "pp." before page numbers of articles in journals and magazines (see items 13 and 14 on pp. 697 and 701).

Breaking a URL or DOI   When a URL or a DOI (digital object identifier) must be divided, break it after a double slash or before any other mark of punctuation. Do not insert a hyphen; do not add a period at the end.

62b Sample APA research paper

On the following pages is a research paper on the effectiveness of treatments for childhood obesity, written by Luisa Mirano, a student in a psychology class. Mirano's assignment was to write a literature review paper documented with APA-style citations and references.

hackerhandbooks.com/bedhandbook

e Researched writing > Sample student writing
   > Mirano, "Can Medication Cure Obesity in Children? A Review of the Literature"
     (literature review)

Running head: CAN MEDICATION CURE OBESITY IN CHILDREN?

1 A running head consists of a title (shortened to no more than fifty characters) in all capital letters. On the title page, it is preceded by the label "Running head." Page numbers appear in the upper right corner.

Can Medication Cure Obesity in Children?

A Review of the Literature

Luisa Mirano

Northwest-Shoals Community College

Full title, writer's name, and school name are centered halfway down the page.

An author's note lists specific information about the course or department and can provide acknowledgments and contact information.

Author Note

This paper was prepared for Psychology 108, Section B, taught by Professor Kang.

Marginal annotations indicate APA-style formatting and effective writing.

CAN MEDICATION CURE OBESITY IN CHILDREN?   2

Abstract

In recent years, policymakers and medical experts have expressed alarm about the growing problem of childhood obesity in the United States. While most agree that the issue deserves attention, consensus dissolves around how to respond to the problem. This literature review examines one approach to treating childhood obesity: medication. The paper compares the effectiveness for adolescents of the only two drugs approved by the Food and Drug Administration (FDA) for long-term treatment of obesity, sibutramine and orlistat. This examination of pharmacological treatments for obesity points out the limitations of medication and suggests the need for a comprehensive solution that combines medical, social, behavioral, and political approaches to this complex problem.

Keywords: obesity, childhood, adolescence, medication, public policy

Abstract appears on a separate page. Heading is centered and not boldface.

Keywords help readers search for a paper on the Web or in a database.

Can Medication Cure Obesity in Children?

A Review of the Literature

In March 2004, U.S. Surgeon General Richard Carmona called attention to a health problem in the United States that, until recently, has been overlooked: childhood obesity. Carmona said that the "astounding" 15% child obesity rate constitutes an "epidemic." Since the early 1980s, that rate has "doubled in children and tripled in adolescents." Now more than nine million children are classified as obese.[1] While the traditional response to a medical epidemic is to hunt for a vaccine or a cure-all pill, childhood obesity is more elusive. The lack of success of recent initiatives suggests that medication might not be the answer for the escalating problem. This literature review considers whether the use of medication is a promising approach for solving the childhood obesity problem by responding to the following questions.

1. What are the implications of childhood obesity?

2. Is medication effective at treating childhood obesity?

3. Is medication safe for children?

4. Is medication the best solution?

Understanding the limitations of medical treatments for children highlights the complexity of the childhood obesity problem in the United States and underscores the need for physicians, advocacy groups, and policymakers to search for other solutions.

What Are the Implications of Childhood Obesity?

Obesity can be a devastating problem from both an individual and a societal perspective. Obesity puts children at risk for a number of

---

[1]Obesity is measured in terms of body-mass index (BMI): weight in kilograms divided by square of height in meters. A child or an adolescent with a BMI in the 95th percentile for his or her age and gender is considered obese.

Full title, centered and not boldface.

Mirano sets up her organization by posing four questions.

Mirano states her thesis.

Headings, centered and boldface, help readers follow the organization.

Mirano uses a footnote to define an essential term that would be cumbersome to define within the text.

medical complications, including Type 2 diabetes, hypertension, sleep apnea, and orthopedic problems (Henry J. Kaiser Family Foundation, 2004, p. 1). Researchers Hoppin and Taveras (2004) have noted that obesity is often associated with psychological issues such as anxiety, depression, and binge eating (Complications section, Table 4).

Obesity also poses serious problems for a society struggling to cope with rising health care costs. The cost of treating obesity currently totals $117 billion per year—a price, according to the surgeon general, "second only to the cost of [treating] tobacco use" (Carmona, 2004). And as the number of children who suffer from obesity grows, long-term costs will only increase.

Is Medication Effective at Treating Childhood Obesity?

The widening scope of the obesity problem has prompted medical professionals to rethink old conceptions of the disorder and its causes. As researchers Yanovski and Yanovski (2002) have explained, obesity was once considered "either a moral failing or evidence of underlying psychopathology" (p. 592). But this view has shifted: Many medical professionals now consider obesity a biomedical rather than a moral condition, influenced by both genetic and environmental factors. Yanovski and Yanovski have further noted that the development of weight-loss medications in the early 1990s showed that "obesity should be treated in the same manner as any other chronic disease . . . through the long-term use of medication" (p. 592).

The search for the right long-term medication has been complicated. Many of the drugs authorized by the Food and Drug Administration (FDA) in the early 1990s proved to be a disappointment. Two of the medications—fenfluramine and dexfenfluramine—were withdrawn from the market because of severe side effects (Yanovski & Yanovski, 2002, p. 592), and several others

---

In a signal phrase, the word "and" links the names of two authors; the date is given in parentheses.

Because the author (Carmona) is not named in the signal phrase, his name and the date appear in parentheses.

Ellipsis mark indicates omitted words.

CAN MEDICATION CURE OBESITY IN CHILDREN?   5

were classified by the Drug Enforcement Administration as having the
"potential for abuse" (Hoppin & Taveras, 2004, Weight-Loss Drugs
section, para. 6). Currently only two medications have been approved
by the FDA for long-term treatment of obesity: sibutramine (marketed
as Meridia) and orlistat (marketed as Xenical). This section compares
studies on the effectiveness of each.

   Sibutramine suppresses appetite by blocking the reuptake of
the neurotransmitters serotonin and norepinephrine in the brain
(Yanovski & Yanovski, 2002, p. 594). Though the drug won FDA
approval in 1998, experiments to test its effectiveness for younger
patients came considerably later. In 2003, University of Pennsylvania
researchers Berkowitz, Wadden, Tershakovec, and Cronquist released
the first double-blind placebo study testing the effect of sibutramine
on adolescents, aged 13-17, over a 12-month period. Their findings
are summarized in Table 1.

   After 6 months, the group receiving medication had lost
4.6 kg (about 10 pounds) more than the control group. But during
the second half of the study, when both groups received sibutramine,
the results were more ambiguous. In months 6-12, the group that
continued to take sibutramine gained an average of 0.8 kg, or
roughly 2 pounds; the control group, which switched from placebo to
sibutramine, lost 1.3 kg, or roughly 3 pounds (p. 1808). Both groups
received behavioral therapy covering diet, exercise, and mental health.

   These results paint a murky picture of the effectiveness of the
medication: While initial data seemed promising, the results after
one year raised questions about whether medication-induced weight
loss could be sustained over time. As Berkowitz et al. (2003) advised,
"Until more extensive safety and efficacy data are available, . . .
weight-loss medications should be used only on an experimental basis
for adolescents" (p. 1811).

In a parenthetical
citation, an
ampersand links
the names of two
authors.

Mirano draws
attention to an
important article.

Mirano uses a table to summarize the findings presented in two sources.

Table 1

Effectiveness of Sibutramine and Orlistat in Adolescents

Medication	Subjects	Treatment[a]	Side effects	Average weight loss/gain
Sibutramine	Control	0-6 mos.: placebo 6-12 mos.: sibutramine	Mos. 6-12: increased blood pressure; increased pulse rate	After 6 mos.: loss of 3.2 kg (7 lb) After 12 mos.: loss of 4.5 kg (9.9 lb)
	Medicated	0-12 mos.: sibutramine	Increased blood pressure; increased pulse rate	After 6 mos.: loss of 7.8 kg (17.2 lb) After 12 mos.: loss of 7.0 kg (15.4 lb)
Orlistat	Control	0-12 mos.: placebo	None	Gain of 0.67 kg (1.5 lb)
	Medicated	0-12 mos.: orlistat	Oily spotting; flatulence; abdominal discomfort	Loss of 1.3 kg (2.9 lb)

A note gives the source of the data.

Note. The data on sibutramine are adapted from "Behavior Therapy and Sibutramine for the Treatment of Adolescent Obesity," by R. I. Berkowitz, T. A. Wadden, A. M. Tershakovec, & J. L. Cronquist, 2003, *Journal of the American Medical Association, 289*, pp. 1807-1809. The data on orlistat are adapted from *Xenical (Orlistat) Capsules: Complete Product Information*, by Roche Laboratories, December 2003, retrieved from http://www.rocheusa.com/products/xenical/pi.pdf

A content note explains data common to all subjects.

[a]The medication and/or placebo were combined with behavioral therapy in all groups over all time periods.

A study testing the effectiveness of orlistat in adolescents showed similarly ambiguous results. The FDA approved orlistat in 1999 but did not authorize it for adolescents until December 2003. Roche Laboratories (2003), maker of orlistat, released results of a one-year study testing the drug on 539 obese adolescents, aged 12-16. The drug, which promotes weight loss by blocking fat absorption in the large intestine, showed some effectiveness in adolescents: an average loss of 1.3 kg, or roughly 3 pounds, for subjects taking orlistat for one year, as opposed to an average gain of 0.67 kg, or 1.5 pounds, for the control group (pp. 8-9). See Table 1.

Short-term studies of orlistat have shown slightly more dramatic results. Researchers at the National Institute of Child Health and Human Development tested 20 adolescents, aged 12-16, over a three-month period and found that orlistat, combined with behavioral therapy, produced an average weight loss of 4.4 kg, or 9.7 pounds (McDuffie et al., 2002, p. 646). The study was not controlled against a placebo group; therefore, the relative effectiveness of orlistat in this case remains unclear.

For a source with six or more authors, the first author's surname followed by "et al." is used for the first and subsequent references.

Is Medication Safe for Children?

While modest weight loss has been documented for both medications, each carries risks of certain side effects. Sibutramine has been observed to increase blood pressure and pulse rate. In 2002, a consumer group claimed that the medication was related to the deaths of 19 people and filed a petition with the Department of Health and Human Services to ban the medication (Hilts, 2002). The sibutramine study by Berkowitz et al. (2003) noted elevated blood pressure as a side effect, and dosages had to be reduced or the medication discontinued in 19 of the 43 subjects in the first six months (p. 1809).

When this article was first cited, all four authors were named. In subsequent citations of a work with three to five authors, "et al." is used after the first author's name.

The main side effects associated with orlistat were abdominal discomfort, oily spotting, fecal incontinence, and nausea (Roche

Laboratories, 2003, p. 13). More serious for long-term health is the concern that orlistat, being a fat-blocker, would affect absorption of fat-soluble vitamins, such as vitamin D. However, the study found that this side effect can be minimized or eliminated if patients take vitamin supplements two hours before or after administration of orlistat (p. 10). With close monitoring of patients taking the medication, many of the risks can be reduced.

Is Medication the Best Solution?

The data on the safety and efficacy of pharmacological treatments of childhood obesity raise the question of whether medication is the best solution for the problem. The treatments have clear costs for individual patients, including unpleasant side effects, little information about long-term use, and uncertainty that they will yield significant weight loss.

In purely financial terms, the drugs cost more than $3 a day on average (Duenwald, 2004). In each of the clinical trials, use of medication was accompanied by an expensive regime of behavioral therapies, including counseling, nutritional education, fitness advising, and monitoring. As journalist Greg Critser (2003) noted in his book *Fat Land*, use of weight-loss drugs is unlikely to have an effect without the proper "support system"—one that includes doctors, facilities, time, and money (p. 3). For some, this level of care is prohibitively expensive.

A third complication is that the studies focused on adolescents aged 12-16, but obesity can begin at a much younger age. Little data exist to establish the safety or efficacy of medication for treating very young children.

While the scientific data on the concrete effects of these medications in children remain somewhat unclear, medication is not the only avenue for addressing the crisis. Both medical experts and

Mirano develops the paper's thesis.

CAN MEDICATION CURE OBESITY IN CHILDREN?   9

policymakers recognize that solutions might come not only from a
laboratory but also from policy, education, and advocacy. A handbook
designed to educate doctors on obesity called for "major changes in
some aspects of western culture" (Hoppin & Taveras, 2004, Conclusion
section, para. 1). Cultural change may not be the typical realm of
medical professionals, but the handbook urged doctors to be proactive
and "focus [their] energy on public policies and interventions"
(Conclusion section, para. 1).

> Brackets indicate Mirano's change in the quoted material.

The solutions proposed by a number of advocacy groups
underscore this interest in political and cultural change. A report by
the Henry J. Kaiser Family Foundation (2004) outlined trends that may
have contributed to the childhood obesity crisis, including food
advertising for children as well as

> a reduction in physical education classes and after-school
> athletic programs, an increase in the availability of sodas
> and snacks in public schools, the growth in the number of
> fast-food outlets . . . , and the increasing number of highly
> processed high-calorie and high-fat grocery products. (p. 1)

> A quotation longer than forty words is indented without quotation marks.

Addressing each of these areas requires more than a doctor armed
with a prescription pad; it requires a broad mobilization not just
of doctors and concerned parents but of educators, food industry
executives, advertisers, and media representatives.

> Mirano interprets the evidence; she doesn't just report it.

The barrage of possible approaches to combating childhood
obesity—from scientific research to political lobbying—indicates
both the severity and the complexity of the problem. While none of
the medications currently available is a miracle drug for curing the
nation's nine million obese children, research has illuminated some of
the underlying factors that affect obesity and has shown the need for
a comprehensive approach to the problem that includes behavioral,
medical, social, and political change.

> The tone of the conclusion is objective.

References

Berkowitz, R. I., Wadden, T. A., Tershakovec, A. M., & Cronquist, J. L. (2003). Behavior therapy and sibutramine for the treatment of adolescent obesity. *Journal of the American Medical Association*, *289*, 1805-1812.

Carmona, R. H. (2004, March 2). *The growing epidemic of childhood obesity*. Testimony before the Subcommittee on Competition, Foreign Commerce, and Infrastructure of the U.S. Senate Committee on Commerce, Science, and Transportation. Retrieved from http://www.hhs.gov/asl/testify/t040302.html

Critser, G. (2003). *Fat land*. Boston, MA: Houghton Mifflin.

Duenwald, M. (2004, January 6). Slim pickings: Looking beyond ephedra. *The New York Times*, p. F1. Retrieved from http://nytimes.com/

Henry J. Kaiser Family Foundation. (2004, February). *The role of media in childhood obesity*. Retrieved from http://www.kff.org /entmedia/7030.cfm

Hilts, P. J. (2002, March 20). Petition asks for removal of diet drug from market. *The New York Times*, p. A26. Retrieved from http:// nytimes.com/

Hoppin, A. G., & Taveras, E. M. (2004, June 25). Assessment and management of childhood and adolescent obesity. *Clinical Update*. Retrieved from http://www.medscape.com/viewarticle/481633

McDuffie, J. R., Calis, K. A., Uwaifo, G. I., Sebring, N. G., Fallon, E. M., Hubbard, V. S., & Yanovski, J. A. (2002). Three-month tolerability of orlistat in adolescents with obesity-related comorbid conditions. *Obesity Research*, *10*, 642-650.

Roche Laboratories. (2003, December). *Xenical (orlistat) capsules: Complete product information*. Retrieved from http://www .rocheusa.com/products/xenical/pi.pdf

Yanovski, S. Z., & Yanovski, J. A. (2002). Drug therapy: Obesity. *The New England Journal of Medicine*, *346*, 591-602.

List of references begins on a new page. Heading is centered and not boldface.

List is alphabetized by authors' last names. All authors' names are inverted.

The first line of an entry is at the left margin; subsequent lines indent ½".

Double-spacing is used throughout.

Writing *Chicago* papers

Most history instructors and some humanities instructors require you to document sources with footnotes or endnotes based on *The Chicago Manual of Style*, 16th ed. (Chicago: University of Chicago Press, 2010). (See 63d for details about *Chicago* documentation style.)

63 *Chicago* papers

You face three main challenges when you write a *Chicago*-style paper that draws on sources: (1) supporting a thesis, (2) citing your sources and avoiding plagiarism, and (3) integrating quotations and other source material.

Examples in this section are written in *Chicago* style and are drawn from one student's research on the Fort Pillow massacre, which occurred during the Civil War. Sample pages from Ned Bishop's paper are on pages 783–88.

TEACHING TIP

Consider building a research proposal into a research paper assignment. One benefit is that writing a research proposal allows students to define their topic as meaningful and relevant. Pitch the proposal as a persuasive piece of writing: Students have to tell you why their topic matters, who the stakeholders are, and what's at stake. A proposal also gives students the opportunity to explore the debate and present different positions in the course of framing their own position.

63a Supporting a thesis

Most research assignments ask you to form a thesis, or main idea, and to support that thesis with well-organized evidence. (See also 1c.)

Forming a working thesis

Once you have read a variety of sources, considered your issue from different perspectives, and chosen an entry point in the research conversation (see 50b), you are ready to form a working thesis: a one-sentence (or occasionally a two-sentence) statement of your central idea. (See also 1c.) Because it is a working, or tentative, thesis, you can remain flexible and revise it as your ideas develop. Ultimately, the thesis will express not just your opinion but your informed, reasoned answer to your research question (see 50b). Here, for example, are student writer Ned Bishop's research question and working thesis statement.

> **MAKING THE MOST OF YOUR HANDBOOK**
>
> It's helpful to start off with a working thesis and a rough outline — especially when writing from sources.
>
> ▶ Draft a working thesis: 1c
> ▶ Sketch a plan: 1d

RESEARCH QUESTION

To what extent was Confederate Major General Nathan Bedford Forrest responsible for the massacre of Union troops at Fort Pillow?

WORKING THESIS

By encouraging racism among his troops, Nathan Bedford Forrest was directly responsible for the massacre of Union troops at Fort Pillow.

Notice that the thesis expresses a view on a debatable issue — an issue about which intelligent, well-meaning people might disagree. The writer's job is to convince such readers that this view is worth taking seriously.

hackerhandbooks.com/bedhandbook

ℯ Researched writing > Exercises: *Chicago* papers: 63–1 and 63–2

TEACHING TIP

Make an appointment with a reference librarian for a session with your class. A reference librarian can help students think about the roles that various sources might play in their college papers.

The thesis usually appears at the end of the introductory paragraph. To read Ned Bishop's thesis in the context of his introduction, see page 784.

Organizing your ideas

The body of your paper will consist of evidence in support of your thesis. It will be useful to sketch an informal plan that helps you begin to organize your ideas. Ned Bishop, for example, used a simple outline to structure his ideas. In the paper, the points in the outline became headings that helped readers follow his line of argument.

> What happened at Fort Pillow?
>
> Did Forrest order the massacre?
>
> Can Forrest be held responsible for the massacre?

Using sources to inform and support your argument

Used thoughtfully, the source materials you have gathered will make your argument more complex and convincing for readers. Sources can play several different roles as you develop your points.

Providing background information or context   You can use facts and statistics to support generalizations or to establish the importance of your topic, as student writer Ned Bishop does early in his paper.

> Fort Pillow, Tennessee, which sat on a bluff overlooking the Mississippi River, had been held by the Union for two years. It was garrisoned by 580 men, 292 of them from United States Colored Heavy and Light Artillery regiments, 285 from the white Thirteenth Tennessee Cavalry. Nathan Bedford Forrest commanded about 1,500 troops.[1]

Explaining terms or concepts   If readers are unlikely to be familiar with a word or an idea important to your topic, you must

---

TEACHING TIP

Assign students to work in pairs or small groups to identify the roles that sources play in a text that you distribute. Choose a text that is fairly brief (no more than three pages) and uses at least three sources, one of which might be visual. The text should be short enough so that students can complete the activity in a single class period or a manageable chat session online. Ask students to identify the sources the writer has used as well as the function of each source in the context of the piece of writing: Does the source provide background? Explain a term? Support the author's claim? Present an objection? Provide an illustration?

explain it for them. Quoting or paraphrasing a source can help you define terms and concepts clearly and concisely.

> The Civil War practice of giving no quarter to an enemy—in other words, "denying [an enemy] the right of survival"—defied Lincoln's mandate for humane and merciful treatment of prisoners.[9]

Supporting your claims   As you draft, make sure to back up your assertions with facts, examples, and other evidence from your research. (See also 6h.) Ned Bishop, for example, uses an eyewitness report of the racially motivated violence perpetrated by Nathan Bedford Forrest's troops.

> The slaughter at Fort Pillow was no doubt driven in large part by racial hatred. . . . A Southern reporter traveling with Forrest makes clear that the discrimination was deliberate: "Our troops maddened by the excitement, shot down the ret[r]eating Yankees, and not until they had attained t[h]e water's edge and turned to beg for mercy, did any prisoners fall in[t]o our hands—Thus the whites received quarter, but the negroes were shown no mercy."[19]

Lending authority to your argument   Expert opinion can give weight to your argument. (See also 6h.) But don't rely on experts to make your argument for you. Construct your argument in your own words and, when appropriate, cite the judgment of an authority in the field to support your position.

> Fort Pillow is not the only instance of a massacre or threatened massacre of black soldiers by troops under Forrest's command. Biographer Brian Steel Wills points out that at Brice's Cross Roads in June 1864, "black soldiers suffered inordinately" as Forrest looked the other way and Confederate soldiers deliberately sought out those they termed "the damned negroes."[21]

Anticipating and countering alternative interpretations   Do not ignore sources that seem contrary to your position or that offer arguments different from your own. Instead, use them to give voice to opposing points of view and alternative interpretations before you counter them (see 6i). Readers often have opposing points of view in mind already, whether or not they agree with you. Ned Bishop, for example, presents conflicting evidence from a biography by Jack Hurst and then counters Hurst's objection to attempt to persuade readers that Forrest can be held accountable for the massacre.

> Hurst suggests that the temperamental Forrest "may have ragingly ordered a massacre and even intended to carry it out—until he rode inside the fort and viewed the horrifying result" and ordered it stopped.[15] While this is an intriguing interpretation of events, even Hurst would probably admit that it is merely speculation.

63b Citing sources; avoiding plagiarism

In a research paper, you will draw on the work of other writers, and you must document their contributions by citing your sources. Sources are cited for two reasons:

1. to tell readers where your information comes from—so that they can assess its reliability and, if interested, find and read the original source

2. to give credit to the writers from whom you have borrowed words and ideas

You must cite anything you borrow from a source, including direct quotations; statistics and other specific facts; visuals such as tables, graphs, and diagrams; and any ideas you present in a summary or paraphrase. Borrowing another writer's language, sentence structures, or ideas without proper acknowledgment is a form of dishonesty known as *plagiarism*. The only exception is common knowledge—information that your readers may know or could easily locate in any number of reference sources.

hackerhandbooks.com/bedhandbook

e Researched writing > Exercises: *Chicago* papers: 63–3 to 63–7

SCHOLARS ON AVOIDING PLAGIARISM

Haviland, Carol P., and Joan A. Mullin. *Who Owns This Text? Plagiarism, Authorship, and Disciplinary Cultures.* Logan: Utah State UP, 2009. Print. The authors pulled together a collection that addresses citation practices in different academic disciplines and how definitions of authorship, plagiarism, and intellectual property are constructed in each discipline. Haviland, Mullin, and others spent three years interviewing college faculty from fields such as biology, sociology, computer science, and visual media. They conclude that faculty should model for students discipline-specific practices for collaboration and "knowledge building" (159).

Using the Chicago system for citing sources

Chicago citations consist of superscript numbers in the text of the paper that refer readers to notes with corresponding numbers either at the foot of the page (footnotes) or at the end of the paper (endnotes).

TEXT

Governor John Andrew was not allowed to recruit black soldiers from out of state. "Ostensibly," writes Peter Burchard, "no recruiting was done outside Massachusetts, but it was an open secret that Andrew's agents were working far and wide."[1]

NOTE

1. Peter Burchard, *One Gallant Rush: Robert Gould Shaw and His Brave Black Regiment* (New York: St. Martin's, 1965), 85.

For detailed advice on using *Chicago*-style notes, see 63d. When you use footnotes or endnotes, you will usually need to provide a bibliography as well.

BIBLIOGRAPHY ENTRY

Burchard, Peter. *One Gallant Rush: Robert Gould Shaw and His Brave Black Regiment*. New York: St. Martin's, 1965.

Avoiding plagiarism when quoting, summarizing, and paraphrasing sources

Your research paper represents your ideas in conversation with the ideas in your sources. To be fair and responsible, you must acknowledge your debt to the writers of those sources. When you acknowledge your sources, you avoid plagiarism, a form of academic dishonesty.

Three different acts are considered plagiarism: (1) failing to cite quotations and borrowed ideas, (2) failing to enclose borrowed language in quotation marks, or (3) failing to put summaries and paraphrases in your own words. Definitions of

SCHOLARS ON RESEARCH WRITING

Shi, Ling. "Rewriting and Paraphrasing Source Texts in Second Language Writing." *Journal of Second Language Writing* 21.2 (2012): 134–48. Print. For most college students, paraphrasing and summarizing texts are difficult skills to master. For multilingual students, such skills are even harder to master, according to the author. Shi concludes that paraphrasing and summarizing are "in fact complex and depend on one's knowledge of the content, the disciplinary nature of citation practices, and the rhetorical purposes of using citations in a specific context of disciplinary writing" (134).

plagiarism may vary; it's a good idea to find out how your school defines and addresses academic dishonesty.

Citing quotations and borrowed ideas
To indicate that you are using a source's exact phrases or sentences, you must enclose them in quotation marks unless they have been set off from the text by indenting (see pp. 749–50). To omit the quotation marks is to claim — falsely — that the language is your own. Such an omission is plagiarism even if you have cited the source.

> **MAKING THE MOST
> OF YOUR HANDBOOK**
>
> When you use exact language from a source, you need to show that it is a quotation.
>
> ► Quotation marks for direct quotations: 37a
> ► Setting off long quotations: page 749

ORIGINAL SOURCE

For many Southerners it was psychologically impossible to see a black man bearing arms as anything but an incipient slave uprising complete with arson, murder, pillage, and rapine.

— Dudley Taylor Cornish, *The Sable Arm*, p. 158

PLAGIARISM

According to Civil War historian Dudley Taylor Cornish, for many Southerners it was psychologically impossible to see a black man bearing arms as anything but an incipient slave uprising complete with arson, murder, pillage, and rapine.[2]

BORROWED LANGUAGE IN QUOTATION MARKS

According to Civil War historian Dudley Taylor Cornish, "For many Southerners it was psychologically impossible to see a black man bearing arms as anything but an incipient slave uprising complete with arson, murder, pillage, and rapine."[2]

Putting summaries and paraphrases in your own words   Summaries and paraphrases are written in your own words. A summary condenses information; a paraphrase uses roughly the same number of words as in the original source to convey the information. When you summarize or paraphrase, it is not enough to name the source; you must restate the source's meaning using your own language. (See also 51c.) You commit plagiarism if you patchwrite—half-copy the author's sentences, either by mixing the author's phrases with your own without using quotation marks or by plugging your own synonyms into the author's sentence structure.

The first paraphrase of the following source is plagiarized—even though the source is cited—because too much of its language is borrowed from the original. The highlighted strings of words have been copied exactly (without quotation marks). In addition, the writer has closely followed the sentence structure of the original source, merely making a few substitutions (such as *Fifty percent* for *Half* and *angered and perhaps frightened* for *enraged and perhaps terrified*).

ORIGINAL SOURCE

Half of the force holding Fort Pillow were Negroes, former slaves now enrolled in the Union Army. Toward them Forrest's troops had the fierce, bitter animosity of men who had been educated to regard the colored race as inferior and who for the first time had encountered that race armed and fighting against white men. The sight enraged and perhaps terrified many of the Confederates and aroused in them the ugly spirit of a lynching mob.

— Albert Castel, "The Fort Pillow Massacre," pp. 46–47

PLAGIARISM: UNACCEPTABLE BORROWING

Albert Castel suggests that much of the brutality at Fort Pillow can be traced to racial attitudes. Fifty percent of the troops holding Fort Pillow were Negroes, former slaves who had joined the Union Army. Toward them Forrest's soldiers displayed the savage hatred of men who had been taught the inferiority of blacks and who for the first time had confronted them armed and fighting against white men. The vision

angered and perhaps frightened the Confederates and aroused in them the ugly spirit of a lynching mob.[3]

To avoid plagiarizing an author's language, resist the temptation to look at the source while you are summarizing or paraphrasing. After you have read the passage you want to paraphrase, set the source aside. Ask yourself, "What is the author's meaning?" In your own words, state your understanding of the author's basic point. Return to the source and check that you haven't used the author's language or sentence structure or misrepresented the author's ideas. Following these steps will help you avoid plagiarizing the source. When you fully understand another writer's meaning, you can more easily and accurately represent those ideas in your own words.

ACCEPTABLE PARAPHRASE

Albert Castel suggests that much of the brutality at Fort Pillow can be traced to racial attitudes. Fifty percent of the Union troops were blacks, men whom the Confederates had been raised to consider their inferiors. The shock and perhaps fear of facing armed ex-slaves in battle may well have unleashed the fury that led to the massacre.[3]

63c Integrating sources

Quotations, summaries, paraphrases, and facts will support your argument, but they cannot speak for you. You can use several strategies to integrate information from research sources into your paper while maintaining your own voice.

Using quotations appropriately

In academic writing, keep the emphasis on your ideas and your language; use your own words to summarize and to paraphrase your sources and to explain your points. Sometimes, however, quotations can be the most effective way to integrate a source.

Limiting your use of quotations Although it is tempting to insert many quotations in your paper and to use your own words only for connecting passages, do not quote excessively. It is almost impossible to integrate numerous quotations smoothly into your own text.

WHEN TO USE QUOTATIONS

- When language is especially vivid or expressive
- When exact wording is needed for technical accuracy
- When it is important to let the debaters of an issue explain their positions in their own words
- When the words of an authority lend weight to an argument
- When the language of a source is the topic of your discussion (as in an analysis or interpretation)

It is not always necessary to quote full sentences from a source. To reduce your reliance on the words of others, you can often integrate language from a source into your own sentence structure.

> As Hurst has pointed out, until "an outcry erupted in the Northern press," even the Confederates did not deny that there had been a massacre at Fort Pillow.[4]

> Union surgeon Dr. Charles Fitch testified that after he was in custody he "saw" Confederate soldiers "kill every negro that made his appearance dressed in Federal uniform."[20]

Using the ellipsis mark To condense a quoted passage, you can use the ellipsis mark (three periods, with spaces between) to indicate that you have left words out. What remains must be grammatically complete.

> Union surgeon Fitch's testimony that all women and children had been
> evacuated from Fort Pillow before the attack conflicts with Forrest's
> report: "We captured . . . about 40 negro women and children."[6]

The writer has omitted several words not relevant to the issue at
hand: *164 Federals, 75 negro troops, and.*

When you want to leave out one or more full sentences, use
a period before the three ellipsis dots. For an example, see the
long quotation on page 750.

Ordinarily, do not use the ellipsis mark at the beginning or at
the end of a quotation. Readers will understand that the quoted
material is taken from a longer passage, so such marks are not
necessary. The only exception occurs when you have dropped
words at the end of the final quoted sentence. In such cases, put
three ellipsis dots before the closing quotation mark.

USING SOURCES RESPONSIBLY: Make sure omissions and ellipsis
marks do not distort the meaning of your source.

Using brackets Brackets allow you to insert words of your own
into quoted material to clarify a confusing reference or to keep a
sentence grammatical in the context of your own writing.

> According to Albert Castel, "It can be reasonably argued that he
> [Forrest] was justified in believing that the approaching steamships
> intended to aid the garrison [at Fort Pillow]."[7]

NOTE: Use the word *sic*, italicized and in brackets, to indicate that
an error in a quoted sentence appears in the original source. (An
example appears on p. 750.) Do not overuse *sic* to call attention
to errors in a source. Sometimes paraphrasing is a better option.
(See 39c.)

Setting off long quotations *Chicago* style allows you some
flexibility in deciding whether to set off a long quotation or run it
into your text. You may want to set off a quotation of more than
four or five typed lines of text; almost certainly you should set off

quotations of ten or more lines. To set off a quotation, indent it one-half inch from the left margin and use the normal right margin. Double-space the indented quotation.

Long quotations should be introduced by an informative sentence, usually followed by a colon. Quotation marks are unnecessary because the indented format tells readers that the passage is taken word-for-word from the source.

> In a letter home, Confederate officer Achilles V. Clark recounted what happened at Fort Pillow:
>
>> Words cannot describe the scene. The poor deluded negroes would run up to our men fall upon their knees and with uplifted hands scream for mercy but they were ordered to their feet and then shot down. The whitte [*sic*] men fared but little better. . . . I with several others tried to stop the butchery and at one time had partially succeeded[,] but Gen. Forrest ordered them shot down like dogs, and the carnage continued.[8]

Using signal phrases to integrate sources

Whenever you include a paraphrase, summary, or direct quotation of another writer's work in your paper, prepare your readers for it with introductory words called a *signal phrase*. A signal phrase names the author of the source and often provides some context for the source material.

When you write a signal phrase, choose a verb that is appropriate for the way you are using the source (see pp. 741–43). Are you providing background, explaining a concept, supporting a claim, lending authority, or refuting a belief? By choosing an appropriate verb, you can make your source's role clear. See the chart on page 751 for a list of verbs commonly used in signal phrases.

Note that *Chicago* style calls for verbs in the present tense or present perfect tense (*points out, has pointed out*) to introduce source material unless you include a date that specifies the time of the original author's writing.

Using signal phrases in *Chicago* papers

To avoid monotony, try to vary both the language and the placement of your signal phrases.

Model signal phrases

In the words of historian James M. McPherson, ". . ."[1]

As Dudley Taylor Cornish has argued, ". . ."[2]

In a letter to his wife, a Confederate soldier who witnessed the massacre wrote that ". . ."[3]

". . . ," claims Benjamin Quarles.[4]

". . . ," writes Albert Castel, ". . ."[5]

Shelby Foote offers an intriguing interpretation: ". . ."[6]

Verbs in signal phrases

admits	compares	insists	rejects
agrees	confirms	notes	reports
argues	contends	observes	responds
asserts	declares	points out	suggests
believes	denies	reasons	thinks
claims	emphasizes	refutes	writes

The first time you mention an author, use the full name: *Shelby Foote argues. . . .* When you refer to the author again, you may use the last name only: *Foote raises an important question.*

Marking boundaries   Readers should be able to move from your own words to the words of a source without feeling a jolt. Avoid dropping quotations into the text without warning. Instead, provide clear signal phrases, usually including the author's name, to indicate the boundary between your words and the source's words. (The signal phrase is highlighted in the second example.)

DROPPED QUOTATION

Not surprisingly, those testifying on the Union and Confederate sides recalled events at Fort Pillow quite differently. Unionists claimed that their troops had abandoned their arms and were in full retreat. "The Confederates, however, all agreed that the Union troops retreated to the river with arms in their hands."[9]

QUOTATION WITH SIGNAL PHRASE

Not surprisingly, those testifying on the Union and Confederate sides recalled events at Fort Pillow quite differently. Unionists claimed that their troops had abandoned their arms and were in full retreat. "The Confederates, however," writes historian Albert Castel, "all agreed that the Union troops retreated to the river with arms in their hands."[9]

Using signal phrases with summaries and paraphrases   As with quotations, introduce most summaries and paraphrases with a signal phrase that mentions the author and places the material in the context of your own writing. Readers will then understand where the summary or paraphrase begins.

Without the signal phrase (highlighted) in the following example, readers might think that only the last sentence is being cited, when in fact the whole paragraph is based on the source.

According to Jack Hurst, official Confederate policy was that black soldiers were to be treated as runaway slaves; in addition, the Confederate Congress decreed that white Union officers commanding black troops be killed. Confederate Lieutenant General Kirby Smith went one step further, declaring that he would kill all captured black troops. Smith's policy never met with strong opposition from the Richmond government.[10]

Integrating statistics and other facts   When you are citing a statistic or another specific fact, a signal phrase is often not necessary. In most cases, readers will understand that the citation refers to the statistic or fact (not the whole paragraph).

Of the 295 white troops garrisoned at Fort Pillow, 168 were taken prisoner. Black troops fared worse, with only 58 of 262 captured and most of the rest presumably killed or wounded.[12]

There is nothing wrong, however, with using a signal phrase to introduce a statistic or another fact.

Putting source material in context   Readers should not have to guess why source material appears in your paper. A signal phrase can help you make the connection between your own ideas and those of another writer by setting up how a source will contribute to your paper (see 52a).

If you use another writer's words, you must explain how they relate to your point. It's a good idea to embed a quotation between sentences of your own. In addition to introducing it with a signal phrase, follow the quotation with interpretive comments that link it to your paper's argument.

QUOTATION WITH EFFECTIVE CONTEXT

In a respected biography of Nathan Bedford Forrest, Hurst suggests that the temperamental Forrest "may have ragingly ordered a massacre and even intended to carry it out—until he rode inside the fort and viewed the horrifying result" and ordered it stopped.[15] While this is an intriguing interpretation of events, even Hurst would probably admit that it is merely speculation.

NOTE: When you bring other sources into a conversation about your research topic, you are synthesizing (see 55c).

63d *Chicago* documentation style

In history and some other humanities courses, you may be asked to use the documentation system of *The Chicago Manual of Style*, 16th ed. (Chicago: University of Chicago Press, 2010).

hackerhandbooks.com/bedhandbook

e Researched writing > Exercises: *Chicago* papers: 63–12 to 63–19

SCHOLARS ON CITATION

Shi, Ling. "Common Knowledge, Learning, and Citation Practices in University Writing." *Research in the Teaching of English* 45.3 (2011): 308–34. Print. Shi's work is based on interviews with seventy-five college students and instructors in a variety of disciplines. Participants in the study commented on examples of writing that included unacknowledged uses of sources, but they could not agree on whether the writers were using common knowledge or were committing plagiarism.

Directory to *Chicago*-style notes and bibliography entries

Directory to *Chicago*-style **notes and bibliography entries** (*cont.*)

In *Chicago* style, superscript numbers (like this[1]) in the text of the paper refer readers to notes with corresponding numbers either at the foot of the page (footnotes) or at the end of the paper (endnotes). A bibliography is often required as well; it appears at the end of the paper and gives publication information for all the works cited in the notes.

TEXT

A Union soldier, Jacob Thompson, claimed to have seen Forrest order the killing, but when asked to describe the six-foot-two general, he called him "a little bit of a man."[12]

FOOTNOTE OR ENDNOTE

12. Brian Steel Wills, *A Battle from the Start: The Life of Nathan Bedford Forrest* (New York: HarperCollins, 1992), 187.

BIBLIOGRAPHY ENTRY

Wills, Brian Steel. *A Battle from the Start: The Life of Nathan Bedford Forrest*. New York: HarperCollins, 1992.

First and later notes for a source

The first time you cite a source, the note should include publication information for that work as well as the page number for the passage you are citing.

> 1. Peter Burchard, *One Gallant Rush: Robert Gould Shaw and His Brave Black Regiment* (New York: St. Martin's, 1965), 85.

For later references to a source you have already cited, you may simply give the author's last name, a short form of the title, and the page or pages cited. A short form of the title of a book or another long work is italicized; a short form of the title of an article or another short work is put in quotation marks.

> 4. Burchard, *One Gallant Rush*, 31.

When you have two notes in a row from the same source, you may use "Ibid." (meaning "in the same place") and the page number for the second note. Use "Ibid." alone if the page number is the same.

> 5. Jack Hurst, *Nathan Bedford Forrest: A Biography* (New York: Knopf, 1993), 8.
>
> 6. Ibid., 174.

Chicago-style bibliography

A bibliography at the end of your paper lists the works you have cited in your notes; it may also include works you consulted but did not cite. See page 782 for how to construct the list; see page 788 for a sample bibliography.

NOTE: If you include a bibliography, *The Chicago Manual of Style* suggests that you shorten all notes, including the first reference to a source, as described at the top of this page. Check with your instructor, however, to see whether using an abbreviated note for a first reference to a source is acceptable.

Model notes and bibliography entries

The following models are consistent with guidelines in *The Chicago Manual of Style*, 16th ed. For each type of source, a model note appears first, followed by a model bibliography entry. The note shows the format you should use when citing a source for the first time. For subsequent citations of a source, use shortened notes (see pp. 755–56).

Some sources on the Web, typically periodical articles, use a permanent locator called a digital object identifier (DOI). Use the DOI, when it is available, in place of a URL in your citations of sources from the Web.

When a URL or a DOI must break across lines, do not insert a hyphen or break at a hyphen if the URL or DOI contains one. Instead, break after a colon or a double slash or before any other mark of punctuation.

General guidelines for listing authors

1. One author

1. Salman Rushdie, *Joseph Anton: A Memoir* (New York: Random House, 2012), 135.

Rushdie, Salman. *Joseph Anton: A Memoir*. New York: Random House, 2012.

2. Two or three authors
For a work with two or three authors, give all authors' names in both the note and the bibliography entry.

2. Bill O'Reilly and Martin Dugard, *Killing Lincoln: The Shocking Assassination That Changed America Forever* (New York: Holt, 2012), 33.

O'Reilly, Bill, and Martin Dugard. *Killing Lincoln: The Shocking Assassination That Changed America Forever*. New York: Holt, 2012.

3. Four or more authors
For a work with four or more authors, in the note give the first author's name followed by "et al." (for "and others"); in the bibliography entry, list all authors' names.

3. Lynn Hunt et al., *The Making of the West: Peoples and Cultures*, 4th ed. (Boston: Bedford/St. Martin's, 2012), 541.

Hunt, Lynn, Thomas R. Martin, Barbara H. Rosenwein, R. Po-chia Hsia, and Bonnie G. Smith. *The Making of the West: Peoples and Cultures*. 4th ed. Boston: Bedford/St. Martin's, 2012.

4. Organization as author

4. Johnson Historical Society, *Images of America: Johnson* (Charleston, SC: Arcadia Publishing, 2011), 24.

Johnson Historical Society. *Images of America: Johnson*. Charleston, SC: Arcadia Publishing, 2011.

5. Unknown author

5. *The Men's League Handbook on Women's Suffrage* (London, 1912), 23.

The Men's League Handbook on Women's Suffrage. London, 1912.

6. Multiple works by the same author

In the bibliography, arrange the entries alphabetically by title. Use six hyphens in place of the author's name in the second and subsequent entries.

Winchester, Simon. *The Alice behind Wonderland*. New York: Oxford University Press, 2011.

------. *Atlantic: Great Sea Battles, Heroic Discoveries, Titanic Storms, and a Vast Ocean of a Million Stories*. New York: HarperCollins, 2010.

7. Editor

7. Teresa Carpenter, ed., *New York Diaries: 1609-2009* (New York: Modern Library, 2012), 316.

Carpenter, Teresa, ed. *New York Diaries: 1609-2009*. New York: Modern Library, 2012.

8. Editor with author

8. Susan Sontag, *As Consciousness Is Harnessed to Flesh: Journals and Notebooks, 1964-1980,* ed. David Rieff (New York: Farrar, Straus and Giroux, 2012), 265.

Sontag, Susan. *As Consciousness Is Harnessed to Flesh: Journals and Notebooks, 1964-1980*. Edited by David Rieff. New York: Farrar, Straus and Giroux, 2012.

9. Translator with author

9. Richard Bidlack and Nikita Lomagin, *The Leningrad Blockade, 1941-1944: A New Documentary from the Soviet Archives*, trans. Marian Schwartz (New Haven: Yale University Press, 2012), 26.

Bidlack, Richard, and Nikita Lomagin. *The Leningrad Blockade, 1941-1944: A New Documentary from the Soviet Archives*. Translated by Marian Schwartz. New Haven: Yale University Press, 2012.

Books and other long works

▶ Citation at a glance: Book, page 760

10. Basic format for a book

a. Print

10. Mary N. Woods, *Beyond the Architect's Eye: Photographs and the American Built Environment* (Philadelphia: University of Pennsylvania Press, 2009), 45.

Woods, Mary N. *Beyond the Architect's Eye: Photographs and the American Built Environment*. Philadelphia: University of Pennsylvania Press, 2009.

b. E-book

10. Drew Gilpin Faust, *This Republic of Suffering: Death and the American Civil War* (New York: Knopf, 2008), Nook edition, chap. 4.

Faust, Drew Gilpin. *This Republic of Suffering: Death and the American Civil War*. New York: Knopf, 2008. Nook edition.

c. Web (or online library)

10. Charles Hursthouse, *New Zealand, or Zealandia, the Britain of the South* (1857; Hathi Trust Digital Library, n.d.), 2:356, http://hdl.handle.net/2027/uc1.b304920.

Hursthouse, Charles. *New Zealand, or Zealandia, the Britain of the South*. 2 vols. 1857. Hathi Trust Digital Library, n.d. http://hdl.handle.net/2027/uc1.b304920.

Citation at a glance

Book *Chicago*

To cite a print book in *Chicago* style, include the following
elements:

1 Author(s)
2 Title and subtitle
3 City of publication
4 Publisher
5 Year of publication
6 Page number(s) cited (for notes)

TITLE PAGE

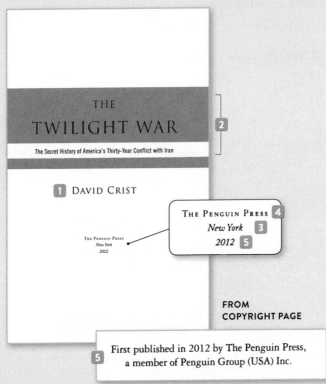

FROM COPYRIGHT PAGE

5 First published in 2012 by The Penguin Press, a member of Penguin Group (USA) Inc.

1. David Crist, *The Twilight War: The Secret History of America's Thirty-Year Conflict with Iran* (New York: Penguin, 2012), 354.

BIBLIOGRAPHY

Crist, David. *The Twilight War: The Secret History of America's Thirty-Year Conflict with Iran*. New York: Penguin, 2012.

For more on citing books in *Chicago* style, see items 10–18.

11. Edition other than the first

11. Josephine Donovan, *Feminist Theory: The Intellectual Traditions*, 4th ed. (New York: Continuum, 2012), 86.

Donovan, Josephine. *Feminist Theory: The Intellectual Traditions*. 4th ed. New York: Continuum, 2012.

12. Volume in a multivolume work
If each volume has its own title, give the volume title first, followed by the volume number and the title of the entire work, as in the following examples. If the volumes do not have individual titles, give the volume and page number in the note (for example, 2:356) and the total number of volumes in the bibliography entry (see item 10c).

12. Robert A. Caro, *The Passage of Power*, vol. 4 of *The Years of Lyndon Johnson* (New York: Knopf, 2012), 198.

Caro, Robert A. *The Passage of Power*. Vol. 4 of *The Years of Lyndon Johnson*. New York: Knopf, 2012.

13. Work in an anthology

13. Janet Walsh, "Unequal in Africa: How Property Rights Can Empower Women," in *The Unfinished Revolution: Voices from the Global Fight for Women's Rights*, ed. Minky Worden (New York: Seven Stories Press, 2012), 161.

Walsh, Janet. "Unequal in Africa: How Property Rights Can Empower Women." In *The Unfinished Revolution: Voices from the Global Fight for Women's Rights*, edited by Minky Worden, 159-66. New York: Seven Stories Press, 2012.

14. Introduction, preface, foreword, or afterword

14. Alice Walker, afterword to *The Indispensable Zinn: The Essential Writings of the "People's Historian,"* by Howard Zinn (New York: Free Press, 2012), 373.

Walker, Alice. Afterword to *The Indispensable Zinn: The Essential Writings of the "People's Historian,"* by Howard Zinn, 371-76. New York: Free Press, 2012.

15. Republished book

15. W. S. Blatchley, *A Nature Wooing at Ormond by the Sea* (1902; repr., Stockbridge, MA: Hard Press, 2012), 26.

Blatchley, W. S. *A Nature Wooing at Ormond by the Sea.* 1902. Reprint, Stockbridge, MA: Hard Press, 2012.

16. Book with a title in its title   Use quotation marks around any title, whether a long or a short work, within an italicized title.

16. Claudia Durst Johnson, ed., *Race in Mark Twain's "Adventures of Huckleberry Finn"* (Detroit: Greenhaven Press, 2009).

Johnson, Claudia Durst, ed. *Race in Mark Twain's "Adventures of Huckleberry Finn."* Detroit: Greenhaven Press, 2009.

17. Work in a series   The series name follows the book title.

17. Lois E. Horton, *Harriet Tubman and the Fight for Freedom: A Brief History with Documents*, Bedford Series in History and Culture (Boston: Bedford/St. Martin's, 2013), 35.

Horton, Lois E. *Harriet Tubman and the Fight for Freedom: A Brief History with Documents.* Bedford Series in History and Culture. Boston: Bedford/St. Martin's, 2013.

18. Sacred text   Sacred texts are usually not included in the bibliography.

18. Matt. 20:4-9 (Revised Standard Version).

18. Qur'an 18:1-3.

19. Government document

19. United States Senate, Committee on Foreign Relations, *Implications of the Kyoto Protocol on Climate Change: Hearing before the Committee on Foreign Relations, United States Senate*, 105th Cong., 2nd sess. (Washington, DC: GPO, 1998).

United States Senate. Committee on Foreign Relations. *Implications of the Kyoto Protocol on Climate Change: Hearing before the Committee on Foreign Relations, United States Senate*, 105th Cong., 2nd sess. Washington, DC: GPO, 1998.

20. Unpublished dissertation

20. Stephanie Lynn Budin, "The Origins of Aphrodite" (PhD diss., University of Pennsylvania, 2000), 301-2, ProQuest (AAT 9976404).

Budin, Stephanie Lynn. "The Origins of Aphrodite." PhD diss., University of Pennsylvania, 2000. ProQuest (AAT 9976404).

For a published dissertation, italicize the title and give publication information as for a book.

21. Published proceedings of a conference   Cite as a book, adding the location and dates of the conference after the title.

21. Stacey K. Sowards, Kyle Alvarado, Diana Arrieta, and Jacob Barde, eds., *Across Borders and Environments: Communication and Environmental Justice in International Contexts*, University of Texas at El Paso, June 25-28, 2011 (Cincinnati, OH: International Environmental Communication Association, 2012), 114.

Sowards, Stacey K., Kyle Alvarado, Diana Arrieta, and Jacob Barde, eds. *Across Borders and Environments: Communication and Environmental Justice in International Contexts*. University of Texas at El Paso, June 25-28, 2011. Cincinnati, OH: International Environmental Communication Association, 2012.

22. Source quoted in another source (a secondary source) Sometimes you will want to use a quotation from one source that you have found in another source. In your note and bibliography entry, cite whatever information is available about the original source of the quotation, including a page number. Then add the words "quoted in" and give publication information for the source in which you found the words. In the following examples, author John Matteson quotes the words of Thomas Wentworth Higginson. Matteson's book includes a note with information about the Higginson book.

> 22. Thomas Wentworth Higginson, *Margaret Fuller Ossoli* (Boston: Houghton Mifflin, 1890), 11, quoted in John Matteson, *The Lives of Margaret Fuller* (New York: Norton, 2012), 7.

> Higginson, Thomas Wentworth. *Margaret Fuller Ossoli*. Boston: Houghton Mifflin, 1890, 11. Quoted in John Matteson, *The Lives of Margaret Fuller* (New York: Norton, 2012), 7.

Articles and other short works

▶ Citation at a glance: Article in a journal, page 766
▶ Citation at a glance: Article from a database, page 768

23. Article in a journal Include the volume and issue numbers (if the journal has them) and the date; end the bibliography entry with the page range of the article. If an article in a database or on the Web shows only a beginning page, use a plus sign after the page number instead of a page range: 212+.

a. Print

> 23. Catherine Foisy, "Preparing the Quebec Church for Vatican II: Missionary Lessons from Asia, Africa, and Latin America, 1945-1962," *Historical Studies* 78 (2012): 8.

> Foisy, Catherine. "Preparing the Quebec Church for Vatican II: Missionary Lessons from Asia, Africa, and Latin America, 1945-1962." *Historical Studies* 78 (2012): 7-26.

b. Web Give the DOI if the article has one; if there is no DOI, give the URL for the article. For unpaginated articles on the Web, you may include in your note a locator, such as a numbered paragraph or a heading from the article.

23. Anne-Lise François, "Flower Fisting," *Postmodern Culture* 22, no. 1 (2011), doi:10.1353/pmc.2012.0004.

François, Anne-Lise. "Flower Fisting." *Postmodern Culture* 22, no. 1 (2011). doi:10.1353/pmc.2012.0004.

c. Database Give one of the following pieces of information from the database listing, in this order of preference: a DOI for the article; or the name of the database and the article number, if any; or a "stable" or "persistent" URL for the article.

23. Patrick Zuk, "Nikolay Myaskovsky and the Events of 1948," *Music and Letters* 93, no. 1 (2012): 61, Project Muse.

Zuk, Patrick. "Nikolay Myaskovsky and the Events of 1948." *Music and Letters* 93, no. 1 (2012): 61. Project Muse.

24. Article in a magazine Give the month and year for a monthly publication; give the month, day, and year for a weekly publication. End the bibliography entry with the page range of the article. If an article in a database or on the Web shows only a beginning page, use a plus sign after the page number instead of a page range: 212+.

a. Print

24. Alan Lightman, "Our Place in the Universe: Face to Face with the Infinite," *Harper's*, December 2012, 34.

Lightman, Alan. "Our Place in the Universe: Face to Face with the Infinite." *Harper's*, December 2012, 33-38.

b. Web If no DOI is available, include the URL for the article.

24. James Verini, "The Tunnels of Gaza," *National Geographic*, December 2012, http://ngm.nationalgeographic.com/2012/12/gaza-tunnels /verini-text.

Verini, James. "The Tunnels of Gaza." *National Geographic*, December 2012. http://ngm.nationalgeographic.com/2012/12/gaza-tunnels/verini-text.

(*continued on p. 767*)

Citation at a glance

Article in a journal

To cite an article in a print journal in *Chicago* style, include the following elements:

1 Author(s)
2 Title and subtitle of article
3 Title of journal
4 Volume and issue numbers
5 Year of publication
6 Page number(s) cited (for notes); page range of article (for bibliography)

FIRST PAGE OF ARTICLE

 Work, Family, and the Eighteenth-Century History of a Middle Class in the American South

By Emma Hart

...TTA WYATT APPEARED BEFORE
...equity in Charleston District,
...ount of her married life, which
...years earlier, when she took
...The daughter of a blacksmith,
...of Charleston from childhood,
...nineteenth century, her experi-
...historical record as those of so
...With her husband at the head of
...he first federal census not as an
...deed, the sole records of her
...neficiary in her father's 1767
...which the documents are now
...ster. Yet, in her lengthy testi-
...rict Chancery Court, the course
...extraordinary detail. Violetta
...ss from their marriage through
...ring the American Revolution,
...naging a household.¹

...the First Census of the United States
...D.C., 1908), 39; Will of James Lingard,
...pts of Charleston County Wills (South
...Charleston, S.C.). The case of *Mary*
...illiam Brisbane, September 23, 1771, is
...th Carolina under the royal government,
...ed., *Records of the Court of Chancery*
...50), 588. The case of *Executors of the*
...tt, Deceased (hereinafter Richardsons v.
...00, is in Folder 20, Box 4, Charleston
...10090 (South Carolina Department of
...AH). The decision in the case is cited as
...m, 1807, Vol. 2, pp. 1–2, Series L10092,

TITLE PAGE OF JOURNAL

 The Journal of **SOUTHERN HISTORY**

 VOLUME LXXVIII AUGUST 2012 NUMBER 3

Contents

1   2

1. Emma Hart, "Work, Family, and the Eighteenth-Century History of a

3   4

Middle Class in the American South," *Journal of Southern History* 78, no. 3

5   6

(2012): 565.

1   2

Hart, Emma. "Work, Family, and the Eighteenth-Century History of a Middle

3   4

Class in the American South." *Journal of Southern History* 78, no. 3

5   6

(2012): 551-78.

For more on citing articles in *Chicago* style, see items 23–25.

24. Article in a magazine (cont.)

c. Database Give one of the following from the database listing, in this order of preference: a DOI for the article; or the name of the database and the article number, if any; or a "stable" or "persistent" URL for the article.

24. Ron Rosenbaum, "The Last Renaissance Man," *Smithsonian*, November 2012, 40, OmniFile Full Text Select (83097302).

Rosenbaum, Ron. "The Last Renaissance Man." *Smithsonian*, November 2012, 39-44. OmniFile Full Text Select (83097302).

Citation at a glance

Article from a database *Chicago*

To cite an article from a database in *Chicago* style, include the following elements:

1. Author(s)
2. Title and subtitle of article
3. Title of journal
4. Volume and issue numbers
5. Year of publication
6. Page number(s) cited (for notes); page range of article (for bibliography)
7. DOI; *or* database name and article number; *or* "stable" or "persistent" URL for article

DATABASE RECORD

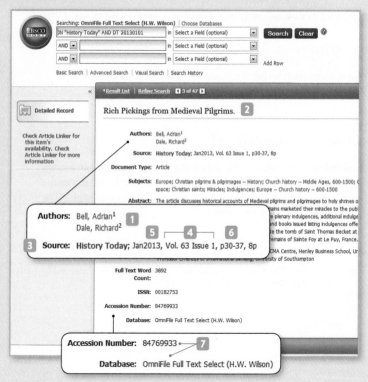

Searching: OmniFile Full Text Select (H.W. Wilson) | Choose Databases
DN "History Today" AND DT 20130101   in Select a Field (optional)   Search Clear
AND   in Select a Field (optional)
AND   in Select a Field (optional)   Add Row
Basic Search | Advanced Search | Visual Search | Search History

◄ Result List | Refine Search ◄ 3 of 47 ►

Detailed Record

Check Article Linker for this item's availability. Check Article Linker for more information

Rich Pickings from Medieval Pilgrims.   2

Authors: Bell, Adrian[1]
Dale, Richard[2]

Source: History Today; Jan2013, Vol. 63 Issue 1, p30-37, 8p

Document Type: Article

Subjects: Europe; Christian pilgrims & pilgrimages -- History; Church history -- Middle Ages, 600-1500; C
space; Christian saints; Miracles; Indulgences; Europe -- Church history -- 600-1500

Abstract: The article discusses historical accounts of Medieval pilgrims and pilgrimages to holy shrines o

Authors: Bell, Adrian[1]   1
Dale, Richard[2]

5 ——— 4 ——— 6

Source: History Today; Jan2013, Vol. 63 Issue 1, p30-37, 8p

CMA Centre, Henley Business School, Ur
University of Southampton

Full Text Word Count: 3892

ISSN: 00182753

Accession Number: 84769933

Database: OmniFile Full Text Select (H.W. Wilson)

Accession Number: 84769933   7

Database: OmniFile Full Text Select (H.W. Wilson)

NOTE

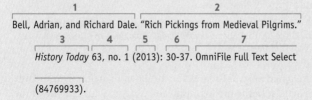

1. Adrian Bell and Richard Dale, "Rich Pickings from Medieval Pilgrims,"

History Today 63, no. 1 (2013): 33, OmniFile Full Text Select (84769933).

BIBLIOGRAPHY

Bell, Adrian, and Richard Dale. "Rich Pickings from Medieval Pilgrims."

History Today 63, no. 1 (2013): 30-37. OmniFile Full Text Select

(84769933).

For more on citing articles from databases in *Chicago* style, see items 23–25.

25. Article in a newspaper   Page numbers are not necessary; a section letter or number, if available, is sufficient.

a. Print

25. Alissa J. Rubin, "A Pristine Afghan Prison Faces a Murky Future," *New York Times*, December 18, 2012, sec. A.

Rubin, Alissa J. "A Pristine Afghan Prison Faces a Murky Future." *New York Times*, December 18, 2012, sec. A.

b. Web   Include the URL for the article; if the URL is very long, use the URL for the newspaper's home page. Omit page numbers, even if the source provides them.

25. David Brown, "New Burden of Disease Study Shows World's People Living Longer but with More Disability," *Washington Post*, December 13, 2012, http://www.washingtonpost.com/.

Brown, David. "New Burden of Disease Study Shows World's People Living Longer but with More Disability." *Washington Post*, December 13, 2012. http://www.washingtonpost.com/.

(*continued on p. 770*)

c. Database Give one of the following from the database listing, in this order of preference: a DOI for the article; or the name of the database and the number assigned by the database; or a "stable" or "persistent" URL for the article.

> 25. "Safe in Sioux City at Last: Union Pacific Succeeds in Securing Trackage from the St. Paul Road," *Omaha Daily Herald*, May 16, 1889, America's Historical Newspapers.

"Safe in Sioux City at Last: Union Pacific Succeeds in Securing Trackage from the St. Paul Road." *Omaha Daily Herald*, May 16, 1889. America's Historical Newspapers.

26. Unsigned newspaper article In the note, begin with the title of the article. In the bibliography entry, begin with the title of the newspaper.

> 26. "Rein in Charter Schools," *Chicago Sun-Times*, December 13, 2012, http://www.suntimes.com/.

Chicago Sun-Times. "Rein in Charter Schools." December 13, 2012. http://www.suntimes.com/.

27. Article with a title in its title Use italics for titles of long works such as books and for terms that are normally italicized. Use single quotation marks for titles of short works and terms that would otherwise be placed in double quotation marks.

> 27. Karen Garner, "Global Gender Policy in the 1990s: Incorporating the 'Vital Voices' of Women," *Journal of Women's History* 24, no. 4 (2012): 130.

Garner, Karen. "Global Gender Policy in the 1990s: Incorporating the 'Vital Voices' of Women." *Journal of Women's History* 24, no. 4 (2012): 121-48.

28. Review If the review has a title, provide it immediately following the author of the review.

> 28. David Denby, "Dead Reckoning," review of *Zero Dark Thirty*, directed by Kathryn Bigelow, *New Yorker*, December 24/31, 2012, 130.

Denby, David. "Dead Reckoning." Review of *Zero Dark Thirty*, directed by Kathryn Bigelow. *New Yorker*, December 24/31, 2012, 130-32.

28. David Eggleton, review of *Stalking Nabokov*, by Brian Boyd, *New Zealand Listener*, December 13, 2012, http://www.listener.co.nz/culture /books/stalking-nabokov-by-brian-boyd-review/.

Eggleton, David. Review of *Stalking Nabokov*, by Brian Boyd. *New Zealand Listener*, December 13, 2012. http://www.listener.co.nz/culture/books /stalking-nabokov-by-brian-boyd-review/.

29. Letter to the editor   Do not use the letter's title, even if the publication gives one.

29. Andy Bush, letter to the editor, *Economist*, December 15, 2012, http://www.economist.com/.

Bush, Andy. Letter to the editor. *Economist*, December 15, 2012. http://www .economist.com/.

30. Article in a reference work (encyclopedia, dictionary, wiki) Reference works such as encyclopedias do not require publication information and are usually not included in the bibliography. The abbreviation "s.v." is for the Latin *sub verbo* ("under the word").

30. *Encyclopaedia Britannica*, 15th ed., s.v. "Monroe Doctrine."

30. *Wikipedia*, s.v. "James Monroe," last modified December 19, 2012, http://en.wikipedia.org/wiki/James_Monroe.

30. Bryan A. Garner, *Garner's Modern American Usage*, 3rd ed. (Oxford: Oxford University Press, 2009), s.v. "brideprice."

Garner, Bryan A. *Garner's Modern American Usage*. 3rd ed. Oxford: Oxford University Press, 2009.

31. Letter in a published collection   Use the day-month-year form for the date of the letter. If the letter writer's name is part of the book title, begin the note with only the last name but begin the bibliography entry with the full name.

▸ Citation at a glance: Letter in a published collection, page 772

31. Dickens to Thomas Beard, 1 June 1840, in *The Selected Letters of Charles Dickens*, ed. Jenny Hartley (New York: Oxford University Press, 2012), 65.

Dickens, Charles. *The Selected Letters of Charles Dickens*. Edited by Jenny Hartley. New York: Oxford University Press, 2012.

Citation at a glance

Letter in a published collection *Chicago*

To cite a letter in a published collection in *Chicago* style, include the following elements:

1. Author of letter
2. Recipient of letter
3. Date of letter
4. Title of collection
5. Editor of collection
6. City of publication
7. Publisher
8. Year of publication
9. Page number(s) cited (for notes); page range of letter (for bibliography)

TITLE PAGE

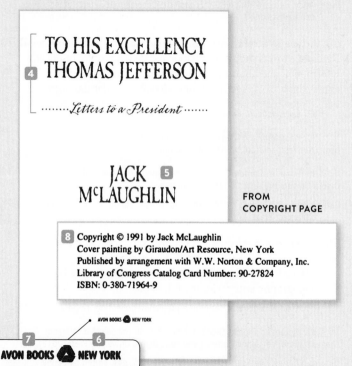

4 TO HIS EXCELLENCY THOMAS JEFFERSON

········ *Letters to a President* ········

JACK **5**
McLAUGHLIN

FROM COPYRIGHT PAGE

8 Copyright © 1991 by Jack McLaughlin
Cover painting by Giraudon/Art Resource, New York
Published by arrangement with W.W. Norton & Company, Inc.
Library of Congress Catalog Card Number: 90-27824
ISBN: 0-380-71964-9

AVON BOOKS NEW YORK

7 AVON BOOKS **6** NEW YORK

Washington 30th. Oct 1805 **3**

His Excellency Ths. Jefferson **2**

Sir,

I have not the honor to be personally known to your Excellency therefore you will no doubt think it strange to receive t
smallest
in as few
a young
partly ec
had beer
sequence
that unh
anything
few yea
[m]isfortu
[I] can a

Patronage   61 **9**

your Excellency this very prolix letter which should it please your Excellency to give me some little Office or appointment in that extensive Country of Louisiana It should be my constant endeavour to merit the same by fidelity and an indefatigable attention to whatever business I should be assigned. May I have the satisfaction in whatsoever Country or situation [I] may be in to hear of your Excellencies long continuence of your Natural powers unempaired to conduct the Helm of this Extensive Country which are the sincere wishes of your Excellencies Mo. Obt. Hum. Servt.

1 John O'Neill

NOTE

    1   2   3

1. John O'Neill to Thomas Jefferson, October 30, 1805, in *To His*
            4   5

Excellency Thomas Jefferson: Letters to a President, ed. Jack McLaughlin
 6   7   8 9

(New York: Avon Books, 1991), 61.

BIBLIOGRAPHY

  1   1   2   3

O'Neill, John. John O'Neill to Thomas Jefferson, 30 October 1805. In
               4

To His Excellency Thomas Jefferson: Letters to a President, edited by
    5   9   6   7   8

Jack McLaughlin, 59–61. New York: Avon Books, 1991.

For another citation of a letter in *Chicago* style, see item 31.

Web sources

For most Web sites, include an author if a site has one, the title of the site, the sponsor, the date of publication or the modified (update) date, and the site's URL. Do not italicize a Web site title unless the site is an online book or periodical. Use quotation marks for the titles of sections or pages in a Web site. If a site does not have a date of publication or a modified date, give the date you accessed the site ("accessed January 3, 2013").

32. An entire Web site

32. Chesapeake and Ohio Canal National Historical Park, National Park Service, last modified November 25, 2012, http://www.nps.gov/choh/index.htm.

Chesapeake and Ohio Canal National Historical Park. National Park Service. Last modified November 25, 2012. http://www.nps.gov/choh/index.htm.

33. Short work from a Web site

▶ Citation at a glance: Primary source from a Web site, page 776

33. Dan Archer, "Using Illustrated Reportage to Cover Human Trafficking in Nepal's Brick Kilns," Poynter, last modified December 18, 2012, http://www.poynter.org/.

Archer, Dan. "Using Illustrated Reportage to Cover Human Trafficking in Nepal's Brick Kilns." Poynter, last modified December 18, 2012. http://www.poynter.org/.

34. Blog post Treat as a short work from a Web site (see item 33), but italicize the name of the blog. Insert "blog" in parentheses after the name if the word *blog* is not part of the name. If the blog is part of a larger site (such as a newspaper's or an organization's site), add the title of the site after the blog title. Do not list the blog post in the bibliography; but if you cite the blog frequently in your paper, you may give a bibliography entry for the entire blog.

34. Gregory LeFever, "Skull Fraud 'Created' the Brontosaurus," *Ancient Tides* (blog), December 16, 2012, http://ancient-tides.blogspot .com/2012/12/skull-fraud-created-brontosaurus.html.

LeFever, Gregory. *Ancient Tides* (blog). http://ancient-tides.blogspot.com/.

35. Comment on a blog post   In the bibliography entry here, the blog is given by title only because the blog has many contributors, not a single author.

35. Didomyk, comment on B.C., "A New Spokesman," *Pomegranate: The Middle East* (blog), *Economist*, December 18, 2012, http://www.economist .com/blogs/pomegranate/2012/12/christians-middle-east.

Pomegranate: The Middle East (blog). *Economist*. http://www.economist.com /blogs/pomegranate/.

Audio, visual, and multimedia sources

36. Podcast   Treat as a short work from a Web site (see item 33), including the following, if available: the name of the author, speaker, or host; the title of the podcast, in quotation marks; an identifying number, if any; the title of the site on which it appears; the sponsor of the site; and the URL. Identify the type of podcast or file format; before the URL, give the date of posting or your date of access.

36. Peter Limb, "Economic and Cultural History of the Slave Trade in Western Africa," Episode 69, Africa Past and Present, African Online Digital Library, podcast audio, December 12, 2012, http://afripod.aodl.org/.

Limb, Peter. "Economic and Cultural History of the Slave Trade in Western Africa." Episode 69. Africa Past and Present. African Online Digital Library. Podcast audio. December 12, 2012. http://afripod.aodl.org/.

37. Online audio or video   Cite as a short work from a Web site (see item 33). If the source is a downloadable file, identify the file format or medium before the URL.

37. Tom Brokaw, "Global Warming: What You Need to Know," Discovery Channel, January 23, 2012, http://www.youtube.com/watch?v=xcVwLrAavyA.

Brokaw, Tom. "Global Warming: What You Need to Know." Discovery Channel, January 23, 2012. http://www.youtube.com/watch?v=xcVwLrAavyA.

Citation at a glance

Primary source from a Web site *Chicago*

To cite a primary source (or any other document) from a Web site in *Chicago* style, include as many of the following elements as are available:

1. Author(s)
2. Title of document
3. Title of site
4. Sponsor of site
5. Publication date or modified date; date of access (if no publication date)
6. URL of document page

WEB SITE HOME PAGE

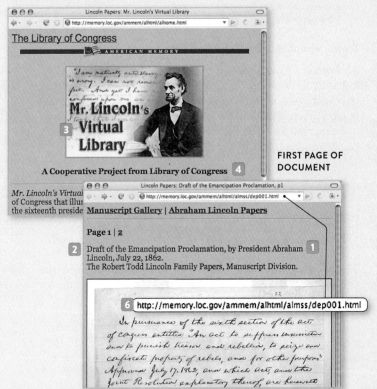

FIRST PAGE OF DOCUMENT

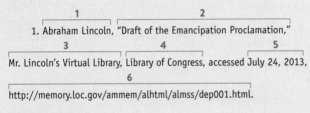

1. Abraham Lincoln, "Draft of the Emancipation Proclamation," Mr. Lincoln's Virtual Library, Library of Congress, accessed July 24, 2013, http://memory.loc.gov/ammem/alhtml/almss/dep001.html.

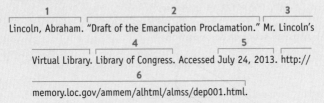

Lincoln, Abraham. "Draft of the Emancipation Proclamation." Mr. Lincoln's Virtual Library. Library of Congress. Accessed July 24, 2013. http://memory.loc.gov/ammem/alhtml/almss/dep001.html.

For more on citing documents from Web sites in *Chicago* style, see item 33.

38. Published or broadcast interview

38. Jane Goodall, interview by Suza Scalora, *Origin*, n.d., http://www.originmagazine.com/2012/12/07/dr-jane-goodall-interview-with-suza-scalora.

Goodall, Jane. Interview by Suza Scalora. *Origin*, n.d. http://www.originmagazine.com/2012/12/07/dr-jane-goodall-interview-with-suza-scalora.

38. Julian Castro and Joaquin Castro, interview by Charlie Rose, *Charlie Rose Show*, WGBH, Boston, December 17, 2012.

Castro, Julian, and Joaquin Castro. Interview by Charlie Rose. *Charlie Rose Show*. WGBH, Boston, December 17, 2012.

39. Film (DVD, BD, or other format)

39. *Argo*, directed by Ben Affleck (Burbank, CA: Warner Bros. Pictures, 2012).

Argo. Directed by Ben Affleck. Burbank, CA: Warner Bros. Pictures, 2012.

(continued on p. 778)

39. *The Dust Bowl*, directed by Ken Burns (Washington, DC: PBS, 2012), DVD.

The Dust Bowl. Directed by Ken Burns. Washington, DC: PBS, 2012. DVD.

40. Sound recording

40. Gustav Holst, *The Planets*, Royal Philharmonic Orchestra, conducted by André Previn, Telarc 80133, compact disc.

Holst, Gustav. *The Planets*. Royal Philharmonic Orchestra. Conducted by André Previn. Telarc 80133, compact disc.

41. Musical score or composition

41. Antonio Vivaldi, *L'Estro armonico*, op. 3, ed. Eleanor Selfridge-Field (Mineola, NY: Dover, 1999).

Vivaldi, Antonio. *L'Estro armonico*, op. 3. Edited by Eleanor Selfridge-Field. Mineola, NY: Dover, 1999.

42. Work of art

42. Aaron Siskind, *Untitled (The Most Crowded Block)*, gelatin silver print, 1939, Kemper Museum of Contemporary Art, Kansas City, MO.

Siskind, Aaron. *Untitled (The Most Crowded Block)*. Gelatin silver print, 1939. Kemper Museum of Contemporary Art, Kansas City, MO.

43. Performance

43. Jackie Sibblies Drury, *Social Creatures*, directed by Curt Columbus, Trinity Repertory Company, Providence, RI, March 15, 2013.

Drury, Jackie Sibblies. *Social Creatures*. Directed by Curt Columbus. Trinity Repertory Company, Providence, RI, March 15, 2013.

Personal communication and social media

44. Personal communication Personal communications are not included in the bibliography.

44. Sara Lehman, e-mail message to author, August 13, 2012.

45. Online posting or e-mail If an online posting has been archived, include a URL. E-mails that are not part of an online discussion are treated as personal communication (see item 44). Online postings and e-mails are not included in the bibliography.

45. Ruth E. Thaler-Carter to Copyediting-L discussion list, December 18, 2012, https://list.indiana.edu/sympa/arc/copyediting-l.

46. Facebook post Facebook posts are not included in the bibliography.

46. US Department of Housing and Urban Development's Facebook page, accessed October 15, 2012, http://www.facebook.com/HUD.

47. Twitter post (tweet) Tweets are not included in the bibliography.

47. National Geographic's Twitter feed, accessed December 18, 2012, https://twitter.com/NatGeo.

63e *Chicago* manuscript format

The following guidelines for formatting a *Chicago*-style paper and preparing its endnotes and bibliography are based on *The Chicago Manual of Style*, 16th ed. (Chicago: University of Chicago Press, 2010). For pages from a sample paper, see 63f.

Formatting the paper

Font If your instructor does not require a specific font, choose one that is standard and easy to read (such as Times New Roman).

Title page Include the full title of your paper, your name, the course title, the instructor's name, and the date. See page 783 for a sample title page.

Pagination Using arabic numerals, number the pages in the upper right corner. Do not number the title page but count it in the manuscript numbering; that is, the first page of the text will be numbered 2. Depending on your instructor's preference, you may also use a short title or your last name before the page numbers to help identify pages.

Margins, line spacing, and paragraph indents Leave margins of at least one inch at the top, bottom, and sides of the page. Double-space the body of the paper, including long quotations that have been set off from the text. (For line spacing in notes and the bibliography, see p. 782.) Left-align the text.

Indent the first line of each paragraph one-half inch from the left margin.

Capitalization, italics, and quotation marks In titles of works, capitalize all words except articles (*a, an, the*), prepositions (*at, from, between,* and so on), coordinating conjunctions (*and, but, or, nor, for, so, yet*), and *to* and *as*—unless the word is first or last in the title or subtitle. Follow these guidelines in your paper even if the title is styled differently in the source.

Lowercase the first word following a colon even if the word begins a complete sentence. When the colon introduces a series of sentences or questions, capitalize the first word in all sentences in the series, including the first.

Italicize the titles of books and other long works. Use quotation marks around the titles of periodical articles, short stories, poems, and other short works.

Long quotations You can choose to set off a long quotation of five to ten typed lines by indenting the entire quotation one-half inch from the left margin. (Always set off quotations of ten or more lines.) Double-space the quotation; do not use quotation marks and do not add extra space above or below it. (See p. 785 for a long quotation in the text of a paper; see also pp. 749–50.)

Visuals *Chicago* classifies visuals as tables and figures (graphs, drawings, photographs, maps, and charts). Keep visuals as simple as possible.

Label each table with an arabic numeral (Table 1, Table 2, and so on) and provide a clear title that identifies the table's subject. The label and the title should appear on separate lines above the table, flush left. For a table that you have borrowed or adapted, give its source in a note like this one, below the table:

Source: Edna Bonacich and Richard P. Appelbaum, *Behind the Label* (Berkeley: University of California Press, 2000), 145.

For each figure, place a label and a caption below the figure, flush left. The label and caption need not appear on separate lines. The word "Figure" may be abbreviated to "Fig."

In the text of your paper, discuss the most significant features of each visual. Place visuals as close as possible to the sentences that relate to them unless your instructor prefers that visuals appear in an appendix.

URLs and DOIs   When a URL or DOI (digital object identifier) must break across lines, do not insert a hyphen or break at a hyphen. Instead, break after a colon or a double slash or before any other mark of punctuation. If your word processing program automatically turns URLs into links (by underlining them and changing the color), turn off this feature.

Headings   *Chicago* does not provide guidelines for the use of headings in student papers. If you would like to insert headings in a long essay or research paper, check first with your instructor. See pages 784 and 786 for typical placement and formatting of headings in a *Chicago*-style paper.

Preparing the endnotes

Begin the endnotes on a new page at the end of the paper. Center the title "Notes" about one inch from the top of the page, and number the pages consecutively with the rest of the paper. See page 787 for an example.

Indenting and numbering Indent the first line of each note one-half inch from the left margin; do not indent additional lines in the note. Begin the note with the arabic numeral that corresponds to the number in the text. Put a period after the number.

Line spacing Single-space each note and double-space between notes (unless your instructor prefers double-spacing throughout).

Preparing the bibliography

Typically, the notes in *Chicago*-style papers are followed by a bibliography, an alphabetically arranged list of all the works cited or consulted. Center the title "Bibliography" about one inch from the top of the page. Number bibliography pages consecutively with the rest of the paper. See page 788 for a sample bibliography.

Alphabetizing the list Alphabetize the bibliography by the last names of the authors (or editors); when a work has no author or editor, alphabetize it by the first word of the title other than *A*, *An*, or *The*.

If your list includes two or more works by the same author, arrange the entries alphabetically by title. Then use six hyphens instead of the author's name in all entries after the first. (See item 6 on p. 758.)

Indenting and line spacing Begin each entry at the left margin, and indent any additional lines one-half inch. Single-space each entry and double-space between entries (unless your instructor prefers double-spacing throughout).

63f Sample pages from a *Chicago* research paper

Following are pages from a research paper by Ned Bishop, a student in a history class. Bishop used *Chicago*-style endnotes, bibliography, and manuscript format.

hackerhandbooks.com/bedhandbook

🅔 Researched writing > Sample student writing
  > Bishop, "The Massacre at Fort Pillow: Holding Nathan Bedford
    Forrest Accountable" (research)

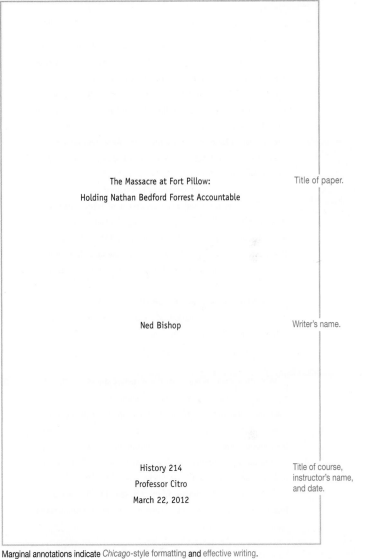

The Massacre at Fort Pillow:
Holding Nathan Bedford Forrest Accountable

Title of paper.

Ned Bishop

Writer's name.

History 214
Professor Citro
March 22, 2012

Title of course,
instructor's name,
and date.

Marginal annotations indicate *Chicago*-style formatting and effective writing.

Bishop 2

Although Northern newspapers of the time no doubt exaggerated some of the Confederate atrocities at Fort Pillow, most modern sources agree that a massacre of Union troops took place there on April 12, 1864. It seems clear that Union soldiers, particularly black soldiers, were killed after they had stopped fighting or had surrendered or were being held prisoner. Less clear is the role played by Major General Nathan Bedford Forrest in leading his troops. Although we will never know whether Forrest directly ordered the massacre, evidence suggests that he was responsible for it.

What happened at Fort Pillow?

Fort Pillow, Tennessee, which sat on a bluff overlooking the Mississippi River, had been held by the Union for two years. It was garrisoned by 580 men, 292 of them from United States Colored Heavy and Light Artillery regiments, 285 from the white Thirteenth Tennessee Cavalry. Nathan Bedford Forrest commanded about 1,500 troops.[1]

The Confederates attacked Fort Pillow on April 12, 1864, and had virtually surrounded the fort by the time Forrest arrived on the battlefield. At 3:30 p.m., Forrest demanded the surrender of the Union forces, sending in a message of the sort he had used before: "The conduct of the officers and men garrisoning Fort Pillow has been such as to entitle them to being treated as prisoners of war. . . . Should my demand be refused, I cannot be responsible for the fate of your command."[2] Union Major William Bradford, who had replaced Major Booth, killed earlier by sharpshooters, asked for an hour to consider the demand. Forrest, worried that vessels in the river were bringing in more troops, "shortened the time to twenty minutes."[3] Bradford refused to surrender, and Forrest quickly ordered the attack.

The Confederates charged to the fort, scaled the parapet, and fired on the forces within. Victory came quickly, with the Union forces

Thesis asserts Bishop's main point.

Headings, centered, help readers follow the organization.

Statistics are cited with an endnote.

Quotation is cited with an endnote.

Bishop 3

running toward the river or surrendering. Shelby Foote describes the scene like this:

> Some kept going, right on into the river, where a number drowned and the swimmers became targets for marksmen on the bluff. Others, dropping their guns in terror, ran back toward the Confederates with their hands up, and of these some were spared as prisoners, while others were shot down in the act of surrender.[4]

In his own official report, Forrest makes no mention of the massacre. He does make much of the fact that the Union flag was not lowered by the Union forces, saying that if his own men had not taken down the flag, "few, if any, would have survived unhurt another volley."[5] However, as Jack Hurst points out and Forrest must have known, in this twenty-minute battle, "Federals running for their lives had little time to concern themselves with a flag."[6]

The federal congressional report on Fort Pillow, which charged the Confederates with appalling atrocities, was strongly criticized by Southerners. Respected writer Shelby Foote, while agreeing that the report was "largely" fabrication, points out that the "casualty figures . . . indicated strongly that unnecessary killing had occurred."[7] In an important article, John Cimprich and Robert C. Mainfort Jr. argue that the most trustworthy evidence is that written within about ten days of the battle, before word of the congressional hearings circulated and Southerners realized the extent of Northern outrage. The article reprints a group of letters and newspaper sources written before April 22 and thus "untainted by the political overtones the controversy later assumed."[8] Cimprich and Mainfort conclude that these sources "support the case for the occurrence of a massacre" but that Forrest's role remains "clouded" because of inconsistencies in testimony.[9]

Long quotation is set off from text by indenting. Quotation marks are omitted.

Bishop uses a primary source as well as secondary sources.

Quotation is introduced with a signal phrase.

Bishop draws attention to an article that reprints primary sources.

Bishop 4

Did Forrest order the massacre?

We will never really know whether Forrest directly ordered the massacre, but it seems unlikely. True, Confederate soldier Achilles Clark, who had no reason to lie, wrote to his sisters that "I with several others tried to stop the butchery . . . but Gen. Forrest ordered them [Negro and white Union troops] shot down like dogs, and the

carnage continued."[10] But it is not clear whether Clark heard Forrest giving the orders or was just reporting hearsay. Many Confederates had been shouting "No quarter! No quarter!" and, as Shelby Foote points out, these shouts were "thought by some to be at Forrest's command."[11] A Union soldier, Jacob Thompson, claimed to have seen Forrest order the killing, but when asked to describe the six-foot-two general, he called him "a little bit of a man."[12]

Perhaps the most convincing evidence that Forrest did not order the massacre is that he tried to stop it once it had begun. Historian Albert Castel quotes several eyewitnesses on both the Union and Confederate sides as saying that Forrest ordered his men to stop firing.[13] In a letter to his wife three days after the battle, Confederate soldier Samuel Caldwell wrote that "if General Forrest had not run between our men & the Yanks with his pistol and sabre drawn not a man would have been spared."[14]

In a respected biography of Nathan Bedford Forrest, Hurst suggests that the temperamental Forrest "may have ragingly ordered a massacre and even intended to carry it out—until he rode inside the fort and viewed the horrifying result" and ordered it stopped.[15] While this is an intriguing interpretation of events, even Hurst would probably admit that it is merely speculation.

Can Forrest be held responsible for the massacre?

Even assuming that Forrest did not order the massacre, he can still be held accountable for it. That is because he created an

Notes begin on a
new page.

Notes

1. John Cimprich and Robert C. Mainfort Jr., eds., "Fort
Pillow Revisited: New Evidence about an Old Controversy," *Civil War
History* 28, no. 4 (1982): 293-94.

2. Quoted in Brian Steel Wills, *A Battle from the Start: The Life
of Nathan Bedford Forrest* (New York: HarperCollins, 1992), 182.

3. Ibid., 183.

4. Shelby Foote, *The Civil War, a Narrative: Red River to
Appomattox* (New York: Vintage, 1986), 110.

5. Nathan Bedford Forrest, "Report of Maj. Gen. Nathan B.
Forrest, C.S. Army, Commanding Cavalry, of the Capture of Fort
Pillow," Shotgun's Home of the American Civil War, accessed March 6,
2012, http://www.civilwarhome.com/forrest.htm.

6. Jack Hurst, *Nathan Bedford Forrest: A Biography* (New York:
Knopf, 1993), 174.

7. Foote, *Civil War*, 111.

8. Cimprich and Mainfort, "Fort Pillow," 295.

9. Ibid., 305.

10. Ibid., 299.

11. Foote, *Civil War*, 110.

12. Quoted in Wills, *Battle from the Start*, 187.

13. Albert Castel, "The Fort Pillow Massacre: A Fresh
Examination of the Evidence," *Civil War History* 4, no. 1 (1958): 44-45.

14. Cimprich and Mainfort, "Fort Pillow," 300.

15. Hurst, *Nathan Bedford Forrest*, 177.

16. Ibid.

17. Dudley Taylor Cornish, *The Sable Arm: Black Troops in
the Union Army, 1861–1865* (Lawrence: University Press of Kansas,
1987), 175.

First line of each
note is indented ½".
Note number is
followed by a
period. Authors'
names are not
inverted.

Notes are single-
spaced, with
double-spacing
between notes.
(Some instructors
may prefer
double-spacing
throughout.)

Last names and title
refer to an earlier
note by the same
authors.

Writer cites an
indirect source:
words quoted in
another source.

Bibliography begins on a new page.

Bibliography

Entries are alphabetized by authors' last names.

Castel, Albert. "The Fort Pillow Massacre: A Fresh Examination of the Evidence." *Civil War History* 4, no. 1 (1958): 37-50.

Cimprich, John, and Robert C. Mainfort Jr., eds. "Fort Pillow Revisited: New Evidence about an Old Controversy." *Civil War History* 28, no. 4 (1982): 293-306.

Cornish, Dudley Taylor. *The Sable Arm: Black Troops in the Union Army, 1861-1865.* Lawrence: University Press of Kansas, 1987.

Foote, Shelby. *The Civil War, a Narrative: Red River to Appomattox.* New York: Vintage, 1986.

Forrest, Nathan Bedford. "Report of Maj. Gen. Nathan B. Forrest, C.S. Army, Commanding Cavalry, of the Capture of Fort Pillow." Shotgun's Home of the American Civil War. Accessed March 6, 2012. http://www.civilwarhome.com/forrest.htm.

Hurst, Jack. *Nathan Bedford Forrest: A Biography.* New York: Knopf, 1993.

McPherson, James M. *Battle Cry of Freedom: The Civil War Era.* New York: Oxford University Press, 1988.

Wills, Brian Steel. *A Battle from the Start: The Life of Nathan Bedford Forrest.* New York: HarperCollins, 1992.

First line of entry is at left margin; additional lines are indented ½".

Entries are single-spaced, with double-spacing between entries. (Some instructors may prefer double-spacing throughout.)

Writing in the Disciplines

College courses expose you to the thinking of scholars in many disciplines, such as those within the humanities (literature, music, art), the social sciences (psychology, anthropology, sociology), and the sciences (biology, physics, chemistry). No matter what you study, you will be asked to write for a variety of audiences in a variety of formats. In a criminal justice course, for example, you may be asked to write a policy memo or a legal brief; in a nursing course, you may be asked to write a case study or a practice paper. To write in these courses is to think like a criminologist or a nurse and to engage in the debates of the discipline.

64 Learning to write in a discipline

Writing in any discipline provides the opportunity to practice the methods used by its scholars. Each field has its own questions, preferred types of evidence, language uses, and citation conventions, but all disciplines share certain expectations for good writing. Becoming a college writer means being able to reflect on earlier lessons learned about writing and to apply these lessons to the writing you are doing in any college course.

64a Find commonalities across disciplines.

If you understand the features that are common to writing in all disciplines, you will have an easier time sorting out the unique aspects of writing in a particular field.

In every discipline, scholars write about texts. For example, in the humanities scholars write about texts such as novels, poems, paintings, and music. In the social sciences, texts

---

TEACHING TIP

Part XI begins by focusing students' attention on the commonalities across disciplines. Students should understand these commonalities because they help students apply what they've learned in a composition class to writing assignments in other academic disciplines. The commonalities also help to establish the value of a composition course, which provides writing skills that help students succeed in other areas. As a class, begin a discussion on the topic by constructing a Venn diagram of expectations for writing in a composition course and expectations for writing in a science or technical course.

include journal articles, case studies, and reports on experiments. In the sciences, researchers write about data taken from reports that other researchers have published and about data drawn from site surveys and laboratory experiments.

A good paper in any field needs to communicate the writer's purpose to an audience and to explore an engaging question about a subject. Effective writers make an argument and support their claims with evidence. Writers in most fields show readers the thesis they're developing (or, in the sciences, the hypothesis they're testing) and how they counter the objections of other writers. In some fields, such as nursing and business, writers do not always state an explicit claim but still communicate a clear purpose and use evidence to support their ideas. All disciplines require writers to document where they found their evidence and from whom they borrowed ideas.

> **MAKING THE MOST OF YOUR HANDBOOK**
>
> When writing for any course, keep in mind the steps needed to write a strong academic paper.
>
> ▶ Communicating a purpose: 1a
> ▶ Determining your audience: 1a
> ▶ Asking an academic question: 64b
> ▶ Making and supporting a claim: 6f–6h
> ▶ Citing sources: 56 (MLA), 61 (APA), 63d (*Chicago*)

64b Recognize the questions that writers in a discipline ask.

Disciplines are characterized by the kinds of questions their scholars attempt to answer. Social scientists, who analyze human behavior, might ask about the factors that cause people to act in certain ways. Humanities scholars interpret texts within their cultural contexts; they ask questions about the society at the time a text was written or about the connections between an author's life and work. Historians, who seek an understanding of the past, ask questions about the causes and effects of events and about connections between current and past events. Scientists collect data and ask questions to help them interpret the data.

TEACHING TIP

If your students don't fully understand the word *discipline* or the term *academic discipline*, show them your college's catalog. Talk about how courses and subjects are divided into disciplines, departments, and divisions.

One way to understand how disciplines ask different questions is to look at assignments on the same topic in various fields. Many disciplines, for example, might be interested in the subject of disasters. The following are some questions that writers in different fields might ask about this subject.

EDUCATION   Should the elementary school curriculum teach students how to cope in disaster situations?

FILM   How has the disaster film genre changed since the advent of computer-generated imagery (CGI) in the early 1970s?

HISTORY   How did the formation of the American Red Cross change this country's approach to natural disasters?

ENGINEERING   What recent innovations in levee design are most promising and most likely to prevent disaster?

PSYCHOLOGY   What are the most effective ways to identify and treat post-traumatic stress disorder (PTSD) in disaster survivors?

The questions you ask in any discipline will form the basis of the thesis for your writing. The questions themselves don't communicate a central idea, but they may lead you to one. For an education paper, for example, you might begin with the question "Should the elementary school curriculum teach students how to cope in disaster situations?" After considering the issues involved, you might draft the following thesis.

> School systems should adopt age-appropriate curriculum units that introduce children to the risks of natural and human-made disasters and that allow children to practice coping strategies.

Whenever you write for a college course, try to determine the kinds of questions scholars in the field might ask about a topic. You can find clues in assigned readings, lecture topics,

---

TEACHING TIP

To help students learn more about writing in a particular discipline, ask them to interview a faculty member in a discipline that interests them or in which they are taking courses. As a class, spend time brainstorming questions for the interviews, such as the following: "How much writing do you require? What are three features of a successful piece of writing in your course? What are some typical writing assignments in your course? Why do you give these particular writing assignments?" In a subsequent class period, have a discussion that allows students to compare notes and share their interview experiences.

discussion groups, and the paper assignment itself. When in doubt, ask your instructor for guidance.

64c Understand the kinds of evidence that writers in a discipline use.

Regardless of the discipline in which you are writing, you must support your claims with evidence—facts, statistics, examples and illustrations, and expert opinion. Familiarize yourself with the kinds of evidence writers use to support claims in your field.

- For an English paper that examines three types of parent-child relationships in Shakespeare's *King Lear*, you would look closely at lines from the play.

- For a psychology paper on the connection between certain medications and suicidal impulses, you might study the results of clinical trials.

- For a nursing practice paper about the medical condition of a particular patient, you would review the patient's chart as well as any relevant medical literature.

- For a history paper on Renaissance attitudes toward marriage, you might examine historical documents such as letters, diaries, and church records.

The kinds of evidence used in different disciplines may overlap. Students of geography, media studies, and political science, for example, might use census data to explore different topics. The evidence that one discipline values, however, might not be sufficient to support an interpretation or a conclusion in another field. You might use anecdotes or interviews in an anthropology paper, for example, but such evidence would be irrelevant in a biology lab report. The chart on page 794 lists the kinds of evidence accepted in various disciplines.

hackerhandbooks.com/bedhandbook

e Writing in the disciplines > As you write: Examining the writing in a particular field

---

TEACHING TIP

Many teachers like to assign readings from different disciplines—especially when the texts offer differing or complementary perspectives on a single topic or question. Ask your students to read two or more such texts and to take notes on the following questions: What key questions does the author ask? What types of evidence does the author use? Does the author provide any citations? If so, what style are they in? What specialized vocabulary does the author use?

Evidence typically used in various disciplines

Humanities: literature, art, film, music, philosophy

- Passages of text or lines of a poem
- Details from an image or a work of art
- Passages of a musical composition
- Critical essays that analyze original works

Humanities: history

- Primary sources such as photographs, letters, maps, and government documents
- Scholarly books and articles that interpret evidence

Social sciences: psychology, sociology, political science, anthropology

- Data from original experiments
- Results of field research such as interviews, observations, or surveys
- Statistics from government agencies
- Scholarly books and articles that interpret data from original experiments and from other researchers' studies
- Primary sources such as maps and government documents
- Primary sources such as artifacts

Sciences: biology, chemistry, physics

- Data from original experiments
- Scholarly articles that report findings from experiments
- Models, diagrams, or animations

64d Become familiar with a discipline's language conventions.

Every discipline has a specialized vocabulary. As you read the articles and books in a field, you'll notice certain words and phrases that come up repeatedly. Sociologists, for example, use terms such as *independent variables* and *dyads* to describe social phenomena; computer scientists might refer to *algorithm design* and *loop invariants* to describe programming methods. Practitioners in health fields such as nursing use terms like *treatment plan* and *systemic assessment* to describe patient care. Use discipline-specific terms only when you are certain that you and your readers fully understand their meaning.

In addition to vocabulary, many fields of study have developed specialized conventions for point of view and verb tense. See the chart on page 796.

64e Use a discipline's preferred citation style.

In any discipline, you must give credit to those whose ideas or words you have borrowed. Whenever you write, it is your responsibility to avoid plagiarism by citing sources honestly and accurately.

While all disciplines emphasize careful documentation, each follows a particular system of citation that its members have agreed on. Writers in the humanities usually use the system established by the Modern Language Association (MLA). Scholars in some social sciences, such as psychology and anthropology, follow the style guidelines of the American Psychological Association (APA). Scholars in history and other humanities typically follow *The Chicago Manual of Style*.

MAKING THE MOST OF YOUR HANDBOOK

You will need to document your sources in the style preferred by your discipline.

▸ Documenting sources: MLA (humanities), 56; APA (social sciences), 61; *Chicago* (history), 63d; CSE (sciences), online at hackerhandbooks.com /resdoc

Point of view and verb tense in academic writing

Point of view

- Writers of analytical or research essays in the humanities usually use the third-person point of view: *Austen presents . . .* or *Castel describes the battle as. . . .*

- Scientists and most social scientists, who depend on quantitative research to present findings, tend to use the third-person point of view: *The results indicate. . . .*

- Writers in the humanities and in some social sciences occasionally use the first person in discussing their personal experience or in writing a personal narrative: *After spending two years interviewing families affected by the war, I began to understand that. . . .*

Present or past tense

- Literature scholars use the present tense to discuss a text: *Hughes effectively dramatizes different views of minority assertiveness.* (See 7e.)

- Science and social science writers use the past or present perfect tense to describe experiments from source materials and the present tense to discuss the writers' own findings: *In 2003, Berkowitz released the first double-blind placebo study. . . . Rogers and Chang have found that. . . . Our results paint a murky picture.* (See 60b.)

- Writers in history use the present tense or the present perfect tense to discuss a text: *Shelby Foote describes the scene like this . . .* or *Shelby Foote has described the scene like this. . . .* (See 63c.)

TEACHING TIP

One way to approach writing in the disciplines is to focus on the similarities and differences among various documentation systems. Review the guidelines for MLA, APA, and *Chicago*. Ask students to list the similarities and differences among the three systems. As a class, discuss what information each of these systems seems to value.

65 Approaching writing assignments in the disciplines

When you are asked to write in a specific discipline, or field of study, start by becoming familiar with the distinctive features of the writing in that discipline. Be curious about the discipline's conventions and expectations for asking and answering questions. Read the assignment carefully and try to identify the purpose of the assignment and the type of evidence you are expected to use. The following sections provide examples of assignments in four disciplines—psychology, business, biology, and nursing—along with excerpts from student papers that were written in response to the assignments.

65a Writing in psychology

Psychologists write with various purposes in mind—to publish research articles, to convince funding agencies to award grants for their research, or to influence the opinions held by the public or decision makers in government, for example. When you take courses in psychology, you may be asked to write reviews of the literature about a particular topic, research papers, theoretical papers, or poster presentations. On page 798 is a typical assignment for a review of the literature.

hackerhandbooks.com/bedhandbook

e Writing in the disciplines > As you write: Examining a writing assignment from one of your courses

e Writing in the disciplines > Sample student writing
  > Charat, "Always Out of Their Seats (and Fighting): Why Are Boys Diagnosed With ADHD More Often Than Girls?" (literature review)
  > Ratajczak, "Proposal to Add a Wellness Program" (business proposal)
  > Johnson/Arnold, "Distribution Pattern of Dandelion (*Taraxacum officinale*) on an Abandoned Golf Course" (lab report)
  > Rist, "Acute Lymphoblastic Leukemia and Hypertension in One Client" (nursing practice paper)

TEACHING TIP

Students benefit from studying writing assignments across the disciplines. You might ask students to bring assignments they've received in their other college courses. Ask students to work in groups to identify the key terms, the purpose, and the expected evidence for each assignment.

ASSIGNMENT: REVIEW OF THE LITERATURE

Write a literature review in which you report on and evaluate the published research on a behavioral disorder.

1 Key terms

2 Purpose: to report on and evaluate a body of evidence

3 Evidence: research of other psychologists

Always Out of Their Seats (and Fighting):

Why Are Boys Diagnosed With ADHD More Often Than Girls?

Background and explanation of the writer's purpose.

Attention deficit hyperactivity disorder (ADHD) is a commonly diagnosed disorder in children that affects social, academic, or occupational functioning. As the name suggests, its hallmark characteristics are hyperactivity and lack of attention as well as impulsive

Evidence from research the writer has reviewed.

behavior. For decades, studies have focused on the causes, expression, prevalence, and outcome of the disorder, but until recently very little research investigated gender differences. In fact, until the early 1990s

APA citations and specialized language (ADHD, comorbid).

most research focused exclusively on boys (Brown, Madan-Swain, & Baldwin, 1991), perhaps because many more boys than girls are diagnosed with ADHD. Researchers have speculated on the possible explanations for the disparity, citing reasons such as true sex differences in the manifestation of the disorder's symptoms, gender biases in those who refer children to clinicians, and possibly even the diagnostic procedures themselves (Gaub & Carlson, 1997). But

Thesis: writer's argument.

the most persuasive reason is that ADHD is often a comorbid condition—that is, it coexists with other behavior disorders that are not diagnosed properly and that do exhibit gender differences.

> It has been suggested that in the United States children are often misdiagnosed as having ADHD when they actually suffer from a behavior disorder such as conduct disorder (CD) or a combination of ADHD and another behavior disorder (Disney, Elkins, McGue, & Iancono, 1999; Lilienfeld & Waldman, 1990). Conduct disorder is characterized by negative and criminal behavior in children and is highly correlated with adult diagnoses of antisocial personality

Two sources in one parenthetical citation are separated by a semicolon.

Marginal annotations indicate appropriate formatting and effective writing.

65b Writing in business

In business courses, you may be asked to create documents that mirror those written in professional settings. Assignments in business courses may include reports, proposals, executive summaries, memos, or newsletters.

Here, for example, is a typical proposal assignment.

ASSIGNMENT: PROPOSAL

Write a proposal, as a memo, for improving or adding a service at a company where you have worked. Address the pros and cons of your proposal; draw on relevant studies, research, and your knowledge of the company.

1 Key terms

2 Purpose: to analyze certain evidence and make a proposal based on that analysis

3 Appropriate evidence: relevant studies, research, personal experience

MEMORANDUM

To: Jay Crosson, Senior Vice President, Human Resources

From: Kelly Ratajczak, Intern, Purchasing Department

Subject: Proposal to Add a Wellness Program

Date: April 24, 2012

Writer's main idea.

Health care costs are rising. In the long run, implementing a wellness program in our corporate culture will decrease the company's health care costs.

Data from recent study as support for claim.

APA citation style, typical in business.

Research indicates that nearly 70% of health care costs are from common illnesses related to high blood pressure, overweight, lack of exercise, high cholesterol, stress, poor nutrition, and other preventable health issues (Hall, 2006). Health care costs are a major expense for most businesses, and they do not reflect costs due to the loss of productivity or absenteeism. A wellness program would address most, if not all, of these health care issues and related costs.

Headings define sections of proposal.

Business terms familiar to readers (costs, productivity, absenteeism).

Benefits of Healthier Employees

Not only would a wellness program substantially reduce costs associated with employee health care, but our company would prosper through many other benefits. Businesses that have wellness programs show a lower cost in production, fewer sick days, and healthier employees ("Workplace Health," 2006). Our healthier employees will help to cut not only our production and absenteeism costs but also potential costs such as higher turnover because of low employee morale.

Implementing the Program

Implementing a good wellness program means making small changes to the work environment, starting with a series of information sessions.

Marginal annotations indicate appropriate formatting and effective writing.

65c Writing in biology

Biologists write reports analyzing the data they collect from their experiments, reviews of other scientists' research or proposed research, and proposals to convince funding agencies to award grants for their research. When you take courses in biology, you may be asked to write lab reports, research papers, literature reviews, or proposals.

Here, for example, is a typical lab report assignment.

ASSIGNMENT: LAB REPORT

Write a report on an experiment you conduct on the distribution pattern of a plant species indigenous to the Northeast. Describe your methods for collecting data and interpret your experiment's results.

1 Key terms
2 Purpose: to describe the methods and interpret the results of an experiment
3 Evidence: data collected during the experiment

CSE style, typical in sciences.

Distribution Pattern of Dandelion (*Taraxacum officinale*)

on an Abandoned Golf Course

ABSTRACT

Abstract: an overview of hypothesis, experiment, and results.

This paper reports our study of the distribution pattern of the common dandelion (*Taraxacum officinale*) on an abandoned golf course in Hilton, NY, on 10 July 2012. An area of 6 ha was sampled with 111 randomly placed $1 \times 1 \, m^2$ quadrats. The dandelion count from each quadrat was used to test observed frequencies against expected frequencies based on a hypothesized random distribution.

[Abstract continues.]

INTRODUCTION

Introduction: context and purpose of experiment. Instead of a thesis in the introduction, a lab report interprets the data in a later Discussion section.

Theoretically, plants of a particular species may be aggregated, random, or uniformly distributed in space [1]. The distribution type may be determined by many factors, such as availability of nutrients, competition, distance of seed dispersal, and mode of reproduction [2].

The purpose of this study was to determine if the distribution pattern of the common dandelion (*Taraxacum officinale*) on an abandoned golf course was aggregated, random, or uniform.

METHODS

Scientific names for plant species.

The study site was an abandoned golf course in Hilton, NY. The vegetation was predominantly grasses, along with dandelions, broad-leaf plantain (*Plantago major*), and bird's-eye speedwell (*Veronica chamaedrys*). We sampled an area of approximately 6 ha on 10 July 2012, approximately two weeks after the golf course had been mowed.

To ensure random sampling, we threw a tennis ball high in the air over the study area. At the spot where the tennis ball came to rest, we placed one corner of a $1 \times 1 \, m^2$ metal frame (quadrat). We then counted the number of dandelion plants within this quadrat. We repeated this procedure for a total of 111 randomly placed quadrats.

Marginal annotations indicate appropriate formatting and effective writing.

65d Writing in nursing

For professional nurses, writing is an important means of communicating with colleagues in the health care profession. As a student in a nursing course, you may be asked to write practice papers, case studies, research papers, or reflective narratives.

Here, for example, is a typical nursing practice paper assignment.

ASSIGNMENT: NURSING PRACTICE PAPER

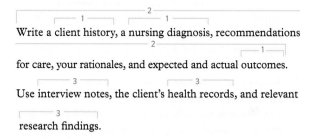

Write a client history, a nursing diagnosis, recommendations for care, your rationales, and expected and actual outcomes. Use interview notes, the client's health records, and relevant research findings.

1 Key terms

2 Purpose: to provide client history, diagnosis, recommendations, and outcomes

3 Evidence: interviews, health records, and research findings

Writer uses APA style, typical in social sciences.

Acute Lymphoblastic Leukemia and Hypertension in One Client:

A Nursing Practice Paper

Physical History

Evidence from client's medical chart for overall assessment.

E.B. is a 16-year-old white male 5'10" tall weighing 190 lb. He was admitted to the hospital on April 14, 2012, due to decreased platelets and a need for a PRBC transfusion. He was diagnosed in October 2011 with T-cell acute lymphoblastic leukemia (ALL), after a 2-week period of decreased energy, decreased oral intake, easy bruising, and petechia. The client had experienced a 20-lb weight loss in the previous 6 months. At the time of diagnosis, his CBC showed a

Specialized nursing language (*echocardiogram, chemotherapy,* and so on).

WBC count of 32, an H & H of 13/38, and a platelet count of 34,000. His initial chest X-ray showed an anterior mediastinal mass. Echocardiogram showed a structurally normal heart. He began induction chemotherapy on October 12, 2011, receiving vincristine, 6-mercaptopurine, doxorubicin, intrathecal methotrexate, and then high-dose methotrexate per protocol. During his hospital stay, he required

Instead of a thesis, or main claim, the writer gives a diagnosis, recom-mendations for care, and expected outcomes, all supported by evidence from observations and client records.

packed red cells and platelets on two different occasions. He was diagnosed with hypertension (HTN) due to systolic blood pressure readings consistently ranging between 130s and 150s and was started on nifedipine. E.B. has a history of mild ADHD, migraines, and deep vein thrombosis (DVT). He has tolerated the induction and consolidation phases of chemotherapy well and is now in the maintenance phase, in which he receives a daily dose of mercaptopurine, weekly doses of methotrexate, and intermittent doses of steroids.

Psychosocial History

There is a possibility of a depressive episode a year previously when he would not attend school. He got into serious trouble and was sent to a shelter for 1 month. He currently lives with his mother, father, and 14-year old sister.

Marginal annotations indicate appropriate formatting and effective writing.

Appendix: A document design gallery

Good document design promotes readability and increases the chances that you will achieve your purpose for writing and reach your readers. How you design a document — in other words, how you format it for the printed page or for a computer screen — affects your readers' response to it. Most readers have certain expectations about how documents should be designed and formatted, usually depending on the context and the purpose of the piece of writing.

This gallery features pages from both academic and business documents. The annotations on the sides of the pages point out design choices as well as important features of the writing.

- ▸ Pages from an MLA-style research paper, 807–08
- ▸ Pages from an APA-style review of the literature, 809–12
- ▸ Page from a business report (showing a visual), 813
- ▸ Business letter, 814
- ▸ Résumé, 815
- ▸ Professional memo, 816
- ▸ E-mail message, 817

Standard academic formatting

Use the manuscript format that is recommended for your academic discipline. In most English and some other humanities classes, you will be asked to use MLA (Modern Language Association) format (see 57). In most social science classes, such as psychology and sociology, and in most business, education, and health-related classes, you'll be asked to use APA (American Psychological Association) format (see 62).

Pages 807–12 show basic formatting in MLA and APA styles. For complete student papers in MLA and APA formats, see 57b and 62b.

Standard professional formatting

It helps to look at examples when you are preparing to write a professional document such as a letter, a memo, or a résumé. In general, the writing done in business and professional situations is direct, clear, and courteous — and documents are designed to be scanned easily and quickly. When writing less formal documents such as e-mail messages in academic contexts, it's just as important to craft the document for easy readability.

MLA ESSAY FORMAT

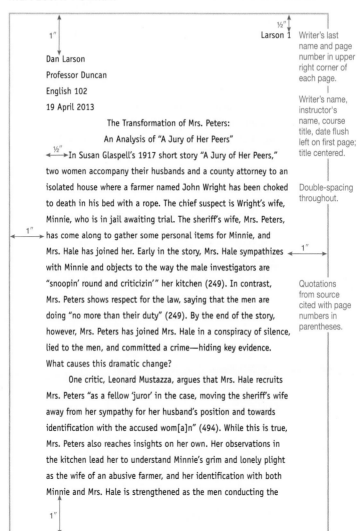

½"
Larson 1

1"

Dan Larson

Professor Duncan

English 102

19 April 2013

The Transformation of Mrs. Peters:

An Analysis of "A Jury of Her Peers"

½"
In Susan Glaspell's 1917 short story "A Jury of Her Peers,"

two women accompany their husbands and a county attorney to an

isolated house where a farmer named John Wright has been choked

to death in his bed with a rope. The chief suspect is Wright's wife,

Minnie, who is in jail awaiting trial. The sheriff's wife, Mrs. Peters,

1"
has come along to gather some personal items for Minnie, and

Mrs. Hale has joined her. Early in the story, Mrs. Hale sympathizes

with Minnie and objects to the way the male investigators are

"snoopin' round and criticizin'" her kitchen (249). In contrast,

Mrs. Peters shows respect for the law, saying that the men are

doing "no more than their duty" (249). By the end of the story,

however, Mrs. Peters has joined Mrs. Hale in a conspiracy of silence,

lied to the men, and committed a crime—hiding key evidence.

What causes this dramatic change?

One critic, Leonard Mustazza, argues that Mrs. Hale recruits

Mrs. Peters "as a fellow 'juror' in the case, moving the sheriff's wife

away from her sympathy for her husband's position and towards

identification with the accused wom[a]n" (494). While this is true,

Mrs. Peters also reaches insights on her own. Her observations in

the kitchen lead her to understand Minnie's grim and lonely plight

as the wife of an abusive farmer, and her identification with both

Minnie and Mrs. Hale is strengthened as the men conducting the

1"

Writer's last name and page number in upper right corner of each page.

Writer's name, instructor's name, course title, date flush left on first page; title centered.

Double-spacing throughout.

1"

Quotations from source cited with page numbers in parentheses.

MLA WORKS CITED PAGE

Works Cited

Heading centered.

Ben-Zvi, Linda. "'Murder, She Wrote': The Genesis of Susan Glaspell's *Trifles*." *Theatre Journal* 44.2 (1992): 141-62. Rpt. in *Susan Glaspell: Essays on Her Theater and Fiction*. Ed. Ben-Zvi. Ann Arbor: U of Michigan P, 1995. 19-48. Print.

List alphabetized by authors' last names (or by title for works with no author).

Glaspell, Susan. "A Jury of Her Peers." *Literature and Its Writers: A Compact Introduction to Fiction, Poetry, and Drama*. Ed. Ann Charters and Samuel Charters. 6th ed. Boston: Bedford, 2013. 243-58. Print.

First line of each entry at left margin; extra lines indented ½".

Hedges, Elaine. "Small Things Reconsidered: 'A Jury of Her Peers.'" *Women's Studies* 12.1 (1986): 89-110. Rpt. in *Susan Glaspell: Essays on Her Theater and Fiction*. Ed. Linda Ben-Zvi. Ann Arbor: U of Michigan P, 1995. 49-69. Print.

Double-spacing throughout; no extra space between entries.

Mustazza, Leonard. "Generic Translation and Thematic Shift in Susan Glaspell's *Trifles* and 'A Jury of Her Peers.'" *Studies in Short Fiction* 26.4 (1989): 489-96. Print.

APA TITLE PAGE

Running head: REACTION TIMES IN VISUAL SEARCH TASKS   1

Header consists of shortened title (no more than 50 characters) in all capital letters at left margin and page number at right margin; on title page only, words "Running head" and colon precede shortened title.

Reaction Times for Detection of Objects

in Two Visual Search Tasks

Allison Leigh Johnson

Carthage College

Full title, writer's name, and school centered halfway down page.

Author Note

Allison Leigh Johnson, Department of Psychology, Carthage

College. This research was conducted for Psychology 2300, Cognition:

Theories and Application, taught by Professor Leslie Cameron.

Author's note (optional) gives writer's affiliation, information about course, and possibly acknowledgments and contact information.

APA ABSTRACT

Shortened title and page number on every page.

Abstract, a 150-to-250-word overview of paper, appears on separate page. Heading centered, not boldface.

Numerals for all numbers in abstract, even numbers under 10.

Keywords (optional) help readers search for paper on the Web or in a database.

Abstract

Visual detection of an object can be automatic or can require attention. The reaction time varies depending on the type of search task being performed. In this visual search experiment, 3 independent variables were tested: type of search, number of distracters, and presence or absence of a target. A feature search contains distracters notably different from the target, while a conjunctive search contains distracters with features similar to the target. For this experiment, 14 Carthage College students participated in a setting of their choice. A green circle was the target. During the feature search, reaction times were similar regardless of the number of distracters and the presence or absence of the target. In the conjunctive search, the number of distracters and the presence or absence of the target affected reaction times. This visual search experiment supports the idea that feature searches are automatic and conjunctive searches require attention from the viewer.

Keywords: visual search, cognition, feature search, conjunctive search

APA ESSAY FORMAT

½″
REACTION TIMES IN VISUAL SEARCH TASKS   1″   3

Reaction Times for Detection of Objects
in Two Visual Search Tasks

> Full title, repeated and centered, not boldface.

½″ Vision is one of the five senses, and it is the sense trusted most by humans (Reisberg, 2010). We use our vision for everything. We are always looking for things, whether it is where we are going or finding a friend at a party. Our vision detects the object(s) we are looking for. Some objects are easier to detect than others. Spotting your sister wearing a purple shirt in a crowd of boring white shirts is automatic and can be done with ease. However, if your sister was also wearing a white shirt, it would take much time ◄ 1″ ► and attention to spot her in that same crowd.

1″ ►

       The "pop out effect" describes the quick identification of an object being searched for because of its salient features (Reeves, 2007). When you look for your sister wearing a purple shirt, for example, you use the pop out effect for quick identification. The pop out effect works when attention is drawn to a specific object that is different from the surrounding objects.

> Sources cited in parentheses with author's last name and date.

REACTION TIMES IN VISUAL SEARCH TASKS   4

conjunctive search because attention is needed for the latter task.

Method

Participants

       Fourteen Carthage College undergraduates participated. Four were male. All were 19 to 21 years old.

Materials

       The experiment was conducted in an environment of each participant's choice, typically in a classroom or library, using the ZAPS online psychology laboratory (2004).

> First-level head centered and boldface; second-level head flush left and boldface; no extra space above or below heads.

APA LIST OF REFERENCES

REACTION TIMES IN VISUAL SEARCH TASKS   8

References

Reeves, R. (2007). *The Norton psychology labs workbook*. New York,
    NY: Norton.

Reisberg, D. (2010). *Cognition: Exploring the science of the mind*.
    New York, NY: Norton.

Treisman, A. (1986). Features and objects in visual processing.
    Scientific American, 255, 114-125.

Wolfe, J. M. (1998). What do 1,000,000 trials tell us about visual
    search? *Psychological Science, 9*, 33-39.

ZAPS: The Norton psychology labs. (2004). Retrieved from http://
    wwnorton.com/ZAPS/

List of references begins on new page; heading centered, not boldface.

List alphabetized by authors' last names.

First line of each entry flush left; additional lines indented ½". Double-spacing throughout.

BUSINESS REPORT WITH A VISUAL

Employee Motivation 5

Doug Ames, manager of operations for OAISYS, noted that some of these issues keep the company from outperforming expectations: "Communication is not timely or uniform, expectations are not clear and consistent, and some employees do not contribute significantly yet nothing is done" (personal communication, February 28, 2006).

Recommendations

It appears that a combination of steps can be used to unlock greater performance for OAISYS. Most important, steps can be taken to strengthen the corporate culture in key areas such as communication, accountability, and appreciation. Employee feedback indicates that these are areas of weakness or motivators that can be improved. This feedback is summarized in Figure 1.

A plan to use communication effectively to set expectations, share results in a timely fashion, and publicly offer appreciation to specific contributors will likely go a long way toward aligning individual motivation with corporate goals. Additionally, holding

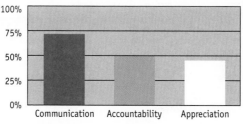

Figure 1. Areas of greatest need for improvements in motivation.

Report formatted in typical business style, with citations in APA style.

Visual referred to in body of report.

Figure, a bar graph, appears at bottom of page on which it is mentioned. Figure number and caption placed below figure.

BUSINESS LETTER IN FULL BLOCK STYLE

LatinoVoice

Date

March 16, 2013

Inside
address

Jonathan Ross
Managing Editor
Latino World Today
2971 East Oak Avenue
Baltimore, MD 21201

Salutation

Dear Mr. Ross:

Thank you very much for taking the time yesterday to speak to the University of Maryland's Latino Club. A number of students have told me that they enjoyed your presentation and found your job search suggestions to be extremely helpful.

Paragraphs
single-spaced,
not indented;
double-spacing
between
paragraphs.

As I mentioned to you, the club publishes a monthly newsletter, *Latino Voice*. Our purpose is to share up-to-date information and expert advice with members of the university's Latino population. Considering how much students benefited from your talk, I would like to publish excerpts from it in our newsletter.

Body

I have transcribed parts of your presentation and organized them into a question-and-answer format for our readers. Would you mind looking through the enclosed article and letting me know if I may have your permission to print it? I'm hoping to include this article in our next newsletter, so I would need your response by April 4.

Once again, Mr. Ross, thank you for sharing your experiences with us. I would love to be able to share your thoughts with students who couldn't hear you in person.

Close

Sincerely,

Signature

Jeffrey Richardson

Jeffrey Richardson
Associate Editor

Indicates
something
enclosed
with letter.

Enc.

210 Student Center University of Maryland College Park MD 20742

RÉSUMÉ

Limit résumé to one page, if possible, two pages at most.

Alexis A. Smith

404 Ponce de Leon NE, #B7   404-231-1234
Atlanta, GA 30308   asmith@smith.localhost

SKILLS SUMMARY
- Writing: competent communicating to different audiences, using a range of written forms (articles, reports, flyers, pamphlets, memos, letters)
- Design: capable of creating visually appealing, audience-appropriate documents; skilled at taking and editing photographs
- Technical: proficient in Microsoft Office; comfortable with Dreamweaver, Photoshop, InDesign
- Language: fluent in spoken and written Spanish

Information organized into clear categories— Skills Summary, Education, Experience, etc.— and formatted for easy scanning.

EDUCATION
Bachelor of Arts, English   expected May 2014
Georgia State University, Atlanta, GA
- Emphasis areas: journalism and communication
- Study Abroad, Ecuador (Fall 2012)
- Dean's List (Fall 2012, Fall 2013, Spring 2014)

Information presented in reverse chronological order.

EXPERIENCE
Copyeditor   Sept. 2013-present
The Signal, Atlanta, GA
- copyedit articles for spelling, grammar, and style
- fact-check articles
- prepare copy for Web publication in Dreamweaver

Bulleted lists organize information.

Writing Tutor   Oct. 2011-present
Georgia State University Writing Studio, Atlanta, GA
- work with undergraduate and graduate students on writing projects in all subject areas
- provide technical support for multimedia projects

Present-tense verbs (*provide*) used for current activities.

OUTREACH AND ACTIVITIES
- Publicity Director, English Department
  Student Organization   Aug. 2013-present
- Coordinator, Georgia State University
  Relay for Life Student Team   April 2013, 2014

PROFESSIONAL MEMO

COMMONWEALTH PRESS
MEMORANDUM

February 26, 2013

To:	Editorial assistants, Advertising Department
cc:	Stephen Chapman
From:	Helen Brown
Subject:	Training for new database software

The new database software will be installed on your computers next week. I have scheduled a training program to help you become familiar with the software and with our new procedures for data entry and retrieval.

Training program
A member of our IT staff will teach in-house workshops on how to use the new software. If you try the software before the workshop, please be prepared to discuss any problems you encounter.

We will keep the training groups small to encourage hands-on participation and to provide individual attention. The workshops will take place in the training room on the third floor from 10:00 a.m. to 2:00 p.m.

Lunch will be provided in the cafeteria.

Sign-up
Please sign up by March 1 for one of the following dates by adding your name in the department's online calendar:

- Wednesday, March 4
- Friday, March 6
- Monday, March 9

If you will not be in the office on any of those dates, please let me know by March 1.

Margin annotations:

Date, name of recipient, name of sender on separate lines.

Subject line describes topic clearly and concisely.

Introduction states point of memo.

Headings guide readers and promote quick scanning of document.

List calls attention to important information.

E-MAIL MESSAGE

| Send | | | | | | | | | | Options... | HTML | | | ? |

To...	watterson.p@northernstate.edu
Cc...	vanessatarsky@gmail.com
Subject:	Two questions about my research project

— Clear, specific subject line gives purpose of message.

| Tahoma | | 10 | **B** *I* <u>U</u> | | | | | | | **A** · | |

Hello, Professor Watterson.

Thank you for taking the time to meet with me yesterday to talk about my research project. I am excited to start the project this week. As we discussed, I am planning to meet with a reference librarian to learn more about NSU's online resources. And I will also develop an online survey to gather my fellow nursing students' perspectives on the topic. In the meantime, I have two questions:

- Do I need approval from the college's institutional review board before I conduct my survey?

- Do I need students' approval to quote their responses in my paper?

I know this is a busy time of year, but if possible, please let me know the answers to these questions before the end of the week.

Thanks for all your help with my project.

Sincerely,

Vanessa Tarsky

Introduction explains reason for writing.

Professional, straightforward tone and formal language appropriate for communicating with professor.

Message formatted to be read quickly. Bullets draw reader's eye to important details.

Desired outcome of message: request stated briefly.

Message ends with brief, friendly closing.

Glossary of Usage

This glossary includes words commonly confused (such as *accept* and *except*), words commonly misused (such as *aggravate*), and words that are nonstandard (such as *hisself*). It also lists colloquialisms and jargon. Colloquialisms are casual expressions that may be appropriate in informal speech but are inappropriate in formal writing. Jargon is needlessly technical or pretentious language that is inappropriate in most contexts. If an item is not listed here, consult the index. For irregular verbs (such as *sing, sang, sung*), see 27a. For idiomatic use of prepositions, see 18d.

a, an Use *an* before a vowel sound, *a* before a consonant sound: *an apple, a peach.* Problems sometimes arise with words beginning with *h* or *u*. If the *h* is silent, the word begins with a vowel sound, so use *an*: *an hour, an honorable deed.* If the *h* is pronounced, the word begins with a consonant sound, so use *a*: *a hospital, a historian, a hotel.* Words such as *university* and *union* begin with a consonant sound (a *y* sound), so use *a*: *a union.* Words such as *uncle* and *umbrella* begin with a vowel sound, so use *an*: *an underground well.* When an abbreviation or an acronym begins with a vowel sound, use *an*: *an EKG, an MRI, an AIDS prevention program.*

accept, except *Accept* is a verb meaning "to receive." *Except* is usually a preposition meaning "excluding." *I will accept all the packages except that one. Except* is also a verb meaning "to exclude." *Please except that item from the list.*

adapt, adopt *Adapt* means "to adjust or become accustomed"; it is usually followed by *to. Adopt* means "to take as one's own." *Our family adopted a Vietnamese child, who quickly adapted to his new life.*

adverse, averse *Adverse* means "unfavorable." *Averse* means "opposed" or "reluctant"; it is usually followed by *to*. *I am averse to your proposal because it could have an adverse impact on the economy.*

advice, advise *Advice* is a noun, *advise* a verb. *We advise you to follow John's advice.*

affect, effect *Affect* is usually a verb meaning "to influence." *Effect* is usually a noun meaning "result." *The drug did not affect the disease, and it had adverse side effects. Effect* can also be a verb meaning "to bring about." *Only the president can effect such a dramatic change.*

aggravate *Aggravate* means "to make worse or more troublesome." *Overgrazing aggravated the soil erosion.* In formal writing, avoid the use of *aggravate* meaning "to annoy or irritate." *Her babbling annoyed* (not *aggravated*) *me.*

agree to, agree with *Agree to* means "to give consent to." *Agree with* means "to be in accord with" or "to come to an understanding with." *He agrees with me about the need for change, but he won't agree to my plan.*

ain't *Ain't* is nonstandard. Use *am not, are not (aren't)*, or *is not (isn't). I am not* (not *ain't*) *going home for spring break.*

all ready, already *All ready* means "completely prepared." *Already* means "previously." *Susan was all ready for the concert, but her friends had already left.*

all right *All right*, written as two words, is correct. *Alright* is nonstandard.

all together, altogether *All together* means "everyone or everything in one place." *Altogether* means "entirely." *We were not altogether certain that we could bring the family all together for the reunion.*

allude To *allude* to something is to make an indirect reference to it. Do not use *allude* to mean "to refer directly." *In his lecture, the professor referred* (not *alluded*) *to several pre-Socratic philosophers.*

allusion, illusion An *allusion* is an indirect reference. An *illusion* is a misconception or false impression. *Did you catch my allusion to Shakespeare? Mirrors give the room an illusion of depth.*

a lot *A lot* is two words. Do not write *alot*. *Sam lost a lot of weight.* See also *lots, lots of.*

among, between See *between, among.*

amongst In American English, *among* is preferred.

amoral, immoral *Amoral* means "neither moral nor immoral"; it also means "not caring about moral judgments." *Immoral* means "morally wrong." *Until recently, most business courses were taught from an amoral perspective. Murder is immoral.*

amount, number Use *amount* with quantities that cannot be counted; use *number* with those that can. *This recipe calls for a large amount of sugar. We have a large number of toads in our garden.*

an See *a, an.*

and etc. *Et cetera* (*etc.*) means "and so forth"; *and etc.* is redundant. See also *etc.*

and/or Avoid the awkward construction *and/or* except in technical or legal documents.

angry at, angry with Use *angry with*, not *angry at*, when referring to a person. *The coach was angry with the referee.*

ante-, anti- The prefix *ante-* means "earlier" or "in front of"; the prefix *anti-* means "against" or "opposed to." *William Lloyd Garrison was a leader of the antislavery movement during the antebellum period.* *Anti-* should be used with a hyphen when it is followed by a capital letter or a word beginning with *i*.

anxious *Anxious* means "worried" or "apprehensive." In formal writing, avoid using *anxious* to mean "eager." *We are eager* (not *anxious*) *to see your new house.*

anybody, anyone *Anybody* and *anyone* are singular. (See 21e and 22a.)

anymore Use the adverb *anymore* in a negative context to mean "any longer" or "now." *The factory isn't producing shoes anymore.* Using *anymore* in a positive context is colloquial; in formal writing, use *now* instead. *We order all our food online now* (not *anymore*).

anyone See *anybody, anyone.*

anyone, any one *Anyone*, an indefinite pronoun, means "any person at all." *Any one*, the pronoun *one* preceded by the adjective *any*, refers to a particular person or thing in a group. *Anyone from the winning team may choose any one of the games on display.*

anyplace In formal writing, use *anywhere.*

anyways, anywheres *Anyways* and *anywheres* are nonstandard. Use *anyway* and *anywhere.*

as Do not use *as* to mean "because" if there is any chance of ambiguity. *We canceled the picnic because* (not *as*) *it began raining. As* here could mean either "because" or "when."

as, like See *like, as.*

as to *As to* is jargon for *about. He inquired about* (not *as to*) *the job.*

averse See *adverse, averse.*

awful The adjective *awful* and the adverb *awfully* are not appropriate in formal writing.

awhile, a while *Awhile* is an adverb; it can modify a verb, but it cannot be the object of a preposition such as *for.* The two-word form *a while* is a noun preceded by an article and therefore can be the object of a preposition. *Stay awhile. Stay for a while.*

back up, backup *Back up* is a verb phrase. *Back up the car carefully. Be sure to back up your hard drive. Backup* is a noun meaning "a copy of electronically stored data." *Keep your backup in a safe place. Backup* can also be used as an adjective. *I regularly create backup disks.*

bad, badly *Bad* is an adjective, *badly* an adverb. *They felt bad about ruining the surprise. Her arm hurt badly after she slid into second base.* (See 26a, 26b, and 26c.)

being as, being that *Being as* and *being that* are nonstandard expressions. Write *because* instead. *Because* (not *Being as*) *I slept late, I had to skip breakfast.*

beside, besides *Beside* is a preposition meaning "at the side of" or "next to." *Annie sleeps with a flashlight beside her bed. Besides* is a preposition meaning "except" or "in addition to." *No one besides Terrie can have that ice cream. Besides* is also an adverb meaning "in addition." *I'm not hungry; besides, I don't like ice cream.*

between, among Ordinarily, use *among* with three or more entities, *between* with two. *The prize was divided among several contestants. You have a choice between carrots and beans.*

bring, take Use *bring* when an object is being transported toward you, *take* when it is being moved away. *Please bring me a glass of water. Please take these forms to Mr. Scott.*

burst, bursted; bust, busted *Burst* is an irregular verb meaning "to come open or fly apart suddenly or violently." Its past tense is *burst.* The past-tense form *bursted* is nonstandard. *Bust* and *busted* are slang for *burst* and, along with *bursted*, should not be used in formal writing.

can, may The distinction between *can* and *may* is fading, but some writers still observe it in formal writing. *Can* is traditionally reserved for ability, *may* for permission. *Can you speak French? May I help you?*

capital, capitol *Capital* refers to a city, *capitol* to a building where lawmakers meet. *Capital* also refers to wealth or resources. *The residents of the state capital protested plans to close the streets surrounding the capitol.*

censor, censure *Censor* means "to remove or suppress material considered objectionable." *Censure* means "to criticize severely." *The administration's policy of censoring books has been censured by the media.*

cite, site *Cite* means "to quote as an authority or example." *Site* is usually a noun meaning "a particular place." *He cited the zoning law in his argument against the proposed site of the gas station.* Locations on the Internet are usually referred to as *sites. The library's Web site improves every week.*

climactic, climatic *Climactic* is derived from *climax*, the point of greatest intensity in a series or progression of events. *Climatic* is derived from *climate* and refers to meteorological conditions. *The climactic period in the dinosaurs' reign was reached just before severe climatic conditions brought on an ice age.*

coarse, course *Coarse* means "crude" or "rough in texture." *The coarse weave of the wall hanging gave it a three-dimensional quality. Course* usually refers to a path, a playing field, or a unit of study; the expression *of course* means "certainly." *I plan to take a course in car repair this summer. Of course, you are welcome to join me.*

compare to, compare with *Compare to* means "to represent as similar." *She compared him to a wild stallion. Compare with* means "to examine similarities and differences." *The study compared the language ability of apes with that of dolphins.*

complement, compliment *Complement* is a verb meaning "to go with or complete" or a noun meaning "something that completes." As a verb, *compliment* means "to flatter"; as a noun, it means "flattering remark." *Her skill at rushing the net complements his skill at volleying. Martha's flower arrangements receive many compliments.*

conscience, conscious *Conscience* is a noun meaning "moral principles." *Conscious* is an adjective meaning "aware or alert." *Let your conscience be your guide. Were you conscious of his love for you?*

continual, continuous *Continual* means "repeated regularly and frequently." *She grew weary of the continual telephone calls. Continuous* means "extended or prolonged without interruption." *The broken siren made a continuous wail.*

could care less *Could care less* is nonstandard. Write *couldn't care less* instead. *He couldn't* (not *could*) *care less about his psychology final.*

could of *Could of* is nonstandard for *could have. We could have* (not *could of*) *taken the train.*

council, counsel A *council* is a deliberative body, and a *councilor* is a member of such a body. *Counsel* usually means "advice" and can also mean "lawyer"; a *counselor* is one who gives advice or guidance. *The councilors met to draft the council's position paper. The pastor offered wise counsel to the troubled teenager.*

criteria *Criteria* is the plural of *criterion*, which means "a standard or rule or test on which a judgment or decision can be based." *The only criterion for the scholarship is ability.*

data *Data* is a plural noun technically meaning "facts or propositions." But *data* is increasingly being accepted as a singular noun. *The new data suggest* (or *suggests*) *that our theory is correct.* (The singular *datum* is rarely used.)

different from, different than Ordinarily, write *different from. Your sense of style is different from Jim's.* However, *different than* is acceptable to avoid an awkward construction. *Please let me know if your plans are different than* (to avoid *from what*) *they were six weeks ago.*

differ from, differ with *Differ from* means "to be unlike"; *differ with* means "to disagree with." *My approach to the problem differed from hers. She differed with me about the wording of the agreement.*

disinterested, uninterested *Disinterested* means "impartial, objective"; *uninterested* means "not interested." *We sought the advice of a disinterested counselor to help us solve our problem. Mark was uninterested in anyone's opinion but his own.*

don't *Don't* is the contraction for *do not. I don't want any. Don't* should not be used as the contraction for *does not*, which is *doesn't. He doesn't* (not *don't*) *want any.*

due to *Due to* is an adjective phrase and should not be used as a preposition meaning "because of." *The trip was canceled because of* (not *due to*) *lack of interest. Due to* is acceptable as a subject complement and usually follows a form of the verb *be. His success was due to hard work.*

each *Each* is singular. (See 21e and 22a.)

effect See *affect, effect.*

e.g. In formal writing, replace the Latin abbreviation *e.g.* with its English equivalent: *for example* or *for instance.*

either *Either* is singular. (See 21e and 22a.) For *either . . . or* constructions, see 21d and 22a.

elicit, illicit *Elicit* is a verb meaning "to bring out" or "to evoke." *Illicit* is an adjective meaning "unlawful." *The reporter was unable to elicit any information from the police about illicit drug traffic.*

emigrate from, immigrate to *Emigrate* means "to leave one country or region to settle in another." *In 1903, my great-grandfather emigrated from Russia to escape the religious pogroms. Immigrate* means "to enter another country and reside there." *More than fifty thousand Bosnians immigrated to the United States in the 1990s.*

eminent, imminent *Eminent* means "outstanding" or "distinguished." *We met an eminent professor of Greek history. Imminent* means "about to happen." *The snowstorm is imminent.*

enthused Many people object to the use of *enthused* as an adjective. Use *enthusiastic* instead. *The children were enthusiastic* (not *enthused*) *about going to the circus.*

etc. Avoid ending a list with *etc.* It is more emphatic to end with an example, and in most contexts readers will understand that the list is not exhaustive. When you don't wish to end with an example, *and so on* is more graceful than *etc.* (See also *and etc.*)

eventually, ultimately Often used interchangeably, *eventually* is the better choice to mean "at an unspecified time in the future," and *ultimately* is better to mean "the furthest possible extent or greatest extreme." *He knew that eventually he would complete his degree. The existentialists considered suicide the ultimately rational act.*

everybody, everyone *Everybody* and *everyone* are singular. (See 21e and 22a.)

everyone, every one *Everyone* is an indefinite pronoun. *Every one,* the pronoun *one* preceded by the adjective *every,* means "each individual or thing in a particular group." *Every one* is usually followed by *of. Everyone wanted to go. Every one of the missing books was found.*

except See *accept, except.*

expect Avoid the informal use of *expect* meaning "to believe, think, or suppose." *I think* (not *expect*) *it will rain tonight.*

explicit, implicit *Explicit* means "expressed directly" or "clearly defined"; *implicit* means "implied, unstated." *I gave him explicit instructions not to go swimming. My mother's silence indicated her implicit approval.*

farther, further *Farther* usually describes distances. *Further* usually suggests quantity or degree. *Chicago is farther from Miami than I thought. I would be grateful for further suggestions.*

fewer, less Use *fewer* for items that can be counted; use *less* for items that cannot be counted. *Fewer people are living in the city. Please put less sugar in my tea.*

finalize *Finalize* is jargon meaning "to make final or complete." Use ordinary English instead. *The architect prepared final drawings* (not *finalized the drawings*).

firstly *Firstly* sounds pretentious, and it leads to the ungainly series *firstly, secondly, thirdly,* and so on. Write *first, second, third* instead.

further See *farther, further.*

get *Get* has many colloquial uses. In writing, avoid using *get* to mean the following: "to evoke an emotional response" (*That music always gets to me*); "to annoy" (*After a while, his sulking got to me*); "to take revenge on" (*I got back at her by leaving the room*); "to become" (*He got sick*); "to start or begin" (*Let's get going*). Avoid using *have got to* in place of *must. I must* (not *have got to*) *finish this paper tonight.*

good, well *Good* is an adjective, *well* an adverb. (See 26a, 26b, and 26c.) *He hasn't felt good about his game since he sprained his wrist last season. She performed well on the uneven parallel bars.*

graduate Both of the following uses of *graduate* are standard: *My sister was graduated from UCLA last year. My sister graduated from UCLA last year.* It is nonstandard, however, to drop the word *from: My sister graduated UCLA last year.* Though this usage is common in informal English, many readers object to it.

grow Phrases such as *to grow the economy* and *to grow a business* are jargon. Usually the verb *grow* is intransitive (it does not take a direct object). *Our business has grown very quickly.* Use *grow* in a transitive sense, with a direct object, to mean "to cultivate" or "to allow to grow." *We plan to grow tomatoes this year. John is growing a beard.*

hanged, hung *Hanged* is the past-tense and past-participle form of the verb *hang* meaning "to execute." *The prisoner was hanged at dawn. Hung* is the past-tense and past-participle form of the verb *hang* meaning "to fasten or suspend." *The stockings were hung by the chimney with care.*

hardly Avoid expressions such as *can't hardly* and *not hardly*, which are considered double negatives. *I can* (not *can't*) *hardly describe my surprise at getting the job.* (See 26e.)

has got, have got *Got* is unnecessary and awkward in such constructions. It should be dropped. *We have* (not *have got*) *three days to prepare for the opening.*

he At one time *he* was commonly used to mean "he or she." Today such usage is inappropriate. (See 17f and 22a.)

he/she, his/her In formal writing, use *he or she* or *his or her*. For alternatives to these wordy constructions, see 17f and 22a.

hisself *Himself* is nonstandard. Use *himself*.

hopefully *Hopefully* means "in a hopeful manner." *We looked hopefully to the future.* Some usage experts object to the use of *hopefully* as a sentence adverb, apparently on grounds of clarity. To be safe, avoid using *hopefully* in sentences such as the following: *Hopefully, your son will recover soon.* Instead, indicate who is doing the hoping: *I hope that your son will recover soon.*

however In the past, some writers objected to the conjunctive adverb *however* at the beginning of a sentence, but current experts allow placing the word according to the intended meaning and emphasis. All of the following sentences are correct. *Pam decided, however, to attend the lecture. However, Pam decided to attend the lecture.* (She had been considering other activities.) *Pam, however, decided to attend the lecture.* (Unlike someone else, Pam chose to attend the lecture.) (See 32f.)

hung   See *hanged, hung.*

i.e.   In formal writing, replace the Latin abbreviation *i.e.* with its English equivalent: *that is.*

if, whether   Use *if* to express a condition and *whether* to express alternatives. *If you go on a trip, whether to Nebraska or Italy, remember to bring traveler's checks.*

illusion   See *allusion, illusion.*

immigrate   See *emigrate from, immigrate to.*

imminent   See *eminent, imminent.*

immoral   See *amoral, immoral.*

implement   *Implement* is a pretentious way of saying "do," "carry out," or "accomplish." Use ordinary language instead. *We carried out* (not *implemented*) *the director's orders.*

imply, infer   *Imply* means "to suggest or state indirectly"; *infer* means "to draw a conclusion." *John implied that he knew all about computers, but the interviewer inferred that John was inexperienced.*

in, into   *In* indicates location or condition; *into* indicates movement or a change in condition. *They found the lost letters in a box after moving into the house.*

in regards to   *In regards to* confuses two different phrases: *in regard to* and *as regards.* Use one or the other. *In regard to* (or *As regards*) *the contract, ignore the first clause.*

irregardless   *Irregardless* is nonstandard. Use *regardless.*

is when, is where   These mixed constructions are often incorrectly used in definitions. *A runoff election is a second election held to break a tie* (not *is when a second election is held to break a tie*). (See 11c.)

its, it's   *Its* is a possessive pronoun; *it's* is a contraction of *it is.* (See 36c and 36e.) *It's always fun to watch a dog chase its tail.*

kind(s) *Kind* is singular and should be treated as such. Don't write *These kind of chairs are rare.* Write instead *This kind of chair is rare. Kinds* is plural and should be used only when you mean more than one kind. *These kinds of chairs are rare.*

kind of, sort of Avoid using *kind of* or *sort of* to mean "somewhat." *The movie was somewhat* (not *sort of*) *boring.* Do not put *a* after either phrase. *That kind of* (not *kind of a*) *salesclerk annoys me.*

lay, lie See *lie, lay.*

lead, led *Lead* is a metallic element; it is a noun. *Led* is the past tense of the verb *lead. He led me to the treasure.*

learn, teach *Learn* means "to gain knowledge"; *teach* means "to impart knowledge." *I must teach* (not *learn*) *my sister to read.*

leave, let *Leave* means "to exit." Avoid using it with the nonstandard meaning "to permit." *Let* (not *Leave*) *me help you with the dishes.*

less See *fewer, less.*

let, leave See *leave, let.*

liable *Liable* means "obligated" or "responsible." Do not use it to mean "likely." *You're likely* (not *liable*) *to trip if you don't tie your shoelaces.*

lie, lay *Lie* is an intransitive verb meaning "to recline or rest on a surface." Its forms are *lie, lay, lain. Lay* is a transitive verb meaning "to put or place." Its forms are *lay, laid, laid.* (See 27b.)

like, as *Like* is a preposition, not a subordinating conjunction. It can be followed only by a noun or a noun phrase. *As* is a subordinating conjunction that introduces a subordinate clause. In casual speech, you may say *She looks like she hasn't slept* or *You don't know her like I do.* But in formal writing, use *as. She looks as if she hasn't slept. You don't know her as I do.* (See also 46f and 46g.)

loose, lose *Loose* is an adjective meaning "not securely fastened." *Lose* is a verb meaning "to misplace" or "to not win." *Did you lose your only loose pair of work pants?*

lots, lots of *Lots* and *lots of* are informal substitutes for *many, much,* or *a lot.* Avoid using them in formal writing.

mankind Avoid *mankind* whenever possible. It offends many readers because it excludes women. Use *humanity, humans, the human race,* or *humankind* instead. (See 17f.)

may See *can, may.*

maybe, may be *Maybe* is an adverb meaning "possibly." *Maybe the sun will shine tomorrow. May be* is a verb phrase. *Tomorrow may be brighter.*

may of, might of *May of* and *might of* are nonstandard for *may have* and *might have. We might have* (not *might of*) *had too many cookies.*

media, medium *Media* is the plural of *medium. Of all the media that cover the Olympics, television is the medium that best captures the spectacle of the events.*

most *Most* is informal when used to mean "almost" and should be avoided. *Almost* (not *Most*) *everyone went to the parade.*

must of See *may of, might of. Must of* is nonstandard for *must have.*

myself *Myself* is a reflexive or intensive pronoun. Reflexive: *I cut myself.* Intensive: *I will drive you myself.* Do not use *myself* in place of *I* or *me. He gave the flowers to Melinda and me* (not *myself*). (See also 24a and 24b.)

neither *Neither* is singular. (See 21e and 22a.) For *neither . . . nor* constructions, see 21d, 22a, and 22d.

none *None* may be singular or plural. (See 21e.)

nowheres *Nowheres* is nonstandard. Use *nowhere* instead.

number See *amount, number.*

of Use the verb *have,* not the preposition *of,* after the verbs *could, should, would, may, might,* and *must. They must have* (not *must of*) *left early.*

off of *Off* is sufficient. Omit *of. The ball rolled off* (not *off of*) *the table.*

OK, O.K., okay All three spellings are acceptable, but avoid these expressions in formal speech and writing.

parameters *Parameter* is a mathematical term that has become jargon for "fixed limit," "boundary," or "guideline." Use ordinary English instead. *The task force worked within certain guidelines* (not *parameters*).

passed, past *Passed* is the past tense of the verb *pass*. *Ann passed me another slice of cake. Past* usually means "belonging to a former time" or "beyond a time or place." *Our past president spoke until past midnight. The hotel is just past the next intersection.*

percent, per cent, percentage *Percent* (also spelled *per cent*) is always used with a specific number. *Percentage* is used with a descriptive term such as *large* or *small*, not with a specific number. *The candidate won 80 percent of the primary vote. A large percentage of registered voters turned out for the election.*

phenomena *Phenomena* is the plural of *phenomenon*, which means "an observable occurrence or fact." *Strange phenomena occur at all hours of the night in that house, but last night's phenomenon was the strangest of all.*

plus *Plus* should not be used to join independent clauses. *This raincoat is dirty; moreover* (not *plus*), *it has a hole in it.*

precede, proceed *Precede* means "to come before." *Proceed* means "to go forward." *As we proceeded up the mountain path, we noticed fresh tracks in the mud, evidence that a group of hikers had preceded us.*

principal, principle *Principal* is a noun meaning "the head of a school or an organization" or "a sum of money." It is also an adjective meaning "most important." *Principle* is a noun meaning "a basic truth or law." *The principal expelled her for three principal reasons. We believe in the principle of equal justice for all.*

proceed, precede See *precede, proceed.*

quote, quotation *Quote* is a verb; *quotation* is a noun. Avoid using *quote* as a shortened form of *quotation. Her quotations* (not *quotes*) *from current movies intrigued us.*

raise, rise *Raise* is a transitive verb meaning "to move or cause to move upward." It takes a direct object. *I raised the shades. Rise* is an intransitive verb meaning "to go up." *Heat rises.*

real, really *Real* is an adjective; *really* is an adverb. *Real* is sometimes used informally as an adverb, but avoid this use in formal writing. *She was really* (not *real*) *angry.* (See 26a and 26b.)

reason . . . is because Use *that* instead of *because. The reason she's cranky is that* (not *because*) *she didn't sleep last night.* (See 11c.)

reason why The expression *reason why* is redundant. *The reason* (not *The reason why*) *Jones lost the election is clear.*

relation, relationship *Relation* describes a connection between things. *Relationship* describes a connection between people. *There is a relation between poverty and infant mortality. Our business relationship has cooled over the years.*

respectfully, respectively *Respectfully* means "showing or marked by respect." *Respectively* means "each in the order given." *He respectfully submitted his opinion to the judge. John, Tom, and Larry were a butcher, a baker, and a lawyer, respectively.*

sensual, sensuous *Sensual* means "gratifying the physical senses," especially those associated with sexual pleasure. *Sensuous* means "pleasing to the senses," especially those involved in the experience of art, music, and nature. *The sensuous music and balmy air led the dancers to more sensual movements.*

set, sit *Set* is a transitive verb meaning "to put" or "to place." Its past tense is *set. Sit* is an intransitive verb meaning "to be seated." Its past tense is *sat. She set the dough in a warm corner of the kitchen. The cat sat in the doorway.*

shall, will *Shall* was once used in place of the helping verb *will* with *I* or *we: I shall, we shall.* Today, however, *will* is generally accepted even when the subject is *I* or *we.* The word *shall* occurs primarily in polite questions (*Shall I find you a pillow?*) and in legalistic sentences suggesting duty or obligation (*The applicant shall file form A by December 31*).

should of *Should of* is nonstandard for *should have*. *They should have* (not *should of*) *been home an hour ago.*

since Do not use *since* to mean "because" if there is any chance of ambiguity. *Because* (not *Since*) *we won the game, we have been celebrating with a pitcher of root beer. Since* here could mean "because" or "from the time that."

sit See *set, sit.*

site See *cite, site.*

somebody, someone *Somebody* and *someone* are singular. (See 21e and 22a.)

something *Something* is singular. (See 21e.)

sometime, some time, sometimes *Sometime* is an adverb meaning "at an indefinite time." *Some time* is the adjective *some* modifying the noun *time* and means "a period of time." *Sometimes* is an adverb meaning "at times, now and then." *I'll see you sometime soon. I haven't lived there for some time. Sometimes I see him at work.*

suppose to Write *supposed to.*

sure and Write *sure to. We were all taught to be sure to* (not *sure and*) *look both ways before crossing a street.*

take See *bring, take.*

than, then *Than* is a conjunction used in comparisons; *then* is an adverb denoting time. *That pizza is more than I can eat. Tom laughed, and then we recognized him.*

that See *who, which, that.*

that, which Many writers reserve *that* for restrictive clauses, *which* for nonrestrictive clauses. (See 32e.)

theirselves *Theirselves* is nonstandard for *themselves. The crash victims pushed the car out of the way themselves* (not *theirselves*).

them The use of *them* in place of *those* is nonstandard. *Please take those* (not *them*) *flowers to the patient in room 220.*

then, than See *than, then.*

there, their, they're *There* is an adverb specifying place; it is also an expletive (placeholder). Adverb: *Sylvia is sitting there patiently.* Expletive: *There are two plums left. Their* is a possessive pronoun. *Fred and Jane finally washed their car. They're* is a contraction of *they are. They're later than usual today.*

they The use of *they* to indicate possession is nonstandard. Use *their* instead. *Cindy and Sam decided to sell their* (not *they*) *1975 Corvette.*

they, their The use of the plural pronouns *they* and *their* to refer to singular nouns or pronouns is nonstandard. *No one handed in his or her* (not *their*) *draft on time.* (See 22a.)

this kind See *kind(s)*.

to, too, two *To* is a preposition; *too* is an adverb; *two* is a number. *Too many of your shots slice to the left, but the last two were just right.*

toward, towards *Toward* and *towards* are generally interchangeable, although *toward* is preferred in American English.

try and *Try and* is nonstandard for *try to. The teacher asked us all to try to* (not *try and*) *write an original haiku.*

ultimately, eventually See *eventually, ultimately*.

unique Avoid expressions such as *most unique, more straight, less perfect, very round.* Either something is unique or it isn't. It is illogical to suggest degrees of uniqueness. (See 26d.)

usage The noun *usage* should not be substituted for *use* when the meaning is "employment of." *The use* (not *usage*) *of insulated shades has cut fuel costs dramatically.*

use to Write *used to*.

utilize *Utilize* means "to make use of." It often sounds pretentious; in most cases, *use* is sufficient. *I used* (not *utilized*) *the laser printer.*

wait for, wait on *Wait for* means "to be in readiness for" or "to await." *Wait on* means "to serve." *We're waiting for* (not *waiting on*) *Ruth to take us to the museum.*

ways *Ways* is colloquial when used to mean "distance." *The city is a long way* (not *ways*) *from here.*

weather, whether The noun *weather* refers to the state of the atmosphere. *Whether* is a conjunction referring to a choice between alternatives. *We wondered whether the weather would clear.*

well, good See *good, well.*

where Do not use *where* in place of *that. I heard that* (not *where*) *the crime rate is increasing.*

which See *that, which* and *who, which, that.*

while Avoid using *while* to mean "although" or "whereas" if there is any chance of ambiguity. *Although* (not *While*) *Gloria lost money in the slot machine, Tom won it at roulette.* Here *While* could mean either "although" or "at the same time that."

who, which, that Do not use *which* to refer to persons. Use *who* instead. *That*, though generally used to refer to things, may be used to refer to a group or class of people. *The player who* (not *that* or *which*) *made the basket at the buzzer was named MVP. The team that scores the most points in this game will win the tournament.*

who, whom *Who* is used for subjects and subject complements; *whom* is used for objects. (See 25.)

who's, whose *Who's* is a contraction of *who is; whose* is a possessive pronoun. *Who's ready for more popcorn? Whose coat is this?* (See 36c and 36e.)

will See *shall, will.*

would of *Would of* is nonstandard for *would have. She would have* (not *would of*) *had a chance to play if she had arrived on time.*

you In formal writing, avoid *you* in an indefinite sense meaning "anyone." (See 23d.) *Any spectator* (not *You*) *could tell by the way John caught the ball that his throw would be too late.*

your, you're *Your* is a possessive pronoun; *you're* is a contraction of *you are. Is that your new bike? You're in the finals.* (See 36c and 46b.)

Answers to Lettered Exercises

Exercise 6–1, page 155

a. hasty generalization; b. false analogy; c. *either . . . or* fallacy;
d. biased language; e. faulty cause-and-effect reasoning

Exercise 8–1, page 203 *Possible revisions:*

a. The Prussians defeated the Saxons in 1745.
b. Ahmed, the producer, manages the entire operation.
c. The tour guides expertly paddled the sea kayaks.
d. Emphatic and active; no change
e. Protesters were shouting on the courthouse steps.

Exercise 9–1, page 209 *Possible revisions:*

a. Police dogs are used for finding lost children, tracking criminals, and detecting bombs and illegal drugs.
b. Hannah told her rock-climbing partner that she bought a new harness and that she wanted to climb Otter Cliffs.
c. It is more difficult to sustain an exercise program than to start one.
d. During basic training, I was told not only what to do but also what to think.
e. Jan wanted to drive to the wine country or at least to Sausalito.

Exercise 10–1, page 213 *Possible revisions:*

a. A grapefruit or an orange is a good source of vitamin C.
b. The women entering the military academy can expect haircuts as short as those of the male cadets.
c. Looking out the family room window, Sarah saw that her favorite tree, which she had climbed as a child, was gone.
d. The graphic designers are interested in and knowledgeable about producing posters for the balloon race.
e. The Great Barrier Reef is larger than any other coral reef in the world.

Exercise 11–1, page 217 *Possible revisions:*

a. Using surgical gloves is a precaution now taken by dentists to prevent contact with patients' blood and saliva.
b. A career in medicine, which my brother is pursuing, requires at least ten years of challenging work.
c. The pharaohs had bad teeth because tiny particles of sand found their way into Egyptian bread.
d. Recurring bouts of flu caused the team to forfeit a record number of games.
e. This box contains the key to your future.

Exercise 12–1, page 222   *Possible revisions:*

a.   More research is needed to evaluate effectively the risks posed by volcanoes in the Pacific Northwest.

b.   Many students graduate from college with debt totaling more than fifty thousand dollars.

c.   It is a myth that humans use only 10 percent of their brains.

d.   A coolhunter is a person who can find the next wave of fashion in the unnoticed corners of modern society.

e.   Not all geese fly beyond Narragansett for the winter.

Exercise 12–6, page 225   *Possible revisions:*

a.   To complete an online purchase with a credit card, you must enter the expiration date and the security code.

b.   Though Martha was only sixteen, UCLA accepted her application.

c.   As I settled in the cockpit, the pounding of the engine was muffled only slightly by my helmet.

d.   After studying polymer chemistry, Phuong found computer games less complex.

e.   When I was a young man, my mother enrolled me in tap dance classes.

Exercise 13–5, page 231   *Possible revisions:*

a.   An incredibly talented musician, Ray Charles mastered R&B, soul, and gospel styles. He even performed country music well.

b.   Environmentalists point out that shrimp farming in Southeast Asia is polluting water and making farmlands useless. They warn that governments must act before it is too late.

c.   We observed the samples for five days before we detected any growth. *Or* The samples were observed for five days before any growth was detected.

d.   In his famous soliloquy, Hamlet contemplates whether death would be preferable to his difficult life and, if so, whether he is capable of committing suicide.

e.   The lawyer told the judge that Miranda Hale was innocent and asked that she be allowed to prove the allegations false. *Or* The lawyer told the judge, "Miranda Hale is innocent. Please allow her to prove the allegations false."

Exercise 13–6, page 232   *Possible revisions:*

a.   Courtroom lawyers need to have more than a touch of theater in their blood.

b.   The interviewer asked if we had brought our proof of citizenship and our passports.

c. Experienced reconnaissance scouts know how to make fast decisions and use sophisticated equipment to keep their teams from being detected.

d. After the animators finish their scenes, the production designer arranges the clips according to the storyboard and makes synchronization notes for the sound editor and the composer.

e. Madame Defarge is a sinister figure in Dickens's *A Tale of Two Cities*. On a symbolic level, she represents fate; like the Greek Fates, she knits the fabric of individual destiny.

Exercise 14–1, page 238   *Possible revisions:*

a. Williams played for the Boston Red Sox from 1939 to 1960, and he managed the Washington Senators and Texas Rangers for several years after retiring as a player.

b. In 1941, Williams finished the season with a batting average of .406; no player has hit over .400 for a season since then.

c. Although he acknowledged that Joe DiMaggio was a better all-around player, Williams felt that he was a better hitter than DiMaggio.

d. Williams was a stubborn man; for example, he always refused to tip his cap to the crowd after a home run because he claimed that fans were fickle.

e. Williams's relationship with the media was unfriendly at best; he sarcastically called baseball writers the "knights of the keyboard" in his memoir.

Exercise 14–2, page 239   *Possible revisions:*

a. The X-Men comic books and Japanese woodcuts of kabuki dancers, all part of Marlena's research project on popular culture, covered the tabletop and the chairs.

b. Our waitress, costumed in a kimono, had painted her face white and arranged her hair in a lacquered beehive.

c. Students can apply for a spot in the leadership program, which teaches thinking and communication skills.

d. Shore houses were flooded up to the first floor, beaches were washed away, and Brant's Lighthouse was swallowed by the sea.

e. Laura Thackray, an engineer at Volvo Car Corporation, addressed women's safety needs by designing a pregnant crash-test dummy.

Exercise 14–8, page 240   *Possible revisions:*

a. These particles, known as "stealth liposomes," can hide in the body for a long time without detection.

b. Irena, a competitive gymnast majoring in biochemistry, intends to apply her athletic experience and her science degree to a career in sports medicine.

c. Because students, textile workers, and labor unions have loudly protested sweatshop abuses, apparel makers have been forced to examine their labor practices.

d. Developed in a European university, IRC (Internet relay chat) was created as a way for a group of graduate students to talk about projects from their dorm rooms.

e. The cafeteria's new menu, which has an international flavor, includes everything from enchiladas and pizza to pad thai and sauerbraten.

Exercise 14–10, page 242   *Possible revisions:*

a. Working as an aide for the relief agency, Gina distributed food and medical supplies.

b. Janbir, who spent every Saturday learning tabla drumming, noticed with each hour of practice that his memory for complex patterns was growing stronger.

c. When the rotor hit, it gouged a hole about an eighth of an inch deep in my helmet.

d. My grandfather, who was born eighty years ago in Puerto Rico, raised his daughters the old-fashioned way.

e. By reversing the depressive effect of the drug, the Narcan saved the patient's life.

Exercise 15–1, page 249   *Possible revisions:*

a. Across the hall from the fossils exhibit are the exhibits for insects and spiders.

b. After growing up desperately poor in Japan, Sayuri becomes a successful geisha.

c. Researchers who have been studying Mount St. Helens for years believe that a series of earthquakes in the area may have caused the 1980 eruption.

d. Ice cream typically contains 10 percent milk fat, but premium ice cream may contain up to 16 percent milk fat and has considerably less air in the product.

e. If home values climb, the economy may recover more quickly than expected.

Exercise 16–1, page 255   *Possible revisions:*

a. Martin Luther King Jr. set a high standard for future leaders.

b. Alice has loved cooking since she could first peek over a kitchen tabletop.

c. Bloom's race for the governorship is futile.

d. A successful graphic designer must have technical knowledge and an eye for color and balance.

e. You will deliver mail to all employees.

Exercise 17–1, page 259 *Possible revisions:*

a. When I was young, my family was poor.

b. This conference will help me serve my clients better.

c. The meteorologist warned the public about the possible dangers of the coming storm.

d. Government studies show a need for after-school programs.

e. Passengers should try to complete the customs declaration form before leaving the plane.

Exercise 17–6, page 267 *Possible revisions:*

a. Dr. Geralyn Farmer is the chief surgeon at University Hospital. Dr. Paul Green is her assistant.

b. All applicants want to know how much they will earn.

c. Elementary school teachers should understand the concept of nurturing if they intend to be effective.

d. Obstetricians need to be available to their patients at all hours.

e. If we do not stop polluting our environment, we will perish.

Exercise 18–2, page 271 *Possible revisions:*

a. We regret this delay; thank you for your patience.

b. Ada's plan is to acquire education and experience to prepare herself for a position as property manager.

c. Serena Williams, the ultimate competitor, has earned millions of dollars just in endorsements.

d. Many people take for granted that public libraries have up-to-date computer systems.

e. The effect of Gao Xingjian's novels on other Chinese exiles is hard to gauge.

Exercise 18–5, page 273 *Possible revisions:*

a. Queen Anne was so angry with Sarah Churchill that she refused to see her again.

b. Correct

c. The parade moved off the street and onto the beach.

d. The frightened refugees intend to make the dangerous trek across the mountains.

e. What type of wedding are you planning?

Exercise 18–8, page 276 *Possible revisions:*

a. John stormed into the room like a hurricane.

b. Some people insist that they'll always be available to help, even when they haven't been before.

c. The Cubs easily beat the Mets, who were in trouble early in the game today at Wrigley Field.

d. We worked out the problems in our relationship.

e. My mother accused me of evading her questions when in fact I was just saying the first thing that came to mind.

Exercise 19–1, page 285 *Possible revisions:*

a. Listening to the CD her sister had sent, Mia was overcome with a mix of emotions: happiness, homesickness, and nostalgia.

b. Cortés and his soldiers were astonished when they looked down from the mountains and saw Tenochtitlán, the magnificent capital of the Aztecs.

c. Although my spoken Spanish is not very good, I can read the language with ease.

d. There are several reasons for not eating meat. One reason is that dangerous chemicals are used throughout the various stages of meat production.

e. To learn how to sculpt beauty from everyday life is my intention in studying art and archaeology.

Exercise 20–1, page 293 *Possible revisions:*

a. The city had one public swimming pool that stayed packed with children all summer long.

b. The building is being renovated, so at times we have no heat, water, or electricity.

c. The view was not what the travel agent had described. Where were the rolling hills and the shimmering rivers?

d. Walker's coming-of-age novel is set against a gloomy scientific backdrop; the Earth's rotation has begun to slow down.

e. City officials had good reason to fear a major earthquake: Most [*or* most] of the business district was built on landfill.

Exercise 20–2, page 293 *Possible revisions:*

a. Wind power for the home is a supplementary source of energy that can be combined with electricity, gas, or solar energy.

b. Correct

c. In the Middle Ages, when the streets of London were dangerous places, it was safer to travel by boat along the Thames.

d. "He's not drunk," I said. "He's in a state of diabetic shock."

e. Are you able to endure extreme angle turns, high speeds, frequent jumps, and occasional crashes? Then supermoto racing may be a sport for you.

Exercise 21–1, page 306

a. One of the main reasons for elephant poaching is the profits received from selling the ivory tusks.

b. Correct
c. A number of students in the seminar were aware of the importance of joining the discussion.
d. Batik cloth from Bali, blue and white ceramics from Delft, and a bocce ball from Turin have made Angelie's room the talk of the dorm.
e. Correct

Exercise 22–1, page 312   *Possible revisions:*

a. Every presidential candidate must appeal to a wide variety of ethnic and social groups to win the election.
b. David lent his motorcycle to someone who allowed a friend to use it.
c. The aerobics teacher motioned for all the students to move their arms in wide, slow circles.
d. Correct
e. Applicants should be bilingual if they want to qualify for this position.

Exercise 23–1, page 318   *Possible revisions:*

a. Some professors say that engineering students should have hands-on experience with dismantling and reassembling machines.
b. Because she had decorated her living room with posters from chamber music festivals, her date thought that she was interested in classical music. Actually she preferred rock.
c. In my high school, students didn't need to get all A's to be considered a success; they just needed to work to their ability.
d. Marianne told Jenny, "I am worried about your mother's illness." [*or* ". . . about my mother's illness."]
e. Though Lewis cried for several minutes after scraping his knee, eventually his crying subsided.

Exercise 24–1, page 324

a. Correct [But the writer could change the end of the sentence: . . . *than he was.*]
b. Correct [But the writer could change the end of the sentence: . . . *that she was the coach.*]
c. She appreciated his telling the truth in such a difficult situation.
d. The director has asked you and me to draft a proposal for a new recycling plan.
e. Five close friends and I rented a station wagon, packed it with food, and drove two hundred miles to Mardi Gras.

Exercise 25–1, page 329
a. Correct
b. The environmental policy conference featured scholars whom I had never heard of. [*or* . . . scholars I had never heard of.]
c. Correct
d. Daniel always gives a holiday donation to whoever needs it.
e. So many singers came to the audition that Natalia had trouble deciding whom to select for the choir.

Exercise 26–1, page 336 *Possible revisions:*
a. Do you expect to perform well on the nursing board exam next week?
b. With the budget deadline approaching, our office has hardly had time to handle routine correspondence.
c. Correct
d. The customer complained that he hadn't been treated nicely by the agent on the phone.
e. Of all the smart people in my family, Uncle Roberto is the cleverest [or most clever].

Exercise 27–1, page 343
a. When I get the urge to exercise, I lie down until it passes.
b. Grandmother had driven our new hybrid to the sunrise church service, so we were left with the station wagon.
c. A pile of dirty rags was lying at the bottom of the stairs.
d. How did the game know that the player had gone from the room with the blue ogre to the hall where the gold was heaped?
e. Abraham Lincoln took good care of his legal clients; the contracts he drew for the Illinois Central Railroad could never be broken.

Exercise 27–5, page 349
a. The glass sculptures of the Swan Boats were prominent in the brightly lit lobby.
b. Visitors to the glass museum were not supposed to touch the exhibits.
c. Our church has all the latest technology, even a closed-circuit television.
d. Christos didn't know about Marlo's promotion because he never listens. He is [*or* He's] always talking.
e. Correct

Exercise 27–9, page 356 *Possible revisions:*
a. Correct
b. Watson and Crick discovered the mechanism that controls inheritance in all life: the workings of the DNA molecule.

c.   When city planners proposed rezoning the waterfront, did they know that the mayor had promised to curb development in that neighborhood?

d.   Tonight's concert begins at 9:30. If it were earlier, I'd consider going.

e.   Correct

Exercise 28–1, page 365

a.   In the past, tobacco companies denied any connection between smoking and health problems.

b.   The volunteer's compassion has touched many lives.

c.   I want to register for a summer tutoring session.

d.   By the end of the year, the state will have tested 139 birds for avian flu.

e.   The golfers were prepared for all weather conditions.

Exercise 28–4, page 368

a.   A major league pitcher can throw a baseball more than ninety-five miles per hour.

b.   The writing center tutor will help you revise your essay.

c.   A reptile must adjust its body temperature to its environment.

d.   Correct

e.   My uncle, a cartoonist, could sketch a face in less than a minute.

Exercise 28–7, page 371   *Possible revisions:*

a.   The electrician might have discovered the broken circuit if she had gone through the modules one at a time.

b.   If Verena wins a scholarship, she will go to graduate school.

c.   Whenever a rainbow appears after a storm, everybody comes out to see it.

d.   Sarah did not understand the terms of her internship.

e.   If I lived in Budapest with my cousin Szusza, she would teach me Hungarian cooking.

Exercise 28–10, page 375   *Possible answers:*

a.   I enjoy riding my motorcycle.

b.   The tutor told Samantha to come to the writing center.

c.   The team hopes to work hard and win the championship.

d.   Ricardo and his brothers miss surfing during the winter.

e.   Jon remembered to lock the door. *Or* Jon remembered seeing that movie years ago.

Exercise 29–1, page 385

a.   Doing volunteer work often brings satisfaction.

b.   As I looked out the window of the plane, I could see Cape Cod.

c.   Melina likes to drink her coffee with lots of cream.

d. Correct
e. I completed my homework assignment quickly. *Or* I completed the homework assignment quickly.

Exercise 30–1, page 390

a. There are some cartons of ice cream in the freezer.
b. I don't use the subway because I am afraid.
c. The prime minister is the most popular leader in my country.
d. We tried to get in touch with the same manager whom we spoke to earlier.
e. Recently there have been a number of earthquakes in Turkey.

Exercise 30–4, page 392 *Possible revisions:*

a. Although freshwater freezes at 32 degrees Fahrenheit, ocean water freezes at 28 degrees Fahrenheit.
b. Because we switched cable packages, our channel lineup has changed.
c. The competitor confidently mounted his skateboard.
d. My sister performs the *legong*, a Balinese dance, well.
e. Correct

Exercise 30–7, page 394

a. Listening to everyone's complaints all day was irritating.
b. The long flight to Singapore was exhausting.
c. Correct
d. After a great deal of research, the scientist made a fascinating discovery.
e. Surviving that tornado was one of the most frightening experiences I've ever had.

Exercise 30–10, page 395

a. an intelligent young Vietnamese sculptor
b. a dedicated Catholic priest
c. her old blue wool sweater
d. Joe's delicious Scandinavian bread
e. many beautiful antique jewelry boxes

Exercise 31–1, page 396

a. Whenever we eat at the Centerville Café, we sit at a small table in the corner of the room.
b. Correct
c. On Thursday, Nancy will attend her first home repair class at the community center.
d. Correct

e. We decided to go to a restaurant because there was no fresh food in the refrigerator.

Exercise 32–1, page 404

a. Alisa brought the injured bird home and fashioned a splint out of Popsicle sticks for its wing.
b. Considered a classic of early animation, *The Adventures of Prince Achmed* used hand-cut silhouettes against colored backgrounds.
c. If you complete the evaluation form and return it within two weeks, you will receive a free breakfast during your next stay.
d. Correct
e. Roger had always wanted a handmade violin, but he couldn't afford one.

Exercise 32–2, page 404

a. J. R. R. Tolkien finished writing his draft of *The Lord of the Rings* trilogy in 1949, but the first book in the series wasn't published until 1954.
b. In the first two minutes of its ascent, the space shuttle had broken the sound barrier and reached a height of over twenty-five miles.
c. German shepherds can be gentle guide dogs, or they can be fierce attack dogs.
d. Some former professional cyclists admit that the use of performance-enhancing drugs is widespread in cycling, but they argue that no rider can be competitive without doping.
e. As an intern, I learned most aspects of the broadcasting industry, but I never learned about fundraising.

Exercise 32–5, page 407

a. The cold, impersonal atmosphere of the university was unbearable.
b. An ambulance threaded its way through police cars, fire trucks, and irate citizens.
c. Correct
d. After two broken arms, three cracked ribs, and one concussion, Ken quit the varsity football team.
e. Correct

Exercise 32–6, page 407

a. NASA's rovers on Mars are equipped with special cameras that can take close-up, high-resolution pictures of the terrain.
b. Correct
c. Correct
d. Love, vengeance, greed, and betrayal are common themes in Western literature.

e.   Many experts believe that shark attacks on surfers are a result of the sharks' mistaking surfboards for small injured seals.

Exercise 32–9, page 411

a.   Choreographer Alvin Ailey's best-known work, *Revelations*, is more than just a crowd-pleaser.
b.   Correct
c.   Correct
d.   A member of an organization that provides job training for teens was also appointed to the education commission.
e.   Brian Eno, who began his career as a rock musician, turned to meditative compositions in the late 1970s.

Exercise 32–11, page 416

a.   Cricket, which originated in England, is also popular in Australia, South Africa, and India.
b.   At the sound of the starting pistol, the horses surged forward toward the first obstacle, a sharp incline three feet high.
c.   After seeing an exhibition of Western art, Gerhard Richter escaped from East Berlin and smuggled out many of his notebooks.
d.   Corrie's new wet suit has an intricate blue pattern.
e.   We replaced the rickety old spiral staircase with a sturdy new ladder.

Exercise 32–12, page 416

a.   On January 15, 2012, our office moved to 29 Commonwealth Avenue, Mechanicsville, VA 23111.
b.   Correct
c.   Ms. Carlson, you are a valued customer whose satisfaction is very important to us.
d.   Mr. Mundy was born on July 22, 1939, in Arkansas, where his family had lived for four generations.
e.   Correct

Exercise 33–1, page 421

a.   Correct
b.   Tricia's first artwork was a bright blue clay dolphin.
c.   Some modern musicians (trumpeter John Hassell is an example) blend several cultural traditions into a unique sound.
d.   Myra liked hot, spicy foods such as chili, kung pao chicken, and buffalo wings.
e.   On the display screen was a soothing pattern of light and shadow.

Exercise 34–1, page 426

a.   Do not ask me to be kind; just ask me to act as though I were.

b. When men talk about defense, they always claim to be protecting women and children, but they never ask the women and children what they think.

c. When I get a little money, I buy books; if any is left, I buy food and clothes.

d. Correct

e. Wit has truth in it; wisecracking is simply calisthenics with words.

Exercise 34-2, page 426

a. Strong black coffee will not sober you up; the truth is that time is the only way to get alcohol out of your system.

b. Margaret was not surprised to see hail and vivid lightning; conditions had been right for violent weather all day.

c. There is often a fine line between right and wrong, good and bad, truth and deception.

d. Correct

e. Severe, unremitting pain is a ravaging force, especially when the patient tries to hide it from others.

Exercise 35-1, page 429

a. Correct [Either *It* or *it* is correct.]

b. If we have come to fight, we are far too few; if we have come to die, we are far too many.

c. The travel package includes a round-trip ticket to Athens, a cruise through the Cyclades, and all hotel accommodations.

d. The news article portrays the land use proposal as reckless, although 62 percent of the town's residents support it.

e. Psychologists Kindlon and Thompson (2000) offer parents a simple starting point for raising male children: "Teach boys that there are many ways to be a man" (p. 256).

Exercise 36-1, page 433

a. Correct

b. The innovative shoe fastener was inspired by the designer's young son.

c. Each day's menu features a different European country's dish.

d. Sue worked overtime to increase her family's earnings.

e. Ms. Jacobs is unwilling to listen to students' complaints about computer failures.

Exercise 37-1, page 440

a. As for the advertisement "Sailors have more fun," if you consider chipping paint and swabbing decks fun, then you will have plenty of it.

b. Correct
c. After winning the lottery, Juanita said that she would give half the money to charity.
d. After the movie, Vicki said, "The reviewer called this flick 'trash of the first order.' I guess you can't believe everything you read."
e. Correct

Exercise 39–1, page 448

a. A client left his or her [*or* a] cell phone in our conference room after the meeting.
b. The films we made of Kilauea on our trip to Hawaii Volcanoes National Park illustrate a typical spatter cone eruption.
c. Correct
d. Of three engineering fields—chemical, mechanical, and materials—Keegan chose materials engineering for its application to toy manufacturing.
e. Correct

Exercise 40–1, page 453

a. Correct
b. Some combat soldiers are trained by government diplomats to be sensitive to issues of culture, history, and religion.
c. Correct
d. How many pounds have you lost since you began running four miles a day?
e. Denzil spent all night studying for his psychology exam.

Exercise 41–1, page 455

a. *MLA style:* The carpenters located three maple timbers, twenty-one sheets of cherry, and ten oblongs of polished ebony for the theater set. *APA style:* The carpenters located three maple timbers, 21 sheets of cherry, and 10 oblongs of polished ebony for the theater set.
b. Correct
c. Correct
d. Eight students in the class had been labeled "learning disabled."
e. The Vietnam Veterans Memorial in Washington, DC, had 58,132 names inscribed on it when it was dedicated in 1982.

Exercise 42–1, page 458

a. Howard Hughes commissioned the *Spruce Goose,* a beautifully built but thoroughly impractical wooden aircraft.
b. The old man screamed his anger, shouting to all of us, "I will not leave my money to you worthless layabouts!"

c. I learned the Latin term *ad infinitum* from an old nursery rhyme about fleas: "Great fleas have little fleas upon their back to bite 'em, / Little fleas have lesser fleas and so on *ad infinitum.*"
d. Correct
e. Neve Campbell's lifelong interest in ballet inspired her involvement in the film *The Company,* which portrays a season with the Joffrey Ballet.

Exercise 44–1, page 471

a. Correct
b. The swiftly moving tugboat pulled alongside the barge and directed it away from the oil spill in the harbor.
c. Correct
d. Your dog is well known in our neighborhood.
e. Roadblocks were set up along all the major highways leading out of the city.

Exercise 45–1, page 476

a. Assistant Dean Shirin Ahmadi recommended offering more world language courses.
b. Correct
c. Kalindi has an ambitious semester, studying differential calculus, classical Hebrew, brochure design, and Greek literature.
d. Lydia's aunt and uncle make modular houses as beautiful as modernist works of art.
e. We amused ourselves on the long flight by discussing how spring in Kyoto stacks up against summer in London.

Exercise 46–1, page 479

a. stage, confrontation, proportions; b. courage, mountain (noun/adjective), climber, inspiration, rescuers; c. need, guest, honor, fog; d. defense (noun/adjective), attorney, appeal, jury; e. museum, women (noun/adjective), artists, 1987

Exercise 46–5, page 481

a. his; b. that, our (pronoun/adjective); c. he, himself, some, his (pronoun/adjective); d. I, my (pronoun/adjective), you, one; e. no one, her

Exercise 46–9, page 484

a. told; b. were, killed; c. brought down; d. Stay, 'll [will] arrive; e. struggled, was trapped

Exercise 46–13, page 486

a. Adjectives: weak, unfocused; b. Adjectives: The (article), Spanish, flexible; adverb: wonderfully; c. Adjectives: The (article), fragrant, the (article), steady; adverb: especially; d. Adjectives: hot, cold; adverbs: rather, slightly, bitterly; e. Adjectives: The (article), its (pronoun/adjective), wicker (noun/adjective); adverb: soundly

Exercise 47–1, page 493

a. Complete subjects: The hills and mountains, the snow atop them; simple subjects: hills, mountains, snow; b. Complete subject: points; simple subject: points; c. Complete subject: (You); d. Complete subject: hundreds of fireflies; simple subject: hundreds; e. Complete subject: The evidence against the defendant; simple subject: evidence

Exercise 47–5, page 496

a. Subject complement: expensive; b. Direct object: death; c. Direct object: their players' efforts; d. Subject complement: the capital of the Russian Empire; e. Subject complement: bitter

Exercise 47–6, page 496

a. Direct objects: adults and children; object complement: weary; b. Indirect object: students; direct object: healthy meal choices; c. Direct object: the work; object complement: finished; d. Indirect objects: agent, us; direct objects: our tickets, boarding passes; e. Direct object: community service; object complement: her priority

Exercise 48–1, page 501

a. In northern Italy (adverb phrase modifying *met*); as their first language (adverb phrase modifying *speak*); b. through the thick forest (adjective phrase modifying *hike*); with ease (adverb phrase modifying *completed*); c. To my boss's dismay (adverb phrase modifying *was*); for work (adverb phrase modifying *late*); d. of Mayan artifacts (adjective phrase modifying *exhibit*); into pre-Columbian culture (adjective phrase modifying *insight*); e. In 2002, in twelve European countries (adverb phrases modifying *became*)

Exercise 48–6, page 504

a. Updating your software (gerund phrase used as subject); b. decreasing the town budget (gerund phrase used as object of the preposition *in*); identifying nonessential services (gerund phrase used as subject complement); c. to help her mother by raking the lawn (infinitive phrase used as direct object); raking the lawn (gerund phrase used as object of the preposition *by*); d. Understanding little (participial phrase modifying *I*); passing my biology final (gerund phrase used as object of the preposition *of*); e. Working with animals (gerund phrase used as *subject*)

Exercise 48–10, page 509

a. so that every vote would count (adverb clause modifying *adjusted*);
b. that targets baby boomers (adjective clause modifying *campaign*);
c. After the Tambora volcano erupted in the southern Pacific in 1815
(adverb clause modifying *realized*); that it would contribute to the
"year without a summer" in Europe and North America (noun clause
used as direct object of *realized*); d. that at a certain point there will
be no more oil to extract from the earth (noun clause used as direct
object of *implies*); e. when you are rushing (adverb clause modifying
are overlooked)

Exercise 49–1, page 512

a. Complex; that are ignited in dry areas (adjective clause); b. Compound;
c. Simple; d. Complex; Before we leave for the station (adverb clause);
e. Compound-complex; when you want to leave (noun clause)

Acknowledgments

Scott Adams, "Dilbert" cartoon. Copyright © 2000 Scott Adams. Used by permission of Universal Uclick. All rights reserved.

Jonathan Adler, excerpt from "Little Green Lies." Copyright © 2012 *Policy Review*. Reprinted by permission of the Heritage Foundation.

AIDS table, data from UNAIDS.

American Heritage Dictionary, entry for "regard." Copyright © 2011 by Houghton Mifflin Harcourt Publishing Company. Reproduced by permission from The American Heritage Dictionary of the English Language, Fifth Edition.

Amherst College screen shot. Courtesy of The Trustees of Amherst College. Reproduced by permission.

Becoming a College Writer photographs (in order of appearance): Copyright © Rich Vintage Photography/istockphoto.com; Copyright © Andresr/Shutterstock.com; Copyright © Jeka/Shutterstock.com; Copyright © michaeljung/Shutterstock.com; Copyright © Maksim Shmeljov/Shutterstock.com; Copyright © Samuel Borges Photography/Shutterstock.com.

Linda Ben-Zvi, excerpt from "'Murder, She Wrote': The Genesis of Susan Glaspell's *Trifles*," *Theatre Journal* 44.2 (1992), 141–62. Copyright © 1992 The Johns Hopkins University Press.

Michelle Berger, excerpt from "Volunteer Army," *Audubon Magazine*, November–December 2010. Reprinted by permission.

Eugene Boe, excerpt from "Pioneers to Eternity: Norwegians on the Prairie" from *The Immigrant Experience*, edited by Thomas C. Wheeler. Copyright © 1971 by Doubleday, a division of Random House, Inc. Reprinted by permission of Doubleday, a division of Random House, Inc.

Isobel Coleman, excerpts from "Technology's Quiet Revolution for Women" in *The Unfinished Revolution: Voices from the Global Fight for Women's Rights*, edited by Minky Worden. Copyright © 2012 by Minky Worden. Reprinted with permission from Isobel Coleman and the publisher.

College graduate infographic. Data provided courtesy of www.postsecondary.org.

EBSCO screen shots. Reprinted by permission of EBSCO publishing.

Education Next, excerpts from 13.1 (Winter 2013): 2, 3, 21. Reprinted by permission.

Equal Exchange, Inc., coffee advertisement. Reproduced with permission.

Stephen J. Gould, excerpt from "Were Dinosaurs Dumb?" *Natural History*, 87.5: 9–16. Reprinted by permission of Rhonda R. Shearer.

Emma Hart, excerpts from "Work, Family, and the Eighteenth-Century History of a Middle Class in the American South" and table of contents from *The Journal of Southern History* 78.3 (August 2012). Copyright © 2012 by the Southern Historical Association. Reprinted by permission.

Health insurance coverage pie chart. Data from the Kaiser Foundation.

Lynn Hunt et al., map, "Castile and Portugal" from *The Making of the West*, Volume II. Copyright © 2005 by Bedford/St. Martin's. Reprinted by permission of Bedford/St. Martin's.

Gary R. Jahn, excerpt from "The Image of the Railroad in Anna Karenina," *The Slavic and East European Journal* 25.2 (Summer 1981): 1–10. Reprinted with permission of AATSEEL of U.S., Inc.

Dorling Kindersley, excerpt from *Encyclopedia of Fishing*. Copyright © 1994 DK Publishing. Reprinted by permission of Penguin Group, Ltd.

Lincoln Papers screen shots. From Mr. Lincoln's Virtual Library.

Jack McLaughlin, excerpt from *To His Excellency Thomas Jefferson: Letters to a President*. Copyright © 1991 by Jack McLaughlin. Used by permission of W. W. Norton & Company, Inc.

Merriam-Webster Online, screen shot of entry for "regard." From *Merriam-Webster's Collegiate® Dictionary*, 11th Edition. © 2013 by Merriam-Webster, Inc. (www.Merriam-Webster.com). Reprinted by permission.

Minnesota Department of Health screen shots. Courtesy of the Minnesota Department of Health. Reproduced by permission.

National Conference of State Legislatures screen shot. Copyright © 2013 National Conference of State Legislatures. All rights reserved.

The *New York Times*, screen shot from "Window into Fed Debate over a Crucial Program" from Inside NYTimes.com. A version of the article appeared in print on October 15, 2009, page B3 of the New York edition. Copyright © 2009 by The New York Times Co. Reprinted by permission.

Patagonia advertisement. Property of Patagonia, Inc. Used with permission.

Peter Popham, excerpts from *The Lady and the Peacock: The Life of Aung San Suu Kyi*. Reprinted by permission of The Experiment, LLC.

"The Pursuit of Property" bar graph. Data from the US Census Bureau.

Anne and Jack Rudloe, excerpt from "Electric Warfare: The Fish That Kills with Thunderbolts," by *Smithsonian* 24.5: 95–105. Reprinted by permission.

David Sacks, "Tororo School, Uganda." Copyright © David Sacks Photography, 2004.

Skin diagram. Courtesy of NIAMS Image Gallery, National Institute of Arthritis and Musculoskeletal and Skin Diseases.

P. D. Smith, excerpts from *The City: A Guidebook for the Urban Age*, Bloomsbury Publishing Plc. Copyright © 2012 P. D. Smith. Reprinted with permission from Bloomsbury Publishing Plc.

Betsy Taylor, "Big Box Stores are Bad for Main Street," from *CQ Researcher* (November 1999). Copyright © 1999 by CQ Press, a division of Sage Publications.

Joseph Turner, "*Sir Gawain and the Green Knight* and the History of Medieval Rhetoric," *Rhetoric Review* 31.4 (2012): 371–88. Reprinted by permission of Taylor & Francis, LLC.

Mark Twain, *Adventures of Huckleberry Finn* screen shot. Courtesy of *Mark Twain in His Times: An Electronic Archive*.

Wilderness flowchart. Data from Arizona Board of Regents.

Garry Wills, excerpt from "Two Speeches on Race," from *The New York Review of Books*, May 1, 2008. Reprinted by permission of The Wylie Agency.

World Wildlife Fund advertisement. Courtesy of World Wildlife Fund, WWF-www.worldwildlife.org.

Fred Zwicky, "Tornado Touch." Photo by Fred Zwicky. Copyright © 2004.

Index

Multilingual Menu

A List of Charts

Revision Symbols

Boldface numbers refer to sections of the handbook.

abbr	abbreviation	40	℘	punctuation	
adj	misuse of adjective	26	∧̓	comma	32
add	add needed word	10	no ,	no comma	33
adv	misuse of adverb	26	;	semicolon	34
agr	agreement	21, 22	:	colon	35
appr	inappropriate language	17	v̓	apostrophe	36
art	article (*a, an, the*)	29	" "	quotation marks	37
awk	awkward		. ?	period, question mark	38a–b
cap	capital letter	45	!	exclamation point	38c
case	pronoun case	24, 25	— ( )	dash, parentheses	39a–b
cliché	cliché	18e	[ ] ...	brackets, ellipsis mark	39c–d
coh	coherence	3d	/	slash	39e
coord	coordination	14	¶	new paragraph	3e
cs	comma splice	20	pass	ineffective passive	8
dev	inadequate development	3b	pn agr	pronoun agreement	22
dm	dangling modifier	12e	proof	proofreading problem	2c
-ed	*-ed* ending	27d	ref	pronoun reference	23
emph	emphasis	14	run-on	run-on sentence	20
ESL	English as a second language, multilingual	28–31	-s	*-s* ending	27c, 21
			sexist	sexist language	17f, 22a
exact	inexact language	18	shift	distracting shift	13
frag	sentence fragment	19	sl	slang	17d
fs	fused sentence	20	sp	misspelled word	43
gl/us	see glossary of usage		sub	subordination	14
hyph	hyphen	44	sv agr	subject-verb agreement	21, 27c
idiom	idioms	18d	t	verb tense	27f, 28a
inc	incomplete construction	10	trans	transition needed	3d
irreg	irregular verb	27a	usage	see glossary of usage	
ital	italics	42	v	voice	8a, 28b
jarg	jargon	17a	var	lack of variety in sentence structure	14, 15
lc	lowercase	45			
mix	mixed construction	11	vb	verb problem	27, 28
mm	misplaced modifier	12a–d	w	wordy	16
mood	mood of verb	27g	//	parallelism	9
nonst	nonstandard usage	17d, 27	∧	insert	
num	use of numbers	41	#	insert space	
om	omitted word	10, 29, 30a–b	⌒	close up space	

A List of Grammatical Terms

Boldface numbers refer to sections of the handbook.

Detailed Menu